THE RENAISSANCE AND
THE REFORMATION

HARPER'S HISTORICAL SERIES
Under the Editorship of
Guy Stanton Ford

THE

RENAISSANCE

AND THE

REFORMATION

SECOND EDITION

Henry S. Lucas

Professor Emeritus of European History
University of Washington

HARPER & ROW, PUBLISHERS

NEW YORK AND EVANSTON

Library of Congress catalog card number: 60-7014

A-R

To My Wife

EDNA S. LUCAS

CONTENTS

PART X

Novel Creations of the High Renaissance

PART XI

Renaissance Art Outside Italy

PART XII

Northern Humanism from Erasmus to Shakespeare

BOOK TWO: THE REFORMATION AND
CATHOLIC REVIVAL

PART I

Breakup of Religious Unity in Western Europe

PART II

Lutheranism Ascendant

PART III

Novel Protestant Teaching

PART IX

Catholic Political Reaction

Contents

MAPS

GENEALOGICAL TABLES

ILLUSTRATIONS

(Following page 248)

EDITOR'S INTRODUCTION

*T*HE WORK that the author had done in scholarly studies of the Low Countries and their civilization in a period covered by this volume interested me, as an editor, in the possibility of his writing a volume on the Renaissance and Reformation. Because of his thorough training under men like Pirenne and Des Marez, his grasp of the basic economic and social factors gave promise of an approach that would relate and interpret movements that were common to western Europe when the civilization of our day took shape.

The commission has been executed in a way to give any student the background of movements that represent in art, literature, and religion some of the most significant achievements of the human spirit. The Renaissance and the Reformation rest upon profound changes in the social and economic activities of the centuries that precede and that compass them. What this volume insistently reveals is the merchant, banker, and artisan whose sturdy interest in material things made possible a civilization that produced artists, poets, and religious leaders.

But the background is for the sake of a foreground crowded in this period with great figures. Around them are many who were typical and vital figures and these the author has fully sketched. He has sturdily insisted on our knowing that great men are great because they did supremely well what others thought worth striving to do.

Of one thing I am sure: the student who masters this text will not only understand better these centuries and his own times but will want to retain his text as one of the best interpretations and guides to the treasures in art, architecture, and literature that he hopes some time to see or study as a European traveler.

GUY STANTON FORD

PREFACE TO THE FIRST EDITION

So important are the Renaissance and the Reformation in the history of our culture that courses in these subjects are justly popular. Notwithstanding the keen interest shown in economic history and in recent events, the achievements of the Renaissance and the issues of the Reformation continue to rouse enthusiasm and excite interest. Making straight the way for youthful inquirers is an arduous task which demands great resourcefulness from the teacher. Therefore a new manual designed to guide students through the intricacies of these periods seems justified. It appears especially imperative to summarize the more significant factors of the social and economic environment in which the far-reaching cultural transformations of those days were effected. If this volume solves some of these problems, I shall be gratified.

My primary care has been to give rather full consideration to psychological factors, particularly in the sections devoted to the Reformation. Believing that we in America have neglected these factors, I have tried to present the problems of life as they appeared to the chief characters of the age; for this reason it was decided to give a more adequate delineation of religious dogma than is to be found in most books of this nature. Basic political and social situations are set forth in some detail; this will require the diligent use of atlas and encyclopedia. A number of genealogical charts and a list of selected literature have been appended.

The writer of a book of this nature is under heavy obligation to a host of laborers who have gone before him. They of course include such illustrious names as Burckhardt, Symonds, and Monnier. But the following pages also reveal a great debt to subsequent writers many of whom are still living. The number of new works is constantly growing and to master them all is well-nigh impossible. No one can keep up with the new facts and ideas which are daily put forward, and I sincerely trust that this fact will temper the judgment of critics.

I wish to thank my students who had the patience to listen to my words; their appreciation and enthusiasm have ever been a genuine inspiration. For reading of proof I am indebted to my friends and colleagues, Professors Allen R. Benham, Donald G. Barnes, and C. Eden Quainton, and I am keenly grateful for their suggestions. To Dean Guy S. Ford, the editor of the series in which this book appears, I would express my sincere thanks. Nor must I omit mentioning the fellowships of the Commission For Relief In Belgium Educational Foundation and the John Simon Guggenheim Memorial Foundation. These have enabled me to form a more concrete conception of European culture than would have been otherwise possible. To my wife whose interest and patient endeavor have lightened the burden of composing these pages I owe more than can be told. I also wish to recall the names of masters at whose feet I have been privileged to sit; these include the departed Professors, Johan Huizinga, Ferdinand Pijper, and Albert Eekhof of the University of Leiden, Professor Henri Pirenne, formerly of the University of Ghent and now of Brussels, and the mentor of my earlier years, Professor Earle W. Dow of the University of Michigan. Lastly, I must refer to a most helpful friend who more than any other has kept me from stumbling where theological and other dangers were greatest and who modestly insists that his name be withheld.

H. S. L.

Seattle, Washington
Midsummer, 1934

PREFACE TO THE SECOND EDITION

*T*HE KINDLY RECEPTION accorded the first edition of *The Renaissance and the Reformation*, which appeared twenty-six years ago, has led the publishers to bring out this revised edition. To rewrite the book entirely appeared impossible, owing to the manifold duties which occupied me as a university teacher. After much reflection it seemed best to revise a large number of paragraphs and short passages, as, for example, pages 526–527, dealing with the activities of Martin Butzer; pages 486–487, which concern the significance of Philip Melanchthon; and pages 539–540, which emphasize the importance of Menno Simons, a man too much neglected by writers. Completely rewritten are the introductions to the Renaissance and to the Reformation as well as Chapters I, II, and III. Chapter IV is practically new.

The point of view remains that of a person who long ago became critical of the masterpieces, however brilliant, of Jacob Burckhardt and John Addington Symonds, who owe much to the thought of the Age of Enlightenment regarding medieval civilization. This revision expresses the belief that the culture of medieval times was a mighty factor in the development of the civilization of the Renaissance, that medieval culture contributed notably to the life, thought, artistic expression, and political and economic activity of our forbears in the age of the Renaissance. The civilization of this great age therefore is not a creation *ex nihilo*, but is due to the great zeal of many centuries of intensive endeavor. Hence my effort to make clear the impact of Flemish and other Low Country medieval art and music upon that of the Renaissance.

I am grateful to my students and to other persons who have called my attention to erroneous statements of dates or facts in the first edition.

H. S. L.

Palm Springs, California
March, 1960

BOOK ONE

The Renaissance

Un événement immense s'était accompli. Le monde était changé.
Pas un état européen, même les plus immobiles,
qui ne se trouvât lancé dans un
mouvement tout nouveau.

J. MICHELET

Italy led the way in the education of the western races, and was
the first to realize the type of modern as
distinguished from classical
and medieval life.

J. A. SYMONDS

Le quattrocento, par quoi il faut entendre le xve siècle d'Italie, est
un des moments les plus considérables
de l'esprit humain.

P. N. MONNIER

Nos vero tempus habentes vindicamus hereditatem nostrorum.

I. MACHABEES

Introduction

WHAT IS THE RENAISSANCE?

*T*HERE ARE MANY definitions of the term *Renaissance*, but not one is really satisfactory. Some definitions exaggerate certain aspects of the Renaissance; some underestimate the import of certain features of it.[1] Certain it is, however, that the Renaissance was an era of striking accomplishment in painting, sculpture, architecture, music, literature, philosophy, science, and technology. It also was an age of change in the economic foundations in the life of our medieval forefathers, in the basic structure of European society, and in the organization of states. And, last but not least, the Renaissance affected the Christian Church, which for generations had presided at the formation of European civilization.[2]

At the outset of our narrative we shall content ourselves with stating that the Renaissance was the civilization of Europe and particularly of Italy during the three centuries following the life of Dante (1265–1321) and includes, besides many other matters, an account of the life, thought, and achievement of Francesco Petrarch (1304–1374), Lorenzo de Medici (1449–1492), Leonardo da Vinci (1452–1519), Raphael (1483–1520),

[1] The term *Renaissance* was borrowed from the French language in 1840. So useful was this word that it soon became popular. The form *Renascence* was employed as early as 1727 but never met with much favor. Matthew Arnold tried to popularize it in the fourth chapter of his *Culture and Anarchy*, for he preferred it to the more foreign *Renaissance*. Few writers, however, have adopted his view and the form *Renascence* is now little used.

[2] The term *Middle Ages* is little more than two centuries old. The humanists of the Renaissance and their successors by 1700 habitually divided the human past into 3 periods: *ancient, medieval,* and *modern* or contemporary. Despising and misunderstanding the culture of the centuries which had elapsed between the decline of classical civilization and the revival of Greek and Latin culture in their own time, they could think of them only as a dreary period separating 2 more brilliant ages. Hence they called them the "middle" or the "medieval" period, or the "Middle Ages." Today this classification is wholly antiquated; it takes no account of the revolutionary discoveries in the realm of prehistory and ignores the cultures of India and China. But the terms *Ancient, Medieval,* and *Modern History* are so deeply entrenched in popular custom that it appears impossible to change them. Throughout this book the term *Middle Ages* comprises roughly the 11 centuries from 400 to 1500.

3

and Michelangelo (1475–1564). It reached its climax about 1500 when Italy was more and more assuming cultural direction of European life and thought—when all Europe came to be what Italy was. This of course is no definition of the Renaissance, but merely a statement when it took place. Descriptions of phases in the movement and definitions of its varied aspects will be offered later whenever necessary.

Culture is a common way in which men live, think, and act—not passively, but dynamically, creatively. It comprises a common organization to satisfy man's material wants necessitated by his social, political, and other needs. Cultural activity includes a general use of the material aspects of man's environment such as economic resources, geographic surroundings, and the products of technological skill. Culture also includes such all-important matters as philosophy, science, art, literature, and religion—mental and moral activities which, more than the forces of material nature, shape the course of civilization.

Culture—whether of the Renaissance, of the Reformation, or of any other period—is uniquely the product of man's creative activity. Culture springs from man's moral nature, from his free will, from the rational character of his being. It does not rise automatically and by necessity out of his material environment of soil, geography, climate, chemical forces, vegetable or animal life, but rather out of his persistently creative capacity more or less independently of the material nature of his existence. Were this not so, the history of civilization would be little more than a subdivision of chemistry, physics, or biology. There would then be no culture. There would be no Renaissance, no Reformation.

The roots of civilization lie deep in the ages gone by. Knowing the past, therefore, helps us to grasp more clearly the character of the present. Some of man's most useful achievements date from the remote past, are, in fact, ageless. Let us here note some of them.

Paleolithic man may not have had much cultural equipment, but he was no brute. He possessed skill as food gatherer, as hunter, as maker of stone knives and hatchets, and had the knowledge how to make fire and use it. Neolithic man, building upon the achievements of his Paleolithic ancestors, made excellent stone tools. He domesticated plants and animals and raised crops. His descendants in the Bronze and Iron Ages discovered copper and iron and used them in making tools.

Setting the spiritual character of our civilization was the contribution of the ancient Hebrews. This tribal and pastoral people of Palestine were poor but virile and developed an ethical monotheism which contrasted with the polytheistic cults of the people about them. The Hebrews believed in Jehovah, infinite in power and majesty, creator and sustainer of all things, and their protector. The prophet Moses proclaimed His nature and presented to His chosen people at Mount Sinai the tables on which were engraved the Ten Commandments. The spiritual experience of the Hebrews is recorded in their Scriptures, a library of small classics, among which are the Five Books of Moses, several books on the history of the Hebrews in the Holy Land, the Book of Job (a masterpiece on the problem of suffering), the utterances of the Prophets, and, finally, the Book of Psalms, a collection of 150 psalms unmatched in the devotional literature of any other people.

Out of this Jewish Palestinian milieu came also the Christian religion. The founder of Christianity was Jesus (crucified in the year 33) who taught a doctrine of salvation based upon the Jewish Scriptures and upon His own teaching that He was divine. His message, told in the Four Gospels, the Acts of the Apostles, the Epistles, and the Apocalypse won followers, not only among the Jews, but also among Greeks and Romans. By the year 500 the Christian community embraced the entire Greco-Roman world. Celts, Germans, Slavs, and other peoples next adopted its teaching about life and eternity, thereby laying the moral and spiritual foundation of medieval life and thought.

Sheer originality characterized the Greeks. To them belongs the credit of laying the foundations of metaphysical thought later so noteworthy a feature of the Middle Ages, the Renaissance, and the Reformation. In philosophy Plato and Aristotle have always been supreme, and the questions raised by the Cynics, Epicureans, and Stoics still are instructive. But the Greeks also were practical; for example, in medicine which was developed by Hippocrates of Cos (d. 356 B.C.). What would medieval and Renaissance medicine have been without Claudius Galen's (d. A.D. 201) encyclopedic system? And succeeding ages without Aristotle's metaphysics and Claudius Ptolemy's geography and astronomy?

The Greeks produced classic forms of art which dazzled the men of the Renaissance. Homer created the *Iliad* and the *Odyssey;* these masterpieces inspired Virgil to write his *Aeneid,* and Francesco Petrarch, nostalgic admirer of all things Greek and Roman, to compose his *Africa.* The tragic drama of Aeschylus (d. 456 B.C.), Sophocles, and Euripides and the comedy of Aristophanes have never been surpassed. Similarly, the historical writings of Herodotus, Thucydides, and Xenophon are paragons of excellence. And how much influence did not Greek sculpture radiate during the Renaissance?

The Byzantine Empire embraced the eastern part of the Roman Empire which survived the ruin of the western provinces during the sixth century. Its power centered in Constantinople on the Golden Horn. It enjoyed great prestige, for its emperors maintained an effective administrative system, kept a strong army, and directed a powerful navy. Down to the year of its destruction in 1453, the Byzantine Empire shielded western Europe from Huns, Slavs, Arabs, and Turks.

Byzantine culture was rooted in the Greek and Roman past. It continued some of the Roman skill in government. Its subjects spoke Attic Greek, derived vital strength from its Christian foundations. It transformed the culture of the Slavs and the Arabs. To these peoples Byzantium taught her achievements in mozaic, fresco, and miniature art, her ivory carving, her architecture, of which the sublimest example is the church of Hagia Sophia in Constantinople, and, last but not least, passed on the tradition of Greek and Roman literature, philosophy, and science, thereby contributing mightily to the Renaissance in Italy.

The significance of the Arabs lay in the fact that this migratory people, divided into discordant tribes whose chief element of unity was the Arabic language, were welded into a mighty united people by the prophet Mohammed. "O ye men!" he said, "Harken unto my words and take ye them to heart! Know ye that every Moslem is a brother to every other Moslem, and that ye are now one brotherhood! It is not lawful for any of you to take what belongs to his brother unless it is willingly given him by that brother!" The Koran containing the prophecies of Mohammed became the Bible of the Arabs.

Unified, the Arab community became a religious-political state under the guidance of Mohammed's successors, the califs. They invaded the lands along the Arabian desert, seized Palestine, took Egypt from the Byzantine Empire, conquered North Africa, and in 711 seized Spain. Eastward they captured Persia and extended their power beyond the borders of China. Soon Islam planted itself in the Philippine Islands and the East Indies. But the triumphs of the Arabs in Europe were stopped by the Byzantine navy at Constantinople.

The desert-dwelling Arabs demonstrated an extraordinary propensity to absorb the civilization of their many neighbors. Their borrowing was greatest from adjoining Byzantium. Eagerly the Arabs appropriated the thought of the Greeks, especially the philosophies of Plato and Aristotle and the scientific and medical knowledge of Galen, and made new contributions to them. They studied the technological skill of the ancients and, as in science, soon equaled them. In trade and industry the world of Islam was most successful, a fact evidenced by the cities of Bagdad, Damascus, Cairo, and Córdoba. Islam united East and West in intimate commercial relations; the volume of trade between them apparently exceeded what it had been in the days of the Roman Empire.

The Middle Ages were most complex in their cultural make-up. Jewish, Greek, Roman, Byzantine, and Arabic peoples had a vital part in it. Into this diverse populace came new peoples, backward as compared with the Greco-Roman world, but nonetheless eager to acquire the culture which that world had to offer. Celts—Irish, Scots, and Britons—besides Germans, Slavs, Bulgars, Finns, and Magyars, became part of a new cultural amalgam welded together by the Christian church, the Latin language, and the tradition of Greece and Rome as the fountain of civilization. During one whole millennium following the death of Constantine in 337 medieval Europe witnessed an extraordinary development in political, social, and religious economic life based in large part upon the achievements of the Greeks and Romans.

For generations it has been thought that medieval life contributed little to civilization. But this view is false. Properly understood, the Middle Ages witnessed a remarkable intellectual, social, political, and economic development. In Romanesque and Gothic art they produced truly classic creations. Gothic painting, sculpture, and music deserve serious study. In metaphysics the Middle Ages had a fruitful revival, a creative adaptation of the thought of Plato and Aristotle. In science, technology, and religion that period also had its great moments. The Middle Ages provided the cultural milieu in which the civilization of the Renaissance developed and the explosion of the Reformation occurred.

PART I

New Secular Foundations

Chapter 1

POLITICAL MILIEU OF THE RENAISSANCE AND REFORMATION: STATES OUTSIDE ITALY

*W*E BEGIN our study of the Renaissance and the Reformation by first noting the political milieu in which these phenomena appeared. Everywhere by the year 1300 state and society were feeling the quickening tempo of a more complicated economy which, developing as early as the eleventh century, had already transformed European life. The newer monarchies were creating centralized administrative organs of government which, compared with older feudal methods, spelled efficient political management, more potent state action. Some of these states were equipping themselves with the newest artillery and firearms. They also possessed a well-trained cavalry and infantry.

The creation of these newer state organizations marked a decisive stage in the political and military history of Europe. These powers, small as well as large, in accordance with their political interests divided into two hostile camps in rapidly shifting combinations. Disastrous wars ensued. There was much military preparation and tortuous diplomatic intrigue. This began in 1494 when Charles VIII of France, to satisfy his Angevin claims upon the kingdom of Naples, invaded Italy. For the states of Italy, as well as for the powers of Europe beyond the Alps, this invasion was a momentous event. Unable to resist the political and military combinations of Spain and its supporters and of France and her allies, the states of Italy proved too weak and divided to expel their invaders and so

9

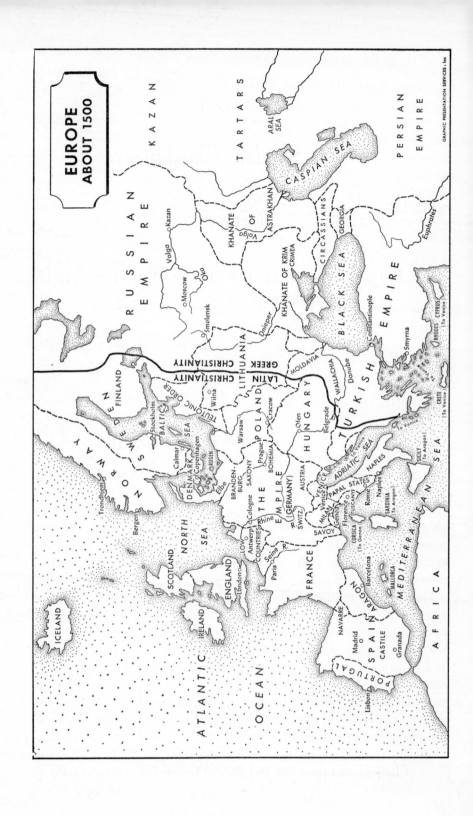

EUROPE
ABOUT 1500

GRAPHIC PRESENTATION SERVICES · Inc

KAZAN

T A R T A R S

ARAL
SEA

PERSIAN
EMPIRE

R U S S I A N   E M P I R E

KHANATE
OF
ASTRAKHAN

CASPIAN SEA

o Kazan

Volga

Volga

o Moscow

Oka

CIRCASSIANS

GEORGIA

Euphrates

o Smolensk

KHANATE OF KRIM
CRIMEA

Dnieper

B L A C K   S E A

Constantinople

o Smyrna

RHODES
CYPRUS
(To Venice)

N O R W A Y

S W E D E N

FINLAND

GREEK CHRISTIANITY

LITHUANIA

LATIN CHRISTIANITY

MOLDAVIA

Danube

T U R K I S H   E M P I R E

CRETE
(To Venice)

Trondhjem

Stockholm

TEUTONIC ORDER

BALTIC

SEA

Wilna

Warsaw

Cracow

T H E   P O L A N D

Olen

Belgrade

H U N G A R Y

WALLACHIA

To Venice

Bergen

Calmar

Copenhagen

RUGEN

DENMARK

Elbe

BRANDEN-
BURG

Prague

BOHEMIA

SAXONY

AUSTRIA

VENICE

Venice

MILAN

ADRIATIC
SEA

PAPAL STATES

NAPLES

SICILY
(To Aragon)

SCOTLAND

N O R T H

S E A

Cologne

Rhine

E M P I R E
(GERMANY)

SWITZ.

SAVOY

Genoa

Florence

TUSCANY

Rome

SARDINIA
(To Aragon)

Naples

M E D I T E R R A N E A N   S E A

ENGLAND

LOW
Antwerp
COUNTRIES

Seine

Paris

R.

R. Rhine

CORSICA
(To Genoa)

London

F R A N C E

Barcelona

A R A G O N

MALLORCA
(To Aragon)

ICELAND

IRELAND

A T L A N T I C

O C E A N

NAVARRE

Madrid

S P A I N

CASTILE

o Granada

A F R I C A

PORTUGAL

Lisbon

Italy became the battleground of forces contending for the mastery of the peninsula. This complex drama in international relations filled the annals of the first half of the sixteenth century.

THE ASCENDANCY OF SPAIN

Of the larger states outside Italy during the sixteenth century none perhaps played so vital a part in European life as did Spain. In military affairs she dominated the political history of western Europe from the days of Ferdinand and Isabella until the death of King Philip II in 1598. In art, she inspired the great age of Baroque painting, sculpture, and architecture. In learning she led in the rejuvenation of the philosophy of Thomas Aquinas and Duns Scotus and contributed significantly to textual biblical criticism by producing the monumental Complutensian Polyglot edition of the Bible (Volume I appeared in 1514). Spanish leadership in the Catholic Revival was of the utmost importance in meeting the religious problems that troubled Europe after Luther broke with the old Church. And, finally, Spain showed the way in discovering the expanses of the Americas, colonizing them, and bringing the elements of European civilization to the Aztecs and Incas and to other peoples in

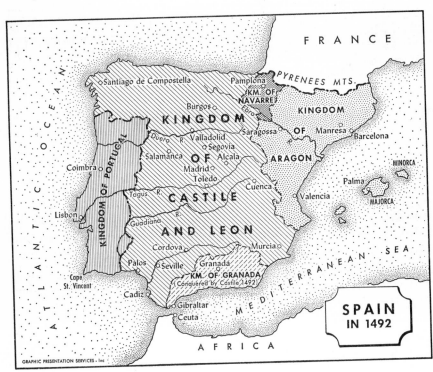

SPAIN
IN 1492

America. These extraordinary achievements, it is vital to note, were accomplished by the Spanish peoples who were never united politically until the reigns of Ferdinand II of Aragon (1479–1516) and Queen Isabella of Castile and León (1474–1504). Bound by common political ties under the leadership of their monarchs, the Spanish peoples now assumed leadership in the life and thought of this period.

Aragon. For ages the Spanish peninsula had been divided into several states, each possessing striking peculiarities. In the northeast was the kingdom of Aragon which embraced Catalonia, Aragon, Valencia, and the Balearic Islands. Through Aragon flowed the Ebro River eastward into the Mediterranean. Barcelona was Aragon's thriving port. The country looked eastward; its commerce was with Mediterranean centers, especially Palermo in Sicily and Genoa on the Italian peninsula.

The kings of Aragon at one time or another also were rulers of Sicily and had a claim upon the crown of Naples. Peter III of Aragon, husband of Constance, granddaughter of the Emperor Frederick II (d. 1250) who had been king of Sicily and Naples, seized Sicily at the time of the Sicilian Vespers in 1282. This was a rebellion of the Sicilians against their French ruler Charles I of Anjou (d. 1285), who had acquired Naples and Sicily after the male Hohenstaufen line of Frederick II became extinct. But neither Peter III nor any of his successors until King Alfonso I of Aragon and Sicily (reign, 1416–1458) was able to lay hands upon the crown of Naples. During the years that had elapsed since the rule of Charles I of Anjou, the Angevins, while wearing the crown of Naples, also claimed the crown of Sicily; and at the same time the Aragonese kings of Sicily insisted on their just title to the crown of Naples. These rival claims produced much confusion and in 1494 led Charles VIII of France, who had inherited the Angevin titles, to seek the conquest of Naples. So, in addition to its geographic position and its prosperous economic connection with the parts of Italy, the crown of Aragon also had a vital dynastic interest in Italian politics which challenged French political ambitions.

Castile and León. These states occupied the central part of Spain extending from the Bay of Biscay on the North to the Atlantic and the Mediterranean on the South. On their eastern borders lay Navarre and Aragon. Along their western boundary stretched the kingdom of Portugal. Castile's southern frontier marched with that of the Moorish kingdom of Granada. León embraced the northwestern part of this area, including Galicia with its pilgrimage center at Santiago de Compostello. The more ancient part of Castile, known as Old Castile, included Santander, San Sebastian, Guipuzcoa, and the country as far south as Avila and Segovia and the mountains of the Sierra Guadarrama. New Castile, so called because it was conquered from the Moors, extended southward to the Sierra Morena.

United in 1230, Castile and León contrasted sharply in their geographical features with those of Aragon. The country was broken by mountain ranges which extend across its territory from east to west. So far as the dictates of geography prevailed Castile and León were orientated toward the Atlantic, from which they were shut off, however, by Portugal. Deprived of contact with the Mediterranean by the Moorish conquerors, Castilian commercial relations with Italian ports were slight.

Portugal. Stretching along the western coast of the peninsula, Portugal possessed no natural frontiers on the east. The country looked out upon the Atlantic and had a great part in the voyages of discovery. Oporto, Coimbra, and Lisbon on the Tagus River drew their prosperity from the Atlantic trade. An energetic dynasty asserted its rights with vigor. Under its leadership the lands from the Minho River to Cape St. Vincent and the Guadiana were united under the crown of Portugal. The monarchs maintained their independence of neighboring Castile and León until 1580 when Philip II of Spain, on the ground that the throne was vacant and that he was its legitimate successor, seized the country. This union, however, came to an end in 1640.

The Kingdom of Navarre. Smallest and least significant of the Spanish states was Navarre. Surrounded on the Spanish side by Castile and Aragon, this diminutive country occupied a portion of the western slopes of the Pyrenees and a smaller area on its northern slopes. Its economic importance was slight, its political power insignificant; but the country provided a corridor (the Pass of Roncesvalles is in Navarre) through which French and Spanish influences moved back and forth. During the wars of the sixteenth century Navarre figured importantly, for the rulers of the country belonged to a French family, a younger branch of the reigning house of France.

CHARACTER OF THE SPANISH STATE AND PEOPLE

In language, the people of Spain developed striking differences. The Portuguese spoke Portuguese; in Castile and León the people used Castilian Spanish, a tongue destined to become classic for all Spanish-speaking peoples; and, finally, Catalan, a form used in Aragon. Portugal's literature, in the *Lusiad* of Camoëns (d. 1580), attained classical perfection. That of Castile and León had long ago acquired excellence as, for example, in the *Poem of the Cid*, an eleventh-century masterpiece of chivalric literature ranking with the *Song of Roland*, its contemporary.

The economic resources of the peninsula also give some insight into the character of the Spanish peoples. The extensive plateaus of Spain, broken by the mountain ridges of Castile and León, had a rough soil, too parched for productive agriculture. In this region between the Guadalquivir River and León and Burgos came into existence one of the most remarkable of medieval organizations, the Mesta. This was a corporation of shepherds and workers and officials who regulated, under the protection of the crown, an extensive sheep-raising industry founded in the thirteenth century. Its flocks grazed up and down this region, once each year. They provided the merino wool which had an excellent reputation.

The Spanish peninsula also was a land of cities, but they were not so large or numerous as those in Italy or in the Low Countries. The most important towns were situated on the seacoast. Aragon possessed the busy port of Barcelona. Granada had a large urban population scattered in numerous towns where fine cloths and metal objects were produced.

Inland areas of Castile had their important urban centers, originally built to protect the country against the Moors. In Old Castile there were Burgos, Valladolid, and Segovia; in New Castile, Madrid, Toledo, and Ciudad Real. The ports of Santander and San Sebastian on the Bay of Biscay were fishing centers, especially whaling. Iron was exported from Bilboa and Guipuzcoa. Choice wines were shipped to the countries of northern Europe and semitropical fruits from Spain found their way to Flemish markets.

But though geographical, political, economic, linguistic, and literary divergencies characterized the life of Spain, there was, on the contrary, one set of circumstances which contributed to unity. This was Christianity and the Church which inspired the people to fight the Mohammedan Moor for the preservation of faith and country. In 711 at Xeres de la Frontera the invader ruined the kingdom of the Visigoths. All Spain seemed to fall under the infidel's yoke. Only at Covadonga, in Asturias, was there power sufficient to oppose the national enemy. The fight was a long one and a determined one. The rulers of Aragon, of Castile and León, and of Portugal all took part in this struggle. Success attended the Christian arms. But it was Castile and León that profited most; gradually their crusading forces pushed the Moors southward over the Tagus, the Guadiana, and the Guadalquivir. Finally, they maintained a precarious hold upon Granada, but this was taken from them in 1492 by Queen Isabella of Castile and León.

One cannot well grasp the character of the Spanish Renaissance, of the Protestant Reformation, or of the Catholic Revival if one does not understand how this struggle with the infidel national enemy affected the Spanish people. It forged a powerful bond of patriotism for the father-land and a deep love for the Christian faith, blending them with the devotion characteristic of feudal nobles proud of long lines of ancestors who always had been faithful to king, to country, and to Church. So St. Francis Xavier, when asked about his ancestry by some person who doubted his true claim to a nobleman's status, declared with spirit that he "came from two castles which were standing before Charlemagne's day and that he belonged to two families which, thanks to God, had never been tainted with heresy." In Portugal every person who had taken part in the battle of Ourique (1139) against the Moors, which had resulted in the establishment of the Portuguese monarchy, was regarded as a noble. Any nobleman who adjured his faith while being a prisoner of the Moors, or who fled while on the field of battle with them, was disgraced and deprived of noble status.

THE SPANISH RULERS AND THEIR STATE

In Spain the Middle Ages may be taken to have ended with the reigns of Queen Isabella of Castile and León (d. 1504) and of King Ferdinand of Aragon (d. 1516). These rulers, united in marriage in 1469, ascended their thrones respectively in 1474 and 1479. They ruled jointly and fol-lowed a common policy. As everywhere else in Europe, so in Castile and León and in Aragon, the rulers found support for their policies among the townsmen. Feuding and independent nobles disturbed the peace of the country. The institution of the "Brotherhood" (*Hermandad*) in Castile originally created by townsmen for their protection, became a royal organization. Having thus strengthened their position, the rulers forced nobles to disgorge crown properties they had seized illegally. Unauthorized castles were dismantled. The headship of the wealthy, knightly crusading orders of Calatrava, Alcántara, and St. James of Compostella passed to the crown.

The government no longer rested in the hands of noble officials of the royal household but in bureaus of laymen drawn by the crown from the bourgeoisie. Broad lines of policy were laid down in the discussions of the royal council over which the sovereign presided. The rulers were careful, however, to preserve old institutions which had grown up under feudal conditions like, for example, the Cortes (a kind of parliament). The new sources of revenue obviated the necessity of going to them for money. The people approved the royal policy of overriding the privileges of the nobility.

Spanish rulers, especially Isabella in Castile, subjected the Church to their policy. The Church had led in the age-long struggle against the infidel invader. But Spaniards doubted the loyalty of the Moriscos (Moors converted to Christianity) and of the Jews who, it was suspected, sympathized with them. The danger was believed to be great because their conversion appeared to be one only in appearance, and, besides, there was much intermarriage between Spaniards and these people. Purity of faith became a passion, the one condition for patriotism and citizenship. To secure uniformity the Inquisition was authorized in 1480. The Spanish Inquisition was a religious institution in form and origin, but it operated as an arm of the state, an instrument of royal policy. Confiscation of the property of the convicted enriched the royal treasury. In addition to the Inquisition the crown also bound the clergy to its policies. The Concordat of 1482 made with Pope Sixtus IV provided that no bishop could be appointed without royal approval and that no papal letters, or bulls, could be announced without royal action. Nor were appeals in ecclesiastical cases to the Roman Curia permitted.

Ferdinand and Isabella's army, symbolic of the might of their new nation-state power, helped win for Spain leadership in European politics and military matters. The Spaniards were excellent soldiers. They believed that fighting the Moors was expected of all men. Spanish shepherd lads, especially those of Castile and León, were tough in physique, abstemious, and able to march and fight with the minimum of comfort regardless of heat or cold. Under Gonsalvo da Córdoba, one of the greatest of military geniuses, Spanish troops were given a new and revolutionary organization. Fighting Moors had been a matter chiefly of besieging fortified cities. But, when Spanish troops were sent to fight the French and their mercenaries in Italy, new methods had to be found.

The basic unit in the new Spanish army was the *cornelia* (later under Charles V called the *tercio*), a group of 6000 infantry divided into twelve companies of 500 soldiers each. Each company, arranged in the form of a square, was a separate unit. Its nucleus was a group of 200 swordsmen surrounded by an equal number of pikemen, each armed with a pike sixteen or eighteen feet long. The musketeers, 100 in number, were placed on the flanks of these squares. The enemy was assailed first by the shot of the muskets, next attacked by the pikemen, and finally confronted by the swords of the soldiers in the center of the square. This disposition of forces proved effective in delivering an attack. Not until the end of the sixteenth century, when Maurice of Orange of the United Provinces developed his army on a scientific engineering basis, did the Spanish *tercio* encounter its equal.

A new type of nation-state diplomacy, characteristic feature of Renaissance political life, went hand in hand with this leadership won by the

Spanish *tercios*. The new diplomacy had its origin in Italy, especially in Venice, and dates back as far as 1400. Practices in the labyrinth of Italian politics, especially in the age of the *signorie*, were copied. Ferdinand of Aragon, deeply immersed in the devious ways of Italian politics, had little to learn from them; his duplicity was as great as that of any successful Italian agent. Management of international matters was more efficient now than formerly because it became the custom to entrust state diplomatic matters to permanent ambassadors resident at a foreign court. Part of the new diplomacy was the negotiation of alliances which were to be secured by matrimonial arrangements.

IMPORTANCE OF THE LOW COUNTRIES

During the Renaissance and the Reformation the Low Countries (the Netherlands) held a unique position among the countries of Europe. Huddled around the mouths of the Scheldt, Meuse, and Rhine, and situated on the North Sea, these lands occupied the geographical center of western Europe. Proximity to thriving neighbors produced rich trade. From the British Isles came wool, hides, and tin; from Scandinavia, fresh and dried fish; from the Slavic east, wood, tar, pitch, and metals; from Spain, Portugal, and France, salt, wool, fruits, and choice wines; and by way of Germany and France, especially along the Rhine and Rhone rivers, there was busy trade with Venice, Genoa, Milan, and Florence, all of which had vigorous commercial contacts with the near and distant Orient.

Each of these Low Country states possessed striking characteristics. Nowhere else in northern Europe was there such flourishing trade and industry, so numerous a population, so many towns, so much wealth, such demand for silks, satins, wines, and articles of luxury. Flanders, situated between the Scheldt River and the North Sea, was predominantly industrial and commercial. Bruges, Ghent, and Ypres were famous for their cloth and leather manufacturing. Bruges had long been noted for its banking activity. But Flanders by 1500 had yielded its leadership to Brabant situated on the opposite side of the Scheldt. Its port of Antwerp at the head of the Scheldt estuary, Mechelen (Malines), and Brussels were eclipsing the towns of Flanders. Holland, between the Zuider Zee and the Meuse River, had long maintained trade with the German and Scandinavian and Slavic east. This trade was the foundation of the prosperity of Amsterdam. Rotterdam at the mouth of the Meuse had extensive business with German lands and also with eastern Europe. Dordrecht grew rich from its trade in wine from the Rhine and Moselle regions and from western France. The cloth industry flourished in Leiden. Middleburg in

Zeeland was a market for salt and other goods from France, Spain, and Portugal. Along the island shores of Zeeland passed much of the sea-borne traffic of northern and eastern Europe.

A number of native dynasties had governed these states before 1400. The Low Countries, excepting the Liégeois which was subject to the prince-bishop of Liége, passed into the hands of the Burgundian family of rulers. King John II of France (1350–1364) had invested his son Philip with the duchy of Burgundy. Philip also acquired the county of Burgundy (within the borders of the Empire, along the duchy of Burgundy) and, besides, married Margaret, heiress of Flanders. Upon the death of Count Louis of Flanders in 1384 Philip acquired Flanders, Artois, Nevers, Réthel, and the two Burgundies. This made him one of the great princes of Europe. His grandson Philip the Good (1419–1467), besides inheriting these titles, acquired (by purchase, by marriage, or by other means) Holland, Zeeland, Hainault, Brabant, Limburg, Namur, and Luxemburg.

From that moment the duke of Burgundy was the equal of any European prince, one to be reckoned with in any military, political, or diplomatic issue of the time. The fact that some of the duke's possessions, like Flanders and the duchy of Burgundy, were fiefs of the French crown, and others, like Holland, Brabant, Hainaut, Luxemburg, and the country of Burgundy, were held of the emperor brought Philip the Good into all sorts of political relations with these powers. These territories did not form a geographic whole, for the Low Country possessions were separated from the two Burgundies by the duchy of Lorraine. To unite these two parts and to form an independent and united kingdom of these lands at the expense of France and the Empire was the desire of Philip the Good's son, Charles the Rash (1469–1477). This dream was shattered by Charles' death at the Battle of Nancy on January 5, 1477. The French king Louis XI seized the duchy of Burgundy and also Charolais, since they were vacant fiefs. Charles' daughter, Mary of Burgundy, succeeded to the county of Burgundy and to her family's Low Country titles.

GERMANY'S STRATEGIC CHARACTER

The kingdom of Germany, situated in the heart of west central Europe and extending from the borders of France to those of Poland, was drained by the Rhine, Weser, Elbe, and Oder. South of these regions, the River Danube flowed east and drained the southern part of the realm. Germany comprised a great variety of states of divergent characteristics and was the largest political entity in Europe west of Russia.

Although a poor land so far as much of her soil was concerned, Germany enjoyed profitable commercial relations with her many neighbors. The great cities of the south, Basel, Strasbourg, Nuremberg, and Frankfort were built along the lanes of traffic between Italy and the Low Countries. As long as the Italians remained in possession of the lucrative trade with the Levant and the Orient, these German centers flourished. But their prosperity declined after Vasco da Gama sailed around the Cape of Good Hope and showed Portuguese traders how they could tap the commerce of the Orient and the Spice Islands by establishing a sailing route to Gôa and Calicut in India. Trade therefore shifted from Italian to Portuguese hands, and the cities of Germany could not compete with the world markets of Lisbon and Antwerp. But they nevertheless retained considerable prosperity, for the mountains of southern Germany supported a vigorous mining industry which furnished a large share of the metals needed in the industry of the day.

The northern parts of Germany, especially the Rhineland, also were an important area of trade and industry. Cologne, centrally situated on the Rhine, stood at the crossroads leading westward to Brabant and Flanders. Eastward the road led to Bremen, Hamburg, Lübeck, Danzig, Wisby, and Slavic ports further east, and Scandinavian towns to the north.

But, compared with the economic activity of northern and western Germany, that of the eastern parts of the country was more modest. While there were towns in those areas as, for example, Frankfort on the Oder, Prague in Bohemia, and Vienna in Austria, the population of eastern Germany was less numerous than in the Rhineland. These cities produced raw materials, wood, grain, and leather for the more populous lands of western Germany. They also delivered copper, salt, fish, and fats, the latter being in demand in the cloth industry of the Low Countries.

It is instructive to note that the mighty progress in economic life which had taken place by the fourteenth century and the social and political transformations in the life of Europe which accompanied it failed to make powerful rulers of the German kings. The long struggle over investitures, the quarrels of the kings with feudal princes, and the extinction of several royal houses, the last being the Hohenstaufen family in the thirteenth century, ruined the crown and robbed it of effectiveness. The sport of rival feudal ambitions, the German monarchy had become elective, unchecked by a crown which kept a firm hand upon governmental activity, and so practically independent feudal states came into existence. Among such were the Low Countries, the Swiss Confederation, and the greater German powers of Bavaria, Saxony, Brandenburg, and Bohemia. In addition, there were petty states and free imperial towns. Besides these secular powers there were great ecclesiastical states such as Mainz, Trier, and Cologne, and also a number of less important ones like Fulda. The rulers of these states, great or small, managed their administration, justice, and coinage with scant consideration of royal wishes. The king of Germany had practically no treasury, no all-embracing political organization, no efficient system of courts, nor an effective royal army. The king lived mainly on his own and paid the expenses of government largely out of incomes derived from his family possessions.

In the government of the Empire, there was, besides the Emperor and his court, the German Diet, a body which represented the states of the realm. The first college of the diet was that of the seven Electors who chose the King. Three of these electors were churchmen: the Archbishops of Mainz, Trier, and Cologne. The other four were secular princes: the duke of Saxony, the margrave of Brandenburg, the count palatine of the Rhine, and the king of Bohemia. Below this first college were two others, one composed of the princes, ecclesiastical as well as lay, and the other made up of free imperial cities. Such was the rivalry in the diet and such the conflict between the Emperor and the diet that there was little effective governmental action. Nevertheless, there was a growing German national sentiment centered in the Emperor as ruler of the empire.

The elected king of Germany became the Emperor of the Holy Roman Empire in a ceremony in which the pope had the traditional right to bestow the imperial diadem. The Emperor also bore the title of king of the Lombards, a dignity which possessed little reality but nevertheless made him an Italian prince and gave him an active interest in the politics of Italy. This dignity of the imperial title represented two remarkable ideas. The first was the continuity of the ancient empire of Rome. The second, and more important idea, was that while the Church, being universal, held sway spiritually and morally, the Emperor was to unite under his temporal rule all men, to enable them to live in charity rendering justice to all. This noble conception failed to be realized in spite of the Christian foundations upon which it rested. Not all Christian rulers of the Middle Ages would recognize the Emperor's headship. The feudal princes within the Empire sought to further their own interests and so prevented the Emperor from successfully ruling all men. Here theory was contradicted by plain facts.

THE SPANISH HAPSBURG COMBINATION

These widely scattered Spanish, Netherlands, and Hapsburg states were destined to have an amazing role in the history of Europe during the Renaissance and the Reformation. For by an extraordinary set of events they were to be inherited by the grandson of Ferdinand and Isabella of Spain and of Maximilian of Austria. This grandson was Charles V who, in addition to bearing these titles, was to be elected King of the Romans, later to be Emperor.

To make clear how the concentration of these states in the hands of Charles V came about we must review the complex family history of the Spanish and Burgundian ruling houses. First, when King Ferdinand II of Aragon died in 1516, title to Aragon and Naples and Sicily passed to his grandson, Charles V. Second, on Isabella's death in 1504 the crown of Castile and León, conquered Granada, and the Americas were acquired by Charles' father, Philip the Fair, who on his death in 1507 passed them on to his son. Third, the Low Countries fell to Charles as being the heir of Philip the Fair (d. 1507) and son of Mary of Burgundy who at her death in 1482 was ruler of most of the states of the Low Countries.

The point to note is that at the Emperor Maximilian's death in 1519 the properties of the Hapsburgs in Germany were acquired by his grandson Charles V. This house had sprung from obscure feudal origins in Switzerland. Acquisition of the duchy of Austria, which occupied a strategic point in the Danube Valley, started the family on its career of aggrandizement. The dukes of Austria in time became also dukes of Carinthia, Carniola, and Tyrol. Since the death of the Emperor Sigismund of the House of Luxemburg in 1437, the Hapsburg rulers were kings of Germany and also bore the crown of the Holy Roman Empire.

Tenacity of purpose brought even greater success to the Hapsburgs when Maximilian, heir-to-be of the Hapsburg properties, in 1478 married Mary of Burgundy. This union with the heiress of the two Burgundies (duchy and county) and of most of the Low Countries was to place the Hapsburg rulers at the pinnacle of power. Their son, Philip the Fair, was to inherit Maximilian's Hapsburg properties, but, as he died in 1507, these were to pass to his son Charles. In 1519, upon the death of Charles' paternal grandfather, the Emperor Maximilian, he received Austria, Carniola, Carinthia, Styria, Tyrol, and other scattered titles in southern Germany. In that same year Charles was elected king of Germany, to be crowned emperor of the Holy Roman Empire in 1530. Thus it happened that Spanish, Burgundian, Hapsburg, and Imperial titles all came to pass into Charles' possession.

The wheel of fortune was to have one more turn in favor of the Hapsburg combination, one that was to add both wealth and power to Charles' position. In 1521 Charles made a division of his properties granting to his younger brother, Ferdinand, the Hapsburg lands of Austria, Styria, Tyrol, Carinthia, and Carniola. In that same year Ferdinand married

Anna, sister of King Louis of Bohemia and Hungary. Once more a turn in family fortunes favored the Hapsburgs. For in 1526 Louis was defeated and slain by the Turks in the Battle of Mohácz, and his crowns thereupon passed to Ferdinand.

TASKS AND LABORS OF CHARLES V

The international political situation bore a menacing aspect. Charles had inherited Naples to which Francis I of France (1515–1547) might revive his claims at any time, for had not the French king claimed the Angevin heritage for which Charles VIII had marched into Italy in 1494? To make matters worse, Francis had inherited the claim of his father-in-law Louis XII (1498–1515) to the duchy of Milan, an imperial fief and as such claimed by Charles on grounds of vacancy. Besides, Charles could not peaceably accept the loss of the duchy of Burgundy which Louis XI had seized upon the death in 1482 of Mary of Burgundy, Charles' grandmother.

Rich and powerful as Charles appeared, his scattered interests demanded more power and greater wisdom than any man possessed. Besides his numerous wars with Francis I which involved the question of ascendancy in Europe's affairs, Charles had to defend imperial interests against the Turks who, as we learned, defeated the Hungarians at Mohácz in 1526. In addition, the issues—religious and political—raised by Luther's break with the Church greatly increased his difficulties.

POWER AND POSITION OF FRANCE

France occupied the part of Europe between the Pyrenees and the Empire, thus isolating the Hapsburg realms of Castile and Aragon from Germany. This division of its territories materially weakened Hapsburg power and successfully challenged its political and military ascendancy in Europe.

In 1453 France had emerged victorious in the Hundred Years' War. This struggle had its origin in the desire of the French crown to absorb the feudal property of the English king who owed homage to the French king for Aquitaine. Philip VI (1328–1350) confiscated Edward III's title to it. Edward (1327–1377) claimed the throne of France on the ground that he was the nearest male heir. But Philip and the French rejected this claim on the ground that Philip was the nearest male heir through male descent. Although the war began with the attack of England and her allies, the Empire and the Low Countries, most princes in western Europe at one time or another were drawn into the struggle. As in the case of most wars the Hundred Years' War had far reaching and unforeseen consequences. The battles of Crécy (1346), Poitiers (1356), and Agincourt (1415), won with the help of the longbow employed in the English army, were disastrous to France, for they placed that country at the mercy of the marauding bands in English pay.

The implications of these victories with the longbow were scarcely realized at the time. Crécy, Poitiers, and Agincourt revealed that the day of military power exclusively in the hands of a mailed chivalry would soon come to a close. For some time peasants armed with scythes, flails, and clubs, especially when protected by swampy terrain, had shown that they could defeat armies of mounted knights. In 1302 at Courtrai on the muddy banks of a creek the guildsmen of Flanders destroyed the finest chivalry of France. During the course of the Hundred Years' War gunpowder began to be used, and firing arms were constantly being perfected. Against these weapons mail-clad mounted chivalry were scarcely a match. Nor were they safe in their castles of stone.

During this war the dukes of Burgundy, once established in the Low Countries, asserted their separatist interests and sided with the English for economic and political reasons. But the tide did not all run in favor of the English. For in the reign of Charles VII (1422–1461) occurred a remarkable manifestation of French patriotism. Joan of Arc, a simple peasant maiden from Lorraine, inspired by her faith, so fired the soldiers with love for their fatherland that, supported by them, she was able to seize Orléans in 1429. Thereafter disaster dogged the English and their Burgundian allies until finally in 1453 at the Battle of Castillon the city of Bordeaux, last remnant of English authority in southern France, fell into French hands.

Following the wonderful deeds of Joan of Arc, the royal power increased rapidly, thanks to the newly developed patriotism among the people, to the blessings of peace, and to the wealth and reviving energy of the towns. The crown developed an army which had none of the drawbacks of feudal levies. In 1445 a force of cavalry was created, known as the *gens d'ordonnance*. Three years later a similar force of infantry was organized, the *francs tireurs*. This manifestation of royal strength enabled the crown to develop an administrative bureaucracy, drawn from the bourgeoisie and the lower ranks of the feudal class. Owing everything to the crown, such persons worked for its advancement, supporting it against the powerful nobility.

With the accession of Louis XI (1461–1483) there was further progress in the direction of royal absolutism. The king quadrupled the taxes. He kept a tight control over internal as well as external affairs. He suppressed the feudal aspirations of the nobility during the War of the Public Weal in 1464 and plotted to overthrow the power of the dukes of Burgundy. He perfected his army, creating the best heavy cavalry in Europe. Such were the resources of the crown that the king could afford a superior artillery. He commanded the best engineering skill in constructing fortresses and defending them.

Economically, France by the close of the Middle Ages had become a wealthy state and was an object of envy to her neighbors during the Renaissance. A large part of her population was agricultural—hardy and vigorous. Her bourgeoisie had developed the commerce and the manufactures of the land. A compact nation-state, economically self-sufficient and militarily powerful, France was able to defend her borders in Burgundy, in the Low Countries, and in Navarre. Such was France's strength that her armies also were able to oppose Hapsburg policy in Italy, especially in the Duchy of Milan. This new military policy, initiated by Charles VIII (1483–1498) and continued by Louis XII (1498–1515), Francis I (1515–1547), and Henry II (1547–1559) was to disturb the life of Europe for many years until the abdication of the Emperor Charles V in 1556.

ENGLAND POLITICALLY INSULATED BUT NOT ISOLATED

We have now to deal with those states of Europe outside Italy which were able to follow a more or less independent policy toward the perennial conflicts between France and the Hapsburg combination. The most important of these was England.

This country had developed a high degree of governmental centralization beginning with the Norman Conquest in 1066. Feudalism in England never was so victorious there in its decentralizing tendencies as it had been in France before Philip Augustus (1180–1223) or in Germany after the death of Emperor Frederick II in 1250. Hence the authority of the royal courts was unquestioned: the king's writs were always obeyed. An administrative system was perfected which strengthened the hands of the king. The English Parliament in which representatives of the towns and counties had their seats, as well as the nobility and the higher clergy, was a powerful body. It was no exaggerated claim, therefore, when Richard II (1377–1399) declared he was an emperor in his own realm, undoubted superior over all his subjects.

Although the kings of England ruled over the most wealthy sections of the British Islands, they never were able to absorb the Celtic parts of the islands. Scotland never was to be conquered by them. The Celtic population of Wales was reduced to obedience during the reign of Edward I (1272–1307), but the Welsh never were incorporated into the English system until the close of the Middle Ages. In Wales the English had been able to show their superiority when fighting on level ground, but they had difficulty in driving the Welsh from their hilly strongholds.

In Ireland the boggy nature of the country made it impossible for the English to profit from superior methods and better equipment. Only around Dublin, the area known as the Pale, was English authority accepted; in other parts Irish tribal life maintained itself, and the people remained defiant toward the intruders. The island became a haunt of the enemies of the crown. Hence came the policy of binding Ireland more closely to the English crown. By Poyning's Law (1494) English parliamentary acts were declared binding upon Ireland, and the Irish Parliament was forbidden to make laws without prior consent of the king. The tie between the two countries, however, was loose, and Ireland remained a dissatisfied land.

England was a prosperous country. Proximity to the Low Countries stimulated her general well-being. Much wool had been produced in the Midlands and in northern counties. Manufacture of cloth was a chief source of wealth. Export of grain was increasing, and tin and lead were produced in important quantities. The English bourgeoisie grew rich and influential from trade in these products. The king taxed his subjects and filled his coffers with cash. As the royal power increased, England stepped forth as one of the most efficiently governed states in Europe.

From the standpoint of military resources England did not measure favorably with France under Charles VIII or with Aragon and Castile under Ferdinand and Isabella. There was no surplus population among the peasantry from which the English crown could draw a large number of infantry. Nor was any great effort made to build up an effective artillery as in France. The ancient longbow remained a favorite weapon. Nor could the English foot soldier equal that of the Spanish. The fact that England was an island gave the crown a feeling of security. An extensive military establishment of the new type was hardly needed, for the English had been ejected from France at the close of the Hundred Years' War. Only Calais remained in their hands. The splendid naval development which marked later Tudor times, especially under Elizabeth (1558–1602), had scarcely begun.

The Wars of the Roses (1455–1485) were a prominent feature in the social history of the time. The English nobility cherished feudal ideals, perpetuated a military tradition, and during the thirty years of these wars the two branches of the royal families of Lancaster and York maintained a feud. Finally Henry Tudor, later Henry VII, defeated the Yorkist Richard III (1483–1485) at Bosworth Field in 1485.

A new age dawned. The feudality was discredited, trade and manufactures increased, and the future lay with the towns and the bourgeoisie. Patriotic Englishmen supported the new Tudor dynasty, for they did not want a return of the troubled days of the Roses. So in England there was a shift from older feudal ways to a more mercantile state. The future was to witness the growth of a navy, the increase of royal power, an outburst of patriotism, and an increase of material wealth.

England's policy toward the perennial contest between the Spanish Hapsburg and the French combinations of power was determined by several factors. Too important to be ignored by either of these political coalitions, and favored by England's geographical position, the king now favored one group, then the other, according to his best interests.

SCOTLAND'S STRENGTH AND WEAKNESS

Although situated in the northern extremity of the British Isles, Scotland was not out of touch with the main currents of European civilization. From the north and east Scotland was in constant contact with Scandinavia. From the south English influences overleaped the Scottish boundary.

The Scottish people of Celtic origin living in the region known as the Highlands still adhered to their Celtic customs and used the Gaelic language. This part of Scotland, mostly mountainous or covered with heath, comprised the region north of the Clyde and west of a line extending northward across the upper waters of the Dee and Spey and westward to Inverness. The population of the Highlands was divided into clans, each of which had a chief, and there was some feuding. They raised cattle and supplemented their income from hunting and fishing. They also raided the farmers of the Lowlands, plundered their fields, and seized their cattle. The Highlanders, intensely loyal to their clans, were good fighters but loath to subject themselves to discipline.

In the Lowlands conditions were very different. English influences were powerful, and the original Celtic ways were profoundly changed so that the Lowlands in social organization and economic life looked much like northern England. Towns came into existence, and there was trade and some manufacture. But the nobles were powerful like the clans and carried on bitter feuds.

The royal power never could subdue its turbulent subjects. Parliament, made up of the nobility (at least in one of its branches), represented these turbulent elements. The kings of the House of Stewart suffered from many minorities and from regencies, so that the royal administration failed to develop in Scotland as it did in England.

Relations of Scotland and France and her allies with the Hapsburg combination were determined chiefly by the policy of the English crown. The Scots carried on an age-long feud with the English kings who insisted they had some title to the throne of Scotland; so, whenever England was leagued against France, Scotland joined France against England.

NEUTRALITY OF THE SWISS

A confederation of small cantons in the Alps, Switzerland was situated between France and lands which formed parts of the Hapsburg combination. Switzerland was part of the kingdom of Germany and so subject to the emperor of the Holy Roman Empire. The invasion of Italy by Charles VIII drew the Swiss into the perennial contest between the kings of France and the rulers of the Hapsburg House, each of whom sought ascendancy in Italy.

Originally the confederation embraced only Uri, Schwyz (from which the name Switzerland is derived), and Unterwalden. These cantons had joined a union for defense in 1291. During the next two centuries fifteen rural and urban communities joined this nucleus, from Lucerne in 1332 to Geneva in 1526 and Vaud in 1536. Each canton managed its internal affairs. The diet representing the entire confederation (each canton sent representatives to it) took care of questions touching all the cantons. In theory this confederation was a league of communities owing obedience to the empire, but such was the weakness of the imperial crown that the Swiss paid little attention to this relationship.

THE STATES OF SCANDINAVIA

The peoples inhabiting the Scandinavian peninsula on the northern confines of the Germanic world had, notwithstanding their geographical remoteness from the centers of European activity, contributed extensively to European wealth and culture. Their sagas tell of the conquering zeal of the Viking heroes of the North who overran much of Europe. Conversion to Christianity had introduced the Scandinavians more directly into the family of European peoples. From them they received the liturgy, art, and thought of the Church. They produced quantities of fish, grain, metals, and timber products, brought to market by the merchants of the German Hanse.

Of the Scandinavian kingdoms, Denmark was the smallest but most influential. It occupied the peninsula projecting from the German mainland, lay between the Baltic and North Seas, and early became prosperous, Copenhagen being the chief mart of the North. The realm of Sweden, to which Finland had been joined in the thirteenth century, occupied the larger part of the northern peninsula, and, facing eastward, provided a link with the Slavic lands. Norway, on the west half of this peninsula, faced the Atlantic and colonized Iceland during the ninth century and Greenland during the tenth.

Queen Margaret of Denmark (d. 1421), as regent, united the states of Scandinavia in the Union of Kalmar (1397). There was to be one crown and a common external policy. Each kingdom was to preserve its own laws and develop its own institutions. But there was much social, political, and economic diversity which kept the three realms from becoming a united kingdom. In Denmark there were an assertive nobility and a half dependent peasantry, but the powers of the crown were well developed. In Sweden there were a powerful nobility and a dependent peasantry, but the crown was less powerful. In Norway, less developed politically and having a freer peasantry, the organs of central government remained embryonic. In none of these lands was the town class as decisive a factor as in other European lands. Much of the wealth of these countries was in the hands of the German Hanseatic League. Copenhagen, Stockholm, Lund, and Bergen were economic outposts of the Hanse.

STATES EAST OF GERMANY

Poland. The Polish people, Slavic in speech and custom, emerged from obscurity during the tenth century. Their kingdom came to extend over the valley of the Vistula (south of Thorn) along the German border as far as the Carpathian mountains. Their social organization was simple —a vigorous peasantry and an assertive nobility which was able to control the king. The conversion of the Poles to the Catholic faith in 966 and the formation of the see of Gnesen in the year 1000 brought them into the family of western European peoples. A town class, largely German, grew up by the side of native Poles. Cracow and Warsaw became important towns. The reign of Ladislaus II (1384–1434) marked a turning point in Poland's history, for that king also was grand duke of Lithuania.

Lithuania. Much obscurity exists about the origins of the non-Slavic Lithuanians who inhabited the region of the Memel east of Prussia and

Poland. The Lithuanians extended their sway over the peoples living in the region drained by the Pruth, Bug, and Dnieper rivers, thus controlling the Ukraine and other parts of what since has become Russian. Like the Poles, the Lithuanians stood in close cultural and economic relations with the German and Christian West. In 1386 when their grand duke Ladislaus II (1384–1434) married the heiress Jadwiga of Poland, the Lithuanians turned to Catholic Christianity and in the following year were given their own bishop at Vilna (subject to Polish Gnesen). In 1413 the Union of Horodeo provided that the kingdom of Poland and grand duchy of Lithuania were to be equal, their king to be chosen by the joint diets of the two states, and that they were to have separate but parallel organization.

Prussia and the Baltic States. The Prussian-Baltic lands, mainly non-Slavic in speech and custom, stretched from the Vistula valley to the Gulf of Finland. From an early date German monks and knights visited them; so these lands, like Poland and Lithuania to the south, were brought under German and Christian influences. During the crusading era the Brothers of the Sword, organized in 1202, established themselves in Lithuania and brought Christianity to Estonia and Kurland. Their success was paralleled in Prussia by another monastic crusading order, the Teutonic Knights, founded in Palestine but transferred to Prussia in 1230. Seven years later the Brothers of the Sword united with them; by 1400 the diverse peoples of these Baltic provinces had become Christianized.

Hungary. The Magyars, speaking a Finno-Ugrian language, lived along the Theiss and Danube rivers and eastward as far as the Carpathian mountains. Like their northern neighbors, the Poles, they too were subject to German influences. German traders visited them. Missionaries from Byzantium and the German West brought them the teachings of Christ. Converted in the year 1000, their king St. Stephen (997–1038) erected the archbishopric of Gran in 1001. In this rich agricultural region lived an industrious peasantry, a politically assertive nobility, and a town element of relatively slight importance. The royal family intermarried with the Hapsburg House, thus strengthening Hungarian ties with the German West. But Hungary was the victim of Turkish assaults from the East. Her army was destroyed on the field of Mohácz in 1526, her king Louis II was killed, and her crown passed to the Hapsburg House.

Russia. The vast area stretching eastward from Lithuania and Hungary to the Ural mountains during medieval times witnessed the emergence of the Russian people. Although obscure in their origins, it is certain that this Slavic people inherited much from the ancient Scythians. But they owed more to Greek Constantinople. So Vladimir the Great

(980–1015), ruling from Kiev, embraced Christianity in 988, which intensified cultural relations with the Byzantine Empire, especially with Constantinople. Trade also grew, and Kiev on the Dnieper and Novgorod on the Volkhov developed along the river route between the Black Sea and the Baltic.

But the Kiev principality, whose prestige Vladimir the Great raised to a high point, succumbed to the might of the Mongols, a Tartar people from beyond the Urals who completed their seizure of southern Russia in 1243. Their power came to an end in 1480, during the reign of Ivan III the Great (1462–1505) who ruled from Moscow, which was to become the center of the new Russian state. Ivan proclaimed himself tsar, regarded himself as successor of the emperors of Constantinople, which had fallen in 1453, married an heiress of the Palaeologue rulers of Byzantium, fought the overextended grand duchy of Lithuania, entered into relations with western European countries, and imported Italian Renaissance architects.

POWER AND THREAT OF THE TURKS

Early in the thirteenth century the Ottoman Turks, a Finno-Ugrian people, moved out of their lands east of the Caspian Sea and assaulted the Byzantine Empire which through the Middle Ages had been a protecting bulwark of the Christian West. But now that impoverished state with its declining agriculture, its vanishing commerce, and depleted treasury was in no position to drive back the invaders. Taking advantage of a bitter struggle in Constantinople between rivals for the throne, the Sultan Orkhan crossed the Dardanelles and established himself in Europe. Succeeding sultans invaded Thrace, proceeded up the Maritza, seized Bulgaria, and set up their government at Adrianople. Constantinople, commanding the narrow waters connecting the Black and Aegean seas and guarding the land passage from Asia Minor to Europe, seemed impregnable. But Sultan Mohammed II (1451–1481) determined to take it. The mighty city fell on May 29, 1453, and thus was closed a long history in one final act of heroic resistance.

It must not be thought that the Turks were a barbarous folk who won their victories only through nomadic violence. Their armies were well organized and excellently equipped. Their generals were as competent as any of the day. The bulk of their army was composed of cavalry recruited from Moslem landholders who owed military service to the sultan. The Janizaries, a group of 8000 professional foot soldiers originally recruited from captives taken in war but later drawn from the subject

Christian population as a kind of tribute, formed the nucleus of the sultan's army and constituted his guard. Turkish artillery, markedly superior to anything European princes could bring into the field, was purchased from Italian and other manufacturers.

Like their army, the government of the Turks during this period was efficient. The sultan, head of the state, was absolute; obedience to him was inculcated by the Mohammedan faith. The Sublime Porte, as the government was called, centered in the sultan's seraglia, or palace. The grand vizier, or premier, the councilors, and other officials formed a supreme advisory body. The grand vizier was head also of the civil and military servants, drawn exclusively from the Moslem subjects. The absolute character of the sultan's rule was due to the absence of influential nobles, clergy, merchants, and conservative peasants determined to keep their rights. The turkish government's income, greater than the income of any other European state, was derived from tribute levied upon its subjects who were mainly Christian.

Following his conquest of Constantinople in 1453, Sultan Mohammed II continued his conquests. In 1462 he warred on Venice's widespread possessions, but did not drive her from the Mediterranean. His successors extended their power over the as yet unconquered parts of the Balkans. Suliman the Magnificent (1520–1566) drove the Knights of St. John from Rhodes in 1522 and assaulted Hungary whose King Louis II he slew in the Battle of Mohácz (1526). The Turkish army now stood at the border of the German empire, poised to kill. The Fleming Augier de Busbecq (1522–1592), diplomatic representative of the Hapsburg rulers at the Sublime Porte, summed up the situation: "When I compare the difference between their soldiers and ours I stand amazed to think what will be the outcome. For on their side there is a mighty, strong, and wealthy empire, great armies, experience in war, a veteran soldiery, a long series of victories, patience in toil, concord, order, discipline, frugality, and vigilance. On our side there is public want, private luxury, soldiers refractory, commanders covetous, a contempt of discipline, licentiousness, rashness, drunkenness, gluttony; and what is worst of all, they are used to conquer, we to be conquered." Small wonder that Europeans trembled at the Turkish threat!

Chapter 2

POLITICAL MILIEU OF THE RENAISSANCE AND REFORMATION: STATES OF ITALY

S TRIKING DIVERSITY characterized the political geography of the peninsula of Italy during the closing Middle Ages, a diversity which contributed significantly to the economic, political, mental, and moral life of each of the Italian states during the Renaissance. These influences, at once subtle and varied, expressed themselves in remarkable ways. In this chapter we shall describe some of the more remarkable social and political peculiarities of each of the states of Renaissance Italy. This will help us understand some of their policies during the great wars of the period.

THE GEOGRAPHY OF ITALY

Three peninsulas jut out from the continent of Europe into the Mediterranean. The Spanish peninsula, westernmost of these, divides the Atlantic from the Mediterranean and is separated from the continent of Africa by the Strait of Gibraltar. The eastern peninsula, the Balkan, divides the Black Sea from the Aegean, an extension of the Mediterranean, and is separated from the continent of Asia by the Dardanelles, the Sea of Marmora, and the Bosporus. Centrally situated in the landlocked Mediterranean are the peninsula of Italy and the nearby Italian islands of Sicily, Sardinia, and Corsica.

Italy is surrounded by the waters of several seas. Its eastern shores are bathed by the Adriatic which extends along the entire length of the peninsula. To the south is the Ionian, separated from the Adriatic by the Strait of Otranto. To the west the coast of Italy is washed by the Tyrrhenian Sea and the Gulf of Genoa. Snow-capped mountains of the Alps set Italy off from the rest of Europe. But though separated from its neighbors by seas and mountains Italy by no means was a country insulated from foreign influences. For external cultural forces of all kinds found lodgment in Italy. In return, Italy taught the rest of Europe many a lesson in the art of civilization.

The boot of Italy, from the Alps to the southernmost tip of the toe, is about 700 miles long. The Apennines, springing from the Alps in the north, bend eastwards, thus with the Alps form the rim of the Lombard plain. Turning southward, the range covers a large part of the peninsula. The Apennines, dominating the peninsula, reach their highest point in Umbria where the Gran Sasso d'Italia has a height of nearly 9500 feet. The width of the boot is about 100 miles except in the region of Tuscany where the distance between Piombino on the Tyrrhenian and Ancona on the Adriatic is about 170 miles.

The northern part of Italy between the Alps and the Apennines comprises the extensive plains of Lombardy. Throughout its entire length of about 170 miles, from Monte Viso in Piedmont to the Adriatic, the Po forms its central waterway, receiving numerous affluents which spring from the melting snows of the Alps.

In addition to this Italian mainland there are a number of Italian islands. The largest of these is Sicily, lying at the toe of the Italian boot, separated from it by the Strait of Messina and having about 10,000 square miles of territory. Next in size is Sardinia, north of Sicily. North of Sardinia lies Corsica, smallest of the three, having an area of about 3750 square miles.

Italy west of the Apennines range possesses a climate resembling that of southern California. Olives grow in Sicily and Naples. Oranges are produced in Sicily and in the peninsula northward as far as Naples. The rivers of Italy are short and useless from the standpoint of commerce. The Apennines, too low to permit perpetual snow to lodge on their peaks, in early spring fill the short streams whose raging torrents soon are drained by the nearby sea. The Po, however, is of some importance as a means of commercial transport, but the streams that pour into it from the Alpine peaks are insignificant from the merchants' point of view. Except in the Po Valley, in Tuscany, in the rich plains behind the cities of Naples and Bari, and in Sicily, agriculture is practiced on a small scale. The extensive hilly slopes produce a wine matchless in quality. Such are the age-old physical features of Italy set before man to challenge his creative skill. At all times a parsimonious nature has bred poverty, a feature of the life of many Italians during the Age of the Renaissance.

ITALY
AT THE TIME OF THE
RENAISSANCE

GRAPHIC PRESENTATION SERVICES · Inc

POLITICAL DEVELOPMENT IN NORTH ITALY
FROM COMMUNE TO SIGNORIA

The communities of Italy, especially those in the northern and central parts of the peninsula, responded vigorously to the mighty social, political, and economic changes that came with the economic revolution during the eleventh century. Under the mighty stimulus of such external forces and the logic of internal contingencies, these communities passed through two stages of growth.

The first of these stages was the commune, a name applied to the self-governing Italian communities of the Middle Ages. Following the disintegration of the Roman Empire, prosperity had declined in Italy. The over-throw of the Ostrogothic kingdom in 553 further ruined the public welfare, even though Sicily and the southern part of the peninsula, including Naples and Bari, and also Ravenna, head of the exarchate, remained subject to Byzantium. The invasion of the Lombards into northern and central Italy, beginning in 568, added disaster to confusion. Joined to the kingdom of Charlemagne in 772, northern Italy shared in the disintegration of the Carolingian state during the next two centuries. The regime of the rulers of the Holy Roman Empire was essentially feudal. However, under the impulse of trade which was noticeable in all parts of Europe at this time numerous towns sprang into existence.

The leaders—merchants, petty nobles, ecclesiastics, and craftsmen—possessed a keen sense of solidarity, dictated by their material interests. They were called upon to defend their communal rights against local princes and noblemen. They jealously protected their fellow merchants against robbers. They built the communal walls, organized the communal soldiery, collected taxes for the communal chest, and enacted statutes to direct the social, religious, economic, and political interests of the commune. The people (*popolo*) met in public squares in *parlamenti* (singular: *parlamento*) convoked by the ringing of bells, to consider political propositions, determine public policy, and elect officials who usually were called consuls. Their number varied from place to place; there might be as many as twelve consuls in any one commune. The consuls, a college of officials, governed the communes in a manner at once aristocratic and popular, at least in earlier times.

A social problem threatened the stability of the rule of the consuls. The *popolo grasso* (wealthier groups) controlled the more important businesses which catered to the ever growing economic wants of Europe. The *popolo minuto* (lesser folk) were composed of the poorer groups who served the demands of the local townsmen, or worked for the *popolo grasso*. To the *popolo minuto* belonged the shoemakers, carpenters, bakers, butchers, oil venders, and also the workers in the silk and woolen cloth industries. The *popolo grasso* and *popolo minuto* dominated the government.

Below these socially and economically favored classes was a group which, for want of a better name, we may call the proletariat. Ill feeling was common; there were violent uprisings fed by factional disputes and dangerous feuds. To put an end to such dissensions it became customary during the thirteenth and fourteenth centuries to entrust the direction of communal affairs to some person, a *signore*, or in some instances to a group of *signori*. Ambitious men often seized the *signoria* (as the government of *signori* was called) and maintained themselves in power, defying every effort to dislodge them. Such rulers, having illegally seized the power of the state, were called "tyrants."

There was another reason for the establishment of the *signoria*. In medieval society which lacked the steadying arm of a powerful state as we have in modern times, feuds were common. In the towns as well as in the country a feuding nobility disturbed the peace. In the cities there were feuds between nobles, between patricians, and between groups of craftsmen. The ancient and bitter hatred of the Montagues and the Capulets in Shakespeare's *Romeo and Juliet* illustrates such a condition.

The *signoria* created the fifteenth-century Italian state of the Renaissance. In the place of the tumultuous communal democracies of thirteenth- and fourteenth-century Italy, the *signoria* adopted an effective policy to promote the interests of townsmen. It subjected the countryside to the regime of cities. Orderly management of political matters (including justice, police, coinage, and war) made states more effective than the communes had been in former feudal days. The *signoria*, frequently under the direction of a tyrant, helped bring on a novel attitude toward life. Government tended to become absolutist, its policy self-sufficient, and its attitude secularist. In these matters the Italian state exerted much influence. This was well summarized by Niccolò Machiavelli (1469–1527) who in his *Prince* (*Il Principe*) took the view that the immediate interests of princes (that is, *signori* and tyrants) should, when it seemed necessary or advisable, be guided by self-interest and not by considerations of morality or religion.

Tyrants usually maintained their authority by the use of professional generals (*condottieri*) who commanded armies of mercenaries (*condotti*). The use of such soldiers became a characteristic feature of late fourteenth- and the fifteenth-century Italian Renaissance life. During communal times in Italy, the citizenry were as incapable of defending themselves as they were incompetent to govern themselves in peace and security. The life of soldiers seemed incompatible with a bourgeoisie eager in the pursuit of wealth; so fighting was left more and more to professional soldiers who sold their services to the highest bidder. Having no loyalties, they had no national interests to serve, knew no political antipathies.

Condottieri did little real fighting, for they sought their objectives by skillful maneuvering. When the citizenry no longer knew how to defend itself, governments became easy prey to ambitious generals. *Condottieri* often were successful tyrants, as in the case of Francesco Sforza, who in 1450 was able to establish his house as dynastic rulers in Milan. This state of affairs boded ill for the freedom of the Italian states. It brought on a catastrophe in Italian political life when a foreign soldiery under Charles VIII of France invaded the peninsula in order to seize the kingdom of Naples (1494–1495).

CITY AND DUCHY OF MILAN

The prosperous city and duchy of Milan, commonly called the Milanese, were situated in the heart of Lombardy between the Ticino and the Adda rivers, streams which connect Lake Maggiore and Lake Como with the Po. From time immemorial Milan had been the center of life in the Po Valley. From Venice to the east, from Genoa to the west, from Florence, Siena, and Rome to the south, and from the towns on the surrounding Lombard plain came goods and traders of all sorts. To the north were the Brenner and Splügen passes through which poured articles of trade and manufacture to and from industrial and commercial centers in France, the Low Countries, Germany, and other northern lands. And far beyond lay the regions of the East, lands of fabulous wealth.

Agriculturally, the Milanese occupied a well-watered plain of immense fertility. From ancient times a numerous and hard-working peasantry had cultivated the land. Villages dotted the plain, and some of them became important centers of commerce and industry. Foodstuffs were produced in abundance. The only necessary article to be imported was salt from the nearby basins at Commachio in the lands subject to the dukes of Ferrara and Modena.

Due to its ecclesiastical connections (for several members of the family held high office in the Church) and due to its "Ghibelline" friendship with the Emperors, the Visconti family were able to seize the *signoria* and establish themselves as tyrants over this powerful community. Their policy was typical of despots, and, as such, few other families of tyrants were so successful. Matteo Visconti, "the Great," who died in 1322, acquired the title of Imperial Vicar from the Emperor Henry VII in 1311. Secure in their ascendant power, the family extended its authority. Gian Galeazzo Visconti who ruled from 1385 to 1402, appeared as a figure of European importance. His wealth enabled him to hire an imposing army of soldiers and purchase the services of Italy's most famous *condottieri*. He annexed many parts of the Lombard plain, including Verona, and even threatened to extend his power over Perugia, Florence, and Siena. Thus by a complicated chain of events the Visconti family was able to bring under its sway the central part of the Po Valley between Savoy to the west and Venice to the east and between the Alps to the north and the Apennines to the south. The seal of Visconti authority was placed upon this wealthy state when the Emperor Wenzel in 1395 raised the Milanese to the dignity of a duchy.

VENICE: QUEEN OF THE ADRIATIC

The Republic of Venice, in contrast to landlocked Milan, built its empire upon the seas. This haughty Queen of the Adriatic was built on a few islands in the shallow waters off the north Adriatic coast. Through these low and sandy islands flows the Canal Grande shaped like an inverted letter S. At the end of the canal and facing the Adriatic are the Piazza of San Marco and the Piazzetta. Here stand the noble basilica of San Marco and facing it the stately *companile*. By the side of the cathedral is the palace of the Doges. On the Piazzetta stand two columns, one surmounted by the winged lion of St. Mark and the other by St. Theodore with the crocodile, both emblematic of Venetian wealth and power, for these two saints point to early relations with the land of the Nile. Halfway up the canal is the Rialto bridge which joins the two halves of the city. On either side of the canal stood the houses and magazines of the wealthy citizenry. There also was the far-famed Fondaco dei Tedeschi, or German Quarter.

Until the fourteenth century Venice had been content to live isolated from the peninsula, secure in her lagoons, and with no possessions on the Italian mainland. Her position, though militarily unassailable, had decided disadvantages, however. She could not command the routes of commerce on the Venetian plain. Chief of these was the one which led to Padua and Verona and up the Brenner northward into Germany, thus tapping the markets of the Low Countries and the Rhineland.

Tyrants of the Della Scala family had established themselves in Verona, Vicenza, and adjoining towns. Commanding the approaches to the Brenner Pass, they might interfere in Venice's life-giving commerce with Europe north of the Alps. Further, the Carrara family which ruled in Padua might cut off Venice's food supply.

Venetian conquests on the peninsula began with the formation of a league to oppose the ambitious tyrant of Verona, Mastino della Scala. The resulting treaty of peace in 1339 gave Venice the towns of Treviso, Castelfranco, and Bassano, which established Venetian control over some of the mainland. But the important Brenner Pass was not yet in Venetian hands, and besides, in the Peace of Turin, made in 1381 after the close of the War of Chioggia, Venice was forced to give up Treviso which soon was acquired by the Carrara despots of Padua.

Soon thereafter Gian Galeazzo Visconti, tyrant of Milan, threatened to subjugate the Lombard plain. For a moment the Venetians coöperated with him, hoping to divide the spoils of conquest with him. So when Gian Galeazzo reduced the Carrara house to vassalage, he gave Treviso to the Venetians (1388). But this common action with the tyrant of Milan could not long serve Venetian interests, and on Gian Galeazzo's death in 1402 this partnership came to an end. In the confusion that followed the Venetians demanded all Milanese properties east of the Adige. By 1405 Venice was in control of Padua, Vicenza, and Verona and ruled up to the Brenner Pass. In a war with Milan, begun in 1425, Venice extended her authority over Brescia and Bergamo, up to Lake Como and the River Adda.

Meanwhile the Venetians had successfully negotiated with the Turks who had captured Constantinople on May 29, 1453. The Turks in the following year granted the Venetians their ports and trading rights. A quarter in Constantinople was assigned to the merchants of Venice who were to be governed by an official sent from Venice. So the proud city managed to retain her ascendancy in the Levant, but only on payment of an annual tribute. But the Turks, fearing Venetian political power and naval might, began a war in 1463 in which Venice lost Albania, Morea, Negropont, and Lemnos. The Peace of Constantinople in 1479 allowed Venice to keep her commercial privileges although she had to pay the Turks a fine of 150,000 ducats in addition to an annual tribute of 10,000 ducats.

The power and position of Venice rested upon her gigantic trading monopoly. Her greatest industry was shipbuilding. So huge was the demand for ships that builders could scarcely satisfy the republic's domestic needs. Because of her location on a group of islands, all foodstuffs had to be imported. Traffic in wheat became important. Vast quantities of it had to be brought from Catania in Sicily, from Bari in the kingdom of Naples, from the Romagna, and from the Levant.

This dependency upon foreign powers entailed significant consequences for the politics of Venice. The king of Sicily could shut off this supply whenever it suited his interests. So also could the Turks who often were hostile. Salt was produced in quantities sufficient for export. But Venetian manufacturers, while important, were less profitable than Venetian commerce. The guilds produced superior silks, brocades, goldsmith's articles, armor, and glass in such forms as beads and eyeglasses.

People admired the character of the Venetian state. Its money was stable. The flow of commerce over its wharves never slackened. Its government was in the hands of experts. The public peace was secure, and there were no riots. This was not because there was no proletariat,

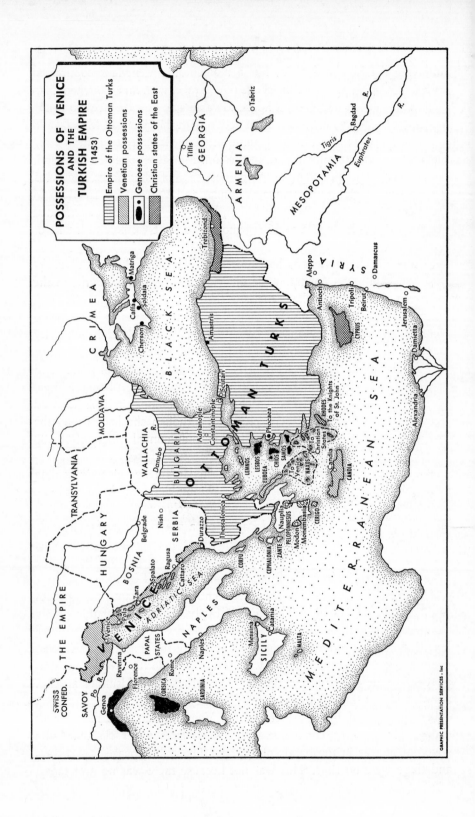

POSSESSIONS OF VENICE
AND THE
TURKISH EMPIRE
(1453)

Empire of the Ottoman Turks
Venetian possessions
Genoese possessions
Christian states of the East

GRAPHIC PRESENTATION SERVICES · Inc

THE EMPIRE

SWISS
CONFED.

SAVOY

Po R.

Genoa

Venice

Ravenna

Florence

Rome

Naples

SARDINIA

CORSICA

SICILY

Messina

Catania

MALTA

PAPAL
STATES

NAPLES

VENICE

ADRIATIC SEA

Pola

Zara

Spalato

Ragusa

Cattaro

BOSNIA

SERBIA

Belgrade

Nish

Durazzo

Thessalonica

CORFU

CEPHALONIA

ZANTE

Modon

Naupli

PELOPONNESUS

Monembasia

CERIGO

Tenos

Venice

NAXOS

SAMOS

CHIOS

LESBOS

EUBOEA

LEMNOS

Negropont

Candia

CANDIA

Christian
States
to the Knights
of St. John

RHODES

Phocaea

Constantinople

Adrianople

Scutari

BULGARIA

Danube R.

WALLACHIA

MOLDAVIA

HUNGARY

TRANSYLVANIA

SwIss

CRIMEA

Caffa

Soldaia

Matriga

Cherson

BLACK SEA

Amastris

Trebizond

OTTOMAN TURKS

MEDITERRANEAN SEA

CYPRUS

Antioch

Aleppo

Damascus

SYRIA

Tripoli

Beirut

Jerusalem

Damietta

Alexandria

GEORGIA

ARMENIA

Tiflis

Tabriz

MESOPOTAMIA

Tigris

Euphrates

Bagdad

R.

R.

but rather because the government was in the hands of men representing the prominent families of Venice, and no rebellion could succeed. There were three great organs of government in Venice: the Great Council (*Maggior Consiglio*); the *Pregadi*, a kind of Senate; and the *Collegio*, a sort of cabinet. The first of these bodies remained unchanged since 1296 when its membership was fixed and restricted to certain noble families.

The chief function of the Great Council came to be restricted to the election of magistrates. The *Pregadi* (Senators) were charged with administration. The *Collegio* was the executive part of the government which initiated policies and guided legislation in the Senate. The doge (or duke), formerly named by the emperor in Constantinople, now was elected according to a curiously complicated plan. A member of the *Collegio*, the doge had little power, and his office was largely ornamental.

The operation of the Venetian government was complicated. The *Collegio* could act only on motion of the Senate (the *Pregadi*), and the Senate could not initiate without the *Collegio* because the preparation of measures passed only through the *Collegio*. To expedite business, especially when there was state urgency, such as war, a Council of Ten (*Dieci*) assumed direction. It was appointed by the Great Council. This description of the government of Venice fails to give an adequate idea of the extraordinarily cumbersome system of elections and the complicated procedure followed. This state organization, controlled by the aristocratic patriciate, was able to curb all incentive to popular or democratic movements. Venice therefore had no class conflicts. Her navy was powerful and effective. But, having no army, she relied upon mercenary *condottieri*. The Venetian diplomatic service became a model of efficiency among the state of the Renaissance.

GENOA: RIVAL OF VENICE

Situated on the narrow strip of land between the Mediterranean and the Ligurian Alps which extend from Nice to Sarzana, the city of Genoa could never become a land power like Milan or Florence. Her geographical position caused her to turn to the sea. Genoa was the product of the great commercial growth of the eleventh and following centuries. On land, in Renaissance times, she served as the water gate for commerce between Sicilian, Aragonese, and western Mediterranean ports and landlocked Milan. Beyond the sea, as in the case of Venice, distant markets—Constantinople, the islands of the Aegean, Antioch, Cairo, and Kaffa and other places on the Crimea—lured her trading citizenry. Genoese success challenged the Pesans whom she defeated in the Battle of Meloria in

1284. But Genoa herself was deprived of her naval ascendancy during the War of Chioggia (1379–1381), as noted above. For a long time, however, Genoa was able to retain a large share of the trade with the Levant. In western Mediterranean waters her relations with Palermo in Sicily and with Barcelona in Spain remained unchallenged.

The public life of Genoa was filled with endless turmoil. Her nobility continued the feuds so dear to that class. The merchants and others of her citizenry were divided into jangling factions. These dissensions weakened her power to resist the Venetians. The Visconti tyrants of Milan, whose territories extended to Genoa's back door, regarded her with covetous eyes, for possession of Genoa would give them access to the sea.

Genoa sold ships and weapons to all who wanted them. Her shipping was at the disposal of the highest bidder. She was courted by the political forces which sought to control Italy after Charles VIII's invasion of the peninsula in 1494. In the ensuing struggle the Spaniards were successful in securing her friendship, for Genoa needed the wheat of Sicily which belonged to Spain, and Spain needed the shipping of Genoa. So the role of Genoa during the Renaissance, aside from her contributions in banking, commerce, and new ideas in business methods, was to serve the purposes of the Spanish crown in its policy of controlling the Italian peninsula.

SAVOY AND ITS STRATEGIC POSITION

Situated partly in the Alps and partly in the upper valley of the Po, the country of Savoy (including Piedmont) modestly shared in the economic development of Lombardy. Its towns were few and small. The country derived its subsistence from agriculture; its customs changed little, and its life remained conservative. Renaissance conceptions could not well thrive in such a region; the country remained feudal in outlook.

Savoy, however, played a considerable part in Italian politics during the age of the Renaissance, mainly because of the military importance of its geographical position. During the interminable wars between France and Spain for the control of Italy, Savoy usually received attention. For the French, the country was strategic because it gave access to Italy; for Spain and the Emperor on the other hand, it served as a bulwark against invasion from France.

MANTUA AND THE GONZAGA FAMILY

The margraviate of Mantua was a small community on the Mincio, an affluent of the Po, which drained Lake Garda. At this strategic point

Mantua controlled the crossing of the deep and rapid Mincio. The town enjoyed some prosperity, for through it passed the trade to Verona on the Adige, at the point where that stream emerges from its Alpine mountain valley into the Lombard plain. But Mantua was an insignificant town, too small to play a great role in the political life of the Renaissance. Its significance derived partly from its militarily strategic position, on the confines of the territories of Milan and Venice.

Mantua also owed much to the vigor and resourcefulness of its rulers of the house of Gonzaga. Being successful *condottieri*, they were paid handsomely for their services. Thus they raised what otherwise would have been a commonplace rule of an Italian despot to the level of a renowned Renaissance court. Although a feudal atmosphere dominated the life of Mantua, the manners of the ruling circle were softened by the new refining influences of the Renaissance.

THE STATES OF THE CHURCH (THE PAPAL STATES)

The States of the Church, or Papal States, comprised a group of diverse communities on both slopes of the Apennines in the central part of the peninsula, from the borders of the kingdom of Naples on the south to the Romagna on the north. Several distinct parts are to be distinguished. The first was Rome on the Tiber which occupied a dominating position in that area. To the south was Latium, famous in the history of classical Rome. North of the Tiber lay the cities of Viterbo and Orvieto. To the east was mountainous Umbria with the cities of Spoleto, Foligno, Assisi, and Perugia. The Marches on the east slopes of the Apennines had a few small towns such as Ancona and Sinigaglia. To the north was the Romagna with the cities of Ravenna, Rimini, Faenza, Cesena, and Imola. Emilia, also part of the Romagna, lay to the west; its chief center, the great and prosperous city of Bologna, was the queen of the lower Lombard plain.

These Papal States for the most part shared but modestly in the commercial and industrial progress in other parts of the Po plain and in Tuscany. Much of the country, especially Umbria and the Marches and also part of the Romagna, is rough and mountainous, fit only for small scale agriculture. A considerable amount of grain, however, was produced in the Romagna and exported to Venice. This surplus brought some wealth into the country and paid for such luxuries as the people desired. Salt was produced at Commachio, in the duchy of Ferrara, and alum, an article prized in the dyeing industry, was produced at Tolfa, south of Viterbo.

The temper of the people of the States of the Church and their artistic and social customs and political ideas were conservative. Feudal ways and manners survived, due largely to the geographical isolation in which the towns and villages lived. Feuds were prevalent, and this condition made orderly government difficult. Especially unstable was Rome, chief center of the States of the Church, whose officials were contentious and quarreled with the Pope, head of the state. Perugia, also, was a prominent city which had a factious population. Possessing little wealth and no peace, the cities of these papal lords could hardly take a leading part in the culture of the Renaissance. Only exceptionally was it possible for them, as in the case of Perugia and Urbino and Bologna, to make some contribution.

The great weakness of the States of the Church, in addition to the scattered character of their territory and the modest economic development of their communities, lay in the nature of their government. Political authority had fallen into the hands of the early popes practically by default during the disintegration of the Roman imperial authority in Italy, the Barbarian invasions, the wars of the Ostrogoths and the Vandals, and the incursions of the Lombards and the Arabs. An effective political regime such as the *signorie* in Lombardy was impossible.

The religious problems of the fourteenth and fifteenth centuries materially weakened the prestige of papal rule. Feudal princes and governments of the States of the Church disregarded the central political authority of the Pope, and so dynasties of local tyrants asserted their freedom. Such rulers were the Este in Ferrara, the Malatesta in Rimini, the Bentivogli in Bologna, the Montefeltri in Urbino, and the Baglioni in Perugia.

After the tumultuous days of the Great Schism (1378–1415), which had rent Christendom and encouraged factional quarrels, Martin V (1417–1431) reestablished Rome as the seat of the papacy, whereupon there followed a restoration of papal authority (at this time papal government was moved from the Lateran to the Vatican). But it proved impossible to raise the Pope's political prestige to the point at which his authority compared favorably with that of his neighbors. Development of central governmental organs was slow, justice was administered independently of papal authority, taxation scarcely existed, there was no army, and scarcely any police. Hence the papal government often was forced to hire mercenaries or seek support from foreign powers. Not until the pontificates of Alexander VI (1492–1503) and of Julius II (1503–1513) was some successful effort made to develop an effective government.

FERRARA AND MODENA

The dukes of Ferrara ruled a strategic area within the States of the Church, along the lower Po and the Adriatic coastline north of Ravenna. They asserted their independence of the Pope more or less consistently. Ferrara possessed some trade and marketed an article of great value, salt, produced in the basins at Comacchio on the Adriatic. The rulers who belonged to the House of Este were of feudal origin. A chivalric outlook long was characteristic of their court. The princes of Ferrara in 1279 acquired the lordship of Reggio and in 1288 appropriated that of Modena. Their territories during the Age of the Renaissance thus extended across the peninsula of Italy, from the mouth of the Po to the Gulf of Genoa. Politically, the dukes of Ferrara were vassals of the States of the Church, a tie which enabled them to resist the encroachments of their mighty neighbor Venice whose lands bordered on those of Ferrara.

THE DUCHY OF URBINO

The state of Urbino, though a fief of the States of the Church, calls for a separate statement. Situated on the upper eastern slope of the Apennines, south of the Romagna, the town of Urbino and its dependent country enjoyed a modest prosperity. Feudal and manorial traditions remained strong among the populace, and here, as in places in neighboring Umbria, the influences of trade were but slightly felt. Urbino was noted for its capable *condottieri*. The ruling house of Montefeltro was characterized by great ability which enabled its members to act in practical independence of papal overlordship. The princes of this house raised Urbino's fame high among Renaissance courts by setting a practical example of courtly nobility.

CITY AND STATE OF FLORENCE

The region known as Tuscany, the principal power of which was Florence, occupied the west slope of the Apennines on both sides of the Arno River which reaches the sea near Pisa. Florence shared in the economic development of the thirteenth century that had also made other Italian communities great and triumphant. By the opening of the fourteenth century she was ruling over all of Tuscany except Siena and Lucca. Pisa, situated on the Arno, at one time seemed to block Florentine contact with the markets of the world. During the thirteenth century Pisa's citizens shared in the trading monopoly of the Venetians. But Genoa, her ambitious rival, shattered the Pisan fleet at Meloria in 1284, as noted above, and ruined her prosperity. But the Pisans could not forget their great days, and the Florentines determined to put an end to any dreams of independence the Pisans might still have. So in 1406 Florence annexed Pisa which thereupon had to be satisfied with the rank of Florence's seaport. But Florence never was able to subdue her northern neighbor Lucca.

Like other Italian towns, Florence too had its complicated social and industrial cleavages which created discontent and rendered its government unstable. The workers in some of the greater as well as in the minor guilds had no voice in the management of affairs, something that rested in the hands of the masters of the greater guilds. The unprivileged workers repeatedly sought to better their lot but each time were repressed. A desperate revolt, that of the Ciompi in 1378, was stamped out in blood. These toilers continued to live in sullen resentment toward their more fortunate fellow citizens. Out of this chronic discontent rose the power of the Medici in 1429.

This family had risen from humble origins and by the fourteenth century had laid the foundation of that fortune which made it possible for them to play the part of tyrants or dictators. Cosimo de' Medici (d. 1464) laid the secure foundations of his power. He knew how to avoid ostentation and show of power. Keeping himself aloof from public office, he contented himself with pulling wires behind the scenes and letting officials elected by the complicated system of government characteristic of most Italian towns of the Renaissance do the dirty work in the open. Having thus laid the foundations of real power, Cosimo established his family as a political dynasty and was succeeded by his astute son Piero (d. 1469) who was followed by Lorenzo the Magnificent (d. 1492).

SIENA AND LUCCA

Siena was situated in the southern part of Tuscany on the much-traveled pilgrim road which crossed the Alps at the St. Bernard Pass, led through Pavia and Lucca, and terminated at Rome. Although Siena's origins are wrapped in obscurity, she shared in the great socioeconomic changes during the twelfth century and for many years was ahead of Florence in these matters.

In Siena, too, the government was unstable. The *popolo minuto* were discontented, and there were innumerable disputes. There also was rivalry with neighboring Florence and political and social contentions were the order of the day. Pandolfo Petrucci became tyrant in 1487, but his unpopular rule proved a dismal failure. Neither he nor other members of his family, unlike the Medici in neighboring Florence, possessed the ability to manage the state successfully in the midst of class and family rivalries. Finally, in 1524, the power of the Petrucci came to an end in a riot. After much dissension, Siena in 1527 passed under the protection of the Emperor Charles V. In 1555 Siena was annexed by the Grand Duke Cosimo I of Tuscany.

Lucca, in the northern part of Tuscany, flourished during the twelfth and thirteenth centuries. The city became famous on account of its silk cloth manufacture. Of this article of luxury Lucca's merchants had a near monopoly and exported it to all parts of Europe. Great sums of money collected in the coffers of the silk cloth guild. Lucchese merchants became bankers, having financial establishments in distant cities such as commercial centers as Bruges. Though attacked by Florence in 1429, Lucca succeeded, in spite of its limited size, in maintaining her independence.

KINGDOMS OF NAPLES AND SICILY

The kingdom of Naples occupied the southern portion of the Italian peninsula. Its surface for the most part was mountainous and rough, for the Apennine range extended through its entire length, to the toe of the boot. The mountain streams were short, and moisture was scarce. There were few extensive agricultural areas. The one in Apulia, in the country around Bari, produced grain for export, and the other, east of Naples, the Terra de Lavoro, was fertile and provided the food supply for Naples. There were few large towns. In former times Amalfi and Salerno had been prosperous economic centers. But at the time of the Renaissance only Naples and Bari figured prominently.

Social and economic life in the kingdom remained static; everywhere there were independent lords, a numerous and poor peasantry, and a small town population. Brigandage was rife, especially in the interior. Nobles recruited their followers from mountain regions such as the Abruzzi and assumed an indifference toward the crown. The rulers had made little progress in developing a centralized government in spite of a brilliant beginning under their Hohenstaufen rulers during the thirteenth century. Taxation remained poorly developed, and the rulers could hardly afford to hire mercenaries. Under these circumstances the Neapolitan infantry and cavalry were ineffective, and the navy was puny. Foreigners controlled most of the shipping. Officials were drawn from the nobility who never became completely loyal to the crown. Revolt was easily successful. Kings might lose their crowns in a moment. This fact explains why Charles VIII in 1494 so easily won the crown of Naples and a year later as easily lost it.

Sicily, a kingdom with a crown distinct from that of Naples, was a populous island of about 10,000 square miles. Its wheat was a prized article in Spain and was in great demand in such cities as Genoa and Venice which had to import foodstuffs. The Sicilian crown derived a rich income from a tax levied on the export of wheat. Olive oil was exported in some quantity. Palermo on the north coast, with its small dependent fertile back country known as the Golden Shell (*Concha d'Oro*), maintained a busy contact with Barcelona and Genoa. From Catania much grain was exported, especially to Venice.

The royal power of Sicily was well developed everywhere save in some of the mountain districts of the north. There were few great barons such as harassed the political life of Naples and the States of the Church. Hence it was unnecessary in Sicily to maintain a large royal army. As long as the rulers of Sicily could call upon the navy of the Genoese, whose shipping was the distributing agency of Sicilian wheat, they were safe in their island kingdom.

Originally the two crowns of Naples and Sicily were held by the same king. But with the passing of the Hohenstaufen House, French support enabled Charles of Anjou, younger brother of St. Louis of France, to seize both Sicily and Naples. His rule, which began in 1266, ran afoul of the Sicilians in 1282, and they invited Peter III, king of Aragon, to assume the crown. Henceforth there was an Aragonese king in Sicily and an Angevin king in Naples, each claiming to be the legitimate ruler also in the other realm. This strained situation continued until 1435 when the Angevin Queen Giovanna of Naples died. Then Alfonso I of Sicily and of Aragon seized Naples and henceforth bore the crown of Naples.

PART II

Spiritual Foundations of Late Medieval Culture

Chapter 3

THE CHURCH: TEACHING ORGANIZATION AND TRIUMPHS

*H*AVING EXPLORED some aspects of the economic foundations, the social structure, and the political organization of European society during the Age of the Renaissance, we next turn our attention to the higher aspects of Renaissance achievement by first noting the part the Christian Church had in molding medieval and Renaissance culture. Clearly, the Church is not the product of material forces such as soil, climate, or geography. For although the Church came into existence in Palestine, she survived the economic and political catastrophes of the Roman Empire, increased the areas of her sway in spite of the Barbarian invasions, outlived the turmoil of feudal society, survived the Renaissance and the Reformation, and still is a force to be reckoned with.

CENTRAL CHRISTIAN TEACHING

It was a momentous event in the history of civilization when the patriarch Moses, drawn by the vision of a sublime monotheism and an austere morality inspired by it, told his people of Israel that God's name was "I Am Who Am," and announced that "He Who Is" (that is, Jehovah) would lead them. This was to be His name forever, His memorial for all generations (Exod. III: 14–16). God, then, was the one eternal and infinitely perfect and self-subsisting Being. On another occasion Moses

49

spoke to Israel these words: "Hear, O Israel, the Lord our God Is one Lord" (Deut. VI: 4). Revolutionary words indeed, for a god whose nature is unicity must be something very different from the gods who swarmed the pantheon of Greece and Rome and of other ancient peoples as well.

The teachings of Mosaic Judaism underwent profound change when Jesus appeared as a prophet among the startled Hebrews telling them that "Before Abraham Was I Am." Jesus moved about Palestine, lived among His people, taught them by means of parables, and uttered precepts of the deepest significance. Like Moses before Him, He preached a lofty ethical religion based upon the Ten Commandments which in His teaching was to be the expression of a supreme love of God as Father of all, which naturally expressed itself in love for all God's creatures. Jesus' oral message was set down in the Gospels and proclaimed by His apostles in whose eyes He was God's anointed, "the Christ." They hailed Him as the Messiah to save man from the effects of sin. A doctrine of redemption unique in history was presented to men, who, weary of vice and an existence which promised nothing, were longing for a nobler way of life.

The Christian Church came into existence among men who had listened to Jesus' discourse and had witnessed His Passion on Calvary, hard by Jerusalem. The report of His Resurrection had an electrical effect. The gods of Greece and Rome were myths, but the founder of the Christian faith was an historical figure. Institutionalized, the Gospel teaching was brought to men whether rich or poor, free or slave. Christian doctrine revolutionized the ancient world and provided the moral and spiritual foundation on which the culture of the Middle Ages was to unfold.

The persecutions to which the Church was subjected during the first three centuries of her existence finally came to an end under the Emperor Constantine (d. 337) who accorded the Church legal equality with the old pagan cults. But within two centuries after that date the Christian faith had embraced the once pagan population of Greece and Rome. During the next ten centuries the Church witnessed many crises in secular culture. It survived the decay and ruin of the Roman Empire in the west of Europe, witnessed the grandeur of the Byzantine Empire and provided it with a firm Christian inspiration, outlived the Feudal Age, and acquired much power and prestige—and also struggled with grave problems—during the vast social and economic changes incident to the rise of towns which helped transform every aspect of European life. At the opening of the Renaissance the Church was shaping much of the culture of the age.

THE CHURCH: CHARACTER AND MISSION

According to the broadest definition the Church was the body who received the teaching Christ gave His disciples and sought to be guided by His precepts. This was a most complex body, one unique in the annals of man. For it comprised not only the Church militant—those who lived here in this milieu of sin and sorrow and struggled to follow Christ's precepts—but also the Church suffering—embracing those momentarily in purgatory to discharge their penalties remaining after the guilt of their sins had been forgiven—and, finally, the Church triumphant—composed of those who had passed into their eternal reward as participants in God's glory. The mystical magnet that bound these three branches of the Church into one palpitating spiritual organism was the person of Christ.

The Church militant was also a visible body. It was a spiritual organism of laymen and clergy, the latter composed of priests and bishops who, it was taught, held authority from Christ to dispense the benefits of Christ's teaching among the faithful. Christ who had founded His Church was head of this body. He had delegated His authority to a vicegerent, as medieval men believed. This was the apostle Simon Peter who sealed his career with the crown of martyrdom when he was executed on the Vatican Hill in Rome by the Emperor Nero about the year 64. To Peter, Christ the Founder had entrusted what was called the keys. This included the power to bind and loosen. On this teaching and on practices based upon it reposed the primacy of Peter and of Peter's successors, the popes, or bishops, of Rome. This basic doctrine was an outstanding feature of the Latin Church in the West. For the faithful in the West the pope was the earthly spiritual head of a vast visible hierarchy. To deny this primacy was thought to be the gravest heresy.

SIGNIFICANCE OF THE LITURGY: THE SACRAMENTS

In her liturgy the Church imparted vital spiritual benefits. This Christian liturgy embraces the whole complex order of the Church's official services—ceremonies, prayers, and particularly her sacraments. These public services are expressed in audible words, in visible actions, and in a set manner. By means of these services the Church perpetuated herself —recruited her faithful, instructed them in the truths of the Christian faith, and guided them in the way of salvation.

The sacraments, seven in number, were outward visible signs of an inner grace instituted by God for the salvation of man. Each sacrament had a special purpose indicated by a special sign which conferred grace on the recipient who put no hindrance to it—and this by the inherent power bestowed by Christ (i.e., *ex opere operato*). The sacraments, of great cultural significance, have molded the thought and morals of generations of Christians. Baptism, for example, was of the utmost importance in the spiritual economy of the Church which recruited its membership by it. On confession of faith (in the case of children, parents or guardians stood sponsors for their faith) candidates at the font received the affusion of water while the priest declared this was done in the name of the Holy Trinity. Their sins forgiven, they became sharers in the spiritual benefits of the Church and entered into communion with it. Later, at the crucial age of mental maturity, the members received the sacrament of confirmation—the imposition of hands by the bishop—thus fortifying the believer's faith as a soldier of Christ. Like baptism, this sacrament could be received only once by each person.

Confession, with penance, also had a great part in the spiritual training of the medieval Christian community. This sacrament was available whenever a member had fallen into sin and needed to recover his favor with God. Examining his conscience, the penitent knelt contritely beside the priest, orally confessed his sins—venial and mortal—was given penalties or satisfactions to discharge, and finally, with admonishment by the priest, he received absolution.

Holy Eucharist, central sacrament in Christian teaching and practical spiritual life, was at once subtle and complex. Instituted by Christ on the evening before His crucifixion, it was an act commemorative of Christ Himself. It also was a sacrifice. It was spiritual food for him who partook of it. And the Eucharist also was a prayer. Inasmuch as Christ had said of the bread "This is My body," and of the wine "This is My blood" the Church taught that Christ was fully present in His humanity and also in His divinity, under the accidents of bread and wine. This is known as the *Real Presence*. Transformation of the substance of bread and wine, the accidents remaining unchanged, into the body and blood of Christ is a mystery which took place at the moment when the words of institution were uttered by the priest. This change is called "transubstantiation." The Eucharist is most important, for much of medieval ethics and culture revolved around it.

Just as baptism was the sacrament of initiation into the Christian communion, so also death and sickness, ever a baffling theme in the life of man, had its special sacrament: extreme unction. This sacrament was conferred on any member of the faithful when in danger of death. The priest heard his confession, shrived him, prayed with him, anointed him with blessed oil, and thus prepared him for his final journey into eternity. Thus, from the cradle to the grave the Church stood ready with its sacraments to guide the faithful in every moment of life's crises.

Family arrangements—the status and duties of husband and wife—are matters of the utmost importance in the life of any society. For much of moral training and preparation for practical life is received in the home. The sacrament of holy matrimony provided a solid and permanent basis for a lasting marriage which was essential in the proper bringing up of children. The matter of this sacrament is the mutual agreement of the parties to renounce all others for the sake of the marital union. Such a marriage, witnessed by the Church and blessed by the priest at a nuptial Mass and elevated to the dignity of a sacrament, possessed special sta- bility. It is easy to see how families so formed contributed mightily toward the social well-being and stability of medieval society.

And, finally, there was the sacrament of ordination, or holy orders. This was most vital for the practice of the Christian faith—the systematic round of religious services, the maintenance of discipline, and the instruc- tion of the faithful. The sacrament of holy orders was instituted for the purpose of providing the Church with priests—official personages who possessed sacramental authority to minister to their followers, especially to celebrate Mass and to hear confessions. Such priestly personages were elevated to holy orders by the episcopal "laying on of hands," a right, it was taught, possessed by the bishops whose authority derived ultimately through episcopal succession to Christ Himself.

THE FUNCTIONS OF PARISH PRIESTS

At the base of the clerical hierarchy stood the parish priest whose sphere of activity was the parish. This, the smallest territorial unit in the organism of the Church, embraced a varying number of souls. In some rural parishes there might be only a handful, but in growing towns mem- bership might reach into the hundreds, even thousands. The parish church, usually dedicated to some saint, was a hallowed place. Here Mass was said, the faithful were married, and their children baptized. Adjoin- ing the parish church was the churchyard where in consecrated ground lay the dead who had passed beyond, fortified by the last sacrament. Socially, also, the parish church was the center of activity, for there parishioners saw their friends and their kin and talked with them about things of common interest.

Parish priests exercised extensive influence. They were set aside from the rest of men by the sacrament of holy orders received at the hand of the bishop who stood in apostolic succession dating back to St. Peter. Priests so marked possessed the right to administer the sacraments, the holy mysteries essential for salvation. They baptized the newly born, instructed children in preparation for their first communion, prepared them for confirmation, heard confessions of the parishioners, celebrated holy Mass and distributed the holy morsel in communion, said the nuptial Mass for the newly wed, and finally, when their charges reached the end of their days, prepared them for a happy death through the prayers of the community and the last sacrament of extreme unction, followed by burial in consecrated ground. Priests also attended the sick, enforced canonical discipline, applied synodal decrees and the commands of the bishops, and looked after the material needs of the parish church, churchyard, priest's house, and anything else belonging to the parish church.

THE BISHOP AND HIS FUNCTIONS

Above the parish priest stood the bishop whose authority extended over a diocese composed of a number of parishes. Dioceses varied in size. So, for example, the diocese, or see, of Utrecht comprised most of the territory at present belonging to the kingdom of the Netherlands, while in Italy some bishops governed areas no larger than a small town as in the case of the bishop of Fiesole, near Florence. The center of the bishop's activity or his see, as it was commonly called, was the cathedral church (from *cathedra,* meaning chair, and symbolizing the bishop's teaching and pastoral authority). A priest in holy orders, the bishop in medieval and Renaissance times was elected by the chapter of the clergy attached to the cathedral church of the see. The bishop was installed by the archbishop or another bishop delegated for that purpose. In that ceremony he received the symbol of his episcopal office—the ring worn on the fourth finger of the right hand. This symbolized the Church whose shepherd he was, the crosier, or shepherd's staff, which reminded the flock of their spiritual shepherd, and the miter which signified that he was acting in behalf of Christ the King.

To the bishop, standing in episcopal succession dating back to the apostles, was given a wide range of power. To him were reserved the sacraments of holy order and confirmation. He visited the parishes of his diocese (something that often had to be left to assistant bishops, or coadjutors) to confirm the youth and guide the older folk of the parish. He convoked diocesan synods to discuss religious matters involving discipline and issued doctrinal and administrative commands. He examined candidates for the priesthood and assigned them to parishes. In his relations with the parish clergy the bishop was represented by his archdeacons who had certain judicial authority, and inducted priests in their office. The archdeacon held a spiritual court in which were tried infractions of discipline and crimes against the Church.

THE ARCHBISHOPS AND THE POPE

Above the bishop stood the archbishop, or metropolitan. Being a bishop, he wore, like other bishops, the insignia of his episcopal office— miter, ring, and staff. But what distinguished him as archbishop was the pallium, or pall, a narrow band of white wool worn on the shoulders and made by the nuns of St. Agnes of Rome and bestowed by the bishop of Rome. His authority extended over the several sees of his archdiocese or province. Over one of these sees he functioned as bishop, the bishops of the other dioceses being referred to as suffragan bishops. The archbishop was elected by his suffragan bishops and his cathedral chapter. He too was assisted in his duties by the clergy of his cathedral who also supervised the affairs of his diocese. The archbishop took special interest in the spiritual affairs of his entire province and to that end convoked provincial synods, instituted inquests, conducted visitations, and received appeals from episcopal courts.

Head of this vast organization extending from Greenland to Finland and southward to the Mediterranean was the pope who occupied a position of extraordinary authority and influence in all parishes, dioceses, and provinces of the Church. Throughout the Middle Ages, as we have noted, it was taught that Peter had spent his last days in Rome and that he had suffered martyrdom on the Vatican Hill. It also was taught that he stood in special relationship to Christ Who in a passage in the Gospel of St. Matthew had declared that Peter was the spiritual rock on which the Church was to be built, that the keys of heaven would be given him, and that he was to have authority to bind on earth what was to be bound in heaven and whatever was loosed on earth was to be loosed in heaven (Matt. XVI: 16–20). From this came the teaching that the pope, bishop of Rome, was the successor of Peter and the vicar of Christ.

As a spiritual and administrative personage, the pope was unique. Like all priests, he was in holy orders possessing powers held by every priest. As metropolitan he was first among equals. Being a successor of St. Peter, as was taught, he was Christ's vicar with authority in faith and morals. He was judge in his own diocese and successfully sustained the right to pass on questions of faith and morals and receive appeals from episcopal and archiepiscopal courts. He had a council, the College of Cardinals drawn from the clergy of certain churches of Rome and its environs. This was the papal curia. Upon the pope's demise the cardinals took over papal duties and prepared for a conclave in which they elected a successor.

CATHEDRAL CHAPTERS

The cathedral chapter was an indispensable element in the practical activities of a diocese. The more important persons attached to a chapter were called canons. Chief of these canons was the dean who had a general oversight of the chapter and other persons associated with the cathedral. Usually there was a subdean. Next in rank was the cantor who had police supervision of the cathedral. He also had charge of music and reading from Scripture. The chancellor, also called *scholasticus*, appointed teachers and supervised the schools of the diocese, especially the school maintained by the chapter. The penitentiary had the care of penitents and instructed, exhorted, and absolved them. The treasurer, or chamberlain, had charge of the cathedral's finances. There also were a sacristan, bell ringer, porter, and assistants. The number of persons attached to the chapter varied greatly; in some cathedrals there were as many as fifty. One of their duties was to elect the bishop or archbishop and assist him as a kind of advisory council.

THE REGULAR CLERGY

The clerical hierarchy here described constituted the secular clergy, so-called because they operated "in the world" (*saeculum*) as priests ministering to the laity. The regular clergy of the Benedictine Order (who, at least in earlier times, were not necessarily in holy orders) lived in religious houses known as convents or monasteries and lived according to a fixed rule (*regula*). They took the irrevocable vows of poverty, celibacy, and obedience. Their common monastic activities centered around a routine of worship—matins at midnight; lauds at daybreak; prime at six, followed by chapter meeting; terce at nine, after which conventional Mass; sext at twelve; nones at three P.M.; vespers at six, after dinner followed by compline. Worship was based upon the breviary and sung in choir. The cloister was the center of their coming and going. The monks slept in a common dortor and had their food in the frater. Such was the rule St. Benedict (d. 543) drew up for the monks at Monte Cassino which was widely followed in western Europe.

A second type of monasticism was that of the Carthusians. Their mode of religious life derived, in part at least, from the early Christian desert fathers who lived solitarily in separate huts under the guidance of a superior. Instead of living in a cloister, meeting in the frater and dortor, and saying their office in the choir, as was the Benedictines' wont, the Carthusians spent most of their time living separately in cells built around the walls of the cloister. They met for conventual Mass on Sundays and on certain feast days. They were noted for their spirituality; their writings stirred the devotions of many a person. Their method of religious life, being most austere, prevented the order from having many houses.

It must not be thought that a rigid uniformity existed among monasteries. Monasticism has generally had a way of meeting the constantly shifting impact of social, political, and intellectual interest of secular society. Repeatedly monks modified their original rule, especially when they founded a new order; but in any case they retained much of the old and traditional in habit, custom, and practice. So, for example, during the heyday of feudalism Benedictine communities (each house had its abbot and was independent of all other Benedictine houses) became the prey of ambitious nobles. To put a stop to this the monks of Cluny in 910 created a new congregation of Benedictine houses ruled by priors appointed by the abbot of the mother house of Cluny which was placed directly under the protection of the bishop of Rome. Another modified Benedictine order was that of the Cistercians who introduced austerities unknown to older houses. They were a closely integrated congregation under an abbot, with a prior ruling each house. Like the Cluniacs, they held annual chapters whose statutes were binding on all houses of the order.

Secular priests often lived according to a rule. Their idea was to combine the advantages of the spirituality of a religious house with the parochial needs of a priest working among men and women "out in the world." This mode of life, combining the regular and secular, dated from the early days of the Church. St. Augustine (d. 430) made use of it in North Africa, and the prestige of his name made this type of monastic life popular. Wherever there were groups of priests (canons) in cathedral chapters or in collegiate churches St. Augustine's rule, or a modified form of it, was likely to be adopted. This type of religious life was widely embraced during the centuries of feudalism. It strengthened the spiritual fiber of priests at a time when laymen sought to enrich themselves at the expense of the Church. Austin Canons, or Augustinian Hermits, became popular, their houses being numerous in town and country. The Premonstratensians, who also, at least in part, adopted the Rule of St. Augustine, were an order of priests organized to labor among the neglected people living in the rapidly growing towns of the twelfth century.

The need of bringing the gospel to the growing population in town and countryside had its response in various ways. In an age when medical practice was most defective disease flourished, and hospitals and lazar houses were to be found everywhere. In England alone there were about 800 such spitals. In most of these the brothers and sisters followed some sort of rule. To teach the youth, engage in practical charity, and cultivate the spiritual life was the object of the Brethren of the Common Life founded by Gerhard Groot (d. 1384) whose houses were to be found everywhere in the Low Countries. The Beguines, first founded in the thirteenth century to minister to the poor in Low Country towns, were organizations of pious lay women living in "beguinages," without taking irrevocable vows. But more effective was the order of Franciscan Friars which came into existence with St. Francis of Assisi (d. 1226). With passionate charity these friars sought out the lame, the halt and blind, helped the sick and unfortunate, and imparted the comforts of the faith among neglected parts of the population. Having nothing, they would gain everything. They lived in cloisters but were not so rigidly bound to service in choir like the Benedictines. The Dominicans, founded by St. Dominic (d. 1221), like the Franciscans, also addressed their efforts to the poor and unfortunate and the sick. Study, spiritual contemplation, and pastoral work were their part in the Christian life of the time.

EFFECTIVENESS OF CHURCH TEACHING

It is difficult to form an adequate idea of the social, moral, and intellectual efficacy of the medieval Church, but that it was great is certain. During the centuries following the collapse of the Roman Empire in the West, the Latin Church had extended her sway from the Mediterranean northward to Finland and westward to Greenland. In this vast region of varied climate and geographic features lived a diversity of peoples speaking a medley of languages, having great variety of social structure and political organization and living in ancient cultural traditions, some of them dating from the late Iron Age. In a time when means of communication were primitive and the most efficient governmental organization was successful usually only on a limited scale, the creation of a far-flung ecclesiastical and administrative system of dioceses, parishes, and monastic organizations capable of directing the thought and practical religious activity of the Church was a most extraordinary achievement.

This Church, founded, as it was taught, by Christ and presided over by His vicar, the bishop of Rome, who held the keys of man's eternal salvation, possessed far greater power than any secular institution then existing. Through her sacramental system explained above it molded the conscience of the faithful. It laid down moral precepts by which social relations were to be guided. A Christian conception of marriage and family life came into existence. A doctrine of business relationships known as the canonists' theory of economics was created, for economic activity, like all other human activity, was regarded as a branch of ethics to be guided by theologians.

A complete doctrine of human relationship was developed. All power, it was taught, came from God. His "eternal law" was His reason or will commanding observance of the entire natural human order and forbidding violations of it. So far as man's eternal fortune was concerned, God had vested supreme ecclesiastical authority in His Church under the headship of the bishops of Rome, successors of St. Peter. God had also founded secular government to restrain man's wicked passions and to direct and control civil society. As head of this power He had appointed the emperor from whom, according to feudal conceptions, princes held their territories in fee. In his secular relationships man was held to be subject to the "natural law"—a body of moral principles taught by reason and binding upon all men. It is that part of the eternal moral law which applied to man's social and political relations. To contravene his "natural rights" was an injustice, a grave sin. Any command contrary to the natural law need not be obeyed and might be resisted even by force. Secular authority in each of these fields was supreme, but, in all moral and religious matters, the secular was to be guided by the sacred.

In her liturgy the Church, as we have learned, had a potent means to teach the mysteries of the Christian faith. The religious calendar of this time clearly reveals its far-reaching influence. All manner of secular events and ordinary business transactions in which religion was not involved were dated according to some saint's day or some holy day. It seemed as if the course of everyday life had shaped itself to religion. An event on 24 June, for example, was said to have happened on the Day of St. John the Baptist; on November 11, St. Martin's Day. Liturgical feasts thus became signposts in the reckoning of time. In France, for example, the new year began with Easter, which seemed proper, for the Resurrection was the central theme in the drama of Christian redemption. In parts of Germany the new year began with Christmas, and in some countries it began on the Feast of the Annunciation (March 25). The two great liturgical festivals—Advent, which announces the Redeemer's coming, and Easter which commemorates the Saviour's crucifixion and resurrection—figured most prominently.

In other ways, besides the liturgy, the spirit of the Christian faith inspired cultural creation. In architecture, for example, Gothic masters produced a style truly as noble and impressive as anything Greece or Rome produced. Gothic miniaturists' work has not yet become sufficiently known for it to win the place it deserves in the history of art. Nor have Gothic painting and sculpture been adequately recognized. Like these plastic arts, Gothic music vibrates with the spirit of late medieval religion. The Church, it is well known, produced an effective dramatic art, for example, in such works as *Everyman* and *Marie of Nijmegen*. A truly remarkable literature came into being as in Malory's *Morte d'Arthur, Piers Plowman,* Chaucer's *Canterbury Tales,* and Dante's *Divine Comedy.* The profundity of the medieval spirit is shown nowhere better than in such manuals of devotion as the *Imitation of Christ.* These medieval masterpieces—architecture, painting, sculpture, prose and poetry, and the literature of spirituality—must be studied if one is to understand the nature of the Renaissance and the spirit of the Reformation.

Besides her powers to teach by means of her liturgy and her priestly ministrations, the Church, in her sentences of excommunication and interdict, possessed extraordinary means to teach and discipline her disobedient children. As a person by sacrament of baptism was admitted to Christ's mystical body, in which there was a communion of spiritual goods, so the unfaithful, by sentence of excommunication, was cast out of the communion of the faithful. Such a person was deprived of ecclesiastical relations with his fellows until he made amends. In an age when religion involved every relationship of life, excommunicates became social outcasts, for they could have no social, political, or economic relations with their fellows. Rulers, for example, dreaded the sentence of excommunication, for feudal ties established by oath were dissolved the moment oaths were relaxed. Interdict, on the other hand, was a censure by which communities of persons were debarred from certain sacraments and from burial in consecrated ground. Parishes, cities, even whole kingdoms, might be placed under interdict. But innocent people in danger of death generally were permitted the use of sacraments, especially baptism.

HERESY AND ITS TREATMENT

Heresy, religious teaching contrary to the universally received faith, seriously challenged the late medieval Church. Our forefathers of that day entertained no kindly sentiments toward it. Medieval society, possessing only elementary political and social organization (at least as compared with modern society), relied upon traditional customs, feudal oaths, ties of kith and kin, and the restraint provided by practical ethics of religion which in countless ways entered into every aspect of medieval life. Following the downfall of the Roman Empire until the twelfth century there had been little heresy. But there rose in southern France the Cathari, also known as Albigenses, who taught that all matter was evil, that the Church was Antichrist, that oaths were wicked, that marriage, even though chaste, was immoral, and that the highest counsel of perfection was suicide. Feudal society, resting on oaths, was outraged, Christian folk were affronted by their conception of marriage, and people abhorred their advocacy of suicide. Albigensian teaching was antisocial, antipolitic, and antichristian. Small wonder that the nobility of France levied war on the Albigenses.

Until then bishops had customarily purged their dioceses of heretics, a policy popular among the people who took a hand in the action which frequently resulted in the extreme penalty—death. But the bishops, especially in southern France, were scarcely equal to the task of cleansing their dioceses. Accordingly, in 1233 a permanent tribunal, known as the Inquisition, was set up. Inquisitors usually were chosen from the Dominicans. Being better educated than the secular clergy, they were more effective in investigating religious opinions. The methods of this court were gentle for first offenders; for lapsed heretics it might be severe. It employed the devices of physical torture derived from Roman Law. As clergymen were forbidden by Canon Law to shed blood, the inquisitors' sentences extended merely to expulsion from the Church. So close, however, was the coöperation between Church and secular government in this matter, that sentences pronounced on heretics were binding in the eyes of princes and automatically condemned the victim to the severe reprisals secular law had invented for the crime of heresy.

No practice of medieval times has been so severely condemned as the infliction of death and other penalties for heresy. But, while we naturally agree in this condemnation, it must, however, be kept in mind that the Middle Ages as well as early modern times were not noted for their indulgent sentiments when heresy was involved. Heresy was held to be a crime equivalent to treason. The penalty of death was always thought proper. In judging the medieval attitude toward heresy we should keep in mind that religion was a basic element in the social, political, and intellectual life of the time, and, if freedom was permitted to hold and apply, subversive opinions like those of the Albigenses anarchy would result.

The practical significance of the Inquisition is to be seen in the successful extirpation of that great heresy.

CANON LAW OF THE CHURCH

The Christian community, embracing more souls than any secular political organism of the day, possessed an elaborate organization of courts. Archdeacons, bishops, archbishops, and the pope had power to try many kinds of cases that rose in the discharge of ecclesiastical business. The law employed in these courts was one of the most remarkable products of medieval culture, and in modern times is known as "Canon Law," or the *Corpus Juris Canonici*, to be distinguished from the great *Corpus Juris Civilis* bequeathed by Roman emperors. Its codification began with the Benedictine monk Gratian in 1151, who arranged precepts drawn from Scripture, the Church fathers, decrees of councils, principles of the natural law, and pronouncements of popes about Church government, some of which contradicted each other. Hence he called his work the *Harmony of Conflicting Canons* (*Concordantia Discordantium Canonum*), or simply, the *Decretum of Gratian*. Bulls of succeeding pontiffs, greatly increasing its bulk, were published under the title *Liber Sextus* by Boniface VIII (1294–1303). To these works later were added the decrees of Clement V (1305–1314) in five books, known as the *Constitutiones Clementinae*, and two other collections, originally not included in the body of the decretals, the *Extravagantes of John XXII* (1316–1334) and the *Extravagantes Communes*. From the standpoint of the history of civilization this Canon Law, whether viewed as a Church legal code or an administrative guide, is a monument of medieval achievement.

Chapter 4

THE CHURCH: PROBLEMS AND CRISES

$\mathcal{T}$HE ELABORATE administrative system of the medieval Church, created to carry on its spiritual labors as described in the foregoing chapter, did not, like Minerva, spring full blown into existence. Founded during the first century of the Christian era when its membership was limited in number, her organization in the beginning was elementary.

But as the centuries passed and the population of the Roman Empire in ever growing numbers identified itself with the Christian community new administrative organs came to be created. By the time of the Emperor Theodosius (d. 395) the Church, theoretically at least, had come to embrace the entire population of the Empire. Such had become the extent of the Church's activity by the close of the Roman Empire in the West (about 500) that everywhere she had become deeply enmeshed in the social, economic, and intellectual political life of the day. For nearly 1000 years thereafter—until the Renaissance and the Reformation—the Church continued in this fashion until the pontificates of Innocent III (1198–1216), Boniface VIII (1294–1303), and those of the popes at Avignon (1309–1378) when the organs and departments of medieval ecclesiastical administration attained their full development. In this chapter we shall trace some of the problems of the Church's political relations with medieval states and with the manorial organization of medieval society.

MANOR AND PARISH ORGANIZATION

Institutions derived from the Roman Empire long provided the material foundations on which the religious and other organizations characteristic of the Middle Ages rested. The manor in some of its aspects, for example, was one of these. It became an increasingly varied and complex organism as the Middle Ages wore on and was most significant in the social, economic, mental, and moral history of those centuries. The manorial village with the lord's barn, mill, press, and smithy, and the strips of land tilled for the lord by the peasants, the strips tilled by the peasants for themselves, and the common woodland and common pasture all provided the material about which revolved the life of a manor.

The parish was the priest's spiritual vineyard. The Church fabric was the center of religious life. Here Mass was said and the sacraments administered. In the churchyard the community's dead, generation after generation, were buried in consecrated ground and with the blessing of the priest. Life on the medieval manor produced a population at once religious, thrifty, practical, and guided by tradition.

The post of the parish priest was called his living, or benefice. He owed his appointment to his bishop. But years ago, when the community had first embraced Christianity, or later, some well-to-do property owner, probably a king or some prince, or some other influential person, set aside lands in the parish for the support of the Church, at the same time reserving for himself the right of presenting to the bishop candidates for the living. This was known as the right of advowson. The practice of advowsons bound the religious life of the village community closely to the lord of the manor. This was to have an important bearing on religious life and practice throughout the Middle Ages.

LANDED PROPERTY AND EPISCOPAL ECONOMIC ORGANIZATION

Archbishops and bishops active in the spiritual affairs of dioceses acquired extensive landed properties. Pious folk—nobles, clergy, and other powerful personages—were lavish with their benefactions. So, for example, the bishops of Rome, most influential because they were successors of St. Peter, received many an estate in his honor. By the time of Pope Gregory I (590–604) this property known as the Patrimony of St. Peter had become so extensive that it covered much of central Italy and also included lands in the Alps, Gaul, Corsica, Sardinia, Dalmatia, Illyria, and Africa. A considerable administrative organism came into existence for the building of churches, managing local village matters, feeding the poor, helping the destitute, and, in addition, taking care of local administration. When bequeathing properties for such purposes to bishops and archbishops or, more accurately, to the patron saint who had founded the see, in this case St. Peter, donors for themselves and for their heirs usually reserved the right of presenting candidates for a living, to be appointed by the bishop or archbishop. Similarly properties were commonly given for the support of cathedral canons in which case also donors kept the right of presenting candidates for some clerical post. Such livings usually were called prebends.

RURAL CHARACTER OF BENEDICTINE MONASTERIES

Monastic orders during the early Middle Ages naturally made use of the methods of agriculture then traditional everywhere. In earlier times Benedictine monks were simple workers of the soil living according to a religious rule under the direction of an abbot. But it was not long before Benedictine monasteries began to receive gifts of prosperous manors tilled by peasant serfs. The abbot then became the managerial head of a complex system of manors. The Cluniac monks followed their example, but few if any of their religious labored in the fields. The granting of such gifts in land to provide endowments for all manner of ecclesiastical persons and institutions became the order of the day. And, as the Church and her organs ever kept on functioning and never died, she accumulated an immense amount of property. During the great economic transformation of Europe in the twelfth, thirteenth, and fourteenth centuries many of these Benedictine monasteries saw towns develop on their lands, as in the case of St. Bavo and St. Peter in Ghent. Many a Benedictine foundation thus became immensely wealthy, a condition contrary to the original monastic ideal of poverty to which St. Benedict's order was dedicated.

COÖPERATION OF CROWN AND CHURCHMEN

In addition to landed property, churchmen also acquired extensive political power. During early medieval times, following the decline of the Roman Empire, state organization in western Europe was elementary and feeble and police forces scarcely existed. There was practically no trained officialdom, and state policy, compared with what we have today, was embryonic, being closely associated with the rulers' household activities which included mainly the care of family estates. Princes of those days were practical men. They asked few questions about the theoretical aim and scope of governmental activity. It was customary for princes to look to churchmen for help in the solution of all manner of secular questions, something quite natural, for at that time churchmen were about the only persons who could read and write and who had any theories of government and what princes should do. As religious leaders, bishops, archbishops, and abbots possessed great prestige, and princes habitually consulted them. Considering the character of social organization and of state management, it was natural that churchmen should take over the role of government. So, the bishop of Rome, when the imperial government no longer was able to carry on in the region around Rome, quite inevitably took over the emperor's political functions. This was the origin of the pope's political power in the region then called the "Duchy of Rome."

During the eighth century this close association of princes and churchmen produced some epochal events. The pope, theoretically dependent upon the emperor at Constantinople, was in 730 ordered to remove all religious statues from his churches. This was the time of the great Iconoclastic Controversy. As head of the Catholic Church, he refused to comply, even when the emperor sent a fleet to Italy with orders, which failed, to bring him to Constantinople, for the fleet was destroyed in a storm. Further, the pope had to meet the attacks of the Lombard kings who had invaded Italy and wanted to expand their territory at the pope's expense.

Meanwhile, members of the Carolingian family, to which the pope had turned for support, themselves also needed help in order to establish themselves as masters of the Franks by replacing the Merovingian house which had ruled the Franks since the days of Clovis (d. 511). The Carolingians showed themselves loyal promoters of the cause of the Church. Charles Martel (d. 741) beat back the Moors at Tours in 732. When his son, Pippin III (d. 768), appealed to the pope for support in putting an end to the reigning Merovingian do-nothing rulers, it was gladly given. So at Soissons in 751 Pippin was elected king and crowned by Bishop Boniface. By this time the Lombard king moved to seize the papal patrimony. Twice the pope journeyed to Frankland to ask for Pippin's help. On his second appearance Pippin restored to him, in a document known as the Donation of Pippin (754), all properties in Italy which the Lombard had taken from the pope. Ruling over the papal states, the pope now was a sovereign prince, a position which he held throughout the Renaissance and the Reformation and which continued to 1871.

The spontaneous and practical coöperation of king and Church, so strikingly exhibited in these activities of Pippin and the pope, received its classic elaboration under Charlemagne who ruled from 768 to 814. Charlemagne dominated the Church by controlling the election of bishops and abbots. He built churches and decreed that tithes were to be raised for their support. He convoked councils, presided over them, and signed their decrees. He enriched the Church by extensive gifts of land, and went to war against pagans, for example, the Saxons. He set forth his theory on the relation of the temporal and the spiritual power in a letter to the pope in 796. In it he declared it was his duty to protect with armed force the Church in her external relations against her enemies. He also considered that it was his duty to "strengthen within the Church knowledge of the Catholic faith." The function of the Church in turn was to assist him with her priestly ministrations and so help him become victorious over his enemies.

The famous events on Christmas day 800 were a part of this policy. The pope had great difficulties in Rome where there was bitter feuding, and he needed help. Charlemagne was an imposing figure dominating the political life of the day. Had he not extended his rule over a large area formerly part of the Roman Empire? Was he not—so it seemed—successor of the great emperors of Rome? Was he not the ever vigilant protector of the Church? And was he not loyal to the Christian faith, something that could not be said of the schismatic Iconoclastic emperor in Constantinople? Why should Charlemagne not be emperor? Such were some of the questions that determined the pope's policy which on Christmas day 800 prompted Pope Leo III to crown Charlemagne and proclaim him Emperor while kneeling during Mass in the Constantinian basilica of St. Peter's in Rome.

FEUDALISM, AND CRISIS IN THE CHURCH

A dangerous crisis confronted the Church during the eleventh and twelfth centuries, one which jeopardized her spiritual calling. Its origins are to be found in the far-reaching changes in the social and political life of Europe since the days of Charlemagne. First, the empire which had been created by him was ineffective in producing order after its founder died. Nor were his successors, Carolingian princes, capable of governing the vast realm over which Charlemagne had held sway. Civil war and anarchy were the order of the day and so political authority slipped out of their hands. The confusion thus caused was increased by the invasion of powerful peoples—Northmen from Scandinavia, Saracens in the Mediterranean area, and Magyars from the Danubian plains. The Carolingian governmental organization was unable to stop them.

As a result of these factors, political power—not only in Carolingian lands, but also in other lands—passed into the hands of powerful personages. Some of these were royal princes while others were officials (counts) in the Carolingian state system, others were successful because they belonged to powerful and ambitious families, and, finally, many others had political power devolved upon them because as bishops, archbishops, or abbots they possessed vast prestige among the people. This revolution, the development of feudalism—a development of the greatest significance in the history of Europe—reached its climax by about the year 1000 and spelled a formidable crisis for the Church.

Charlemagne, as noted above, had shown by example how a ruler might coöperate with the Church. But while the latter received protection from him and was granted all manner of political favors, churchmen were effectively controlled and even appointed by him. During the heyday of feudalism princes everywhere—in such Carolingian lands as France, Italy, and Germany, and in non-Carolingian countries like England—controlled the spiritual activities as well as the temporal acts of bishops, archbishops, and abbots.

So, for example, in Germany it was the policy of the Emperor Otto I (936–973) to keep a firm hand upon the nobility by controlling the election of prelates. The sacred symbols of high ecclesiastical office—ring and staff—were bestowed by the king at the same time as the scepter which symbolized a churchman's temporalities, or fiefs, held of the king by feudal oath. Similarly, German emperors, who also ruled over northern Italy, controlled papal elections. Originally the clergy of Rome had elected the popes. But with the development of feudalism election passed into the hands of the Roman nobility who carried on blood feuds whence ensued great scandals. So the German kings sought to establish regularity in papal appointments. But their interference in papal elections meant the subjection of the Church to a secular ruler.

THE TWO POWERS: SPIRITUAL AND TEMPORAL

This subordination of the Church to the policies of feudal princes and feudal kings, and to the emperor of the Holy Roman Empire in particular, was intolerable. For in practice it meant that the things that were God's would be subjected to secular expediency, or simply to politics. Long before Charlemagne's day there had been protests against this practice. So, for example, Pope Gelasius I (492–496) had laid down the classical theory of the relationship of the temporal and the spiritual powers. He declared that there were ". . . two powers by which this world is chiefly ruled: the sacred authority of the popes and that of princes. Of these the priestly is much more important, because it has to render account for the kings of men themselves at the divine tribunal."

Naturally, this theory could not be forgotten by churchmen in spite of the practical success which Charlemagne's theory and practice subsequently had throughout the feudal period. Gelasius' theory, as we shall see, was constantly used in arguing for the superiority of Christian principles over secular political activities. Later, this teaching was expressed by the symbolical use of the two swords—spiritual and temporal—and the superiority of the former over the latter. This theory was to acquire classical importance throughout the Middle Ages.

THE STRUGGLE OVER INVESTITURE

Subserviency of the Church to feudal society in general and to the Holy Roman Empire in particular was objectionable. There were protests. For example, the Cluniac congregation of Benedictine monks, established in 910, which sought to exalt the Church in every walk of life saw the danger of a Church subjugated as a handmaid to political power.

Especially did that order oppose the persistent policy of feudal interests of invading the Church and using it for secular ends. But it was not until the eleventh century that it became possible for the popes to free themselves from imperial control. Bishop Bruno of Toul, although an appointee (1028) of the emperor, was a zealous churchman who, as Pope Leo IX (1048–1054), traveled far and wide, holding councils and vigorously banishing from the ecclesiastical organization all kinds of simoniacal abuses that had crept into the Church. Nicholas II (1059–1061), chosen by the Roman clergy, continued the movement of reform. In 1059 he struck a blow for the freedom of papal elections. His decree reserved the election of popes to a college of cardinals, thus eliminating imperial influences.

But it was not until the pontificate of Hildebrand, or Gregory VII (1073–1085), that the struggle for the liberation of the Church from lay feudal control really burst forth. Hildebrand had come to maturity as a Benedictine monk in Rome. Upright in character, austere in morals, skillful as an administrator, he had during many years—ever since the days of Leo IX—been associated with the reforming clergy of Rome. He was wholly in sympathy with the Cluniac ideas concerning reform. The Church, he believed, should be exalted above all men and all human institutions. The points of his program were set forth in the *Dictatus Papae*, a document apparently from Hildebrand's hand. It stated that the Church was of divine foundation and could not err in faith and morals. The pope, being the successor of St. Peter, vicar of Christ, had supreme authority and could depose, reinstate, and translate bishops; and his legates of any grade could depose them. Appeals might be made directly to the Holy See, and the pope could even depose emperors. To achieve these ends the clergy were to be celibate. Under feudal and manorial conditions of society it had been impossible to enforce ancient teaching on this matter. Through clerical marriage ecclesiastical properties were in danger of being alienated; parishes and dioceses accordingly might become purely secular institutions tied to the feudal system. Therefore, Gregory opposed lay investiture.

As soon as he was elected Gregory VII in 1073, he sought to reform the Christian community according to his cherished ideas. The "City of God" was to be established. He appealed to the princes of Europe to submit to Peter "whom Christ had established as Prince over all the kingdoms of the world." At a council convoked at Rome in 1075 Gregory forbade marriage of the clergy and threatened to excommunicate bishops and abbots who should receive investiture at the hands of laymen, whether emperor or any other ruler of whatever rank. Soon the pope excommunicated some of the councilors of the Emperor Henry (1056–1106) and cited the latter to appear in Rome, to be excommunicated should he refuse.

A bitter struggle ensued, one in which all Germany took sides. Henry "deposed" Gregory, whereupon the pope excommunicated Henry. Such was the force of Gregory's appeal to the German people that Henry was deserted. His princes convoked a council to Augsburg at which Gregory was to preside. The result could only be disastrous to the emperor. So Henry, resolved to lift the sentence of excommunication, journeyed to Gregory. For three days Henry, garbed as a penitent, stood in the snow at castle Canossa in the Apennines where Gregory was staying. The pope, much against his will—for his duty as a priest of course took precedence —received him in his presence and after imposing some hard terms granted absolution. This meeting of pope and emperor at Canossa on January 28, 1077, is one of the most dramatic events in history.

But the struggle continued, for Henry reopened it. His strength, however, was limited to the support of a clique of wealthy nobles who battened on the properties of the Church. The pope's policy, on the other hand, found favor among the people. How enthusiastic they were for papal leadership was shown by the way they thronged at the Council of Clermont in 1095 when the first crusade was proclaimed. Finally Henry V (1106–1125), weary of the struggle he could not win, agreed to a practical settlement with Calixtus II (1119–1124) in what is known as the Concordat of Worms (September 23, 1122).

Henceforth bishops and abbots were to be elected freely, without simony, and in the emperor's presence. They were to take the ring and staff, not from the emperor, but from the Church's legitimate representatives. They were to receive the temporalities, diocesan or monastic, by touch of the royal scepter. This latter ceremony was to be but a supplementary rite in no way influencing the election and investiture with ring and staff.

The Concordat of Worms definitely put an end to a crying abuse in the life of the Church. For centuries it had been the practice of princes to appoint Church officials directly and invest them with the symbols of their religious office. Henceforth they no longer possessed such rights. The Concordat, however, could not stop illegal investiture, nor did it put an end to lay influences indirectly exercised. And, of course, the rights of lay patrons in conferring benefices remained a serious problem.

Administratively, Pope Innocent III (1198–1216) was successful in exalting the papacy in the life and thought of this age. He conducted a vigorous management and sent out a stream of legates to represent him in Church matters. He maintained a well-organized chancery. In the Fourth Lateran Council (1215) he laid down measures to combat simony and pluralism in ecclesiastical posts, and ruled against the taxation of Church property by secular governments; ordered the holding of annual diocesan synods; insisted that priests should be celibate and have a measure of education; issued decrees regarding heresy, required annual confessions, defined the classical teaching of transubstantiation in the Real Presence, and encouraged crusades.

Although successful in his spiritual program, Innocent III had much opposition from the princes of the day. He had the same lofty conception which Gregory VII held regarding the superiority of the spiritual over the temporal. He wrote "As God has placed two great lights in the starry heavens—a greater light to preside by day and a lesser to preside by night—so he has established two great powers in the realm of the universal Christian community—one to rule the souls of men and another to rule their bodies. And as the moon—inferior in size and quality—draws its light from the sun so the power of kings derives its splendor from the priestly." But although all men at the time believed in the theory of the two powers governing man's actions, it was difficult to direct human activities accordingly. There was bound to be conflict between the world of material interests and the general principles of ethics, as Machiavelli later was to demonstrate in his *Prince*. So Innocent had to contend with King John of England (1199–1216) over the royal appointment of the archbishop of Canterbury. Innocent also had a bitter struggle with King Philip Augustus of France (1180–1223) who sought to repudiate his lawfully wedded wife and attempted to remarry.

THE STRUGGLE WITH THE HOHENSTAUFEN

The most determined opponents of papal political theories and policies were the emperors of the Hohenstaufen House, the second of whom, Frederick Barbarossa (1152–1190), sought to rule the empire in the tradition of Charlemagne. But he also was inspired by the principles of Justinian's *Civil Law*, the study of which had recently been revived at the university of Bologna. This study of civil law sharpened Barbarossa's desire to act independently of papal principles. His son Henry VI (1190–1197) followed his example and, in addition, married Queen Constance of Naples and Sicily, thereby politically uniting the Hohenstaufen and Neapolitan and Sicilian political aims, something that threatened to ruin all possibility of peace for the papacy. A bitter struggle broke out between Frederick II (1212–1250) and the popes. Ruling the most highly organized and autocratic state on the continent of Europe west of the Byzantine Empire, Frederick was absolutist in policy, disdainful of papal ethical principles, determined to follow his own ideas, and unscrupulous in formulating his own independent policies.

During the course of the struggle Pope Innocent IV (1243–1254) convoked a General Council to Rome. But Frederick's navy, patrolling the Mediterranean, seized a number of the prelates while on their way to the council and imprisoned them on his ships. The pope, however, escaped from Rome and called the council to Lyons. There, on July 17, 1245, Innocent issued his famous bull deposing the emperor and freeing his subjects from their oaths of fealty to him as Gregory VII had done in 1076 and 1080.

But it was easier to depose Frederick than to be rid of him, and the contest continued. Frederick died in 1250 in full possession of his titles. His son Conrad IV (1250–1254) and grandson Conradino (1254–1268) continued the contest. The royal line was perpetuated, in an illegitimate branch, by Conrad's natural brother, Manfred (d. 1266), whose descendants, as we have learned, played a vigorous role in the subsequent history of Sicily.

RISE OF NATIONALISM: BONIFACE VIII AND PHILIP THE FAIR

The thirteenth century marked the culmination in European life of a tremendous transition—socially, economically, and politically. Under feudalism, dominant from 900 to about 1200, government was elementary, usually an extension of the household activity which managed some landowners' extensive estates. By about 1300, however, government was becoming departmentalized and administration more efficient, collection of revenue more systematic, the work of justice more regular, and the military more responsive to royal commands. Powerful princes adopted ambitious national policies. Henceforth the subtle forces of national sentiment often challenged ecclesiastical theories. New political theories were produced, new crises presented themselves. The first serious contest with these new powers took place during the pontificate of Boniface VIII (1294–1303). The occasion was the war between Philip IV, the Fair, king of France (1285–1315), and Edward I Plantagenet, king of England (1272–1307).

Philip was an able and unscrupulous prince. Although not a great warrior, he was an effective ruler. At his court he retained men trained in Roman law who taught that a king's will should be supreme in his realm. He was ambitious to bring into his hands such great fiefs of his crown as Flanders and Guienne. He was especially eager to secure Guienne, of which the English king was duke; it was the last remnant of that splendid empire over which Plantagenet Henry II (1154–1189) had ruled. The unity of France and the pride of its king demanded this possession. The ancient rivalry between Norman and English sailors suddenly broke out in 1293. Philip accused Edward I and demanded reparation. Summoned to present himself before his peers in Paris, Edward sent his brother who unwisely surrendered some border strongholds of Guienne into Philip's hands for a period of 40 days until Edward should make formal submission in a personal interview. Philip at once poured large numbers of troops into the land, clearly intending to keep it. When the 40 days were over, he argued that Edward had not obeyed his summons and had forfeited the duchy.

Edward I was an energetic ruler who enjoyed the confidence of his subjects. He did much to make the will of the crown effective, laid the basis for many reforms in administration, and was aware of the new power in the hands of the bourgeoisie. When he mounted the English throne, he realized the danger that lurked in Guienne and began to organize alliances against Philip III (1270–1285) and Philip the Fair. He made matrimonial connections with princes in the Low Countries. Commercial and industrial Brabant, commercial Holland and Zeeland, and the county of Bar were cultivated. In 1274 Edward had done homage for Guienne but only with suppressed bitterness. A chronicler described his relations with Philip as "the love of a cat and a dog." When the fight between English and French mariners in the English Channel brought on the long-threatened war, Edward turned to Count Guy of Flanders (1278–1305).

Flanders, as fief of the French crown, was required to support Philip. But industrially it was dependent on English wool which kept its weavers employed in manufacturing cloths for the markets of Europe. Its towns possessed a large population which could be fed only by foodstuffs imported from all parts of Europe. The Flemings paid for these out of the profits from the manufacture of cloth. Social antagonisms were rife in Flemish towns and greatly influenced the course of the struggle. Count Guy was opposed by his aristocratic townsmen (patricians) because he championed the craftsmen who were exploited by their more favored brethren. These craftsmen violently opposed their industrial and political masters. The patricians therefore appealed to Philip who, eager for an opportunity to interfere in the county, summoned Guy before the Parlement of Paris (1296). Meanwhile Edward perfected his alliance with the archbishop of Cologne, his friends in the Low Countries, and Emperor Adolph. Guy listened to Edward's suggestions and in December 1296, agreed to an alliance whereby his daughter, Philippa, was to become the wife of Edward, the Prince of Wales. The Scottish crown had fallen vacant in 1290, and Edward had succeeded in establishing his claim as overlord, but the Scottish lords were discontented and joined Philip.

A war of such proportions demanded funds. Edward found that his usual income, even though supplemented by grants of the Commons, was far from sufficient. He forced the clergy, regular and secular, to give him large sums. Philip pursued an identical policy in France and secured grants from his clergy in their provincial synods held in the autumn of 1294. A few prelates protested to the pope. In 1296 the clergy granted further subsidies and again complained of the royal pressure. In reply to these protestations Boniface, when he found that his efforts to arbitrate between the two kings were threatened with failure, issued the bull *Clericis Laicos* (February 24, 1296), in which he forbade secular princes, under pain of excommunication, to collect contributions from the clergy without authorization from the Holy See. It was, as we have learned, an ancient principle (which had caused much contention in earliers days) that the Church's property should not be taxed for secular purposes.

Boniface was an able pontiff. Trained in every point of canon law, he was above all things a lawyer. He adopted the traditional view of ecclesiastical property. He could scarcely comprehend the transformations of the day in social, economic, and political life. His reply to the policy of taxation adopted by Edward I and Philip the Fair was characteristic. It consisted simply in a reassertion of legal and ecclesiastical rights with special vigor and unpleasant emphasis. It antagonized kings who believed they possessed some right to tax the clergy for the defense of their realms. The question was whether the hierarchy should insist on its privileges and prevent the taxation of its goods by secular princes. In other words, should the hierarchy be permitted to challenge the acts of a ruler when he violated the ancient privileges of the Church, rights Boniface held as supreme pontiff, vicar of Christ?

The answer to the pope was prompt and decisive. Edward outlawed the clergy who, when the bull was published in England, refused to contribute. The clergy thought it best to redeem their outlawry by a fine, and soon all but the archbishop of Canterbury and the bishop of Lincoln yielded. In France a storm of nationalistic antipapal feeling was unleashed. Philip the Fair, not thus to be crossed, forbade the exportation of precious metal. This hurt the activities of Italian bankers who were acting as agents in transmitting payments made by people in France to the Holy See.

A war of pamphlets began in which the most radical statements were made about the relation of papal and royal power. One of these, the *Dialogue between a Cleric and a Knight,* attacked the immunities of the clergy, declared that lay society was superior to that of the clergy, and held that the latter were bound for patriotic reasons to pay a subvention for their lands to the king for the national defense. Even the clergy in France wavered. Finally, Boniface retraced his steps and in August, 1297, issued the bull *Etsi de Statu,* in which he recognized the right of the crown in case of necessity to tax ecclesiastical property without papal permission. Meanwhile Edward's campaign in Flanders (1297) came to naught and, faced with serious difficulties at home, the king made a truce with Philip.

Soon Boniface was involved in another quarrel with Philip. Bishop Bernard Saisset of Pamiers was seized in Paris and accused of treasonable negotiations with Philip's enemies. The pope broke into violent language against the king for thus proceeding against a religious person. The bull *Salvator Mundi* of December, 1301, rebuked Philip and revoked concessions made to him since the issuance of the bull *Clericis Laicos.* Then followed *Ausculta Fili* in which he complained against Philip's conduct in the purely temporal affairs of his government. Philip knew he could appeal to the townsmen in his struggle with the papacy. He summoned the clergy, nobility, and bourgeoisie who met at Paris in April, 1302. The issue was clearly drawn. Philip was supported by the growing nationalist sentiment among the bourgeoisie who disliked interference by any external power, especially the papacy. The king's agent, Pierre Flotte, harangued the gathering with much heat. False papal bulls were produced, insulting letters were written to the Holy See protesting against the pope's policies.

Meanwhile Philip, having made peace with Edward, invaded Flanders. But the Flemings did not want to be incorporated into France. The men of Bruges rose against the French mercilessly massacring Frenchmen within the walls. Other towns accepted this rising as a signal for revolt, and the French were expelled from Flanders. Philip called out the levies of the realm. The flower of French chivalry marched forth to put down the rebels, but the handicraftsmen defeated them outside the walls of Courtrai on June 11, 1302.

This misfortune to French arms came at an opportune moment for Boniface. When news of the disaster reached him, the pope took courage and in November, 1302, issued the bull *Unam Sanctam*. It set forth the traditional theory of papal relations with secular princes. It declared that the two swords symbolizing religious and secular authority had been confided by God to His Vicar on earth. The former was wielded by the hierarchy subject to God alone, the latter by princes and their officials but under the instruction of the priests who also had authority to judge their conduct. At the close of the document appeared the emphatic words: "Moreover, we declare, state, define, and pronounce that it is altogether necessary to salvation for every human creature to be subject to the pontiff of Rome." Philip was incensed, but Boniface threatened him with excommunication.

But Philip was to have speedy revenge, planned and executed by Guillaume de Nogaret, the king's prominent adviser. He was a doctor from the University in Toulouse, had been trained in Roman law, and bore in his bosom some of the hatred of Albigenses toward the hierarchy. He proposed to seize the pope, convey him to France, convoke a council before which he was to be tried, and choose a new pontiff. The plan was supported by Sciarra Colonna and some bankers of Florence who were also bitter toward the pope. Nogaret proceeded to Italy. Colonna received support among his Tuscan and Roman friends. One morning in September, 1303, they broke into the presence of the aged pope in Anagni. Nogaret told him of his mission, but it was impossible to carry the old man off in the face of his rallying supporters who conducted him to Rome where he died on October 11. The humiliation inflicted upon Boniface marked the beginning of the end of papal control over the policies of secular princes. It also marked a stage in the growth of the sovereign power of secular princes.

Benedict XI (1303–1304), who succeeded Boniface, was a wise and circumspect pontiff from whom much might have been expected. He sought to still the strife with Philip by moderate measures couched in kindly tones. The censures of Boniface were remitted, and the bull *Clericis Laicos* was given an interpretation which did not clash with royal interests. Even the Colonna cardinals were restored to their dignities and properties. But Philip entertained further designs; he insisted upon a general council to try the acts of the departed Boniface. Benedict now showed firmness and issued a bull in June, 1304, in which he complained of the outrage of Anagni and excommunicated fifteen persons implicated in it, among whom were Guillaume de Nogaret and Sciarra Colonna. When the pope died in Perugia in the same month, it was whispered that he had been poisoned.

There was much contention in the conclave to choose his successor. The Colonna party, supported by French money, resisted the election of a member of the Orsini family which opposed foreign influences in the *curia*. Finally, Archbishop Bertrand de Got of Bordeaux was chosen and succeeded as Clement V (1305–1314). It is said that before his election he had an interview with Philip, who demanded complete reconciliation, a grant of taxes on church lands, condemnation of Boniface's memory, and restoration of the Colonnas. Clement was crowned at Lyons and Philip played an important role in the ceremonies. The pontiff offered absolution to the king, yielded in the matter of taxes, restored the Colonnas to favor, and appointed ten new cardinals, all members of the king's party. "A French pope was to be surrounded by a French court."

Clement continued to show himself compliant to Philip. The bull *Clericis Laicos* was rescinded, and *Unam Sanctam* was declared to imply no prejudice to the realm of France. Philip made further demands upon the harassed pontiff. Guillaume de Nogaret was given full absolution for bullying Boniface to his death, and for penance was required to go to the Holy Land to fight the infidel. Suppression of the Knights Templars was to be Philip's next step. This crusading order, founded in 1118, had performed heroic service by protecting pilgrims in Palestine. The expulsion of the Christians from the Holy Land at the fall of Acre in 1291 robbed the Templars of their theater of activity. They had accumulated much property in Europe and had become bankers. Philip eyed their resources with jealousy and trumped up extraordinary accusations. He arrested all of them in October, 1307, and subjected them to torture. Confessions confirming the royal accusations were wrung from the unfortunates.

Philip seized the possessions of the order in France and put its members in prison. Clement reluctantly agreed that the order should be discussed at the council to be held at Vienne beginning October, 1310. Meanwhile Clement was weak enough to believe the sworn statements extorted by torture. His bull *Faciens Misericordiam* of August, 1308, commanded that trials be instituted in all states. A papal commission investigated the activities of the order in Paris, and four proctors were named to defend the order. The questionings of the commission revealed the frightful tortures to which the knights had been subjected in order to extract incriminating evidence. Thinking that they would receive justice from the papal commissioners, many of them boldly retracted their confessions. Their faith was misplaced, for the archbishop of Sens went so far as to condemn as relapsed heretics those knights who retracted their confessions. Those who persisted in their retractions were burned in Paris near the gate of St. Antoine in May, 1309. Others were burned later, until the number mounted to more than a hundred.

The archbishop of Sens was the brother of Enguerrand de Marigny, one of the king's councilors; this helps explain why the prosecution was successful in France. Elsewhere, except in England, the order was acquitted. Philip left no stone unturned to obtain the desired end. On March 12, 1312, the pope yielded and dissolved the order. Its properties were given to the Knights of St. John, but Philip claimed such great indemnities that little escaped his coffers. Thus Philip sought to advance his power by crushing all that stood in his way. Since the Templars were hardly powerful enough to endanger the safety of the crown, Philip's action was dictated by covetousness and desire for revenge.

Meantime Philip insisted on the prosecution of the departed Boniface. Clement was frightened and wished to evade the royal demands. He dared stay no longer in France and in the spring of 1309 sought residence in Avignon, a town situated on the left bank of the Rhone in the county of Venaissin, a fief of the papacy. To Avignon the pope summoned the king and several of his supporters to appear before him in February, 1310. The consistory opened in March, and arguments were heard. Accusations against Boniface varied greatly and at points contradicted each other. Philip finally abandoned his plea and left it to Clement's judgment. The bull of May, 1311, is a pitiful example of the papal weakness: in it Philip was extolled for his zeal in behalf of the Church; his charges against Boniface were declared to spring from pious fervor; and the bulls against Philip and his subjects were annulled or mitigated. This was the beginning of the long residence of the papacy in Avignon, from 1309–1378, a period of great trial, as we shall now learn.

PART III

Trials Confronting the Church

Chapter 5

THE PAPACY AT AVIGNON. THE GREAT SCHISM AND THE COUNCILS

ᖴOLLOWING THE humiliation of the papacy inflicted upon Pope Boniface VIII by the royal power of France came a series of new and more formidable crises which rocked the Church. The first of these was the residence of seven popes at Avignon from 1309–1378. The second was the Great Western Schism which began in 1378. The third, no less severe than the two preceding, was the Age of the Councils, from 1409 to 1449.

THE PAPACY AT AVIGNON

Thinking that he could not safely live in Rome amid its turbulent population, Pope Clement V (1305–1314) had stayed on in France. So involved and urgent were his negotiations with Philip the Fair that he could not well leave France. Although established at Avignon, on the left bank of the Rhone outside the boundaries of France, he did not live beyond the French king's influence. What had been intended as a temporary sojourn dragged on during seven pontificates, from 1309–1378. This period, generally referred to as the Avignonese Papacy, is also called the "Babylonian Captivity."

The next pontificate, that of John XXII (1316–1334), was seriously disturbed by the pope's contest with Louis the Bavarian, emperor from 1314–1347. John was a native of Cahors in southern France, a member of a family of bankers. Though a septuagenarian when elected, he was an able financier as fantastic and exaggerated statements attest of how he amassed colossal sums of money in the papal treasury. But as spiritual shepherd of the Church who should have understood the mighty changes that had come over European society during several centuries past, he failed.

Being a canon lawyer and fiery tempered, John XXII was given to excessive legalism and insisted upon rights that were obsolescent. For example, when the imperial throne fell vacant on August 24, 1313, John's predecessor Clement V had claimed the right of guardianship. Two rival factions among the electors elected two hostile emperors, Louis the Bavarian and Frederick of Austria; but John, being elected pope in 1316, ignored both of them and as guardian sought to arbitrate between the two claimants. When Frederick was defeated in 1322 John insisted that Louis receive the empire as a papal gift. Louis refused, whereupon a bitter struggle ensued. Superficially it looked like a renewal of the old quarrel between popes and emperors. The empire, however, was but a shadow of its former self, and the papacy had fallen from the lofty heights it had occupied during the previous century. The grand contests between popes and emperors were finished. The old traditions survived, however; both sides were shadow boxing. A more serious contest was impending, one at best faintly comprehended by the pope, the emperor, or the writers of the day, in spite of the fact that Philip the Fair had staged his audacious attack on the papacy at the opening of the century. The future was to resound with the struggles between the papacy and national monarchs.

THE THEORIES OF MARSIGLIO OF PADUA
AND WILLIAM OF OCKHAM

The quarrel between Louis the Bavarian and the papacy produced a crop of revolutionary theories which have echoed down to our own time. The first of these was propounded by Marsiglio of Padua (d. 1342?) who had studied at the University of Padua and had become Master of Arts at the University of Paris and finally rector in 1312. In 1327 Marsiglio took up his residence at the court of the emperor. He had imbibed some of the bitterness of his fellow townsmen of Padua toward clerical immunities and the interference of churchmen in secular affairs. His animosity was colored by a lawyer's contempt for such privileges. The quarrel between John and Louis gave him an opportunity to write his book entitled *The Defender of the Peace*, which contained revolutionary ideas on the relations of Church and state.

Instead of conceiving of mankind as a Christian community ruled by the two powers—empire and Church—of which the Church was superior, Marsiglio thought of the community of man as being a purely secular thing and politically organized. The Christian legislator, the total body, or the majority of the people or citizenry, makes the law. To be sure, the community was thought of as being Christian. But the Church was to be shorn of all independent powers in the life of the citizenry. Although it was conceded that the clergy were to administer the sacraments, all disciplinary acts touching religion were to be controlled through the prince named by the Christian legislator. The clergy could not even exercise any authority in questions of heresy. The Christian legislator, or the prince alone, had authority to convoke councils. It also had authority to interpret Scripture. Based on Aristotle's *Politics*, this book taught that sovereignty in political affairs lay with the people. The prince as their representative had authority over all political functions within the community. The Church had no jurisdiction in this field.

Marsiglio boldly asserted that there was no political distinction to be drawn between clerics and laymen. Both were subject to the laws of the land. Weighty matters should be decided in councils composed of laymen and clerics appointed by secular communities. Princes should guide the procedure of these councils. The pope was merely an agent of the council. The Church, though divinely instituted, was to be run by laymen, the members of a secular political organism. This revolutionary book was to exert much influence in shaping the state-controlled Church arrangements of the Age of the Reformation.

The philosopher, William of Ockham (d. 1349?), also had some radical things to say about empire, Church, the pope, and the nature of the Christian faith. Ockham was a Franciscan friar who naturally was acquainted with current Franciscan criticisms of papal activities. In 1328 he took up residence at the imperial court and made himself obnoxious to the pope by publishing several radical pamphlets. (For his philosophical views see Chap. 9.) In regard to the Christian faith, the pope possessed no authority, either spiritually or temporally. And as the pope, general councils, and the Church fathers may err, the only infallible guide was Scripture. Further, he argued, the emperor had the right to depose the pope if the latter fell into heresy. Like the opinions of Marsiglio of Padua, those of Ockham too were to prove revolutionary. They exerted much influence, as we shall learn, on late medieval thought, and particularly on that of Martin Luther.

TRIBULATIONS OF THE AVIGNONESE PAPACY

A precarious peace existed in Europe when Benedict XII (1334–1342) succeeded to the papacy. The struggle with Emperor Louis the Bavarian, begun in 1323 when John XXII excommunicated and "deposed" him, continued. The struggle threatened to become more dangerous when the Hundred Years' War began in 1336. For Louis the Bavarian and Edward III of England, being brothers-in-law, formed an alliance directed against Philip VI of France (1328–1350). Benedict labored to quiet the contestants. None of the quarreling parties would hearken to him, however. His acts were questioned partly because of the quarrel with Louis the Bavarian. The imperial electors were incensed at his policy. They wished to retain the right of choosing their emperor. But Benedict, being a Frenchman, was suspected of favoring France.

In general, growing German national sentiment was opposed to foreign "interference." Finally, in July, 1338, the electors met at Rense and drew up a document stating that the "emperor duly elected . . . does not need the nomination, approbation, confirmation, assent, or authority of the Apostolic See in order to assume the administration of the rights and property of the empire or the royal title."[1] Three weeks later, at Frankfort, Louis, in a letter known as *Licet Juris*, gave this doctrine the sanction of imperial law. The empire was declared to be received from God alone and its bestowal was in no wise dependent on the will of the pope.

Nor did the English listen to Benedict's admonishments in behalf of peace. Rightly or wrongly, they distrusted him because of his French nationality and because of his residence in Avignon, believing that he was dominated by the French crown. Nor was Benedict liked by the French people, for, swayed by warlike passions, they regarded him as being too friendly toward the national enemy. The nascent spirit of nationalism threatened the papacy.

Naturally, Benedict continued his struggle with the excommunicated Louis, and his successor Clement VI (1342–1352) raised against him Charles, heir apparent of the crown of Bohemia. Charles was elected emperor by the pope's help, in 1346, but only after acknowledging the papal right to confirm the election of emperors (1346). He also promised to stay but a day in Rome, to go there only with the pope's consent, and to submit to the pope all differences between the empire and the crown of France. Germans called him the "pope's king."

An outstanding event of Clement's pontificate was the career of Rienzi, a Roman patriot. Italy was torn by dissensions of Guelphs and Ghibellines, *popolo minuto* and *popolo grasso*, rival states, and hostile nobles. In spite of her commerce and industry, Italy did not develop unity. Dante longed for this unity and thought that it would come through the

---

[1] G. D. Laffan, *Select Documents of European History*, I, 147–148.

emperor. Petrarch, the poet, was charmed by the tradition of Roman greatness. His lyrical soul was stirred by the anarchy of the peninsula. Rienzi also thought about such themes. Born about 1314, this son of a poor innkeeper spent much time musing over the glories of departed Rome eloquently proclaimed by the ruins on the Palatine Hill, the half-buried structures in the Forum, the dilapidated Colosseum, and other monuments to be seen at every hand. He read Livy and other Roman classics. He pondered the fallen state of the Eternal City; nobles lived in feud, prosperity had vanished, and insecurity reigned everywhere. Rome was no longer the capital of the world! The emperor lived among the barbarians, and her chief glory, the papacy, had long resided in France! (For an account of Petrarch's ideas, see Chapter 12.)

Rienzi dreamed of restoring Rome to its former glory and expounded his views to eager listeners. His oratory was magic to their ears, for they had not forgotten the ancient greatness of their city. Rienzi spent the night of May 18, 1347, before the altar in the church of Sant' Angelo. In the morning he appeared clad in armor, attended by twenty-five conspirators. The procession was full of symbolism. The townsmen had been summoned to the Campidoglio, the ancient Capitoline Hill. They burst into cheers and approved the laws which had been prepared beforehand. These laws had something of the wild justice of wild times. They declared the establishment of good government: strict punishment to be meted out to murderers, a force of 125 men from each of the thirteen wards to be appointed to police the city, the communal laws to be honestly managed, and rigid justice to be applied even to the baronage.

Rienzi was acclaimed dictator to enforce these laws. In a few days he took the title of tribune, apt reminder of the defenders of the rights of common folk in ancient Rome. He called himself "Tribune of Liberty, Peace, and Justice, and Liberator of the Holy Roman Republic." The astounded nobles dared not move. He invited the princes and cities of Italy to send envoys to Rome for a national parliament. But his dream of restoration was visionary. The revived republic could be no more than a confederation of states with Rome as nominal head. Rienzi declared Rome to be the capital of the world. The election of emperors was asserted to be a right of the Roman people, the *populus Romanus*. He summoned Louis the Bavarian, Charles IV of Bohemia, prelates, kings, and princes to appear before him as judge. But his impractical character caused the bold stroke to fail. The nobles were biding their time. Rienzi's assumption of authority over imperial elections stirred the pope to resentment. The mighty Colonna from their stronghold at Tusculum cut off the city's supply of corn. This caused revolt, and Rienzi, who could no longer command the people, abdicated on December 15. He retired to the Apennines where he spent two years with devout and excited Spiritual Franciscans, or Fraticelli, from whom he imbibed strange heresies.

Meanwhile, the terrible Black Death came and went. Devout folk, thankful for being spared, crowded to Rome in 1350, the year of the great jubilee. Rienzi also went, to muse over fallen Rome and revive the memories of his brief successes. Returning to the mountains, he met a hermit whose mind was kindled with the heretical prophecies of Abbot Joachim of Fiore, that God's judgment was imminent and that the reign of the Holy Spirit was to begin. God would reveal His Chosen One to rule the children of man by the side of the emperor! Rienzi went to Prague to apprise Charles IV of his fantastic plans and bring him back to Rome. He declared that the pontiff in Avignon would be slain, and a new pope, a poor priest after the heart of the Fraticelli, would be named who would at once return to Rome. Rienzi himself was to be king of Rome and all Italy! Pope, emperor, and Rienzi were to rule the earth together, a reflection of the Holy Trinity! Charles eyed him in amazement and sent him to Pope Clement in Avignon who placed him in confinement. The pontiff died in December, 1352, and his successor, Innocent VI (1352–1362), resolved to use Rienzi to help his lieutenant, Cardinal Albornoz, establish papal authority in the States of the Church.

The Romans speedily repented their ill-judged desertion of the tribune. The rule of the nobles was unbearable; all Rome yearned for the laws established by Rienzi in 1347. Rienzi reappeared in Rome in 1354 and again cast the spell of his ideas over the Romans. In August he was appointed senator by the papal legate and, collecting a few troops, soon put the unpopular government to rout. Again he paraded as master on his beloved Capitoline Hill. But he had learned nothing from his years of wandering. He was tyrannical and ill counseled. He seized the *condottiere* Fra Moreale and ordered him executed, in spite of the fact that he owed his success largely to Moreale's two brothers who had provided him with money. Rienzi antagonized the Romans; seeing that nothing could be gained from his rule, they rose and thrust a sword into his bosom (October, 1354).

Meanwhile Cardinal Albornoz, who had won fame in the crusades against the Moors in Andalusia, fulfilled his mission to reduce the tyrants in the States of the Church. In 1357 he issued the code of laws known as the *Constitutiones Egidienae* which remained the basis of papal government until the nineteenth century. They put an end to the feuds which troubled the land. A papal representative was to act as adviser to the

towns and communities of the country. For the moment Rome was con-
ciliated, and papal authority was again established. The Campagna was
cleared of freebooting bands. When recalled to Avignon to give account
of his stewardship, Albornoz pointed with pride to the submission of all
the papal towns. Never had papal authority been so generally respected.

PAPAL ADMINISTRATION AND FINANCE

The Roman Church, as we have learned, long ago had extended her
spiritual sway over the peoples of western and central Europe. Practically
everywhere—from Scandinavia to Corinthia and westward to Spain and
Iceland, even to distant Greenland—were to be found fully developed
parish, diocesan, archdiocesan, and monastic organizations. Considering
the distances of the dioceses from Rome, difficulties incident to travel at
that time, the impossibility of maintaining an ever effective supervision,
we are convinced that the creation of this vast organization to instruct the
people in the truths of the Christian faith, administer the sacraments, and
maintain religious discipline must be regarded as one of the most remarkable creations of medieval times.

The development of a permanent and effective force of administrative
officers attained its apogee about 1350. The large personnel of the papal
administration is evident when we study the magnificent, spacious, and
crenellated palace in Avignon. There were, to carry on the papal business,
four main departments each served by a staff of clerks. The *Camera
Apostolica* was charged with the financial business of the Holy See. The
Chancery also had a large staff of clerks charged with the task of drawing
up official letters and documents. The *Rota* was a court of appeals, and
the *Penitentiarius* took care of ecclesiastical censures and discipline.

The Avignonese papacy showed itself clever in organizing and perfecting a new system of taxation. As long as life rested on a manorial basis,
incomes from properties sufficed to support the Church. But when coined
money supplanted manorial methods of exchange, wealth grew rapidly,
the cost of living mounted, and fixed incomes declined in value. Like other
organizations, the hierarchy was forced to change from a manorial to a
financial basis. The system of ecclesiastical taxation was reorganized.
New taxes were developed, and an elaborate mechanism for collections
was perfected. Christendom was divided into districts called *collectoria*.
These varied in size, sometimes comprising several dioceses. Collectors
were chosen from among the clergy. They swore an oath of obedience to
the papal chamberlain and, accompanied by notaries and assistants, left
Avignon for the scene of their duties. On their arrival they notified

ecclesiastical authorities of their purpose and organized a personnel for the task of collecting the taxes.

The variety of taxes gathered in the collectories were, first of all, the tithe (decima), originally a crusade tax but now levied also for other purposes. The annates, or first fruits, were a part or the whole of the income of a benefice during the year following its bestowal. Vacancies were incomes from benefices the collation of which belonged to the Holy See. Purveyance, or procuration, was an ancient tax in feudal society, but now also levied by the clergy when visiting benefices under their jurisdiction. Right of spoil (jus spolii), the appropriation by the papal camera of goods belonging to an ecclesiastic who died when absent from his benefice and who had not disposed of them by will, brought in large sums. Charitable contributions, originally given to meet special needs, by this time had become a special tax. And finally, there was the census, sums paid to the Holy See by ecclesiastical persons (such as archbishops, bishops, abbots and priors), for the special protection of St. Peter.

Besides these taxes collected in the dioceses and parishes there was a smaller and less important group that were collected at the Holy See. These comprised gratuities paid by bishops and abbots upon their nomination, confirmation, consecration, or translation to another post; gratuities given to the personnel of the curia, dues charged for the issuance of bulls, gifts by pilgrims to the tombs of the apostles, and dues paid by archbishops for the pallium and by vassal states and legacies.

Collectors coöperated with the banking houses of Siena, Lucca, and Florence which dispatched the sums to the papal treasurer. The papal chamberlain was chief minister of finance and directed the financial policy of the papacy. He had a large number of assistants, and the treasurer was also under his direction. Vast quantities of documents were preserved relating to the finances and rights of the papacy. Even today one is impressed by their number, orderly character, and the details they reveal about parishes, dioceses, and other religious properties.

The papacy not only developed "one of the earliest and best of medieval financial systems, but by means of its operations influenced profoundly the general economic development of Europe . . . with an almost modern system of taxation covering all Western Europe [it] furnished one of the principal forces which aided the establishment of money and credit transactions on a great scale."[2]

Historians point to the unfortunate influence the crown of France exerted upon pope and cardinals. They often assume that the papal policy

[2] W. E. Lunt, "The Financial System of the Mediaeval Papacy in the Light of Recent Literature," Quarterly Journal of Economics, XXIII (1909), 251–252.

during the so-called "Babylonian Captivity" was dictated chiefly by French interests. This is an exaggeration. A survey of the documents leads one to think that as a rule pontiffs faithfully sought to uphold papal superiority. Yet it remains true that the French parties among the cardinals exerted a baneful influence on papal policy. The papacy was overwhelmed by secular interests. Whatever the truth, it was what the people believed or were led to believe by critics and enemies of the papacy that weighed most heavily.

POPULAR CRITICISM OF THE AVIGNONESE PAPACY

And what did people think about the popes in Avignon? Wealth flowed to the Holy See, cardinals lived in affluence, and the men in Church offices became worldly and corrupt, it was said. Originally, the pope was simply Christ's vicar on earth, the shepherd of His flock, but the demands of economics and politics reduced him more and more to the level of an administrator. The papacy became enmeshed in the secular life of the day. All this was regarded as a scandal. Popular views of life were religious, colored by traditional ascetic ideals. The devout uttered notes of despair because the popes had forsaken the tombs of the apostles in Rome to live in Avignon. Idealists vented their feelings in mordant satire.

The men and women living in the Franciscan tradition—asceticism and practical mysticism taught by St. Francis of Assisi—were inspired with an other-worldly conception of life. That great saint had sought to solve the problem of riches and their unequal distribution in a manner based upon traditional and ascetic ideals of religion. His father was a well-to-do cloth merchant of Assisi. Brought up in the lap of luxury, Francis was a worldly youth. Like many another religious spirit, he abandoned the ways of the world and resolved to carry out to the letter Christ's injunctions about poverty as written in the tenth chapter of St. Matthew. He espoused "poverty" as his bride. He gave his clothes to the poor. Rejected by his father, he retired to a cave where he spent his days in prayer. He adopted as his habit a single brown tunic of woolen cloth, girt by a hempen cord. His personality is revealed to us in his *Canticle of the Sun* and in the *Flowers of St. Francis*. He organized a brotherhood which was authorized in 1216 by Pope Innocent III. The Franciscans, as they were called, labored in complete poverty among the urban folk who were miserably poor. St. Francis believed that complete poverty was the solution of the problems caused by inequalities in the distribution of wealth. The humble friars taught and comforted the lowly with sermons in the mother tongue. Sharing the sufferings of the poor, the friars became popular. The ministry of St. Francis and his friars was an event of great importance in the social history of the Middle Ages.

Franciscan asceticism, however, could not resist the claims of this material world. Wealth was heaped upon the friars. Hardly was the breath out of St. Francis' body when his successor, Brother Elias, began building the splendid basilica in his honor at Assisi. Many friars followed Elias' example and surrendered to riches, luxury, and ease. Those whose convents held property were called "Conventuals." Others who adhered to St. Francis' teaching and example were called Fraticelli or Spiritual Franciscans. "The lofty and spacious convents were their abomination; they housed themselves in huts and caves; there was not a single change in dress, in provision for food, in worship, in study, which they did not denounce as a sin—as an act of apostasy. Wherever the Franciscans were, and they were everywhere, the Spirituals were keeping up the strife, protesting, and putting to shame these recreant sons of the common father."[3] In order to put an end to their bickerings, Nicholas III (1288–1292) issued the bull *Exiit qui Seminat* which defined apostolic poverty for the order and for individuals. Title to property was to be vested in the Roman See. This solution was adopted by most of the friars, but it did not please the more zealous brethren who insisted upon complete poverty, corporate as well as individual.

The Spirituals were ever busy with their lamentations about the sinful state of the hierarchy. They consistently inveighed against the worldliness of the Conventuals. Jacopone da Todi, a Spiritual Franciscan poet who died in 1306, was trenchant in his criticisms:

> The Church is weeping, weeping bitterly,
> Feeling the torments of her evil state.

[*The Church speaks*]

> My son, good cause have I these tears to shed,
> I see my spouse, my Father, lying dead:
> Sons, brothers, kinsmen, all alike are fled;
> My friends are prisoned and disconsolate.

> Now none but bastard sons around me press,
> False cowards who desert me in my stress;
> My true sons, in their fervent tenderness
> Feared neither sword nor dart nor foeman's hate. . . .

[3] H. H. Milman, *History of Latin Christianity, Including that of Pope Nicholas V*, New York, 1903, VII, 27–28.

> Now holy poverty they scorn and slay;
> For pomp and place alone they strive and pray,
> My true sons lived austerely in their day
> And trampled on the world and the world's estate. . . .
>
> Where are the prelates, just and vehement?
> To feed their flocks their ardent lives were spent:
> False pomp and ostentation now are bent
> This noble order to attenuate. . . .
>
> O ye religious whose austerities
> In days gone by gave pleasure to mine eyes,
> Vainly I seek a cloister whence arise
> The virtues that I love to contemplate.

The Spirituals enthusiastically greeted the election of Celestine V (July–December, 1294) because he was a poor hermit. Jacopone warned him of the difficulties in his path:

> And the cardinals are fallen low,
> In an evil course their longings flow,
> Never one his kinsmen will forego
> To enrich them all by perfidy.
>
> Of the prebends, too, thou must beware,
> Great their hunger for unlawful fare,
> Fierce their thirst, fierce even to despair,
> For no draught can quench its cruelty.

A person of such temper hated Boniface VIII, that statesman and master of canon law who understood only too well the ways of man. The pontiff imprisoned Jacopone for his violent criticisms; this explains the poet's bitterness:

> O Boniface, who art the pope,
> Thy ban is heavy on my hope;
> Thy malediction and thy hate
> Have made me excommunicate.
> Thy forky tongue, so like a snake's,
> This wound upon my spirit makes:
> There let thy tongue again be laid,
> To staunch the hurt itself hath made.[4]

Even practical men like Dante shared some of this enthusiasm for

---

[4] E. Underhill, *Jacopone da Jodi, Poet and Mystic, 1228–1306: A Spiritual Biography.* London, 1919, pp. 433–437, 431, 439.

poverty. At the mouth of hell he saw among others Celestine V, and wrote of him as follows:

> After I had recognized some amongst them, I saw and knew the shadow of him who from cowardice made the great refusal.[5]

As became a great enemy of Boniface VIII, for political reasons he put the following words in the mouth of St. Peter:

> . . . If I transform my hue, marvel thou not; for, as I speak, thou shalt see all of these transform it too.
>
> He who usurpeth upon earth my place, my place which in the presence of the Son of God is vacant,
>
> Hath made my burial ground a conduit for that blood and filth whereby the apostate one who fell from here above is soothed down there below.[6]

The prophetic utterances of Abbot Joachim of Fiore (d. 1202) were eagerly appropriated by the Spirituals. He was a visionary and lived as a hermit, studying *Scripture* and writing theological treatises. He brooded upon the teaching of the Revelation of St. John and upon the state of the Church. He believed that mankind's history was divided into three ages: the first, that of the Father, had come to an end with Zacharias; the second was that of the Son; and the third, that of the Holy Spirit, had begun with St. Benedict and would supersede the age of Christ in 1260. This third age was to be an era of perfection in human beings and their affairs. In their troubles the Spirituals resorted, like Joachim, to prophecy. They believed that a golden age would come with complete poverty such as the apostles were supposed to have practiced. "No omens of the coming of the new kingdom of the Holy Ghost were so awful or so undeniable as the corruptions of the Church; and those corruptions were measured not by a lofty moral standard but by their departure from the perfection, the poverty of St. Francis. The pope, the hierarchy, fell of course."[7]

A Provençal Franciscan, John Peter Oliva (d. 1297), prophesied the coming end of the world. The last age had arrived! Christ's law would be carried out. Christ would rise and the pristine purity of the Franciscan rule be revived, the very rule under which Christ and His apostles, it was said, had lived. Papacy and hierarchy, utterly rotten and useless, would fall. All mankind would live according to the rule of St. Francis.

Another friar named Gerald Segarelli founded a special brotherhood of

---

[5] *The Inferno of Dante Alighieri* (Temple Classics), Canto III, 58–60.

[6] *The Paradise of Dante Alighieri* (Temple Classics), Canto XXVII, 19–27.

[7] Milman, *op. cit.*, p. 32.

Apostolic Brethren who lived in extreme austerity according to the Franciscan rule. He was put under the ban, seized, and burned in 1300.

Dolcino of Novara, one of his followers, also taught that mankind's history was divided into a number of ages. The third age was the era in which the Church had amassed great wealth and had become corrupt. Dolcino bitterly denounced the papacy, for of all popes since the earliest days, only Celestine V had been righteous. St. Benedict's order had lost its holiness; those of St. Francis and St. Dominic also had declined. The end was at hand; papacy, hierarchy, and friars would all be swept away! The fourth age was one of apostolic perfection; it had begun with Segarelli. In the last days there were to be four popes. The first, they thought, was the poor and holy Celestine V. The second and third they seemed to think were Boniface VIII and Clement V, respectively. They passed by Benedict XI, and John XXII had not yet begun his pontificate. His worldliness might have appeared to them as proof of their prophesyings, for the last pontiff would be the very negation of righteousness and herald the end of all things.

Dolcino's followers formed a religious community in Piedmont, and, like other groups, looked about for political help. They were Ghibellines; in their opposition to the papacy they hoped to enlist secular power. They prophesied that in 1335 the king of Aragon would enter Rome and destroy pope and hierarchy. Apostolic poverty was to be established, and Dolcino was to be pope. Such radicalism could not be tolerated by priest or secular lord. Bitter war developed against the sect. Its members retreated into mountainous recesses where they defended themselves with desperation. Driven to the sorest straits, they ravaged the country. Besieged and worn out by hunger, the decimated group was massacred or taken prisoners. The prisoners refused to recant and so perished at the stake, the leaders, including Dolcino, being executed by mutilation and fire (1307).

A crisis arrived when the papacy was transferred to Avignon. John XXII was a practical individual, and his financial policy antagonized many. Dante denounced the Gascon Clement V and the Cahorsin John XXII: "In garb of pastors ravening wolves are seen from here above in all the pastures. Succor of God! Oh wherefore liest thou prone?

Cahorsines and Gascons make ready to drink our blood. Oh fair beginning, to what vile ending must thou fall!"[8]

The Spirituals and their allies were bitter. One Ubertino da Casale was continuing the prophecies of Oliva and others. John XXII moved to

---

[8] *The Paradiso of Dante Alighieri*, Canto XXVII, 55–60.

uproot the uncomfortable doctrine of apostolic poverty. The Franciscans held a chapter at Perugia in 1322 which declared for the doctrine. John issued a bull on December 8 in which he declared in the name of the Roman See that all property held for the order should be remitted to the original donors. Since this practically deprived the friars of the economic basis of their life, there was much consternation. Michael of Cesena, general of the order, once a strong enemy of the Spirituals, opposed the pope. A bitter struggle developed. The Spirituals had often revealed a tendency to join forces with the Ghibellines; now they hastened to support Louis the Bavarian, king of the Romans, whom John XXII had driven to take up arms against him. Michael of Cesena issued his *Tractate Against the Error of the Pope*. He was so bold as to appeal from the pope to a general council which, he maintained, was superior to popes in faith and morals. Like Marsiglio of Padua, he argued that a council could not err. William of Ockham used his keen logic in Michael's behalf and issued many treatises. He argued that popes, councils, and the fathers of the Church might err; but there was one infallible authority, *Scripture*, and it should be the basic rule of faith. Marsiglio of Padua's *The Defender of the Peace*, described in the foregoing, was a significant document in the history of this struggle.

Few, if any, of these critics ever raised the question how in an age when revolutionary changes had taken place in business, commerce, and industry, and, when a money economy had greatly modified the feudal and manorial manner of life, the far-flung spiritual empire of the Church was to be managed and financed. With some, patriotism was the chief reason for criticism. So, for example, the poet Francesco Petrarch (1304–1374), an Italian patriot and nostalgic admirer of ancient Rome, censured the popes of Avignon and lamented the loss which his country suffered because the bishop of Rome had taken up residence in Avignon. How great was the decline since the days of majestic Rome! And when he saw how temporal concerns dominated papal action, he wrote in poetic exaggeration:

> May fire from heaven rain down upon thy head,
>> Thou most accurst; who simple fare casts by,
>> Made rich and great by others' poverty;
> How dost thou glory in thy vile misdeed!
> Nest of all treachery, in which is bred
>> Whate'er of sin now through the world doth fly;
>> Of wine the slave, of sloth, of gluttony;
> With sensuality's excesses fed!
>> Old men and harlots through thy chambers dance;

> Then in the midst see Belzebub advance
> With mirrors and provocatives obscene.
>> Erewhile thou wert not shelter'd, nursed on down;
>> But naked, barefoot on the straw wert thrown:
> Now rank to heaven ascends thy life unclean.[9]

THE GREAT SCHISM

Would the pope return from Avignon? The people of Rome, the Italian cardinals, and many a pious soul longed to see the universal shepherd again take up his abode at the tombs of the apostles. John XXII and Benedict XII had thought of taking this step, but such was the turmoil in Rome and in the States of the Church that the curia prevented it. Neither Clement VI nor Innocent VI had cared to return to Rome, for they belonged to the French Limousin party (i.e., from Limoges). They were deaf to the yearning of Italians and to the fervid prayers of the devout.

Pope Urban V (1362–1370) was an able and holy man whose life was guided by spiritual aims. He wanted to return the papacy to Rome. He was urged by the emperor Charles IV, and the poet Petrarch seconded the project. But Charles VI of France (1364–1380) and the French cardinals sought to dissuade Urban. Nevertheless he set out, landed at Corneto in June, 1367, and marched to Rome where he was greeted by the enthusiastic shouts of the citizenry. But Albornoz died and confusion reigned everywhere. There were riots in Viterbo and revolt threatened in other places. The French cardinals pressed for return to comfortable Avignon. St. Brigitta of Sweden predicted the dire wrath of God if the pope should yield; Petrarch besought him to stay. Prophecy and prayer were in vain, and in September, 1370 Urban left Italy for Avignon, only to die there on December 19. Small wonder people saw in this a mark of divine displeasure!

The next pope was Gregory XI (1370–1378), a Frenchman who belonged to the Limousin faction. Would this prevent him from returning to the city on the Tiber? Papal relations with France and England went from bad to worse. It appeared that the Holy See had lost all prestige. Italy was rife with feuds and turmoil; adventurers plundered the peninsula. Chief among them was the Englishman John Hawkwood or, as the Italians called him, Giovanni Acuto. The Visconti family of Milan sought to encroach on the States of the Church. Towns in this section were in the wildest confusion. Force could reduce this factional life, but the papal

---

[9] *The Sonnets, Triumphs, and Other Poems of Petrarch,* London, 1897, 136.

treasury was not equal to the task. The governors appointed by Urban and Gregory were Frenchmen who little understood the people and their institutions. Theirs was an impossible mission, for nationalist resentment flared up whenever the agents sought to put down local tyrants. Only by returning to Rome could the pope hope to instill obedience and institute effective government.

Pious people urged Gregory to return. St. Catherine begged him to take this step, and St. Brigitta's visions impressed everybody. Italians whose patriotic feelings were wounded longed to see the papacy restored to Italy. Finally, Gregory set out for Italy and landed at Corneto where he spent Christmas (1377). He resumed his journey by sea, sailed up the Tiber, and landed on the bank near the basilica of St. Paul-outside-the-Wall. Large crowds joyfully greeted him and his attendants as he approached the gate of St. Paul on January 17. But the aged pontiff died on March 27. People instinctively believed that the Church and Italy faced another crisis. Who would be elected to the chair of St. Peter? Would he be an Italian? Or, if a foreigner, would he retire to the banks of the Rhone?

There were sixteen cardinals in Rome at this juncture, four Italian, one Spanish, and eleven French. Six tarried in Avignon, and one was on mission in Tuscany. The sixteen cardinals entered conclave on April 7. The French party was divided into two factions, the Limousins, now six in number, who had dominated the papacy for 36 years, and the Gallicans who were opposed. This was a dangerous division, for it seemed that difficulties experienced in former conclaves might be revived. Needless to state, the Italian cardinals were not sympathetic to the Limousins. They were outvoted from the first; it was clear that a compromise candidate would have to be produced. Such a person was found in Archbishop Bartolomeo Prignano of Bari. He was not a member of the curia, thus not an adherent to any faction. The fact that he was an Italian won the approval of the Italian cardinals. He had been a protégé of one Limousin group, which appears to have led the Limousins to support him. They no doubt thought that a person of such humble origin could readily be controlled, especially if he owed his elevation to them.

Meanwhile the Romans made their wishes known in no uncertain manner. The government of Rome had taken all necessary steps to prevent irregularities. The Piazza in front of St. Peter's on the Vatican was filled with people vociferously crying for a Roman pope. They broke into some of the buildings and found their way to the papal cellars which increased their vivacity and turbulence. The cardinals feared the displeasure of the crowd when it should learn that a person other than a

Roman had been elected. They fled to various places; but this proved needless, for the people decided to accept with good grace Prignano, or Urban VI as he was called. They were glad that an Italian was pope. When all things are considered, it appears that the excitement of the crowd may have hurried the election; but did the uproar on the Piazza unduly influence the conclave? This speedily became a burning question.

Urban was an unfortunate choice. Elevated to an exalted position, this man of little acquaintance with the world possessed no tact. He was fiery and outspoken. He determined to stay in Rome and dismayed the cardinals by insisting on simplifying their mode of life. He estranged them without considering the consequences. This was a serious mistake, for the Limousin group was supported by their Gallican brethren who resented Urban's incivilities. They formed a party of opposition and retired to Anagni while Urban remained at Tivoli. They questioned the legitimacy of his election and on September 20 proceeded to choose one of their number, Robert of Geneva, who assumed the name of Clement VII.

Urban established himself in and about Rome with some difficulty. Clement, who for a while tarried in the environs of Rome, had in his service some mercenaries who roved through the environs of the city and held the castle of Sant' Angelo. Urban enlisted the services of Alberigo da Barbiano. This Italian *condottiere* led a group of soldiers exclusively Italian in nationality. They defeated Clement's troops and forced the surrender of the castle of Sant' Angelo which had held the populace in awe.

Driven from Rome by the soldiery of Alberigo da Barbiano, a *condottiere* in the service of Urban VI, Clement ensconced himself in Avignon. In earlier years he had been a worldling. Vigorous and ambitious, his directness of manner had caused the cardinals to designate him for the papacy. He had won a dubious reputation from the businesslike manner in which he put down an insurrection of the people of Cesena when he was papal legate in the Romagna in 1377. The vigor with which he reduced the town could not be forgotten; it made any support of his claims by Italians impossible. In a few years he won the obedience of Castile and Aragon.

Two popes claimed to be pastors of Peter's flock. Which would people accept? St. Catherine of Siena adhered to Urban; St. Vincent Ferrer to Clement. But it was the new spirit of nationalism which determined the attitude of many. The great contest in the political world of the day, the Hundred Years' War, was being waged between England and France. The French king supported Clement, as did his political allies, the Scots; and eventually the Spanish also accepted Clement. The English king, on the other hand, accepted Urban. States in the Low Countries, with the exception of Liége, joined Urban's supporters. The emperors did likewise, partly out of enmity toward France. Italians were Urbanists from national motives. The religious division of nations, thus made along the lines of major political antagonisms, rent the peace of Europe.

THE CONCILIAR MOVEMENT

Christendom now was divided into two obediences—the Roman, which was legitimate, and the Avignonese, which was illegitimate, as the future would show. The establishment of two curias was disastrous alike to papacy and religion. Each pope refused to recognize the other as the successor of Peter. Each maintained a staff of officials so that the total burden of Christendom was increased. Urban appointed twenty-eight new cardinals in September, 1378. Clement also maintained a staff in Avignon but on a less elaborate scale. To pay for the luxury of so large an organization, the machinery of tax collection perfected in the days of the Avignonese papacy was employed to produce the greatest possible revenue. Furthermore, the papacy in its endeavor to collect sufficient income tended more and more to treat the hierarchy as a source of taxation. Benefices were disposed of with the view of bringing as much money into the papal coffers as possible. They might be divided to create several livings. Translation, the transfer of prelates from one see to another, was common. Dispensations were readily granted for any canonical irregularity. The papacy interfered in the internal affairs of bishoprics. Diocesan arrangements suffered especially because of the practice of reservations of appointments. Expectatives, or rights to livings which had not yet fallen vacant, were granted for a monetary consideration in anticipation of vacancies. Cases tried in diocesan courts were withdrawn to the tribunals in Avignon or Rome for the sake of fees.

When Urban VI died (1389) the cardinals at Rome chose Boniface IX who ruled until 1404. He led a blameless life but approached the papal office in so base a spirit that genuine religious devotion among the higher clergy became impossible. He needed money above all things. Hence the spiritual power of the papacy was addressed unblushingly to the task of extracting the maximal revenue without which the pope could not hope to dominate Italy, especially Naples. Everything had its price, and spiritual offices were treated in the most mercenary manner.

Much resentment was shown in Germany toward collectors of papal taxes. Imperial authority was feeble, and the state was divided into numerous feudal principalities. There was little to prevent the papacy from drawing large sums from German sees and using the Church for secular advantages. Such was the anger of the Germans that "collectors were hunted down, thrown into prison, mutilated, and even strangled. The excitement among the clergy in the dioceses of Cologne, Bonn, Xanten, Soest, and Mainz reached such a pitch that in 1372 they bound themselves by oath not to pay the tenth demanded by Gregory XI, and to support all against whom action was taken; any incumbent who betrayed his pledge was to be deprived of his benefice and declared ineligible to possess one again in the future." In France also the clergy resisted papal officials sent to collect taxes.

Nationalist feeling was especially strong in England, a land where the royal power was more highly developed than anywhere else in Europe. Englishmen viewed the papacy in Avignon with suspicion after they began the war with their perennial enemy, France. William Langland opposed the sending of sums to the papal treasury:

> Till Rome-runners carry no silver over sea
> Graven or ungraven, for the robber pope of France . . .

Parliament took action in 1343 when it forbade anyone to bring into the realm letters from Rome, as Avignon was called, which in any way might be prejudicial to the rights of the crown. The *Statute of Provisors,* passed in 1351, forbade granting benefices by papal letters and provided that bearers of such letters were to be fined and imprisoned. Next came the *Statute of Praemunire* (1353) which forbade under severe penalty appeals from Church courts in the realm to the tribunals of the curia in Avignon. It can cause no surprise, therefore, that Englishmen in 1366 refused the demand of Urban V for the payment of tribute of 1000 marks annually, which had been begun by King John (d. 1216) but had rarely been paid since the accession of Edward I. A spirit of political anti-clericalism was rife in the land.

The Great Schism produced a dangerous crisis. How to end the strife it occasioned became a burning question. Ways and means were discussed in university circles. From Paris came practical suggestions. Three solutions were offered: abdication of the popes to be followed by the election of a successor by the cardinals of both parties, arbitration by impartial judges, or a general council representing the Church universal.

Objections were raised to each of these plans. Abdication, to be valid, would have to be spontaneous because the pope as Christ's vicar recognized no one superior to himself. It was impossible to secure a voluntary surrender from the obstinate rivals, each of whom was bent on asserting his rights and was supported by his cardinals. Arbitration also proved impossible, for no pope would accept the decision of arbiters. Nor was it possible to find impartial judges whom all could approve. A committee of cardinals would not be impartial. The same objection would also be made against any group of prelates or lower clerics. Finally, arbitration by laymen was out of the question. Churchmen could not accept this expedient because it implied that the laity possessed authority over the clergy.

The third suggestion, which had been advanced by Parisian scholars as early as 1379, proved most popular. They argued that a council representing the entire Church possessed authority higher than that of the pope. The bishop of Rome was Christ's vicar; but Christ had always been considered as living in the entire Church. An appeal to a general council representing the Church universal was an appeal to Christ Himself and therefore superior to the word of popes. The difficulty with this theory was that it denied the pontiff's supreme position in the Church. Rival popes would not submit tamely to such a theory. Its advocates knew that this procedure was of doubtful legality, but they argued that it was a case of necessity.

Clement VII died in September, 1394. The University of Paris, the French crown, and the clergy wanted to end the schism. The problem was also discussed by the cardinals, who feared that if they did not elect a pope they would raise doubts as to the validity of their own election. A document was drawn up wherein each promised, if elected, to abdicate in case a majority of the cardinals should ask him to do so. The French court requested the cardinals not to choose a successor, but the king's missive and a letter from the university came too late. The Aragonese Peter de Luna who had declared, "I can abdicate as easily as take off my hat," was elected and took as his name Benedict XIII. There was much disappointment in Paris. Furthermore, the cardinals' choice proved unfortunate. Trained in canon law, Benedict took a legal view of the crisis and refused to abdicate.

Chagrined that these well-meant plans for reconciliation had failed and disgusted at the pontiff's obstinacy, the University of Paris insisted on his abdication. Finally the clergymen, backed by the university, met at Paris from May to August, 1398. They argued that the pope was Christ's vicar only as long as he preserved unity. Since Benedict was prolonging the schism, they decided upon the bold step of withdrawing the allegiance of France. This measure was taken on July 27. The crown issued an ordinance in the same tenor early in September. By taking away support from Benedict they hoped to force him into submission. This withdrawal of obedience proved a fiasco because appointments to clerical posts now

began to be filled by nominees of king and nobles, and they were peculiarly able to swell their own purses. The clergy now found to their
sorrow that taxes were much heavier and were more rigidly exacted by
royal than papal authorities. Dissatisfaction led to reaction. Even the universities resented the new policy whereby the bishops bestowed livings
upon their supporters and not upon the professors.

Nor was royal power able to formulate a more successful policy. The
French king Charles VI had frequent spells of lunacy. Emperor Wenzel
(1378–1400) had promised him to withdraw the obedience of his lands
from Boniface IX, but he spent his last days in drunken stupor. The duke
of Orléans, a royal uncle, vigorously opposed the treatment given Benedict. Finally, in May, 1403, the French crown renewed its obedience to
the pope in Avignon.

Innocent VII (1404–1406) succeeded Boniface IX as pope of the
Roman obedience. He was an aged man, dominated by a nephew, and
too indolent to end the schism. He was followed by Gregory XII (1406–
1415), a man of eighty and of blameless life. He asserted his intention of
working for unity if elected. He would abdicate if Benedict would do
likewise. It was decided that the rivals should meet at Savona north of
Genoa, but certain states in Gregory's obedience were loath to see a
conclave there. This was dangerously near France and Venice, and
Naples and England feared that French influences might again dominate.
The irresolute Gregory was controlled by their wishes and by his
nephews. He also was afraid to leave Rome because King Ladislaus of
Naples (1386–1414) stood ready to seize the Eternal City. He moved
from Rome to Siena but would go no farther.

Safely ensconced in Avignon, Benedict was in a position to make a
great show of zeal for negotiation. He offered to meet his rival between
Pietra Santa and the Gulf of Spezia. "One pope, like a land animal,
refused to approach the shore; the other, like a water beast, refused to
leave the sea." Finally, in January, 1408, Gregory appeared in Lucca,
but, when he heard that Ladislaus had seized Rome in April, he changed
his policy. Benedict plotted against his rival by seeking a foothold in
Rome. Gregory yielded to his nephews and to others in his following who
feared that they might lose from his abdication. He declared that he
would oppose the machinations of the French pope and in May named
four new cardinals, two of whom were his nephews.

The cardinals of the Roman obedience were wroth at Gregory's change
of front for he had sworn to abdicate if his rival would do likewise.
Embittered, they fled from Lucca, met in Pisa, and published an appeal to

a general council (May, 1408). Benedict, feeling insecure in Avignon, fled to Perpignan.

Negotiations between Gregory's and Benedict's cardinals were opened at Livorno. They, as well as Christendom, were disgusted with the quarrel and in July issued a request to the clergy to appear in a general council to be held at Pisa in March, 1409. Gregory retired to Rimini and sought to take a leaf from the cardinals' book by convoking a council in the province of Aquileia or in lands subject to Ravenna. It actually convened at Cividale but was so poorly attended that its sessions were of no consequence. Benedict also summoned a council to Perpignan which sat from November, 1408 to February, 1409. Over one hundred prelates attended, and a commission was named to discuss the matter of unity. Instead of justifying Benedict, as the pontiff had expected, it urged that he resign. Benedict was obdurate and in March excommunicated the council just as the clergy were coming from all parts to Pisa in response to the invitation of the cardinals.

The cathedral of Pisa was famed for its beauty. Equally noteworthy were the campanile or leaning tower, the baptistery, and the Campo Santo decorated by some of the great painters of the early Renaissance. The cathedral, today still supreme in its loveliness, was the scene of the trial. Here representatives of the Church met cardinals of both parties, archbishops, generals of the great orders, bishops, abbots, delegates of cathedral chapters or their proctors, professors of canon law and theology, ambassadors of secular princes, and envoys of universities. The legal bases of the council troubled the churchmen. Well might they hesitate, for popes would not admit that councils had supreme authority in faith and morals. There was danger that Christendom would disown whatever they might seek to accomplish. Finally, it was agreed that, if the popes persisted in the schism which they had sworn to bring to an end, they were guilty of heresy, and the cardinals as representatives of the Church should provide a new pope. Gregory and Benedict were cited before the council, but, when they failed to appear, were declared contumacious and deposed. The cardinals therefore proceeded to elect a new pope. Choice fell upon a Franciscan, Peter Philargi, who took the name of Alexander V. For a moment it was fondly hoped that the schism had come to an end.

A few members of the Pisan council were eager for reform of abuses, and consideration of this matter had been set for July 15, 1409. The cardinals were quite willing to depose the two popes and elect a third, but reform of abuses on which they themselves throve proved unpopular. Nevertheless, they protested against annates, tenths, exemptions from episcopal visitorial authority, translation of bishops from one see to another without consulting them, the practically unlimited appeal to papal courts, and the complicated character of procedure in the papal chancery. Many of the fathers wished to return home; they could not be interested in something which would hurt their own interests. A sop was thrown to the advocates of reform. Alexander V made a few trivial concessions and announced that another council would be held in April, 1412. The council closed on August 7. Now there were three popes, three curias, three obediences! The evils under which the Church had labored for a generation had only been aggravated.

Alexander V died in May, 1410, and was succeeded by John XXIII, an unworthy choice. Benedict had retired to Peñiscola. Gregory retired to Rimini. John soon had the support of most Italians. He next sought the help of Emperor Sigismund, a hearty supporter of the conciliar theory who recognized John as the true pope who believed his wishes would prevail at the next council, to be held in Rome in 1412. It accomplished nothing beyond ordering a new council to meet at Constance in November, 1414.

THE COUNCIL OF CONSTANCE

The Council of Constance (1414–1418) was opened on November 5, 1414. It was a magnificent assemblage: 29 cardinals, 3 patriarchs, 33 archbishops, about 150 bishops, more than 100 abbots and 50 deans from all quarters of Christendom. The English group led the way and formed a nation, and the Germans and French followed their example. The Italians could only do likewise. A fifth nation, the Spanish, was added, and their cardinals as a group were also granted one vote. A unanimous vote of all the nations was necessary for a conciliar decree.

The council was influenced by the spirit of the age. The Hundred Years' War was in progress. England and Germany were hostile toward France. Pope John and his Italian cardinals were distrusted. The lower clergy, secular princes, and representatives of the universities were allowed to vote on all questions in the nations. Nationalism thus threatened to overwhelm the council, which was supposed to be ecumenical. The universal and nonnational Church of the Middle Ages seemed about to founder among the new states of the Renaissance.

The theoretical basis of conciliar action was laid down on April 6, 1415, in the revolutionary decree *Sacrosanct*. It stated that a council, duly formed, had full authority to legislate for the Church and that the pope was subject to its decisions.

> This sacred synod of Constance . . . declares first that itself, lawfully as-
> sembled in the Holy Spirit, forming a general council and representing the
> Catholic church, has its power immediately from Christ; and everyone, of
> whatever status and rank he may be, and even the pope, is bound to obey
> it in matters pertaining to the faith, and to the abolition of the said schism,
> and to the general reformation of the church of God in head and members.
> Further it declares that anyone of whatever condition, status, or rank, and
> even the pope, who contumaciously shall refuse to obey the orders, decrees,
> ordinances, or instructions, made or to be made by this sacred synod and by
> any other general council lawfully assembled, concerning or in any way re-
> lating to the aforesaid objects, shall, unless he comes to a right mind, be
> subjected to due penance and appropriately punished. . . .[10]

Three questions confronted the fathers: schism, heresy, and reform.
The first of these was easily disposed of, for all were agreed on this point.
John XXIII was eager to place the question of heresy in the foreground
in order to put off reform and the question of unity. John Hus' ideas
were popular in Bohemia. Just as Wycliffite heresy in England was associated with nationalism, so Hus' doctrines stimulated Czech nationalist
feeling. (For the teachings of Wycliffe and Hus see following chapter.)
Hus was summoned to the council, and Emperor Sigismund granted him
a safe-conduct. The great leader, hoping to bring the fathers to his point
of view, appeared in Constance early in November, but was arrested and
put in prison. Sigismund, though irate at the violation of his safe-conduct,
was zealous to make the council a success and, rather than endanger it
for the sake of a heretic, yielded to the arguments of theologians and
canonists. Hus was condemned to be burned. This sentence, carried out
in July, 1415, raised a storm of nationalist passion in Bohemia directed
against Germany and the papacy.

Schism was a more difficult matter, for each of the three popes had his
supporters. Everybody was disgusted with Benedict's legalism. He had
few supporters outside Navarre, Castile, and Aragon. As for Gregory XII,
the years had taken their toll. Besides, his nephews upon whom he had
relied so much had weakened his position. He still had a few supporters
but was ready to yield to the inevitable. He abdicated in July, 1415 when
the council legalized his pontifical acts. But John proved more obstinate.
When stories of his unpriestly character were passed about, the council
induced him to promise to resign if his rivals would also take this step.
But John fled in March, whereupon the council proceeded against him.
Every transaction of his past was laid bare. It was no enviable record,
and he was deposed in May, 1415. Emperor Sigismund now proceeded as

[10] Laffan, *Documents*, p. 195.

agent of the council to meet Benedict's proctors in Perpignan, but that pontiff refused to have anything to do with him. And his supporters, the kings of Castile, Navarre, and Aragon, were weary of the obstinate pope and threatened to withdraw their obedience and came to an understanding with Sigismund. The Council at Constance, no longer in fear of division and dissension, deposed Benedict in July, 1417 on the ground that he supported schism and acted as a heretic.

To reform the Church was more difficult than to deal with the three popes, for reform involved the interests of many parties. The cardinals were loath to see their privileges taken away, whereas the lower clergy were eager for reformation "in head and members," as they expressed it. The matter could not be put off after Huss had been executed and the three popes deposed. A commission had been appointed to draft a program of reform. But cardinals and other prelates wanted to postpone action. A new commission, composed of five men from each of the five nations, was named. The policy adopted by the curial party, on the other hand, was to press for the election of a pope. The reform party opposed this step, knowing that a pontiff might close the council and thus avoid curtailment of "abuses" on which the curia throve. Finally, the emperor was forced to agree to an election, with reformation to be undertaken immediately after. To pacify the opposition, the decree *Frequens* was issued in October, 1417.

This decree, one of the most striking documents issued by the Council, aimed to provide a parliamentary government for the Church.

> The frequent holding of general councils is one of the chief means of cultivating the Lord's field. It serves to uproot the briars, thorns, and thistles of heresies, errors, and schisms, to correct excesses, to restore what is marred, and to cause the Lord's vine to bring forth fruit of the richest fertility. Neglect of councils spreads and fosters the said evils. This is clearly proved by the records of the past and consideration of the present. Wherefore, by this perpetual edict, we provide, decree, and ordain that henceforth general councils shall always be held every ten years in places which the supreme pontiff shall be bound to appoint and assign, with the approval and consent of the council, one month before the conclusion of the preceding council. In the absence of a pope, the council itself shall appoint the place of meeting. Thus, with a certain continuity, a council will always either be functioning or be awaited at the end of a definite period.[11]

Martin V, a member of the Roman family of Colonna and a cardinal, was elected pope in November, 1417. The nations preferred him because he stood aloof from all factions. He professed a desire for reform, but it

[11] Laffan, *op. cit.*, pp. 196–197.

soon became apparent that the nations could not agree. In January, 1418, he announced some changes in curial and episcopal government. In March a decree was issued containing a few mild reforms. Other points were settled by concordats or treaties between the pope and the English, French, and German nations. The council was weary; its members were eager to return home. Martin dissolved the council on April 22.

The Church rejoiced over the healing of the schism. Many now looked forward to the new council which was to reform the Church. According to the decree *Frequens* it was to meet five years after the closing of Constance. Martin issued a bull for its meeting in Pavia in 1423. It was an impressive assembly but accomplished nothing. After being organized into nations, the council was transferred to Siena because of the plague. The curial party cared little for reform, and its intrigues were so skillful that the nations were set against one another. Nothing could be accomplished, and the council was dissolved in March, 1424.

THE COUNCIL OF BASEL: FAILURE OF THE CONCILIAR IDEA

Meanwhile the Christian community was rocked by the Husite heresy in Bohemia. Czech national feeling stood arrayed against the Church and against German nationalism. Sigismund and his subjects could not cope with the situation and appealed to pope Martin V who proposed a crusade. But instead, on February 1, 1431, he convoked a council to meet at Basel. Martin was succeeded by Eugenius IV (1431–1447). The new pope at his election promised extensive reforms of the Church in head and members. But curial leadership showed itself hostile to conciliar pretensions. Cardinal Cesarini, appointed by Martin to preside as papal delegate, appealed to the Bohemians to return to the Church.

Pope Eugenius was frightened when the council began negotiating with the Husites. He disliked the note of radicalism which could clearly be heard. Accordingly in December he issued a bull dissolving the council, but it refused to obey. Cesarini was disappointed because the papal policy did not take into consideration the gravity of the Husite question. Finally, in February, 1432, the council reasserted the principles advanced at Constance in the decree *Sacrosanct*. This was a remarkable step because it was taken in opposition to a pope who was universally accepted, whereas the fathers as Pisa and Constance had to deal with pontiffs, regarded in most quarters as schismatic.

The council now proceeded with its organization. To avoid the difficulties presented by nationalist interest which had wrought much damage at Constance, it was decided to form four deputations or committees for faith, peace, reformation, and general business. Each deputation was to consist of an equal number of representatives of the four nations, Italian, French, German, and Spanish. Cardinals, prelates, masters, and doctors, and also lower clergy were admitted to the deputations. Approval of three deputations was necessary for a conciliar decree. Each member possessed one vote regardless of his rank in the Church. Membership was changed each 4 months. A committee of twelve prepared the general business. At the head stood the president, Cardinal Cesarini.

This organization made it possible for the lower clergy to insist upon reform. Emperor Sigismund's support gave strength to the council, especially when the pontiff withheld his approval. The work of reform began early in 1433. Much of it was consistent with the provisions of canon law. Diocesan and provincial synods were to be held regularly. Clerical conduct, care of Church properties, and all matters pertaining to public services were to be scrutinized. An effort was made to restore the autonomous character of the Church by ordaining that capitular and other elections should be final. Papal incomes from the collation of benefices thus came to an end. These and other measures were not at all radical. Only one can be classed as such: the decree of June 26, 1434, which placed general councils above popes. It declared that councils should meet every ten years and that each newly elected pope was to take an oath that councils were superior to popes.

Eugenius, displeased at this revolutionary spirit, sought to transfer the council to some city in Italy. The quarrel with the council became so bitter that Eugenius dissolved it on September 18, 1437, and fixed Ferrara as the place of future meetings. This choice was dictated by the papal desire to win a diplomatic triumph over the council at Basel. The Greek Orthodox Church, after having maintained an existence independent of the Latin Church ever since 1054, now sought help against the Turks. The Greek fathers appealed to Eugenius and the council, but soon perceived that the pope was the acknowledged head of the Church. Eugenius favored them by naming a place in Italy more readily accessible than Basel. By thus winning Greek recognition of his headship, Eugenius won a signal advantage over the council. Cesarini abandoned the schismatic council in January and joined the curial party. The more democratic element now triumphed at Basel. Cardinal Louis de l'Allemand, bishop of Arles, succeeded to the presidency. The papal bull of dissolution was annulled on the ground that councils were superior to popes. Eugenius was deposed.

The Council of Ferrara opened in January, 1438. It was organized in three groups, or *status:* the first comprised cardinals, archbishops and bishops; the second, abbots; and the third, doctors and lower clergy. A vote of two-thirds was necessary for a decision in a *status.* Thus the upper clergy were certain to dominate the proceedings. It was a most remarkable assembly. Grave and proud dignitaries of the Greek Church who disliked to beg favor of the Latins mingled and debated with the theologians of the West. Business was prepared by two committees representing the Latin and Greek Churches. In January, 1439 the council was transferred to Florence because of the pest. In June the Greeks agreed with reservations to the supremacy of the pope and to other points. The results were drawn up in the bull *Laetantur Coeli* which was proclaimed in the Church of Santa Maria del Fiore over which the proud monument of the Renaissance, the dome of Brunelleschi, had just been erected.

The Council of Florence came to an end in 1439. While its decisions were later repudiated by the Greeks, nevertheless Eugenius won substantial benefits from it. His prestige was enhanced throughout Christendom; that of the Council at Basel was lowered. After Eugenius had been deposed, the fathers in Basel proceeded to elect a new pope. Choice fell upon Amadeus, formerly count of Savoy, who had renounced his earthly titles to live a religious life. He took as his name Felix V. But the council met with much opposition. Sigismund disapproved of this radical step, and, after his death in December, 1437, his electors and other subject princes with few exceptions declared their neutrality in the struggles between the contestants. France also rejected Felix. A number of universities pronounced in his favor, which was natural because the conciliar idea sprang from academic circles.

The reform movement seemed to end in a debacle. Disgusted at the rebuffs at Pisa, Constance, Siena, and Basel, the champions of the conciliar theory at Paris now looked to the French king to adopt the reforming decisions made at Basel. These were incorporated in the twenty-three decrees of the Pragmatic Sanction of Bourges in 1438. Annates were discontinued, and, instead, payments, only about a fifth as large as former contributions, were to be paid to the Holy See. Chapters were to be free in episcopal elections. This was an attempt to make the Church autonomous as it once had been and still was in theory. But it had other results. The Church fell under the power of the crown, for in securing these privileges the clergy acted as a French and not as a Catholic and non-national clergy. At Basel nationalism asserted itself successfully because of the quarrel between pope and council. It rested upon the new forces in economics and statecraft characteristic of the age of the Renaissance.

The Germans followed the French example and in March, 1439, accepted some of the decrees.

The Council of Basel now degenerated rapidly. Its extreme hostility to the pope and its schismatic actions alienated most people. The discordant fathers of the council were no match for the curia with its harmonious policy. Eugenius' cause was well represented by Aeneas Sylvius Piccolomini. In 1447 this clever Italian with persuasive language induced Frederick III (1440–1493) to abandon neutrality and recognize Eugenius. The Concordat of Vienna followed in 1448 and renewed the terms laid down in a concordat made at Constance between Martin V and Germany. By this time the Council of Basel was abandoned by all. Felix V, weary of his office, abdicated. Eugenius died in February, 1447 and was succeeded by Nicholas V (1447–1455). In 1449 the schismatic fathers of Basel, conceding their failure, also elected Nicholas, made Felix a cardinal, and decreed their own dissolution.

The conciliar movement thus ended in victory for papal supremacy. It heralded the end of local autonomy in the Church. Sometimes writers have deplored this turn in its fortunes, but it was inevitable. Church foundations had long been exposed to the greed of princes. Abuses became rampant, and the papacy in its solicitude for the freedom of the Church had sought to control local offices. Thus had been founded the papal rule of the thirteenth and fourteenth centuries. But in the age of the Renaissance there arose a new species of ruler, powerful because of the support which the bourgeoisie gave him. New economics made possible new autocratic princes whose desire to control the Church in their realms threatened the unity of Christendom. Universal Christian conscience therefore supported popes against councils because popes alone could insure unity in the Church.

This sentiment enabled Pius II (1458–1464) to issue his bull *Execrabilis* on January 18, 1460. It put an end to the theories enunciated in the decrees *Sacrosanct* and *Frequens*:

> An execrable abuse, unheard of in former ages, has grown up in our time. Some persons, embued with the spirit of rebellion, not in order to obtain more equitable judgment but to escape the consequences of their misdeeds, presume to appeal to a future council from the Roman pontiff, the vicar of Jesus Christ. . . . Anyone not wholly ignorant of the laws can see how contrary this is to the sacred canons and how injurious to Christendom. And who will not pronounce it ridiculous that appeal should be made to what does not exist and the time of whose future existence is unknown? Therefore . . . we condemn such appeals and denounce them as erroneous and detestable. . . . If anyone . . . shall act contrariwise, he shall *ipso facto*

incur sentence of excommunication, from which he cannot be absolved but by the Roman pontiff and when at the point of death.[12]

The Great Schism and the conciliar movement thus ended in triumph for the papacy because people wanted to see but one successor of Peter as vicar of Christ. Reform so urgently needed was sacrificed for unity, and the Renaissance papacy came into existence, wealthy and corrupt. This was a dangerous condition, for sooner or later some intrepid spirit like Wycliffe or Hus would rise to protest against this worldliness. Two generations after the bull *Execrabilis* Martin Luther, an Augustinian friar, voiced a national protest and broke with the Church.

[12] Laffan, *op. cit.,* p. 120.

Chapter 6

POPULAR RELIGION AT THE CLOSE
OF THE MIDDLE AGES

T HE FOREGOING CHAPTERS have presented in brief outline the central teaching of the medieval Church and the political, social, and cultural activities created on account of it. The question now to be considered is: How did the Church succeed in imparting to the faithful its doctrines and ethical concepts? The answer to this query is one of paramount interest, for the medieval Church spiritually fructified the cultural milieu in which the Renaissance appeared and against aspects of which the leaders of the Reformation revolted.

FASHIONING THE PEOPLE'S FAITH

The medieval Church successfully taught the faith of Christ to its children. In fact, the Church was surprisingly efficient, considering the practical difficulties that had to be overcome in teaching the youth. The average layman could not understand the Latin of the Church's liturgy. But this was not so serious as might be supposed. The Mass, central ceremony in the liturgy, was a prayer service. Worshipers attending Mass did so to adore the Real Presence of Christ under the species of bread and wine. Also it is to be noted that the Mass, except on rare formal occasions, was a low Mass, one in which the celebrant inaudibly and without accompaniment of music read the service while the worshipers silently adored the Body and Blood of Christ and partook of it, for which no literary ability was necessary.

Medieval Christian homes were successful in inculcating a love for the faith. Having baptized their children "into Christ's mystical body," they proceeded to teach them by precept and example the external and the interior acts of the faith. Children learned almost spontaneously to make the sign of the cross (which really was a prayer) and to make it correctly. They were taught to say the *Our Father* and the *Hail Mary*. They learned about their spiritual friends, the great body of saints, and that they should set up candles before their images. They acquired such pious practices as fasting, carrying palms and candles, taking ashes, going on pilgrimage. They also learned to go to church, that they should be confirmed, confess their sins, do penance, and go to communion. When ill or in danger of death, they were taught that they should be shriven and, after death, be buried in consecrated ground. This was the ordinary program for a layman. If, however, he wanted to become a priest, he knew he should be celibate, seek some education, and eventually receive the sacrament of holy orders. In all these pious efforts the home had the coöperation of the parish priest and the community.

The Bible has been correctly described as being the "most studied book of the Middle Ages." This does not mean that the Bible was read by everybody, however. The medieval peasant population of Spain, France, and Italy as well as the Germanic peoples, the Celts, the Magyars, and the Slavs, except in rare exceptions, were illiterate. But social changes of vast import were taking place in European life from the year 1000 onward. A veritable revolution in trade and manufacture took place during the next three centuries. The volume of cash money increased markedly. New towns appeared in all areas ideally situated for commerce and industry. By 1300 there were more towns in the Rhineland, the Low Countries, and France than ever existed in this area under the Roman Empire.

This phenomenal increase in population profoundly modified the life and habits of the people. Formerly, for the larger part, they had lived by tilling the soil either as freemen or as unfree serfs. The rest, a small percentage, belonged either to the ruling class or to the clergy. But because of the socioeconomic changes listed above, old existing organizations or new ones—monarchies, feudal states, the Church, towns, guilds, and business concerns (banks)—were in constant need of helping hands. This expanding business activity in turn stimulated the study of Latin, the language in which not only ecclesiastical but also records and official orders of secular governments were drawn up. Later, after about 1300, officials more and more kept their accounts in the vernaculars.

Widely read literary works written by laymen appeared in the mother tongue. Among them, to mention only a few of the more prominent, were the Flemish *Historical Mirror* by Jacob Van Maerlant (d. 1291?), the Italian *Divine Comedy* by Dante (d. 1321), the *Chronicle* by Matteo Villani, and the incomparable *Canterbury Tales* by Chaucer (d. 1400). The large number of books written in Latin attests to a widespread ability to read books in that tongue. Among examples may be mentioned the

Life of Christ by Ludolphus of Saxony (d. 1377) and the *Imitation of Christ* by Thomas à Kempis (d. 1471), two of the most widely influential books written during this period.

PIETY AND THE THEME OF DEATH

Nowhere is the spirit of our late medieval forebears applied to religious teaching better illustrated than in the perennial theme of death. This was quite natural in view of the fact that all men are destined to die. The Church kept the thought constantly before her children, teaching them ever to pray for a happy death as, for example, in the petition *Ave Maria*. And had not St. Paul in I Corinthians stated the Christian hope of immortality by writing that the children of the faith shall, at the final resurrection, "put on immortality," for it was written "Death is swallowed up in victory. O Death, where is thy victory? O Death, where is thy sting?" The popular view of death as held at that time was not so much one of pessimism as one of hope mingled with fear and despair and trust based on divine promises.

The practical artistic skill of the closing Middle Ages, utilized to express the prevailing faith, produced a number of popular artistic motifs. The representation of the "Three Living and the Three Dead" became common. In this, three young men or women are suddenly confronted by three departed beings. Sometimes these latter expressed pious sentiments intended to emphasize the fleeting character of this life. Such figures were put into manuscripts and printed books. Pictures of decomposing human forms also became universal. The "Dance of Death" was another pictorial favorite, and may be regarded as the completed development of the theme of the "Three Living and the Three Dead." It represented dead forms of leading living popes, bishops, cardinals, princes, knights, and laborers in process of decomposition. Mottoes were commonly employed to impress religious truths. Some of these still linger with us, a legacy of this age in which the thoughts of man were so deeply concerned with death. Probably the best known is *Memento Mori*.

A number of books designed to instruct the layman attained a great circulation. *The Mirror of Human Salvation* was written before 1300 but became increasingly popular during the closing Middle Ages because of its growing appeal to the laity. It was an illustrated life of Christ and the Virgin. Each scene was accompanied by three pictures from the Old Testament which were supposed to foreshadow the mission of Christ. Thus the Annunciation was shown with pictures of Mary kneeling and a white lily nearby, Gideon and the fleece, and the meeting of Rebecca and Eleazar. A commentary was prepared for each scene.

Another best seller, the *Bible of the Poor*, older probably than *The Mirror of Human Salvation*, also won great popularity in the fourteenth and fifteenth centuries. It was a series of pictures representing the life of Christ, each of which was accompanied by two from the Old Testament. Brief descriptions were placed at the side of these pictures. When the art of printing became common, these books were lavishly embellished by woodcuts. It is in such books rather than in the *Summa Theologica* of Thomas Aquinas that one gets glimpses of what fed the minds of the simple and devout faithful.

The *Art of Dying*, composed at the opening of the fifteenth century, is especially illuminating from the standpoint of common beliefs. In it were written the hopes, fears, and terrors of the human heart. Life's drama was retold in the realistic and somber accounts of the age. Editions filled with woodcuts of the devil and his minions were studied, and many a child must have derived vivid impressions from them. One such picture shows a dying man surrounded by spirits of sinister aspect who recall to him the sins which disfigure his past. One tells him that he has lived in immorality, a second declares that he has borne false testimony, a third recounts to him other sins, a fourth reminds him that he has killed a man, and a fifth demon, a strange creature half human and half ox, tells him that he has lived a stingy life. Other pictures show the dying man being comforted by his priest, or oppressed by the thought of his house and treasure which he is about to leave, the last determined onslaught of the devil and his evil company, and, finally, the departure of the soul which is received by the angels in heaven while the demons, enraged and in confusion, stand helplessly by the bedside crying, "Our hope is gone," "We have lost a soul," "I am consumed with wrath," and "O the shame of it!"

These ideas also savored of the preaching in the vernacular tongues, for there was more preaching in medieval times than is often assumed by modern writers. As the populations in towns increased and the power of the laity became greater, it was inevitable that preachers should seek to teach and exhort in the vernacular. Friars often preached in this way. Practical manuals showing how sermons should be drawn up became popular. The gloomy view of life and the insistence upon the theme of death led preachers to become ghoulish in their homiletic oratory. Of one exhorter it is reported that he would "point his audience to the skulls and bones of the departed, bidding them reflect how through the mouth once so delectable to kiss, so delicate in its eating and its drinking, through eyes but a short while before so fair to see, worms now crawl in and out. The body of the head once so richly attired, so proudly displayed, now boasts no covering but the soul, no bed of softness, no proud retinue save worms for the flesh, and, if its life was evil, demons for the soul. Therefore let all going forth to God's eternal banquet prepare themselves before-hand—by looking into the mirror of the dead."[1] These appeals remind one of the methods employed by present-day revivalists.

Such sermons were popular, and the preacher who drew the most vivid picture of life's horrors won fame and attracted followers. Savonarola, the great revivalist priest of Florence, made the same kind of graphic appeal to the humble folk and with tremendous success.

POPULAR CULT OF THE SAINTS

Saints played a great part in the religious life of medieval folk. They were spiritual friends, members of Christ's mystical body ever ready with prayers to help petitioners in all kinds of needs. Most important and most effective was the Blessed Virgin, St. Mary. Next came St. Anne, St. Joseph, St. John the Baptist, and the disciples of whom St. Peter was the most significant. Very important also were a group whose fame was well-nigh universal: St. Martin, St. Augustine, St. Jerome, St. Denis, St. Nicholas, St. Catherine, St. Barbara, and St. Ursula. But the vast multi-tude of saints was composed of men and women of more or less local importance. Thus St. Gudule was honored in Brussels, St. Donatian in Bruges, St. Bavo in Ghent and Haarlem, St. Omer in St. Omer, St. Gertrude in Nivelles, and St. Geneviève in Paris.

Saints were patrons of churches, countries, and cities. During the closing Middle Ages this patronage became more specialized, and there was scarcely a human ailment or problem which did not have some special intercessor with God. This development forms an interesting chapter in the history of religion and culture. Thus St. Clarus of Albi was supposed to be helpful for eye trouble. Later St. Clare (d. 1253), the follower of St. Francis, was supposed to possess the same qualities for the same reason. More interesting is the protection which St. Wolfgang in Germany and St. Lupus in France were supposed to give against wolves. Another example of this belief is furnished by the practice in some parts of France of making St. Sebastian the patron of the hosiers because the saint's name sounded like the words *ses bas se tiennent*—his stockings hold up![2]

[1] G. R. Owst, *Preaching in Medieval England*, Cambridge, 1926, p. 344.
[2] S. Hauraucourt, *Medieval Manners Illustrated at the Cluny Museum*, Paris, n.d., p. 72.

St. Vincent was the patron of vinedressers in parts of southern France for no other reason, it appears, than that his name contained the French word *vin*, wine.

St. Roch was a fourteenth-century saint who won fame in stopping the pest. Sanitary science was almost completely unknown in the closing Middle Ages. Disease was common and pestilence often spread with terrifying rapidity among the crowded populace of towns. His power to stay its spread explains the great popularity of St. Roch. The Venetians particularly prized his intercessory powers because they were especially exposed to the diseases of the Orient. Small wonder that they finally stole St. Roch's body from Montpellier in the hope that it would protect their city from the plague! It became customary in towns to place a figure of St. Roch on the side of houses facing the street. St. Denis was petitioned for help in headache and insanity because he was beheaded. St. Apollonia was thought to be efficacious in relieving toothache. St. Lucy could help in eye trouble. St. Agatha, popular in Sicily, was supposed to prevent earthquakes.

The cult of the Fourteen Helpers in Need was popular. It was mentioned for the first time toward the close of the thirteenth century and spread from Germany to other lands. Of this group, St. Barbara was petitioned for help against sudden death by lightning, St. Blaise for troubles of the throat, St. Christopher against sudden death in storms and accidents, St. Denis against headache and rabies, St. Erasmus against intestinal troubles, St. George against fever, St. Margaret against insanity and for aid in pregnancy, St. Pantaleon against tuberculosis, and St. Vitus against epilepsy. The other saints of this group were Cyriacus, Achatius, Giles, Catherine, and Eustachius.

The Virgin Mary was the most popular of all saints, for everyone could understand her. She was believed to have special influence with her Son. She became a veritable queen of heaven, and men and women thought lovingly of her and addressed their prayers to her for help in their appeals to God and to Christ. Some of the sweetest faces ever created were made of her in stone for the churches. The one on the south porch of the transept of Amiens cathedral is especially famous. The *Stabat Mater Dolorosa*, one of the noblest hymns ever penned, deals with her sorrows. The mournful view of life characteristic of the age naturally led pious folk to reflect long and sympathetically upon the Virgin's Seven Sorrows. They also loved to think about her Seven Joys. The hymn *Stabat Mater Speciosa* also became widely known. The Virgin's hold upon piety was also strengthened by the Franciscans and Dominicans, the former of whom advocated the dogma of her immaculate conception. Many shrines and churches were dedicated to her. Her Feasts of the Visitation (July 2), Assumption (August 15), Nativity (September 8), Presentation (November 21), Purification (February 2), and Annunciation (March 25) were widely celebrated. St. Anne, traditionally supposed to have been the Virgin's mother, also was popular. A large number of chapels and churches were dedicated to her. Women appealed to her when in travail. She became immensely popular among the mining population of Saxony. It was even argued that her conception was immaculate, but this belief never secured much support.

Belief in miracles was another striking feature of the age. Man's mind constantly dwelt upon the direct action of God. Untaught by natural science, man adopted an all too simple view of the world. Storm, drought, flood, pestilence, earthquake, war, and famine were manifestations of God's displeasure. The miracles in connection with the Holy Host are interesting. One of these is the pious story of how a priest in Bolsena near Rome disbelieved the teaching that the bread in the sacrament became the body of Christ. Suddenly he was amazed to see the Host bleed and discolor the corporal. This altar cloth was ever after preserved as a relic. St. Catherine of Siena (d. 1380), receiving the sacrament, in rapture saw the crucified Christ surrounded by a bright light coming to her. From His five wounds issued rays of light which fell upon the corresponding parts of her own body. She prayed that she might not see Christ's wounds and immediately the red color of the rays was changed into a brilliant gleam of color which fell upon her heart, hands, and feet.

Many tales are told of Jews who sought to desecrate the Host and were miraculously confounded. A Jew, it was said, on Good Friday of 1370 stole consecrated wafers from the Church of St. Gudule in Brussels. Cut with knives and poniards, the wafers bled, and the Jews were frightened. They sent the wafers to Cologne, but a converted Jewess, stricken in conscience, returned them. The miraculous Host was brought back to St. Gudule in a magnificent procession, and the Jews, tortured with glowing pincers, were executed. The wafers long after were said to have worked miracles.

The morality plays were allegories in which appeared such characters as Hope, Faith, Fear, Holiness, and Death. The liturgical drama, or mystery and miracle plays, dealt with scenes from the Bible, portrayed the story of the Christian scheme of redemption, and depicted the faith of the saints and the marvels wrought by their intercession. These plays were enacted by the craftsmen on saints' and holy days. It was customary for each guild to be responsible for one or more scenes to be presented in various parts of the town in such manner that in each place a complete enactment of the play was given. The acting and production of these unprofessional players did not constitute a very exalted form of dramatic art. Often the crudity and naïveté of the untutored townsman appeared throughout. On the other hand, a refined purity breathed through some of the better ones. Townsmen also loved to stage magnificent religious processions. Many a town had its annual celebration during which the clergy bore relics about the streets. Such were the processions of the Holy Blood in Bruges, Corpus Christi in Antwerp, and the Miracle in St. Mark's Square in Venice.

Pilgrimages were immensely popular. It is said that in the county of Norfolk in England there were as many as seventy shrines. That of Our Lady of Walsingham enjoyed more than local repute. Pilgrims flocked to it from distant parts, even from the continent. The tombs of St. Edward the Confessor in Westminster Abbey and of St. Thomas in Canterbury were famous shrines. The latter has been immortalized by Chaucer:

> And specially, from every shires ende
> Of Engelond, to Caunterbury they wende,
> The holy blisful martir for to seke
> That hem hath holpen, whan that they were seke.[3]

More famous still were the shrines of St. James at Compostella in Spain and St. Peter's in Rome. Roads leading to them were among the busiest highways in Christendom. To these shrines came a constant stream of men and women to ask the saints to help them in their difficulties. Relics were kept in reliquaries and shrines. At Cologne a magnificent golden receptacle studded with precious stones contained the bones of the Three Magi. The tomb of St. Thomas in Canterbury was decorated with lavish care. Turin was famous because it contained the Holy Shroud which had covered Christ's body. The Holy Girdle which, it was believed, the Virgin dropped at her Assumption was preserved at Prato. Great zeal was displayed in collecting relics. Elector Frederick of Saxony brought together into his church in Wittenberg more than 5000 of them. In the elector's treasury there were a part of the burning bush which Moses saw and a piece of the true cross on which Christ suffered. An uncritical collector was willing to buy anything labeled as the relic of a saint.

POPULARITY OF MYSTICAL THOUGHT

Mysticism was a natural type of religious thought of the Middle Ages. During the height of this period theologians and philosophers had reared

[3] *The Complete Works of Geoffrey Chaucer*, Oxford, n.d., p. 419.

an imposing system of thought mainly on the basis of Aristotle's philosophy. Neoplatonism also had found its way into scholastic thought and had assumed a dominant role before the death of Thomas Aquinas (1274). Whenever mysticism entered the thought of the great thinkers, it remained subordinated to the rational part of scholastic philosophy. But many people, immersed in the multitudinous cares of their life, found it easier to follow the intuitive and mystical thought in theology and philosophy than the more abstruse and logical parts of the systems.

Master Eckhart (d. 1329), a learned German Dominican, adopted an intuitive Neoplatonic view of life. He taught that God, who is a spirit working in all things and creating all things, is the life and being of all things. The soul possesses a spark of this divine intelligence. The supreme end of man is to bring about the birth of God in his soul. Only in complete abandonment to Him can this be accomplished. The presence of God kindles a burning love of virtue. Love, feeling, and character appeared more valuable to Eckhart than theology and the ordinances of the Church. Eckhart had two famous pupils, Tauler (d. 1361) and Suso (d. 1362). The Friends of God, a group of German mystics, derived much inspiration from them and included laymen as well as nuns and friars.

The popularity of mysticism in this century was partly due to the feeling that the visible Church of Christ was not what it ought to be. Ecclesiastics were engrossed in secular concerns, and the papacy was becoming a great tax-gathering institution. Mystics set little store by external rules, preferring rather to seek immediate understanding of God and personal union with Him. They felt little need of priestly intercessors. The hierarchy did not approve of this type of piety because it lessened respect for the visible organ of salvation established on earth by Christ who intended that the sacraments should be the means of salvation. This manner of mystical thinking often savored of heresy, and Eckhart's teachings were condemned as heretical.

The greatest of these mystics was the Brabançon John Ruysbroeck (1294–1381). It is not certain, but it is probable that he was related to the mystics of the Rhenish valley. This "ecstatic doctor" was a simple priest in Brussels where he carried on a vigorous polemic against the pantheistic excesses of a woman named Bloemardine. Later he retired to a convent at Groenendael near Brussels where he wrote treatises in which he systematized his teachings about the mystical life. *The Adornment of the Spiritual Marriage*, the *Sparkling Stone, the Kingdom of the Lovers of God*, and other of his works are of the highest importance in studying the spread and influence of the mystical doctrine among the townsmen.

With Gerard Groot (d. 1384), a Netherlander, this mystical teaching passed into a new phase, the *devotio moderna,* or new devotion. He studied at Paris, taught at Cologne, and worked at Deventer. He collected around him a group of admirers who were deeply impressed by his piety. Groot was practical in his religious thought and labor. His simplicity prevented him from adopting the complicated spiritual ways of Ruysbroeck and the Rhenish mystics. He disliked the refined subtleties of scholastic philosophy, and insisted upon a direct application of Christ's teaching as set forth in the Sermon on the Mount. Groot's influence was exercised mainly through the Brethren of the Common Life and the Augustinian Canons of Windesheim in the Netherlands.

The Brethren of the Common Life were an order of laymen living according to a rule, leading a life of service among the poor and unfortunate, and teaching the young. Their practical piety impressed all who came in contact with them. They did not take irrevocable vows. This was a novel idea, and certain Dominicans at the Council of Constance demanded legislation forbidding lay communities such as the Brethren to live according to rule. But the fathers of the Council refused, and the order established houses throughout the Low Countries, France, and Germany. The congregation of Windesheim was a cloistered group with ideas very like those of the Brethren. This order grew until it numbered over one hundred houses. Their practical devotional life produced a remarkable classic, *The Imitation of Christ,* by Thomas à Kempis (d. 1471) who spent many years in a cloister at Mount St. Agnes near Zwolle.

The Brethren were not the only semimonastic body called into existence by the spiritual needs of the day. Communities of women called Beguines appeared in Flanders as early as the thirteenth century. Their houses were centers of religious instruction and urban welfare work. The sisters promised to obey a superior but did not take the vows of poverty and celibacy. They became popular and their houses, called beguinages, were established in all towns of the Low Countries and in many places in France, Germany, and elsewhere. The Alexians were a group of lay brethren engaged in caring for the sick and burying the dead with appropriate services. They became widely known among the people of the pest-ridden towns. The Brigittines also were important. Their original house at Vadstena in Sweden became the center of an intense popular mysticism which was preached to the populace in the vernacular. St. Brigitta's influence was felt in nearly all parts of Europe. There also were many smaller groups organized to work in hospitals, give charity, and emulate the pious deeds of saints.

THE HERESIES OF WYCLIFFE AND HUS

The spirit of budding nationalism which accompanied the Hundred Years' War, the residence of the Pope in Avignon on the borders of France, and the Great Schism evoked widespread criticism which in the case of John Wycliffe and John Hus brought forth heresy.

Englishmen viewed the papacy in Avignon with suspicion after they began the war with their perennial enemy, France. William Langland, who died about 1400, criticized the papacy and opposed the sending of sums to its treasury:

> Till Rome-runners carry no silver over sea
> Graven or ungraven, for the robber pope of France . . .[4]

Parliament had taken action in 1343 when it forbade anyone to bring into the realm letters from Rome, as Avignon was called, which might be prejudicial to the rights of the crown. In the following year the Commons made the first of their protests against the privileges of the clergy whom they suspected of divided allegiance. The *Statute of Provisors*, passed in 1351, forbade granting benefices by papal letters and provided that bearers of such letters were to be fined and imprisoned. Next came the *Statute of Praemunire* (1353) which forbade under penalty appeals from Church courts in the realm to the tribunals of the curia in Avignon. It can cause no surprise, therefore, that Englishmen in 1366 refused the demand of Urban V for the payment of 1000 marks annually, which had been begun by King John but had rarely been paid since the accession of Edward I (1272–1307). Political anticlericalism was rife, and it came to a climax in the teachings of John Wycliffe (d. 1384).

Wycliffe was born in Yorkshire, studied at Oxford, became master of Balliol College, and was appointed to several posts, the most important being that of chaplain to the king. He was sent on a diplomatic mission to Bruges in 1375 to discuss provisions and reservations to English benefices. His association with the papal nuncios on this occasion, his acquaintance with the views of English officials on ecclesiastical abuses, and his knowledge of the popular sentiment in England against malpractices prepared him to speak out for the national cause. He wrote a treatise, the *Determinatio*, in which he marshaled arguments advanced by seven lords in parliament against the demands of the papacy for tribute from the English crown. From a patriotic point of view his statements were a crushing answer to the pope's demands.

[4] W. Langland, *Piers Plowman, the Vision of a People's Christ* (Everyman's Library), p. 57.

A wider sphere of activity was opened to Wycliffe when he began championing the right of the crown to tax ecclesiastical property. The long war with France was a heavy drain on the royal treasury and new taxes had to be found. National interests were blocked by the privileges of the clergy. Wycliffe supported the demands of the nationalist party headed by John of Gaunt, duke of Lancaster, who had attracted the support of poverty-loving Franciscans. With them, Wycliffe argued that the clergy should possess no property, nor should they be permitted any voice in secular affairs. He taught that the Church should be poor as it had been in the days of Christ and the Apostles. He went so far as to affirm that in all temporal matters the king stood higher than the clergy. These points were advanced in a series of pamphlets of which two, *On Civil Dominion* and *On Divine Dominion*, were the most important. Furthermore, all title to property should be dependent on whether the holder was in a state of grace. Thus Church possessions might be appropriated by the crown if the clergy misused their privileges or were corrupt or spiritually deficient. Wycliffe argued that the crown possessed the right to determine these points. This exaltation of secular over ecclesiastical authority bore the impress of Marsiglio of Padua's ideas. Gregory XI issued five bulls in May, 1377 to Wycliffe's civil and ecclesiastical superiors in which he drew up a list of eighteen theses taken for the most part from Wycliffe's *On Civil Dominion*. In former days Wycliffe had written covertly; now he preached in the open, advancing arguments against a property-owning clergy, all in the interest of the authority of the state.

Thus far Wycliffe had said nothing specific regarding the official doctrinal teachings of the Church. Deeply impressed by the ills into which it had fallen and the corruption which had crept into it, he proceeded to examine its nature. What was the Church? To answer this question he wrote his *Tractate on the Church* in which he argued that the Church was the company of those predestined from all eternity to salvation. The Church was not the hierarchy as was popularly believed. It was a purely religious association and should have no authority in political affairs, which belonged entirely to the princes. Outside this Church there was no salvation. He also wrote *On the Truth of Sacred Scripture*. Contrary to accepted doctrine, authority was placed not in the pope but in Scripture alone. The Bible was intended to be the sole norm of faith, and it set forth the norm of political action for secular rulers.

Wycliffe also attacked the central citadel of the faith, the power of the pope. Besides the treatise *On the Power of the Pope*, he wrote a number of pamphlets on special topics, such as *On Apostasy*, *On Simony*, and *On*

Blasphemy. Christ was the head of the Church, not the pope. In the primitive Church there had been no distinction between bishop and priest. The bishop of Rome might be followed, but only because of his greater devotion, not because of any power of binding and loosing. The doctrine of papal infallibility was an error. Because of Constantine's donation the pope had become a prince, rich and powerful. This was contrary to the counsel of perfection preached from time immemorial, that is, apostolic poverty. The pope was Antichrist! Each true priest should preach the gospel, for, as compared to a faith founded on the gospels, relics, pictures, pilgrimages, and external practices were of no value. Monkish orders had no justification according to Scripture, and Wycliffe became a determined enemy against his one-time allies.

During the first years of the Great Schism Wycliffe regarded Urban VI as the true pope, but the political character of his pontificate soon undeceived him. The propagandist became an active reformer. His followers translated the Vulgate, the Latin translation of the Bible commonly used in the Middle Ages, into the vernacular. He instituted the "poor priests," for the most part laymen, to go in groups of two among the people, barefoot, provided with staff, to preach the gospel and the "law of Christ," that is, a life of poverty such as Franciscans had preached. These Lollards, as they were called, carried everywhere their hatred of papacy and hierarchy and denounced a property-owning clergy.

Wycliffe's doctrine regarding the place and power of princes was an important element in his teaching. Kings ruled by right divine. Scripture contained many examples of divine appointment, such as Saul and David. Royal power and priestly power, both of divine appointment, should cooperate with each other. The priesthood should honor secular authority just as Christ had done, and secular power should show deference and humility toward the priestly office. Whenever priests fell from grace and became "traitors to God," secular power should judge and deprive them of property and authority. Wycliffe thought that a council of theologians should advise the king about his duties which, he believed, should conform to the teachings of Scripture.

These teachings reached their climax when Wycliffe advanced his conception of the Eucharist. His attack upon the doctrine of transubstantiation came in 1381 and marks the last great onslaught of the reformer. He taught that Christ was present in the sacrament, but not by virtue of the priest's words. Christ's body was present in the Host just as the king was present in every royal court of the realm. This revolutionary conception reduced the power of the clergy. Pious practices of which the Mass was the center now became an object of attack.

Wycliffe died in 1384, after his doctrines had been condemned by the University of Oxford and the archbishop of Canterbury. But Lollardy continued to be popular. Richard II (1377–1399) showed little inclination to enforce judgments pronounced in Church courts. The Lollards in 1395 even petitioned parliament to aid them in "reforming religion according to the precepts of Scripture." Apostolic poverty was to be introduced. But Richard refused to entertain this petition. With the accession of Henry IV (1399–1413) as the result of a dynastic change, the fate of the Lollard movement was sealed. Henry needed the support of the hierarchy in order to establish his authority, for he had grasped at the crown and won it by an act of violence. The Lollards were sacrificed. The statute *De Haeretico Comburendo*, passed in 1401, placed the secular arm at the service of ecclesiastical justice. Many executions followed, but it proved difficult to uproot the heresy taught in secret meetings. The pressure of the government nevertheless was effective and Lollardy dwindled but never wholly disappeared.

Wycliffe's heretical teaching, compounded of nationalism, antagonism to Rome, and certain traditional ideals about a possessionate clergy also had some influence in Bohemia. The close connection between the royal families of both lands—King Richard II had married Anne, a daughter of King Wenzel of Bohemia—made the passage of Wycliffe's ideas to Bohemia easy. In Bohemia as in other Slavic lands the native populace was dominated by the Germans who had settled among them. A renaissance of nationalist feeling was in the making, and John Hus (1369?–1415) became its exponent. He was born of lowly parents, studied at the University of Prague, and began lecturing in 1398. He was a man of deep piety and exemplary morals, was interested in the practical aspects of religion, and became a popular preacher when he was appointed priest of Bethlehem Chapel in Prague. He addressed his hearers in the Czech tongue. His eloquent pleadings and trenchant criticisms of clerical morality won him many supporters. He thus became an apostle of Czech nationalism.

The struggle which ensued was to last half a century and was as dangerous a threat to the German Empire as to the Church. Archbishop Zbynek of Prague, a well-meaning but rather illiterate prelate, at first favored Hus, but soon became fearful of the practical consequences of his teaching. In 1408 the clergy of the diocese induced the prelate to suspend Hus from preaching. Zbynek also condemned Wycliffe's teachings. Meanwhile Emperor Wenzel sought support from the university to withdraw obedience from Gregory XII. The Czech masters and students agreed but the others refused. Thereupon the German masters and students withdrew and founded a university in Leipzig (1409). This was a triumph for Czech nationalism. Huss was excommunicated and cited before the fathers of the council in Constance (1414–1418) where he dignified his ideas by dying for them at the martyr's stake.

Hus must be regarded as a remarkable man, like Wycliffe, a herald of the dawning spirit of nationalism. His ideas of reform in the Church were set forth in his treatise *On the Church*, written in 1413. Although it criticized many things in the life of the Czech Church, it must not be assumed that his views were merely an echo of Wycliffe's teaching. He did not, for example, accept Wycliffe's denial of the Real Presence but vigorously insisted on it. Like Wycliffe, Hus exerted much influence on the Reformation, both being significant as pointing the direction of future revolts.

SUPERSTITION DURING THE LATE MIDDLE AGES

Magic flourished during the Renaissance and the Reformation. It had been inherited from the superstitions of the Germanic, Celtic, Slavic, Greek, and Roman past, and the Church, in spite of its persistent efforts, found it impossible to eradicate these notions. Such was the virility of the belief in witches and what they could effect that Shakespeare, to heighten the appeal of his *Macbeth*, opened that play with a witch scene.

A regular cult of witchcraft grew up. It was thought by many that, as God was the creator of all things beneficent, so the devil, His opposite, possessed a corresponding power over evil. Small wonder that the people called upon the devil to aid them against their enemies, real or fancied! The worship of the evil one was carried on in many communities by groups of witches or warlocks, called covens. Witches were active agents of the devil. They conducted meetings known as sabbats, to which they were said to fly through the air on broomsticks. In their ritual there were singing, dancing, and ceremonies in which the devil, as either a man or an animal, preferably a goat, was worshiped with disgusting rites. Witches possessed all sorts of power to do extraordinary things. They could cause rain or hail, blight fields or make them fertile, cause babes to be stillborn, and make invalids of children. Strange sexual irregularities occurred, such as the union of men with succubae and women with incubi. The offspring was half devil, half human. Pacts by witches or wizards with the devil were commonly made, it was alleged.

These vulgar practices were opposed to the faith, and churchmen became frightened at the prevalence of this cult. Hence Church tribunals condemned warlocks and the secular arm applied a fitting penalty. Pope

Innocent VIII (1484–1492) issued his famous bull *Summis Desiderantes* in 1484, condemning the practice of witchcraft especially in Rhenish Germany and adjacent lands.

The Church did not create the witchcraft delusion, nor is this bull a dogmatic statement about witchcraft. The pope merely moved to put an end to something which had existed a long time and was growing in intensity. Two Dominican friars, Jacob Sprenger and Henry Kramer, were appointed as inquisitors. They produced a remarkable book called *The Witches' Hammer* (1487), the classic treatment on the subject and the source of many later works. It is a bulky compendium divided into three parts, the first dealing with the agents of witchcraft, the second showing the methods employed by witches in their nefarious work, and the third setting forth the judicial steps in combating the evil. Witchcraft, like heresy, was regarded as a crime by the state. To league with man's archenemy, the devil, deserved punishment. Torture was regularly invoked in continental Europe, and the rack was employed in England. Condemned witches were strangled, hanged, beheaded, and their bodies cast into the fire; often they were burned alive.

PART IV

Late Medieval Chivalric Life and Letters

Chapter 7

THE PASSING OF CHIVALRIC IDEALS

C HIVALRIC IDEALS dominated the thought, manners, and customs of the declining Middle Ages. These ideals had been created by the aristocratic feudal elements of the population who guided their life according to knightly principles. Townsmen flattered their lordly superiors by adopting chivalric views, ideals, and manners. The clergy likewise shared these conceptions. Such ideals tended to become obsolete in the urban and commercial environment of the vanishing Middle Ages. But deeply entrenched, they continued to exercise great influence. Though the age of the Renaissance witnessed the passing of chivalric manners and ideals, it nevertheless produced at the court of the Este princes of Ferrara three great classics, all based upon chivalric tradition. These are the *Orlando Innamorato* by Matteo Maria Boiardo (1434?–1494), the *Orlando Furiosa* by Ludovico Aristo (1474–1533), and the *Gerusalemme Liberata* by Torquato Tasso (1544–1595).

RISE OF CHIVALRY

Chivalry has been defined as that "body of sentiment and practice, of law and custom, which prevailed among the dominant classes of Europe between the eleventh and sixteenth centuries; and which, more completely developed in some countries than others, was so far universal that a large portion of its usages is common to all the nations of western Europe." To comprehend the nature of chivalry it is necessary to trace the social history of Europe. Four stages may be distinguished: first, the age of predominantly manorial economy to about 900; second, the period in which feudal institutions and chivalric customs were created, which lasted to about 1100; third, the era of the full florescence of chivalric customs to about 1300; and fourth, a time of overripeness and decadence which lasted into the sixteenth century.

The first of these stages, beginning with the fall of the Roman Empire, was an age in which towns, commerce, and the use of coined money were practically absent in northern Europe. A limited amount of this mercantile activity, however, existed in the Mediterranean area. The greater portion of society lived as serfs on estates. They tilled land assigned to them by their lords and in return for this also worked on the part reserved for the lord's use. They were bound to the soil on which they were born and were subjected to all sorts of limitations upon their freedom. They were not in this respect equal before the law with other members of the population such as nobles and royalty. Manorial servitude provided the economic support for feudalism and chivalry.

The second stage in the formation of chivalry is marked by the creation of feudal institutions. Central government collapsed after the death of Charlemagne because of weakness in the organization of the state, the ambitions of local officials (counts and dukes) to become rich and powerful, and the incursions of Saracens, Northmen, and Magyars. Powerful local magnates usurped governmental activities and the more successful established themselves as feudal princes. This was an age of anarchy in which only a nobility could control the country. By the year 1000 much of western Europe was in the power of such princes.

Chivalry began with the crystallization of feudal customs about the year 1000. The severest fighting was finished but much of the former roughness persisted. Loyalty of vassal to lord and of lord to vassal had been a chief virtue during the old days of violence and was emphasized even to the point of death. This personal fidelity brought a measure of security to many communities, a measure of repose wanting ever since the early days of anarchy. As soon as this stage was reached, refining influences began to transform the rough life of the baronage. The first of these was the Church and the truths she taught. The fighting ardor of knights henceforth was enlisted in behalf of the Church which had to defend her far-flung borders against the infidel in Spain, in the Mediterranean area, and in the Holy Land. Pilgrims were wont to visit the shrine of St. James at Compostella. Since the route thither was beset with dangers, it was inevitable that pilgrims should become crusaders. They went also to the sepulcher of the Saviour in Jerusalem. Thus was born the martial ardor of the crusading ages. Religion cast its spell upon these fighting chevaliers and softened their rough manners.

THE IDEALS OF CHIVALRY

To these formative influences was added the refining example of woman. This was inevitable because of the revolution in economic life and social organization which gained momentum during the twelfth century. Commerce revived, money became more plentiful, and the material bases of life were broadened. Men were no longer satisfied with the rough life of former days. When favorable social conditions appeared, woman's subtle influence invaded the castle. She became the object of song and romance and the center of an elaborate etiquette known as courtly love. Feminine influence became more and more important in chastening the asperities of feudal life. Tournaments took the place of the combats of former days. Thus chivalry came to possess its three classic ideals: service to one's lord, service to God, and service to women.

In this age marked by the rise of chivalric literature, the laity possessed little higher culture. The baronage was illiterate and often superstitious. Only the clergy were learned. But the experiences of feudal life had taught men a theme—that of service and loyalty—which they could readily understand. During the troublous days after the ninth century political life had been dominated by a race of fighting men such as the dukes of Normandy and the counts of Flanders. There arose a worship of heroes whose deeds were sung in poetry. Chief of these romances is the incomparable *Song of Roland* composed shortly before the First Crusade. Others followed in rapid succession such as *Raoul of Cambrai, Renaud of Montaubon, Bertha with the Large Feet,* and *Ogier.* These accounts of heroes are legendary. Men even began to look to classical antiquity whose civilization had perished but could not be effaced entirely from the memory of a turbulent baronage. Alexander and Theseus became inspiring heroes. The story of Troy fascinated nobles.

The Arthurian romances became popular. In 1148 Geoffrey of Monmouth finished a romance, the *History of the Kings of Britain.* It told of a King Arthur who held a Round Table to which gathered a company of noble knights who rendered perfect service to God, their king, and the ladies. Practically nothing in this tale has any historical foundation, although it is possible that some person named Arthur won fame in fighting the Angles and Saxons during those dismal centuries when Roman power became extinct in Britain. But a greater truth than mere fidelity to dates and events animates the long cycle of stories which grew up around the Round Table. They expressed the perfection of the chivalric ideal extolled in every human relationship.

Introduced into France, these stories soon became popular. They were elaborated by such writers as Chrestien de Troyes, whose romances were admired at the court of the count of Flanders, and Marie de France, whose tales were read by the chivalrous of England and France. Hartmann von Aue introduced them into Germany. His example was followed by Wolfram von Eschenbach whose *Parzifal* became a masterpiece of this type of literature. Gottfried von Strassburg's *Tristan and Isolde* (about 1210) is one of the last of these romances.

Unswerving fidelity was a basic motif in this literature. Nobles liberally received knights attracted from all parts to their halls to participate in the splendors of chivalric entertainment. Fighting remained an essential part of knightly activity but henceforth was exalted to an ethical basis. Knights stood ready to fight against every wrong. For God, king, country, and right they fought with passionate zeal. The finest expression of this ideal is found in tales dealing with the quest for the Holy Grail "wherein the precious blood of the Saviour was received on the day that He was put on rood and crucified in order that He might redeem His people from the pains of hell." Many a valiant knight sought the Grail, but most of them failed because they were not pure in life. Sir Galahad was successful because he was free from all moral blemish.

SOCIAL ASPECTS OF CHIVALRY

Towns and economic life made leisure and artistic cultivation possible in southern France, which was marked by greater refinement than northern Europe. Not war but themes of love and social intercourse prevailed there. "Courts of love," in which sat the noblest ladies guided by a spirit of exalted gallantry, were common. The poetry of the south is composed of short pieces, light in character, devoted not to the deeds of great heroes but to such human passions as jealousy, hatred, and love. It was cultivated in the castles, and many a seignior took a hand in composing songs and ballads. This literature vanished in the thirteenth century during the Albigensian wars. Some of the old-time gaiety persisted, however, in the songs of the troubadours. This literature became popular in Italy and also in Germany where it was taken up by the minnesingers. In northern France these poets were called *trouvères* and the people who sang the songs, *jongleurs*. The conception of love embodied in this literature exerted an abiding influence upon writers of the Renaissance.

Elaborate social conventions grew up around the central theme of chivalry. Preparation for a life of service became an important matter. Youths were placed in the household of some lord to acquire chivalric practices. For seven years they lived under the supervision of the women in the castle who taught them that service was ennobling. At fourteen the page or *damoiseau* became an esquire and passed under the direction of chivalric men. He learned to use weapons, ride horseback, and take part in such sports as hawking. He tried his hand at courtly poetry, played chess and backgammon, and prepared himself for a courtier's career. At twenty-one the young man was ready to become a knight.

This was an elaborate ceremony composed of the following steps: taking a bath, dressing in white tunic, red robe, and black hose, fasting for twenty-four hours, a night's vigil in the chapel, confession and Mass, blessing of the sword, taking of vows, being invested with sword, spurs, and armor, receiving the accolade, placing the helmet on the head, mounting the horse, and showing by dextrous management of the mount that he was worthy to become a knight. Secular and religious elements were brought together in this ceremony. The bath symbolized purity, while the white tunic, red robe, and black hose stood for purity, self-sacrifice, and death. Often, however, the ceremonies of conferring knighthood took place on the field of battle when the recipient had given concrete evidence that he was worthy of the honor. In such cases a knight would strike the kneeling candidate on the back with the flat of the sword and pronounce the words which made him a member of the fraternity of knights.

Chivalric culture was bound to produce lofty ideals. In an age of social insecurity, when violence was rife and life crude and uncouth, it was natural that men should set great store by high precepts. An elaborate code of knightly conduct grew up among the chivalric groups of Europe as universal as the manorial foundations upon which feudal society rested. Leon Gautier reduced the obligations of knights to a code containing ten points. Every chevalier was to believe the teaching of the holy Church and observe her commandments, protect the Church, defend the feeble, love the land of his birth, shrink from no enemy, wage implacable war against infidels, treat vassals according to feudal justice, never lie and always cleave to his plighted word, be liberal in largess to all, and act at all times and everywhere as champion of what is right and good against injustice and evil. These ideas were exemplified in the heroes of chivalric romances. History can also point to individuals who won renown as exemplars of chivalric ideals. Such were Godfrey of Bouillon who became ruler of the crusading state founded in the Holy Land at the time of the First Crusade (1096–1099), Frederick Barbarossa, Emperor of the Holy

Roman Empire (d. 1190), and John Hawkwood (d. 1394), a dashing and successful *condottiere* in Italy.

The great military orders perpetuated the spirit of chivalry during the closing Middle Ages and remained popular even during the age of the Renaissance. The Knights of St. John of Jerusalem were a crusading order which maintained a hospital in the Holy City. They fought the Saracens and cared for sick and weary pilgrims who visited the Holy Land. The Knights Templars, or Knights of the Temple, rendered heroic service in defending the conquests of the crusaders against the Saracens. Similar work was performed in Spain by the orders of Alcántara, Calatrava, and St. James of Compostella. Important also were the Knights of the Sword, who worked against the pagans in Estonia, and the Teutonic Knights, who forced the Prussians and Lithuanians to accept Christianity.

The chivalric ideal was nourished by many illustrious examples of chivalric nobility nearer home than the frontiers of Christianity. Such was the force that model fraternities were organized to emulate the knightly ideal. Thus Edward III created the far-famed Order of the Blue Garter, eloquently described by Froissart:

> In this season the king of England took pleasure to new re-edify the castle of Windsor, the which was begun by King Arthur, and there began the Table Round, whereby sprang the fame of so many noble knights throughout all the world. Then King Edward determined to make an order and a brother-hood of a certain number of knights, and to be called knights of the Blue Garter, and a feast to be kept yearly at Windsor on St. George's Day [April 23]. And to begin this order the king assembled together earls, lords, and knights of his realm, and shewed them his intention; and they all joyously agreed to his pleasure, because they saw it was a thing much honorable and whereby great amity and love should grow and increase. Then was there chosen out a certain number of the valiantest men of the realm, and they swore and sealed to maintain the ordinances, such as were devised; and the king made a chapel in the castle of Windsor, of St. George, and established certain canons there to serve God, and endowed them with fair rent. Then the king sent to publish this feast by his heralds into France, Scotland, Burgundy, Hainault, Flanders, Brabant, and into the empire of Germany, giving to every knight and squire that would come to the said feast fifteen days safe-conduct before the feast and after, the which feast to begin at Windsor on St. George's Day next after in the year of our Lord 1344, and the queen to be there accompanied with three hundred ladies and damsels, all of noble lineage and apparalled accordingly.[1]

Another ideal order was the Golden Fleece, founded in 1430 by Philip

[1] *The Chronicles of Froissart*, London, 1913, p. 2.

the Good, duke of Burgundy and ruler of the Low Countries. This example proved contagious, and many similar orders were founded.

Certain knightly accouterments were a striking feature of the declining Middle Ages. It became a custom among noble families to possess some heraldic device by which they might be identified on the field of battle, in tournament, and in social life. These devices were of manifold origin and were composed of symbols whose original meanings soon became lost. Often they were puns upon the name of the family or town. Thus the arms of Oxford show an ox crossing a river at a ford. Even folk of humble degree adopted such devices. The Rijnvisch (Rhine fish) family of Ghent, for example, bore on its shield two fishes. Mottoes invented by nobles and townsmen became popular—the motto of the proud house of Luxemburg was *Ich dien* (I serve). Liberal use of such devices and mottoes became a feature of the art of the closing Middle Ages.

MILITARY EQUIPMENT IN THE AGE OF CHIVALRY

Enjoying an ascendent position in medieval society, the chivalric class created cultural forms which even in this day speak eloquently of their one-time leadership. So, for example, medieval armor underwent an interesting evolution, following the development of social, political, and economic institutions. During the earlier days of feudalism knights wore simple hauberks composed of iron rings woven together. This shirt-like garment fitted loosely and fell to the elbows and knees. Instead of this shirt of mail, knights often wore a shirt of cotton or wool covered with scales of iron or leather, for many a nobleman could not afford a hauberk of mail. A conical helmet was worn to which was fastened a piece of metal to protect the nose and face. Shields, javelins, axes, and maces were the chief weapons.

As generations passed great changes were introduced. First to be modified was the conical helmet which during the thirteenth century was supplanted by a great box-like helmet with a device of iron completely covering every part of the face. Plates of metal were added to the hauberk of mail. Kneecops, shinpieces (*jambs*), legpieces (*cuisses*), armpieces (*vambraces* and *rerebraces*), elbowcops, breastplates, and backpieces gradually appeared. Over all was worn a surcoat which served to keep the armor dry and on which were emblazoned heraldic devices. Under the hauberk of mail was worn a thick shirt of wool, cotton, or silk. Constant improvement is apparent to one who studies the monumental brasses and armor in museums. The fourteenth century was an age of transition. In 1300 knights equipped themselves from head to foot in mail, but by 1400 the use of plate had become general.

To this day the castles erected by the nobility of medieval Europe dot the landscape. Many of them were built at spots uniquely situated for trade and so encouraged the development of commerce. Castle building began with the simple structures of the eleventh century. A circular plot of ground known as the bailey was raised above the surrounding land by the earth dug from the ditch around it, which was called the moat. Another but smaller area known as the motte was raised to a higher level and was also surrounded by a moat which adjoined the bailey. Such structures were common in England and Normandy. Elsewhere there were fortified areas surrounded by palisades and ditches; within were erected wooden fortresses. By the twelfth century the wooden stockade had been replaced by a wall of stone. In Norman lands great rectangular keeps of four or more stories were erected.

The construction of castles reached its highest perfection during the later Crusades. The impregnability of the structures was increased by use of the advanced principles which crusaders saw employed in the Byzantine Empire. An inner and outer ward within the walled area became common. Machicolations, crenels, and turrets were added to the walls. Some castles were provided with homocentric walls, each of which had to be seized before the attack upon the donjon could be undertaken.

Technologically, medieval castle building also had a striking part in the history of architecture. During the crusades the chivalry came in contact with the instruments of warfare in Byzantine and Arabic lands. From them they learned to make the trebuchet, onager, and the battering ram, machines capable of demolishing the most powerful walls.

THE PASSING OF THE CHIVALRIC IDEAL

Chivalry had its justification. There was much crudity in the Middle Ages. Assertion of lofty ideals of conduct exerted influence even though they were honored in the breach as much as in the observance. In so far as it upheld an ideal of propriety in social intercourse, of refinement in manners, and of a greater measure of self-sacrifice among the nobility than among other classes of lay society, chivalry had a worthy mission. Without it the world would have been poorer. The standards of gentility which it brought remained a permanent acquisition even after feudalism and chivalric convention had passed. Thus chivalry made a direct contribution to refinement among the bourgeoisie of the Renaissance.

The social ideas of a class may persist long after the real power of the class itself has crumbled. A French scholar has described the nobleman's idea of society from 1000 to 1200, the heyday of feudalism, as follows:

> Society is divided by Divine Will into three classes or castes, each of which has its proper function and which is necessary to the existence and life of the social bodies: the priests, who are charged with prayer and conducting mankind to salvation; the nobles, on whom devolves the mission of defending the nation by arms against its enemies and causing justice and order to reign; the people, peasants and burghers, who by their labor nourish the two upper classes and satisfy all their desires for luxuries as well as necessities. It was extremely simple. Sometimes, however, the clergy varied the formula and gave it a metaphorical turn. . . . Society was like the human body: the priests were the head and eyes, because they were the spiritual guides of humanity; the nobles were the hands and arms, charged with protecting the others; the people of the country and the towns formed the legs and feet—that is to say, the base upon which all the rest stood.[2]

Such conceptions were held to the very end of the Middle Ages and even in the sixteenth century. The nobility and others seemed to believe that this hierarchical organization of society was instituted of God and would last forever. It is remarkable how people can hold views on social questions founded on authority and tradition long after they have become antiquated. For centuries townsmen had steadily forged to the front and by the fifteenth century they may be regarded as the most significant part of European society. But none of the writers of that time could make this deduction. Thus the chronicler Georges Chastellain (1404?–1475), a native of Alost in Brabant, held the old views without modification. This is the more remarkable when one considers that he was brought up in a land of many towns, vast commerce, and industry. His failure to comprehend the importance of the bourgeoisie is revealed in the following passage taken from his chronicle. After describing the role of the clergy and the nobility, he says: "Coming to the third part of the realm [of France] we note that it is the estate of the good towns, of merchants and laborers. It is not necessary to make so long an exposition of them as of the other two because it is scarcely capable of high qualities because it is composed of men who do not belong to the nobility."[3]

If these social conceptions of the chivalric classes were obsolescent, what is one to say about their political views? The nobleman was brought up in a tradition of self-sufficiency. The manor had provided nearly all of his needs. But his economic independence was being destroyed by the new money economy. He became dependent upon the town and its ways.

[2] A. Luchaire, *Social France at the Time of Philip Augustus*, New York, 1912, p. 382.
[3] *Oeuvres de Georges Chastellain*, Brussels, 1865, VII, 13.

In earlier days he had been politically independent. But this also was rapidly changing. It became more and more impossible to exercise a nobleman's political feudal rights in the face of the king's growing power. Towns were wealthy and townsmen readily supported the crown when it sought to restrain the nobility. Feudal and manorial law were set aside for the ideas about government found in Roman law. The individualism of knights and their belief in the right of private war were obsolete. Their military conceptions also were antiquated. In former days contests were decided by sheer force. Knights rushed at each other at full speed. Tactics and strategy were unknown to them. It was only after long experience in adversity during the closing centuries of the Middle Ages that they were able to subject themselves to discipline. Knightly education was mainly a practical affair, designed to fit the youth for a noble's career. It was inadequate to meet the demands of the growing complexities of life during the closing Middle Ages and the Renaissance.

The passing of chivalry was hastened by certain important events. Fighting in the Middle Ages was done for the most part on horseback. When foot soldiers began to contend with nobles as equals, the day of the common man arrived. The battle of Legnano (1176) was won by the communal levies of Lombard towns against the feudal soldiery of Frederick Barbarossa. This victory registered in military annals a significant social change in European life. The battle of Courtrai (1302) had the same significance, for on that field Flemish handicraftsmen destroyed the flower of French chivalry. Soon after this, Swiss freemen with long pikes successfully withstood the onslaughts of Hapsburg nobility in the battles of Morgarten (1315) and Sempach (1386). The longbow, introduced by the English during the Hundred Years' War (1336–1453), made simple yeomen henceforth the equal of knights in fighting. Such battles as Sluys (1340), Crécy (1346), Poitiers (1356), and Agincourt (1415) proved that the mounted knight in armor was no certain victor in battle. The invention of gunpowder placed him at a still greater disadvantage. Its effectiveness grew as precision in guns became greater. Soon it was difficult to make armor thick enough to protect the wearer against bullets and at the same time light enough to permit him to move. This decline was furthered by the development of scientifically managed armies. The success of Edward III's fighting forces was due in part to better business methods than those of his opponents. Finally Charles V of France (1360–1380) organized his *bandes d'ordonnance,* a force of fighting men, an example followed by the dukes of Burgundy who ruled the Low Countries.

At last the people became disgusted with the fighting zeal of the nobility which kept the country in turmoil and prevented prosperity. The savage struggles between the Burgundian and Armagnac factions under Charles VI (1380–1422) made the common man eager to support a king who could maintain peace and put down brigandage. In England the Wars of the Roses (1455–1485) brought ruin to the nobility. That struggle was waged with such brutality that men longingly looked back to the romantic days of King Arthur and the Round Table and the noble knights who desired justice and set a splendid example by their conduct. Thus William Caxton (d. 1491) wrote, lamenting the decline of chivalry:

> O ye knights of England, where is the custome and usage of noble chivalry that was used in those days? What do ye now but go to the baynes and play at dice? And some not well advised use not honest and good rule against all order of knighthood. Leave this, leave it, and read the noble volumes of Saint Graal, of Lancelot, of Galahad, of Tristram, of Perseforest, of Perceval, of Gawayn, and many more. There shall ye see manhood courtesy and gentleness. And look in latter days of the noble actes with the conquest as in King Richard's days Coeur de Lion, Edward the First and the third and his noble sons Sire Robert Knolles, Sir John Hawkwood, Sir John Chaundos, and Sir Walter de Manny. Read Froissart. . . .[4]

But the days of chivalric glory were gone forever. Knighthood was a conception possible only in the Middle Ages. It proved inadequate in the new age. The Renaissance did not put it wholly aside, however, for social conventions cannot be destroyed in a moment. It continued to live in the new age but was adapted to new situations.

[4] Adapted from *The Book of the Ordre of Chyvalry*, translated and printed by William Caxton, Early English Text Society, Original Series, No. 168, London, 1926, pp. 122–123.

Chapter 8

LATE MEDIEVAL LITERARY
EXPRESSION

M EDIEVAL LITERATURE of the fourteenth and fifteenth centuries may, if properly understood, be regarded as one of the most remarkable to have come into existence. This literature is at once complex and practical. Its complexity is due to the fact that it flourished among a variety of peoples—Germans, Celts, Magyars, and Slavs—who had come in contact with the western Roman Empire after its wreck during the fifth and sixth centuries. An amalgam of new peoples possessing new ideals, speaking new languages, having different social, political, and economic problems dating from the late Iron Age and borrowing heavily from the defunct western Roman Empire, came into existence. Beginning with Bede's *Ecclesiastical History of the English People, The Anglo-Saxon Chronicle*, and the *Song of Roland*, to mention only a few classics of the Middle Ages, these new peoples helped bring forth a literature which tells of the life and problems of medieval times.

This literature also bore a telling practical ethical aspect. During centuries of tutorship under the direction of the Church, these peoples brought forth a wealth of spiritual books dealing with interior devotion. We need refer to only two names to illustrate this fact. One of these is the Carthusian monk, Dionysius the Carthusian, from Cologne whose *Life of Christ* long was a guide to an understanding of Christian interior spiritual life, the other Thomas à Kempis whose *Imitation of Christ* was for generations, next to the Bible, the most read book among all groups— Catholic, Lutheran, or Calvinist.

POPULARITY OF CHRONICLE LITERATURE

Chronicles were a popular literary production ever since the year 1000, and a large number of such histories were penned. John le Bel (d. 1370?), for example, produced a chronicle which covers events of the Hundred

Years' War from 1329 to 1361. Born about 1290, he belonged to one of the powerful noble families in the neighborhood of Liége and became a canon in the cathedral of that city. In the service of the ruling house of Hainault which played an active role during the first decades of the Hundred Years' War, Le Bel possessed unique opportunity to become acquainted with the stirring events of those years. His chronicle is a vivacious account in French of the war, especially as it concerned the Low Countries. Probably his most striking passages are those which recount his personal observations of the campaign in Scotland in 1329. His accurate account reveals throughout a purely feudal point of view.

John Froissart (1337?–1405?) was a great chronicler. Although born of a bourgeois family in Valenciennes, his point of view is feudal and reveals a remarkable inability to understand the significance of the bourgeoisie. The reason for this is that townsmen like him looked at life from the traditional chivalric point of view. Froissart entered the service of Queen Philippa of England in 1361 and later received encouragement from some princes in the Low Countries. Thus he was brought up in the stereotyped feudal environment of his day, and his long chronicle reveals the chivalric tastes and prejudices of the fourteenth century. It is a classic account of the Hundred Years' War and is a favorite book with many readers.

The earlier part of Froissart's work is little more than a paraphrasing of John le Bel's chronicle, but from 1356 his account is based upon his own experiences. His account is couched in a vivacious and picturesque style. Unable to understand the great transformations through which society was passing, Froissart saw everything from the point of view of the nobility whom he served and for whom he wrote. He sought to perpetuate the memory of the chivalric achievements of great men. This is stated at the opening: "To the intent that the honorable and noble adventures of feats of arms, done and achieved by the wars of France and England, should notably be enregistered and put in perpetual memory whereby the prewe and hardy may have ensample to encourage them in their well-doing, I, Sir John Froissart, will treat and record an history of great louage and praise."[1]

Georges Chastellain, another great historian or chronicler, was a Fleming, born in Alost in 1404 or 1405, and served the dukes of Burgundy who were also counts of Flanders. He wrote a chronicle extending from 1419 to 1475, of which, unfortunately, only fragments have come down to us. Like Froissart he traveled extensively, visiting courts, conversing

[1] *The Chronicles of Froissart*, p. 1.

with the notables of his day, and taking part in military expeditions. His chronicle is a rich quarry for the student of the fifteenth century when the dukes of Burgundy, made powerful by the wealth of Flemish and Brabançon commerce and industry, played a leading role in the life of Europe. His style is direct, simple, and truthful. He accepted the common belief that the feudal element was the noblest part of society. He was oblivious to the significance of the bourgeoisie whose labor supported the brilliant following of the Burgundian rulers of the Low Countries. Olivier de la Marche (d. 1502), following the example of Chastellain, wrote a chronicle covering the period from 1435 to 1467. It also extols the chivalry of the Burgundian court and illustrates the feudal manners and customs of the vanishing Middle Ages. John Molinet (1435–1507) continued the narrative of Chastellain, bringing the account down to 1506. It has less merit as an example of the chronicler's art, but is important as revealing thoughts and manners of the time.

John de Bueil (d. 1478?) was a captain who served under King Charles VII of France (1422–1461) in the wars against the English. His experiences are recorded in his *Jouvencel*. This chronicle describes the new military methods which the French adopted during the closing decades of the Hundred Years' War against the English. Soldiers no longer are impetuous as in the days of Froissart. The hero of this account is an efficient captain who can obey orders and who carefully plans how he may lead his men to victory. The chronicle breathes the new spirit that has come over a rejuvenated France which under the command of her king is achieving national unity, repression of the feudality, and the expulsion of her national enemy. This book devotes less attention to the accouterments of chivalry than its predecessors and contemporaries.

A remarkable Flemish chronicle, the *Gestes of the Dukes of Brabant*, written by John Boendale of Antwerp (1280–1365) illustrates the point of view of a bourgeois living in a rapidly growing metropolis. His chronicle is less dominated by chivalric ideals and reflects the writer's bourgeois environment. It deals with the history of the ducal house of Brabant. Its rhymes, though doggerel, express a healthy respect for truth and concrete fact.

The *Florentine Chronicle* begun by Giovanni Villani (d. 1348) is even more remarkable as an example of chronicle writing. Florence was becoming a city of world importance, and its citizenry had unrivaled opportunities to form an extended acquaintance with all of western Europe. Villani traveled far and wide, gathering information which he used in writing a chronicle. His narrative is vivacious and concrete, characteristic of an energetic bourgeois curious in all things which concerned his business interests. The chronicle begins with early Biblical times and ends with 1348. It was continued by Giovanni's brother Matteo until the year 1363. The latter's son, Filippo, brought it down to 1364. The authors were content to observe events honestly without the excessive veneration for chivalric life.

Town chronicles were popular, especially in Germany. Fable and fact were recounted at length, and, when printing became an established industry, magnificent editions with elaborate woodcuts appeared. One such work is the *Book of the Holy City of Cologne*. Nuremberg, Augsburg, Magdeburg, Strasbourg, Basel, Bremen, Lübeck, Hamburg, and others possessed chronicles. Of wider scope were the *Universal Chronicle of Saxony (Sachsenchronik)*, John Twinger of Königshofen's chronicle, and Eberhard Windeck's account of the deeds of the Emperor Sigismund.

SPIRITUALITY OF MEDIEVAL HYMNS

Hymns were a natural product of this religious environment. The liturgy of the Church employed many songs. The *Dies Jrae*, written by the Franciscan Thomas of Celano (d. 1255), appealed to an age keenly interested in the day of judgment. Its sonorous and stately verses cannot be translated adequately:

> Day of wrath and doom impending,
> David's word with Sibyl's blending!
> Heaven and earth in ashes ending!
>
> O, what fear man's bosom rendeth,
> When from heaven the judge descendeth,
> On whose sentence all dependeth!
>
> Wondrous sound the trumpet flingeth,
> Through earth's sepulchers it ringeth,
> All before the throne it bringeth.
>
> Death is struck, and nature quaking,
> All creation is awaking,
> To its Judge an answer making. . . .
>
> Ah! that day of tears and mourning!
> From the dust of earth returning,
> Man for judgment must prepare him;
> Spare, O God, in mercy spare him!
> Lord all pitying, Jesu blest,
> Grant them Thine eternal rest.[2]

[2] M. Britt, *The Hymns of the Breviary and Missal*, New York, 1948, pp. 343–345.

Few of the songs dealing with death are as beautiful and stirring as St. Francis' *Canticle of the Sun* written in Italian. It reveals true poetic insight and genuine religious sentiment.

> Most high, omnipotent, good Lord.
> Thine be the praise, the glory, the honor, and all benediction.
> To Thee alone, Most High, they are due, and no man is worthy to
>   mention Thee.
>
> Be Thou praised, my Lord, with Thy creatures, above all Brother Sun
> Who gives the day and lightens us therewith.
> And he is beautiful and radiant with great splendor,
>   of Thee, Most High, he bears similitude.
>
> Be Thou praised, my Lord, of Sister Moon and the stars,
>   in the heaven host Thou formed them
>   clear and precious and comely . . .
>
> Be Thou praised, my Lord, of Brother Fire,
>   by which Thou hast lightened the night,
>   and he is beautiful and joyful and robust and strong. . . .
>
> Be Thou praised, my Lord, of our Sister Bodily Death,
>   from whom no man living may escape.
>   Woe to those who die in mortal sin;
>
> Blessed are they who are found in Thy most holy will,
>   for the second death shall not work them ill.
>
> Praise ye and bless my Lord, and give Him thanks,
>   and serve Him with great humility.[3]

St. Thomas Aquinas (d. 1274) wrote five remarkable hymns which have occupied an honored place in the liturgy of the Church. They were specially prepared at the request of Pope Urban IV (1261–1264) for the Feast of Corpus Christi instituted in 1264, and summarize Catholic teaching on the sacrament of the altar. They are *Lauda, Sion, Salvatorem* (Praise, O Sion, Praise thy Savior), *Pange, lingua, gloriosi* (Sing my tongue, the Savior's glory), *Sacris solemniis juncta sint gaudia* (At this our solemn feast, let holy joys abound), *Verbum supernum prodiens* (The heavenly Word proceeding forth), and the *Adoro te devote, latens Deitas* of which the following are the first two stanzas:

> Hidden God, devoutly I adore Thee
>   Truly present underneath these veils:
> All my heart subdues itself before Thee,
>   Since it all before Thee faints and fails,

---

[3] *The Little Flowers and Life of St. Francis* (Everyman's Library), pp. 294–295.

> Not to sight, or taste, or touch be credit
> Hearing only do we trust secure;
> I believe, for God the Son hath said it—
> Word of Truth that ever shall endure.

Especially appealing were the *Stabat Mater Speciosa* and the *Stabat Mater Dolorosa*, liturgical hymns by Jacopone da Todi (d. 1306) unsurpassed in expressing the deepest piety of the Middle Ages. The following translation (of the first stanzas of the record of these hymns) gives but a faint idea of the tender pathos conveyed by it:

> At the Cross her station keeping
> Stood the mournful Mother weeping.
>   Close to Jesus to the last
> Through her heart, His sorrow sharing,
> All his bitter anguish bearing,
>   Now at length the sword had passed.[4]

Many a hymn sprang from the lower classes and expresses the piety of simple folk. The following Christmas song, popular in the fifteenth century, was translated into many vernaculars, including Scottish:

> To us is borne a barne of blis,
>   Our King and Empriour:
> Ane gracious Virgin Mother is,
>   to God hir Saviour.
> Had not that blissit bairne bene borne,
> We had bene everie ane forlorne,
> With sin and feindis fell.
> Christ Jesus, loving be to the,
> That thow ane man wald borne be,
>   To saif us from hell.[5]

A popular carol was the *In dulci jubilo* which interspersed Latin words in the mother tongue:

> In dulci jubilo   O Jesus Parvule,
> Now let us sing with myrth   O thirst sair after Thee;
>   and jo!   Comfort my hart and mind,
> Our hartis consolation   O puer optime!
> Lies in presepio,   God of all grace so kynde,
> And shynes as the sonne,   Et Princeps Gloriae,
> Matris in gremio,   Trahe me post Te,

---

[4] Britt, *op. cit.*, pp. 76–78, 172–174, 178–189.
[5] *A Compendious Book of Godly and Spiritual Songs* (Scottish Text Society), Edinburgh, 1897, pp. 51–52.

Alpha es et O,   Trahe me post Te![6]

Alpha es et O!

CHRISTIANITY TAUGHT BY ALLEGORY AND IN DREAM LITERATURE

Dream and allegory literature was popular. This was natural because men viewed the world as fallen from the primitive righteousness of Paradise. Was not this life a vale of tears, and was there not a perfect order beyond? Writers often arranged their productions in the form of dreams. Probably the most remarkable example of this type of literature is William Langland's *Piers Plowman* written in the English vernacular of the fourteenth century.

> In a summer season, when soft was the sun,
> In rough cloth I robed me, as I a shepherd were,
> In habit like a hermit in his works unholy,
> And through the wide world I went, wonders to hear.
> But on a May morning, on Malvern hills,
> A marvel befel me—sure from Faery it came—
> I had wandered me weary, so weary, I rested me
> On a broad bank by a merry-sounding burn;
> And as I lay and learned and looked into the waters
> I slumbered in a sleeping, it rippled so merrily,
> And I dreamed—marvellously.[7]

The poet dreams that he sees the society of his day divided into ranks. He beholds laboring peasants, townsmen, wandering friars, poor and rich, happy, and unfortunate. He sees that there are many wrongs in society, such as greed, violence, and all manner of injustice. These he judges from the standpoint of the conventional ideals of the time. The first part of his poem is a satirical picture of the world as he knew it, the second presents the world made ideal by the application of Christian ethics as taught in theology.

The *Pearl* is an allegorical poem written at about the same time by an unknown author. He is sad because he has lost his daughter Marguerite, a name derived from the Latin word *margarita* meaning pearl. She is buried in the churchyard, and one August day when he visits the spot he has a vision of a radiant landscape like that in John Van Eyck's altarpiece, the Mystic Lamb.

[6] *Ibid.*, pp. 53–54.
[7] W. Langland, *Piers Plowman* (Everyman's Library), p. 3.

> Wondrously the hill-sides shone
> with crystal cliffs that were so clear;
> and all about were holt-woods bright,
> with trunks as blue as hue of Inde;
> and close-set leaves on every branch
> as burnish'd silver sway'd and swung;
> when glided 'gainst them glinting gleams,
> splendent they shone with shimmering sheen;
>> and the gravel I ground upon that strand
>> were precious pearls of Orient;
>> the sunbeams were but dim and dark,
>> if set beside that wondrous glow!

Soon he beholds the pearl, his daughter:

> More marvels then did daunt my soul;
> I saw beyond that merry mere
> a crystal cliff that shone full bright,
> many a noble ray stood forth;
> at the foot thereof there sat a child,—
> so debonair, a maid of grace;
> glistening white was her rich robe;
> I knew her well, I had seen her ere.
>> As gleaming gold, refin'd and pure,
>> so shone that glory 'neath the cliff;
>> long toward her there I look'd,—
>> the longer. I knew her more and more.

Recognizing her, he exclaims:

> "O Pearl!" quoth I, "bedight in pearls,
> art thou my Pearl, that I have plain'd,
> bewept by me, so lone, a-night?
> Much longing have I borne for thee,
> since into grass thou hence didst glide;
> pensive, broken, forpined am I;
> but thou hast reach'd a life of joy,
> in the strifeless home of Paradise.
>> What fate hath hither brought my jewel,
>> and me in dolorous plight hath cast?
>> Since we were sunder'd and set apart,
>> a joyless jeweller I have been."

The pathetic note, so marked a feature of late medieval art and literature, is nowhere more effectively rendered. Though crushed by the tragedy of his daughter's death, the author takes comfort that she lives in heaven among the angels and the happy host gathered around the throne of God.

> "Immaculate," said that merry queen,
> "Unblemish'd I am, without a stain;
> and this may I with grace avow;
> but 'matchless queen'—that said I ne'er.
> We all in bliss are Brides of the Lamb,
> a hundred and forty-thousand in all,
> as in the Apocalypse it is clear;
> Saint John beheld them in a throng,
> On the hill of Zion, that beauteous spot,
> the Apostle beheld them, in dream divine,
> array'd for the Bridal on that hill-top,—
> the City New of Jerusalem."[8]

Allegorical tales were widely read and often employed in sermons. The anonymous *Gesta Romanorum* or *Tales of the Romans*, written in the first half of the fourteenth century, were known throughout Europe. They consist of 181 short stories, each of which is followed by a moral application. The following tale deals with adultery:

A certain king had a lion, a lioness, and a leopard, whom he much delighted in. During the absence of the lion, the lioness was unfaithful, and colleagued with the leopard. And that she might prevent her mate's discovery of the crime, she used to wash herself in a fountain adjoining the king's castle. Now the king having often perceived what was going forward, commanded the fountain to be closed. This done, the lioness was unable to cleanse herself; and the lion returning, and ascertaining the injury that had been done him, assumed the place of a judge,—sentenced her to death, and immediately executed the sentence.

Application: My beloved, the king is our heavenly Father; the lion is Christ, and the lioness the soul. The leopard is the devil, and the fountain is confession, which being closed, death presently follows.[9]

CULTIVATION OF INTERIOR PIETY

An extensive literature was created by the saints and religious men and women of the fourteenth and fifteenth centuries, of whom St. Catherine of Siena (1347–1380) was perhaps the most remarkable. Born of poor Sienese parents, the youngest of twenty-five children, she early developed a deep piety. Mystic exaltation characterized her devotion. By sheer

[8] *Pearl, an English Poem of the XIVth Century*, London, 1921.
[9] *Gesta Romanorum*, London, 1905, p. 349.

strength of character she attracted contemporaries who were much influenced by her letters. About 400 of these are addressed to popes, princes, and governments, and constitute a remarkable monument of fourteenth-century Italian culture. Her published prayers were widely read. She wrote the *Book of Divine Doctrine*, a series of dialogues in which she poured out her mystical devotion.

Practical manuals for the cultivation of mystical religious sentiment flourished. The greatest of these, *The Imitation of Christ*, ascribed to Thomas à Kempis, became one of the most widely read books of the closing decades of the fifteenth century.

Thomas taught that fashioning one's inner spiritual life after the model of Christ was the Christian's highest counsel of perfection:

> He that followeth Me, walketh not in darkness, saith the Lord. These are the words of Christ, by which we are taught to imitate His life and manners, if we would be truly enlightened and be delivered from all blindness of heart. Let therefore our chief study be to meditate upon the life of Jesus Christ.

Imitation of Christ did not consist in repeating empty phrases or in acquiring worldly wisdom but rather in creating an inner and edifying love of the Master:

> What will it avail thee to be engaged in profound discussions concerning the Trinity, if thou be void of humility and art thereby displeasing to the Trinity? Truly, sublime words do not make a man holy and just; but a virtuous life maketh him dear to God. . . . I had rather feel compunction than know how to define it. If thou knowest the whole Bible by heart and the sayings of all the philosophers, what would it profit thee without the love of God and without grace?
>
> Vanity of vanities, all is vanity, except to love God and Him only to serve. This is the highest wisdom, by contempt of the world to tend toward the kingdom of Heaven.[10]

This devotional literature was especially popular among all classes. Its cultural significance is incalculable.

THE FAITH TAUGHT IN LITURGICAL DRAMA

An extensive liturgical drama consisting of miracle and mystery plays also was created by the piety of the late Middle Ages. While many of these plays are decidedly inferior as literature, they were significant in the

[10] *The Imitation of Christ*, ed. by Brother Leo, New York, 1930, pp. 1–2.

evolution of the Renaissance drama. The Towneley Plays contain scenes from the life of Noah. God instructs Noah to build an ark for the animals to be saved from the flood. All is well until Noah tells his wife what he has been ordered to do. She proves intractable, and the scene descends into broad comedy. They enter the ark, but Noah's wife rushes out, distaff in hand, and nothing will induce her to return:

> Sir, for Jack nor for Gill will I turn my face,
> Till I have on this hill spun a space on my rock.
> > Well were hem mygt get me!
> > Now will I down set me;
> > Yet reede I no man let me,
> > for dread of a knock!

She refuses to come into the ark when the torrents descend. Not until the waters rise does she rush into the ship. But she remains intractable and Noah cannot manage her. Finally, the scene degenerates into a fight which no doubt pleased the spectators.

The devil also provided an element of comedy. Sometimes he would jump off the stage, after having tormented the damned, and rush about among the onlookers playing practical jokes. Genuine pathos was occasionally displayed, as in the scenes of Abraham sacrificing Isaac in the Brome plays. As the solemn moment draws near, Abraham puts a cloth over his son's eyes:

> Now fare-wyll, my child, so full of grace,
> A! fader, fader, turne downward my face,
> For of your scharpe sword I am ever a-dred![11]

Morality plays in which virtues appeared as actors were popular. Although handicapped by such abstract characters as Faith, Penance, and Good Deeds, moral plays sometimes developed rare power. Thus *Everyman*, written in England toward the close of the fifteenth century, is a remarkable literary monument of the closing Middle Ages. Death and the last dread ordeal when the soul appears before its Judge are the end toward which the action moves. Death speaks:

> Lord, I will in the world go run over all,
> And cruelly out search both great and small.
> Everyman will I beset that liveth beastly
> Out of God's laws, and dreadeth not folly.
> He that loveth riches I will strike with my dart,

---

[11] Adapted from J. M. Manley, *Specimens of Pre-Shakespearean Drama*, Boston, 1897, I, 23, 51.

> His sight to blind, and from heaven to depart,
> Except that alms be his good friend,
> In hell for to dwell, world without end.
> Lo, yonder I see Everyman walking;
> Full little he thinketh on my coming;
> His mind is on fleshly lusts and his treasure,
> And great pain it shall cause him to endure
> Before the Lord Heaven King.—
> Everyman, stand still; whither art thou going
> Thus gaily? Hast thou thy Maker forgot?

Called by Death, Everyman learns that the things upon which he has relied desert him. Fellowship, Kindred, and Goods leave him; only Good Deeds stands by him and recommends his sister Knowledge to accompany him. She leads him to Confession, who says that God will grant His mercy:

> When with the scourge of Penance man doth him bind,
> The oil of forgiveness then shall he find.

Finally, when he is contrite, his strength ebbs:

> O all things faileth, save God alone;
> Beauty, Strength, and Discretion;
> For when Death bloweth his blast,
> They all run from me full blast.

The Angel comes and bids Everyman:

> Come, excellent elect spouse to Jesu;
> Here above thou shalt go
> Because of thy singular virtue;
> Now the soul is taken the body fro;
> Thy reckoning is crystal-clear.
> Now shalt thou into the heavenly sphere,
> Unto the which all ye shall come
> That liveth well before the day of doom.[12]

FORCE AND THOUGHT OF DANTE

These examples must suffice to illustrate the character of the extensive and flourishing literature which grew up in the vigorous life of the closing Middle Ages. Above them tower certain great writers whose works occupy a high place in the history of literature. Outranking all writers and taking an assured place among the creative authors of all time is

[12] *Everyman, a Morality Play* (Select English Classics), Oxford, pp. 9, 22, 30, 31–32.

Dante Alighieri (1265–1321). He was a Florentine citizen who boasted an ancient and noble lineage. His family possessed some real estate in Tuscany. Dante was a member of the physicians' and apothecaries' guild of Florence and held office as one of the city's six priors. A violent feud between two factions, the Whites and the Blacks, broke out in November, 1301. As Dante was an influential member of the defeated Whites, he was banished. He spent the remainder of his life in exile, wandering over northern and central Italy. His hopes of ultimately returning to Florence were never realized for he proudly spurned to come back as a penitent. He died in 1321 and was buried in Ravenna.

The *Vita Nuova*, or *The Youthful Life*, was Dante's first work. It is an autobiographical account of the poet's profoundest experiences in early manhood and centers around his love for Beatrice. She was his junior by 1 year, and he first met her in 1274 when he was but 9. He rarely saw her after this first meeting, and remained practically unknown to her. "Her dress, on that day, was of a most noble color, a subdued and goodly crimson, girdled and adorned in such sort as best suited her very tender age. At that moment, I say most truly that the spirit of life, which hath its dwelling in the secretest chamber of the heart, began to tremble so violently that the least pulses of my body shook therewith; and in trembling it said these words: 'Here is a deity stronger than I; who, coming, shall rule over me.' "[13] The poet wrote sonnets and other verse about this passion, and after the death of Beatrice in 1290 he brought them together, joining them by a poetic prose narrative in which he set forth what his love for her meant to him. "There is no book of the sort which reveals to us a spirit so profound, so tenacious of its thought, so loyal in its feeling, so rare and radiant and strong in spite of feminine tremulousness of emotion."[14]

Deeply bereaved by the death of Beatrice, Dante dreamed of her. Once in his anguish he called her, but he only seemed to see some ladies about him who sought to comfort him. The poet's lyrical soul described the incident in the following verses:

> A very pitiful lady, very young,
>> Exceeding rich in human sympathies,
>>> Stood by, what time I clamor'd upon Death
> And at the wild words wandering on my tongue
>> And at the piteous look within mine eyes
>>> She was affrighted, that sobs choked her breath.

[13] D. G. Rossetti, *Dante and his Circle, with the Italian Poets Preceding him, 1100–1200–1300*, London, 1908, p. 31.

[14] J. A. Symonds, *An Introduction to the Study of Dante*, London, 1899, p. 45.

> So by her weeping where I lay beneath,
> Some other gentle ladies came to know
> My state, and made her go:
> Afterward, bending themselves over me,
> One said, "Awaken thee!"
>   And one, "What thing thy sleep disquieteth?"
> With that, my soul woke up from its eclipse,
> The while my lady's name rose to my lips:
> But utter'd in a voice so sob-broken,
>   So feeble with the agony of tears,
>   That I alone might hear it in my heart;
> And though that look was on my visage then
>   Which he who is ashamed so plainly wears,
>   Love made that I through shame held not apart,
>   But gazed upon them. And my hue was such
> That they look'd at each other and thought of death;
> Saying under their breath
> Most tenderly, "O let us comfort him. . . ."[15]

Visions were a common literary device during the Middle Ages and many a poet and prose writer employed them. But Dante rose above the limits of this formal convention and in the *Vita Nuova* created one of the tenderest pieces of literature.

Dante's next work was *The Banquet*, or *Il Convito*. The poet intended to produce a great philosophic treatise, but he never finished it. Only the introduction and three of the fourteen treatises planned were penned. Dante borrowed his views of the world from the system of Thomas Aquinas. Even if there is nothing original in his thought, one must not assume that it was unimportant. This was the first medieval book wherein a layman wrote on a subject which hitherto had been the peculiar province of professors in the schools. Furthermore, it was written in Italian instead of Latin. The work reveals how the lay bourgeoisie was advancing in culture so that it could express in its mother tongue the highest scientific and philosophic thought.

The *De Vulgari Eloquentia*, or *On the Mother Tongue*, written at about this time, is a defense of the native Italian language. It was held during the Middle Ages that all serious thought should be expressed in Latin. No one of any intellectual standing believed that the language of the common people could be used to express the thought of theologians and philosophers. But the unprecedented growth of trade and industry raised the prestige of townsmen so that sooner or later they would possess

---

[15] Rossetti, *op. cit.*, p. 65.

a literature in their mother tongue. Being a citizen of Florence which was rapidly growing in wealth, Dante was the proper person to express the profoundest thoughts in the native idiom. For a time in the thirteenth century, poets wrote in Provençal, thinking that it was the only medium in which the theme of love could be treated. A few Italian poets had revolted against this idea; they and especially Dante championed the vernacular of Tuscany or, as it was called, "the sweet new style" (*dolce stil nuovo*).

The *Divine Comedy*, a poem in three parts, was Dante's greatest work and the poetic masterpiece of the Middle Ages. Although filled with biographical facts and personal experiences, it is in reality a mirror of the Middle Ages. After the death of Beatrice, Dante wrote in the *Vita Nuova*: "It was given unto me to behold a very wonderful vision: wherein I saw things which determined that I would say nothing further of this most blessed one, until such time as I could discourse more worthily concerning her. And to this end I labor all I can; as she well knoweth." This is plainly an allusion to the *Divine Comedy* which was not finished until the last days of the poet's life. "The subject of the whole work, taken literally, is the state of souls after death, regarded as fact; for the action deals with this, and is about this. But if the work be taken allegorically, its subject is man, in so far as by merit or demerit in the exercise of free will he is exposed to the rewards or punishments of justice." With these words Dante himself described the vision to his friend Can Grande della Scala, tyrant of Verona.

The first part of the *Divine Comedy*, the *Inferno*, deals with Dante's journey among the souls forever lost. The poet began by relating metaphorically how the great miseries of his life began, that is, with his banishment from Florence:

> In the middle of the journey of our life I came to
>   myself in the dark wood where the straight way was lost.
> Ah, how hard a thing it is to tell what a wild, and rough,
>   and stubborn wood this was, which in my thought renews
>   the fear!
> So bitter is it, that scarcely more is death. . . .

Oppressed by the woes which overwhelmed him, Dante spied the poet Vergil:

> Whilst I was rushing downwards, there appeared before my
>   eyes one who seemed hoarse from long silence. . . .
> "Art thou then that Vergil, and that fountain which
>   pours abroad so rich a stream of speech?"

The shade of the ancient poet explained to him the meaning of the fierce beasts he met in the wood on the side of the hill. He offered to guide Dante so that the poet might comprehend more clearly the moral scheme of things:

> Wherefore I think and discern this for thy best, that
>   thou follow me; and I will be thy guide and lead
>   thee hence through an eternal place. . . .[16]

The two accordingly set out to view hell and its suffering souls. Over the gate leading into it was the inscription:

> Through me is the way into the dole city; through me
>   into the way of eternal pain; through me the way
>   among the people lost . . .
> Leave all hope, ye that enter![17]

After Dante had seen the souls of famous men and women suffering for the evil they had wrought while in the flesh, Vergil led him out of the dim nether realm into the brighter world of purgatory, the temporary abode of the saved who must be purged of imperfections before they may be admitted into the bliss of heaven. The two poets came to a stream, and Dante saw a boatman approaching, guiding his craft with open wings. After being ferried across, they began the ascent of the hill of purgatory, on the various circles of which Dante saw the proud, the envious, the avaricious, the prodigal, the gluttonous, and the lustful passing through the purging process. Vergil, who until now had guided him, deserted him. The greatest poet of Roman paganism knew nothing of heaven for he had died without learning of Christ's mission as Saviour. He said:

> Son, the temporal fire and the eternal hast thou seen,
>   and art come to a place where I, of myself discern
>   no further.

Sorrowfully Dante moved on alone and approached the river Lethe which flowed before paradise. The appearance of Beatrice, his guide to divine wisdom and Christian revelation, profoundly moved him:

> I saw the lady, who first appeared to me veiled beneath
>   the angelic festival, directing her eyes to me on
>   this side the stream.
> Albeit the veil which fell from her head, crowned with
>   Minerva's leaves, did not let her appear manifest,
> Queenlike, in bearing yet stern, she continued, like

---

[16] *The Inferno of Dante Alighieri* (Temple Classics), Canto I, 1–7, 61–63, 79–81, 113–114.

[17] *Ibid.*, Canto III, 1–3, 9.

> one who speaks and holdeth back the hottest words
> till the last:
> 'Look at me well; verily am I Beatrice. How didst thou
> deign to draw nigh the mount? knewest thou not that
> here man is happy?'
> Mine eyes drooped down to the clear fount; but beholding
> me therein, I drew them back to the grass, so great
> a shame weighed down my brow.

After being bathed in the waters of the Lethe, Dante clambered upon the bank. Beatrice in all her heavenly glory now appeared close to him.

> O glory of living light eternal, who that so pale hath
> grown beneath the shade of Parnassus, or hath drunk
> at its well,
> that would not seem to have mind encumbered, on trying
> to render thee as thou appearedest, when in the air
> thou didst disclose thee, where heaven in its harmony
> shadows thee forth?[18]

Dante now learned first the secret of the divine economy of all things. The hidden truths of theology were disclosed to him, the story of creation, man's fall from his pristine purity, the crucifixion, the scheme of redemption. Finally, he gazes upon the hosts of the Church triumphant, multitudes of the saved who occupy tiers enjoying the presence of the living God.

> They had their faces all of living flame, and wings of
> gold, and the rest so white that never snow reacheth
> such limit.

Beatrice next summoned St. Bernard, greatest exemplar of Cistercian monasticism and the master of contemplative theology, to prepare Dante to look upon the Godhead.

> In the profound and shining being of the deep light
> appeared to me three circles, of three colors and
> one magnitude . . .
> O Light eternal who only in Thyself abidest, only thyself
> dost understand, and to thyself, self-understood,
> self-understanding, turnest love and smiling![19]

[18] *The Purgatorio of Dante Alighieri* (Temple Classics), Cantos XXX, 64–78, and XXXI, 139–145.
[19] *The Paradiso of Dante Alighieri* (Temple Classics), Canto XXXIII, 115–117, 124–126.

The *De Monarchia,* or *On Monarchy,* written in Latin, sets forth the poet's ideal of government. The world was governed by two supreme orders, the spiritual and the temporal. The former was presided over by Christ's vicar, the bishop of Rome; the latter was given to the emperor. The thirteenth century had witnessed fierce struggles between these two divinely constituted powers, to the great scandal of Christendom. Italian society was rent with factional strife. Dante had suffered much and longed for peace. His heart ached when he saw popes descend into the political arena. Believing that God had instituted the empire for human welfare, he thought that the rumored coming of Henry of Luxemburg, elected emperor in 1308, would prove the dawn of peace when all strife would be stilled. To establish such quiet was not the pope's task. In temporal matters he was inferior to the emperor. Did not Christ teach His followers to submit to the power of the emperor?

Dante better than any other poet summed up the aspirations of the time. The Middle Ages were rapidly nearing their decline, for the Renaissance was approaching. Although his ideas were medieval, Dante remained a mighty influence among the humanists of the following centuries. And for students of every land and of every century his works will be a classic expression of the Middle Ages, like St. Thomas' *Summa Theologica* and Van Eyck's great altarpiece, the Mystic Lamb.

GENIUS OF CHAUCER AND SPIRIT OF SATIRE

Next to Dante as interpreter of the fourteenth century stands Geoffrey Chaucer (d. 1400), an Englishman. Born about a dozen years after Edward III ascended the throne of England in 1327, he witnessed the stirring scenes of the Black Death, the war with France, the career of Wycliffe, and the rise of the Lollards. His father was a vintner in London, and therefore Chaucer, like Dante, belonged to the bourgeoisie. He formed an intimate acquaintance with life and traveled extensively. No one, save Shakespeare, two centuries later, has better expressed the English life of his day. Chaucer, unlike Dante, was not occupied with the idealist tendencies of the age. His nimble and eager mind saw life through clear eyes. He investigated everything past and present, and possessed a ready sympathy for all human things. His works faithfully depict the thought of the declining Middle Ages. On the other hand, he expressed the dawning spirit of English nationalism which was evolving from the economic and social conditions of the day.

Chaucer exerted a mighty influence on the formation of English literature. He exhausted the literary motifs of previous writers. He translated the *Romance of the Rose,* a French poem of the thirteenth century which had profoundly influenced him. Study of this poem helped him to forge new poetic forms. Soon he was vastly superior to all French writers. When he had exhausted all that they could teach him, he began to feel a strong attraction to the Italian writers, Dante, Petrarch, and Boccaccio. Hitherto he had made translations of the work of his predecessors and contemporaries. But this was only a prelude to the composition of his brilliant masterpiece, the *Canterbury Tales* in which he described a group of pilgrims on their way to the shrine of St. Thomas in Canterbury. The *Prologue* of this literary masterpiece probably has never been surpassed as a picture in words. Thirty pilgrims (of whom Chaucer was one), representing almost every class in English society and described with the greatest truthfulness, met at a hostel in Southwark in London. The tales they recount while on the road give us a bright and realistic picture of the life of that day.

Among the bright passages Chaucer lays before us in his *Prologue* none is so pleasing as his portrait of what in the mind of that day constitutes an ideal priest.

> A good man was ther of religiun
> And was a povre parsoun [parish priest] of a toun;
> But riche he was of holy thoght and werk.
> He was also a lerned man, a clerk,
> That Cristes gospel trewely wolde preche,
> His parisshens devoutly wolde he teche,
> Benigne he was, and wonder diligent,
> And in adversitee full pacient. . . .
> Wide was his parish, and houses fer a-sonder,
> And he never lafte nat, for rain nor thonder
> In sikness nor in meschief, [mishap] to visyte
> The ferreste [farthest] in his parisshe; much and lyte,
> Up-on his feet, and in his hand a staf.
> This noble ensample to his sheep he yaf, [gave]
> That first he wroghte [wrought] and afterward he taughte,
> Out of the gospel he the wordes caughte,
> And this figure he added eek there-to
> That if gold ruste, what shall iren do?
> For if a preest be foul, on whom we truste,
> No wonder is lewed [ignorant] man to ruste . . .
> Well ought a priest ensample for to give . . .
> By his clennesse [purity], how that his sheep shold live.
> He sette not his benefice to hyre
> And leet his sheep encombred in the myre

And ran to London, un-to seynt Poules,
To seken him a chaunterie [chantry] for soules . . .
A bettre preest I trowe that nowher noon is,
He wayted after no pompe and reverence,
He made he him a spyced conscience,
But Cristes lore, and His apostles twelve,
He taughte, and first he folwed it himselve.[20]

Satirical criticism, like lofty idealization of human conduct, such as Chaucer expressed in his portrayal of an ideal priest, was quite common in late medieval literature. The gap between the real and the ideal in all of life's practical relations provokes satire. So Sebastian Brant (d. 1521) in his *Ship of Fools* held up to ridicule the abuses which featured life of his day. He denounced usurers as "vile and rash, the man of poverty they thrash, they'd care not if the world should crash." He denounced every forestaller, regrater, and engrosser in the approved manner of the day:

We'd punish him for all his tricks,
From him we must remove the ticks
And pluck his pinions with elation
Who buys up goods on speculation,
The wine and corn in all the land,
No sin, dishonor stays his hand,
So that a poor man cannot flee
Starvation with his family.
Thus prices mount, it must be clear,
They're higher now than those last year,
If wine now costs a scant ten pound,
Next month 'twill certainly be found
You'll pay full thirty when you buy.
The same is true of wheat, spelt, rye.
The great abuse need not be stressed
Of money, kind, and interest,
Of loans, pawn business oft unsound:
In one day some will earn a pound
More profit than a year should hold,
They lend in silver, ask for gold,
You borrow ten, eleven's due,
They're more usurious than the Jew.
Their business now the Jews may lose,
For it is done by Christian Jews.
With Jewish spears they run about,

---

[20] The Complete Works of Geoffrey Chaucer, Oxford, n.d., p. 425.

> I could name many such a lout,
> Unsavory are their transactions
> Yet are not stopped by legal actions.
> With joy they greet the hailstorm's might
> And see the hoarfrost with delight,
> But often too, deprived of hope,
> You'll find men hanging from a rope.
> Harm common weal and help your own,
> And you're a fool, but not alone.[21]

Medieval literature, as the selections here given show, touched practically every aspect of the life and thought of the Middle Ages. (For the literature of Philosophy, see Chapter 7, for that of Chivalry, Chapter 5.) The variety and unity of inspiration of this literature are evident at every hand. When viewed in its genetical relations with the Age of the Renaissance, as we shall learn, this literature was to prove influential.

[21] *The Ship of Fools*, tr. by E. H Zeydel, New York, Columbia University Press, 1944, pp. 302–303. Quoted with permission of the publisher.

PART V

Late Medieval Practical, Philosophical, and Artistic Achievement

Chapter 9

MEDIEVAL BUSINESS AND TECHNICAL SKILL

*T*HAT ITALIAN RENAISSANCE PAINTING, sculpture, architecture, literature, music, and forms of polite social intercourse are among the
most impressive cultural creations of European civilization is taught by all
scholars. Also, it is held that this ascendancy of Italian cultural forms is
due to the creation of magnificent form inspired by the revived study of
ancient Greek and Latin art, thought, and letters which, as we shall
learn, began with Francesco Petrarch. But unique as the contributions of
the ancient classical world may have been, a proper understanding of the
Italian Renaissance is possible only if we study the technological, political, and socioeconomic labors of our medieval forebears. Due credit
should be given to the achievements of medieval times which genetically
brought forth the Renaissance, for those achievements in many ways
have been as significant as was direct borrowing from classical antiquity.

THE LATE MEDIEVAL TRADING AREA

Europe of the Renaissance was smaller than it is today. Its eastern
boundary lay beyond the important towns of Reval, Dünaburg, Cracow,
Lemberg, and Budapest; this line separated Finns and Estonians, Latvians
and Lithuanians, and Poles and Slovaks from the vast plains to the east

occupied by Russians and other peoples. Southward the line followed the Carpathian Mountains, separating Rumanians from Hungarians. It passed eastward of the Croatians, Slovenes, and the Italians of the Adriatic coast as far as the Gulf of Arta.

Throughout this area, beginning with the eleventh century, great economic changes were in progress which profoundly modified ways of living. Formerly, life had been based upon an essentially agrarian economy. Manors provided the chief means of support of all groups— clergy, nobles, and peasants. Local production for local consumption was its striking feature. But when trade developed and industry came into being, men began to adopt new conceptions of state, society, and the practical concerns of life. Revival of trade and industry, use of coined money, and the rise of towns which began in the eleventh century were among the most significant social and economic events in the entire history of the Occident. If one were to compare a map of Europe in 500 with another about 800 years later he would be impressed by the vast number of towns that had sprung up. Such busy centers of commerce in the Low Countries as Bruges, Ypres, Ghent, Antwerp, and Brussels grew up in the Middle Ages. In France, Spain, and Italy great trading communities, which seemingly date back to the Roman Empire, were recreated at this time.

One reason for this revival of urban life was that feudal kings and nobles began to develop orderly government in their petty states. Trade had never been wholly extinct even in the darkest days of the tenth-century turmoil. At all times there had been some demand for spices, drugs, silks, precious stones, and metals. When greater public security was developed, business increased and soon again became important. Local trade sprang up at many points favorable to commerce. It was stimulated by the never ending stream of oriental articles demanded by noblemen and wealthy townsmen, and the demand by churchmen for vestments, sacred vessels, and reliquaries.

For centuries Constantinople had been the economic bridgehead between Europe and the East. But during the age of the Crusades this changed. Venetians, Genoese, and Pisans began competing with Byzantine merchants, thus steadily sapping their monopolies. The Byzantines lost this monopoly forever when Constantinople fell in 1204. Henceforth Italian merchants became the distributors to western Europe of the choice products of the East.

Quickening pulsations of trade were felt along the great river routes of commerce, the Rhine, Rhone, Meuse, and Scheldt. Places marked by nature as advantageous for economic life developed into towns. Urban communities grew up at the mouths of rivers as in the case of Dordrecht and Rotterdam on the Meuse, Bordeaux on the Garonne, Antwerp on the Scheldt, Bruges on the Zwin, London on the Thames, Hamburg on the Elbe, and Bremen on the Weser. Others rose at or near the junction of rivers as in the case of Coblentz, Lyons, Paris, and Ghent; or where land routes met rivers as at Cologne, Maastricht, Frankfort on the Main, Berne, Milan, and Orléans; or where a lake poured into a river as Geneva, Zurich, and Lucerne; or at favorable points along a river as Troyes, Langres, Provins, Bonn, Basel, and Mainz. Many a town grew up in the center of a fertile agricultural region if situated on or near a river, as in the case of Brussels, Milan, Florence, and Leiden. Sheltered harbors along the coast became sites of towns, as in the case of Venice, Naples, Marseilles, and Barcelona. Without a knowledge of such geographical conditions the growth of commerce and the rise of towns would be difficult to explain.

This extensive economic activity in western Europe stood in constant contact with distant lands. From China—where Mongol rule held sway over much of Asia, extending from the Russian plains eastwards as far as the Sea of Japan and the South China Sea—had been brought the art of raising silkworms and the secrets of producing silk.

Meanwhile Nestorian Christian missionaries from Asia Minor had been active in propagating their teaching in the Mongol empire. Later, in the thirteenth century, Dominican and Franciscan missionaries appeared at Karakorum and Peking (Kambulac). During this time the three Venetian merchants, brothers of the Polo family, traveled far and wide in the Mongol empire, visiting Karakorum and Kambulac and other places. Marco Polo (d. about 1323) recorded their thrilling experiences in his *Book of Marco Polo*. At this time northern Africa was part of the European trading empire, and distant Greenland stood in commercial and other relations with northern Europe. Although its export of tusks (from which artists carved religious objects) was limited, this trade nevertheless gives some hint of the vigorous commercial and colonizing activities of our medieval European ancestors.

LATE MEDIEVAL TOOLS AND TECHNOLOGY

Medieval workers were most industrious and practical. From the Stone, Bronze, and Iron Ages they inherited some of the more important features of civilization such as agriculture, metal and stone working, pottery, spinning, and weaving. Practical skill acquired through generations characterized the medieval laboring man in every kind of work.

There was a time when writers on the Renaissance misprized the manual operations of medieval guildsmen, peasants, and other workers, holding that their manner of production had a deleterious effect upon the artistic creative activity. The truth is, however, that this practical character of medieval man's achievement prepared the material foundation and technical skill which made possible much of the brilliance of the Renaissance. So, mechanically, medieval man made significant progress. The crank shaft, for example, was in common use as early as the eighth century. This invention may be regarded as being as significant as that of the wheel, for it came to be applied to many machines. Without this device medieval tools such as the roasting spit, the famous Dover mechanical clock of the fourteenth century, and many other inventions would not have been possible. The invention of the clock may be regarded as a most significant achievement, for it was the first mechanical device for measuring time accurately.

During this time Europe also acquired the secret of making guns and gunpowder. These inventions tended to make obsolete the trebuchet, springal, and onager—machines introduced from the Byzantine East and designed to batter down the walls of castles. Windmills came to the Low Countries from the Arab East and revolutionized agriculture in areas where the country lay at sea level or below. By this time the horse collar, stirrup, and saddle, devices which enabled men to equip horses for plowing, travel, and feudal fighting, also had become common.

The rapid growth of towns after the year 1000 must have been a powerful stimulus to the building industry. This was accompanied by a steady increase in population and a constant demand for builders and carpenters. Late medieval folk possessed a plentiful assortment of manual tools. All this, it appears, was expressed with telling effect by the organization of workers and guildsmen. Gothic structures—churches, town walls, bridges, belfries, gates, houses—bear testimony to the medieval builders' skill. The tools these artisans used were the hammer, nail, axe, mallet, adze, saw, knife, T square, auger, chisel, jointer, pincer, tongs, plane, ruler, level, ladder, lathe, and derricks—tools still to be found in builders' and carpenters' collections. Similarly, peasants, brewers, tanners, dyers, bakers, smiths, and iron mongers, to name but a few, possessed their own special tools.

Medieval Europe also witnessed the rise of revolutionary business establishments, for example in the manufacturing of cloth. In the beginning spinning was done by means of the ancient distaff, but in the silk industry of Lucca, as early as the fourteenth century this and other operations were performed by mechanical devices, and Lucca's silk cloth industry became truly a big business. The Florentine silk cloth guild, it appears, also used the methods of manufacture which had enriched Lucchese merchants.

But it was the mining business that was truly remarkable. During the fifteenth century it, too, was a big business. Its machinery reached a high degree of efficiency. Giant wheels, sometimes run by water, sometimes by the treading of men, provided power for operating suction pumps, hoisting buckets filled with ore, stamping ingots, and manufacturing trip hammers. Particularly important in supplying the need for metal tools in the society of the times was the ancient forge. This tool looked much like the forges we used to see in blacksmith shops and which were described by Longfellow in his *Village Blacksmith*. Such forges were operated by bellows, the historical origin of which seems to be unknown. Beside such a forge usually stood the smith's anvil, hammer, and tongs. Truly, this age was one of the most remarkable of all medieval times.

LATE MEDIEVAL BUSINESS AND FINANCE

The extraordinary development of social and economic activity during the thirteenth and fourteenth centuries also brought forth new business methods and provided the necessary material foundation for the brilliant pageant of cultural achievement we call the Renaissance.

Commercial relations between Italy and the Levant early led to great changes in trading methods. Trading corporations such as the *commenda*, or *societas*, arose. This was a type of partnership in which investors provided two-thirds of the capital and factors or agents one-third. The factor or agent took the entire stock of goods to Syria or other parts, sold it, and on his return home divided the profits with the investor. Each received one-half. These associations were common in the twelfth century in Genoa and other Italian towns. It is probable that the *commenda* was originally an Arabian institution. Sometimes there were several investors, each of whom probably was too poor to provide twice as much capital or goods as the factor. In this case the investors jointly received half of the profits. In another type of *commenda* the factor carried goods of his own in addition to those of the partnership which had been formed for the venture. Or the investor might contribute more than two-thirds. Finally it became customary for the factor to manage capital or goods entrusted to him by merchants who were not partners in the *commenda*. This form of association varied according to business needs. During the Crusades and in subsequent centuries, opportunities for trade were constantly expanding, and modifications in the form of these early societies were inevitable.

Another type of partnership came into existence at the time when the *commenda* was popular. This was the *accommodatio* in which the investor provided all the capital. The factor carried the goods to the place of business, acted as agent of the investor in selling the goods and collecting the money, and received a fourth of the net proceeds for his labor. Like the *commenda*, this association dissolved after the voyage was finished. The *commenda* and the *accommodatio* were temporary organizations which marked the beginning of trading groups which finally developed into the joint-stock company with limited liability.

The *maone* were an important stage in the evolution of these trading groups. These were associations formed by Genoese merchants for trade in Chios, Cyprus, Ceuta, and Corsica. The *maona* organization in Chios may be regarded as typical. In 1346 the Genoese conquered the island of Chios. Finding that the city's exchequer did not have the funds to pay the expenses of this military expedition, it was suggested that a company should be formed of the men who had advanced the initial expenses, and this company should be given the sole right to exploit the taxes and commerce of Chios. This was done in the next year. It was an association of shareholders who received dividends and the shares could be sold. The company of twenty-nine shareholders was to last 20 years, during which it was expected that the debt of the republic would be liquidated and the *maona* would come to an end. Finally in 1362 only twelve owners were left who formed the "Casa [House] of the Giustiniani." Varying fortunes attended the history of this *maona* which lasted until recent times. Out of these business methods grew the joint-stock company.

This organization of a number of stockholders was usually authorized by a charter and possessed limited liability. The earlier development of this type of corporation has never been carefully studied. It appears to have had a number of predecessors. Some form of joint-stock company was known before 1300 even in remote Scandinavia where economic development lagged far behind that of Italy. The Merchant Adventurers of England, who received a royal charter in 1404, are a noteworthy example. The chartered companies of the sixteenth and seventeenth centuries were built directly upon the practical experience derived from medieval business in northern Europe.

The rapid growth of trade and industry which made the cities of northern Italy the capitalist center of Europe led to the establishment of banking. Merchants were in the habit of handling large sums of money, the management and transfer of which presented many problems. To facilitate payment of debts in distant places, letters of exchange or credit were invented. Their origin is obscure, but they appeared early in the greater centers of trade. Letters of exchange (*lettres de foire*) were plentiful in Flanders, Brabant, and Artois, and at the fair of Champagne as well as in Italy.

Great sums of money were accumulated by Italian families in Piacenza, Asti, Siena, Lucca, and especially Florence; this early induced them to engage in banking. A striking feature of this banking activity was its organization into companies or *case* (houses). Such were the Bardi, Peruzzi, and Frescobaldi of Florence in the early part of the fourteenth century. They lent enormous sums to princes who had to finance wars which could no longer be fought with the old feudal methods of the eleventh century. They also financed the popes in their many undertakings such as crusades and wars in Naples and Sicily. Thus Pope Boniface VIII borrowed to the limit of his credit in order to reduce the king of Sicily to obedience.

Borrowers usually paid exorbitant rates of interest or heavy bonuses and commissions. Lending of money became exceedingly profitable, and many fortunes were made. Lenders demanded good security; this consisted in manorial incomes, customs, taxes, or in mortgages on lands and valuable mining properties. The bankers of Siena waxed rich in the thirteenth and fourteenth centuries from the great profits of their loans to the papacy. The house of Medici supplanted them in the fifteenth century and in turn grew to be immensely wealthy. Their monopoly passed to the German house of the Fugger, established in Nuremberg in the fifteenth century. They played an increasingly important part in European affairs. They and other German houses financed the rapidly expanding business life of the closing Middle Ages. They lent vast sums to Charles V in his many undertakings; without their aid the great wars for the balance of power in the age of the Reformation could hardly have been fought.

The Bank of St. George (*Casa di San Giorgio*) of Genoa, composed of a number of shareholders who were creditors of the city of Genoa, was formed in 1407 in order to fund the public debt which the republic at the moment found difficult to pay. Venice also possessed such an institution, the Bank of St. Mark. These were private institutions which managed state debts and loans in the form of bonds. Barcelona appears to have been the first to establish a state-owned bank (1401). Banking was thus by no means an uncommon phenomenon in the age of the Renaissance. These banks did not merely handle commercial obligations and public debts, but also, contrary to common opinion, received sums of money on deposit. This financial activity became the indispensable element in the cultural life of the age.

The Renaissance also produced a system of bookkeeping. Each type of economic activity presupposes some method of keeping accounts. In the earlier Middle Ages when life was essentially agrarian and manorial, accounting was a simple matter. Manorial lords kept lists of dues which serfs owed them. Monastic houses and episcopal establishments also possessed such manorial rolls. Feudal lords drew up lists of feudal obligations due them. Sometimes princes caused to be drawn up records of incomes from their states. Such were the *Domesday Book* of William the Conqueror and the *Book of Hearths* of Duchess Johanna of Brabant (1374). A new type of accounting came into existence when agrarian economy was being supplanted by a money economy. Town and commercial life required a new kind of bookkeeping.

The first bookkeeping developed was that of the single entry. It was practicable only for small businesses but was long employed by large organizations. Thus the accounts of Flemish and other Low Country towns were kept in this manner throughout the fifteenth century, in spite of the fact that large towns like Brussels and Antwerp became very important commercial and banking centers. These town accounts were drawn up year by year. Each year was divided into sections devoted to some class of the constantly growing expenditures or receipts. The original accounts of Bruges and Ghent, still extant, contain much statistical data. The accounting of the English crown and of the counts of Holland and Hainault was done in much the same manner.

Italian towns also kept accounts by single entry but soon outgrew the limitations of this method. As economic life became more complicated and trading operations varied, double entry bookkeeping was invented. This is a system whereby every transaction is entered twice, under assets and liabilities. It provides a constant check on the arithmetical accuracy of the record and is a much more scientific system than that provided by the single entry. By 1340 Genoa began to keep its records in this manner and found it a great improvement upon the older method. It enabled officials to ascertain at a glance the exact financial status of every public activity. This method with some variations was also employed in Venice, the earliest specimens extant dating from 1406. The remarkable part played by that republic in the development of accounting causes no surprise, for Venice remained the commercial capital of Europe down to the time when Vasco da Gama sailed to Calicut by way of the Cape of Good Hope.

From Venice double entry bookkeeping passed to all parts of com-

of morality, for it involved sustenance of life, clothing the poor, support of churches and hospitals, and charity. It was incumbent upon Christians to provide more equitable distribution so that necessary consumption might be possible.

Just as laymen could not ignore the progress of economic life, so too were clergymen constrained to take cognizance of it. From the thirteenth century writers on canon law agreed that certain charges might be made in connection with loans. These were not usurious because they were supposed to be made not for the use of money but for labor and risks. There were four of them: *periculum sortis,* or risk of loss; *poena conventionalis,* or fine for failure to pay at a specified time; *damnum emergens,* for loss incurred at the moment the loan was made by the lender because he could not himself use the principal in order to make money; and *lucrum cessans,* for loss of money incurred after the loan was made because the lender was for the moment not in a position to employ the principal in gainful pursuit. It is evident that such rules readily evaded as economic relations became more complex.

Meanwhile, as governments expanded and grew more powerful they became efficient in the collection of taxes. The Exchequer of England early showed the way how taxes could be gathered in the most business-like manner. The treasury of the French crown likewise developed the most practical methods of raising taxes. The Kingdom of Naples and Sicily created a highly centralized state organism, including a system of taxation, during the fourteenth century. But striking as these governmental successes were, it was the Papacy that developed the most remarkable system of administration. Its widespread sway extended to Scandinavia (and Greenland), to Mediterranean lands, and eastward as far as Poland, Bohemia, and Hungary. The papal chancery maintained correspondence with the most distant bishops, priests, and parishes. The Papal treasury stood in regular financial relations with the Church's tax collectors. From the standpoint of human achievement during the entire Middle Ages no other organism can compare with it.

Because of its far-flung activities the Church itself needed great sums of money with which to finance its operations. It appealed to bankers and submitted to the traditional methods of financial groups. Theologians and moralists might denounce usurers, but in spite of all they could do, the world of business persisted in its course. Wealthy merchants and merchant princes troubled themselves little about the restrictions which canon law imposed upon business. This explains in part the secular character of the period. People disregarded religious discipline and were concerned, in part at least, with secular interests. The secularity of the age of the Renaissance was the natural result of medieval economic progress. Economic and social realities to some seemed more compelling than churchly teaching in a world in which the layman was taking his place beside the cleric and the knight.

Chapter 10

BEQUEST OF MEDIEVAL THOUGHT
AND EDUCATION

$\mathcal{T}$HE CIVILIZATION of the Renaissance, and that of the Reformation as well, is not to be understood without some knowledge of the philosophic thought of the Middle Ages and of the educational practices developed during those times. To suppose that the thirty or more generations that elapsed since the reign of the Emperor Constantine (d. 337) have contributed nothing to the culture of the Renaissance has been shown to be fallacious. And the attempt to explain the Renaissance, the Reformation, and the Catholic Revival simply as social or economic phenomena has lost the simple charm it once possessed. After all, man is a rational creature who guides his acts by his free will and imposes his culture upon his material environment as he deems proper. The consequences of such activity naturally vary from place to place and from time to time.

THE SEVEN LIBERAL ARTS AND THE UNIVERSITIES

Catastrophic as was the disintegration of the Roman Empire in the West, that disaster nevertheless presented some constructive aspects. The "barbarians" of early medieval Europe living along the confines of the Roman Empire were destined to become the ultimate heirs of the splendors of Rome. Germanic Goths and Vandals, already Christianized but, being Arians, were heretical, established their kingdoms in Roman lands. Pagan Franks, Anglo-Saxons, and Arian Lombards also founded states within the ancient boundaries of the Empire. The Celts of Ireland, of Wales, and of Scotland acquired their Christianity directly from Roman soil and without invading the Empire. By the year 1000 the Magyars, Poles, and Germanic Scandinavians also had accepted the Christian faith. This acquisition of Christianity from the Romanized population of the Roman Empire in the West was of decisive importance in the life and thought of these peoples, for through the Church they were to receive not only the teachings of Christianity but also the more or less incidental things of civilization such as painting, sculpture, architecture, letters, and other aspects of culture as theology and monasticism.

These "barbarian" folk, then, possessing a variety of economic life, social organizations, political systems, and religious activities—much of them derived in part at least from the late Iron Age culture of their ancestors—were destined to help lay the socioeconomic foundations of later medieval civilization. Moving into Roman lands, they came in contact with the manorial system obtaining in the late Roman Empire, and in many areas became part of it, living as unfree men in economic subjection to lords (forerunners of the later feudal nobles). But manorial institutions were not exactly universal in western Europe. Much of this "barbarian" population never became serfs but retained their ancient tribal freedom as we see among the Celts, Scandinavians, and north Germans. Whether serfs or freemen, these people cultivated strips or plots of soil according to methods which changed little from generation to generation. Conformity to time-honored custom was the life of such folk. Little mental training was required of people living in such a social organization; custom regulated economic activities and social relationships. Serfs, free peasants, and nobles were illiterate. The secular clergy, recruited for the most part from the lower levels of this population, could barely read or write. Only with difficulty could they move through the Latin of the divine service. Princes and lords also were illiterate and felt little attraction to literature, philosophy, or science. Even so prominent a personage as Charlemagne, who was much interested in learning and supported scholars, could not write.

In a society thus constituted there was only limited need of schools and formal education. The age, however, had preserved a fraction of classical learning and methods of teaching. The seven subjects of the Liberal Arts—curriculum of studies for Greek and Roman youths designed to prepare them for public life—were indeed continued, but in an emaciated form. For example, rhetoric, which was of basic importance for the Roman boys because it taught eloquence in oratory, possessed less practical value in this manorial agricultural age and was accordingly simplified and adapted to other uses. The *trivium*—grammar, rhetoric, and logic—the three first subjects of the Liberal Arts, long bore the character of elementary and beginners' studies. The *quadrivium*—geometry, arithmetic, astronomy, and music—were also studied, but on the whole less thoroughly, excepting possibly music which was necessary in religious services. Knowledge of the Greek language had died out in western Europe. Of the vast bulk of Greek literature only the *Timaeus* of Plato and such parts as were imbedded in Latin letters were available. The Bible, writings of some of the Church Fathers, accounts of saints' lives, and some of the Latin classics, especially St. Augustine, provided the intellectual pabulum of the time. Its poverty must not, however, be exaggerated. The age produced some remarkable examples of learning, for instance, the Venerable Bede (d. 735), who may be considered as having mastered most of the learning available at that time and Alcuin (d. 804), famous teacher and scholar at the court of Charlemagne.

The schools of that time, clearly, were designed to meet the needs of the day. In monastic schools monks learned to read the breviary and to chant the Mass. Most episcopal centers offered some instruction to candidates for holy orders. Charlemagne and his successors realized the need of education and made it the subject of royal legislation. Especially noteworthy was his palace school. Designed chiefly for the nobles of the realm living at the court, this school was successful in tapping the best learning of the day. The palace school, however, came to an end when the Carolingian royal family could no longer maintain its leadership in the political life of the time. But the liberal arts nevertheless continued to be the accepted medium by which such scholarship as the age possessed was passed on to succeeding generations. Indeed, it has become the fashion to refer to the age of Charlemagne as the "Carolingian Renaissance."

Similarly, there was much intellectual activity in Germany during the tenth century while Otto I (936–973), Otto II (973–983), and Otto III (983–1002) guided the German Empire. Monastic and cathedral schools flourished, and there was some copying of ancient Roman artistic objects. All this was directly inspired by the example of the Carolingian Renaissance. Some scholars, struck by the creative energy of that age, have called it the Ottonian or Saxon Renaissance.

During the three centuries following the year 1000 Europe experienced an extraordinary intellectual as well as a social and economic revolution. Feudal monarchies became powerful, commerce and industry throve, population increased noticeably, towns became abundant, and the volume of coined money grew conspicuously. Some writers have declared these material changes to be the most remarkable in the entire history of mankind before the Industrial Revolution of the eighteenth and nineteenth centuries. Others have called this expanding culture the *Twelfth-Century Renaissance.*

Great changes now were made in the curricula of many a liberal arts school. The *trivium* and the *quadrivium* were expanded to include newly developed studies. Noted teachers, like Abelard (1079–1142) in the cathedral school at Paris, attracted flocks of students. Gradually teachers were grouped into faculties, each faculty representing a separate group of studies as liberal arts, medicine, law, and theology. The practical organization of the liberal arts faculty obviously was suggested by the crafts which were a normal feature of the bustling, expanding towns of the age. Students were apprentice teachers and the teachers were masters. Hence the degree of Master of Arts. In medicine, law, and theology the degree was that of doctor. These degrees conferred the right to teach (the *licentia docendi*).

Schools so organized and composed of several faculties were called *studia generalia*, a term which indicates the encyclopedic character of its instruction, an ideal which the ancient program of the liberal arts had cherished ever since the Roman Empire. Later the *studia generalia* were called universities, from the Latin *universitas*, meaning corporation, a word that might be applied to any organization as, for example, a town government, a guild, a cathedral chapter, or a synagogue. The first university of teaching and learning to be founded in medieval Europe was Salerno, during the twelfth century, really a medical school and not a *studium generale*. Four other universities came into existence during this period—Bologna, a law university; Montpellier, a school of law and medicine; Paris and Oxford, both of which more definitely were *studia generalia*. As time wore on the number of such institutions increased in all countries of Europe. This fact alone demonstrates the vigor of intellectual life in Europe during the closing centuries of the Middle Ages.

MEDIEVAL TRADITION OF PLATONIC THOUGHT AND LEARNING

Throughout the Middle Ages down into the Renaissance and the Reformation, the thought of Plato was a constant influence springing mainly from study of that philosopher's *Timaeus*. The greater part of medieval Platonic influence, however, is ultimately traceable to Plotinus (d. A.D. 270), one of the last pagan philosophers of the ancient world. He taught that the Infinite was "One" and the "Good" and that this unity transcends all rational nature. He rejected the idea that the Infinite was "Being" and that it was to be styled "intelligent," for intelligence implies a knower and something known. This duality Plotinus thought contradicted the idea that God was "One." This doctrine had important consequences, for, instead of being created, things come into existence through an "overflow" of the perfection of the "One" and are known through intuition or illumination.

St. Augustine (d. 430) was the fountainhead through which Platonic philosophic thought, Christianized by that great master, made its way into Europe. Because of his extensive influence, theology and philosophy took on a Platonic character. His *City of God*, written in accordance with this philosophy, is one of the world's great books. It deals with the social, political, and moral life of man and traces God's ruling and guiding hand in the march of human events. In the successive steps which mark the development of human society St. Augustine insists that there are two cities or societies, namely: an earthly city built by love of self, and the heavenly city created by the love of God. The two cities are mingled. Babylon is St. Augustine's apt designation of the earthly city; Jerusalem is the name of the other. Ultimately the citizens of Jerusalem will reign with God forever, and the subjects of Babylon will suffer the punishment with the Evil One. The course of humanity is nothing but a portrayal of the uninterrupted outpouring of God's grace upon man. This philosophy of history was to occupy the minds of men to the close of the Middle Ages and beyond.

One of the foremost propagators of Augustinian Platonism during the ninth century was John Scotus Erigena (d. 875?), an Irishman who spent most of his years on the continent of Europe in charge of the Carolingian palace school. Although a brilliant intellect, his philosophic teachings, especially pantheism, naturally proved unacceptable. Later, during the twelfth century, the school of Chartres taught philosophy and theology to its many students, imparting to them a Neoplatonic view of these subjects. At this time the schools were the scene of vigorous debates over the problem of universals. Men who held to Neoplatonic conceptions were called Realists. Neoplatonic thought was widely embraced by the friars of the Franciscan Order. Among the greatest of these was St. Bonaventure (d. 1274). Neoplatonic mysticism and teaching that all knowledge takes place by illumination fitted the spirituality of their order. The influence of Christian Neoplatonic thought during the closing years of the Middle Ages was almost universal.

ARISTOTELIAN REVIVAL: SCIENCE AND METAPHYSICS

The intellectual and scholarly antecedents of this new age are complex and difficult to explain adequately. In western Europe before the year 1000 there naturally was much practical interest in the Christian faith.

The development of a systematic theology, however, was yet to begin. Similarly the elaboration of philosophic thought had scarcely started, and the first steps in the advance of science and medicine had yet to be taken. Knowledge of Roman law was rare. But all this was to change among our medieval forebears when they first acquired some knowledge of the cultural achievements of the peoples of the Near East. Byzantium, living on its classical Greek heritage, had much to contribute to the intellectual world of the Jews and Arabs. These peoples added to the Greek heritage discoveries of their own, thus enriching science, philosophy, and technology. In addition, the Hindus contributed their system of arithmetical notation, a practical device destined to be universally received. Even the distant Chinese were to make their contributions in the art of making paper, the craft of block printing, and the harnessing and saddling of horses.

It seems surprising that while Platonic thought was well known in Christian Europe down to the twelfth century, Aristotelian philosophy which certainly had been studied as assiduously as was Plato's during the days of Greece and Rome almost completely died out. Only in the Moslem world—in Mesopotamia, Syria, Egypt, and Spain—did some of it survive as a living system. The Arab Averroës (1126–1198), of Córdoba, was specially instrumental in reviving the study of Aristotle in the Christian West during the thirteenth century. His great contribution to Aristotelian study consisted in producing a commentary on Aristotle's philosophy (with some elements of Plato's thought included). The impact of Averroës' speculations was profound and was long to be felt.

Gerard of Cremona (d. 1197) had a leading part in making available through translation many scientific and philosophical texts from Greek and Arabic into Latin. Among these were a number of the works of Aristotle and Ptolemy's *Almagest*, the translation of which was finished at Toledo in 1175. Much of this translation was defective, and it was not until the middle of the next century that better texts became available. William Van Moerbeke (d. about 1286), an active churchman who spent much time in Greece where he acquired mastery of the Greek tongue, presented scholars with better translations. It was of him that St. Thomas Aquinas in 1260 requested a translation of Aristotle's *Politics*, a book whose existence was unknown even to the Arabs.

Of the many scholars who busied themselves with the newly recovered philosophical ideas of Aristotle one of the first and most influential was the Englishman, Robert Grosseteste (d. 1253). Born in Suffolk, he studied in Paris where he received the degree of Master of Arts, entered the Franciscan order, became bishop of Lincoln, and was actively associated with studies at Oxford where as chancellor he exerted great influence. He appears to have translated Aristotle's *Ethics* directly from the Greek. He also produced a series of treatises on theology, philosophy, and the sciences. In the development of his ideas Grosseteste drew chiefly from St. Augustine, but also utilized some of Aristotle's ideas.

Of the scholars who thus busied themselves with the newly recovered philosophical principles of Aristotle the most influential was the Bavarian Dominican, Albertus Magnus (1193–1280). Since he spent his days in the order's houses of study, we may be sure that his theological and philosophical knowledge was as thorough and complete as was possible in that day. But his greatest interest was science, and to that end he mastered such ancient Greek scientific knowledge as had been preserved in the works of Aristotle and Ptolemy, and added much information from direct observation. He studied plants so successfully that he is regarded as the greatest botanist since the Greek Theophrastus (d. 287 b.c.). He speculated on the nature of sap, the relation of leaves, vines, buds, and flowers, and described many plants that grew in his native Bavaria but had not been noticed by students before him. He was interested in zoology and supplemented the writings of Aristotle on animals with his own observations. People of his day read bestiaries, inaccurate, fanciful descriptions of animals, intended to illustrate moral lessons. But Albertus Magnus was above such folklore. In addition, he critically studied astronomy, meteorology, climatology, physics, mechanics, chemistry, mineralogy, and anthropology. Being something of an experimenter, he knew how to make gunpowder. "The aim of the natural sciences," he declared, "is not merely to accept statements by others, but to investigate the causes at work in nature."

Although Albertus Magnus shines forth as a genius of encyclopedic learning, the great intellectual triumph of the age was the formulation of a system of philosophic thought known as Thomistic Scholasticism. Though all thinkers were interested in such elements of Platonic speculation as had survived the neglect of philosophy and learning during the first centuries, the decisive factor in building scholastic philosophy was the recovery of the long lost texts of Aristotle. A peculiar feature of this system of thought was its universality, for it became as universal as Christianity, its main tenets being accepted in all the lands of western Europe. It occupied much the same relation toward religion as did Gothic art. It was the intellectual complement of Catholicism. Another feature of Scholasticism was its perfected structure which offered a place for all things human as well as divine.

This system of thought, which spoke with unique authority to every questioning mind of the age, was perfected and completed by Thomas Aquinas (1225–1274). He was born into a Neapolitan family of counts and was educated in the famous Benedictine abbey of Monte Cassino near his parental home. Later he studied in the newly founded University of Naples where the works of Aristotle were eagerly read and discussed. In 1244 he entered the Dominican order and was sent to Paris, the capital of scholastic studies, where he listened to the lectures of Albertus Magnus. After studying in the University of Cologne, whither Albertus had been sent by his superiors, he returned to the schools of Paris in 1252 and began lecturing on theological subjects. From this time until his death 22 years later he wrote a large number of books, a veritable philosophical and theological library, a most impressive monument of medieval thought and learning.

The significance of Thomas' scholarly work, set forth in his *Summa Theologica* and the *Summa contra Gentiles*, consisted in the synthesis which he made of the revived philosophical doctrines of Aristotle and the theological convictions of the Middle Ages. At the base of his system lay the Aristotelian classification of knowledge. Here the different sciences dealing with man's environment found their appropriate place. These branches of learning expanded the work of Aristotle and, after some observation of nature and rudimentary experimentation, subjected them to Aristotle's philosophical conceptions. At the summit of this vast pyramid of learning appeared the doctrines taught by the divinely instituted Church and entrusted to her. Thus the entire realm of human learning, sacred or profane, was brought together into one harmonious system. Christian principles animated thought on all human activities, economic, artistic, and political. This philosophic and theological system which enjoyed unquestioned ascendancy during the Middle Ages continued to exert the greatest influence throughout the Renaissance and the Reformation. Such is its virility that even in recent years it has received the intellectual assent of many.

Thomas' Aristotelian intellectualism, as illustrated in his psychology and his metaphysics, inaugurated a revolution in all branches of philosophy and challenged the opinions of scholars who had gone before him. Ever since the days of St. Augustine (d. 430) philosophers and theologians, as we have noted, had adopted the idea that the divine order could be known best through special divine illumination. Thomas, however, held that all knowledge of that order was made known through man's intellectual faculties.

Bonaventure (1221–1274), however, was the most noteworthy of all who followed Augustinian ideas, minimizing the importance of the natural order and exalting the supernatural. Aristotelian intellectualism he rated inferior to Platonic wisdom, in which as a Franciscan friar he had been brought up. As a mystical theologian his fame was unsurpassed. Duns Scotus (d. 1308), a Scottish Franciscan, followed in the footsteps of Bonaventure but borrowed from Thomas whose ideas, however, he viewed critically. While remaining faithful to his Augustinian views, Scotus was greatly influenced by the scientific ideas taught in Oxford— ideas he interpreted in a positivist and voluntarist manner. Thomas taught that the omnipotence of God and the immortality of the human soul were demonstrable by reason, which Scotus denied. The new Scotist school developed a chasm between the divine order and the human order when it taught that the former could not be known by the processes of the mind and that any knowledge of it rested solely on revelation.

Following Albertus Magnus, Thomas Aquinas, Robert Grosseteste, and Roger Bacon, came William of Ockham (d. 1349?), a Franciscan friar who followed his master Scotus. Born in Surrey, England, and trained at Oxford, he too fell under the influence of the scientific spirit which flourished in the English university. In his attacks upon the traditional Thomistic philosophy he developed extraordinary subtility. His scepticism led him to deny the existence of types outside the mind. Thus, he would argue that *horses* indeed did exist, but the general concept *horse* possessed no objective validity. In psychology he argued against the existence of the possible intellect, that part in the ideogenetic train which expresses abstract ideas. He therefore was something of a nominalist and was opposed to Thomas who was a moderate realist. Ockham also denied the power of the mind to penetrate into the secrets of God. Thus he claimed that philosophy and theology were so distinct that the first could not serve as handmaid to the second. Theology was the science of God's authoritative revelation and could not be accounted for by human reason. Two schools of theological thought sprang up: the Realists who followed the old way, or *via antiqua,* as taught by St. Thomas, and the Nominalists who adopted the new way, or *via moderna,* as it was developed by William of Ockham. The dissensions of these groups divided the schools of the closing Middle Ages.

The philosophy of Averroës (not to be classified as "scholastic"), long troubled the schools of Europe, for its materialism threatened the foundations of traditional Christian thought. Averroës taught that the power whereby the potentially intelligible became the actually intelligible, moving through the "agent intellect" and the "possible intellect," acted physically separate from the human body and independently of it and is *one* in all men. This is what is meant by the "unity of the intellect." This "universal intellect" only is immortal. Individual immortality is an illusion. The individual therefore possessed no freedom of will, something Christian thinkers opposed, for this doctrine destroyed the basis of Christian ethics and also Christian teaching of the immortality of the soul. Confronted by Christian philosophers like Albertus Magnus and Thomas Aquinas, the Averroists argued that what was true in philosophy might be false in theology and vice versa. They thought that religion was good enough for the many, but philosophy was something loftier to be cultivated by the intellectually elite. Averroism remained influential down into the Renaissance, especially in Italy.

SOME SCHOLASTIC TEACHINGS

In view of the fact that scholastic teaching as presented by Albertus Magnus, Thomas Aquinas, and other philosophers of their day was widely disseminated and most influential during the Renaissance and the Reformation, let us note a few of the characteristic teachings of these men. Following Aristotle, Thomas erected an imposing logical structure upon an elaborate analysis of "being." Seeing that the mind is confronted by a multitude of existing things and noting that they are in change (movement), Thomas taught that they are in "potency" toward the full realization of their "being," their "act." So an acorn is an oak in potency. The scholastic philosophers also took over Aristotle's teaching regarding "form" out of which by formal cause beings are produced. "Form" and "matter" are related to each other as "act" and "potency." "Matter" limits and individuates; "form" specifies and completes. Thomas, like Aristotle, held that "being" is a compound of "substance" and "accidents." A "substance" is a being that needs only itself to exist in; an "accident" can exist only in a substance. Shape and size exist in John as in a subject; but John himself is an ultimate thing which does not again exist in anything else.

Psychology was an important branch in scholastic study, for its theories of knowing involved every system of philosophic thought. Its purpose was metaphysical—the better understanding of "the whole man." Psychological theory as held by Albertus Magnus and Thomas Aquinas ultimately derived from the scientific labors of Plato and particularly from the thought of Aristotle. The central problem was to explain how the "potentially intelligible" is rendered "actually intelligible."

According to Thomas ideas are not innate. Rather, they are the product of the human mind reacting to stimuli. Hence to bring about a union between the intellect and the thing, the following ideogenetic data were conceived to explain the subtly complex phenomena of human thought. An object stimulates the mind through the five external senses—sight, hearing, taste, smell, and touch. These stimuli impinging upon the mind are a complex stream of many impressions and form a kind of a rudimentary image. These stimuli are unified by the "synthetic," "common," or "central" sense, the first of the "interior" senses whose function it is to perceive and distinguish the sense data presented, combining them and referring them to their proper objects. A completed, or formal cognitive phantasm, results. This phantasm next comes under the action of the second interior sense—the imagination.

The reproductive imagination pictures things as copies of original experiences, which elaborate phantasms of things. Next, the memory, the third interior sense, preserves the phantasm and recalls it. And, finally, there is the fourth interior sense, instinct, by means of which man perceives the useful or harmful nature of particular things not merely in sensory fashion but also by means of collating ideas. So far, the phantasm still is a sensory thing but through the action of the "agent intellect" its substantial being, or nature, is "abstracted" and the "idea" is expressed. This immaterial idea brought forth by the possible intellect corresponds to the original object, the stimuli which we have traced through this ideogenetic track. The reader will of course note that these are but two parts of scholastic teaching, the others being passed by because of their lengthy and involved character.

MEDIEVAL EMPHASIS ON EXPERIMENTATION

Scholars during the early days of the great medieval scientific revival realized the necessity of systematic observation, experimentation, and rational interpretation. They had some appreciation of the need of tools and mechanical devices, but such means of scientific investigation were either totally absent, or so elementary as to prevent rapid progress. Nevertheless the advances in science during the fourteenth century were truly remarkable. This is well shown by Roger Bacon's enthusiastic appreciation of his teacher, Peter of Miracourt (fl. 1269), at the Parisian *Studium Generale:*

> One man I know, and one only, who can be praised for his achievements in this science. Of discourses and battles of words he takes no heed: he follows the works of wisdom, and in these finds rest. What others strive to see dimly and blindly, like bats in twilight, he gazes at in the full light of day, because he is a master of experiment.
>
> Through experiment he gains knowledge of natural things, medical, chem-

ical, indeed of everything in the heavens or earth. He is ashamed that any things should be known to laymen, old women, soldiers, ploughmen, of which he is ignorant.

Therefore he has looked closely into the doings of those who work in metals and minerals of all kinds; he knows everything relating to the art of war, the making of weapons, and the chase; he has looked closely into agriculture, mensuration, and farming work; he has even taken note of the remedies, lot-casting, and charms used by old women and by wizards and magicians, and of the deceptions and devices of conjurers, so that nothing which deserves inquiry should escape him, and that he may be able to expose the falsehoods of magicians.

If philosophy is to be carried to its perfection and is to be handled with utility and certainty, his aid is indispensable. As for reward, he neither receives nor seeks it. If he frequented kings and princes, he would easily find those who would bestow on him honors and wealth. Or, if in Paris he would display the results of his researches, the whole world would follow him. But since either of these courses would hinder him from pursuing the great experiments in which he delights, he puts honour and wealth aside, knowing well that his wisdom would secure him wealth whenever he chose.

For the last three years he has been working at the production of a mirror that shall produce combustion at a fixed distance; a problem which the Latins have neither solved nor attempted, though books have been written upon the subject.[1]

Such was the famed teacher to whom Roger Bacon (d. 1294) was obligated for much of his ideas and methodological skill. Bacon was a Franciscan friar who seems to have spent many of his mature years at Oxford. Under the tuition of such masters as Peter of Miracourt, Bacon was inspired not only to master the science of the day but also to add to it. He studied plants and animals, refraction, astronomy, the rainbow, mechanics, navigation, and the calendar. His views of nature were marked by a positivist spirit. At the same time, however, he imbibed some of the Augustinian spirit which dominated Bonaventure and Grosseteste.

PRACTICAL NOTE IN EDUCATION

Our medieval forebears were a most practical folk. The swelling volume of trade and manufacture and consequent rise of towns, development of commerce and new inventions, and the creation of centralized and efficient monarchies provided the socioeconomic milieu for practical studies, not only in elementary schools, the number of which increased rapidly during the fifteenth century, but also in the new universities.

[1] J. H. Bridges, *The Life and Work of Roger Bacon*, London, 1914, pp. 21–22.

To keep the vocational spirit out of the universities proved impossible. So manifold were the needs of the business world for men trained to write letters that a practical rhetoric shorn of linguistic and literary study came into existence. It was known as the *Ars Dictaminis* and first grew up in northern Italy which in the twelfth century was leading Europe in commercial and industrial development. This "business rhetoric" was successfully taught by one Boncompagni (d. 1240?) in the University of Bologna. He published a practical manual which became popular. This new rhetoric spread to other universities. The niceties of Latin writings and the curious details of Latin classics were scorned by students who demanded instruction in practical things. This vogue of the "business rhetoric" explains, in part at least, why the study of Latin literature and language declined in the universities of the late Middle Ages. It also gives a partial explanation why so much of the medieval Latin writing is devoid of literary grace. Genuine appreciation of the beauties of ancient Latin classics was rare among university professors in the fourteenth century. Later, enthusiasm for the classics was to be kindled outside the schools by humanists, the most noteworthy example being set, as we shall learn, by humanists such as Francesco Petrarch.

Such practical and vocational interests also obtained in the universities north of the Alps. An instructive example was one Thomas Sampson who as teacher was active at Oxford during the middle decades of the fourteenth century, giving lessons in what, for lack of a better term, we may call practical training for a business career. For his students he wrote short manuals on practical letter writing, especially in French and Latin, on the notary's craft, on heraldry, conveyancing, drawing up of wills, how to keep household and business accounts, and how to hold court.

The vocational spirit likewise invaded other studies. Churchmen found that a knowledge of canon and civil law was a surer guarantee of advancement in the Church than was theology. Positions in the Church were bestowed upon administrators and not so much upon learned theologians. The great religious people of the day rarely sat in high places. Why should one toil long years to acquire a doctorate in theology when a knowledge of civil and canon law might lead to the episcopal dignity or perchance even to a cardinalate?

A new body of law was needed to fit the demand of town and commercial life, and accordingly the ancient Roman civil law was revived. Study of the civil law, inaugurated in the University of Bologna, was subsequently introduced into other schools. Mastery of this law proved a sure road to a profitable career, and fathers solicitous for their sons' welfare introduced them to its study. This was the case with Petrarch,

Luther, and Calvin. As monarchical government became more effective and administrative agencies increased and broadened the scope of their activities, it was necessary to recruit officials from a class which possessed legal training. Rulers sought the services of men skilled in Roman law. These were drawn from the townsmen and were more loyal servants of the crown and more efficient administrators than the sons of the nobility. For this reason many a youth hurried to school to prepare himself for a splendid career. He impatiently studied the elementary liberal arts, and plunged into the precepts of Roman law.

LATE MEDIEVAL REVOLUTION IN PHYSICS AND CELESTIAL MECHANICS

The death of William of Ockham marked the close of an era in the intellectual history of the Middle Ages. Many of the works of Aristotle had been recovered and made available in adequate translations. These books stirred the metaphysical interest of Christian Europe, quickened the scientific temper of the age. Although a metaphysician, Albertus Magnus won fame as student of nature. Thomas Aquinas, a greater philosopher than Albertus, had a lively interest in scientific matters. This is shown in his *Summa Theologica* in which he discusses the rotundity of the earth and the problem of causality, showing that there are five kinds of causes each of which demonstrates the existence of God (*Summa Theologica*, Question 1, Art. 1). And Roger Bacon, besides his studies in philosophy and theology, exhibited a strong penchant for the study of mechanics, medicine, and the sciences in general, all in a pronounced scientific manner, prophetic of future development.

The new age which followed—from about 1300–1500—witnessed remarkable growth in scientific matters. Scholars, particularly theologians, busied themselves with basic phenomena of physics, including optics, statics, astronomy, and motion. Most fruitful was their idea that these things should be studied by rational methods—by means of mathematics, systematic observation, and the use of instruments specially adapted to the study of natural phenomena. So, for example, Theodoric of Freiburg (d. 1311), won fame from his study of optics and the formulation of the laws of refraction in connection with his study of the rainbow. Soon physics, including optics, statics, astronomy, and the study of motion, was dominated by mathematics. More accurate instruments of measuring appeared, such as the quadrant and the astrolobe. Among the great scientific names of the new age, to name only a few, was Nicholas d'Oresme (d. 1382), bishop of Lisieux, who studied mathematics, physics, and astronomy, was critical of Aristotelian physics and suggested that the earth was not stationary, but was in motion, an idea later accepted by Nicolas Copernicus (1473–1543). Later, Peter d'Ailly (d. 1420) produced his *Ymago Mundi* (1410), a study of the earth, which soon was to be perused by Christopher Columbus.

New and significant discoveries in celestial mechanics were made as the age drew toward its close in the 1500's. The early Middle Ages had inherited its ideas about astronomy from Aristotle, who taught that the universe was composed of a series of homocentric spheres. At the center was the earth, an immobile mass, surrounded by a region of air beyond which lay another of fire. Next were seven spheres in each of which one of the seven planets revolved around the earth. The Moon was nearest the earth, and next in order were Mercury, Venus, Sun, Mars, Jupiter, and Saturn. Beyond was the eighth sphere, that of the fixed stars which composed the zodiac. Next lay the ninth or crystalline sphere, also known as the *Primum Mobile,* and thought to be the abode of the Infinite. Above it was the empyrean or paradise. Each of the planets was set in motion by the *Primum Mobile* and revolved about the earth in solemn grandeur.

This simple system failed to satisfy observers. It was noticed that the planets seemed not to revolve in their spheres in a steady homocentric course, but appeared to wander from their course and to return later. Critics of Aristotle's theories increased rapidly about 1277, and soon the ideas of Ptolemy, author of the *Almagest* and philosopher of the second century, became accepted by the scholars of Paris. The course of the planets in their spheres was explained by a system of epicycles and eccentric spheres. John of Béthune (d. 1358?) disproved Aristotle's doctrine and taught that motion was not due to the air which surrounded the moving object but to an *impetus* imparted directly to the object. Albert of Saxony (d. 1390) and Nicholas d'Oresme continued these studies in Paris, but after the latter's death creative ability in that university appears to have subsided. Interest in mathematics and the problems of celestial mechanics, however, persisted in German universities. George Peurbach (d. 1461), for example, produced a new and better text of Ptolemy's *Almagest.* Johannes Müller (Regiomontanus), who died in 1476, helped him in accomplishing this significant task. Nicholas of Cusa (d. 1464), a figure prominent in the ecclesiastical and scientific life of the fifteenth century, continued this critical treatment of scientific data derived from classical Greek and Roman times. Clearly, this age was a noteworthy one in the study of science. Soon men were to hear of Copernicus' discoveries. Next came the revolutionary doctrines in celestial mechanics by Galileo Galilei (d. 1542), Tycho Brahe (d. 1601), and Johann Kepler (d. 1630).

LATE MEDIEVAL MEDICAL SKILL

From earliest times man had reflected on his numerous maladies and sought cures for them. Great figures in the history of medical practice like the Greek Hippocrates and Galen had consolidated medical knowledge and practice. Systematic medical study was resumed in the eleventh century and, following this example, instruction was begun at Montpellier, Bologna, Padua, and Paris. Medical scholars borrowed extensively from nearby Arab lands. The ancient Greek had relied chiefly on drugs, and now practitioners prescribed such new mineral drugs as camphor, naptha, borax, arsenic, sulphur, and mercury. They also introduced the *spongia soporifica* which, for want of a better means, was to serve as an anesthetic. Surgery also throve; operations for hernia and the stone were common. Eye glasses were invented, and in dentistry teeth were extracted, filled, and the disease of caries was treated. Wounds were cauterized. All considered, the science and theory of medicine progressed in medieval times and by 1400 had probably equaled that of the Greeks, Romans, and Arabs.

Diagnosis was surprisingly effective in such diseases as the bubonic plague, diphtheria, leprosy, tuberculosis, rabies, diabetes, gout, cancer, and epilepsy. Hospitals were plentiful and surprisingly well equipped, even from our modern standpoint. Such hospitals as the Hotel Dieu in Paris, the one at Beaune in France, and St. Bartholomew's in London reveal the influence of Christian charity.

A curious feature of medieval medical practice was the influence of astrology and alchemy. Astrology, which teaches that the stars influence terrestrial affairs, is of ancient origin, either Chaldean or Egyptian. It was appropriated by the Greeks and Romans and became part of the speculations of Jews and Arabs in the Middle Ages. The Christian Church was opposed to astrological science because it seemed to contradict the principle of free will; nevertheless, astrology had devotees among Christians. During the closing Middle Ages, especially in the fourteenth century, it appears to have been accepted almost universally. The theory that stars exerted much power for good or ill was given a scientific basis by the Ptolemaic system of the universe then in vogue. The planets in their course around the immobile earth were moved by the elements which surrounded them. Obviously all earthly things came under the sovereignty of stars.

These influences were further complicated by the planet which happened to appear at the moment when any zodiacal sign was in the ascendant. The influence was not fixed, but varied according to the sign with which it happened to be associated. A complicated science was evolved in the effort to explain everything in human life from this point of view. Wars, famines, pestilences, revolutions, and deaths of monarchs could be predicted. This is the reason why medieval chroniclers never failed to note meteors and eclipses in connection with catastrophes. Traits of human beings were influenced, it was believed, in the arrangement of stars at the moment of birth. Casting horoscopes became a profitable business. Princes often consulted the stars before undertaking any important matter of state. So popular was this science that students who had graduated from the universities made a professional practice of contemplating the stars.

It became important to ascertain which stars were in the ascendant at the moment of birth. This was called *judicial astrology* and was closely akin to divination. A horoscope was drawn up consisting of a diagram of the heavens showing the position of the stars at the date of birth. The sky was divided into twelve sections called *houses,* each containing some fixed stars. These constituted the zodiac. Each house was designated by the name of some animal, except one which was called the *scales.* Each of these had a fancied influence upon human actions at the moment when it was in the ascendant. Thus the Ram exerted control over the head, the Bull over the neck, the Twins over the shoulders and arms, Cancer over the breast, Leo over the sides of the body, Virgo over the bladder, the Balance over the buttocks, the Scorpion over the genitals, Sagittarius over the thighs, Capricorn over the knees, Aquarius over the legs, and Pisces over the feet.

Like astrology, alchemy flourished mightily throughout medieval times and during the Reformation. Alchemy, like astrology, sprang from Babylonian, Egyptian, and Greek origins. It corresponded to our chemistry, but as it was based upon erroneous theories and a scanty knowledge of facts, it was little better than astrology. Its basic conception was that the foundation of our material life was provided by a *primal matter.* This was always associated with some form in varying degree, thus producing the different elements with which we are familiar—air, earth, fire, and water. Human imagination, led by its innate inquisitiveness, asked why, if the material world was so constituted, one could not create some primal matter and then add to it the things necessary to make gold; this became the chief aim of alchemists. It was thought that this primal matter had to be treated with some substance called the philosopher's elixir or stone which consisted in the first principle of sulphur. When applied to primal matter, gold would result. Only in modern times under the influence of chemistry have these scientific fantasies been dispelled, but in our own day quacks still seek to exploit them.

Chapter 11

THE ACME OF GOTHIC ART

$\mathcal{T}$HE TREMENDOUS changes effected in the intellectual, social, economic, and political life of Europe from the eleventh century onward also occasioned numerous changes in the moral and religious thought of the time. The activities of an expanding society demanded new structures of all kinds. Castles had to be erected, town walls and town gates were needed, new streets had to be laid out. The crusades helped broaden the basis of economic activity and enriched the philosophic and scientific thought of European scholars. Because of their closer contact with Byzantium and Arab lands they acquired the thought of Aristotle and Plato, Jews and Arabs, and so laid the bases of a new material and intellectual life. These influences brought many changes to western Europe. In architecture they contributed to the development of Romanesque and Gothic art.

SALIENT FEATURES OF ROMANESQUE AND GOTHIC BUILDING

The Middle Ages attained lofty expression in the arts, especially in architecture. The medieval building tradition is to be traced back to the political wreck of the Roman Empire. That was the period in which were built stately Roman basilicas such as Santa Maria Maggiore, St. John Lateran, and St. Peter in Chains. Later, during the eleventh century, evolved the Romanesque style inspired by Roman basilicas. The classic cathedral, baptistry, and leaning tower of Pisa, dating from about the First Crusade (1096–1099), reveal how vital the ancient tradition still was.

It can cause no surprise that a great Romanesque style in architecture should evolve during the eleventh century in the early upswing of trade, industry, and town life. This is shown by the many extant Romanesque (in England called Norman) structures as, for example, the Tower of

London and stately churches at Canterbury, Norwich, Shrewsbury, and Durham. Besides these imposing structures parishes erected smaller churches, also in the Romanesque manner. The heavy stone walls of these churches, their barrel vaulting, and their small windows, clearly echo the rough fighting life of feudal Europe of the tenth and eleventh centuries. A striking example of a church with its west front like a castle is St. Servatius' in Maastricht in the Netherlands.

The great era of building in the Romanesque style produced another and even greater type of construction—the Gothic. Its origins are difficult to trace, and it is not possible to set an exact date for its appearance. But elements of Gothic were employed in France during the last half of the twelfth century. By about 1200 they were spreading to all parts of western Europe. To define Gothic art in a few words is impossible. Usually it is stated that the basic device in Gothic architecture was the pointed arch on which the stone ribs of the vaulting rested. The weight of the stone ceiling was distributed to the heads of the columns and not to the lateral walls as in Romanesque buildings. Flying buttresses sometimes were added to neutralize the lateral thrust of the ribs in the vaulting. It was no longer necessary to erect massive walls as in the Romanesque manner. Gothic artists inserted windows, usually filling the space between lateral columns with stained glass, thereby flooding the interior with light.

SYMBOLS AND CEREMONIES INSTRUCTED
MEDIEVAL MAN

Back in the so-called Dark Ages the basic economy was agriculture and the raising of cattle. The making of cloth and other necessaries was limited to household production. Government remained elementary, being associated with the rulers' domestic property as, for example, in the case of Charlemagne. In a society thus constituted the family was most important, for to it was entrusted the teaching of religious concepts and moral obligations. And the Church stood by, ever ready to instruct the people.

Practically all men at that time, excepting the clergy, were unable to read or write. Nevertheless, they cannot be said to have been ignorant of the guiding ideas of the day. The Church, in a manner all could understand, presented traditional Christian teaching in her liturgy. All men learned about the seven Sacraments and their efficacy. In vivid stories the Church told of Christ's life from the Annunciation and Nativity to the Last Supper, Crucifixion, and Ascension. And the Church also pointed to a great company of saints, the greatest of whom was the Virgin Mary, heading the list of men and women who, like St. Stephen and St. Catherine of Alexandria, had lived for the faith.

Rulers, when they appeared officially before their public, made use of symbols and ceremonies. The emperor, for example, appeared crowned, seated on a throne, bearing a sword or scepter in his right hand and a round object surmounted by a cross signifying his Christian rule over this earth. Kings also appeared with such symbols; dukes and counts on public occasions also bore sword and globe with cross. The clergy also made use of symbols. The pope, for example, appeared wearing a triple crown. Bishops carried croziers (which signified their function as shepherds of their Christian flocks) and wore rings which signified their union with their Church. Every priest wore a stole, a bit of vestment which signified his authority as a priest.

Gothic art employed many symbols and conventions. Since the earliest days of the Church Christians had elaborated a symbolical art. In the catacombs where they buried their dead one can still trace the early evolution of this art. For example, Christ was commonly represented as a good shepherd bearing a sheep on His shoulders; the Nativity was pictured by an infant in a manger with St. Mary and St. Joseph adoring Him. The Trinity was represented by the Father with a patriarchal beard, the Son, and the Holy Spirit in the form of a dove. The four disciples, writers of the Gospels, are represented by four symbolic creatures: St. Matthew by an angel, St. Mark by a lion, St. Luke by an ox, and St. John the Evangelist by an eagle. The synagogue, false church of the Jews, was represented by a young woman blindfolded, leaning upon a broken spear. These devices became traditional and rarely varied.

The saints also had their symbols. St. Peter bore two keys; St. Andrew, a cross; St. John the Baptist, clothed in camel's hair, a lamb; St. James carried a pilgrim's staff; St. Mary Magdalene wore long hair and carried a jar of ointment. St. Veronica held the sacred kerchief; St. Lucy, a pair of eyes on a salver; St. Barbara, a tower; St. Appolonia, a tooth in a forceps; St. Christopher the Christ Child on his shoulders. St. Catherine is shown with a wheel or a sword; St. Lawrence with gridirons; and St. Anthony with a bell and accompanied by a pig. St. Denis appeared with head struck off and held in his hands. St. Sebastian was portrayed pierced with arrows. St. Mary was often shown holding the infant Jesus in her lap. Sometimes she appeared with St. Anne. St. Joseph was always an old man standing near Mary. St. Agatha was shown undergoing mutilation of her breasts. St. Erasmus, who suffered martyrdom by having his vitals drawn from his body, was shown carrying them over his arm or with a windlass winding them on a reel. St. Stephen, protomartyr, carried rocks on his head, which indicated that he died by being stoned. These conventions also dominated the art of the Renaissance and are repeated endlessly. Some of them are employed even in our own day.

RELIGIOUS INSPIRATION OF GOTHIC ART

The artistic forms which man has given to buildings, furniture, clothing, jewelry, and other objects have always been closely related to his economic, social, political, moral, and intellectual development. The religious life of the Middle Ages created abbeys, cathedrals, baptisteries, hospitals, and parish churches. Feudal society produced castles, manorial halls, and granges. Towns erected walls, gates, belfries, and halls for officials and guildsmen. Each class in medieval society developed its costume: the fighting nobility carried expensive armor; peasants and townsmen wore working clothes; and priests had a habit of their own. Furniture possesses similar interest. The Church had her altars, chairs, choir stalls, reredoses, reliquaries, and all sorts of special objects needed in her services. Noblemen and townsmen combined use and varying degrees of utility and artistic excellence in chairs, tables, chests, dressers, and bedsteads. The humble peasants possessed few things, barely sufficient to prepare their food and satisfy their simplest needs.

Of the arts, architecture, literature, painting, sculpture, and music best reveal the spirit of an age. People are always eager to beautify practical objects. To do this they must use their imagination, and what they create is in the truest sense part of their lives. Pictures, sculpture, and decoration disclose in innumerable ways what they think of themselves, the world, and their destiny. These arts therefore cannot be understood without a knowledge of the religious and intellectual life of the age.

Universal in northern Europe after the twelfth century, Gothic art revealed remarkable diversity. Every community exhibited something distinctive in its buildings so that the study of Gothic architecture reveals a bewildering variety of forms. In general, however, its chief characteristics were the use of the pointed arch in windows, doorways, and the vaulting. It achieved classical perfection during the twelfth and thirteenth centuries, especially in the cathedrals of France, England, and Germany. Its early excellence is explained in part by the great increase in population due to the revival of trade, industry, and town life. New and larger churches were constantly demanded. It was possible to pay for them because of the striking increase of wealth which attended the growth of towns.

Some of the great parish churches such as St. Gudule in Brussels and

St. John (the present St. Bavo) in Ghent rivaled the sumptuous churches of many bishoprics. Sculpture followed hard upon architecture, and some of its best examples were created during the thirteenth century. We need only recall the figure of Christ and that of the Virgin with the Christ Child on the cathedral of Amiens, the statues in the south porch of the transept of the cathedral of Chartres, and the many carved forms on the portals and other parts of the cathedral of Rheims. Sculptors carefully studied their models and succeeded in combining tender maternal solicitude with exactitude in anatomy. They copied the fruits and plants of the countryside and decorated capitals of columns and other parts of buildings with them. Spaces on the walls of churches, chapels, and town halls were decorated with pictures illustrating the Christian faith. Painters also illuminated religious books with scenes from the life of Christ, the apostles, or the saints, and employed decorative motifs taken from natural or everyday life. Similarly artists beautified windows by using colored glass. Splendid designs were made in harmonious hues which even today delight visitors of such cathedrals as Chartres.

The themes of this Christian art illustrated the dramatic incidents of the story of man's fall and redemption. From the Old Testament were drawn such subjects as the creation of Adam and Eve, the fall of man, the expulsion from Paradise, the flood, the building of the Tower of Babel, scenes from the life of Moses, and others. Far more numerous were the episodes drawn from the earthly career of the Saviour. One finds countless examples of the Nativity, the Magi, adoration of the shepherds, slaughter of the innocents, presentation in the temple, flight into Egypt, teaching in the temple, and baptism. Certain scenes from Christ's suffering were particularly popular—the kiss of Judas, the appearance before Caiaphas, the denuding, the scourging, the division of His garments, the carrying of the cross, the nailing of the Saviour to it, the crucifixion, the descent from the cross, the entombment, the resurrection, and the ascension. There also were pictures illustrating the Trinity. Finally, the catastrophic events of the last days found expression in a large number of pictures of the last judgment and the rejection of the damned.

Besides these central themes there were many others. The Church derived her teaching not only from Scripture but also from ancient tradition. The Virgin Mary was popular, especially at the height of the Middle Ages. Her cult appealed with particular power to the imagination of the people of the fourteenth and fifteenth centuries. The scenes of her activities became popular themes in art. Artists often depicted her birth, assumption, coronation, purification, immaculate conception, and the annunciation. The *pietà*, especially interesting, is a picture or a statue showing the Virgin seated, holding the dead body of the Lord in her lap while she grieves in silent resignation over the cruel death of her Son. Her seven joys and seven sorrows also became popular subjects. The Church boasted a large number of saints, holy men and women who had sealed their faith with martyrdom or who had lived lives of eminently Christian virtue. Chief among these were the apostles who had spread the Gospel. Next came a large company of men and women who had labored for the faith. Episodes from their lives, especially their martyrdom, became popular themes for pictures.

GOTHIC COMPETITION WITH RENAISSANCE SKILL

Gothic painting did not reach its highest point of excellence until the fifteenth century. Artists in the Gothic tradition sought to create the illusion of concrete things on a flat surface. Mastery of form and realistic action required accurate knowledge of anatomy. And, besides perspective and anatomy, psychological unity was required. The ancients had been successful in developing these features in the art of painting. But classical painting had disappeared in western Europe during the demise of the Roman Empire.

The artistic spirit of ancient Rome, however, lived on during the Middle Ages when artists at Constantinople created excellent miniatures and mural forms. There was demand for devotional pictures called icons. Under Byzantine influence a miniaturist art developed in Romanesque times and flourished during the Gothic period which followed. In open spaces of capital letters, in margins, and in paragraph headings in manuscripts all sorts of scenes were painted with much realism. This new art form was to exert much influence, especially in northern Europe, in the formation of easel painting out of which came the work of Hubert and John Van Eyck (d. 1441), both painters in the Gothic tradition in Flanders.

To understand the evolution of pictorial art in southern Europe, especially in Italy, one should first study how pictures were produced. The methods employed in the Byzantine East were followed. A panel of wood was smoothed and sized with sticky gum on which was applied a layer of gold leaf. Colors mixed with the white of eggs were applied according to a previously prepared cartoon. This was called *tempera* painting. It produced pure and pleasing colors of a jewel-like beauty.

Another characteristic feature of the painting of that time was the use of models. In Romanesque days artists seem to have made little or no use of them. But Gothic ideals demanded that artists study objects with an exacting fidelity to truth. Human figures and other objects were to be noted with meticulous exactitude. From the early days of the miniaturists in the thirteenth century down to the close of the Middle Ages Gothic artists made effective use of models. This does not signify, however, that they studied anatomy, perspective, and expression scientifically. A painting, *St. Luke Painting the Portrait of the Virgin,* by the Fleming John Gossaert (d. 1535) may be taken to illustrate how models at that time were used in painting. The Virgin is shown seated in the lap of her mother. St. Luke is seated nearby drawing the Virgin's profile. Following such methods Gothic masters, especially the Flemings, succeeded in rendering figures with great fidelity. John Van Eyck, for example, produced excellent portraits of himself and his wife. Especially successful was his *Man with a Pink,* a portrait unexcelled by such Italian Renaissance contemporaries as Piero della Francesca (1416–1492).

Fresco painting was especially common in southern Europe. It did not flourish so profusely in the north because the walls of Gothic churches were pierced by many windows. The Romanesque basilicas of the south possessed few windows, and artists thus had a chance to produce great pictures on the walls of these buildings. This art presented peculiar difficulties. Water colors were applied to the wet plaster and penetrated it so that the picture became part of the plaster. This method necessitated rapid execution because color could not be applied when the plaster was dry. It demanded exact work because any mistake necessitated scraping the plaster. The fresco artist therefore was required to have his cartoons ready when the plaster was applied. He emphasized detail less than bold, quickly executed composition, a fact which had an important bearing upon the development of Italian painting. The artist of the north, on the other hand, began as a miniaturist and never wholly abandoned his habit of studying details and depicting them with meticulous regard for detail.

ART AND SPIRITUAL EXERCISE

The chief function of Gothic art was to instill a spirit of piety, to stimulate spirituality. This is well shown by the following quotation from the *Vision of God* by Nicholas of Cusa (1401–1488), a remarkable theologian and philosopher of the time. It shows how finite believers may conceive the Infinite:

> If I strive in human fashion to transport you to things divine, I must needs use a comparison of some kind. Now among men's works I have found no image better suited to our purpose than that of an image which is omnivoyant—its face by the painter's cunning art, being made to appear as though

looking on all around it. There are many excellent pictures of such faces—for example, that of the archeress in the market-place of Nuremberg; that by the eminent painter, Roger [Van der Weyden], in his priceless picture in the governor's house at Brussels; the Veronica in my chapel at Coblenz, and, in the castle of Brixen, the angel holding the arms of the Church, and many others elsewhere. Yet, lest ye should fail in the exercise, which requireth a figure of this description to be looked upon, I send for your indulgence such a picture as I have been able to procure, setting forth the figure of an omnivoyant, and this I call the icon of God.

This picture, brethren, ye shall set up in some place, let us say, on a north wall, and shall stand around it, a little way off, and look upon it. And each of you shall find that, from whatsoever quarter he regardeth it, it looketh upon him as if it looked on none other. And it shall seem to a brother standing to eastward as if that face looketh toward the east, while one to southward shall think it looketh toward the south, and one to westward, toward the west.

First, then, you will marvel how it can be that the face should look on all and each at the same time. For the imagination of him standing to eastward cannot conceive the gaze of the icon to be turned unto any other quarter, such as west or south. Then let the brother who stood to eastward place himself to westward and he will find its gaze fastened on him in the west just as it was afore in the east. And as he knoweth the icon to be fixed and unmoved, he will marvel at the motion of its immovable gaze.

If now, while fixing his eye on the icon, he walk from west to east, he will find that its gaze continuously goeth along with him, and if he return from east to west, in like manner it will not leave him. Then will he marvel how, being motionless, it moveth, nor will his imagination be able to conceive that it should also move in like manner with one going in a contrary direction to himself. If he wish to experiment on this, he will cause one of his brethren to cross over from east to west, still looking on the icon, while he himself moveth from west to east; and he will ask the other as they meet if the gaze of the icon turn continuously with him; he will hear that it doth move in a contrary direction, even as with himself, and he will believe him. . . . And while he observeth how that gaze never quitteth any, he seeth that it taketh such diligent care of each one who findeth himself observed as though it cared only for him, and for no other, and this to such a degree that one on whom it resteth cannot even conceive that it should take care of any other. He will also see that it taketh the same most diligent care of the least of creatures as of the greatest, and of the whole universe.

'Tis by means of this perceptible image that I purpose to uplift you, my most loving brethren, by a certain devotional exercise, unto mystical theology . . .[1]

[1] Nicholas of Cusa, *Vision of God*, London, 1928, pp. 3–6.

BEGINNINGS OF GOTHIC ART AT PISA AND SIENA

Gothic art appeared in Italy and became a formidable competitor of the yet dominant Romanesque. The new art form, here too, revealed the unity and diversity it had shown north of the Alps. An outburst of building zeal produced large numbers of new Gothic churches. Among the greatest creations of Gothic inspiration were the Lower and Upper churches of St. Francis at Assisi, the cathedral of Siena, three great churches—Santa Maria del Fiore, Santa Croce, and Santa Maria Novella —of Florence, Santa Maria della Spina at Pisa, and Santa Maria sopra Minerva at Rome. The imposing cathedral of Milan, larger than any of the above mentioned, was built about 1400. There also were civic structures in Gothic as, for example, the Palazzo of the Doges at Venice and the Palazzo Vecchio at Florence.

A new school of sculpture with partly Gothic inspiration appeared in the thirteenth century in Pisa. Pisa's glorious cathedral with baptistry and campanile had long ago been finished when Niccola Pisano, also known as Andrea of Apulia (d. 1282?), was commissioned to construct a pulpit for the baptistry. This hexagonal pulpit of marble is supported by six columns, three of which rest on the backs of lions and alternating with each of these, three which stand on the floor. A flight of steps leads up to the pulpit box. Scenes on the panels represent the *Nativity, Adoration of the Magi, Presentation in the Temple, Crucifixion,* and the *Last Judgment.*

These panels give rise to much thought. Niccola was an artist of great independence. The figures on the panels obviously reveal that the artist had an eye for Gothic workmanship. The panels are overcrowded, the figures are draped in heavy cloth, and they all have matted hair. They possess a certain realism which unmistakably classifies them as Gothic in style. At the same time we note Roman features. It is certain therefore that Niccola studied ancient Roman models. Thus the *Virgin of the Adoration* of the Magi looks like a reclining Roman matron. Classical influence is definitely proved by the totally nude, muscular *Hercules* carrying two lions' skins. This figure is placed on the spandrel of one of the arches supporting the pulpit box. This *Hercules* is incongruously placed among scenes of Christ's nativity.

Niccola's pulpit in the cathedral of Siena is even more remarkable. It is an octagonal structure, five of whose panels are devoted to the themes which appear in the pulpit in the baptistry of Pisa. The two which were added represent the *Massacre of the Innocents* and the *Torments of the Damned.* The execution of the work in Siena is finer, the proportions more exact, and the dramatic rendering truer. Thus the matrons in the *Massacre of the Innocents* gaze fixedly upon the wounds of their babes or clasp their agonized forms to their bosoms.

Giovanni Pisano (d. 1320), son and pupil of Niccola, continued the work of his father. He assisted him in the construction of the pulpit at Siena and probably is responsible for the greater delicacy which makes this work more remarkable than that in the baptistry of Pisa. Giovanni's masterpiece is the pulpit in Sant' Andrea of Pistoia. The reliefs reveal little of the classical manner, but possess rare tenderness and delicacy. The *Virgin in the Nativity* is a beautiful matron, weak after the trying ordeal, whose heart is aglow with solicitude for the holy infant. The *Massacre of the Innocents,* a magnificent panel, is dramatic in all its parts: women stricken with grief over the death of their babes and others calling the curse of heaven upon Herod. Giovanni filled his panels with vibrant life. The calm of classic sculpture is not to be found in his work; it is really inspired by the Gothic work which had come into Italy from beyond the Alps. Aside from better modeling, the classical inspiration of Niccola Pisano appears to have been but a momentary matter. The Pisan school, however, was to exert much influence upon Italian, especially Tuscan, sculptors of the fourteenth century.

Meanwhile, at Siena, a new school of painting came into existence. Gothic ideas must have been widely cherished at a time when Siena's magnificent Gothic cathedral was being built and its pulpit constructed by the Pisani. In painting, Byzantine ideas were popular. But Duccio di Buoninsegna (1265?–1319) appears to have adopted some Gothic realism which placed Sienese painting in the forefront of painting in Italy. Duccio, however, retained the practice of gold leaf backgrounds and the tempera method of painting. The *Rucellai Madonna* is one of his first masterpieces. In it the painter portrayed the Virgin in an intensely reverent manner. More significant in the formation of the Sienese school of painting is Duccio's *Madonna in Majesty,* a work designed to adorn the altar of the cathedral. On the front of this altarpiece is shown the Virgin enthroned and surrounded by a number of angels. On the back of this altarpiece is an extraordinary group of twenty-five scenes illustrating the life of Christ.

GIOTTO FOUNDS A NEW ARTISTIC SCHOOL

While the Pisani were thus founding their school of sculpture at Pisa and Duccio that of painting at Siena, a third and more important school was being developed—that of the Florentine Giotto di Bondone (1266–1337). Giotto's mental formation lay in those days when the Pisani were becoming famous. And he could not fail to note how Duccio combined the jewel-like workmanship of artists who worked after the Byzantine manner with the effort of Gothic masters to portray figures realistically. Giotto also, while working at Rome, saw the mosaics by Pietro Cavallini (1251–1330) in the church of Santa Maria at Trastevere which reveal facial naturalness and exactitude in depicting folds of garments and much ability to arrange groups. Cavallini's art, apparently independent of Byzantine traditions, appears to echo local ancient Roman artistic conceptions.

Giotto's master from whom he learned the elements of painting was Cimabue (1240–1302), a Florentine artist of originality and skill. His masterpiece is the *Virgin Enthroned*. Like Duccio's great work of similar design, the Virgin is shown seated and surrounded by angels. But Cimabue's great work reveals an artist's endeavor to arrange them perspectively. The angels are placed around the throne with a suggestion of some space between them. Giotto's *Virgin Enthroned* reveals an artist preoccupied with the basic principles of painting, the full solution of which was not to be achieved until the days of Andrea Mantegna (1431–1506) and Leonardo da Vinci (1452–1519).

There was at least one other influence that contributed toward Giotto's artistic eminence. This was the phenomenon of what may be called *Franciscanism*, after all that St. Francis of Assisi (1182–1226) did, stood for, and achieved. St. Francis was a holy, simple man ever practicing utter denial of self. His life was lived for the most part in his native Umbria, and there was hardly a community in that hilly country which did not have its traditional stories about him. Two magnificent churches were built in his honor. The lower church was his tomb, the upper church told the story of his life in a series of frescoes on its walls. Painters in the tradition of Franciscanism produced innumerable pictures of St. Francis living his life in his homeland of Umbria.

Among the first painters to illustrate the life of St. Francis was Giunta Pisano (d. 1265?) who produced a crucifix decorated with a series of pictures of the life of the popular saint. Later, Cimabue and his pupil Giotto decorated the walls of the Lower Church with pictures illustrating St. Francis' life. Being so commissioned, they had to paint the popular saint's life as he had lived it in his native Umbria. This demanded a powerful impulse toward realism, something that persisted in Italian artistic endeavor throughout the Renaissance.

Giotto was a man of remarkable ability as poet, sculptor, architect, and above all as painter. He appears as a forerunner of the host of artistic geniuses in Italy whose personality and achievements fill the next two centuries of Italian life. He so astounded his countrymen that they told many stories about him. One of these relates that he drew the picture of a fly so perfectly that his master Cimabue, mistaking it for a real fly, tried to brush it away with a motion of his hand. Giotto's ready wit endeared him to all.

Giotto was engaged to do some frescoes in the Upper Church at Assisi. A few years before the close of the century Giotto assumed direction of the great frescoes which already were in progress. These pictures show that he sought to impart the corporeal reality which Cimabue had attempted. They are also characterized by a striking vivacity of action. One of these pictures is the famous incident of *St. Francis Preaching to the Birds* and another portrays the saint's *Renunciation of His Father.* It is evident that Giotto had made great progress by this time, but he still had much to learn. His crowds are not always well arranged, and the backgrounds possess little unity. For example, buildings are placed at the sides of the pictures, leaving a gap in the middle. Giotto's next work was done at Rome, whither he went in 1300 to prepare for St. Peter's the design of the mosaic which was to represent Christ walking on the sea.

Giotto's next great work was done in the Arena Chapel at Padua. On its barrel-shaped ceiling and its sides he painted in fresco the story of the Christian scheme of redemption. Besides pictures of *God the Father* and the *Last Judgment,* there is a long series depicting the life of Christ. Here again the artist reveals his realism and vivacity, but he has gained dramatic unity. This is well illustrated by the fresco of the *Lamentation over the Body of Christ.* The actions of the grief-stricken mourners around the rigid body harmonize with their sorrow. The movements of the *Virgin and St. Mary Magdalene* are surprisingly realistic. These pictures also reveal Giotto's progress in portraying mass, a progress inevitable the moment he began to give greater dramatic unity and intensity to his scenes.

During the next few years Giotto tarried at Florence, but by 1312 was again at work at Assisi. This time he produced a number of pictures in the lower church. Giotto possessed a marvelous capacity for growth, for these pictures reveal great improvement in his ability to give symmetry to groups. The four frescoes on the vaulting illustrating *Poverty, Chastity, Obedience,* and the *Apotheosis of St. Francis,* mark an important advance upon all his previous achievement. Other pictures in the left arm of the transept of this church show similar progress. In the *Massacre of the Innocents* the horror of this episode and the vigorous action demanded by it evoked the artist's dramatic ability.

Giotto was one of the greatest of artistic geniuses, boldest of initiators.

Most artists of the fourteenth century were, directly or indirectly, his pupils. Even the great masters of Florence found that they could profitably study his work. Giotto's influence was strongly felt in Siena which was to produce a remarkable school of painters during the fourteenth century. They improved the traditional Byzantine methods by adapting Giotto's realism.

THE GREATNESS OF FLEMISH ART

Gothic art in northern Europe reached its highest excellence in the Low Countries. By the end of the fourteenth century the art which had flourished in Paris was transferred to the Low Countries. The dukes of Burgundy who ruled in Flanders and the neighboring Low Countries were a younger branch of the Valois house which had occupied the French throne since 1328. These princes brought with them an appreciation of the best art of the Seine region. Thus John Maelwael, a native of Guelders who worked in Paris, became painter to Duke Philip the Bold (1368–1404). Under Burgundian patronage was born the magnificent art of Flanders.

The earliest pictorial work for the Burgundian princes which has come down to us is the *Très Riches Heures,* a book of hours preserved in the museum at Chantilly. Its miniatures were made by Paul of Limburg and his two brothers, nephews of Maelwael, who were related to the Parisian school of miniaturists. In these little pictures the figures are drawn with that regard for realism we associate with Flemish painting and which in lesser degree characterized all Gothic pictorial art. The colors are delicate; flowers, plants, and trees are exquisitely drawn and reveal a keen love of nature. The skies are tinted a delicate blue. The themes are religious: the coronation of the Virgin, the Three Magi, and so forth. Gold leaf is abundantly used. Another choice work was the *Très Belles Heures,* destroyed in a fire in Turin in 1904. Its miniatures also reveal close study of nature. Their themes were of the traditional sort but were executed with greater skill and freedom. These pictures have been ascribed for the most part to John Van Eyck (d. 1441). They reveal startling naturalism, knowledge of form, artistic unity, and some skill in creating illusion of space.

The next great masterpiece to claim our attention is the triptych of *The Mystic Lamb* in Ghent. It was painted by Van Eyck at the request of Jodocus Vyt, a wealthy citizen of Ghent who wished to decorate a chapel in the present church of St. Bavo. Its theme is drawn from the seventh chapter of the Revelation of St. John. The central panel presents a pleasant landscape of hill, wood, and meadow spangled with flowers. In the distant background rise the towers of the heavenly Jerusalem. In the center is erected an altar on which stands a lamb, emblematic of Christ. Its breast is pierced, and a stream of blood flows into a chalice. Around the altar are gathered angels, while farther in the background is assembled a host of saints and martyrs. In the foreground on each side of a fountain with flowing water emblematic of the living faith in Christ, the fountain of life, is a group of priests, monks, and laymen praying and singing. In a smaller panel above is a magnificent picture of God in all His glory. In the panel at His right sits the Virgin, a creation of unsurpassed beauty. On His left is St. John the Baptist with an open book in his lap. On each side of this group of three are St. Cecilia at the organ and a choir of singing angels. Below them and on the sides of the central panel showing the mystic lamb are companies of judges, hermits, pilgrims, and crusaders.

This great classic of Flemish art reveals even more fully the remarkable excellences of Van Eyck's miniatures in the *Très Belles Heures* of Turin. Here realism, careful study of anatomical detail, and religious zeal are more perfectly combined than in any other contemporary Flemish work.

Of the other pictures from the hand of John Van Eyck, equally as interesting is the *Virgin and Canon Paele*. The Virgin is seated on a carpeted throne. She wears a robe of the finest cloth embroidered and set with jewels. The child Jesus on the right side of her lap is an interesting study. Painters before Van Eyck and even in his day were wont to portray a stiff child incapable of motion, but Van Eyck produced a natural child. The donor of the picture, a canon of St. Donatian's church in Bruges, is shown kneeling in a white surplice at the Virgin's left. His service book and spectacles are carefully executed. His face is a remarkable bit of realism; the wrinkles, eyes, ears, and half-bald head are models of excellence. By his side stands St. George clad in armor, bearing the traditional banner of white with a cross on it. At the Virgin's right stands St. Donatian, patron saint of the church in Bruges, bearing his traditional wheel to which lighted candles are fixed. Van Eyck also painted a number of portraits, the most striking of which is the *Man with a Pink*. Realism could go no further in depicting anatomical detail. The portrait of *John Arnolfini and His Wife* shows a couple standing in a room lighted by a window. Van Eyck, like all Flemish painters, noted every detail and reproduced it faithfully. The perspective may be faulty at times, but the colors and feeling for reality are an abiding glory.

The next important artist of the Flemish Low Countries to be noted is Roger van der Weyden (d. 1464). He drew his inspiration from Van

Eyck and spent much of his life in Brussels. Van Eyck's religious pictures are characterized by serious thought, and all objects are subordinated to it. There is little motion in them. All is quiet as if hushed by the sanctity of the solemn scene. But van der Weyden was dramatic. He was interested in the concrete expression of religious conviction. His *Descent from the Cross* shows Christ being taken down by Joseph of Arimathea. At the left of the cross stands Mary Magdalene in deep sorrow; at the right is the Virgin who has dropped to the ground swooning. She is supported by St. John and another woman.

Van der Weyden's *Last Judgment*, to be seen in the hospital at Beaune in France, tells the story of the final scenes on this earth as they were popularly conceived during the Middle Ages. Christ is seated on a rainbow with the sword of justice at His right. His feet rest on a globe, emblematic of the world He is to judge. Below Him stands St. Michael with scales in his hands weighing two human beings. The picture represents the moment when the call of the angel has been heard by the dead who rise from their graves. Some have emerged completely, others are struggling to free themselves from the clay. Here and there the ground cracks and upheaves as a body pushes its way up; in one place an arm and part of the head are visible. Some of the souls adore Christ, but others flee in terror to the torment prepared for them. Around Christ are seated holy men and women, including the Virgin and St. John the Baptist, in attitudes of prayer. Angels sounding their trumpets fly around St. Michael. The artist has succeeded in creating a certain unity through the vigorous actions of the resurrected in response to the dread summons.

Bold and original in his execution, Hugo Van der Goes (d. 1482) followed in the footsteps of Van Eyck and van der Weyden. His work possesses the same qualities of realism, careful study of detail, and a certain dramatic vigor. In his picture *Death of the Virgin* the mother of Christ lies on a bed diagonally to the observer. The artist thus sought to solve the problem of depth by employing foreshortening with a boldness never before attempted by his Flemish predecessors. He made an effort to give to each person at the bedside an appropriate expression and proper action. Van der Goes' triptych, the *Adoration of the Shepherds* (Portinari altarpiece), is his masterpiece. The central panel shows Mary in adoration before her Son. The child is inferior to similar figures by Van Eyck and van der Weyden, but the shepherds are unsurpassed. In them one sees the tendency toward realism so pronounced a feature in Flemish art, especially in the case of Peter Brueghel (d. 1569), in the next century. These shepherds were drawn from those the artist saw around him every day. In the foreground stand two vases, one containing iris and the other columbines. The fifteenth century never produced finer floral studies.

Low Country artists also produced noteworthy sculpture. The dukes of Burgundy beautified the Carthusian monastery at Champmol near Dijon in Burgundy. This was to be a mausoleum for the Burgundian house. Philip the Bold secured the services of a sculptor named Claus Sluter. Very little is known of this artist's origin, but tradition has it that he came from Zeeland. Sluter was commissioned to decorate the monastic well and prepare a crucifix above it. The finished work is known as *Moses' Well.* On each of its six sides was placed one of the great prophets of the Old Testament. The figures are swathed in cloth which falls in thick folds about the forms. The statue of Moses is particularly impressive. Its facial expression is worthy of the great leader of God's chosen people. Moses peers into the distance, his soul kindling with wrath as he sees his people worshiping false gods. David is crowned and leans sadly upon his harp as he thinks of the great sacrifice which a distant descendant, Jesus, must make for the sins of the world. On Jeremiah's face sorrow is written; on Zachariah's, bitter anguish. Daniel stands erect giving his prophecy; and Isaiah, old, bald, bearded, and oppressed by the tragedy of Christ's coming sacrifice, prophesies this supreme event. The words of each of these figures are inscribed on a long scroll, a frequent device in Gothic art. The prophets are wrought with great fidelity to life. They are Jews such as Sluter no doubt had seen in some ghetto. The somber note, the realization of the awful drama of man's fall, Christ's crucifixion, and the final judgment, are characteristic of the mournful view of life at the close of the Middle Ages. The Calvary above this group was destroyed during the French Revolution. Only the mutilated figure of Christ crowned with thorns remains. It is unsurpassed in naturalness and in the expression of infinite suffering. The other figures of this group were the Virgin, St. Mary Magdalene, and St. John the Baptist. In executing this work, Sluter had the assistance of his nephew, Claus de Werve, likewise an able sculptor.

Sluter also decorated the door of the monastery. In the center he placed a Virgin with the child Jesus in her left arm. Her garments fall in flowing folds. She gazes with tender adoration upon the Infant. At the right of the door is the figure of Duke Philip kneeling in prayer, and behind him stands St. John the Baptist. On the opposite side is the kneeling figure of the duchess, behind whom stands St. Catherine. The duke's face is an excellent portrait. Two other works at Champmol, the tombs of Philip the Bold (d. 1404) and John the Fearless (1404–1419), continue the ideas of Sluter. The carved figures of the departed rulers swathed in heavy garments with hands folded in prayer lie on marble slabs. Along the sides of the tombs, between Gothic pillars, as in a church, passes a cortege of mourning monks.

Especially remarkable is the treatment of landscape by the Haarlem artist Geertgen tot St. Jans (George of St. John) who died about 1495. In his picture *St. John the Baptist* he placed the figure of the saint in the immediate foreground. This enabled him to fill the background with a series of grassy hillocks covered with grass, and plants, and flowers. The water in the creeks flows into a shallow marsh. Beyond stands a clump of trees. In the distance over the trees and against a range of hills may be seen the towers of a town. This landscape so meticulously executed is anything but exceptional among painters of the Gothic school. But few if any produced larger scenes of nature, not even Leonardo da Vinci at the close of the fifteenth century.

Hans Memling (d. 1494) was the last of the great Flemish painters of the Middle Ages. He produced numerous pictures in which the characteristic Flemish methods were employed. A delicate psychological expression and a subtle refinement dominate his pictures. The reliquary with scenes from the *Martyrdom of St. Ursula* is justly famous. Memling also painted a *Last Judgment* which was obviously inspired by Roger van der Weyden. The *Mystic Marriage of St. Catherine* shows Mary seated on a sumptuously decorated throne. The rich clothing of the figures is carefully portrayed, the pattern of the cloth of St. Catherine's robe being reproduced with laborious fidelity. At the saint's feet lies the traditional wheel which figured in her sufferings. At the Virgin's left is seated St. Barbara with the customary tower behind her. Back of the Virgin stand St. John the Baptist with his lamb and St. John the Evangelist with a chalice in his hands.

GOTHIC ART IN GERMANY AND ELSEWHERE

Germany, too, could boast of excellent churches, remarkable sculptures, and impressive paintings, all created by Gothic inspiration. Such, for example, was the cathedral of Naumburg, which, though Romanesque, was finished in the Gothic style. The female figures to be found there are most expressive. Uta, for example, gazes thoughtfully into the distance, Reglindis is smiling broadly, and Gerlindis has a pensive look. Surely these German masters of the Gothic style had an inspired eye for reality and knew how to execute impressively all they observed.

There is a remarkable landscape scene from the hand of Conrad Witz (d. 1447), a painter from Basel who had professional relations with John

Van Eyck. The bishop of Geneva commissioned him to decorate a retable, one of the panels to represent the *Marvelous Catch of Fish*. Witz executed his commission with great fidelity to the biblical account. Christ is shown standing on the north shore of Lake Geneva, six of His disciples are in the boat, and Peter has just leaped into the water to come to the Master.

The landscape in this picture is especially interesting, for it contradicts statements often made that late medieval Gothic painters and their patrons had no interest in landscape. In this painting, however, Witz followed the example of Van Eyck and devoted more than half the space of his picture to landscape in the background. He portrayed the placid water, the trees growing on the bank opposite, the sloping hill with fruit trees dotting its surface and rows of trees dividing it into fields. In the distance looms Mt. Salève. The spot where Witz stood when studying the setting for his painting of the *Miraculous Catch of Fish* can easily be found today. The structures at the right clearly are those of Geneva.

Although the Germans produced excellent examples of Gothic art during the opening decades of the sixteenth century, we shall note only two of the most remarkable. The first of these is the group of statues in the Hapsburg court chapel in Innsbruck guarding the tomb in which the Emperor Maximilian was to have been buried. In 1502 he commissioned one Gilg Sesselschreiber to draw up a plan upon which this masterpiece of Gothic funeral architecture is based. These stately, life-sized figures in bronze stand along the aisle leading to the empty tomb. The women are clad in the bejeweled regal clothing of the time, the men are in full armor. By their sides appear (as in case of some of the women) armorial shields bearing heraldic devices. The figures are most realistic. Those of Maximilian's immediate relatives are genuine portraits while the statues representing King Arthur, King Theodoric, and Godfrey of Bouillon—all famous in chivalric tradition—though not portraits, are copied after living models.

The *Altarpiece of Isenheim*, largely the work of Mathias Grünewald (d. 1530), surely is one of the most extraordinary masterpieces of late Gothic painting, combining naturalistic expression in its figures with Gothic sadness and mourning. Composed of many panels and separate scenes, this is one of the most complex examples of altar furniture in existence. When opened the central panel presents the viewer with a remarkable *Crucifixion*. The crucified Christ is shown racked with pain, scourged with thorns; His figure is contorted. The dolorous character of this scene of suffering is heightened by the somber sky which serves as a background. Mary swoons, yielding to an access of grief, St. John the

Evangelist supports her tenderly, and St. Mary Magdalene, with hair disheveled, kneels praying fervently. Among the other noteworthy scenes of this altarpiece are the *Temptation of St. Anthony, Annunciation,* and *Ascension.* Typically Gothic are the carefully studied plants and decorative backgrounds showing glimpses of the open country beyond.

In France, as in the Low Countries, Germany, and elsewhere north of the Alps, Gothic art also flourished, everywhere revealing kinship with the ideas, themes, and techniques of Gothic masters. The note of pathos, for example, is well illustrated in the *Virgin of Pity* (by an unknown artist) from Villeneuve-les-Avignon and is to be dated about 1400. This picture shows the form of the crucified Christ supported by the grieving Virgin. Mary Magdalene is kneeling at His feet, and the third Mary is seated at His head. But the work of Jean Fouquet (1420?–1481?) of Touraine is more broadly representative of Gothic painting. As an artist he had many contacts with persons of all stations in the life of his day— royalty, nobility, officials, clergy, soldiers, and common folk—and his paintings therefore cover a wide range of subjects. His *Juvenal des Ursins,* a royal chancellor, is photographically realistic.

But Fouquet's miniatures illustrating the text of Josephus' *Jewish Antiquities* reveal him at his best. One of these, the *David Lamenting over Saul's Death,* is most skillfully conceived. A closely huddled group of soldiers stands behind the grief-stricken David. Near them flows a placid river rising in the distance among castle crowned hills and winding back and forth through the plain. Fouquet's art reveals some Italian Renaissance trends in painting. While on a visit in Italy Fouquet learned how to portray meandering rivers by studying the masterpieces of Piero della Francesca (1416–1492). By this time the art of Europe north of the Alps, having reached its highest development, was about to succumb to the skill of the great masters of the *Quattrocento.*

Music had received serious attention during the entire Middle Ages. It was one of the studies in the quadrivium. Unisonous chant, or plainsong, had long been used in the liturgical services of the Church. But there also was much secular music among the people; minstrels were common, and there was a plentiful supply of musical instruments such as organs, lutes, psalteries, viols, and cymbals. One influential musician, an early master of counterpoint, was John Dunstable (1370–1453) of England. Polyphony and counterpoint advanced rapidly after him, especially in the Low Countries. Guillaume Dufay (d. 1474), of Hainault, Johannes Okegem (d. 1495) from Ninove in Brabant, and Josquin Des Prez (d. 1523) from Hainault, carried this art to great perfection, especially in Italy.

With this brief review of Gothic art—music, painting, and sculpture—we conclude our survey (Chaps. 1–11) of the more salient features of late medieval culture and, following our definitions given in the Introduction (pp. 3–7), we now proceed to trace their development and the creation of new ones, during the Italian Age of the Renaissance.

PART VI

The Early Renaissance

Chapter 12

THE BIRTH OF HUMANISM

*H*UMANISM WAS a revolt against many features of medieval thought and society. Much of the culture of the Middle Ages was thought to be obsolete or inadequate. The center of life had shifted from the manor to the town. An ancient natural economy based upon the manor had been supplanted by a new economy supported by trade and industry and urban population. Capitalism had come into existence. Townsmen were supplanting the nobility as leading members of society. When the material bases of the social structure had grown vastly more complex, traditional ideals were to undergo profound transformation. Humanists were the midwives of a new culture, the culture of the Renaissance.

THE WORD *RENAISSANCE:* ITS ORIGIN AND MEANING

The meaning of the word *Renaissance* has varied from time to time. At the close of the sixteenth century it meant the revival of Latin and Greek letters. The Italians called this movement the *Rinascimento,* or rebirth of the classical languages and literatures. The word also connoted dislike of the culture of the Middle Ages and even hostility to it. It was believed that Greek and Roman life was the source of all true culture. Humanists often thought that the Middle Ages were an empty void, a dreary waste which could profitably be ignored.

This depreciatory view of the age which witnessed the rise of towns, the growth of industry and commerce, and the development of the bourgeoisie—one of the greatest economic revolutions in the history of man—

created the majestic institutions of the Holy Roman Empire and the Church, brought forth scholastic philosophy and theology, composed great poems like *Reynard the Fox* and the *Lay of the Nibelungs*, produced Gothic cathedrals and sculpture, developed Flemish painting and music, and evolved new and original institutions of government such as juries, communes, and parliaments, is still all too common even in our own day. It derives not only from the prejudices of humanists, but from writers nearer our own day who scorned the medieval Church and the culture with which she was associated.

The Age of Enlightenment which preceded the French Revolution renewed and sharpened this prejudice toward the Middle Ages. Philosophers of the eighteenth century were hostile to revealed religion and to established churches. They hated dogmas and condemned forms of culture which revealed religious influence. They regarded the Middle Ages as a period of faith and superstition which came to an end in the rationalism of the Renaissance. Their views were most unjust and unhistorical, being based upon ignorance of the true character of the Middle Ages.

A change came with the Romantic Movement at the opening of the nineteenth century. In their opposition to the rationalism of their predecessors its adherents emphasized sentiment and feeling. They believed in historical processes and were particularly interested in religion and the historical origins of institutions. They often displayed keen interest in the Middle Ages. Thus Sir Walter Scott (1771–1832) laid the scenes of some of his historical romances in that period. His example proved contagious, for in every country there sprang up schools of writers who exploited the noteworthy deeds of medieval princes and people.

The Romantic Movement also was interested in the problem of human liberty. From this standpoint the Romantic historians viewed the Renaissance as an age which liberated mankind from the supposed tyranny of medieval dogma and superstition. Jules Michelet (1798–1874) devoted the eighth volume of his *History of France* to this theme. This work gained great favor and established the universal use of the word *Renaissance*. His conceptions were adopted and popularized in the English-speaking world by John Addington Symonds (1840–1893), whose volumes are numbered among the historical classics in our language. More important than either of these writers was Jacob Burckhardt (1818–1897). His *Civilization of Italy in the Renaissance* (1860) may be regarded as a great historical classic. The author was something of a poet gifted with a fine ability to comprehend the significance of forms of art in relation to their economic, social, and political environment. This book may be said to lay a secure basis for the history of culture.

Even while Burckhardt and Symonds were still active, a firmer foundation was laid for the study of Renaissance culture. Numerous scholars were exploring the Middle Ages and exposing to our scrutiny the civilization of a much abused and misunderstood period. Viollet-le-Duc (1814–1879), for example, studied the evolution of Gothic architecture. Émile Mâle (b. 1862) revolutionized our knowledge of Gothic and Renaissance sculpture and painting. Other scholars have patiently investigated the economic, social, and political evolution of the Middle Ages. Scholastic philosophy, theology, and medieval science are better understood today. The result of all this scholarship is that we can now place the civilization of the Renaissance in its proper relation to the Middle Ages. Today we know that this brilliant culture was the fulfillment of the medieval promise and not simply a "return to classical antiquity." It marked the close of a significant chapter in history.

How shall we define the word *Humanism*? It was the chief of the new conceptions of the Renaissance. Cicero discussed it in his *On the Orator*, stating that boys who some day would assume leadership in state and society should prepare themselves for this task by studying literature, philosophy, rhetoric, history, and law. A man so trained was said to be *humanus*, or *human*. "We are all called men," wrote Cicero, "but only those of us are human (*humani*) who have been civilized by the studies proper to culture." This kind of culture—Roman or Greek—was called *humanitas*, a Latin word more or less equivalent to our *humanism*. As we shall use this word in the following pages it implies a certain criticism of medieval forms stimulated by the cultivation of the pagan and other aspects of Greek and Roman life ignored in the Middle Ages. Scholars and literary men who cultivated a knowledge of classical Greek and Roman life and thought, of whom there were many, were called *Humanists*.

So complex and varied is the culture of the Renaissance that it seems advisable to divide it into periods. We shall subdivide the age into centuries as is usually done in Italy. So we shall call the thirteenth century the *Duecento*; the fourteenth century the *Trecento*; the fifteenth century the *Quattrocento*; and the sixteenth century the *Cinquecento*.

PETRARCH'S MENTAL FORMATION

The first person to give expression to the new spirit of Humanism and attract attention was Francesco Petrarch (1304–1374). He was born of Florentine parents in Arezzo, whither the family had fled from Florence because of the feuds in which the father had a share. They moved to Pisa when Petrarch was about 8 years old. After further wanderings the family settled in Carpentras near Avignon. Petrarch's father was a thrifty and industrious merchant who had some appreciation for Cicero. He fondly cherished a rare manuscript containing that master's orations *On Glory* and *On the Laws*. Like many practical men who well understood life's hard road, the father decided to send his son to school to study law. Petrarch accordingly went to the University of Montpellier in southern France.

The study of law proved irksome to the boy. He found comfort in the stately hexameters of Vergil and the noble sentences of Cicero. His father disapproved of this unusual ardor for the Latin classics and rebuked the boy for wasting his time. Once the irate parent discovered these writings, drew them forth from their hiding place, and, before the eyes of the youth, cast them into the fire. The boy burst into a plaintive wail, whereupon the stern father relented and snatched a copy of Vergil's *Aeneid* and Cicero's *Rhetoric* from the flames. He allowed the youth to keep them, but with the injunction that he should use them for recreation only and not allow himself to be drawn from the study of law. From 1323–1326 Petrarch studied at the chief school of law, the University of Bologna, but his love for the classics did not perish.

Petrarch's father died in 1326, and Francesco was summoned home to Avignon. His mother died shortly after, and he was free to do as he pleased. The next important event occurred one day in Holy Week in 1327. He saw the lady Laura whom his verse was to make forever famous. Little is known about her beyond what Petrarch himself tells. She did not accept his attentions, but this did not chill his ardor. She became the passion of his life, the inspirer of his song. Petrarch was a sensitive spirit, and this sensitiveness dominated his entire life. He became one of the greatest of lyric poets. Rarely has an artist given the world song so pure, lofty, and perfect. The depth of his feeling forced him to use his native Tuscan Italian, for Latin seemed an inadequate vehicle for his sentiments. This was significant because with Dante's *Vita Nuova* and *Divine Comedy* it heralded the end of the reign of the Latin tongue which at best was but a learned idiom and probably could not well become the artistic medium of modern thought.

Petrarch's poems about Laura are in the form of sonnets. This type of verse was not his creation, but its perfection was due entirely to him. In his hands it ceased to be a complicated and labored form and became a delicate instrument capable of expressing the deepest sentiments. This lyric verse form consists of fourteen rhyming lines divided into two parts, the octet and the sestet. A profoundly moving thought stated in the first four lines of the octet is repeated with some variation or elaboration in the second four lines. The thought then turns reflectingly in the first half of the sestet; in the second half, it ends in hope, despair, resolution, consolation, or some such emotion. Many of the world's greatest poets, among them Michelangelo, Spenser, Shakespeare, Milton, and Wordsworth, have used this form of verse.

A tender, languid melancholy breathes through Petrarch's sonnets. Thus in his third sonnet he described his meeting with Laura:

> 'Twas on the blessed morning when the sun
>   In pity to our Maker hid his light,
> That, unawares, the captive I was won,
>   Lady, of your bright eyes which chained me quite;
> That seem'd to me no time against the blows
>   Of love to make defence, to frame relief:
>   Secure and unsuspecting, thus my woes
> Date their commencement from the common grief.
> Love found me feeble then and defenceless all,
>   Open the way and easy to my heart
>   Through eyes, where since my sorrows ebb and flow:
> But therein was, methinks his triumph small,
>   On me, in that weak state, to strike his dart,
>   Yet hide from you so strong his very bow.

The following sonnet, like the preceding, though translated, preserves some of Petrarch's poetic finesse:

> The eyes whose praise I penned with glowing thought,
>   And countenance and limbs and all fair worth
>   That sundered me from men of mortal birth—
> The clustering locks, with golden glory fraught;
>   The sudden-shining smile, as angel's mirth,
>   Wonted to make a paradise on earth;
> Are now a little dust that feels not aught.
> Still I have life, who rail and rage at it,
>   Lorn of love's light that solely life endears,
>   Mastless before the hurricane I flit.
> Be this my last of lays to mortal ears;
>   Dried is the ancient fountain of my wit,
>   And all my music melted into tears.[1]

Petrarch's Laura will always be one of the world's literary heroines. She was something wholly new. Poets in the earlier Middle Ages had

---

[1] *The Sonnets, Triumphs, and Other Poems of Petrarch*, London, 1909, pp. 3–4, 15–16.

sung of love, but the object of their affections had usually been insubstantial. Her personality was submerged in the elaborate conventions of courtly love which had grown up in feudal society. This idealization was associated with strong religious sentiment. Thus Dante views Beatrice as noble beyond compare among human beings, fit to guide him through heaven. But Petrarch's Laura is a flesh and blood woman. The poet's treatment of love is human, therefore modern, and was to be imitated by many subsequent writers.

PETRARCH'S ATTITUDE TOWARD NATURE

The character of Petrarch's poetic interests is further shown by his keen interest in nature. He retired occasionally to Vaucluse, a mountain dell near Avignon through which flowed the river Sorgue. In this calm and lonely spot he had a house and garden where he loved to reflect and write. One day in 1335 he climbed Mount Ventoux, an elevation near Avignon. The ascent occupied an entire day. At the summit the poet was entranced by the beauty of the prospect. His apostrophe to Vaucluse is one of unforgettable beauty:

> Ye limpid brooks, by whose clear streams
> My goddess laid her tender limbs!
> Ye gentle boughs, whose friendly shade
> Gave shelter to the lovely maid!
> Ye herbs and flowers, so sweetly press'd
> By her soft rising snowy breast!
> Ye Zephyrs mild, that wreathed around
> The place where Love my heart did wound!
> Now at my summons all appear,
> And to my dying words give ear.[2]

To many an admirer of Petrarch this ascent of Mount Ventoux appeared especially significant. They thought Petrarch disapproved of the medieval view of nature. So, for example, John Addington Symonds thought that medieval man could not because of his Christian faith even look at nature:

During the Middle Ages man had lived enveloped in a cowl. He had not seen the beauty of the world, or had seen it only to cross himself, and turn aside and tell his beads and pray. Like St. Bernard traveling along the shores of the Lake Leman, and noticing neither the azure of the waters, nor the luxuriance of the vines, nor the radiance of the mountains with their robe of sun and snow, but bending a thought-burdened forehead over the neck

---

[2] *Ibid.*, pp. 116–117.

of his mule; even like this monk, humanity had passed, a careful pilgrim, intent on the terrors of sin, death, and judgment . . . and had scarcely known that they were sightworthy or that life is a blessing. Beauty is a snare, pleasure a sin, the world a fleeting show, man fallen and lost, death the only certainty, judgment inevitable, hell everlasting; ignorance is acceptable to God as a proof of faith and submission.[3]

But this view must be rejected. We have noted in the foregoing Chapter that Gothic art, contrary to what Symonds thought, was based on much study of reality. When decorating backgrounds in illuminations, artists usually reproduced scenes from nature. Especially expressive are the scenic background painted by the Van Ecyk brothers in the *Milan Book of Hours* which mark the culmination of the art of making illuminations. We have noted Conrad Witz's view of the Rhone above Geneva, a bit of scenery today still recognizable—after the passage of five centuries. Similarly, in the Isenheim altarpiece by Grünewald, should be noted the magnificent rose plant. Its branches, leaves, and blossoms must have been observed by an artist of consummate skill. The picture of St. John the Baptist in the *Wilderness* would do credit to any Italian artist of the early Renaissance. Geertgen tot St. Jans' *St. John the Baptist*, noted above, has a large background of swamp, hillock, distant wood, a city, and beyond its outlines, a range of hills. Clearly, Gothic artists took note of physical nature in planning their artistic creations.

Nor is it correct to assume with Symonds and other nineteenth-century writers on the Renaissance that the Middle Ages, being religious and hence theological, were unfavorable to the development of science. There was great progress in science at the hand of Albertus Magnus, Robert Grosseteste, and Roger Bacon—and all these were scholastic philosophers as well as theologians. Also, it is to be noted, our medieval forefathers made skillful inventions such as the mechanical clock, guns and gunpowder, and the printing press. Petrarch, being a poet, well expressed the appeal Nature made to him and, no doubt, to others as well.

PETRARCH AND THE FAITH

It must not be thought that Petrarch was an unbeliever. On the contrary, much that was specifically medieval filled his spirit. This is shown over and over again in his poems as, for example:

> The day must come, nor distant far its date,
> Time flies so swift and sure,
> Oh, peerless and alone!

[3] J. A. Symonds, *Renaissance in Italy: The Age of Despots*, p. 9.

When death my heart, no conscience struck, shall seize;
Commend me, Virgin! then to thy dear Son,
    True God and Very Man,
That my last sigh in peace may in His arms be breathed![4]

Much that was specifically medieval persisted in Petrarch's thought and work. This is shown in his *Secret*, dialogues between St. Augustine and himself. The saint as chief teacher of Christian doctrine converses with the penitent Petrarch, a Christian who is torn between traditional ideals, his love of fame, and affection for Laura. In the first dialogue the saint shows how the poet's melancholy and restless spirit rises from his many desires. These worldly interests have caused him to forget his Creator. There is a traditional remedy—ascetic self-denial and contemplation of God. The second dialogue deals with Petrarch's specific faults—his love of glory, his pride, ambition, and melancholy. These disturb his quiet; rest might be secured from thinking upon the drama of Christian redemption.

The last dialogue concerns Petrarch's infatuation for Laura and his avid love for fame. To the poet's protest that the passion has proved an ennobling influence, St. Augustine replies:

Nothing so much leads a man to forget or despise God as the love of things temporal, and most of all this passion that we call love. . . .

The saint's advice to the penitent in regard to the books he was writing in order to win renown is in the same tenor:

Throw to the wind these great loads of histories; the deeds of the Romans have been celebrated quite enough by others, and are known by their own fame. Get out of Africa [alluding to Petrarch's *Africa* which celebrated the deeds of Scipio] and leave it to its possessors. You will add nothing to the glory of your Scipio or to your own. . . . Therefore leave all this on one side, and now at length take possession of yourself; and to come back to our starting-point, let me urge you to enter upon the meditation of your last end, which comes on step by step without your being aware. Tear off the veil; disperse the shadows; look only on that which is coming; with eyes and mind give all your attention there: let nought else distract you. Heaven, earth, the sea—these all suffer change. What can man, the frailest of all creatures, hope for? . . . Therefore . . . say to yourself: 'The seasons pass, yet they will come again; but I am going, never again to return.' As often as you behold at sunset the shadows of the mountains lengthening on the plain, say to yourself: Now life is sinking fast; the shadow of death begins to overspread the scene; yonder sun to-morrow will again be rising the same, but this day of mine will never come back.

4 *The Warner Library*, XIX, 11374–11375.

Petrarch accepted these admonitions. But life's secular interests continued to draw the poet's mind away from his thoughts of eternity and God. The reader feels that in the end the saint will fail and that Petrarch will remain a spiritual wanderer:

> I will pull myself together and collect my scattered wits, and make a great endeavor to possess my soul in patience. But even while we speak, a crowd of important affairs, though only of the world, is waiting my attention.[5]

PETRARCH AS AN ITALIAN PATRIOT

Petrarch, like Dante, was a patriot. His lyrical soul was sensitive to the glories of his native Italy. He lamented the fate that started his family's wanderings into exile. He bewailed the feuds which disturbed the peace of his land and made it the sport of foreign adventurers and Holy Roman emperors:

> O my own Italy! though words are vain
> The mortal wounds to close,
> Unnumber'd, that thy beauteous bosom stain,
> Yet may it soothe my pain
> To sigh forth Tiber's woes,
> And Arno's wrongs, as on Po's saddened shore
> Sorrowing I wander, and my numbers pour.
> Ruler of heaven! By the all-pitying love
> That could thy Godhead move
> To dwell a lowly sojourner on earth,
> Turn, Lord! on this thy chosen land thine eye:
> See, God of charity!
> From what light cause this cruel war has birth:
> And the hard hearts by savage discord steel'd,
> Thou, Father! from on high,
> Touch by my humble voice, that stubborn wrath may yield!

Petrarch's love for Italy calls for careful study. He was conscious of his country's glorious past, and he conceived an ardent love for Rome. Everything in her history became interesting. His love for her extended to every detail and often degenerated into an indiscriminate praise of all things connected with ancient life and letters, a vice apparent among his successors. Rome had been the seat of the empire, the head of all government, the parent of civilization. How had the great city fallen! Foreigners, whom in classical fashion he called "barbarians," swayed her destiny.

---

[5] *Petrarch's Secret: or, the Soul's Conflict with Passion*, London, 1911, pp. 184–185, 191.

How different had it been in ancient times! Thus the poet's lyrical feelings mingled with his patriotism. Comparing Rome as it had been with Rome as it was when abandoned by the papacy at Avignon, he voiced the melancholy sentiments of a patriot's burning hope that better times would come.

> Ah! is not this the soil my foot first pressed?
> And here, in cradled rest,
> Was I not softly hushed?—here fondly reared?
> Ah! is not this my country?—so endeared
> By every filial tie!
> In whose lap shrouded both my parents lie!
> Oh! by this tender thought
> Your torpid bosoms to compassion wrought,
> Look on the peoples' grief!
> Who, after God, of you expect relief;
> And if ye but relent,
> Virtue shall rouse her in embattled might,
> Against blind fury bent,
> Nor long shall doubtful hang the unequal fight;
> For no,—the ancient flame
> Is not extinguished yet, that raised the Italian name!

When Rienzi seized the government of Rome in 1347, Petrarch hoped that a change for the better had come. He supported Rienzi's cause with enthusiasm and addressed to him his noble *Spirto Gentil.*

> Spirit heroic! . . .
> Since, rightly, now the rod of state is thine
> Rome and her wandering children to confine,
> And yet reclaim her to the old good way:
> To thee I speak, for elsewhere not a ray
> Of virtue can I find, extinct below,
> Nor one who feels of evil deeds the shame.
> Why Italy still waits, and what her aim
> I know not, callous to her proper woe.
> Indolent, aged, slow,
> Still will she sleep? Is none to rouse her found? . . .
>
> Forth on thy way! my song, and where the bold
> Tarpeian lifts his brow, shouldst thou behold,
> Of others' weal more thoughtful than his own,
> The chief, by general Italy revered,
> Tell him from me, to whom he is but known
> As one to virtue and by fame endear'd,

Till stamp'd upon his heart the sad truth be,
That, day by day to thee,
With suppliant attitude and streaming eyes,
For justice and relief our seven-hilled city cries.[6]

PETRARCH AS COLLECTOR OF CLASSICAL AUTHORS

From youth Petrarch collected the writings of classical authors, searching monastic and episcopal libraries with the zeal of a pilgrim, and copying old manuscripts in his beautiful handwriting. In time he secured a large collection of Latin authors, and brought together many of Cicero's extant works. Medieval scholars had read the ancient classics, but not in the spirit of Petrarch, for they were not attracted to the human interests of the ancients because the ancients were pagans. They were not interested in collecting copies of all the old writings and usually neglected them.

Besides being a collector, Petrarch was famous as a writer on classical subjects. Hoping to produce a great epic rivaling Vergil's *Aeneid*, he wrote the *Africa* in which he celebrated the greatness of Scipio Africanus. He always thought that this was his best work. While from the point of view of humanism the poem was significant, it can lay no claim to greatness as compared with his sonnets and songs and letters. It did not possess the true spirit of spontaneous creativeness, but it played an important role in the revival of interest in classical letters. Petrarch's consuming passion for Roman antiquity is illustrated also in his *Lives of Illustrious Men*, a collection of thirty-one biographical accounts of persons famous in Roman history.

Petrarch was in the habit of addressing his thoughts to the great writers of classical antiquity such as Homer, Livy, Ovid, Cicero, Varro, Vergil, and Seneca. These *Familiar Letters*, which were greatly admired by Petrarch's friends, breathe the very spirit of the new devotion to pagan classics. The following letter addressed to Quintilian is typical:

I had formerly heard of thy name, and had read something of thine, wondering whence it was that thou hadst gained renown for keen insight. It is but recently that I have become acquainted with thy talents. Thy work entitled the *Institutes of Oratory* has come into my hands, but alas how mangled and mutilated! I recognized therein the hand of time—the destroyer of all things—and thought to myself, "O destroyer, as usual thou dost guard nothing with sufficient care except that which it were a gain to lose. O slothful and haughty Age, is it thus that thou dost hand down to us men of

[6] *The Sonnets, Triumphs, and Other Poems of Petrarch*, pp. 124, 126, 54–56.

genius, though thou dost bestow most tender care on the unworthy? O sterile-minded and wretched men of today, why do you devote yourselves to learning and writing so many things which it were better to leave unlearned, but neglect to preserve this work intact?"

However, this work caused me to estimate thee at thy true worth. As regards thee I had long been in error, and I rejoice that I have now been corrected. I saw the dismembered limbs of a beautiful body, and admiration mingled with grief seized me. Even at this moment, indeed, thy work may be resting intact in someone's library, and, what is worse, with one who perhaps has not the slightest idea of what a guest he is harboring unawares. Whosoever more furtunate than I will discover thee, may he be sure that he has gained a work of great value, one which, if he be at all wise, he will consider among his chief treasures.

In these books [whose number I am ignorant of, but which must doubtless have been many] thou hast had the daring to probe again a subject treated with consummate skill by Cicero himself when enriched by the experience of a lifetime. Thou hast accomplished the impossible. Thou didst follow in the footsteps of so great a man, and yet thou didst gain new glory, due not to the excellence of imitation but to the merits of the original doctrines propounded in thine own work. By Cicero, the orator was prepared for battle; by thee he is molded and fashioned, with the result that many things seem to have been either neglected or unheeded by Cicero. Thou gatherest all the details which escaped thy master's notice with such extreme care that [unless my judgment fail me] thou mayest be said to conquer him in diligence in just the degree that he conquers thee in eloquence. Cicero guides his orator through the laborious tasks of legal pleading to the topmost heights of oratory. He trains him for victory in the battles of the courtroom. Thou dost begin far earlier, and dost lead thy future orator through all the turns and pitfalls of the long journey from the cradle to the impregnable citadel of eloquence. The genius of Cicero is pleasing and delightful, and compels admiration. Nothing could be more useful to youthful aspirants. It enlightens those who are already far advanced, and points out to the strong the road to eminence. Thy painstaking earnestness is of assistance, especially to the weak, and, as though it were a most experienced nurse, offers to delicate youth the simpler intellectual nourishment.

But, lest the flattering remarks which I have been making cause thee to suspect my sincerity, permit me to say [in counterbalancing them] that thou shouldst have adopted a different style. Indeed the truth of what Cicero says in his *Rhetorica* is clearly apparent in thy case, namely, that it is of very little importance for the creator to discourse on the general, abstract theories of his profession, but that, on the contrary, it is of the very highest importance for him to speak from actual practice therein. I do not deny thee experience, the second of these two qualities, as Cicero did to Hermagoras, of whom he was treating. But I submit that thou didst possess the latter in only a moderate degree; the former, however, in such a remarkable degree that it seems now scarcely possible for the mind of man to add a single word. . . .

I have nothing more to say. I ardently desire to find thee entire; and if thou art anywhere in such condition, pray do not hide from me longer. Farewell.[7]

PETRARCH AS MAN OF FAME

Petrarch knew no Greek; his knowledge of that literature was gleaned from the Latin classics. Roman writers had borrowed profusely from the Greeks, and only through their eyes did he discern faintly the wonders of the vanished Hellenic world. He wanted to learn Greek and even began its study, but his tutor, Barlaam, a Calabrian who had learned some Greek in southern Italy where it was still spoken, was not able to help him. It is striking that, as yet, no Italian appeared to be versed in both Latin and Greek. So Petrarch gave up the attempt and to the end of his life contented himself with gazing at the pages of Homer which he could not read. He remained an Italian patriot; Rome to him was the basis of civilization. Thus the humanist movement launched by him was directed first of all toward the recovery of Latin culture.

Petrarch was the first man to illustrate the traits of the Renaissance. He attained high excellence in many things. He was fond of music and played the flute. His lyrical verse in the mother tongue has never been surpassed. He loved Latin antiquity as did no other man of his day. He was fond of nature and liked gardening. Everything of human interest, especially if it could be found in classical antiquity, attracted his sympathy. This temper of mind was an example of what Italians called *virtù*, a prime characteristic of the Renaissance. This word had none of the connotations of *virtue*. It implied great vigor combined with extraordinary ability crowned with striking success. His many-sided interests made him a truly universal man or *uomo universale*, a term in which is summed up the Italian fifteenth- and sixteenth-century conception of what a great man should be.

Petrarch's restless spirit led him to travel. To satisfy his consuming passion for scholarship, he set out on long journeys, beginning in 1329. On these peregrinations he met admirers and made numerous friends. In 1337 he visited Rome for the first time. His poetic soul was at the same time thrilled and cast into despair by the sight of the material ruins of a majestic past. His fame spread, and distinguished visitors in Avignon were

[7] *Petrarch's Letters to Classical Authors*, tr. by M. E. Cosenza, Chicago, 1910, pp. 84–89.

eager to make his acquaintance. He learned to know the Della Scala family which was then ruling Verona. Among his intimate friends was the influential Cardinal Giovanni Colonna who showed him many favors. In 1340 the senators of Rome asked Petrarch to come to the ancient city to receive a crown of laurel which they were eager to bestow upon him in recognition of his poetic achievements. The cardinal urged him to accept the invitation and to decline a similar one from the University of Paris. The ceremony was performed on the ancient Capitoline Hill in April, 1341, before a concourse of citizens who little understood the meaning of these proceedings. This public recognition of his merits pleased him greatly.

From this time Petrarch was a famous man. He passed from court to court; sovereigns delighted in his company and were eager to bid for his friendship. He visited the Correggio family in Parma, the Visconti in Milan, and the Emperor Charles IV in Prague. Petrarch became an itinerant scholar dependent on the favor of princes who were flattered by the praise he gave them and the luster he shed on their courts. This patronage of scholars was a characteristic feature of the Renaissance, but it sometimes led to servile flattery, even to blackmail as in the case of Pietro Aretino of Venice (d. 1556). Petrarch's last years were spent in a villa at Arquà in those Euganean hills which the poet Shelley has made famous.

Petrarch was one of the world's most interesting men. Much of what he did or sought to do was significant for the history of culture. A rebel against convention and outworn conceptions, he hated the practicality of medieval education which neglected the cultivation of the intellect through the study of classical letters. Disgusted with the Latin style of his day, he hated the study of Roman law because it was presented in practical and business-like Latin. Above all he loathed the medicine and astrology of the day because it was dominated by quackery and dead tradition. His lyrical soul abominated all these banal and unintellectual things. He sought a fuller artistic life, a loftier culture.

BOCCACCIO AS HUMANIST

Giovanni Boccaccio (1313–1375) was the most remarkable of Petrarch's friends, and the master's mantle fell upon him. He was the natural son of a Florentine merchant and a French woman and was probably born in Paris. His father early apprenticed him to a man of business in order to prepare him for a practical career. The youth was sent to Naples to serve in a branch of the Florentine banking house of the Bardi (1323),

but these activities disgusted him. For some years he had shown a preference for literature, especially poetry. Naples was a fitting environment
to stimulate the soul of a sensitive youth. At the court of its kings
flourished the poetic and chivalric ideals imported from France by the
house of Anjou. The house of the Bardi had many connections with the
court which led a gay and carefree life under languorous skies. One day
in March, 1330, Boccaccio saw in church a beautiful lady whom he
afterwards celebrated in his writings under the name of Fiammetta. She
is said to have been a natural daughter of King Robert of Naples. She
long rejected the importunate youth, but finally yielded to him in spite
of the fact that she was already married.

Encouraged by Fiammetta, Boccaccio wrote a number of romances
and poems, of which the *Filocolo* was his first. A youth's labor of love, it
told the story of the long thwarted love of Floris and Blanchefleur. The
second was the *Filostrato*, which recounted the agonizing experience of
two lovers, Troilus and Criseyde; and the third, *Teseide*, dealt with the
rivalry of Palamon and Arcite for the favor of a lady named Emilia. Each
of these is to be regarded as part of the poet's own experience with
Fiammetta. These tales were known to everyone who had any contact
with the literary life of the times. Boccaccio perfected himself in the art
of telling stories; in fact, the world knows no greater master of this type
of literature. His extraordinary skill with his native tongue made him the
founder of Italian prose. But Fiammetta at length turned from him, whereupon he left Naples in 1341 and went back to Florence. He sought solace
in poetry and the study of Vergil and Ovid.

Boccaccio's greatest work without doubt is the *Decameron*, a collection of one hundred tales arranged in groups of ten. Three young men
and seven young women had abandoned Florence at the time of the
Black Death (1348) and retired to a villa nearby. Ten tales were told
each day. The subject matter ot most of them was drawn from old
fabliaux and chivalric romances, but the spirit was different. No longer
were the old stories told with the seriousness of knightly epics which the
bourgeoisie felt were alien to their own experiences. Towns and industry
had made the feudality obsolete. Its tales were retold by townsmen, but
in their own way. Banter, mocking, and biting sarcasm became the
dominant note. None of the old ideals, chivalric, monkish, or priestly,
were spared. This note of irreverence was heightened by the lucid prose
in which Boccaccio couched these stories. One serious defect marked the
stories of the *Decameron*—an utter disregard for the ordinary demands
of morality. But in spite of this the *Decameron* by reason of its style alone

expresses one of the chief characteristics of the Renaissance—the creation of magnificent artistic form.

The story of Abraham told in the *Decameron* is a sardonic account of how a Jew became a Christian, a friend having importuned him to take this step. Abraham consented, but specified that he would first go to Rome to see the pope's manner of life. His friend regretted this decision, for he thought that the wickedness at the papal court was such that the Jew would be turned from Christianity. But on his return Abraham announced his desire to be baptized, because so evil was the Holy Father's life that he must needs be holy, for otherwise he would not be able to continue so wicked a life! Another story was about Ciappelletto who had lived in a very evil way. But when he came to die the Franciscan confessor marveled greatly at his holiness, for he feigned remorse for his deeds and confessed only the most harmless sins, omitting entirely his lascivious past. The story of his pious death spread among the people who venerated him as a saint!

Jaunty irreverence developed in the chaffering of the market place pervades these stories. Holy things were treated with a familiarity spiced by the author's libertinism. The stories turn on some clever fraud or trick. The sexual note is dominant. Husbands are deceived, wives are outwitted, nuns cleverly evade the restrictions of their rule, and monks often are immoral. It would be erroneous, however, to assume, as is done sometimes, that these stories described the society of the day. They probably have no more historical basis than the chivalric romances. Nor should one accept them as true pictures of moral conditions. This is especially true in the case of women, for they appear in quite another light when one remembers that the women of Florence stayed at home during dangerous plagues taking care of their families and perishing with them.

Boccaccio did not become acquainted with Petrarch until 1350. It proved an important event, for the humanist imparted to him some of his passion for classical culture. In 1360 Boccaccio befriended Pilato, a Calabrian Greek, from whom he tried to learn Greek, but Pilato's knowledge of the tongue and the literature was slight. Boccaccio, however, managed to get him appointed to a teaching post in the University of Florence. The West had to wait another generation for a qualified teacher of Greek, and Boccaccio and his contemporaries had to be content with the Latin classics. Between 1350 and 1360 he wrote *On the Genealogy of the Gods,* an encyclopedia of mythology. This was followed by *On Famous Women* and *On the Fortunes of Great Men,* biographical dictionaries which began with Adam and Eve but dealt mostly with Greek and Roman subjects. Another work, *On Names of Mountains, Woods, Lakes, Rivers, Swamps, and Seas*, was a manual of classical geography.

Besides writing these manuals which were useful to humanist admirers of the classics, Boccaccio was also a keen student of Tacitus and Livy. He discovered several rare classical works. On one occasion when he visited the library of Monte Cassino he was saddened to find its classical treasures being neglected. The story of how the monks sold the parchments to be made into amulets in total disregard of their contents apparently is false. It is probably here that Boccaccio found the copy of Tacitus' classic *Histories* and part of the *Annals*. Thus he followed in the steps of Petrarch, and, when master and pupil died, the study of classical culture was making rapid strides.

Chapter 13

THE CULT OF CLASSICAL LETTERS

FRANCESCO PETRARCH's perfervid zeal for classical literature fired his admirers, especially students, with enthusiasm. Thus was created the cult of Greek and Latin classical letters which was to become so striking a feature of the intellectual life of the closing Middle Ages and shaped school and college curricula down to our own day. This passionate devotion to Latin and Greek thought and letters is known as the *Revival of Learning*. Just what is the meaning of this expression? Many have assumed that there was literally a revival of learning. It has been taken for granted that there was no intellectual cultivation during the Middle Ages and that mental progress was initiated by Petrarch and his followers when they undertook the study of the Latin and Greek classics. Then mankind once more took up the work of civilization where the ancients had abandoned it.

CLASSICAL CULTURE IN MEDIEVAL TIMES

The ten centuries that passed between the decline of the classical world and the birth of humanism were not barren of noteworthy achievement. Barbarians—German, Celtic, Slav, and Finno-Ugrian—had been introduced to the declining culture of Greeks and Romans. They received from them the elements of civilization: the basic manorial life of the Middle Ages; the Latin language, medium of intellectual life; church, religion, theology, and elements of philosophic thought; fundamental artistic ideas, the work of the goldsmith, and manuscript decoration; the science of Ptolemy and medicine of Galen; and church organization which became a dominant factor in the life of medieval man. Rome in decay was better able to give the Barbarians her culture than in the heyday of her power. It was the new peoples who perpetuated the elements of Roman civilization.

But the Barbarians also created a great deal. The mighty economic changes of the eleventh, twelfth, and thirteenth centuries which gained some momentum in the age of the Renaissance owed little to the ancient world, of course, and nothing to the Revival of Learning. More towns sprang up in medieval Europe than ever existed in Greek or Roman days. Capitalist society was created in the Middle Ages. Upon this basis were founded new bureaucratic states, absolute, efficient, and orderly. Desire for the life beautiful also was satisfied in the Middle Ages. Gothic architecture and sculpture attained classic perfection. Illumination of manuscripts evolved into Gothic painting which reached its climax in the Flemish masters of the fifteenth century. A large number of universities came into existence. Scholastic philosophy reached its fullest perfection in Thomas Aquinas (d. 1274). The mother tongues were acknowledged and vernacular literature boasted many noble classics. Science also received attention and made remarkable progress. In short, the bases of much of modern civilization were laid in the Middle Ages long before any so-called Revival of Learning.

If the Revival of Learning was not the sole factor in the founding of our modern life, why was it important? Because it provided the studies which helped men in the last centuries of the Middle Ages to break with outworn traditions. Vast changes in social, economic, and political organization had rendered old conceptions obsolete. Wealth had created new and greater social responsibilities. Prevailing ideals of life, chivalric ideas of what constituted a gentleman, the unintellectual life of the nobility, the practicality of bourgeois life no longer fitted the requirements of the new Renaissance urban life. Secular, artistic, and intellectual conceptions were certain to rise. The pagan literature of classical antiquity helped men form a more secular outlook on life.

It was inevitable that townsmen of the Renaissance should feel at home with the ancients. Throughout the Middle Ages men had never wholly lost touch with the Roman world. Latin language and literature at no time were completely neglected. A fervid zeal was shown in appropriating the doctrines of Plato and Aristotle which had been neglected during the simple manorial times after the dissolution of the Roman Empire. When economic and social life progressed so far that old legal customs were outworn, men of the Middle Ages looked back to the ancients for guidance. Thus already in medieval times was born the revival of Roman law which provided a ready set of rules whereby to guide new states and urban society. And in the Renaissance men again looked to the ancients and found inspiration in their culture.

PETRARCH'S HUMANISM STRIKES ROOT

Arduous tasks confronted the disciples of Petrarch, for they possessed none of the facilities which smooth the path of modern students of the classics. Teubner of Leipzig and the Oxford University Press had not yet begun their work. The Loeb Classical Library in which texts are accompanied by parallel translations was not to be projected for five centuries. None of the texts had been carefully studied from a philological point of view and compared with extant manuscripts. Nor were the lines of these writings numbered to facilitate scientific discussion. There were no grammars, manuals, or dictionaries. Manuscripts were widely scattered so that few students could hope to read all the ancient authors. And for a long time few could read Greek. Monastic and cathedral libraries contained some of the classics, but few people paid attention to them. Greek masterpieces were supposed to be plentiful in Constantinople. Greek learning of the eleventh and twelfth centuries was given a disastrous blow in the sack of Constantinople in 1204, and such ancient literature as had survived was threatened with complete loss because of the poverty and decline of Byzantine life. Pressed by the Turk without and weakened by Venetian and Genoese economic competition within, the people had little possibility of continuing the study of ancient lore. Greek classics were in danger of disappearing forever.

Petrarch's influence was strongly felt in Padua and Verona, cities situated in lands governed by the Carrara family, for Francesco I (ruled 1355–1388) was a warm admirer of the great humanist and entertained him at his court. Arquà where Petrarch spent his last days was not far distant, and from this retreat his influence was felt far and wide. Universities and other institutions of learning usually were hostile to the new humanist conceptions, and a whole century had to pass before they obtained a hearing. The University of Padua was an interesting exception, for the Carrara family of despots through their interest in Petrarch's ideas exerted a beneficial influence on its curricula.

In 1392 Giovanni Conversini (1347–1406), a native of Ravenna, was appointed to teach rhetoric at Padua. He was a devoted follower of Petrarch and possessed unbounded zeal for the study of Cicero's writings. Although he taught only one year, his influence in behalf of the new conceptions continued after he became chancellor of the university. His pupils included most of the great humanists of the early part of the fifteenth century. Among them were men like Poggio Bracciolini, Francesco Filelfo, Vittorino da Feltre, Guarino da Verona, and Palla Strozzi.

Gasparino da Barzizza (d. 1431) began to teach in 1397 and won renown as a master of rhetoric. He passionately admired Cicero and instilled in his students profound respect for this master.

It was in Florence, however, that the ancient classics were cultivated with the greatest zeal. Here lived Coluccio Salutati (1331–1406), a great admirer of Petrarch and Boccaccio with whom he corresponded actively. He became Latin secretary to the government of Florence, eagerly searched for Latin manuscripts, and in 1389 discovered Cicero's *Ad Familiares* in Vercelli. Being the center of a humanist coterie, he exerted wide influence. Although his tumid prose was filled with useless erudition, it was stylistically superior to much of the Latinity of the Middle Ages. His manner of writing was keenly admired and led to the composing of state documents, orations, and addresses in an ornate style which became characteristic of the Renaissance. Luigi Marsigli (d. 1394), an Augustinian friar in the church of San Spirito, gathered together a group of men interested in humanist studies. He was a friend of Petrarch, from whom he had received his humanist zeal. Many Florentines became devotees of the classics while listening to Marsigli's discourses.

But the supreme task of humanism—the recovery of classical Greek language and literature from which Latin culture had sprung—remained unfinished. Petrarch had tried to learn Greek, but failed. Boccaccio was more successful. No one in Italy, it appears, really knew the language. Humanists in Padua contented themselves with the study of Cicero and his style. The appearance of Manuel Chrysoloras (1350?–1415) in Florence was an event of the greatest importance in the Revival of Learning.

This Byzantine Greek boasted a long line of ancestors extending back to the time when Constantine settled on the Bosporus. Chrysoloras was sent by the emperor of Constantinople to secure from the Latin West help against the Turks. He arrived in Venice in 1393 and at once found favor among the humanists. Three years later Palla Strozzi and Niccolò Niccoli, prominent Florentines deeply interested in the classics, authorized Salutati to invite Chrysoloras to come to Florence as teacher of the Greek classics, and for 4 years the youth and mature men of Florence enjoyed his tuition. To them Chrysoloras was a sort of apostle of that distant and glorious world which through the Middle Ages had shone with romantic splendor. His knowledge was superior to that of every humanist in the West. He fired his auditors with zeal to make themselves masters of the new learning.

SHINING EXAMPLES OF EARLY HUMANISTS

Leonardo Bruni (1370–1444) was typical of Chrysoloras' pupils. He had been inspired by Salutati to perfect his Latinity and knowledge of Latin classics. He threw himself enthusiastically into the study of Greek.

> At that time I was studying the civil law and had gained some proficiency in other subjects. Naturally I burned with love for learning and studied logic and rhetoric. When Chrysoloras came to Florence I found myself in a quandary because I did not like to give up the study of law, nor did I think that so fair an opportunity of studying Greek letters should be neglected. Young as I was I was wearied by the question: 'Will you know when it is possible to become acquainted with Homer, Plato, and Demosthenes and other poets, philosophers, and orators about whom many wonderful things are said, master their thoughts in their own tongue or give them up and keep yourself aloof? Will you allow this heaven-sent opportunity to escape? Seven hundred years have passed since anyone in Italy paid any attention to Greek letters; and yet we admit that all knowledge sprang from them. How useful in your studies would be the mastery of this tongue, what opportunities to become famous would it offer and what a source of satisfaction would it give you! There are doctors of civil law in plenty and everywhere. You possess a *flair* for study. Here now is but one doctor of Greek letters; he is in Florence, when he leaves no one will be able to teach you.' Persuaded by this reasoning I devoted myself to Chrysoloras' instruction with such glowing zeal that whatever I learned from him at day occupied my mind at night.[1]

Bruni became an influential man in the Revival of Learning. Such was his mastery of Greek that his translations of Plato and Aristotle were hailed as important achievements. They marked a milestone in the history of classical philology. Throughout the Middle Ages translations had been made into faulty Latin by men who did not possess an adequate knowledge of Greek. Many Greek works were translated from the Arabic into which they had been translated from the original. Bruni's critical attitude greatly influenced classical scholars of the time. He also wrote a *History of Florence* in which he abandoned the methods of medieval chroniclers and sought to write an account of his native city in ordered exposition after the manner of such ancient historians as Livy.

Niccolò Niccoli (1363–1437) was a friend of Salutati. With him he frequented the meetings of the Augustinian friar Luigi Marsigli, an enthusiastic humanist. Niccolò was brought up as a merchant but, like

---

[1] Adapted from *Rerum suo Tempore Gestarum Commentarius*, in *Muratori Rerum Italicarum Scriptores*, XIX, 920.

Boccaccio, showed little zeal in business. He preferred the study of the classics and labored earnestly to promote the Revival of Learning.

> He collected a fine library, not regarding the cost, and was always search-
> ing for rare books. He bought all these with the wealth which his father had
> left, putting aside only what was necessary for his maintenance. He sold sev-
> eral of his farms and spent the proceeds on his library. . . . He held his
> books rather for the use of others than of himself. . . . If he heard of stu-
> dents going to Greece or elsewhere he would give them the names of books
> which they lacked in Florence. . . . When it happened that he could only
> get the copy of a book he would copy it himself. . . . He procured at his
> own expense the works of Tertullian and other writers which were not in
> Italy. He also found an imperfect copy of Ammianus Marcellinus and wrote
> it out with his own hand. The *On the Orator* and the *Brutus* of Cicero were
> sent to him from Lombardy. . . . The book was found in a chest in a very
> old church; this chest had not been opened for a long time, and they found
> the book . . . while searching for evidence concerning certain ancient rights.
> The *On the Orator* was found broken up, and it is through the care of Nic-
> colò that we find it perfect today. He also rediscovered many sacred works
> and several of Cicero's orations. . . . A complete copy of Pliny did not
> exist in Florence, but when Niccolò heard that there was one in Lubeck, he
> secured it . . . and thus Pliny came to Florence.

Niccolò welcomed eager students to his house and opened to them the many literary treasures upon which he had expended his time and fortune.

> [He] always encouraged promising students to follow a literary life, and
> he nobly aided all those who showed merit in providing them with teachers
> and books, for in his time teachers and books were not as numerous as they
> are today [*i.e.*, about 1390]. It may be said that he was the reviver of Greek
> and Latin letters in Florence; they had for a long time lain buried, and al-
> though Petrarch and Boccaccio had done some things to rehabilitate them,
> they had not reached that height which they attained through Niccolo's culti-
> vation of them for divers reasons. First, because he urged many in his time
> to take to letters, and through his persuasion, many scholars came to Florence
> for study and teaching. . . . After having done so many good deeds, and
> gathered together a vast number of books on all the liberal arts in Greek
> and Latin, he desired that these should be made accessible to everyone. He
> directed that, after his death, they should continue to be at the service of all,
> so in his will he designated forty citizens to see that his books in question
> should be made a public library in order that all might use them. There were
> eight hundred volumes of Greek and Latin.

Most Florentines of wealth and position took part in the Revival of Learning and liberally employed their fortunes in its behalf. Especially interesting was Palla Strozzi (d. 1462), who gave great sums for the university at Florence and paid Chrysoloras to come there to teach.

> He never wasted time by loitering, but returned home after business and spent his time in studying Greek and Latin. Being greatly devoted to letters, he bought a fine collection of books which he housed in a handsome building in Santa Trinita for the use of the public. He wished to furnish it with books on all subjects, but this project came to nothing on account of the misfortunes which befell him. . . . Palla, in his study in Padua, found a tranquil port after many years of shipwreck. He engaged at a liberal salary John Argyropoulos [1416–86] to read Greek with him, and another Greek scholar as well. With Argyropoulos he read Aristotle's *Natural History*, and the other Greek read certain other works he selected. He wasted no time, but undertook the translation of Chrysostom from Greek into Latin.[2]

One of the most remarkable of the early humanists was Poggio Bracciolini (1380–1459). He studied under Chrysoloras and enjoyed the friendship of Niccolò Niccoli. He entered the papal service and appeared at the Council of Constance in the following of John XXIII. After that pontiff's deposition he was free to do as he wished and began to satisfy his desire to collect manuscripts. His success is one of the romantic tales in the story of the Revival of Learning. In the summer of 1415 he visited the monastery of Cluny and was rewarded by finding a number of Cicero's orations. A year later he directed his steps to the famous foundation of St. Gall whose monks cared little for their classical treasures. His most important discovery was Quintilian's *Institutes of Oratory*. Part of this work had for some time been known to humanists, but a complete copy had not yet been found. Its discovery was a capital event in the age of the Renaissance. So eager was Poggio to possess the complete text that he copied it in 32 days.

Poggio renewed his searches in 1417, visiting the abbeys of St. Gall, Einsiedeln, and Reichenau. These expeditions were especially fruitful, for he found the works of the poet Lucretius and a copy of the historian Ammianus Marcellinus. He also secured eight of Cicero's orations at Langres and other places in France and Germany. For years Poggio persisted in his hunt for ancient authors, and probably had something to do with the discovery of Tacitus' shorter works, *Agricola, Germania,* and the *Dialogues.* He found the text of Vitruvius, the letters of Pliny the Younger, and nine new comedies by Plautus. The total number of manuscripts collected is amazing, but only a few of the most important can be

---

[2] Adapted from *The Vespasiano Memoirs,* London, 1926, pp. 396–397, 400–401, 237–243.

mentioned here. As papal secretary, Poggio introduced a refined Latinity such as the chancery had never seen. Cicero's stately prose served as model for his writings.

Attention was soon directed to Constantinople where examples of Greek masterpieces were said to exist. A few had arrived in Italy, and a desire to find others now sprang up. Guarini da Verona (1370–1460) followed Chrysoloras to Constantinople and stayed there from 1403 to 1408. On his return he carried with him fifty-four manuscripts, many of which were Greek. He was very proficient in Greek and was offered a number of posts. In Venice he found 124 letters by Pliny the Younger, a welcome addition to those found by Poggio.

But it was Giovanni Aurispa (1374–1450) who was to do for Greek letters what Poggio accomplished for Latin letters. He visited Chios in 1413 and on his return to Italy carried with him some of the works of Sophocles, Euripides, and Thucydides. In 1421 he went to Constantinople and in 1423 returned with an astounding collection of 238 codices, almost all of which contained Greek classics. Another choice collection of about forty codices was made by Francesco Filelfo (1398–1481) who spent several years as secretary to the Venetian legation at Constantinople.

Thus most of the Greek classics which had survived the sack of Constantinople in 1204 were saved for posterity. It is certain that not much was lost in the catastrophe of 1453, for the Turks soon learned that manuscripts were worth money in the Italian market. A number of scholars, among them John Argyropoulos, John and Constantine Lascaris, and Demetrius Chalcondyles, came to Italy after 1453, but by this time the impulse to study Greek classics had already reached its zenith. The story so often told in textbooks of how frightened Greeks fled from Constantinople with coffers packed with manuscripts and first disclosed to wondering Italians the glories of Hellenic culture is not correct. It was the desire of the Latin West to explore the sources of its civilization that caused some of its scholars to go to Byzantium in quest of Greek learning.

The Council of Ferrara and Florence (1438–1439) advanced the revival of classical studies. It brought 500 Greeks to Italy, and Italian scholars were privileged to listen to their mellifluous Attic Greek. Humanists of Florence heard with wonder the discourses in Plato's philosophy given by the Greek scholar Gemistos Plethon (d. 1450), who gave a new direction to classical study. Henceforth the cult of Plato became the passion of Renaissance society. Plethon's philosophic teaching was largely a re-organization of medieval doctrines filled with Neoplatonic teaching. Nevertheless, it was done in a new spirit, contained something fresh and poetic, and revealed extensive knowledge about ancient Greek life. This stirred the Florentines who had been fed the traditional pabulum of late medieval philosophers, and they turned eagerly from arid scholastic syllogisms to Platonic mysticism. With Plethon came his disciple Bessarion (d. 1472), a fiery defender of Plato's reputation who went over to the Latin Church. Pope Eugenius IV made him a cardinal in 1439, in which capacity he was able to exert wide influence in Church and secular society.

HUMANISTS TURN TO ARCHAEOLOGY

An important evidence of the humanist interest in the classical past was the love for archaeological study. The search for manuscripts soon was extended to include the material remains of antiquity. Niccolò Niccoli collected bronzes, sculptures, coins, and antique figures in bronze and marble. Ciriaco of Ancona (d. 1451), a merchant, traveled widely in the interests of his business and took pains to find relics of ancient days wherever he went. He enjoyed little formal instruction and owed his success in studies to his own initiative. Stirred by what he saw in Rome, he decided that inscriptions were better sources of information than literary works and made transcripts which filled three large volumes. Although he was uncritical toward antique objects, his work was important, for it was in a very true sense the beginning of the study of archaeology.

Flavio Biondo (1392–1463) was a humanist who wrote a number of important books of an archaeological nature. *Roma Instaurata* was a description of the Eternal City, in which Biondo combined inscriptions, monuments, historical anecdotes, and topography in order to give a living and real picture of the ancient city. *Italy Illustrated* did the same for Italy. *Rome Triumphant* described the life and political institutions of the great city. Biondo's histories were written with a humanist's love for the classical Greek and Roman tradition. Other men showed similar interests. Thus Poggio Bracciolini wrote his *Description of the City of Rome*. He was the first to rely upon data given by classical authors in elucidating inscriptions. He became well acquainted with ancient classical coins, in which study he found the works of Pliny the Younger useful.

This cult of classical letters had its limitations. Study of ancient culture became so mighty a vogue that writers cast their thoughts into sonorous sentences like those of Cicero. It was part of the Italian passion for magnificent and significant form. Ciceronianism, however, became something of a vice. Prose of this type was too academic, often devoid of life. A simple style such as that of chroniclers of the Villani family possessed more life than many a humanist production. Such medieval poems as the *Song of Roland*, the *Reynard the Fox*, and the *Divine Comedy* were superior to the often jejune and stylistically perfect Latinity of fifteenth-century writers. Passion for the life beautiful became dominated by classical literary forms. Imitation, not original creation, all too often characterized the literary efforts of the so-called Revival of Learning.

PART VII

Quattrocento Renaissance Culture Under Florentine Leadership

Chapter 14

THE ADVENT OF *QUATTROCENTO* RENAISSANCE ART

*F*EW THEMES in the history of the Renaissance are so instructive as the rise of the new art which flourished in Italian towns, and especially in Florence, during the *Quattrocento*. The triumphs in Romanesque and Gothic art had been associated with northern Europe as much as with Italy. Everywhere churches as well as civic buildings and private homes had been erected in the Gothic manner. But during the *Quattrocento* leadership in these arts, including painting, passed to the wealthy and populous cities of Italy. It can cause no surprise, therefore, that Italians now created novel artistic forms pleasing to the new social groups in the cities of Italy. They tended to abandon the methods dominant in Byzantine, Romanesque, and Gothic schools. Before studying the art of the new masters, let us first note a type of pictorial art especially popular during the *Trecento*.

DIDACTIC AND PANORAMIC ART OF THE *TRECENTO*

Duccio, of Siena, at the time of his death in 1319, definitely had founded a new school of painting. His combination of gold backgrounds, jewel-like colors, and warm faith won for him great admiration. Among his followers was the Sienese Simone Martini (1285–1344) who combined with Duccio's ideas and methods some grasp of Giotto's realism. Martini's justly famous *Annunciation* may be regarded as his greatest work. In it the angel Gabriel has descended most gently, and Mary, surprised, draws back in humility on hearing in the angelic salutation the stupendous news of the Messiah's coming birth. Jewel-like beauty and devout simplicity characterize this and other masterpieces of the Sienese school. The artistic achievement of Duccio and Martini marked the highest development of painting in Siena.

Very different was the school of painting Giotto left upon his death in 1336 (see Chap. 11). A large number of admiring artists were dazzled by his originality. Would these pupils continue in the master's steps and improve upon his art? Throughout the rest of the *Trecento* no artist, it appears, was able to develop the germinal principles we have noted in Giotto's works. The artists who now appeared sought to imitate the particular achievements of Giotto without asking, it appears, how they might develop the master's ideas scientifically. In general, traditionalism developed in painting, and little change was made before the advent of the Florentine Masaccio (1401-1428).

But a number of remarkable paintings were nevertheless produced during the middle of the *Trecento*. One of these is Andrea Bonaiuti's fresco *Dominican Allegory of Church, State, and Society*, to be seen in the Dominican Church of Santa Maria Novella in Florence. This fresco is an excellent example of the didactic, episodic, and panoramic works of art which taught all who beheld them man's relations with his Creator, the Church, the state, and society.

At the top of Bonaiuti's fresco Christ is shown seated with the Virgin at His right. She is offering her petitions in behalf of praying mankind. Before Him stands an altar and on it lies a slain lamb, proclaiming His sacrifice in behalf of sinful mankind. Before the altar stand the symbols of the four Gospels which tell the story of divine redemption. Below is a conventional "Garden of Delights." The people in it are having a happy time; they are satisfied with life's superficial pleasures. But some are moved to confess and are received at the portals of heaven by St. Peter who holds two keys. Behind him are the saints, recognizable because they carry the instruments of their martyrdom. Below is a church, the background for the acts of a group of rulers, ecclesiastical and secular, and a number of pilgrims and monks. In the lower right corner stand St. Dominic teaching the people and St. Thomas Aquinas refuting the errors of pagans and heretics. Dogs spotted black and white run about fighting evil spirits in the form of wolves. These dogs so spotted are Dominican dogs (a pun on the word *Dominicani*) protecting the faithful from the wiles of heretics.

Another example of the didactic and panoramic art of that time is to be found in the Campo Sancto at Pisa. Its sermonic theme is the *Triumph of Death*, the work of an unknown artist. A splendidly arrayed hunting party of men and women has moved into the wilderness. Abruptly the leaders halt on seeing three coffins containing three bodies in various degrees of decomposition. Sad moment for a party bent on pleasure! A desert monk nearby calls their attention to the fact that death is inexorable, no respecter of persons! In the middle of the picture is a group of the world's lame, halt, and blind. The Grim Reaper is flying low, scythe in hand and poised to slay. They ask to be freed from their miseries, saying, "Since happiness has left us, may death, cure of all grief, give us our last meal!" But the Reaper takes no notice of them. He is more interested in the "Garden of Delights" where men and women are indifferent to the fate that awaits them. In the background are good and evil spirits flying about struggling to take souls to Paradise or to holes filled with fire, in the background. In the center of the fresco is a scroll held by two angels. On it are the words: "Knowledge and wealth, birth and valor—all these are powerless against the Reaper's strokes." This, as we have seen, was a characteristic theme of late medieval sermonic literature.

It has been asserted that this kind of art lacks taste and skill, is tiresome, and is not worth serious study. This is a mistake, for to the people living during the *Trecento* these pictures spoke eloquently of man's ethical, religious, philosophical, political, and economic activities. This fact is demonstrated by Ambrogio Lorenzetti (d. 1348) who created a series of frescoes on the walls of the Palazzo Pubblico in Siena. They deal with the nature and function of government. Unfortunately, they have suffered at the hand of time and in places cannot readily be deciphered. The one on *Good Government*, however, is practically intact. It consists of a number of figures arranged according to current philosophical (scholastic) ideas and not merely according to esthetic concepts. It should be pointed out that this panoramic type of art found favor even in the High Renaissance when Raphael produced his magnificent *Disputa* showing the reverence all men have for the Sacrament, and the *School of Athens*, a pictorial history of the philosophies of man.

> Justice, with Wisdom overhead and carrying two suspended scales, one at each side of her, is shown seated at the left end of the composition. Her hands rest on the scales, steadying them. One angel stands in each of the scales administering justice, the one at the left dispenses commutative jus-

tice in settling a suit between two persons; the one at the right of Justice administers distributive justice [justice between society and persons] is executing a person and crowning another.

Two cords descending from each of the angels in the scales are united by Concordia, seated below Justice, who passes them between a double line of men standing before the dais [the twenty-four representing the government of Siena] who, grasping the cord, help it on its way to the stately and bearded sovereign seated on an elevated portion of the dais. He receives the cord attached to the scepter in his right hand. In his left hand he holds a shield on which is blazoned the symbol of Siena. At his feet lie a wolf with two children, emblematic of Siena.

At this point the allegory becomes more complex, as it must account for the motives and acts of government. Above the Ruler hovers Charity bearing an effigy of the face of Christ. Faith bearing a cross and Hope in attitude of adoration gaze prayerfully upon it. Five temporal virtues, serving as councillors, are seated on the dais beside the Ruler. At the Ruler's right sits aged and serious Prudence, pondering on things past, present, and future. At her right is Fortitude holding a shield and a mace and wearing a thorny crown, for her part in human affairs is difficult. At the Ruler's left are three seated figures—Magnanimity, the first, paying the worker and crowning the hero. Temperance is next and watches her hourglass. And, finally, Justice appears again holding a sword in her right hand, a crown in her left. On her tray rests the head of an executed man. And, finally, on the same dais, on Fortitude's right sits Peace, a noble figure bearing an olive branch and her feet resting on a shield and helmet. Before the Virtues on the dais are mounted and standing guards watching over some prisoners.[1]

RENAISSANCE SCULPTURE FROM JACOPO DELLA QUERCIA TO LORENZO GHIBERTI (d. 1455)

To what extent did the Renaissance cult of classical antiquity fathered by Petrarch contribute to the development of the new sculpture? It has often been assumed that the "rediscovery of antiquity" was the chief factor in the creation of the new art. Some have gone so far as to suppose that there was no sculpture worthy of the name during the Middle Ages. Such views are erroneous. The works of Claus Sluter and Claus de Werve at Dijon, for example, reveal mastery of the chisel in the service of the religious ideas of the fourteenth century. It is therefore not true that sculpture was reborn in Florence. It received a new bias. Although this new secularism was not due immediately to Greek or Roman ideas, it certainly was assisted by the secular and pagan motifs which artists found

[1] Adapted from W. M Conway, *Early Tuscan Art*, London, 1902, pp. 160–163.

on antique gems and statuary and in decoration. This process meant that sculptors studied the human form more closely and discarded such conventions of Gothic sculpture as heavy draperies, angular figures, scrolls with legends, and the frequently mournful expression of man about to hear the trumpet call of judgment.

The Pisan school of sculpture (dating from about 1300), which we noticed above, exerted much influence among Italian artists of the fourteenth century. So, for example, Arnolfo del Cambio (d. 1302), a pupil of Niccola Pisano, carried the art to Florence where he was the architect of Santa Maria del Fiore. Andrea da Pontedera (d. 1349) produced the south bronze doors of the baptistry in Florence. The twenty-eight bronze panels of the door tell the story of St. John the Baptist's life in a harmoniously lyrical and realistic manner. Andrea Orcagna (d. 1368) was a representative of this school. His fame rests mainly on the sculptured work of the tabernacle in the Florentine church of Or San Michele.

At the threshold of the *Quattrocento* appeared an artistic luminary of great magnitude, the most noteworthy sculptor that Siena was to produce. Jacopo della Quercia (1374–1438) was an independent genius who not only absorbed the realism which had become traditional since the rise of the Pisan school of sculpture but also studied classical models. He had a passion for portraying mass and form which gave to his art striking full-ness and vigor. His masterpiece, the *Fonte Gaia*, or *Merry Fountain*, of Siena, is famous because of his treatment of the *Virgin of the Seven Virtues*. Especially remarkable are Jacopo's marble reliefs at the principal door of the church of San Petronio in Bologna. His manner here is highly personal. The relief representing the *Expulsion of Adam and Eve from Paradise* is dramatically rendered. So eager was the sculptor in this and other works to portray mass effectively that he exaggerated the sinewy figures and their dramatic action. His interest in the classical ideal is shown in the tomb of Ilaria del Carretto in the cathedral of Lucca. The sides bear in high relief figures of angels supporting a heavy wreath of fruit and leaves. The figures look like cupids; the entire design seems to have been inspired by some ancient sarcophagus. On the top rests the stately figure of Ilaria wrapped in flowing garments. Her face is serenely beautiful, her hair falls in gracious locks over her temples. This work is a triumph of realism chastened by the ideal beauty of classical sculpture.

The next step forward was taken in Florence by Lorenzo Ghiberti (1378–1455). In a competition in 1401 for models of the north doors of the baptistry in Florence, he was pronounced winner and given the contract. His early training as a goldsmith caused him to treat his panels as delicate pictures. The finished doors have twenty-eight scenes from the life of Christ, the disciples, and the four great Church fathers, each of which is placed in a geometrical frame. Like the doors by Andrea da Pontedera on the opposite side of the building, they are executed with strenuous realism. Each scene is limited to a few figures.

But Ghiberti's fame rests on the marvelous east doors facing the cathedral church of Santa Maria del Fiore. Each door has five scenes. The larger size enabled the sculptor to introduce more detail and to treat his subject according to the laws of perspective which engrossed his attention. He created the illusion of depth. The figures are reproduced with great fidelity to nature and with a delicacy and elegance which have pleased every generation since. Ghiberti gave them an idealized form which may be due to study of classical statuary. A good example of the artist's work is the torso of Isaac who is kneeling on the pile of wood waiting for the thrust of his father's knife. A fitting dramatic vigor characterizes the panels. The doors were finished in 1452, and artists of the time acclaimed them. Michelangelo, it is said, declared that they were worthy to be placed on the gates of Paradise.

DONATELLO AND HIS FOLLOWERS: TRIUMPH OF RENAISSANCE SCULPTURE

Donatello (1383–1466) was the greatest Florentine sculptor of the *Quattrocento*. He freed his art from Gothic mannerism, gave his figures an unconventional naturalness, and applied some of the ideas learned from antique statuary. According to Vasari, Donatello went to Rome with his friend, the architect Filippo Brunelleschi (1377–1446), when they were disappointed in not getting the contract for the doors of the baptistry.

[Filippo] . . . first sold a small farm which he possessed at Settignano when both artists departed from Florence and proceeded to Rome where, when Filippo beheld the magnificence of the buildings and the perfection of the churches, he stood like one amazed and seemed to have lost his wits. They instantly made preparations for measuring the cornices and taking the ground-plans of these edifices, Donatello and himself both laboring continually and sparing neither time nor cost. No place was left unvisited by them, either in Rome or without the city, and in the Campagna; nor did they fail to take the dimensions of anything good within their reach.[2]

How much influence this archaeological study had upon Donatello is difficult to tell. His first works reveal a firm sense of realism, but of the

[2] G. Vasari, *Lives of the Most Eminent Painters, Sculptors, and Architects* (Bohn Library), I, 422.

Gothic rather than the classical. Among them are the statues in the niches of the campanile of Florence. *Job* and *Jeremiah* are famous for their rugged naturalism and perfection of anatomy. The statue of *St. George* in a niche in the church of Or San Michele at Florence is justly noted for its fine facial expression, for the stone features seem animated with thought. The body is correct but does not match the graciousness of the face. Donatello again visited Rome in 1432 and 1433 and on his return to Florence was employed to make the medallions which one may see today in the courtyard of the Medici Palace. He modeled them after ancient gems.

At this time Donatello also made his bronze figure of *David*, the first image of the *Quattrocento* to be cast in bronze. This statue is famous not only for its modeling and evident classical inspiration but also because it was made to stand in the open and not in a niche as was traditional with Gothic sculpture. Thus sculpture was emancipating itself from the domination of architecture. The form of the hero is that of a slender youth. Every part of the body is vibrant with energy as the youthful face contemplates the severed head of the giant Goliath. The body might pass for that of an Olympian god; in spite of the idealization of form which Donatello owed to antique models, there are unmistakable touches of Gothic naturalism. Another work, likewise placed in this courtyard, was the bronze *Judith Killing Holofernes*. Donatello made the eight medallions which may be seen above the columns in this courtyard. They were copied after antique gems in Cosimo's collection. His *Singing Choir*, made for the cathedral of Florence, is especially worthy of study, for the group of singing and dancing youths is of unsurpassed beauty. Classical influences are to be seen in the decoration. The sculptor possessed complete knowledge of the human form, disposed of drapery in an effective manner, and, what is more important, gave to the group unity, appropriate action, and facial expression.

Donatello's maturity was spent in Padua (1443–1453). His most important work of this period is the bronze equestrian statue *Gattamelata*, the first of its kind since antiquity. The idea of making such a statue seems to have been inspired by the four horses on the façade of St. Mark's in Venice. The horse seems to stride like a mighty animal. On it sits the *condottiere Gattamelata*, accoutered as a Roman general, stately in figure, and sure of his power to command. In this work Donatello obtained complete harmony of form, action, and thought, a unity toward which the masters of the *Quattrocento* were striving. None attained it more completely than did Donatello. Emotionally his work owes something to older Gothic influences as illustrated by the Pisan school. At the same time it is chastened by the simplicity and accuracy of form which he noticed in classical models.

The portrait bust *Niccolò da Uzzano,* exemplifies Donatello's novel skill in expressing human thought in sculpture. Niccolò, prominent in the public life of Florence, was a calm and dignified man. Donatello presents him in a fleeting moment of thought. Something above him, to the left, attracted his attention. In a rapid, oblique movement he raised his left shoulder, turned his face to his left, and raised his eyes to see what had attracted his attention. Donatello's vigorous plastic power appealed to the new artistic age of the *Quattrocento.* The men and women of his day saw that he owed his triumphs to his genius alone. Donatello's inspiration was to lay the foundations of *Quattrocento* art.

During this time the Della Robbia family also became prominent as leaders in the art of sculpture. Luca della Robbia (1400–1482), a younger contemporary of Donatello, did not possess the mighty energy of this great master. He is nevertheless famous for the singers' loft made for the cathedral and placed opposite Donatello's. The eight panels representing singing and dancing boys and girls are of matchless beauty. Although the action is less vigorous and the expression less forceful than in the figures by Donatello, the singers are extraordinarily appealing. In fact, no other sculptor succeeded in rendering children as well as these two masters. Luca also worked in terra cotta to which he gave a delightful glaze of white and blue. These works usually represent the Virgin and the Christ Child with angels. Andrea della Robbia (d. 1525), Luca's nephew, produced many works, especially in terra cotta. Della Robbia artistic work bore a distinctly popular note. Thus Giovanni, son of Andrea, produced the famous frieze on the hospital porch of the Ceppo in Pistoia. It is about 4 feet high and extends along the entire front of the porch. On it Giovanni portrayed the *Seven Corporal Works of Mercy.* This great work illustrates the popular social aspects of della Robbia art.

Like Donatello, Andrea del Verrocchio (1435–1488) owed much to the workshops of Ghiberti. He became a complete master of anatomy and possessed superior skill in imparting to his creations appropriate thought and action; he sought also to combine this action with grace and delicacy. He thus carried to greater perfection the ideas advanced by Donatello. Verrocchio's *David* has many of the characteristics of Donatello's *David.* Its youthful body is as perfectly modeled, and the lithe frame is filled with vigorous energy. The sculptor succeeded in giving to the face a thoughtful expression which characterizes all his works. The smile, the expression of the lips, and the bearing of the boy's head represent a momentary thought which the beholder expects to change in a second. These qualities are also found in his equestrian statue of *Colleone* at Venice. This monument is even more successful than the great work of Donatello at Padua. The play of muscle, the posture of the legs, and the whole bearing of the forward marching steed express keen nervous energy. *Colleone* wears the armor of the day. His facial expression is an interesting study. In it is concentrated the thought which dominates the entire work and gives it unity. Verrocchio's great desire to combine excellence of anatomy and action with beauty made him a significant artist in the third quarter of the *Quattrocento,* and he became the inspiration of Leonardo da Vinci's youthful efforts.

Antonio Pollaiuolo (1429–1498) who, as painter as well as sculptor carried forward the ideas of Donatello, aimed to give accurate muscular expression to thought. Trained as a goldsmith and accustomed to working with small quantities of costly metal, he developed extraordinary accuracy. He was very successful in anatomical details, especially hands and feet and the play of muscle. He liked to portray energetic themes because it gave him opportunity to study facial expression and the play of sinews. His *Martyrdom of St. Sebastian* admirably illustrates his manner. The saint is fastened to a tree at some distance above the ground, and six archers are shooting arrows into him. They are placed in varying positions and poses which gave the artist a chance to display his powers. He created a small bronze statue of the struggle between *Hercules and Antaeus,* classical mythology being so popular at that moment that sculptors found it profitable to borrow themes from it. This sculptor successfully rendered this difficult theme in a manner impossible a generation before. The clasp of Hercules, the backward sway of his powerful body, and the frantic efforts of Antaeus to force himself out of the giant's grasp are all correctly represented. The student should compare the muscular expression of this group with the greater placidity of Donatello's figures.

Pollaiuolo's greatest works are the tombs of Sixtus IV and Innocent VIII in St. Peter's in Rome, the first being the more famous. The pontiff's figure, surrounded by the Seven Virtues which reveal careful study of ancient statuary, expresses resignation in death, and his face is a masterpiece of anatomical realism. His vestments are arranged in complicated folds and conform to the curves of his body. The design in the cloth is faithfully noted. Innocent's seated figure set an example which was to be followed very often by future sculptors. Even in death the exuberance of life seemed real. These two tombs are remarkable illustrations of the great progress made in sepulchral art during the *Quattrocento.* The Gothic rigidity of figures has disappeared; they are now anatomically perfect.

BRUNELLESCHI AND ALBERTI: CREATORS OF
THE NEW ARCHITECTURE

The development of a new architecture began with the Florentine Filippo Brunelleschi (1377–1446). His visit to Rome enabled him to study ancient buildings and learn many things about construction, proportion, and decoration. On his return to Florence he began a splendid career as builder. The silk guild entrusted him with the construction of its foundling hospital. A loggia with wide arches, supported by columns with modified Corinthian capitals, adorns the front. Terra cotta medallions of infants in swaddling clothes, the work of Andrea della Robbia, are placed on the spandrels between the arches. This structure is an interesting example of the benevolent institutions which wealthy guilds of Italian towns were in the habit of building.

More significant is the Pazzi chapel which Brunelleschi constructed about 1420 in the cloisters of the church of Santa Croce in Florence. It is a rectangular building with a loggia as wide as the main part of the chapel. This loggia has six columns surmounted by modified Corinthian capitals. A high arch divides the façade into two halves and leads to the door of the chapel. The dome covering the central part of the chapel is evidently modeled upon Roman or Byzantine originals. The decorations of the moldings are copied after late Roman originals. This chapel "is unmatched by any previous building that we know of, and none can contend that in this instance Brunelleschi was merely copying Roman work." The chapel in the church of San Lorenzo of Florence is also Brunelleschi's work. It is a noble structure in which the architect employed the traditional ceiling of Roman antiquity and adapted decoration derived from classical sources.

The most famous work of Brunelleschi is the lofty dome of the cathedral of Santa Maria del Fiore in Florence, begun in 1296 by Arnolfo del Cambio. By the opening of the *Quattrocento* the dome over the intersection of nave and transept remained to be added. The space was about 140 feet across, and much misgiving was felt as to the best method of constructing so large a dome. After some hesitation the task was given to Brunelleschi in 1420. He constructed two concentric and octagonal domes on an octagonal drum built upon the walls of the church. The domes were joined at the corners by means of ribs. Girdles composed of great oak beams fastened together by iron clamps bound the segments of the inner dome together and held the outer in place. The work was finished in 1436. The lantern, constructed according to the architect's plans, was not completed until 1445. The dome is a highly original creation and reveals Brunelleschi's skill. There is little truth in the story that he copied it after the dome of the Pantheon which he studied when in Rome.

The palaces of the *Quattrocento* are typical of the Renaissance. They were built by wealthy townsmen as fitting abodes in which they could have the greatest possible comfort and gratify their passion for higher artistic satisfaction. They were not like the old square and lofty towers with few windows such as may still be seen in San Gimignano, a town near Siena. They are airy and well-lighted structures, and their military character for the most part has been abandoned. In the center is an open sunlit space or courtyard, surrounded by columns which support the stories above. A flight of stairs leads to the living quarters. Often a garden is laid out adjoining the building.

The first to merit study is the Medicean palace built for Cosimo de' Medici and typical of domestic architecture during the *Quattrocento*. It was begun after 1440 by Michelozzo de' Michelozzi (1396–1472) who was both sculptor and architect and was often associated with Brunelleschi. Michelozzo was successful in giving to relatively small buildings a grace and beauty which all posterity has acclaimed. The ground story of the palace is constructed with roughly finished stones in what is known as "rusticated style." The story above is made of smooth stone with beveled edges, and the next story has a perfectly smooth surface. Each window of the two upper stories is divided into two sections by a column supporting arches over each half. A cornice 8 feet deep crowns this imposing structure.

León Battista Alberti (1405–1472) was the next great innovator in architecture. He was a member of an exiled Florentine family and only with difficulty carried on his studies. He entered the service of Eugenius IV, and, when that pontiff moved his court to Florence, for the first time visited the city of his fathers. Alberti was truly a *uomo universale*. His boundless curiosity led him to study all things, and the range of his ability and knowledge was marvelous. He was a mathematician, jurist, poet, philologist, and musician. He also wrote a treatise on painting and another on sculpture. He was interested in archaeology and wrote *Description of the City of Rome*.

Alberti's love for ancient objects, derived in part from Vitruvius' work on Roman architecture, influenced his architectural labors. This author was not read in the Middle Ages, but, when Poggio Bracciolini found a manuscript of this work, humanists began to study it feverishly. Its ideas provided norms for the new architecture of the classical revival. An indiscriminate use of columns and pilasters began. This has been severely criticized because forms employed in classical temples could not be adapted effectively to the secular buildings of the *Quattrocento*. Alberti used pilasters in each of the three stories of the Rucellai palace in Florence. They are surmounted by capitals, but do not satisfy the observer, for he feels that they are purely ornamental since they appear to support no weight. The windows of the upper stories are constructed in the same manner as those of the palace of Cosimo de' Medici, except that the architect placed a heavy crosspiece over the column. On this transverse beam rest the arches over the halves of the window. This device is unfortunate, for it violates the principle that columns must bear burdens.

Alberti also applied his knowledge to church architecture. He constructed the façade of Santa Maria Novella at Florence. Some of its parts, especially the central arch and the columns, were suggested by the triumphal arch of Augustus at Rome which Alberti had studied. Another example of this type of work is the façade of Sant' Andrea at Mantua. But the most curious work from Alberti's hands is San Francesco of Rimini. This church was built in the Gothic style of the thirteenth century, and from 1447–1456 it was revamped in the new style. It was never completed, and the dome which Alberti intended to construct over the choir was never begun. It is a curious structure and well illustrates the great change which took place in artistic taste as a result of the classical revival. This new style was to reach maturity during the next century in the work of Bramante (d. 1514) and Sansovino (d. 1520).

THE NEW REALISM IN PAINTING: MASACCIO, 1401–1428

Among painters, Masaccio (1401–1428) was the first bold innovator of the *Quattrocento*. When we consider that his mental formation lay in the artistic theories and practices of the *Trecento*, we are astounded by his originality. He appears to have been practically a self-made man. His frescoes are to be found in the Brancacci chapel of the Carmelite church in Florence. He knew Giotto's works thoroughly and soon progressed beyond that painter's innovations. In Masaccio's pictures space is realistically treated; one is conscious of the air which surrounds each figure. An effect of thickness is imparted to objects by the use of light and shadow. Foreshortening and an effort to give groups unity of action are far more successful than in the case of Giotto. Buildings in the background are in better proportion and seem habitable. Facial expression and hands and arms are rendered according to life. Groups are arranged with charming naturalness.

Painting of the *Quattrocento* was concerned with one great idea, the scientific solution of the problem of creating the illusion of reality on a flat surface. The painter's task was to place three-dimensional objects on a two-dimensional surface. This involved many questions which perplexed artists throughout the century. They were called upon to study anatomy, perspective, foreshortening, dramatic unity, thought conveyed in posture and facial expression, arrangement of individuals in a crowd, effect of light and shade, and the significance of color. Naturalism triumphed. All this magnificent progress was accomplished, except for the contributions of Mantegna (1431–1506) and a few other masters, by the artists of Florence from Masaccio (1401–1428) to Botticelli (1444–1510).

Masaccio's greatest work, *The Tribute Money*, is taken from Matt. XVII: 24–27. A tax gatherer dressed in a short tunic demands tribute for Caesar. The disciples, being poor, turn to Christ in their dilemma. Christ directs Peter to go to the water's edge. There Peter finds a coin in the mouth of the fish. Next Peter is shown giving the coin to the tax collector. The central part especially reveals the painter's originality, for neither Giotto nor anyone since had so successfully represented a group. The action of Christ and Peter dominate the scene, and the disciples who stand around concentrate their attention upon the Master. *Peter Healing the Sick* is a street scene. The buildings are represented in their proper proportions. The saint moves past a cripple lying on the ground without looking down upon him. One of the afflicted men gazes reverently up at the saint and makes a gesture of adoration, hoping to be cured by him. Most remarkable is the *Expulsion of Adam and Eve*. As the first parents are driven forth from the portals of paradise they present a picture of complete despair. Adam in sorrow hides his face in his hands; Eve's face, stained with tears, is the very expression of grief. Their nude bodies are correctly modeled and dramatically portrayed.

Masaccio's naturalism did for painting what Donatello's did for sculpture, but Masaccio was probably not inspired by that sculptor. His influence was enormous, as was testified by Vasari:

> This [Brancacci] chapel has indeed been continually frequented by an infinite number of students and masters for the benefit to be derived from these works, in which there are still some heads so beautiful and life-like that we may safely affirm no artist of that period to have approached so nearly to the manner of the moderns as did Masaccio. His works do indeed merit all the praise they have received, and the rather as it was by him that the path was opened to the excellent manner prevalent in our own times; to the truth of which we have testified in the fact that all the most cele-

brated sculptors and painters since Masaccio's day have become excellent and illustrious by studying their art in this chapel. Among these may be enumerated . . . Fra Filippo Lippi, who completed the work; Baldovinetti, Castagno, Verrocchio, Ghirlandaio, Botticelli, Da Vinci, Perugino, Bartolommeo, . . . and the sublime Michelangelo. Raphael also made his first commencement of his exquisite manner in this place. . . .[3]

None of the younger artists, however, possessed the bold genius of Masaccio. But they did have talent, and they successfully worked out some of the problems indicated in the frescoes in the Carmelite church in Florence. So Paolo Uccello (1397–1475) made a specialty of perspective. In the *Route of Romano* he arranged the forces contending in the battle to illustrate this difficult problem. Bodies and broken spears are placed at right angles to the spectator, thus the illusion of depth. Horses with men on them are drawn as cubes. Even the landscape is forced into this scheme. This problem of perspective was Uccello's special interest; and Vasari relates how he would mutter, "Oh, what a delightful thing is this perspective," when his wife entreated him to go to sleep.

To give reality to space was a difficult task, and it is not strange that painters following in the footsteps of the great master experimented with the problem. Domenico Veneziano (d. 1461), who is noted for portraits in profile and detailed designs in cloth, covered his pictures with a coating of varnish resembling oil in order to give a pale tone to backgrounds. His pupil, Piero della Francesca (1410?–1492), filled pictures with light and air by giving silvery tones to backgrounds. He was a careful student of form and endeavored to reduce perspective to a mathematical science. His contributions led to the final triumph over the problem of space by Perugino and Raphael and to a treatment of atmosphere which culminated in the use of light and dark effects (*chiaroscuro*) by Leonardo da Vinci (d. 1519).

Piero's zeal in solving the problem of space and light led him to neglect motion—the figures in his pictures stand still as if hewn out of stone. His portraits in profile are especially fine, those of Guidobaldo da Montefeltro of Urbino and his wife Battista Sforza being famous examples. His great pictures relating the story of the Holy Cross are in the choir of the church of San Francesco at Arezzo.

Andrea del Castagno (1390–1457) concentrated his energies upon another aspect of painting, that of powerful physique vibrating with energy. He did not aim at graciousness but emphasized form and mass, and his pictures therefore show sinewy, energetic figures. A good example

[3] *Ibid.*, pp. 410–411.

Basilica of St. Mark, Venice.

Burning of witches.

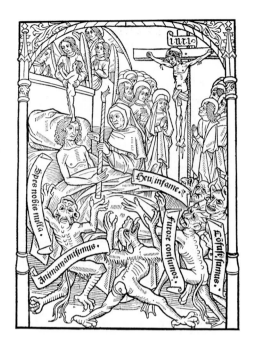

Page from *The Art of Dying*.

A medieval tilt.

St. Lazarus' Gate, Avignon (about 1364).

Lucca brocade, about 1400: Christ appearing before Mary Magdalene.
(Courtesy, Museum of Fine Arts, Boston)

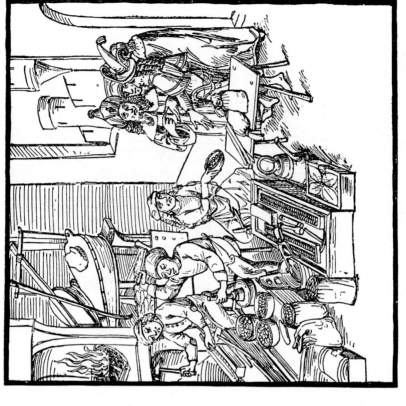

Late medieval mint.

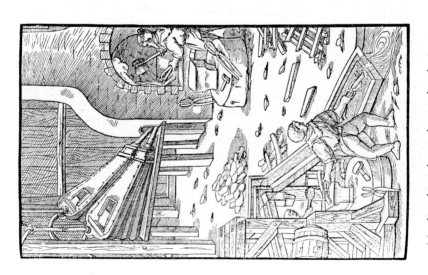

Metal-working shop in late medieval mine.

Cathedral of Pisa.

Farnese Palace, Rome. (Courtesy, The Bettmann Archive)

Lamentation over the Body of Christ, by Giotto, Padua. (Courtesy, Alinari)

Colleoni, Venice, by Verrocchio. (Courtesy, The Bettmann Archive)

CAROLVS, ROMA.IMPE, QVINTVS.

Emperor Charles V wearing crown, sword, and globe with cross.

Portrait drawing, by Van Eyck.

Descent from the Cross, by van der Weyden.

Allegory of Good Government, by Lorenzetti, Siena.

The Triumph of Death (fresco on the walls of the Campo Santo, Pisa).

Part of the Triumphs of Julius Caesar, by Mantegna, Hampton Court.

The Corporal Works of Mercy, by Della Robbia.

The Tribute Money, by Masaccio.

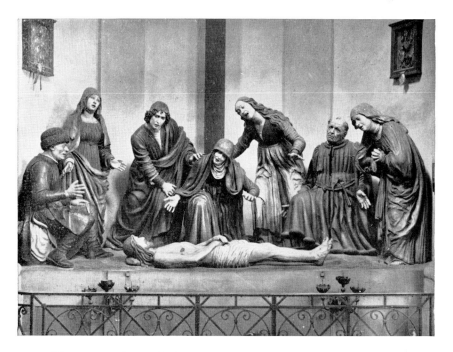

Weeping over the Dead Christ, by Mazzoni, Modena. (Courtesy, Alinari)

Madonna Shielding Citizens of Perugia from the Plague, by Bonfigli, Perugia.
(Courtesy, Alinari)

The Last Supper, by da Vinci, Milan.

Pieta, by Michelangelo, Rome. (Courtesy, Alinari)

Moses, by Michelangelo, Rome.

Madonna with the Child Jesus, by Bellini, Venice.
(Courtesy, The Bettmann Archive)

The Fair Gardener, by Raphael, Paris.
(Courtesy, Alinari)

Nymphs from the Fountain of Innocents, sculptures by Goujon, Paris.
(Courtesy, The Bettmann Archive)

is his portrait of the *condottiere, Pippo Spano,* who was employed by the Hungarian King Sigismund against the Turks. This picture is interesting also from the point of view of social and cultural history, for it is a splendid likeness of a *condottiere.* Castagno also painted an equestrian portrait of *Niccolò da Tolentino.* The vigorous step and energetic move- ment of the horse are emphasized by powerful muscles.

One of the first artists to be guided chiefly by what he saw about him in everyday life was Fra Filippo Lippi (1406–1469). He learned the secrets of his craft from his master Masaccio but abandoned the latter's heroic themes drawn from Scripture. He took his models from the people among whom he had been reared. His *Madonna in Adoration* shows a maiden filled with maternal adoration kneeling before the Christ Child. St. John is a youth such as Fra Filippo saw every day in the streets of Florence. The background is filled with woods and rock such as his native Tuscany presented on all sides. In the foreground is a green carpet of grass spangled with bright flowers. Another picture, a *Madonna and Child,* illustrates the social interest of his pictures in a different way, for here the Holy Mother is a Florentine matron dressed in the manner of the women of that day. Her headdress, an elaborate study of folds, is skill- fully done. The Christ Child is a chubby, lusty infant who is likely to overpower His mother. What a difference between him and his Gothic predecessors! The face of the angel is that of a street gamin from whom one can expect any impish prank.

Similar tendencies were revealed in the art of Benozzo Gozzoli (1420– 1497). He lavished his skill upon scenes of nature, crowds, cavalcades, and interesting incidents rather than on the investigation of basic prob- lems in painting. He was a superb storyteller. The world justly admires his pictures of the life of St. Augustine in the church of St. Augustine in San Gimignano. Critical moments in the saint's life are depicted as if they took place in the Tuscan milieu during Renaissance days. His *Visit of the Magi* on the walls of the Medici palace in the Via Larga in Florence possesses similar qualities. The Magi and their attendants on horse and afoot are making their way along a mountain road to do homage to the Christ Child. Trees, plants, rocks, buildings, animals, trappings, and clothing are treated with loving attention to detail. The artist wished to create an interesting picture, and he succeeded. Gozzoli's portrait of Cosimo—portrait of a shrewd and clever man of the world—is justly famous; the smooth-shaven face of the gray-haired man, once seen, cannot be forgotten. Such cavalcades must have been common in real life, for the Medici often visited their villas. There is something especially appropriate in Cosimo's patronage of Gozzoli, for his popular tastes were well expressed by the use of ordinary folk as models.

Similarly Domenico Ghirlandaio (1449–1494) won fame as a painter of frescoes. His style, like that of Gozzoli, was narrative, at once popular and descriptive. He understood the genius of artists like Masaccio, but added little of his own. He faithfully portrayed religious themes as if in local Florentine settings. His best frescoes depicting the life of St. John the Baptist are to be found in the choir of Santa Maria Novella in Florence.

Very different in spirit and technique was the work of Fra Giovanni Angelico (1387–1455), a Dominican friar. He fully mastered the skill and technique of his contemporaries, and so his creations remind us of the school of Masaccio and his followers.

Fra Angelico's pictures belong to the vanishing Middle Ages when popular imagination still clung to traditional Gothic methods of presenting the world of saints, angels, heavenly choirs, and the final judgment. He loved to portray objects for their religious values; indeed, a certain "sacramental earnestness" may be said to pervade his work. "It was the custom of Fra Angelico [according to Vasari] to abstain from retouching or improving any painting once finished. He altered nothing but left all as it was done the first time, believing, as he said, that such was the will of God. It is also affirmed that he would never take pencil in hand until he had first offered a prayer. He is said never to have painted a crucifix without tears streaming from his eyes; and in the countenances and attitudes of his figures it is easy to perceive proof of his sincerity, his goodness, and the depth of his devotion to Christ."[4]

The backgrounds of his pictures are natural, buildings assumed proper proportions, and draperies were arranged according to a better knowledge of the human form. Yet, in spirit, Fra Angelico ranked with the great Gothic masters of the *Trecento*. His paintings possess an ineffable charm and sweetness. Their colors are fresh and like gleaming jewels, and the scenes are arranged with infinite care. His great work was done for the convent of San Marco at Florence. At the head of the stairs leading to the cells is his famous *Annunciation*; smaller frescoes are to be found in each of the cells. His *Coronation of the Virgin* is also famous. A host of saints stand around the throne on which Christ is seated while he places a crown on Mary's head. The artist's smaller pictures are resplendent with gold and delicate colors.

With the career of Sandro Botticelli (1444–1510) we come to the

[4] *Ibid.*, II, 34–35.

culmination of Florence's great *Quattrocento* art. His mental formation was received from that most remarkable galaxy of artists who followed the teaching of Donatello and Masaccio. His painting is interesting not only as art but as an expression of the thought and life of his day. He received his first lessons from Fra Filippo Lippi, owed much to the vigor of Antonio Pollaiuolo's creations, and was deeply impressed with the dainty and incisive work of Verrocchio. He combined their merits in a satisfactory manner. His figures often have a languid expression and are clothed in billowy garments which flutter with the movement of limbs or the stirring of breezes. *An Adoration of the Three Magi* illustrates his earlier style. The popular note of Fra Filippo Lippi is evident in its *Virgin and Christ Child* and in the ruined structure which serves as the stable. The group of adorers is a collection of Florentine notables, some of whom are members of the Medici family. The artist's interest lay as much with secular things as with religion. The theme is traditional and affords the opportunity of displaying in one group the celebrities of the day. Here is a touch of the narrative manner so popular at the moment. The *Madonna of the Magnificat* is a beautiful picture with a view of nature in the background. An infinitely tender expression pervades the delicate face of the Virgin, a tenderness which may be described as maternal and human.

Botticelli's *Primavera,* an allegory of spring, has a purely secular theme drawn from such pagan poets as Lucretius and Vergil, and illustrates how secular interests had crowded out old religious conceptions. It also illustrates the cult of classical forms which had now reached its zenith. The scene is laid in an orange and olive grove, the green leaves of the trees attractively contrasting with the gleam of golden fruit. In the foreground is a thick carpet of grass studded with flowers. More than thirty-five varieties of plants have been discerned, all reproduced with great fidelity. This illustrates a characteristic of the Renaissance, the interest in mundane things which led to a more patient study of the details of nature. Venus is placed in the center, with a flying cupid aiming his arrows at her from above. Zephyr appears amid the branches driving forward Spring from whose mouth issues a garland of flowers and plants. Before her advances Flora bearing flowers which she scatters with her right hand. Three dancing Graces are at the right of Venus. Next, and leading the procession, advances Mercury with baton in hand clearing away lingering Winter.

The *Birth of Venus* further illustrates what has been said about the allegory of spring. It retells the ancient story of how Venus was wafted upon the shore by the waves of the sea. She is standing in a sea shell borne forward by breezes blown by two winged creatures. Her radiant body, nude and beautifully modeled, lithe and sinuous, is ready to step ashore where a maiden awaits her, ready to cover her with a mantle. Her golden hair falls in profuse masses over her shoulders or flutters rhythmically in the breeze. Flowers are blown about in the breeze and on the right stand a few trees which suggest an idyllic grove. These two pictures of Botticelli, inspired by an age which yearned for the vanished beauty of the ancient pagan world might well illustrate the verse of a Theocritus.

It was fortunate that no matter how much the narrative style of artists like Ghirlandaio pleased the people of Florence, they did not allow themselves to be drawn from the path marked out by Masaccio. Great painting indeed must be truthful and must consider the life of the age. Its mission is not primarily to make pretty pictures or merely to illustrate life. Florence owes her supreme position in painting and sculpture to the fact that her workers cared most for the intellectual solution of the technical problems which confront artists. In this way Florentine artists laid the foundation of modern painting and sculpture. They became instructors first of other Italians and finally of the whole world. Their labors led directly to the achievements of the *Cinquecento,* to works of the mighty geniuses of the High Renaissance.

Chapter 15

MEDICI RENAISSANCE PATRONS

*W*HERE WERE artists and scholars of the *Quattrocento* to find patrons to support them? Not among the nobility, for that class still lived according to traditions created in the feudal age. Preferring the chase and an elaborate code of chivalry, it cared little for the development of the new culture. Nor among churchmen, for they were either occupied in theological studies of the old type or engrossed in practical details of monastic or episcopal administration. The lay culture of the early Renaissance made little appeal to the rank and file of the clergy. Nor could humanists find posts in universities, for these institutions were, for the most part, governed by old conceptions which allowed little opportunity to cultivate humanist learning. And the economic problems of life precluded the lower and middle classes of townsmen from participating in the new secular culture.

The patrons of the Renaissance were, as a rule, townsmen who had grown wealthy from trade and industry. This is especially true of the aristocratic *popolo grasso* of Florence, among whom were the Strozzi and the Medici. They had the wealth and leisure necessary to cultivate new ideas, and devoted their energy to this end. Renaissance culture therefore was not only secular but also aristocratic. Possessing the greater share of the world's capital, this class inevitably appropriated social and political power. By becoming sponsors of the art, letters, and learning of the *Quattrocento*, its members played a chief part in the formation of the new lay civilization.

EMERGENCE OF THE MEDICI FAMILY

Of all patrons of the Renaissance the House of Medici was the most active and the most distinguished. For over a century its members were intimately associated with the new culture of the Renaissance. This family had long lived in Florence; its origins are lost in the dimness which enshrouds the early annals of medieval towns. But in the fourteenth century Salvestro de' Medici assumed an important position in communal affairs. He was known to be sympathetic with the *popolo minuto*, and especially the unenfranchised proletariat. The bitter antagonisms of the lowest classes toward the *popolo grasso* who controlled their destinies, politically as well as economically, led to the violent outburst of the Ciompi in 1378. Salvestro sympathized with them, but the uprising failed miserably, and the yoke of the aristocracy was fastened upon the unfortunates more firmly than before.

The Medici did not play a large part in the politics of Florence for some decades after that ill-fated rising, but their espousal of the popular cause was never forgotten and later proved a solid foundation for their policy against the oligarchy. It was Giovanni (d. 1429) who made possible the family's future greatness. He was a typical product of an environment of plots and counterplots. A man of great penetration and resourcefulness, he avoided public intrigues. Instead, he devoted his energy to trade and banking, thus laying the bases of wealth which made possible the later success of Cosimo and Lorenzo. His house lent money to foreign princes, both lay and ecclesiastical, financed businesses, and reaped great profits. From all quarters of Europe wealth poured into the coffers of the Medici.

Giovanni enjoyed the confidence of the Florentines, especially the aristocracy, and held several offices. Toward the end of his life he sided with the popular element. From 1422–1427 Florence was involved in a war against Milan. It necessitated taxation which, because of the methods employed by the aristocracy, weighed heavily upon the lower classes while the wealthy escaped with small contributions. Giovanni supported the famous *catasto*, a proposal to shift the burden to the shoulders of the rich. "This system of taxation in some degree checked the tyranny of the upper classes, because they were not able to browbeat the plebeians and with threats make them silent at the council, as they formerly did. Thus it followed that whilst this taxation was approved by the generality of men, it was regarded with great displeasure by the rich." The enemies of this successful measure concentrated their venom upon Giovanni's son, Cosimo, while the people looked with increased favor upon the Medici.

Cosimo ruled as head of the family from 1429 to 1464. He was a splendid example of a bourgeois statesman. Never swayed by impossible or fantastic ideas, he addressed himself only to things which could be realized. He understood the treacherous quicksands of Florentine politics and therefore abstained from intrigue and officeholding, preferring to control the organs of government through henchmen. At the same time he was accessible to all men and was always considerate of the needs of the poor and unfortunate, to whom he lent money, thereby increasing his popularity. So successfully did he manage the fortune which his father had left him that the family's wealth increased enormously. He was rarely deceived in his relations with men because he had an uncanny ability to estimate character. "He understood people even before looking at them," it was said. His wealth, circumspection, and political finesse enabled him to play the role of one of the greatest of Renaissance princes.

Cosimo's success and popularity aroused the hostility of the aristocrats, and they resolved to crush him and his family whose democratic associations might sooner or later destroy the oligarchy. Rinaldo degli Albizzi, one of the jealous patriciate, led them in an effort to get rid of the Medici ere it was too late, and in 1433 they brought about Cosimo's arrest by high-handed methods. It was their intention to kill him, but, fearing the wrath of the people, they secured a decree of banishment instead. The family was ordered into exile, Cosimo finding shelter in Venice. But a war with Lucca, undertaken in 1432, went from bad to worse, and Rinaldo lost control of the government. In 1434, just one year after the expulsion, the *signoria* reversed its decree and recalled the Medici. On their return Rinaldo was exiled, and with him Palla Strozzi and others. Now began the ascendancy of the Medici in Florentine affairs which was to last without interruption until 1494.

Under Cosimo de' Medici Florence continued to be governed by a clumsy system of boards of magistrates. The manner of appointment, functions of officers, and all forms of government were left unchanged. Cosimo controlled public policy by manipulation because he well understood how his fellow citizens detested tyranny and overweening ambition. By keeping democratic forms inviolate, he was able to control the destinies of Florence far more effectively than if he had been an absolute prince.

While Cosimo thus ably ruled the internal affairs of Florence and extended the commercial successes of its citizens and incidentally increased his own wealth, he also managed its foreign relations. This was a difficult matter because of the intense jealousy of Italian states. Milan was the chief disturbing element. Its Visconti despots sought to expand their lands at the expense of the States of the Church, especially in the Romagna. They allied themselves with the exiled Rinaldo degli Albizzi and his friends, opposed Florentine, designed upon Lucca, and coveted Florentine territory. Besides, they were engaged in a perennial struggle with Venice, which had successfully encroached upon Milanese territory in Lombardy. Florence was allied with Venice and the papacy. But the Venetians, jealous of Florentine commercial and political success, were cool allies; and Cosimo soon determined to support Francesco Sforza, who, as we have seen (see Chap. 2) had married the daughter of Filippo Maria Visconti and aspired to the lordship of Milan after the latter's death in 1447. Cosimo lent him considerable sums with which Sforza established himself as tyrant of Milan (1450). Venetian schemes were defeated, and any danger of hostility to Florentine trade in Lombardy and Germany vanished.

Alliance with Milan implied alliance with the King of Naples. King Alfonso of Sicily (d. 1458) had conquered Naples in 1435 and held it in defiance of his enemies, the heirs of the Angevin line. Sforza feared Angevin ambitions might at any moment be backed up by French force. The house of Orléans held Asti and claimed to have the best title to Milan because Valentina Visconti, daughter of Gian Galeazzo (1378–1402), had become the wife of Duke Louis of Orléans. This was a stronger claim than Sforza could advance, because his wife was only a natural daughter of Filippo Maria. Florence had long been an active sympathizer with French policies, but under Cosimo's guidance she gave this up and accepted the friendship of Milan and the Aragonese kings of Naples. This triple alliance, which became the corner stone of Cosimo's foreign policy, placed in his hands the balance of power in the peninsula and maintained the peace of Italy by keeping out the French until the days of his great-grandson Piero (1492–1503). The success of Cosimo's policy greatly enhanced his wealth and prestige.

COSIMO PATRON OF RENAISSANCE ART AND LEARNING

This fortunate balance of internal and external political affairs and the possession of unlimited wealth enabled Cosimo to become the patron *par excellence* of the new Renaissance culture. Giovanni had shown some leanings toward art, but he was an old-fashioned man. Nevertheless, he had encouraged Masaccio and had given liberally toward the construction of the foundling hospital which Brunelleschi had designed. He was one of the judges of the competition for the south doors of the baptistery which was won by Lorenzo Ghiberti. Cosimo was the first of the Medici to concern himself actively with letters, painting, sculpture, and architecture. Not only did he show a vital interest in these arts but also displayed an amazing insight. Whatever he approved and supported, the world has agreed was worthy of patronage. Few rulers in medieval or modern times have so completely and so worthily associated themselves with art and learning as did Cosimo de' Medici.

Cosimo was but 7 years old when Manuel Chrysoloras began teaching Greek in the University of Florence. Although Giovanni apparently had no part in bringing this scholar to the banks of the Arno, it is probable that Cosimo was one of Chrysoloras' first auditors. He received instruction from the chief teachers of Latin and Greek and attained proficiency in both. He early sought the society of humanists and encouraged them by his keen interest. In the monastery of San Spirito in Florence he often met with Luigi Marsigli and others to discuss theological and philosophical topics. The monastery of Santa Maria degli Angeli of the order of Camalduli was another center where many of the new spirits met. There Ambrogio Traversari spent long hours in his cell reading to Cosimo his translations of St. Paul's epistles and some of the works of the Church fathers.

Cosimo was intimate with Michelozzo de' Michelozzi (1396–1472), builder of his palace in the Via Larga. It is characteristic of the cautious Cosimo that he accepted Michelozzo's modest plans rather than the more elaborate ideas of Brunelleschi. Michelozzo accompanied him while in exile. In 1437 Cosimo employed him to construct the Dominican convent of San Marco in Florence, paying for this work and also endowing the house. He employed Brunelleschi in the renovation of his parish church of San Lorenzo which sadly needed repairs. Vast sums were expended on the old sacristy and other parts of the building. San Spirito was given the same attention. The cloisters of the Badia of Fiesole were erected. Cosimo built country villas at Careggi and Trebbia, very different in style from the castles of nobles. They were bourgeois abodes in the country. The Middle Ages were gone; the townsmen had usurped the place occupied by the nobles.

An avid collector of manuscript books, Cosimo provided help for Niccolò Niccoli (1364–1437), for, when the latter had exhausted his patrimony and was bankrupt, Cosimo took over his obligations, and Niccolò on his death gave him his great collection. Ciriaco of Ancona, the antiquarian, collected ancient books for Cosimo who also gave orders to other agents to watch for manuscripts. Thus he brought together a large number of important works. He also gave many books to the library of San Marco. His own collection, begun in 1444, became the foundation of the Medici library which finally in 1524 was housed in the cloisters of San Lorenzo. It is now called the Laurenziana and is one of the world's most important collections.

Cosimo left an indelible impress upon the new scholarship by initiating a revival of Platonic philosophy. He persuaded Pope Eugenius IV to move to Florence the council which had convened at Ferrara in 1438. Cosimo was induced to found the Platonic Academy by the Greek scholars to whom he acted as host while they were attending the council. Membership in this academy was restricted. The group met in his villa at Careggi to discuss the great problems of life. Some of Plato's works were not accessible in Latin, and Cosimo determined to remedy this by subsidizing Marsilio Ficino (1433–1499) to make translations. Born near Florence, the son of a physician in Cosimo's service, and educated in the Universities of Pisa and Florence, Ficino made rapid progress in humanist studies. His great affection for Plato's teaching induced Cosimo to help him. Rooms were assigned to him in the palace in the Via Larga, and all his needs were provided for so that he could pursue his studies untrammeled. In 1458 Ficino assumed the presidency of the Platonic Academy which was destined to become the prototype of similar foundations of the *Quattrocento* and subsequently of all modern academies. The Platonic revival was the philosophic copestone of Humanism.

As the years of his life wore on, Cosimo prepared for the moment when his eldest son Giovanni would succeed him. But the young man died in 1463. This was a sad blow to the aging man who could not find comfort in Platonic teaching to dissolve his grief. Cosimo was carried through his house in the Via Larga after Giovanni's death and was heard to say with a sigh, "This is all too large a house for so small a family." Cosimo died in the following year and was buried near the altar in his parish church of San Lorenzo. On his tomb, according to public decree, were inscribed the words *Pater Patriae* (Father of his Country).

Governing Florence and the task of guiding the Medicean heritage devolved upon his younger and physically weak son Piero. A group of Florentines led by Luca Pitti, jealous of the Medicean position in politics, sought to overthrow Piero in 1466, but failed. Piero died in 1469. His son Lorenzo, known in history as *Il Magnifico* (the Magnificent), and his younger brother Giuliano succeeded to the Medicean inheritance.

MEDICI LEADERSHIP CHALLENGED

As in the reign of Piero, their father, so also Lorenzo and Giuliano were called to defend the position of Florence in the politics of Italy. Ever since the days of Cosimo, Florentine leadership in Italian politics rested upon an alliance with Milan and Naples. But now the political security of the peninsula was threatened. In one of the worst examples of nepotism Sixtus IV (1471–1484) sought to aggrandize his nephew, Girolamo Riario, his sister's son. Sixtus bestowed upon him the city of

Forlì in the Romagna, and there was talk that Imola and Faenza might also be given him.

Lorenzo opposed Sixtus' desire to strengthen papal control in the Romagna and did what he could to block the transfer by refusing to let the pontiff have the necessary sums from the Medici bank in Rome. The enraged pope, however, received the necessary money from a rival Florentine banking firm, that of the Pazzi. This was a proud and haughty family which had failed to ingratiate itself with the public. Sixtus transferred to it all of his banking business which till then had been transacted by the firm of the Medici. In September, 1474, the triple alliance of Venice, Milan, and Florence was announced, which was soon followed by a counter alliance between Sixtus and Naples. Galeazzo Maria was assassinated in December, 1476, and the government of Milan fell into the hands of his widow Duchess Bona, mother of an infant son, Gian Galeazzo. But the dead duke's brothers proved troublesome, and it appeared that Milan could not be counted upon as a support of Florence.

Sixtus, angry with Lorenzo, determined that the Medici should be expelled. Florence would then be innocuous, and the papacy could resume its policies with every prospect of success. Sixtus wanted to bring about the fall of the Medici but was opposed to bloodshed. The conspiracy of the Pazzi in 1478 was modeled on the one in which Galeazzo Maria was slain. The Pazzi were willing tools. Riario was bitter because Florence, which had opposed his getting Forlì, would certainly refuse to let him extend his authority over nearby Faenza and Imola. An attempt was made to execute the plot on Sunday, April 26, 1478. At an impressive moment during Mass Giuliano, Lorenzo's brother, was killed, pierced with nineteen wounds. Lorenzo was wounded but escaped. The Pazzi sought to rouse the city. The people angrily came forward to defend the Medici. The attempt of the conspirators to seize the town hall (*Palazzo Vecchio*) failed. Archbishop Salviati of Pisa, one of the plotters, was seized and hanged from the windows amid approving jeers from the public.

The pope pronounced excommunication against all who had a share in the death of the archbishop, and Florence was placed under the interdict. These measures reveal how worldly papal politics had become, for the pope employed religious measures to further purely political projects. It was his purpose to induce Florence to expel "that son of perdition, Lorenzo dei Medici." But the city's government rallied to Lorenzo's support. Neapolitan troops entered Florentine territory in support of papal politics, and a desultory war ensued which lasted until the next year. Louis XI of France sought to argue with Sixtus in behalf of Florence, but the pontiff was obdurate and persisted in placing all the blame upon Lorenzo and his government.

Lorenzo now resolved upon a bold move—to go to Naples in person, entrust himself to King Ferrante, and seek peace. This famous visit, undertaken in December, 1479, proved successful and in the next year led to the establishment of peace. After long manipulation Lorenzo alienated the king from the papal side. The treaty stipulated the surrender by Naples of towns captured in the previous campaigns and specified that Florence should beg pardon from the pope for its offenses against the Holy See. Ferrante made peace easy and certain by yielding on the question of the towns. The Turks had landed in Italy in 1480, seized Otranto, slaughtered the people, and harried the countryside. Ferrante needed all his resources and showed himself generous. The comedy of an apology was worked out, and a formal ceremony was arranged in St. Peter's (December 3, 1481). The pontiff was represented, because of divine guidance, as having better knowledge of their enormities than the Florentines themselves. For all these crimes they begged to be forgiven. Thus Sixtus, whose policy had been a great mistake, made a virtue of necessity, and reconciliation was complete.

MEDICEAN ESTHETIC PATRONAGE

Such were the petty, ferocious, and vindictive wars that rocked the public peace and private life of *Quattrocento* Italy. But these violent outbursts scarcely interfered with the cultivation of significant form and the life beautiful which characterized the ruling Medici. We have noted how Cosimo encouraged artists during his long and active life. And as far as health permitted, his son Piero endeavored to continue his policy toward art and letters. For example, he gave commissions to the important painter Domenico Veneziano. Piero's wife, Lucrezia Tornabuoni, was one of the noblest women of the *Quattrocento*. She exerted much influence upon the society of the Medici and especially upon her sons, Lorenzo and Giuliano. She was a model mother and in no wise neglected the duties of her home. She identified herself with the intellectual life of Florence and wrote lyric poems. Her poetic reputation rests chiefly upon renderings of the stories in the Apocrypha which are pervaded by a genuine religious fervor. The fact that they are written in the Italian tongue is significant, for this was in harmony with the popular sentiments which had always characterized the Medici house. She took an active interest, as did Piero and Cosimo, in the education of her sons who were placed under the tuition of noted humanists. They were educated in accordance with

Renaissance conceptions formed by the influence of Cicero, Plutarch, and especially Quintilian.

Of all the princes of the Renaissance, Lorenzo the Magnificent was the most influential. His position was never again questioned after the failure of the Pazzi in 1478. Henceforth he continued the policy which had become traditional in the Medici family of bestowing patronage upon scholars, painters, sculptors, and literary men. The age of Lorenzo was characterized by a particular step: the union of old and popular cultural traditions with the new Humanist movement which had begun with the arrival of Chrysoloras in Florence and the rule of Cosimo. This was inevitable, for no age can thrive on its archaeological past alone, no matter how significant that culture may be. León Battista Alberti had long ago begun the protest against the exclusive use of Latin. He had written a number of works which were to become important in the revival of the Italian mother tongue, the chief of these being his *On the Family*, or *Della Famiglia*, published in 1434. He argued that the ancient Romans who, according to humanist conceptions, were truly great men, never used any idiom but their mother tongue. They did not have a learned language apart from that of the people. Others argued that Italian was eminently worthy as a vehicle of thought—witness the great names of Dante, Petrarch, and Boccaccio! Alberti planned a literary contest for the citizens of Florence. They were invited to write poems on *True Friendship*, and the best compositions were to receive prizes which were to be donated by Piero de' Medici. The judges did not understand Alberti's motive and were disappointed that the poems were serious efforts and not popular ditties such as were sung in the streets.

The popular traditions of his family instilled by his mother inclined Lorenzo to the cultivation of the mother tongue and popular themes as well as those which derived from antiquity. He believed that his native Tuscan was more perfect than other languages because of its rich vocabulary, its harmony, the large number of excellent works written in it, and because it had become a widely used idiom. He believed that it would some day be the speech of the entire Italian people. When the great patron of the *Quattrocento* spoke thus, can one wonder at the popularity which the vernacular began to enjoy? Lorenzo himself set up the fashion by writing a liturgical play entitled *St. John and St. Paul*. It was inspired by the popular religious poetry which had grown up among townsmen under Franciscan influences, especially in Umbria. Lorenzo's work was produced for the edification and entertainment of the people by the Company of the Evangelist, a sort of chamber of rhetoric to which younger members of the aristocracy belonged. The poetic efforts of townsmen were thus drawn into the loftier artistic life of the new age. Therewith began a splendid evolution which was to lead to the drama of the Renaissance.

Lorenzo's carnival songs must be noticed, for he raised these productions to a high artistic level without sacrificing their spontaneity. His *Bacchus and Ariadne*, the best of them, was written for one of the floats in a carnival procession which he helped organize:

> Fair is youth and void of sorrow;
> But it hourly flees away.
> Youths and maids, enjoy today;
> Naught ye know of tomorrow.
> This is Bacchus and the bright
> Ariadne, lover true!
> They, in flying time's despite,
> Each with each find pleasure new;
> These their nymphs, and all their crew
> Keep perpetual holiday.
> Youths and maids, enjoy today;
> Naught ye know about tomorrow.

Next follow other stanzas about satyrs and nymphs, Silenus and Midas, etc. Then again it returns to the main theme:

> Listen well to what we're saying;
> Of tomorrow have no care!
> Young and old together playing,
> Boys and girls be blithe as air!
> Every sorry thought forswear!
> Keep perpetual holiday.
> Youths and maids, enjoy today;
> Naught ye know about tomorrow.
> Ladies and gay lovers young!
> Long live Bacchus, live desire!
> Dance and play, let songs be sung;
> Let sweet Love your bosoms fire;
> In the future come what may!
> Youths and maids, enjoy today;
> Naught ye know about tomorrow.

O Chiara Stella is one of Lorenzo's most charming songs, possessing something of the spirit which we find in the poems of Petrarch. This sonnet laments the passing of the famous beauty, Simonetta Cattaneo, who died in the prime of youth.

O lucid star, that with transcendent light
    Quenchest of all those neighbouring stars the gleam,
    Why thus beyond thine usage does thou stream,
    Why art thou fain with Phoebus still to fight?
Haply those beauteous eyes, which from our sight
    Death stole, who now doth vaunt himself supreme,
    Thou hast assumed: clad with their glorious beam,
    Well may'st thou claim the sun-god's chariot bright.
Listen, new star, new regent of the day,
    Who with unwonted radiance gilds our heaven,
    O listen, goddess, to the prayers we pray!
Let so much splendour from thy sphere be riven
    That to these eyes, which fain would weep alway,
    Unblinded, thy glad sight may yet be given![1]

His love for popular themes is well illustrated by his *Hunting with the Falcon*, a poem of 350 verses. It is a vivacious account of a hunting party. Originally the chase was the pastime of the nobles and was almost as important as the tilting yard. The wealthy bourgeoisie of the closing Middle Ages aped the nobility in many ways. The Medici and their friends were fond of hunting. Lorenzo's treatment is devoid of chivalric elements and is couched in the most artistic Italian. The hunters make ready at the first streak of dawn and start amid the baying of hounds. The falconers talk, and one of the hunters, still drowsy, falls from his mount and breaks the wing of his falcon. After many episodes, the hunters return home where, as is fitting, they satisfy their hearty appetites with food and wine. Then begins a great hubbub, each talking about the course of the hunt and praising his bird. And the one whose hawk has accomplished little, seeks to make up for it by drinking and talking about it.

In *La Nencia da Barberino* Lorenzo presents another aspect of his love for the countryside. It is the speech of Vallera, a rustic lad, addressed to Nencia, a country lass, to whose charms he has succumbed. He declares that he has not seen anyone so pretty at the market places which he has visited. She is like a pearl, and he is never weary of describing the details of her dress. She is industrious and weaves beautiful things—God only knows how beautiful! Poor Vallera is so disturbed by all this that he cannot do any work. He fears that he has a rival, and he mutters that he too has a knife—how like the peasant youth—and it would be well for his rival to have a care. Again he sings her charms, but pain returns when he reflects that Nencia does not care for him at all. Farewell, he says, and turns to his task, the tramping on grapes. In this poem Lorenzo created a

---

[1] J. A. Symonds, *Renaissance in Italy*, 'I, 93–94, 84.

new literary character, a peasant lad who speaks his sorrow in the language of the country. In this he succeeded completely. The great literary lights of the second half of the *Quattrocento*, Lorenzo, Poliziano, Pulci, and Savonarola, all wrote in Italian.

Lorenzo was a product of the Renaissance, especially when viewed in the light of social history. He was lively, energetic, and richly endowed with imagination. He typified the spirit of the newly risen bourgeoisie and was the born leader in everything to which this class aspired. Not only was he the wealthiest citizen of Florence but also the foremost among her intellectual sons. The culture of the townsmen demanded a more artistic rendering of the vernacular, and it is to Lorenzo's glory that he more than any other person gave expression to this wish. Thus the secular and pagan humanism was introduced to the townsmen who could read Latin only with difficulty.

The popular note of Lorenzo's day was furnished by the poetry of Luigi Pulci (1432–1487). Born of an impoverished Florentine family of magistrates, he won the friendship of Lorenzo who employed him on diplomatic and business missions. Lucrezia Tornabuoni requested him to write a metrical romance, for she knew how popular the tales of Charlemagne and Roland were among common folk in the market place. In writing his *Il Morgante*, Pulci drew upon the wealth of medieval tales as Boccaccio had done in the previous century. The poem at once met with favor. Its social significance lay in the appeal which it made to the bourgeoisie. The account often descends to the kind of comedy one finds in Don Quixote. Margutte, wicked, clever, and unscrupulous, is just the character to please ordinary folk. There is plenty of fun here and no exalted respect for traditional knightly virtues. Thus chivalric accounts of great heroes became popular bourgeois tales.

Lorenzo also encouraged Angelo Poliziano, or Politian (d. 1494). Born in Montepulciano in 1454, he studied at the University of Florence and in his twenty-sixth year was appointed professor of classical languages. Lorenzo had earlier relieved his dire wants and made him one of his secretaries and tutor of his son Piero. A great scholar, who won fame by his translations of Homer, Politian was led by Lorenzo's example to write in Italian. In producing the *Giostra*, or *The Tournament*, Poliziano wrote as a court poet of the Medici. This poem celebrated a tournament given in Florence in 1475 after the formation of an alliance between Florence, Venice and Milan. The poet glorified the success of Giuliano and the popularity and beauty of his favorite, Simonetta Cattaneo. Poliziano worked with zeal, but soon Simonetta died and Giuliano was slain in the

Pazzi conspiracy of 1478. The unfinished masterpiece nevertheless is a striking monument of the Medicean Renaissance.

His *Orfeo* is a more important creation. It is a tragedy dealing with the love of Orpheus and Eurydice. Drawn from Greek mythology, copied after classical models, and written in the vernacular, it was peculiarly typical of the Renaissance. The form suggests descent from the old liturgical plays. Its cultivated literary expression betrays the humanist's work. This purely pagan theme marks the secularization of the old religious drama, and the play occupies an important place in the history of drama. It also illustrates the victorious career of the mother tongue as the vehicle of the new culture of the bourgeoisie. The cult of classical Latin style henceforth was to be the vocation of scholars and pedants. Latin itself became the language of the learned few.

Like his grandfather Cosimo, Lorenzo was deeply interested in Plato. On one occasion he confessed his faith in that philosopher's doctrine as set forth in the *Phaedo*. Marsilio Ficino labored incessantly at the translation of the Platonic dialogues into humanist Latin. He began publishing them in 1482 and soon after undertook the translation of Plotinus' works. The Florentine academy continued to flourish under Lorenzo's patronage. Many meetings were held in the Villa at Careggi where such themes as the highest good and the greatest beauty were discussed.

In this circle there were, besides Ficino and Lorenzo himself, Cristoforo Landino and Pico della Mirandola (1463–1494). Pico was an extraordinary man, truly a universal genius of the Renaissance. Born of the family of the counts of Mirandola who lived in the Po Valley, he early displayed a zeal for Platonic doctrine. While at the Sorbonne in Paris, the very citadel of scholasticism, he conceived his ideas about the unity of all things. He believed that the chief propositions of Platonic philosophy could be traced to more ancient sources, especially the Mosaic code of the Old Testament. The philosophic lights of classical antiquity possessed the one eternal truth in fragments. A philosopher could bring all these together into a great system. Plato and Aristotle could be made to harmonize. Pico labored long to unify the two systems and wrote a number of treatises on the subject. He also studied the Jewish Talmud and the Cabbala.

Pico was strongly opposed to astrology which was widely esteemed in the Middle Ages. Petrarch had expressed hatred of this fraudulent science. The members of the Platonic academy accepted it, but Pico

made an epoch in the subject by his famous refutation. He detected in this belief the root of all impiety and immorality. If the astrologer, he maintained, believes in anything at all, he must worship not God, but the planets, from which all good and evil are derived. All other superstitions find a ready instrument in astrology, which serves as handmaid to geomancy, chiromancy, and magic of every kind. As to morality, he maintained that nothing can foster evil more than the opinion that heaven itself is the cause of it, in which case faith in eternal happiness and punishment must also disappear. Pico even took the trouble to check off the astrologers inductively, and found that in the course of a month three-fourths of their weather prophecies turned out false.[2]

But Pico's orthodoxy was suspected. He had the hardihood to draw up in Rome 900 theses about all sorts of questions which he offered to defend. As was natural, the pope and *curia* condemned some of them. Pico thereupon fled and settled in Florence where he spent his few remaining years.

Botticelli was commissioned to paint a picture to commemorate Lorenzo's return from Naples in 1480 after the conclusion of an alliance with King Ferrante. Pallas is shown leading the centaur by the lock. She is crowned with a chaplet of olive branches, and her skirt is adorned with the device of the Medici, the *palle* or balls. This picture typifies the triumph of Lorenzo's house over all obstacles of war and treachery. Botticelli was the truest counterpart of the literary tendencies of his day, and more especially of those of his chief patron.

[2] T. Burckhardt, *The Civilization of the Renaissance in Italy* (Oxford Univ. Press), p. 272.

PART VIII

Quattrocento Renaissance Culture Outside Florence

Chapter 16

RENAISSANCE IN NORTHERN ITALY (OUTSIDE TUSCANY) AND IN UMBRIA

*H*UMANISM ALSO flourished in the valley of the Po, from Milan to the Adriatic. While the Renaissance was essentially the cultural product of the vigorous urban life of this region, its history was also influenced by important princely and feudal families. The fertile soil of Lombardy and Venetia produced a hardy peasantry and a powerful nobility. From this feudal aristocracy had sprung many of the tyrants who seized the lordship (*signoria*) of the towns in the Lombard plain when the bourgeoisie proved incapable of ruling themselves. A rank growth of feudal and bourgeois habits and ideas, made possible by the economic progress of the Middle Ages, flourished in the towns.

RENAISSANCE CULTURE IN MILAN

The new humanist learning and novel ways of viewing life did not thrive noticeably at the Visconti court of Milan. Duke Gian Galeazzo (1378–1402), however, showed some interest in the new scholarship and collected a library. Filippo Maria (1412–1447) was a typical despot of the Renaissance. His craft, autocratic rule, and boundless cruelty were, in part at least, dictated by political necessity. He ruled by terrorism and kept himself aloof from his subjects. He could not, therefore, play the role of a beneficent Maecenas. Nevertheless, he devoted some study to Latin classics. His secretary, Pier Candido Decembrio (1392–1477), a pupil of Chrysoloras, worked at the Milanese court from 1419 to 1447. Although engaged in diplomatic activities, he found time to write a colossal number of books, translations as well as treatises, most of which, however, were never printed.

The Milanese, as told above, sought to recapture their freedom after Filippo's death in 1547 and established the Ambrosian Republic, named after St. Ambrose, the popular saint of the city. But they soon (1450) fell under the tyranny of a parvenu, Francesco Sforza (d. 1466), the son of Muzio Attendolo Sforza, successful *condottiere* of the troublous days of the Great Schism. Duke Francesco did not share fully in the humanist life of the time, but so important was the vogue of the new letters that he found it necessary to play the patron. His treasury was empty, his family boasted no ancient lineage, and he personally cared little for the Muses. He believed, however, that these defects could be remedied by inducing humanists to fill the world with praise of his house. Francesco Filelfo (1398–1481), the most important humanist at his court, was the right man to do this. He was born near Florence, studied at Padua where he showed ability to absorb an astonishing amount of learning, was appointed secretary to the Venetian embassy in Constantinople (1419–1427), became a master of Greek, and married a niece of Manuel Chrysoloras who, as we have learned, had taught Greek in Florence.

Filelfo possessed a photographic memory but little creative ability. He was inordinately vain and boasted that he had read all Greek and Latin writers from beginning to end. He moved to Florence in 1429 where his humanist achievements were fully appreciated. Great numbers attended his lectures. Devoid of tact and good sense, he antagonized Niccolò Niccoli and other Medicean protégés. Soon he began to oppose Cosimo and support his political opponents. Poggio Bracciolini lashed Filelfo with scathing language, accusing him of all sorts of crimes. When Cosimo returned from exile in 1434, Filelfo was forced to flee and until 1439 found refuge with the Piccolomini of Siena. In 1440 he entered the service of Filippo Maria Visconti who supported him liberally. When Francesco Sforza assumed control of Milan, Filelfo found in him a desired patron.

For years Filelfo labored over his great epic poem, the *Sforzias*, in which he sang fulsome praises of the house of Sforza just as Vergil once had recited the deeds of Aeneas. The poem, however, lacked inspiration and was filled with endless allegories. Filelfo confidently expected that this work would make him eternally famous (such often was the Renaissance zeal for *gloria,* or fame). But posterity decreed otherwise, for of the twenty-four books, eleven were finished and only eight have survived. Filelfo's fame rests solely upon his cult of classical letters. How different was Sforza's patronage from that of Cosimo and Lorenzo! Few men in any age have been able to choose the best creative spirits for patronage, and Sforza was not one of them. Consequently in this respect his court never equaled in splendor that of the Medici.

The Certosa, a Carthusian convent near Pavia, is the one great Renaissance architectural monument associated with the Visconti and the Sforzas. It was begun by Gian Galeazzo Visconti, the ruler who planned and began the Gothic cathedral of Milan. This cathedral shares in the late medieval tendency to overrich ornamentation. The edifice, however, is by no means inferior in its structural aspects to its Gothic sisters of northern Europe. The Certosa was planned originally according to the Romanesque style of Lombardy, but under the Sforzas plans were altered. Construction was inspired by the new studies of classical Roman architecture, and Roman decoration was used. Thus in the lower story one finds rectangular windows while elsewhere galleries and windows have round arches. The hybrid character of this building well illustrates how architectural ideas were changing.

Galeazzo Maria Sforza (1466–1476) succeeded his father Francesco. He and his sister Ippolita were educated according to the new humanist conceptions. They became proficient in Greek and Latin in their early teens and were repeatedly called upon to give orations or addresses before visiting princes or their delegates. These speeches created a deep impression. Galeazzo Maria thus in a way approximated the Renaissance ideal of a prince. Humanist ideas throve among his subjects. Classical literature possessed great fascination for young men who hated the duke's cruelty and were eager for a republic.

Fired by the tales of republican Rome, three of them resolved to kill the tyrant. Their design was carried out on December 26, 1476, when they stabbed the duke at the door of the cathedral. One of the assassins escaped but was seized and put to torture. To his confessor he said, " 'I know that by my sins I have deserved even greater torments, could my body but bear them . . . but I trust that the holy deed for which I die will obtain mercy for me at the hands of the Supreme Judge. And were I reborn ten times and ten times to perish in these torments, I would give my blood and all my strength for this sacred end.' . . . Mangled, under the knife of the executioner, a loud cry escaped the unfortunate man. 'Be of good cheer, Girolamo [his name was Girolamo Olgati]! Death is bitter, but fame is eternal! The memory of this deed will live long!'"[1] Such was the influence ancient classics frequently exerted upon men of the *Quattrocento*. Piling up treasure in heaven was desirable, but secular fame (*gloria*), according to Renaissance conceptions, was especially coveted.

Ludovico Sforza next succeeded to the government which his nephew Gian Galeazzo Sforza (d. 1494), the son of Galeazzo Maria, was too weak to assume. He has been variously judged and many unfavorable things have been said of him—for example, that he poisoned his nephew. This can readily be disproved. We are to regard him, however, as "the most perfect type of the despot of that age, and, as a kind of natural product, [he] almost disarms our moral judgment. Notwithstanding the profound immorality of the means he employed, he used them with perfect ingenuousness; no one would probably have been more astonished than himself to learn that, for the choice of means as well as of ends, a human being is morally responsible; he would rather have reckoned it as a singular virtue that, so far as possible, he had abstained from too free a use of the punishment of death."

Court life in Milan was especially interesting. Lombardy was an immensely fertile region teeming with wild life. The Sforzas possessed hunting lodges and palaces at Vigevano, Pavia, and other places. The castle at Pavia sometimes lodged as many as 400 persons besides envoys from foreign princes who came to the duke on business. Isabella of Aragon, wife of Gian Galeazzo, and Ludovico's wife, Beatrice d'Este, usually attended the gay hunting parties. On such occasions ladies wore their dazzling gems which in those days of poor artificial lighting could not be displayed in the evening so well as in the sunlight. Scholars, painters, and sculptors were brought to the court. Bramante (1514) was employed to improve the little church of Santa Maria delle Grazie in Milan. Omodeo (d. 1522) constructed the façade of the Certosa. Romano (1465–1512) carved a number of busts of the ducal family. Solari (d. 1525) was commissioned to prepare the decorations on the famous tomb of Ludovico and Beatrice. For 60 years it rested in Santa Maria delle Grazie until it was moved to the Certosa.

Leonardo da Vinci (1452–1519) was the one great light at the court of Milan. He was invited thither to create an equestrian statue of Francesco Sforza like Donatello's *Gattamelata* and Verocchio's *Colleone*. The statue was to immortalize the great duke. Leonardo worked on it for many years, and his patron grew weary of his endless experimentation. Nevertheless, Leonardo ingratiated himself by his brilliant conversation

[1] P. Pasolini, *Catherine Sforza*, New York, 1898, pp. 29–31.

and gave Ludovico advice about all sorts of engineering projects. Although the model of the statue was nearly completed, it was never cast in bronze. After Ludovico's fall in 1499, French soldiers destroyed it. Leonardo also painted some famous pictures, portraits of Ludovico's circle. Other works executed at this time are the *Virgin of the Rocks, The Virgin and St. Anne,* and the *Last Supper,* the last a fresco in Santa Maria delle Grazie. It is striking that the Sforzas did not, like the Medici, create artists, but preferred to patronize men who had won reputation in other places.

CONTRIBUTION OF MANTUA: EDUCATION AND PAINTING

Mantua played a special role in the Renaissance. Gain Francesco I (d. 1444) made it the most significant center of the new Renaissance education when he invited Vittorino da Feltre (d. 1446) to open a humanist school at his court. One of the first contributions of the classical revival was a new conception of education. Traditional methods and ideals were too banal and too practical to be truly educative. Classical ideas about learning, superior to contemporary methods, again became practicable. Pier Paolo Vergerio (d. 1419), who wrote *De Ingenuis Moribus,* or *On Good Manners,* was one of the first to draw his ideas from practices developed in the city life of Greece and Rome as set forth by Plato, Plutarch, and Cicero. Gasparino da Barzizza had opened a humanist school in Padua as early as 1408. Progress was slow, however, until princes became sufficiently interested to establish schools at their courts. It is for this reason that Vittorino's school, opened in 1425, was so important.

Vittorino believed that boys and girls alike were to be educated in the higher activities of man and prepared to play a part in the environment in which the new humanist learning and refined bourgeois manners were becoming more and more important. Hence they were to be educated in those studies which the men of the *Quattrocento* regarded as supremely important. They were not to be given a simple vocational training as was all too customary among the nobility, bourgeoisie, and peasantry. Vittorino believed that Greek, Latin, and Italian literature, together with mathematics, drawing, and music should receive major attention. Physical education in the form of horseback riding, swimming, fencing, and marching was emphasized and made obligatory. His students were drawn from the household of the Gonzaga princes and the nobility of Mantua. Children from the lower classes also were admitted, for such education was not to be restricted to any one class; it was as broad as humanity which embraced every man, woman, and child. Vittorino required the same mental effort from all regardless of social status. Equality was an effective motto. All were subjected to common rules regarding dress, food, and comforts. Good manners were stressed. Character was emphasized and religion was not neglected, for the students were required to study the Bible and the Church fathers, especially St. Augustine. The school was situated in attractive surroundings; hence it was named *La Casa Gioiosa* (Happy House). Vittorino was probably the most effective teacher of modern times. He exercised unusual influence upon his pupils and shaped their moral and intellectual life to a surprising degree. Many of the finest characters of the age came from this school, and some of the ablest scholars of the Renaissance were trained by him.

Ludovico Gonzaga, who succeeded Gian Francesco in 1444, was one of Vittorino's pupils. Ludovico never ceased studying the classics and carried a copy of Caesar's *Commentaries* on his campaigns. He was also interested in art. He brought Mantegna (d. 1506) to his court, thereby adding luster to his little state. Born in 1431 in Vicenza, Mantegna was at ten years of age adopted by Francesco Squarcione (d. 1474) of Padua. Squarcione started his career as a tailor and maker of brocades, but he also shared in the popular enthusiasm for classical Greek and Roman antiquities and soon became an artist. Although not a genius in painting, he became very influential, for he started the popular fad of introducing classical bric-a-brac in his pictures. Such was his enthusiasm for archaeological themes that he painted living objects as if made of stone. An enthusiastic antiquarian, he traveled as far as Greece, collecting fragments of ancient statuary which he believed artists should use as models. Squarcione introduced the archaeological note into painting, the vogue of placing ruins of classical structures in backgrounds.

Between 1454 and 1459 Mantegna painted a series of frescoes in the Augustinian church of Padua and was at once hailed as the leader of painting in northern Italy. In 1459 he moved to Mantua at the request of Ludovico who needed a good painter. His great work, a group of paintings showing the court circles of the Gonzaga princes, is in the bridal room in the Mantuan castle. "The roof decoration is of unrivalled beauty. It is entirely in grisaille and gold, except the center which is painted in most delusive imitation of an opening through which we look up to the brilliant blue sky. Round it runs a parapet in marvellous perspective, and over this lean and look laughingly down into the room, a group of women, among them a negress; portraits, probably, of some of the favorites of the court *personale*."[2] Mantegna mastered most of the problems which the artists of the *Quattrocento* struggled to solve. Perspective was reduced to

[2] M. Cruttwell, *Andrea Mantegna*, London, 1901, p. 70.

a science, space was given unwonted reality, and foreshortening was audaciously practiced. He loved to give his pictures a classical setting, as is illustrated in the *Triumph of Julius Caesar* in Hampton Court Palace at London.

Nowhere is Mantegna's consummate artistry better revealed than in his *Madonna della Vittoria*. This masterpiece commemorates the Battle of Fornovo on July 6, 1495, in which the French forces of Charles VIII cut their way through the Italian troops under the *condottiere* Francesco Gonzaga, marquis of Mantua. For the French this was an empty victory, because it was the last stage of an inglorious and enforced withdrawal begun some months before at Naples. But to the Italians it seemed like a great victory, for it freed their country from a foreign invader, and the Virgin's prayers were solicited that they might be freed of this threat to their liberties. This became the theme of Mantegna's great painting. The virgin is seated on an elevated throne before a leafy arbor decorated with pears and other fruits. Two warrior saints—St. Michael at her right and St. George at her left—hold up her protecting mantel, thus drawing the eye of the beholder to the central figures of the picture. Here the Christ Child is standing in His mother's lap. Mother and Son are keeping their eyes fixed upon the Gonzaga hero kneeling at the Virgin's right. Her right arm is extended, in subtle foreshortening, over His head. On her left, is a kneeling figure of St. Anne intently observing the Virgin giving her blessing. Above St. Anne, at the Virgin's left knee, stands the child-like figure of St. John the Baptist gazing intently upon the Christ Child above him. In this masterpiece Mantegna combined all the studied artistry of the *Quattrocento*—effective anatomy, excellent composition, subtle foreshortening, chiaroscuro, and perfect unity.

Isabella of Este (d. 1539), wife of Francesco I (1484–1519), was one of the noteworthy personalities of the Mantuan court. Trained in the best humanist traditions, she was an ardent lover of the classics and the new art. She collected objects of classical antiquity, pictures by recent painters, and all sorts of objects of art and placed them in her *grotta*. These rooms became famous throughout Italy and even in northern Europe. She patronized Leonardo da Vinci, showed great interest in the writings of Ariosto and Castiglione, and enjoyed the homage of noted personalities of the day.

THE RENAISSANCE AT THE COURT OF FERRARA AND IN MODENA

The court of Ferrara also made characteristic and noteworthy contributions to the culture of the Renaissance. The origins of the Este family are lost in the dimness of the Middle Ages. Fratricidal strife filled its annals because the popes from whom it held Ferrara in fee often preferred to bestow the fief upon younger sons, a procedure which violated the feudal principle of primogeniture. Niccolò III (1393–1441) was a man of the transition. In manners and ideas he belonged to the Middle Ages, but he also revealed the character of a Renaissance prince. He was cruel and violent, a man of vicious life. He knew little Latin but preferred the courtly romances of Roland and King Arthur. Love for these and other medieval themes remained a trait of the court of Ferrara throughout the Renaissance. In 1429 Niccolò succeeded in bringing Guarino da Verona to Ferrara. This humanist schoolmaster established a court school for the Este family as Vittorino da Feltre had done in Mantua.

Lionello (1441–1450), who succeeded his father, was trained by Guarino and showed greater sympathy for the new ideas. He knew the Latin classics well, and his physical training consisted in riding, swimming, running, jumping, fencing, and dancing. Only later did he receive instruction in arms. He corresponded with the chief humanists of his day, but withal kept alive a keen affection for his mother tongue and, inspired by Petrarch, wrote sonnets. He married Margherita Gonzaga, a pupil of Vittorino da Feltre's school in Mantua. She also was an admirer of Latin and Greek classics.

Thus were laid the secure bases of humanist culture in Ferrara. Lionello collected a library of classical authors, appointed humanist scholars to teach in the University of Ferrara, supported itinerant scholars who sought his patronage, and associated with men like the Greek Theodore Gaza who composed the first Renaissance Greek grammar, León Battista Alberti, and the Strozzi family who had been exiled from Florence. He formed a club for the discussion of humanist themes. Refined social intercourse dominated the court; the rudeness of older feudal manners rapidly disappeared, for Guarino taught that man was created not only to live (*vivere*) but to live with (*convivere*) his fellow men. Even in governmental policy the urbanity of humanism is to be traced. Lionello aimed to make his state a happier place for his subjects.

Borso (1450–1471), Lionello's brother who succeeded him, is an interesting example of cultural atavism in that he cared nothing for humanism but preferred traditional chivalric conceptions. He did not cultivate Latin, and the humanist circle which had been formed in the days of Lionello gradually melted away. Borso loved his native Italian language, and scholars who sought his favor translated Latin works into Italian or wrote original compositions in it.

His brother Ercole (1471–1505) succeeded him. He married Eleonora, daughter of King Ferrante of Naples, a typical woman of the Renaissance. She was fond of music, collected pictures by Mantegna and Bellini, and was interested in Latin classics. She became the mother of two remarkable daughters, Isabella and Beatrice, who married Francesco Gonzaga and Ludovico Sforza, respectively. They were educated by Battista da Guarino (1370–1460), son of Guarino da Verona, and made their courts in Mantua and Milan famous as centers of Renaissance culture.

Ercole was especially fond of music and dramatics. Flemish musicians, the best in Europe at that moment, had long been welcome at the court of Ferrara. Eleonora, who cultivated letters far more than did Ercole, formed a literary coterie. The exiled Strozzi family continued to be important in Ferrara. Tito Strozzi (1422–1505), Ercole's court poet, was employed in diplomatic missions. He and Battista da Guarino championed the view that Latin and not Italian was the proper vehicle of ideas. The younger generation preferred Italian, and finally the mother tongue triumphed in court circles of Ferrara, as it had done in Medicean Florence. But humanism was becoming pedantic in some quarters and losing its pristine freshness.

Chivalric customs and conceptions, however, retained great vigor in Ferrara. Feasts, tournaments, and the chase were the order of the day. Borso built a summer palace called Schifanoia, or Sans Souci. Its walls were decorated according to that prince's taste by Cosimo Tura (d. 1495) and Francesco Cossa (d. 1477), both of whom were influenced by Mantegna. Their frescoes are interesting portrayals of the Renaissance life of Ferrara; they reveal Borso's interest in horses, hunting, embassies, and astrology. There is also a beautiful allegory of *Autumn* by Cossa, which shows a young woman tending a vineyard. She carries a spade in her right hand, her left hand, holding a vine with trusses of grapes, rests on a hoe over her left shoulder. In the background are green hills. Schifanoia was a villa like the one at Careggi built by Cosimo. But how different was its life! The Medici were bourgeois, but the Este were an old feudal family who could not forget their knightly ideals.

Boiardo (1434–1494) was vassal of the dukes of Ferrara and a member of an old feudal family. He represented Duke Ercole in various capacities, studied the classics, wrote poetry for the court, but nevertheless cherished medieval themes above those cultivated by humanists. He wrote verses which were inspired by his love for one of the court beauties who rejected him. This experience influenced his *Orlando Innamorato*, a story drawn from the cycle of tales about Roland and Charlemagne. Angelica, daughter of the Tartar king, appears in Paris at a tournament given by Charlemagne and proposed that the person who defeats her brother in the lists shall claim her hand in marriage. Angelica employs magic to prevent her brother's defeat and plans to bring some of the bravest knights of Charlemagne's court captive to Tartary. She disappears by means of a magic ring but is pursued by Rinaldo and Orlando through the Ardennes. Angelica drinks from the fountain of love and is seized with a violent passion for Rinaldo who, however, has quaffed from the fountain which extinguishes love. Orlando is desperately enamored with the entrancing princess.

Orlando is a Renaissance character. He is no hero, as was Roland at Ronceval, nor a pure hearted knight who did no wrong, but a man of unbounded passion who stops at nothing in order to possess Angelica. Orlando practically declares that medieval chivalric virtues are obsolete. Angelica's father says that he crushed the skull of a teacher who had tried to teach him to read and write. A knight should be bold in battle, true to his word; he should not read or study.

> I think there's little chivalric virtue
> In poring over a book and racking one's brain,
> But it befits a knight noble and fair
> To be strong in body and dextrous at arms;
> For a doctor 'tis well to have knowledge
> But others should know only what is necessary.
> Responded Orlando, "With you I too testify
> That arms are most honorable for man
> But knowledge does not make one less worthy
> It adorns him as flowers deck a field."[3]

Angelica may be regarded as the coquettish type of woman common in Renaissance courts. Freed from the restraints of feudal society, women became more independent.

Modena, situated in the western part of the Romagna and ruled by the dukes of Ferrara, produced a remarkable master of terra cotta *pietàs* in the person of Guido Mazzoni (d. 1518). As a practical craftsman he made masks for theatrical plays, directed public festivals, and was skillful in the art of pantomime. His remarkable *pietà*, preserved in the church of San Giovanni in Modena, reveals a master of the art of the High Renaissance. At the foot of the cross are arranged in balanced composition seven figures weeping over the dead figure of the crucified Christ before them. The dramatic fervor of St. Mary, St. Mary Magdalene, and St. John the Baptist is most effectively expressed.

[3] *Orlando Innamorato*, Part I, Canto XVIII, no. 43.

RENAISSANCE CONTRIBUTION OF URBINO

The narrow limits of the duchy of Urbino and the modest wealth of its mountainous territory kept it from playing a leading part in the Renaissance. Such was the character of its rulers, however, that the court became famous under Duke Federigo (1444–1482), a humanist prince. Educated at the court of Mantua, he was deeply influenced by the tuition of Vittorino da Feltre. He was fond of Greek and Latin classics but never lost his interest in practical military affairs, for as a *condottiere* he was the equal of the best generals of his day. When on campaigns, he read ancient historians and the works of Aristotle. He was well versed in the church fathers. As became a humanist prince, he made gifts to scholars in want; indeed, it is stated that there were few literary men who did not receive generous gifts from him.

Duke Federigo had one great ambition:

> He alone had a mind to do what no one had done in a thousand years or more; that is, to create the finest library since ancient times. He spared neither cost nor labor, and when he knew of a fine book, whether in Italy or not, he would send for it. It is now fourteen years ago since he began the library, and he always employed, in Urbino, in Florence, and in other places, thirty or forty scribes in his service. He took the only way to make a fine library like this: by beginning with the Latin poets, with any comments on the same which might seem merited; next the orators, with the works of Tully and all Latin writers and grammarians of merit; so that not one of the leading writers in this faculty should be wanted. He sought also all the known works on history in Latin, and not only those, but likewise the histories of Greek writers done into Latin, and the orators as well. The duke also desired to have every work on moral and natural philosophy in Latin, or in Latin translations from Greek. As to the sacred doctors in Latin, he had the works of all four, and what a noble set of letters and writings we have here; bought without regard to cost. . . . He had an edition of the Bible made in two most beautiful volumes, illustrated in the finest possible manner and bound in gold brocade with rich silver fittings. . . . There were all the works of modern writers beginning with Pope Pius; of Petrarch and Dante in Latin and in the vulgar tongue. . . . He added to the books written by ancient and modern doctors on all the faculties all the books known in Greek. . . . The duke, having completed this noble work at the great cost of thirty thousand ducats . . . determined to give every writer a worthy finish by binding his work in scarlet and silver.

As a connoisseur of art, Federigo showed remarkable taste. "To hear him talk of sculpture you would deem it was his own art." He was at great pains to bring to his palace the finest products of Flemish looms. Justus of Ghent, a Flemish artist (d. 1480?), painted a famous picture of him "which only wanted breath." The palace which Federigo built in Urbino is especially famous.

> [It was] . . . to the opinion of many men, the fairest that was to be found in all Italy, and [he] so furnished it with all necessary things belonging thereto, that it appeared not a palace, but a city in form of a palace, and that not only with ordinary matters, as silver plate, hangings for chambers of very rich cloth of gold, of silk, and other costly materials, but also for their beauty: and to deck it out withal, placed there a wondrous number of ancient images of marble and metal, very excellent paintings and instruments of music of all sorts, and nothing would he have there but what was most rare and excellent.[4]

Federigo was succeeded by his son Guidobaldo (1482–1508), who married Elisabetta Gonzaga, one of the noblest of Renaissance women. Her court is famous because the masterpiece of humanist chivalry, the *Courtier*, was composed there by Baldassare Castiglione.

SIGISMONDO MALATESTA—RENAISSANCE PATRON

The princes of Rimini and Cesena here also are worthy of some attention. Sigismondo Malatesta (1417–1468) was the most significant of them. Brought up in the Romagna amid the tumultuous and violent life of that region, he was early initiated into the secrets of Italian *condottiere* warfare. Bold, resourceful, utterly unscrupulous, he was a typical product of the chaotic political life of the *Quattrocento*. Furthermore, he possessed a nimble mind delicately sensitive to the great artistic revolution of the age. He visited Florence, eager to play the part of a Maecenas in his ancestral capital of Rimini. He surrounded himself with servile courtiers who heaped adulation upon him with their poetry. His own poems give us a vivid conception of a Renaissance despot's many interests and worldly character.

Himself an admirer of the universal geniuses of the day, Sigismondo invited one of the greatest of them, León Battista Alberti, to live with him in Rimini:

> And with him Sigismondo talked of many things: of his ambition, which was boundless; of his dreams for Rimini that was to be a city of palaces and fortresses in the new manner; of war and arms and the art of government; of sovereign remedies against fatigues and wounds; of swords and engines of

---

[4] Adapted from *The Vespasiano Memoirs*, pp. 102–104.

war; of difficult feats of engineering; of the taking and destroying of castles, and of the building of them too; of the beauty and strength of horses and their swiftness; of hunting and of dogs; of women and the stars; of love, lust, and death—those three agonies for which there is no remedy; of family life, of which Messer Leon Battista was so hopeful, in which he was to be so fortunate; of art and painting and sculpture, and of the learning of Petrarch and Boccaccio; and he promised to show Sigismondo the house of the latter in the village of Corbignano, the which he did, and his discourse there led me first to think of these writers rather as men who had given us back the dead than as poets or novelists themselves.

Sigismondo indulged his every passion without restraint. Although married to a princess of the house of Este, he formed, as was common in the morally lax age of the Renaissance, a famous and illicit attachment to Isotta, one of the noteworthy women of the *Quattrocento*. His disregard of Christianity is revealed in his plans to revamp the old church of St. Francis—the Templum Malatestianum as it became known—in honor of Isotta and himself.

> If the spirit of Alberti impressed every part, it was the genius of Sigismondo that gave it life; and there again and again around the marble platform, in a frieze of dancing *putti* [or boys], Messer Matteo da Pasti carved his head as in a medal, and between these medallions others bearing his shield, and others bearing his sign, in the which the "S" of Sigismondo and the "I" of Isotta, while there were beautiful and marvellous leaves, flowers, and devices. . . . It was a temple built to the ever-living God, who hides Himself in the beauty of the world, whom men called Zeus, whom we call the Father, who is to be found in the philosophy of Plato as well as in the gospel of Jesus. . . . This temple raised to the everliving God was also to be the monument and symbol of his life. Therein he himself was to be buried, and Madonna Isotta whom he had loved; here too lay his ancestors, and many holy men who had been attached to his family; while around them, in those tombs under the arches without, philosophers, artists, and soldiers of his court were to sleep in death, even as they had wakened in life, for his glory and for witnesses of his dream.[5]

Nor did Sigismondo have any regard for traditional morality. He murdered, or caused to be murdered, his wives, was said to be guilty of rape and arson, openly insulted the Host, profaned churches, and mocked the teachings of the Church. As a prince he might have played a resplendent part in Renaissance history had he had sufficient moral seriousness and had his means permitted. Nevertheless, he was one of the most

[5] F. Hutton, *Sigismondo Pandolfo Malatesta, Lord of Rimini,* London, 1906, pp. 69–70, 203–204.

remarkable men of this period of transition from the Middle Ages to modern times.

THE CONTRIBUTION OF UMBRIA

The hilly country of Umbria and such neighboring lands as the Marches lying east of Tuscany, in addition to Perugia, possessed many small communities which served as centers of a simple pastoral and small-scale agricultural life. Social development and outlook naturally were conservative. Artistic tradition went back to the *Duecento* and the *Trecento*. An interesting example of Umbrian art is Benedetto Bonfigli's *Plague Banner* showing a city attacked by the arrows of a plague. Above and beyond the city, surrounded by plague saints like St. Sebastian, stands the majestic Virgin, clad in a widespreading mantle under which mankind finds protection. (For arrows representing plagues, see Psalms 64:4 and 91:5 in the King James' version.) Another painting speaking of the same Umbrian environment is the *Adoration of the Magi* by Gentile da Fabriano (1360–1450?). He loved the gleam and color of the Gothic tradition still powerful in Umbria and delighted to paint scenes suggestive of the intense and vivacious religious life of his native Umbria. The *Adoration of the Magi* portrays a magnificent and crowded cavalcade just come to a halt at the crib to do obeisance to the Christ Child. The picture reveals many influences—of Giotto, the Sienese school, and the Gothic tradition generally.

But Umbrian art would have signified little had it not been for the impulse given to painting by Piero della Francesca, born in Borgo San Sepolcro (d. 1492). He studied in Florence and was influenced by Antonio Pollaiuolo's muscularity and statuesque immobility of body. One of Piero's pupils, Melozzo da Forli (1438–1494), readily overcame this feature of his master's work. His *Sixtus IV and his Court* in the Vatican gallery is a noteworthy masterpiece.

Luca Signorelli (1450?–1523), born in Cortona, also reveals the influence of Pollaiuolo. Caring little for color, he sought to portray effective action. His famous works are the frescoes in the cathedral of Orvieto, representing events at the final judgment: *Preaching of Antichrist, Resurrection, Rejection of the Wicked,* and *Acceptance of the Saved.* The *Resurrection* is instructive, for it gave the artist a chance to display his skill in anatomy. Bodies are rising from the graves, skeletons acquire missing parts, and the fully resurrected stand around nude, gazing upward into the skies whence angels are calling to the dead to rise from their graves.

Pietro Perugino (1446–1524) remained a more faithful follower of the Umbrian manner. He chastened Byzantine traditions by studying Fra Angelico and other Florentine masters, and knew how to distribute his figures and coördinate the pose of hands and feet. His success in these things gave him a great reputation. However, there is much traditionalism in his paintings. Hands and feet are too small; the pursed lips and rotund faces seem unreal. On the other hand, his landscapes are delightfully reminiscent of the upper Tiber. Branches of trees have a feather-like effect. His treatment of space is interesting; the countryside disappears in the dimness of the horizon, and color is employed to heighten this effect of distance. These devices later became important in Raphael's work.

One of Perugino's masterpieces is a *Crucifixion* in the convent of the Santa Maddalena in Florence. Especially famous is the Sistine fresco of *Christ Giving the Keys to St. Peter* in which the artist shows himself superior to his rivals. The besetting faults of the latter were overcrowding, inability to give unity to a multitude, and formal arrangement of groups. Not so in Perugino's masterpiece. A broad space is presented with a relatively small number of figures in it so carefully arranged that not one is superfluous. In the immediate foreground stands Christ giving the keys to St. Peter. Behind them are some people so arranged as to make an interesting group. In the background is a temple surmounted by a dome. On each side stands a triumphal arch, and in the far distance are trees and mountains. No painter of the eighth decade of the *Quattrocento* so well created the illusion of space.

BEGINNINGS OF VENETIAN RENAISSANCE CULTURE

The Venetian Renaissance also had a course all its own. Situated at the confluence of the trade routes of the Occident, Venetians were accustomed to seeing the wealth of east, west, and north flow into the Grand Canal. Never had the sea failed in bringing to them everything they needed. They acted as if their monopoly would last forever, and became satisfied, complacent, self-centered. Economically and politically, their state was one of the most successful in the Middle Ages. It played a predominant part in the lives of its citizens. Revolution never marred the quiet and even tenor of its life. The wealthy patriciate found that all aspirations for honor and power were satisfied in serving the "most serene republic." The state with its grand functions, ceremonies, and festivals dominated the life of its subjects. It is necessary to grasp this if one is to understand the character of the Venetian Renaissance.

From nearby Padua, a city under the authority of Venice, came certain humanist impulses. Giovanni Conversini, Gasparino da Barzizza, Guarino da Verona, and Vittorino da Feltre all had friends and acquaintances in Venice. From the Greek East came many a codex containing works of classical pagan authors and the Greek church fathers. But Venetian patricians viewed the new vogue of humanist studies as a luxury in which they might indulge but which would never become a dominating passion with them as it did with the Medici and their coterie. Many Venetians such as the Giustiniani and Barbari favored humanist studies, but they rarely progressed beyond simple dilettantism. It is not surprising therefore that the great lights of humanism were attracted to other centers where enthusiastic patrons supported the new learning. Not until the *Cinquecento* did Venetians make their significant contributions to the Renaissance. The University of Padua remained a fosterling of the state where young Venetians went for instruction. The study of Greek was not accorded official recognition until 1463 when Chalcondyles was appointed to teach the language.

Venetians took a practical attitude toward humanism, as was shown by the way in which they received the invention of printing. This great craft was imported from Germany where it had been developed and perfected. Realizing its practical value, the Venetian Senate in 1469 decreed "that this peculiar invention of our time, unknown to those former, is in every way to be fostered and advanced." John of Speier was granted the privilege of plying his craft for 5 years, and Nicolas Jensen, another German, was given similar rights in 1470. Others followed their example, and Teobaldo Manuzio, or Aldo Manutius, became Venice's chief printer. Books were in growing demand. Not only were religious books and chivalric romances desired, but texts and translations of the classics were eagerly sought. Many humanists disliked the new craft, preferring the old handwritten codices, but the rapid multiplication of inexpensive texts assured victory for the printers. Many a person of modest fortune could now afford the luxury of some classical texts. Soon presses were flourishing in many Venetian provincial centers, chief of which were Padua, Verona, Brescia, Vicenza, and Bergamo.

During this time also Venetians began to develop a native art which was to attain undreamed perfection in the next century. At the beginning of the *Quattrocento* Venetian artists showed little inclination to follow Giotto and the Florentines. Byzantine traditions remained vigorous, and Venetian architecture was a hybrid of Gothic and Romanesque styles. The doges' palace and the Casa d'Oro, the magnificent palace of a wealthy merchant family situated on the Grand Canal, are famous examples of this manner. Classical influences in Venetian building were not to triumph until Sansovino began his work in 1527.

Painting, however, started on a magnificent career in the middle of the fifteenth century. At first the ideas and methods of Squarcione of Padua exerted much influence. The stiffness of his pictures and the sculpturesque manner for which the Paduan group is noted are observable in the earlier productions of Jacopo Bellini (1395–1470), founder of the famous Bellini family of artists. But Jacopo was also influenced by Florentine masters, for he visited the city on the Arno and learned to admire the scientific advance in painting made since the days of Masaccio. Mantegna's influence also was a strong factor in the evolution of the art of the Bellini; in fact, Jacopo's daughter Niccolosia became Mantegna's wife. The Bellini, Jacopo, and his two sons, Gentile (1429–1507) and Giovanni (1430–1516), laid the firm foundations of Venetian painting.

Other influences were helping to shape the growing school of art. Chief of them was the work of Antonello da Messina (d. 1479), a Sicilian who was well acquainted with the choice works of Flemish masters. He had an opportunity, it appears, to study them in Sicily and learned some of the secrets of their success, especially painting in oil. He was a skilled draughtsman, drew faces in three-quarters view, and profoundly affected all who studied his work. The Bellini brothers assumed leadership in Venetian painting about 1480. Gentile Bellini's famous *Corpus Christi Procession* in the Piazza of St. Mark's depicts one of the many civic festivals which make Venetian painting so interesting and instructive. The crowds are realistically portrayed, splendid clothes are carefully studied, and the buildings of the city are reproduced with loving fidelity. Another of his pictures is the *Recovery of the Cross* which, according to legend, had fallen into the water and was recovered miraculously. The scene is one of Venice's many canals. The flow of light upon the groups who stand about on the bridge and on the side of the canal, the shadows on the water, and the realism of the spectators make this a striking picture.

Mantegna's influence is more palpable in the works of Giovanni Bellini who copied features of the great Paduan such as the rigidity of drapery and landscape. But he painted his pictures in a more mellow manner. His madonnas possess an ineffable sweetness which distinguishes them from all the pictures of the century. The portrait *Doge Loredano* has a pleasing glow of soft and rich color and a feeling for quality of fabric typical of Venetian luxury. Vittore Carpaccio (d. 1523?) acquired the secret of luminous coloring from the Bellini. His canvases portrayed most eloquently the life of the time as he knew it in its varied aspects. His unwearied attention to detail, his sense of the dramatic, his skill with color, and his mastery of technique justly give his pictures an abiding place among the great paintings of the early *Cinquecento*. His greatest achievement is the scenes from the life of St. Ursula, painted for the guild of St. Ursula of Venice. Carpaccio may be regarded as the last of Venice's great masters of *Quattrocento*.

No brief account can do justice to the creative achievements of the exuberant life of the communities of northern Italy. The painting of Mantegna, the Bellini, and Carpaccio; the architecture of Alberti and his followers; the educational ideals of Vittorino da Feltre, and the cultivated life in the courts of the Lombard plain are some of the noblest accomplishments of the Renaissance in northern Italy. These creative achievements of the *Quattrocento* contributed their share to the brilliant accomplishments of the High Renaissance of the *Cinquecento*.

Chapter 17

RENAISSANCE ROME AND NAPLES:
ITS PAGAN NOTE

*W*HAT WAS THE attitude of humanists toward religion? To them cultivation of classical letters implied a fuller participation in ancient thought, although they did not propose to revive a purely pagan conception of life. Many of them remained loyal to the Church; but others like Valla and Platina, however, abandoned her teachings and became devotees of paganism. It seemed that the Church had lost its prestige with the elite of the bourgeoisie; its doctrines could scarcely compete with the charm of reviving pagan thought. The Renaissance in Rome therefore is significant. From the pontificate of Nicholas V (1447–1455) to the death of Clement VII (1523–1534) the papacy was called to face the economic, political, and cultural problems of the Renaissance. Situated in the Eternal City amid the ruins of the palaces of the Caesars, would it escape the spirit of reviving paganism?

HUMANIST ATTITUDE TOWARD CHURCH
AND RELIGION

When Pope Martin V (1417–1431) returned from the Council of Constance he found the ancient city in ruins. The long absence of the papacy during the Avignonese period and the subsequent wars of the Great Schism had wrought much damage. Trade was stagnant, population was dwindling, and the city and its environs were infested with brigands and predatory barons. Many of the churches threatened to crumble to ruin; the rain beat upon the paved floors of St. Peter's. The Palatine Hill was a mass of debris covered with a rank growth of vegetation. The Forum, choked with sand and refuse, served as pasture for cattle. The Viminal, Quirinal, and Pincian Hills were uninhabited. The ancient aqueducts had crumbled, and the inhabitants depended upon the Tiber and shallow cisterns for their water. The population was crowded into the narrow area between the Capitoline Hill and the Campus Martius

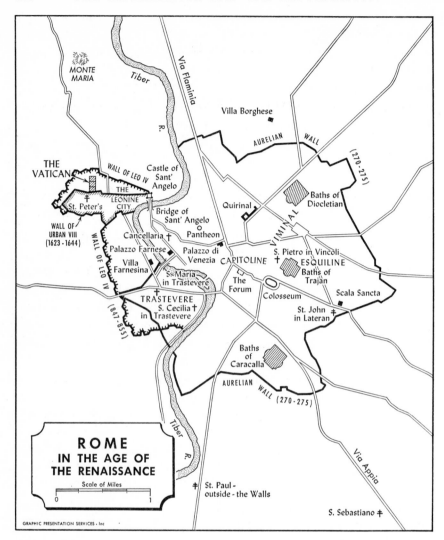

MONTE MARIA

Tiber

Via Flaminia

R.

Villa Borghese

AURELIAN WALL

(270-275)

THE VATICAN

WALL OF LEO IV

Castle of Sant' Angelo

THE LEONINE CITY

St. Peter's

Quirinal

Baths of Diocletian

WALL OF URBAN VIII (1623-1644)

Bridge of Sant' Angelo

Pantheon

VIMINAL

Cancellaria

Palazzo Farnese

Villa Farnesina

Palazzo di Venezia

CAPITOLINE

S. Pietro in Vincoli

ESQUILINE

Baths of Trajan

WALL OF LEO IV

S. Maria in Trastevere

The Forum

Colosseum

Scala Sancta

TRASTEVERE

S. Cecilia in Trastevere

(847-855)

St. John in Lateran

Baths of Caracalla

AURELIAN WALL (270-275)

ROME
IN THE AGE OF
THE RENAISSANCE

Scale of Miles

0   1

GRAPHIC PRESENTATION SERVICES · Inc

Tiber R.

St. Paul - outside - the Walls

Via Appia

S. Sebastiano

and along the streets which led to the bridge connecting the old city on the left bank with the castle of Sant' Angelo and the Vatican on the right. The Lateran palace and church, the abode of former popes, had suffered severely during the fourteenth century. Beginning with Martin V, pontiffs made the Vatican their habitual residence.

Martin V and Eugenius IV (1431–1447) were occupied chiefly with the problems of the schism, the question of reform, and their relations with Rome and the papal states. Neither of these pontiffs therefore took much interest in classical studies. Some humanists, however, had found service in the curia, chief of whom was Poggio Bracciolini (1380–1459).

Born of poor parents who lived near Florence, he became acquainted with Coluccio Salutati by a lucky chance and thus was enabled to share in humanist studies. Poggio entered the papal service and, as has been noted previously, was wonderfully successful in collecting manuscripts. He was famed as a letter writer. One of his most striking letters contains an animated description of a bathing establishment which he visited at Baden Baden in Germany (1416), and another related the spirited defense which Jerome of Prague, a follower of John Hus, made before the fathers of Constance.

Poggio also wrote a collection of stories, or *Facetiae*, typical of the jokes told by people in inns and market places. Poggio states, however, that these anecdotes originated in the convivial evening gatherings which began at the papal court in the days of Martin V. These meetings were held in a room called the *Bugiale* or "Chamber of Lies." All sorts of themes were discussed in these stories, and their cynical criticism spared nothing, sacred or profane. Some of them, couched in good Latin, are as salacious as Boccaccio's tales; others are innocuous. The clergy are often made the butt of ridicule. The following may be taken as typical:

> One of those friars who wander about and ask alms in the name of St. Anthony, persuaded a peasant to give him some grain, promising him in return that all his belongings, and his sheep especially, should be free for a year of any harm or damage. The peasant, believing in the promise, allowed his sheep to stray freely, so that a wolf came and ate many of them. When next year, the friar returned and asked for his ration of grain, the peasant indignantly refused to give it him, lamenting how vain had proved the friar's promise. Asked by the religious the reason, the countryman replied that a wolf had gone off with several of his sheep. "A wolf!" said the other. "The wolf is an evil beast, which you must not trust. He would not only deceive St. Anthony but even Christ himself, if he could." It is a foolish thing to put trust in those whose business is deceit.[1]

Poggio was the first humanist to write a *Description of Rome (Descriptio Urbis Romae)* based upon first-hand observation. He also made a collection of Roman inscriptions which still possesses some value, and gathered and classified Latin coins. But it was in pamphlets above all that Poggio displayed his humanist ideas. In his encounters with Filelfo and Lorenzo Valla he had the fullest opportunity to employ all the qualities of humanist wit. Filelfo had run afoul of Niccolò Niccoli, as related above. Poggio rushed into the lists with the most vituperative invective. He spared nothing in Filelfo's past and gave to everything the worst possible

---

[1] *The Facetiae of Poggio*, London, 1928, pp. 105–106.

interpretation. He declared that Filelfo had fled from Italy because of some unworthy offense, and that at Constantinople he had seduced the daughter of John Chrysoloras in order to force her into marriage with him, and so on to the end. He concluded one of his tirades as follows: "Is there anyone, Filelfo, who does not despise and loathe you? Who of the guests you receive in your home has any consideration for you except those who put up with your boresome conversation in order to be entertained by the favors of your wife? You reeking goat, you horned monster, you evil-minded libeler, you, father of lies and fountain of every dissension, may divine wrath destroy you, the enemy of all virtues, you parricide, you who strive to damage wise and good folk by means of your lies and vices, your senseless and false accusations!"[2]

The reader should not take such apostrophes seriously. Often they were only rhetorical exercises which pleased the public and were soon forgotten. Poggio's literary encounters with Lorenzo Valla were as violent as those with Filelfo. One of his diatribes against Valla is a classic in vituperative literature. Valla was represented as having fallen into hell because of his evil deeds. The devils soon discovered how wicked a being had come into their hands and decided that it would be better to return him to earth where he might make conquests for Satan. Valla agreed to be faithful to them and swore an oath of fealty to Lucifer, the words of which are too indecent to be translated. In the vestibule of hell a gigantic statue of Valla was erected; on it appeared the words: "To Lorenzo Valla, their worthy comrade, by the inhabitants of hell!" Valla was not slow in answering this diatribe. He asserted that Guarino da Verona's cook and stable boy had set an examination in Latin for Poggio whose knowledge of that tongue was inferior to theirs!

Poggio's attitude toward churchmen was typical of many humanists. He was indifferent to the truth of Christian teaching. Although he served the curia for half a century, he felt no hesitation in lashing the clergy and friars for their alleged moral shortcomings. His *Dialogue against Hypocrites*, a diatribe on the faults of monks and friars, aroused no protest, not even in the curia itself. This work, as well as his *Facetiae*, was widely read and helped undermine traditional respect for the clergy. In his private life Poggio himself was far from perfect—he was the father of fourteen natural children. His superiors disliked this irregularity and suggested that he mend his ways. He was unfeeling enough to reject his faithful mistress, and, when 55 years of age, he married a maid of 18.

---

[2] Adapted from T. Soderhjelm and W. Soderhjelm, *De Italiaansche Renaissance*, Utrecht, 1903, p. 133.

In 1453 he was appointed chancellor of Florence and retired to a villa near his native Terranova where he spent his declining years.

THE HUMANISM OF POPE NICHOLAS V

Martin V and Eugenius IV were conservative men and took little interest in the revival of classical studies. Nevertheless, zeal for these studies was stimulated at the curia by Poggio and others, and their efforts were duly recognized when the humanist Thomas Parentucelli ascended the chair of St. Peter as Nicholas V (1447–1455). Born of an obscure family of Sarzana in 1398 and too poor to continue his education, he served as tutor to the sons of Rinaldo degli Albizzi and Palla Strozzi, members of the Florentine patriciate. Thus he was introduced into the humanist circles of Florence; this connection exercised an abiding influence upon his life. He studied at the University of Bologna, entered the service of the bishop of Bologna, succeeded to that office, and finally, in 1446, became cardinal. His election as pope was greeted with satisfaction by all humanists, for now they could expect the patronage of the Church.

The jubilee of 1450 brought many pilgrims to Rome and filled the impoverished coffers of the papacy. This money enabled Nicholas to conceive great projects. Rome was to be improved and beautified. Pope Nicholas V repaired the aqueduct Aqua Vergine and built the famous Trevi fountain. Bridges were renovated. Churches were repaired. On the Capitoline Hill Nicholas built the palace for the conservators and refinished that of the senators, as the officials of Rome were called. Filth and rubbish were carted away. Streets were straightened and paved. Vast building projects were conceived. A new St. Peter's was to be constructed, and broad avenues were to be laid out leading toward it. Important changes were effected in the Vatican palace. Similar projects were executed in provincial cities of the States of the Church.

To carry out these schemes Nicholas brought artists to Rome. They were for the most part Tuscans; thus the artistic ideas of Florence began to transform the Eternal City. Leon Battista Alberti was employed as architect. Fra Angelico decorated the walls of the Vatican chapel of St. Lawrence with scenes from the lives of that saint and of St. Stephen in which he attained his highest excellence. In these activities Nicholas displayed the passion for artistic embellishment so typical of Renaissance rulers.

Nicholas wished to make Rome again the proud capital of the world. It was necessary, therefore, to bring the greatest scholars within its walls.

Gianozzo Manetti (1406–1455) was invited to become apostolic secretary. He was a friend of Cosimo de' Medici and belonged to the coterie of humanists in Florence during the early part of the *Quattrocento*. He was a man of wide learning and was especially interested in the church fathers and the great moral works of antiquity such as Aristotle's *Ethics*. His religious interests led him to study Hebrew, and no other Italian of his day knew that language as well. He was a practical man and his services as orator, diplomat, and administrator were much esteemed. Nicholas was fond of him because of his piety and nobility of character. The best papal posts were bestowed upon men of this type and not upon monks and priests as had been the rule. Humanist activity in Rome was chiefly concerned with the translation of Greek classics into Latin. This was laudable, for, in spite of the work of Chrysoloras and his humanist disciples, knowledge of the Greek language remained a rare accomplishment. Poggio, for example, who never could read it fluently, came to blows with George of Trebizond (1396–1486), a Greek of overbearing conceit, who had found favor at the papal court and who twitted him because of his defective knowledge of Greek and Latin.

Poggio's scurrilous assault upon Lorenzo Valla (d. 1457) may well be forgotten, but not the scholar who repudiated the faith of his fathers and subjected papal claims to the sharp acid of historical criticism. Valla received his humanist education from Aurispa and Leonardo Bruni and obtained an appointment as papal secretary under Martin V. He was one of the humanists who abandoned Christian teaching and ethics, substituting for them the thought of ancient philosophers. Such was Nicholas V's zeal to make Rome a great center of humanist learning that men like Valla were eagerly welcomed. While professor of rhetoric in the University of Pavia, he published a book, *On Pleasure* (1431). This treatise is divided into three parts in which three persons advocate the point of view of the Christians, the Stoics, and the Epicureans. It taught that all natural desires should be gratified fully. Conventions of morality were not binding; in fact, Valla suggested that marriage should be abolished. His conception of pleasure was purely Epicurean.

Valla soon became secretary to King Alphonso I of Naples (1435–1458) and in 1440 wrote his treatise *On the Donation of Constantine*. According to accepted teaching throughout the Middle Ages, Constantine had given the bishop of Rome extensive temporal powers and had confirmed his grant in a document the authenticity of which was never questioned until the fifteenth century when Nicholas of Cusa and Reginald Pecock each had revealed its unhistorical character. Valla, however, made his critique a political pamphlet. As servant of the king of

Naples, he was interested in showing that papal suzerainty over the kingdom of Naples was without foundation in law or history. He held that Constantine's forgery was of recent date and that the papal claims were sheer usurpation. In common with all men of that day, Valla had an exaggerated idea of the significance of this document. For this reason the treatise occupies an important place in later controversies over papal power as well as in the development of historical criticism. Valla also wrote bitterly against monks and friars, but Nicholas disregarded these writings, welcomed him to Rome, and asked him to make translations of Homer, Herodotus, and Thucydides. Could the Holy Father have chosen a stranger guest or any other career than Valla's to throw so lurid a light upon the Rome of the early Renaissance?

Nicholas was eager to form a library of classical authors. Formerly popes had collected books on theology and canon law. Now a complete collection of the hitherto neglected Latin and Greek works was to be made for the papal library. Nicholas when a young priest had arranged the collection which his friend Cosimo de' Medici had made for the convent of San Marco in Florence. As pope, he bought as many manuscripts as he could find. Commissions were given scribes to make copies of rare works. Far and wide the search was made for new writings. Vespasiano da Bisticci, noted bibliophile of the day, was invited to Rome to build up the collection intended for public use and to be an adornment of the papacy which Nicholas wished to place at the very pinnacle of culture. He was eager to make his collection the largest in existence, and, when he died, it numbered over 1000 volumes. Unfortunately his successor did not carry out his plans and allowed the books to be scattered so that later under Sixtus IV the Vatican library had to be reëstablished.

These humanist activities resulted in an interesting political revolution. Emphasis upon the glamour of ancient Rome and the study of its literature stirred up hope for independence. The fickle populace was provoked to rebellion by one Stefano Porcaro who prepared a plot to establish a republic. A rising took place in January, 1453, but the plans miscarried and Stefano was seized and beheaded in the castle of Sant' Angelo. The conspiracy clearly showed the incompatibility of republican sentiments with papal leadership. The two could not exist side by side, and Nicholas put down the rising with a ruthlessness characteristic of the age but quite foreign to his nature.

Another event which grieved Nicholas was Mohammed II's final assault upon the Byzantine Empire. As head of the Christian world, the pontiff felt that he should do something to help the Greeks. True, they persisted in their schismatic ideas in spite of the agreements made at the Council of

Florence, but their dire extremity was a concern of Christian Europe. Nicholas fitted out a fleet of galleys, but it was captured by the Turks. Constantinople fell, on May 29, 1453, and Italy was stunned. Christendom suffered a serious blow, and humanists lamented that the ancient capital of letters had fallen into the hands of the infidel. Nicholas summoned all princes to prepare for a crusade, but the age of such undertakings was past. They were no longer possible since powerful centralized governments had taken the place of feudal principalities. Princes were jealously watching one another, fearful lest someone should gain an advantage. The French king was struggling with the duke of Burgundy, the king of England was ranged against France, the Spanish kingdoms were hostile to each other, and Poland was at war with the Teutonic Knights. The emperor of the Holy Roman Empire, the head of all earthly government, could do nothing, for the Congress of Ratisbon which he convened (April, 1454) to discuss plans for a crusade proved a dismal failure. No one came at the imperial request except Duke Philip of Burgundy, the ruler of the Low Countries. In March, 1455, Nicholas died, sorrowfully realizing that he had not been equal to the strenuous task.

RENAISSANCE ROME FROM 1455

Alfonso Borgia succeeded as Calixtus III (1455–1458). He was an old-fashioned man, impetuous, and determined upon immediate action against the Turks. He declared war, prepared a fleet, and announced that an army and a fleet would set out on the first of March in the next year. But such was the absorption of secular governments in their political interests that nothing came of the project, and the papal fleet accomplished no more. The Hungarians bore the brunt of battle and stayed the Turks' progress at the siege of Belgrade in April, 1456. Calixtus thus signally failed to accomplish anything. He discontinued the policy initiated by Nicholas in behalf of the new learning. Humanists began to leave Rome, and Nicholas' library was dissipated. Some attention, however, was given to the renovation of Roman churches.

Aeneas Sylvius Piccolomini became pope as Pius II (1458–1464). Born in 1405, he studied in Florence under Filelfo. He entered the service of a number of prelates, supported in his writings the claims of the Council of Basel, and was made secretary to the schismatic Felix V. When the proper moment arrived, he adroitly changed to the side of Eugenius IV. During youth and early manhood he led a dissolute life like some of the humanists and many high-placed persons of his day. He wrote a novel, *Lucretia and Euryalus*, which in salaciousness was not outdone by

Boccaccio. But toward the close of Eugenius IV's pontificate he turned against his former way of living. A remarkable change is observable after he was priested, for he became a deeply pious man; no moral fault can be found in his life as minister of the Church. Bitterly repenting his past, he sought to undo the evil he had done and tried to recall the books he had penned.

Aeneas Sylvius was a character typical of the Renaissance. He possessed vivacity of intellect, broad knowledge of mankind, and capacity to take delight in the thoughts and acts of men with whom he came in contact—characteristics one notes so often in the bourgeoisie of the *Quattrocento.* Yet he was not recognized by his contemporaries as one of the great men of his day. He did not employ the new classical learning to win a living or acquire position as did other humanists, nor did he care for the servile adulation which they sought to give him. Hence he did not measure up to what was expected of a Renaissance patron. But his writings are fully as significant as those of his humanist contemporaries. His *Commentaries* are important as a record of the events of his life; he projected a universal history, composed treatises on education, and was especially interested in history and geography.

Humanists were disappointed because he possessed the taste and good sense to value their fulsome flattery at its true worth. He was a genuine patron, but within limits. He gathered manuscripts, spent money on the embellishment of St. Peter's and the Vatican, and encouraged a few literary men. His passion for building is shown by his efforts to beautify the town of his birth, to which he gave a new name, Pienza, or "City of Pius."

The Turkish problem called for immediate action, and Pius laid plans for a crusade. He called a council of princes which met at Mantua from September, 1459, till the following January. The pontiff arrived early, but the princes were slow in appearing. It was found after deliberations had begun that although all might applaud the idea of a crusade, few cared to assume its responsibilities. "Christians prefer to war against one another rather than against the Turks. The beating of a bailiff, even of a slave, is enough to draw kings into war; against the Turks, who blaspheme our God, destroy our churches, and strive to destroy the whole Christian name, no one dares take up arms,"[3] ruefully remarked the pope.

To grasp the difficulties confronting the papacy, one must bear in mind the incompatibility of the pope's position as Italian prince with his post as head of Christendom. As feudal overlord of Naples, he was frequently

[3] M. Creighton, *A History of the Papacy from the Great Schism to the Sack of Rome,* III, 224–225.

called upon to deal with the Angevin claims which were opposed by the Aragonese incumbents. The attitude of France was always an important consideration because it supported the Angevin claims, and the emperor might at any moment interfere in Italian affairs. At the Congress of Mantua the French envoys urged a settlement of the Neapolitan problem. They even argued that their king had the right to appeal to a council against the pope's action. Nor were the Germans satisfied with the papacy. They had urgently asked for reform at Constance and Basel, and the imperial diet might at any moment suggest the calling of a council.

Pius was resolved to prevent any repetition of the confusion caused by the theory that councils were to govern the Church. He thought it desirable to declare once for all against the idea, and accordingly on January 18, 1460, issued his bull *Execrabilis*. It was the one tangible result of the Mantuan congress and placed the copestone on the edifice of papal power. Ambitious princes were forbidden to appeal to a council in the future and thus endanger the religious quiet of Christendom.

Paul II (1464–1471), the next pope, displayed only moderate enthusiasm for humanists. He distrusted their agile rhetoric which he knew might be employed against himself at any moment. He showed favor to Flavio Biondo and a few other scholars. He was an ardent collector of gems, stones, medals, tapestries, and carved objects, and placed them in the museum of the Palazzo Venetia built by him and still standing as a monument of the early Roman Renaissance. He was interested in printing which had been established at Subiaco as early as 1465.

Probably the most interesting episode of the pontificate was the pope's difficulty with the Roman Academy. Its head was Pomponio Leto (d. 1498), a pupil of Valla, from whom he imbibed enthusiasm for classical antiquity and hostility to Christianity. He affected a preference for *Stoicism*. A sentimental fanatic, he would burst into tears whenever he reflected upon the vanished glories of Rome. He had a garden on the Quirinal Hill which he tried to cultivate according to the precepts of Varro and Columella, Roman writers on agriculture.

Soon after his elevation Paul abolished the College of Abbreviators, or scribes, who drew up the public documents of the popes. This was a measure of economy, but it proved embarrassing because many of the scribes were humanists who knew how to use their power of language against the pontiff. Their chief, Bartolommeo Platina (d. 1481), was especially acrid and threatened to appeal to a council. Many of the abbreviators aired their grievances in the Academy of Pomponio Leto. There was much atheistic talk, and a desire was expressed for a republican government copied after the ancient Roman model. Remembering

Porcaro's conspiracy, Paul threw a number of the members of the Academy into prison (1468); but, as there really was no conspiracy, Leto and Platina were set at liberty. The Academy was suspended but was revived during the next pontificate, to be extinguished forever in the disaster of 1527.

Sixtus IV (1471–1484), a Franciscan friar it is interesting to note, was the first of Peter's successors to assume openly the manner and methods of secular Italian princes. As a ruler of a principality, the States of the Church, he found it necessary to strengthen his political power, and he relied upon his nephews whom he advanced to the highest positions in the gift of state and Church. Thus he inaugurated the baneful practice of nepotism which was to discredit the papacy during the next half century. By making himself an absolute prince he felt safe within his own borders. He knew that the papacy no longer enjoyed the full respect and affection of the people, for everywhere princes and states were bent on extending their power and possessions. This policy is well summed up by Bishop Mandell Creighton:

> Previous popes had trusted for the maintenance of their dominions to the respect generally felt toward the papacy, and to the support of the powers of Europe; Sixtus felt that neither of these was secure. He resolved no longer to shelter himself behind the claims of the papacy as an institution, but as a man to enter into Italian politics, and establish his temporal sovereignty by means of men, their weapons, and their enterprise. When he looked around him he found the papacy without friends in Italy. The pacific policy and the moderating position of Paul II had only been maintained by a resolute effort of self-restraint; it was not understood by other powers, and there was no guarantee that it could be safely continued. Sixtus did not think it worth while to give it a trial, but decided that he would use the resources and the authority of his office for the protection and extension of its temporal possessions.[4]

The great political venture of Sixtus' pontificate was the establishment of his nephew Girolamo Riario as prince in Imola and Forlì, a policy opposed by the Medici, as has been related above. The complete ascendancy of political interests over sacred concerns in the papal mind is revealed in Sixtus' connection with the murder of Giuliano de' Medici in 1478. In this episode Sixtus acted like a secular prince and did not scruple to employ his religious powers to advance his political interests. In other respects also he revealed the Renaissance prince. He labored to beautify Rome by straightening, widening, and paving streets, and building bridges, churches, walls, gates, and other structures. He repaired the

[4] *Ibid.,* IV, 71.

Hospital of Santo Spirito near the Vatican. He was an indefatigable collector of coins, gems, and precious objects of art and was the first to open a museum for the public.

Sixtus also favored humanist writers. Platina was commissioned to write a *History of the Popes*, a significant work in the development of historical writing because it marks a complete departure from the old method of arranging data by years and not according to their logical relations. John Argyropoulos was the chief Greek scholar in Rome, and Pomponio Leto continued to be the chief lecturer at the Academy. In 1471 Sixtus revived the Vatican Library which had suffered so sadly after the death of Nicholas V. Every effort was made to collect manuscripts. So successful was Sixtus that by 1484 his collection contained over 3500 volumes.

But it is as patron of painting that Sixtus is to be remembered. Melozzo da Forlì was employed to paint a fresco in the Vatican Library in which are shown Sixtus IV seated, with his four nephews standing and the librarian Platina kneeling before him. This picture is a magnificent artistic achievement and a most instructive document of the Renaissance. The Sistine Chapel was built by Sixtus, for whom it was named. The best painters of the day were invited to come to Rome and decorate its walls. The twelve frescoes on the side walls of the chapel are eloquent of the pontiff's taste and understanding. To the left, as one faces the altar, are six dealing with the career of Moses; opposite are six which illustrate Christ's mission on earth. These works are by Pinturicchio (an Umbrian painter who died in 1513), Signorelli, Botticelli, Ghirlandaio, and Perugino. The most significant, without doubt, is Perugino's great picture in which Christ gives the keys to St. Peter.

But all this patronage of art and learning did not of course compensate for the loss in moral prestige which the papacy suffered. The frank acceptance of the traditional methods of Italian politics nearly bankrupted the spiritual authority of the prince of the Church. The next pope, Innocent VIII (1484–1492), was not a man of edifying character. He allowed himself to drift with circumstances, and reversed the policy of Sixtus IV in regard to Florence, even making Lorenzo de' Medici his intimate adviser. As we shall learn, this secular policy, continued by subsequent pontiffs, contributed materially to the rise of Protestantism.

THE RENAISSANCE IN NAPLES

It remains to consider the Renaissance in Naples. The social structure and economic progress of that realm were not favorable to the new culture. The country remained feudal in social organization and manorial in economic life. A turbulent baronage, wedded in old chivalric conceptions, controlled the state. Towns were small, and a vigorous bourgeoisie did not exist there as in the urban centers of Tuscany and Lombardy. Naples therefore was too poor and conservative to become the home of Renaissance art and letters. Alfonso I (1435–1458), who succeeded in getting control of the realm in spite of Angevin claims, desired to be ranked among the Italian princes. It was necessary, therefore, to play the patron. Although untutored, he professed keen interest in learning and welcomed scholars to his court. An interesting artistic monument of his region is the triumphal arch over the entrance to the great castle in Naples.

Chief among Alfonso's favorites was Lorenzo Valla, who entered the royal service as secretary, and whose *Donation of Constantine*, directed against papal claims in Naples, has been described. Alfonso was succeeded by his natural son, Ferrante (1458–1494), a vindictive tyrant who stirred his baronage to revolt. He was interested in the new culture and befriended Antonio Beccadelli (1394–1471), a disciple of Valla who continued that scholar's hostility to religion and the clergy. He is famous because of his *Hermaphroditus*, epigrams of the grossest obscenity. Another humanist was Giovanni Pontano (1426–1503) who produced a number of histories, a type of literature which gave humanist flatterers opportunities to heap fulsome praises upon delighted despots. In common with most men of the day, Pontano was interested in astrology, in spite of Pico della Mirandola's disbelief in that science, and he taught that mathematics and astronomy were branches of astrology. Beccadelli and Pontano founded an academy in which humanist ideas were cultivated. But Renaissance culture did not flourish vigorously in Naples. Supported entirely by royal munificence, the new culture enjoyed only a precarious existence which came to an abrupt end in the destructive wars which disturbed the peace of the realm after its conquest by Charles VIII of France in 1495.

Chapter 18

ARTISTIC EXPRESSION DURING THE
HIGH RENAISSANCE

*T*HE CULMINATION of artistic expression during the High Renaissance —whether in painting, sculpture, or architecture—is one of the glories of the Italian High Renaissance. The thought and experimentation of a multitude of artists since the days of Giotto and Duccio were merged in a great creative triumph, one of the most brilliant in all art history. The great painters of the *Quattrocento*—Masaccio, Uccello, Francesca, Veneziano, Fra Filippo Lippi, Pollaiuolo, Verrocchio, Ghirlandaio, Mantegna, Botticelli, and Perugino—were forerunners of the artists of the High Renaissance as the first generation of the *Cinquecento* is frequently referred to.

THE GENIUS OF LEONARDO DA VINCI

Leonardo (1452–1519) was born in Vinci near Florence. His father was a notary, his mother a plain woman—a waitress, it is related. But the boy was endowed with extraordinary powers. He possessed courtly manners, ready wit, great physical strength, and an insatiable desire to investigate all things. These led to endless experimentation which occupied most of his time. He wished to know all things before he sought to recreate them in art. Leonardo was perhaps the best example of a universal man—a *uomo universale*—of the Renaissance. More than any other, he expressed the unceasing energy, creative impulse, and artistic temper of the creative minds which at the close of the Middle Ages found themselves in possession of the world's resources.

Recommended by Lorenzo the Magnificent, Leonardo went to Milan in 1480 to work for Duke Ludovico who was seeking a sculptor to prepare a bronze equestrian statue of his father, Francesco Sforza. The artist made many studies of horses and drew innumerable sketches illustrating the anatomy of the horse, for such was his thirst for knowledge that he could never be satisfied. But he made little progress with the model of the statue. Finally, about 1493, when the model was ready to be inspected, it was considered too large to be cast in bronze. The statue was never completed, and the model was destroyed by the soldiers of Louis XII when they entered Milan in 1499. Leonardo spent many years at the Milanese court as companion to the duke who consulted him on such things as war, fortifications, administration, drainage, and court festivities.

About 1490 the artist produced his *Madonna of the Rocks*, an altarpiece for a church in Milan. This famous painting shows the Virgin seated, with John the Baptist adoring the Christ Child, and an angel behind the latter pointing to St. John. In this picture the artist gave the results of his study of other masters and his reflections upon the problems of painting. First we should note his successful treatment of the problem of light and shadow, or chiaroscuro. *Quattrocento* painters had relied especially upon line, but Leonardo preferred to represent objects by degrees of light and shadow, for his observations had taught him that we see things in this manner. The arrangement of the figures in the form of a triangle also is noteworthy. This best satisfied his aesthetic feelings and so pleased contemporaries that it became a favorite device with painters of the *Cinquecento*. This masterpiece well illustrates Leonardo's conception of beauty. He believed that the artist would find beauty in the objects which he was called upon to represent. Scientific study of structure must precede the use of the brush. He endowed human objects with an ideal beauty which has won enthusiastic praise from generations of artists. Leonardo, unlike Michelangelo, believed that ideal beauty was associated with the feminine figure, and he endowed even male figures with this delicate female beauty. Rocks, plants, flowers, and anatomy are treated with the utmost virtuosity.

The *Last Supper*, Leonardo's greatest triumph, was painted in oil on the walls of the refectory of Santa Maria delle Grazie in Milan. A masterpiece of composition, it marks the culmination of two centuries of experimentation and announces the advent of the magnificent style of the High Renaissance. Christ, seated at the middle of the table facing the room, has just told His disciples that one of them will betray Him. The psychological effect of these terrible words was carefully worked out by Leonardo. The Master's face is serene; He seems resigned to the terrible ordeal which He must undergo. Six disciples are seated on each side of Him. They are arranged in groups of three, Leonardo being especially fond of this triangular arrangement. At Christ's right are John, Judas, and Peter. John, the Lord's favorite, seems to swoon at the dreadful words, and his head inclines toward his right shoulder. The impulsive Peter leans forward placing his hand upon John's shoulder—the statement seems almost unbelievable to him. Judas, seated between them, leans on the table and looks around to them. He seems oppressed with guilt. In paintings of the Last Supper by previous artists Judas is seated on the opposite side as if to emphasize the fact that he really does not belong to the Lord's following. The next three figures are in the act of receiving the import of Christ's words. Andrew's hands are raised in astonishment and horror. James also is deeply moved, and Bartholomew, who has sprung to his feet, leans forward as if to verify what he has heard. At Christ's left are James the Elder, Thomas, and Philip. James with hand upraised seems to counsel Christ, Thomas recoils in horror, and Philip has jumped to his feet protesting that he will not betray Him. At the end of the table Matthew is telling the dire news to Thaddeus. Simon has not yet grasped the full import of Christ's words. Thus the artist painted a living drama.

Unfortunately, Leonardo experimented with oil and, as the surface was not properly prepared, the colors in the picture faded. Within a generation after the artist's death his pictures were nearly ruined. The room has since been put to miscellaneous uses and the picture has suffered grievously. The head of Christ, which disappeared entirely, was restored by another painter; but the original must have been one of sublime beauty if we may judge from a drawing in the Brera Gallery of Milan.

The invasion of Milan by the French in 1499 drove Ludovico Sforza into exile. Leonardo went to Florence and in 1502 as a military engineer served Cesare Borgia in his wars against the princes of the Romagna. On his return to Florence he painted the portrait of *Mona Lisa*, or *La Gioconda*. This picture marks an important stage in portrait painting.

Portraits bore a peculiar relation to Renaissance civilization. The bourgeoisie desired likenesses of themselves and their relatives as decorations for their homes; hence portraits were among the first purely secular pictures of the Renaissance. Piero della Francesca had produced remarkable portraits of Duke Guidobaldo da Montefeltre of Urbino and his wife Battista Sforza in 1472. Similar progress had been made in Flanders by John Van Eyck and Roger Van der Weyden. Donatello created a remarkable portrait bust of Niccolò da Uzzano, and other sculptors like Desiderio da Settignano (1428–1464) also produced portrait busts. But even prior to these artists, Vittore Pisano or Pisanello (c. 1395–1455?) had won fame from his medals. He gave us likenesses of many great men of the *Quattrocento*, such as Vittorino da Feltre, Guarino da Verona, Sigismondo Malatesta, Borso of Este, and Lionello of Este. Artists before Donatello had succeeded in reproducing the facial characteristics in a portrait, but they did not endow their pictures with the subtle charm of personality. Later artists experimented with this problem, but it was left to Leonardo to produce in *Mona Lisa* the first distinctly psychological portrait of the Renaissance.

The subject of this portrait was the young wife of a Neapolitan named Francesco del Giocondo. Leonardo, struck by her beauty and charm, studied her face long and carefully and sought to convey to his canvas the subtle smile which played on her lips from time to time. To induce her to smile he entertained her with music and stories. Here Leonardo showed himself a master of psychological moods. The subject sits in a chair in two-thirds profile with her head slightly turned to the observer. Her left arm rests upon the chair, her right arm is drawn forward and rests upon her left hand—an interesting example of foreshortening. Beauty of posture and detail of clothing are brought out by skillful use of chiaroscuro. In the background are streams, pools, and rugged crags. Leonardo never finished this masterpiece. Shortly after this he painted another noteworthy picture of *St. Anne, the Virgin, and the Christ Child*, which also remained unfinished. Here the artist again reveals his conviction that ideal beauty is to be found primarily in the feminine form. Subtle smiles play upon the faces of the two women.

Leonardo was a genius distracted by many interests. He possessed supreme skill in everything he undertook, and this unfortunately led him to disperse his energies. His experimentation prevented him from finishing all but a few of his conceptions. His last years were spent at the court of Francis I of France. He died at Amboise in 1519.

THE CREATIONS OF MICHELANGELO

Sculpture, which, like painting, achieved its greatest development during the High Renaissance, was practically the work of one man, Michelangelo Buonarroti (1475–1564). His impoverished father sent him to school in Florence; but, preferring to draw sketches, the youth made little progress in his studies. The attention of Domenico Ghirlandaio was drawn to him, with the result that Michelangelo became his apprentice. He frequented the Medicean gardens near San Marco to study the collection of antique statuary which Lorenzo the Magnificent had brought together. One day the youth's skill caught Lorenzo's eye. With the sure insight of a connoisseur, Lorenzo brought him to his palace in the Via Larga, gave him rooms, and generously opened his purse to him. Never has a patron been so richly rewarded.

Michelangelo at first studied the work of previous sculptors. He knew the great creations of Donatello, the dainty but less perfect work of Mino da Fiesole (d. 1484), the exquisitely delicate carvings of Desiderio da Settignano, the dramatic realism of Antonio Rosselino (d. 1478), and the productions of many minor artists. Michelangelo also studied classical carvings and understood the basic characteristics of ancient sculpture, from which he acquired ideas about form and expression. He studied nature assiduously, and carefully dissected bodies in order to possess the mechanical secrets of bodily action. But Michelangelo transcended the teachings of his predecessors, ancient as well as modern.

Michelangelo believed that the highest art consisted in thought wrought in stone. His art always embodies a central thought to which everything else is subordinated. He subordinated all nature to his ideas. It may be said, therefore, that his art transcends nature herself. It exalts human thought above everything material and physical and is therefore the highest expression of man in the Renaissance. Michelangelo was a *uomo universale*. He illustrates the *Quattrocento* conception of *virtù*, and his boundless energy exemplifies its idea of *terribilità*. His achievements include sculpture, painting, architecture, and sonnets of surpassing beauty.

Among Michelangelo's earliest work is a marble statue called *The Bathers*. It reveals poetic feeling for significant form based upon careful study of nature. To the last days of his long life, after he had completed his great works, the artist contemplated this first achievement with intense satisfaction. The sculptor mourned the passing of his generous patron Lorenzo in 1492 and soon left Florence, seeming to have a presentiment of the approaching misfortunes of the Medicean house. His wanderings took him finally to Rome where at the age of 24 he finished his first masterpiece, the *Pietà*. The Virgin, a beautiful young woman, is seated at the foot of the cross. She bears in her lap the form of the dead Christ whose shoulders are gently supported by her right arm. Her left hand is free and with a graceful gesture calls attention to her sorrow. The Virgin's face is of matchless beauty; her whole bearing is one of repose in grief. These effects are enhanced by the smallness of her face and her powerful frame. The body of Christ looks like the form of some Olympian god. "It is a sober and harmonious composition, combining the profoundest religious feeling with classical tranquility of expression," remarks Symonds. The Virgin is younger than her Son. Speaking of this fact, Michelangelo said, "The mother must be young, younger even than the Son to show that she is eternally the Virgin; while the Son, who took on our human character, should appear as any other man in his mortal frame."

The artist returned to Florence in 1501 and was requested by the authorities of the city to execute a statue of *David* from a block of marble which had been spoiled by another sculptor. Attacking this task with his wonted energy, he successfully completed the statue in 1504. It is a stupendous work, far larger than a human form. Its proportions, the size of its hands and the way the figure stands on its feet have been widely criticized. But the striking thing about the statue is the subjection of mass to thought. David stands peering into the distance where he sees Goliath. In his right hand he holds a sling ready for action. The sling passes over the left shoulder, and the stone in it is held in the left hand. As we look upon this figure we expect it to move and send the deadly missile. In the *Pietà* we note calm resignation, but in the *David* we first behold something of Michelangelo's mighty energy.

Although Michelangelo regarded himself as being a sculptor, he was most successful as a painter. While yet in Florence he was commissioned to produce a *Holy Family*, a masterpiece, finished in 1505. Executed in tempera, the *tondo* (a framed circular space) presents Mary, a vigorous and muscular form, in a most difficult position—sitting and reaching backward over her right shoulder to receive the Christ Child as He is being raised by Joseph. In the background stands John the Baptist, and behind him are a number of nudes who appear to be disciples. The introduction of these nudes, so characteristic of the age, is due to classical influences as, for example, in Botticelli's *Birth of Venus*. Unity of action, supported by vigorous muscular power paired with masterly physical and psychological expression characterizes Michelangelo's creations. Michelangelo's figures are bearers of ideas. These conceptions were exemplified in his frescoes in the Sistine Chapel. Michelangelo did not want to do these frescoes, insisting that he was a sculptor, not a painter. But he was overborne by the impetuous pontiff and finally consented. To decorate a ceiling of 6000 square feet from a lofty scaffold was no easy task. The artist had not wielded a brush for some years, and his conceptions of art and his personality made it difficult to work with assistants. Nevertheless, in 4 years he painted 145 pictures comprising 394 figures, a large number of which are as much as 10 feet high. In addition to these pictures there was much purely decorative and geometrical design. Only a man of superhuman strength could have executed so vast a work.

The middle portion of the ceiling contains nine pictures representing the chief points in the story of redemption. They are of unequal size, the second, fourth, sixth, and eighth being larger than the rest. They depict: *God Dividing the Light from the Darkness, God Creating the Earth, Creation of the Waters, Creation of Adam, Creation of Eve, Fall of Man, Sacrifice of Noah, Deluge,* and *Fall of Noah*. These scenes are placed in a heavy framework which the artist painted on the bare surface. At the corners of each of the smaller scenes appear nude male figures which are popularly known as "athletes." They are drawn in every possible pose, thus revealing the painter's matchless knowledge of the human form and how it moves. On the turn of the vaulting are Jewish prophets who foretold the coming of the Messiah, and sibyls who imparted this knowledge to the pagan world. Above the windows is a series of triangular pictures showing Christ's ancestors. Michelangelo's painted figures look like statues in the round.

Soon after these tasks were completed, the sculptor was invited to Rome by Pope Julius II. That ambitious pontiff, with characteristic Renaissance disregard of Christian humility, had conceived the idea of constructing a gigantic tomb for himself to be placed in a new St. Peter's on the spot occupied by the tomb of the great apostle himself. This presumptuous plan was modified, however, and it was decided to place the tomb against the wall. Many drawings of this projected work are extant. Interruption and other delays prevented him from completing the tomb. The great artist was bitter at being interfered with in this manner. Julius' tomb was the tragedy of his life and continued to haunt him years afterwards. Finally the tomb, greatly reduced in size and far less sumptuous than originally planned, was erected in the church of St. Peter in Chains. It has only three completed figures: *Rachel*, *Leah*, and the famous *Moses*. It appears that the gigantic *Moses* was finished after 1542. The mighty form is seated, gazing into the distance, filled with wrath, probably at the defection of the children of Israel. The two unfinished captives, or slaves as they have been popularly called, finally found their way to Paris. One of these bound figures chafes under his bonds; the other sleeps. Another unfinished group which is in Florence has been much discussed, for it is not known exactly what these figures were intended to signify or where they were to stand on the monument.

Equally famous are the groups in the new sacristy of San Lorenzo in Florence. Michelangelo, commissioned by Pope Clement VII to prepare appropriate tombs for members of the Medici family, practically completed the figures for two tombs, one for Giuliano, brother of Leo X, and another for Duke Lorenzo of Urbino. On the first of these are two recumbent figures known as *Day and Night*, above which is seated the effigy of Giuliano clad as a Roman general. There has been much discussion of *Day and Night*, and various interpretations have been advanced. They were finished during troubled days when wars disturbed the quiet of Florence; the Medici, driven out in 1527, again secured control of the city after a determined attack. Michelangelo's patriotism was sorely tried by these events, and it is supposed that his feelings are embodied in these statues of *Day and Night*. Day is a male figure. From behind his upraised shoulder glowers his menacing face. Michelangelo linked Night with the misfortunes of the time. It is a female figure, "so sorrowful, so utterly absorbed in darkness and the shade of death, that to shake off that everlasting lethargy seems impossible." The following verses by Michelangelo, translated by Symonds, show how Night expresses her grief over the misfortunes which have engulfed Florence and Italy:

> Sweet is my sleep, but more to be mere stone,
> So long as ruin and dishonor reign;
> To hear naught, to feel naught, is my great gain;
> Then wake me not, speak in an undertone.

The figures of *Dawn and Sunset* decorate the tomb of Lorenzo; his effigy, one of the noblest creations of the artist, is seated above in deep reverie. *Dawn*, a female figure, is turning and raising her head "as though some painful summons had reached her sunk in dreamless sleep, and called her forth to suffer. Her waking to consciousness is like that of one who has been drowned and who finds the return to life agony. Before her eyes, seen even through the mists of slumber, are the ruin and the shame of Italy" (Symonds). *Sunset* is the figure of a powerful man who seems to sink under the load of human troubles around him. Unfortunately the tombs were never finished, and the complete idea which the sculptor wished to portray by means of these stones was never made known. The *Madonna and Child* for the tomb of Lorenzo the Magnificent was nearly completed and is usually regarded as surpassed only by the *Pietà* executed more than 25 years before.

The artist also painted a *Last Judgment* on the wall and behind the altar in the Sistine Chapel. This fresco is excessively crowded with gigantic figures. That of Christ is simply immense, and St. Peter has the size of an ox. Finished in 1541, when the artist was 66 years old, the picture represents the artist in life's decline. This mighty creation of figures more than human in size in which the artist's vigorous manner is greatly exaggerated, seems out of place back of the altar.

Michelangelo was a sad and lonely person. A genius of the first order, his ideas about art and life were strikingly individual. He outlived his relatives, friends, patrons of his youth, and even pupils. He spent his days in solitude, aloof from men. His greatest friendship was for Vittoria Colonna, perhaps the noblest woman of the age. A deep platonic feeling bound them together. Her death in 1547 left him a lonely man. Yet such was his creative instinct that he kept on working. Weary with life, he prepared his own tomb. He made a *pietà*, a pathetic thing in which he himself in the form of Nicodemus assists in taking Christ from the cross. Mary is a pitiful woman as she shows her solicitude for her Son. It is evident that the sculptor was turning to religion for comfort, for the group reminds one of the somber themes which dominated Gothic art during the previous century. Although he was displeased with it and broke it up, its fragments were saved and put together, and the statue finally was set up in the cathedral of Florence. Like the figure of *Sunset* which he carved for the tomb of Duke Lorenzo, Michelangelo sank under the weight of life's burdens and died in 1564 at the advanced age of 89. Contemporaries realized that a genius had passed from the earth. His body was buried with pomp in the church of Santa Croce, the mausoleum for some of Florence's greatest men.

Michelangelo's influence upon the artists of his age was decisive. The mighty energy of his vigorous creations dwarfed all competitors. To save themselves it seemed necessary to do what Michelangelo was doing, but this was impossible, for the works of genius are unique and can only be imitated. Nevertheless they sought to copy his manner. Decline inevitably resulted, and a labored perfection and technical accuracy began to dominate sculpture and painting. The quickening force of thought failed. Hence Michelangelo's death in 1564 marks the end of the Renaissance.

RAPHAEL'S ARTISTIC MASTERSHIP

Raphael's creations rank with Leonardo's as an expression of the High Renaissance. Raphael was born in Urbino in 1483 and died in 1520. His father was court painter and poet to Duke Guidobaldo. The boy thus possessed the advantage of living in a refined atmosphere to which his adaptability responded with natural ease. Readiness to absorb novel ideas and methods characterized Raphael; it is the keynote of the strivings of his brief life. He was left an orphan at the age of 11 and began studying painting under a local artist. Soon he had exhausted what his master could teach him and in 1500 went to Perugia to study under the celebrated Perugino. Raphael had much to learn from this great master, such as the treatment of space and the disposition and limitation of objects in a painting. He imitated the pictures of his master so closely that, as Vasari states, "his copies cannot be distinguished from the original works of the master, nor can the difference between the performances of Raphael and those of Pietro Perugino be discerned with any certainty." This affinity is well illustrated by the similarity of Perugino's *Christ Giving the Keys to St. Peter*, a fresco in the Sistine Chapel, to Raphael's *Betrothed of the Virgin*, a painting in the Brera Gallery in Milan.

Having exhausted the possibilities of Perugino's tuition, Raphael resolved to go to Florence, for he had heard of the magic work of Leonardo da Vinci and Michelangelo and had determined to learn from them. He arrived in Florence in 1504 and at once began studying with these painters. A noteworthy evolution took place in his painting. Leonardo's influence is clearly visible in the magnificent Madonnas which Raphael began to paint, of which perhaps the first was the *Madonna of the Grand Duke*. Perugino's influence may be detected in the placid oval face of the Virgin, but the Christ Child reveals careful study of Leonardo's pictures. Other Madonnas followed: the *Madonna of the Goldfinch*, the *Fair Gardener*, the *Madonna of the Meadow*, and the *Madonna of the Chair*. The carefully studied triangular arrangement in these pictures likewise reveals Leonardo's influence.

Raphael's Florentine period came to an end in 1508 when Pope Julius II asked him to come to Rome to redecorate some rooms in the Vatican palace. The *Camera della Segnatura* occupied Raphael from 1509 to 1511. Its walls contain the so-called *Disputa*, the *School of Athens*, and the *Parnassus*, described in a previous chapter in connection with Julius' interest in art. In this room also was painted the *Jurisprudence*. In the adjoining Room of Heliodorus were the *Expulsion of Heliodorus from the Temple*, the *Mass of Bolsena*, the *Deliverance of St. Peter*, and the *Meeting of Leo IV and Attila*. These frescoes are some of the noblest monuments of the High Renaissance. Like the work of Leonardo da Vinci, they are a synthesis of much that was noteworthy in Italian painting of the *Quattrocento*.

Meanwhile Raphael's art was being influenced by the tumultuous genius of Michelangelo. Raphael, always sensitive to the great achievements of other masters, absorbed many ideas from them. The calm serenity of the Umbrian tradition which he had acquired from Perugino was transformed by Leonardo's intellect, as is shown in the grouping of subjects, careful study of form, skillful use of chiaroscuro, and audacious foreshortening. To these was added the spirit of Michelangelo's works.

Before taking leave of the artistic geniuses we have just considered, it remains to note several masters who, while they can hardly be rated among the first rank of artists, nevertheless have occupied the sustained attention of appreciative critics ever since. First of these is the Dominican Fra Bartolomeo (1469–1517), member of the monastic community of San Marco in Florence and an admirer of Savonarola. His spirituality was Dominican, and his mental formation was the same, at least in religious principles, as that of Fra Angelico (d. 1455). His *Pietà*, now hanging in the Pitti Palace, has always been admired. It shows the disciple John gently raising the shoulders of the dead form of Christ, while the Virgin is tenderly embracing His head, and Mary Magdalene, whose hair is disheveled, embraces His feet.

Like Fra Bartolomeo, Andrea del Sarto (1486–1531) learned the clever tricks of painters like Raphael and Michelangelo and employed them with success. His *Madonna of the Harpies* is a masterpiece of deft arrangement. The Christ Child is a smiling boy clinging to His mother. On her right stands St. Francis, on her left is John the Baptist. The *Madonna of the Sack* in the convent of the Servites in Florence has attracted many admirers. The Virgin holding her playful Son is the center of attraction. Joseph, seated at her right, is leaning against a sack and reading a book, probably Christ's genealogy in the first chapter of St. Matthew. Undoubtedly perfect from the standpoint of technique, the picture somewhat seems to lack the spirit of devotion.

Our attention lingers for a moment to contemplate the work of Benvenuto Cellini (1500–1572), Florentine goldsmith of great versatility who grew to maturity during Michelangelo's ascendancy. His reputation rests upon a number of remarkable works such as the salt cellar which he made for King Francis I of France. His *Perseus*, finished in 1554, and particularly famous, shows a vigorous figure holding in its right hand a sword, in its upraised left, the head of Medusa. At its feet lies the extinct body with blood gushing from its neck. The statue usually is criticized as being mannered, a fault into which sculptors of Michelangelo's declining days fell. The pedestal is exquisitely wrought in its details, but most critics feel that it is too ornate. Great as he was as an artist, his fame rests still more upon his memoirs, or *Autobiography*, in whose pages he reveals himself as a restless, conceited, and boastful ruffian who never hesitated to carry out his impulses. It is an amusing account of a multitude of escapades and a valuable source book for the manners and morals of the *Cinquecento*.

THE ACME OF NORTH ITALIAN ART DURING THE *CINQUECENTO*: THE VENETIAN SCHOOL

Before noting the achievements of the great painters of Venice we pause for a moment to contemplate the work of Correggio (d. 1534) at Parma. The heir to many traditions, his art seems to reveal study of Mantegna, Leonardo, and Michelangelo. A psychological note dominates his creations; his art was sensuous, feminine, and subtle. Smiling madonnas, playful babies, and ecstatic saints were familiar topics. He was fond of woods, glades, plants, sky, and clouds. His madonnas are filled with the tenderest solicitude, and the Christ Child has become a vivacious babe.

These characteristics were combined with great virtuosity. In this way Correggio became an important influence in the grand manner of the *Cinquecento*, especially in the second half of the century. In the words of Symonds:

> Every cupola throughout the length and breadth of Italy began then to be painted with rolling clouds and lolling angels. What the wits of Parma had once stigmatized as a ragout of frogs now seemed the only possible expression for celestial ecstasy; and to delineate the joy of Heaven upon those multitudes of domes and semi-domes was a point of religious etiquette. False lights, dubious foreshortenings, shallow colorings, ill-studied forms, and motiveless agitation suited the taste that cared for gaudy brightness and sensational effects. The painters, for their part, found it convenient to adopt a mannerism that enabled them to conceal the difficult parts of the figure in featherbeds of vapor, requiring neither effort of conception nor expenditure of labor on drawing and composition.

Thus the manner of Correggio contributed to the baroque style of the closing *Cinquecento*.

It was Titian (1477–1576) who more than any other artist created the superb school of Venetian painting during the *Cinquecento*. These artists made effective use of what the Florentines had achieved—perspective, adequate anatomy, facial and bodily expression, *chiaroscuro*, painting in oil, and eloquent posture. Titian's genius evolved slowly with constant application. He possessed all the secrets of his predecessors and became the most perfect interpreter of the luxurious and pleasure-loving life of Venice. Symonds regards his *Assumption of the Virgin*, painted in 1518, as "the greatest single oil painting in the world, if we except Raphael's *Sistine Madonna*." This picture in Santa Maria Gloriosa in Venice marks the advent of the monumental style in Venetian painting. The Virgin is rising amid a bevy of nude boy angels. Above her is the Father suspended in a pearly haze of glory, and below, on earth, are the apostles who gaze upward. The picture is a symphony of color. "The grand manner can reach no further than in this picture—serene, composed, meditated, enduring, yet full of dramatic force and of profound feeling." Other noteworthy pictures by Titian are *Bacchus and Ariadne*, *Sacred and Profane Love*, the *Pesaro Madonna*, the *Venus of Urbino*, some portraits, and many religious subjects.

The Venetian school is the most complete expression of the secularization of Renaissance art. This appears inevitable, for Venice was the greatest commercial center of the Occident. Its artists sought to satisfy a luxurious and pleasure-loving public. Venetian painting reflected the beauty, sensuous joy, and secular appeal of Venice. Incidents from Venetian life, patriotic stories, and pastoral scenes were popular. Small pictures to decorate the walls of bourgeois dwellings were in demand. Religion naturally was of restricted importance in this art.

The technical excellence of Florentine, Roman, and other artists became the basis of Venetian painting. Oil painting had been perfected in the days of Antonello da Messina (d. 1479), a painter of the Venetian *Quattrocento*, and became the accepted medium of this school. Leonardo's skill with chiaroscuro was eagerly appropriated. The great contribution to painting made by this school was the skillful use of color and chiaroscuro.

Giorgione (c. 1478–1510) was the first Venetian painter to fall completely under humanist influences. He was fond of idyllic landscapes, fitting abode of the Muses, and he gave to his pictures a soft deep glow of satin and lucent color. His art might serve to illustrate the poetry of Theocritus. Palma Vecchio (d. 1528), a Venetian trained in Rome, was a superb colorist. The luxurious garments of his subjects are painted in harmonious browns, blues, reds, and other colors which shimmer as the light falls upon them. He was an affable painter and knew the secret of pleasing patrons who delighted in superficial beauty.

The manner of Titian was continued by Tintoretto (1518–1594). Like his great master, he painted sumptuous silks, satins, and brocades. But he abandoned the harmonious action of Titian's subjects and developed a vigorous, impulsive, and often precipitate style which seems to herald the coming Baroque style about to sweep Europe. Among his more noteworthy creations are a *Presentation of the Virgin, Miracle of the Slave,* and *Bacchus and Ariadne.* His slightly younger contemporary, Paolo Veronese (1528–1588) also followed in the footsteps of Titian. But his work shows the peculiar complexity and grandiose composition of the later decades of the *Cinquecento*. His pictures are filled with handsome men clothed in richly colored satins and velvets, women in satin with fair white skin, and there is no end of spacious palaces and blue skies. His *Marriage at Cana* and his *Feast in Levi's House* reveal him in his proper element. Other famous pictures are the *Rape of Europa, Marriage of St. Catherine,* and the ceiling decorations in the palace of the doges.

The Venetian school occupies a unique place in history, for it gave the most adequate expression to the artistic, luxurious, and secular tastes of a purely bourgeois society. With Tintoretto and Veronese we say farewell to the painting of the Italian High Renaissance.

PART IX

Political Crises in High Renaissance Italy

Chapter 19

ITALY INVADED BY FRENCH KING CHARLES VIII, 1494–1495

THE INVASION of Italy by Charles VIII of France in 1494 and 1495 was an event of prime importance in the history of the Renaissance. Hitherto, ever since the decline of the Holy Roman Empire, Italians had been allowed to solve their political problems with little interference from external powers. Now, however, began a period which lasted until the Treaty of Cateau-Cambrésis (1559) during which Italian states became the sport of foreign interests. French and Spanish armies fought out their quarrels on Italian soil. It was the beginning of an age of conflict over what later became known as the Balance of Power, a conception typical of Renaissance politics. Two great powers faced each other, the crown of France and the Hapsburg house, and caused Europe to resound with their clashing interests. States might range on one side or the other, but the hostility of the French and Hapsburg powers remained a constant fact in European and Italian life regardless of transient shiftings.

PROBLEM OF MAINTAINING THE PEACE IN *QUATTROCENTO* ITALY

The fate of Italy, as we have noted above, rested with five large states: Milan, Venice, Florence, Naples, and the States of the Church. Peace was maintained by the triple alliance formed by Cosimo de' Medici in the Treaty of Lodi (1454). Its central idea was that Florence, which hitherto had supported Venice in her quarrels with Milan, should ally with her northern neighbor to restrict Venetian economic and political dominance. Florence and Milan admitted Naples into this union, thus securing valuable support in their relations with the papacy whose territories bordered upon their own lands. This alliance was diligently maintained by Lorenzo the Magnificent. But in 1478 a group of the discontented, especially the Pazzi family of Florence, encouraged by Sixtus IV and King Ferrante of Naples, failed to destroy Medici leadership in the peninsula. In 1480 Lorenzo visited King Ferrante—even while the war was going on—and recovered the king's alliance. The peace, thus reëstablished, was further strengthened by an understanding between Lorenzo and Pope Innocent VIII (1484–1492) who elevated Giovanni de' Medici, later Pope Leo X, to the cardinalate.

But as Lorenzo's term of life drew near its close, there were signs that his combination would not last much longer. Duke Galeazzo Maria Sforza of Milan had been slain in 1476, leaving the governance of his lands to his widow, Bona of Savoy, who ruled in the interests of her youthful son, Gian Galeazzo. But she was no match for the ambitions of Galeazzo Maria's brothers, of whom Ludovico, called the Moor, was the most astute. He thrust her out of the government and took into his hands the total management of affairs. He was careful, however, to rule in the name of his nephew who was not expected to live long. Gian Galeazzo's wife, Isabella, daughter of King Alfonso II of Naples, was a high-spirited woman who resented the power which Ludovico arrogated to himself. She was furious because public recognition of her rights was withheld from her and bestowed upon Beatrice of Este, Ludovico's wife. This ill feeling was shared also by King Alfonso, and amity between the courts of Milan and Naples visibly cooled.

Other events seemed to foreshadow a change in the political system of Italy. Lorenzo the Magnificent died in 1492, and the leadership of Italy fell into the unpracticed hands of his son, Piero, who possessed none of the astuteness of his father. He was interested in athletics and possessed physical charm and cultivated manners as befitted a member of his famous house but was devoid of insight in politics. It was difficult for anyone to guide Italy through the approaching crisis. The banking house of Medici had many branches in France whose king was soon to invade the peninsula. It was Piero's duty to conserve his wealth and business organization and at the same time maintain the equilibrium of political forces established by his great-grandfather Cosimo. This seemed to dictate close sympathy for France, or even menial subserviency. On the other hand, the peace of the peninsula demanded that no foreign military power should set foot on its soil. Both these policies could not easily be maintained because the king of France was determined to enforce his claims to the crown of Naples.

Piero drew closer to the Neapolitan king on the advice of his Orsini relatives who were friends of Alfonso. On the other hand, Pope Alexander VI (1492–1503) quarreled with the king of Naples about some lands and drew closer to Venice and Ludovico Sforza. Thus the balance of power was ruined, for Florence and Naples formed one combination, while the pope, Milan, and Venice constituted a second. Duke Ludovico of Milan was deeply concerned for the safety of his authority. That great exemplar of Renaissance political and diplomatic methods calmly surveyed the situation which threatened to overwhelm him and decided that he could rely upon his subtle intellect and clever methods to save himself from the danger which lurked in a French attempt against Naples. "He began to tickle King Charles (who was but 22 years of age) with the vanities and glories of Italy, demonstrating the right which he had to the fine kingdom of Naples, which he knew well enough to blazon and display. He addressed himself in everything to the seneschal Étienne de Vesc and to Guillaume Briçonnet, who was rich and well skilled in the management of the finances, and a great friend of De Vesc, by whose means Ludovico persuaded Briçonnet to turn priest, and he would make him a cardinal; but the seneschal was to have a duchy."[1]

Ludovico's policy, as the issue was to show, was a stupendous blunder. It was dangerous to urge the French (militarily vastly more powerful than any one of the states of Italy) to establish themselves in Naples, because they also had a claim upon Milan which had its origin in the marriage of Valentina, daughter of Gian Galeazzo Visconti, duke of Milan (d. 1402), to Duke Louis of Orléans, grandfather of Louis of Orléans, who stood very near the crown. Should Charles VIII die leaving no heirs of his body, Louis would become king. Before he actually did become king, as Louis XII (1498–1515), Louis argued that the legitimate line of the Visconti had come to an end with the death of Filippo Maria in 1447 and that according to feudal legal conceptions his natural daughter Bianca could not transmit legal title to her husband, Francesco Sforza, the *condottiere* who had seized the government and installed himself as tyrant without regard to the rights of the house of Orléans.

The kings of France had never forgotten their claims upon the crown of Naples; in fact, they had been keenly interested in that land ever since

[1] P. de Comines, *Memoirs* (Bohn Library), II, 107–108.

Charles I of Anjou, brother of Louis IX, became its king in 1266 and founded the line of the Angevin kings of Naples. This family came to an end when Queen Giovanna died in 1435. She had bequeathed her rights to a representative of the younger Angevin house still flourishing in France, but King Alfonso I of Sicily seized her realm and established himself therein in defiance of the claims of the Angevin heir, René. Charles VII of France (1422–1461) had married Marie, a daughter of Louis II of Anjou who was king of Naples (d. 1417), and sister of René, but because of his war with England he could not interfere in behalf of his brother-in-law. There was no lack of interest on his part, however, and his son, Louis XI (1461–1483) tried through negotiations to secure some foothold in Milan. René of Anjou died in 1480. On the death of the next heir, Charles of Maine, in 1481, title to Naples was devised by testament to Louis XI. But this sagacious prince preferred to stay at home and look after the interests of the crown which were jeopardized by the ambition of powerful nobles.

Charles VIII (1483–1498), however, did not hesitate. During the earlier years of his reign his sister Anne controlled the royal policy, but as soon as he was freed from her tutelage he resolved to secure his rights in Naples. At his court were to be found some of the Neapolitan princes who had been dispossessed by King Ferrante (d. 1494). They labored to incite the young king's desires. He should be king of Naples, they said, and lead an army against the Turk who was threatening Christendom. It was a foolish project and detrimental to the interests of the realm, for the royal duty lay at home where the crown needed to be strengthened. It was important to secure control over lands along the Pyrenees and the Netherlands border. But Charles disregarded these interests. The glory of distant achievement, the conquest of Naples, and a crusade against the infidel turned his head. Tales of chivalry, the crusading tradition so strong in the history of the rulers of France, and the encouragement of eager courtiers weighed more than the national needs of the state.

Before setting his army in motion Charles had to settle certain questions with his enemies who had attacked him when he married Anne, heiress of Brittany. They objected to the addition of the Breton duchy to the French crown without securing some compensations for themselves. Henry VII of England had laid siege to Boulogne, and, to be rid of him, Charles paid him an enormous sum of money (Treaty of Étaples, November, 1492). Ferdinand of Spain threatened to move because he was interested in the rights of the Aragonese house of Naples whose titles might devolve upon him, whereupon Charles hurriedly offered him Cerdagne and Roussillon, two counties situated on the northern slope of the Pyrenees, as the price of his neutrality (Treaty of Barcelona, January, 1493). There was grave danger that the Emperor Maximilian also might interfere if Charles should invade Italy, for, as we have noted, he possessed some rights in Lombardy, a fief of the empire. Furthermore, Maximilian was aggrieved because his wife, Mary of Burgundy, had been deprived of Artois and the Franche-Comté by Louis XI at the death of her father, Charles the Bold. Accordingly these lands were now returned (Treaty of Senlis, May, 1493).

CHARLES' RECEPTION IN ITALY

Having thus sacrificed his territorial interests in northern Europe, Charles was ready for the conquest of Naples. He collected a well-equipped army of 20,000 men and set out in July, 1494. He expelled the branches of the Medici banking house from his realm and broke relations with the king of Naples. A troop of soldiers under the duke of Orleans was sent to occupy the Italian coast, including Genoa, while Charles crossed the Alps. The king reached Asti on September 9 and passed through the Milanese territory by way of Pavia, Piacenza, and Pontremoli where he crossed the Apennines. Piero de' Medici had not prepared the strongholds which guarded the way and which might have checked the French, and, thoroughly frightened, he sought to come to terms. He weakly surrendered Sarzana, Pietra Santa, Livorno, and Pisa which had been won by Florence with great effort. The Pisans, men and women alike, greeted Charles with tears of joy, crying "Liberty, Liberty!" and cast into the Arno the marble Marzocca, a sculptured lion emblematic of Florentine domination. The king made vague promises to restore their liberties. Charles next advanced toward Florence where a remarkable revolution had just taken place, for when Piero de' Medici returned after the surrender of the Florentine fortresses, the people, inspired by the words and example of the Dominican friar Girolamo Savonarola, rose and forced Piero to leave the city on November 9.

Smarting under the terms which Piero made and fearful of a disastrous occupation by the French, the Florentines sought definite terms from the French king. "We shall arrange everything within the great city," said Charles. Savonarola was one of the ambassadors sent to interview him. As a religious he was able to impress the susceptible king, making him believe that he was coming into Italy at the will of God. Consequently, on the royal banners were inscribed the words *Missus a Deo* (Sent from God). Charles wanted to treat Florence as a conquered city, but this was impossible because of the strongly built houses which looked like fortresses. At length it was agreed that Charles should be recognized as protector of Florence, that he should occupy her fortresses for 2 years, and receive a sum of money. But this demand for money seemed excessive, and the Florentines demurred. "Then we will sound our trumpets," said Charles. "And we will ring our bells" was their rejoinder, alluding to the custom common in Italian cities of calling the citizenry to war by the ringing of bells. Thereupon an agreement was reached, 100,000 ducats were paid, and on November 28, after a stay of 11 days, the king marched out of the city, to the great relief of its citizenry.

Charles next advanced upon Rome. Pope Alexander VI was in a difficult position. He had cast his lot with King Alfonso when Charles entered Italy, and Neapolitan troops had been sent to block the French advance through Romagna. This had compelled the French to proceed along the west coast by way of Pontremoli and Pietra Santa. The papal policy was encumbered by the hostility of Cardinal Giuliano della Rovere, a nephew of Sixtus IV, who hated the reigning pope and had gone to France in order to whet Charles' desire for the crown of Naples. Cardinal Ascanio Sforza hated Alexander because of his espousal of Neapolitan interests to the prejudice of Ludovico and the Sforza. These two cardinals urged the king to summon a general council to try the pontiff and depose him for his acts.

But Charles was not capable of such far-reaching policies. Besides, his councilor Briçonnet wished to become cardinal, which might be impossible if they proceeded violently. Alexander corresponded with the Sultan Bajazet II who offered to help him with arms if the pope would put to death Djem, the sultan's brother who was staying in Rome and threatened the quiet of Turkey. When the pope's negotiations with the enemy of Christendom were known, the cry for a council became more determined. Charles was eager to be on his way and finally an agreement was reached. Djem was delivered to him, a number of papal towns were surrendered till the close of the war, and Alexander's son, Cesare Borgia, was to accompany Charles as a hostage. On December 27 the French king entered Rome, and on January 28, 1495, set out for Naples.

King Alfonso II who had succeeded to the throne on the death of his father, Ferrante II, at the close of 1494 did not know how to resist the powerful invader and on February 3, 1495, surrendered his crown. The writer, Comines, states that Ferrante,

> who was so cruel and terrible, and in such reputation for his experience in military affairs before the king of France's departure from Rome, renounced the crown, and was seized with such a panic fear, that in the night he would cry out he heard the French, and that the stones and trees shouted 'France,

France!' Nor durst he ever stir boldly out of Naples; but upon his son's return from Rome he resigned the government of his kingdom to him, and caused him to be crowned, and carried on horseback through the streets of Naples, attended by the chief persons of the city . . . and all the foreign ambassadors that were there; and after all this pomp and solemnity was performed, Alfonso himself fled into Sicily—Charles entered Naples on February 12 and within a few days the entire kingdom fell into his hands.[2]

Charles found, as did many another after him, that it was easier to conquer a part of Italy than to hold it. He was victorious because of his prowess; beside him the best of Italy's *condottieri* seemed puny opponents. Another reason for his success was that the divided state of the peninsula made concerted action in a common cause impossible. Although they were helpless to resist him, Italians despised Charles because he was a barbarian, inferior in culture. Nor did he perceive the precarious nature of his progress. His head was turned by the ease with which he had conquered. Comines declared:

> We may conclude this whole expedition, both going and coming, was conducted purely by God: for . . . the wisdom of the contrivers of this scheme contributed but little.[3]

He marveled that

> this expedition into Italy was performed with so much ease, and so little resistance, that our soldiers scarce ever put on their armor during the whole expedition, and the king marched with his army from Asti to Naples in four months and nineteen days; an ambassador with his retinue could hardly have got thither sooner.[4]

The Neapolitans greeted Charles with characteristic volatility. He gave himself over to a life of gaiety, and his officers and soldiers followed his example. Charles bestowed many offices upon his French favorites. However, the natives soon grew tired of him, and elsewhere in Italy appeared ominous signs of hostility. Pope Alexander still feared a council. The Venetians believed that the freedom of the peninsula was at stake and were encouraged in this belief by the sultan who disliked Charles' ambition to play the part of crusader. Ludovico was eager to drive the French out after irreparable damage had been inflicted upon his rivals in Naples. The Emperor Maximilian was jealous of any extension of French power which he deemed harmful to his interests. King Ferdinand of Spain also had a lively interest in Naples, for he was next in succession should the

---

[2] *Ibid.*, p. 155.
[3] *Ibid.*, p. 94.
[4] *Ibid.*, pp. 153–154.

present family come to an end. Charles' enemies accordingly drew together, and the League of Venice was formed on March 31. They agreed to defend Christendom against the Turk, restore the Roman see to its former prestige, and guarantee the integrity of each member of the coalition. It was also understood that they would expel the French from Italian soil.

Perceiving that his military connections with France were endangered by this hostile coalition, Charles resolved to return. He hurriedly put his affairs in order, appointed officials to rule the newly conquered land, and on May 20 began his hasty retreat along the route of his triumphant invasion. As he was descending the Apennines at Fornovo he found drawn up to resist him the army of the league commanded by Duke Francesco Gonzaga of Mantua. A battle took place on July 6 in which Charles with great difficulty managed to thrust his enemy aside. Charles and Ludovico Sforza came to an agreement in October. As soon as Charles disappeared beyond the Alps, his conquests in Naples melted away. King Ferdinand sent thither his able general Gonsalvo da Córdoba, who began an aggressive campaign against the French. All Italian states save Florence forsook Charles.

Milan, Venice, the pope, and the emperor were discontented with the public policy of Florence under the guidance of Savonarola. Florence clung to the French in the vain hope that their king would restore Pisa to them. Meanwhile the city was ruled by the new constitution put into effect in December, 1495. It was a copy of the Venetian constitution, the envy of all who desired stable government. A Great Council (*Maggior Consiglio*) was organized, composed of every citizen above 30 years whose father, grandfather, or great-grandfather had been elected an officer of Florence. Savonarola continued to guide the city as a reformer. He persisted in preaching in prophetic strains and even claimed direct revelations and inspiration from heaven. Meanwhile Alexander labored to secure the adherence of Florence to the national Italian policy of the League of Venice. Savonarola in his denunciations did not spare the papal policy which in reality was purely secular. Alexander took a political view of the matter and in October ordered the friar to cease preaching.

LIFE AND MISSION OF SAVONAROLA

The moving cause of the rising in Florence against Charles VIII was Girolamo Savonarola, a Dominican friar born in Ferrara in 1452 of a family which lived in close contact with the new Renaissance culture fostered by the Este family. He did not as a youth evince much interest in the new culture and was pensive and inclined to melancholy. Brooding on religious and theological questions, he more and more opposed the paganism of the Ferrarese court. Bruised in spirit by the worldliness which he saw everywhere around him, he retired to a Dominican convent in 1475, whence he wrote to his father: "The reasons which drove me to become a religious are these: the miserable condition of the world and the evils of which men are guilty such as rape, immorality, robbery, pride, idolatry, cursing, all in so grave measure that it may be said that almost no one can be found who has any regard for what is good. Each day, therefore, weeping, I often repeated the line of Vergil's Aeneid: 'Alas, flee these cruel lands, flee this avaricious shore.'" These words from a classical author show clearly that Savonarola had been touched by the new humanist culture, even though its paganism repelled him so that he sought refuge in traditional religious and moral ideas.

During his novitiate in Bologna he wrote two odes, *On the Fate of the Church* and *On the Fall of the World*, in which he lamented the sad decline of religion and morality. He became a forceful penitential preacher. In 1482 he was transferred to San Marco in Florence and was appointed public preacher and reader of Scripture. His discourses in the church of San Lorenzo brought him more and more closely in contact with the new cultural tendencies. This was the parish church of the Medici, the family which more than any other was identified with the Renaissance. With a mind turned toward mysticism, Savonarola studied intently the Christian scheme of redemption and especially the events which St. John in his Revelation declared would happen during the last days of the world. He studied the prophets of the Old Testament and took their fiery denunciations to heart. Presently he began to talk as if he had received revelations from God. His sermons announced that the Church would soon be chastised for its worldliness, after which it would be cleansed of its faults.

Savonarola spared neither pope nor prince. Sixtus IV passed away in 1484, but Innocent VIII was no better a shepherd. The canker which infected all was the new secular culture of which the Medici were the chief promoters. Savonarola inveighed against the "tyranny" of that house and was eager to substitute for it the rule of the people. A righteous people should establish a righteous rule, a sort of theocracy! His power over the crowd was immense; men and women hung intently on his words. Lorenzo died in 1492, and his son Piero was not able to cope with the situation. Savonarola had become a practical reformer. He aimed at eradicating public vices and the private immoralities of the citizenry. Meanwhile Charles was moving into Italy. The king seemed to be the sword of wrath sent to vindicate God's cause, and the coming of the French seemed to prove the truth of Savonarola's vaticinations.

Savonarola's influence with the Florentines continued to grow. Men, women, and even children fell under the spell of his ideas. He organized the latter into bands to purify the carnival of its licentiousness. They were arranged in graded ranks and paraded the streets. They conducted themselves in a decorous manner and no longer gambled, threw stones, or played mischievous pranks. No longer did they sing the worldly carnival songs which Lorenzo the Magnificent had composed; instead, Savonarola substituted religious compositions, often in the same meter. Pictures which were thought to be improper from a religious point of view, playing cards, vanities, cosmetics, false hair, and immoral books were thrown into bonfires.

The people longed to hear the sermons of the prophet whose voice had been hushed by papal prohibition. After many requests had been made to the *signoria* and to the pope, the officials permitted Savonarola to resume his sermons in Lent of 1496. He boldly asserted his liberty to preach. "We are not bound to obey all commands. If they come through false information, they are not valid. If they contradict the law of love set forth in the Gospel, we must understand them as St. Paul understood St. Peter. We cannot suppose such a possibility: but if it were so, we must answer our superior, 'You err; you are not the Roman Church, you are a man and a sinner.' " Alexander was angered by these bold words chiefly because of the friar's political influence as shown in his appeal to a council. He next sought to undermine his power by bringing the house of San Marco, and with it Savonarola, under superiors more directly subject to papal control (November, 1496).

Finally on May 15, 1497, Savonarola was excommunicated. He held, however, that the pope had proceeded on erroneous grounds, and in February of the following year boldly resumed his sermons in the cathedral. "God governs the world by secondary agents, which are instruments in His hand. When the agent withdraws himself from God, he is no longer an instrument, he is a broken iron. But you will ask how I am to know when the agent fails. I answer, compare his commands with the root of all wisdom, that is, good living and charity; if they are contrary thereto the instrument is a broken iron, and you are no longer bound to obey. Those who by false reports have sought my excommunication wished to do away with good living and good government, to open the door to every vice." The *signoria* was loath to prohibit Savonarola from preaching, but Alexander was determined to silence the excommunicate and finally in March, 1498, he was ordered to cease.

The pope had many enemies, but none more determined than the Cardinal Giuliano della Rovere, who incessantly urged that a council should try the pontiff. Charles was inclined to support the proposition, and the University of Paris sided with him. Savonarola had talked about a council for the regeneration of the Church and had written about the grounds for convoking it. If one were called under French auspices, the friar, because of his great following, might become a dangerous adversary of the pope. Meanwhile the friar's enemies within Florence who resented his moral dictation began their bitter attacks. The jealous Franciscans were especially hostile, and one of them announced that he would gladly submit to the ordeal by fire to prove that Savonarola was no true prophet of God. Trial by fire and similar methods of establishing proof were forbidden by canon law, but popular belief in their efficacy still flourished.

There was much excitement in Florence as the proposition was discussed, and finally the *signoria* agreed that Savonarola's claims should be tested in this way. Pope Alexander disapproved of the procedure and sought to interfere, but to no avail. Many of Savonarola's supporters believed in the sanctity of his cause and were certain that he would emerge unscathed. The trial did not take place, for it was impossible for both sides to agree to the conditions proposed. In the midst of the discussion, a rainstorm passed over the city which increased the delay. The Franciscans insisted that Savonarola should not be allowed to carry the Host with him through the flames, but Savonarola was adamant. The *signoria* was weary and announced that the ordeal was postponed. On April 8 the friar's enemies assaulted San Marco, and the *signoria* decided to arrest Savonarola in the interest of the public peace.

Savonarola was subjected to torture and in the midst of his agonies confessed that he had received no communications from God as he had declared in his sermons. It is said that he retracted all claims. His followers were stunned by these official reports; even his fellow friars began to forsake him. The pope now wished to punish him as a disobedient priest, but the *signoria* refused to countenance any such recognition of papal judicial rights in their city. Papal commissioners were sent to Florence, and on May 22 they declared Savonarola guilty of heresy. The magistrates of the city thereupon condemned him and two companions to be hanged and then consumed by fire on the following day. When the time came, they were stripped of their vestments, degraded from their sacred office, and handed over to the secular arm for punishment. A gallows had been erected in the *Piazza* in front of the *Palazzo Pubblico*. The sentence was at once carried out, and the bodies were reduced to ashes. Savonarola's sorrowing followers watched for a miracle, but none came.

The ashes were collected and cast into the Arno that no relic might be had of them (May 23, 1498).

Thus died Savonarola, a victim of the vicious political circumstances which dominated Italian life at the close of the *Quattrocento*. In sentiment he was a true son of the Church. He sought to revamp public and private life in Florence according to the law of Christ. He wished to establish a sort of theocracy. There comes a time when reformers must resort to political means, and it came to Savonarola. He believed that Charles was the scourge of God come to purge the Church of its evils. This advocacy of Charles' cause ran counter to Italian national interests as championed by the League of Venice. The pope was opposed to him because of his friendship toward France, which desired a council. Not his religious ideas, but his political role set the pope against him. Alexander's policy was purely secular, carried out according to the methods traditional in Italian politics. So he excommunicated Savonarola which made possible the success of the friar's enemies.

In a sense Savonarola was a man born out of his time. His conception of life belonged to the later Middle Ages. This is shown by his apocalyptic views and his prophetic inspiration as well as by his poems on the fall of the Church and the end of the world and his treatise on revelations. But he also belonged to the Renaissance. He was deeply influenced by the doctrines popularized by the revival of Platonism. He loved the Latin and Greek classics as became a child of the Renaissance, but he did not care for the pedantic absurdities of some humanists who thought that the sum of learning was contained in copying accurately the form of Cicero's writings. He keenly admired the work of Fra Angelico whose noble productions he saw every day in San Marco. He objected to the cult of the nude human form which such artists as Verrocchio and Pollaiuolo had cultivated; he protested against the exclusive study of secular beauty. But he was no ignorant disparager of everything in the new art, as is proved by the fact that Botticelli and so religious a spirit as Michelangelo were deeply influenced by his ideas. Even in his writings Savonarola showed himself to be a child of his age. His *Triumph of the Cross*, in spite of its typically medieval theme, was written in the direct manner of the humanists, stripped of scholastic verbiage. It was addressed to the people and therefore put in the vernacular. This, as we have noted, was a characteristic of the age of Lorenzo the Magnificent.

Chapter 20

THE PAPACY OF THE HIGH RENAISSANCE: POLITICAL AND ARTISTIC

*T*HE TERM High Renaissance is applied to the culmination of Italian civilization in the early sixteenth century. It marked the zenith of artistic, literary, and other cultural activities which were so noteworthy a feature of the *Quattrocento*. After the death of Lorenzo the Magnificent in 1492, Florentine leadership was transferred to Rome where culture flourished under the patronage of the popes. Before describing these activities it is necessary to review the political history of the papacy from the accession of Alexander VI (1492–1503) to Clement VII (1523–1534). They form an important part of the long and complicated history of the Balance of Power.

During this period the Papacy was confronted with peculiar political problems. The States of the Church had preserved the now antiquated organization which had grown up during the Middle Ages. The countryside was predominantly agricultural. Towns were numerous but small and served merely as economic centers for the adjacent country. Feudal and communal authorities controlled the States of the Church. The bishop of Rome failed to concentrate political authority in his hands. Centralization of political functions, a prime feature of the Renaissance in Italy as well as in other lands, remained rudimentary in the States of the Church.

THE PAPACY OF ALEXANDER VI, 1492–1503

The popes adopted several policies to strengthen their rule. Unlike other Italian rulers, they possessed no adequate officialdom or bureaucracy such as many princes had developed in their efforts to establish absolute power. They resorted to nepotism, that is, the advancement to important posts of nephews and other relatives upon whom they could rely. Thus Pope Calixtus III (1455–1458) promoted his nephew, Rodrigo Borgia. Another expedient was to bestow upon nephews political power

323

over important lands. This was done by Sixtus IV (1471–1484) who gave his nephew Girolamo Riario the lordship of Imola and Forlì. A third plan was to seize political authority from petty princes and place it in the hands of the bishop of Rome. This policy, successfully prosecuted by Julius II, gave him greater control over the States of the Church than any of his predecessors had enjoyed.

This growth in temporal power had an important influence upon the character of the papacy. Centralization implied a large staff of officers, organization of an army, and development of a system of taxation. The papacy was primarily a religious institution, but these latter policies emphasized temporal interests at the expense of its spiritual calling. This is the reason, in part at least, why the papacy of the Renaissance seemed to become a secular institution. Its acts were scarcely distinguishable from those of secular princes. Alexander VI (1492–1503) completely secularized the papacy. Before his elevation he was known as Rodrigo Borgia, nephew of Calixtus III, a man with none of the spiritual qualities required of a pope. He was the father of a number of children, the offspring of Vanozza dei Catanei. So worldly had the papal environment become, that this apparently produced little criticism in the morally lax environment of the Renaissance.

Alexander, who dearly loved his children, sought to enhance their welfare, but at the same time used them to strengthen papal political authority. He therefore offered his daughters in marriage to princes who would give him support. The eldest of these children, the duke of Gandia, was named captain of the Church and given the duchy of Benevento. Alexander's daughter Lucrezia Borgia was united in marriage with Giovanni Sforza, seignior of Pesaro, a connection believed advantageous because it linked the fortunes of the house of Borgia with the powerful Sforza rulers of Milan. When no longer useful from a political point of view, this union was dissolved, and Lucrezia was married to Duke Alfonso of Bisceglia, a son of Alfonso II of Naples, who was killed in 1501. Thereupon she became the wife of Duke Alfonso I of Ferrara, a union which, it was hoped, would further papal schemes in the Romagna.

But it was in Cesare Borgia that Alexander's fondest hopes were placed, and he resolved to use Cesare in building up a political principality in the Romagna. This part of the States of the Church gave the pope much trouble. The pope wanted to get rid of the petty but vigorous princes who ruled in Bologna, Rimini, Urbino, Faenza, Pesaro, Sinigaglia, Camerino, Ferrara, Imola, and Forlì. He determined to place their properties in the hands of Cesare, to be held directly of the Church. Plans for the advancement of Cesare went hand in hand with the negotiations with France.

King Charles VIII had died in April, 1498, and was succeeded by his relative Duke Louis of Orléans, grandson of the duke of Orleans who had married Valentina Visconti. King Louis XII's designs upon Milan were known to all men.

Cesare had been made a cardinal in 1493 when but 18 years of age; and, since this dignity was thought to stand in the way of his political career, the pope induced him to renounce the cardinalate and gave him a dispensation which enabled him to abandon the clerical estate. (He was a subdeacon, not a priest.) Cesare set out for France, and an agreement was soon made whereby King Louis' marriage to Jeanne, a sister of Charles VIII, would be annulled. He would marry Anne of Brittany and thus gain the great Breton fief for the crown. A cardinal's hat was bestowed upon Louis' favorite, the Archbishop George d'Amboise of Rouen. Cesare was given two French fiefs, the counties of Diois and Valentinois, and the hand of Charlotte d'Albret, a sister of the king of Navarre. Louis promised to help Cesare secure the Romagna. This mercenary political transaction caused a great scandal, but the papacy was indifferent to the moral incompatibility of its religious position and its political policy.

Louis' policy in making this agreement with the Borgia family needs explanation. He wanted to get control of Milan, and to do so it was necessary to break up the League of Venice formed in 1495 to protect Italy against further encroachments by France. Pope Alexander was won by the promise of help in the Romagna. In return for help, Venice was promised Milanese Cremona and a small stretch of land on the left bank of the Adda. Thereupon Louis invaded Milan in August, 1499, assisted by the Venetians who advanced from the east. Ludovico Sforza who was not in a position to defend his duchy, fled to Innsbruck. The French thus occupied the land, but the populace hated Louis. Ludovico returned in 1500, and the French were forced to evacuate the city of Milan, but only temporarily, for Ludovico was defeated in the Battle of Novara (April, 1500), taken prisoner, and spent his remaining days in a French fortress. The French king again controlled Milan.

Louis also claimed the crown of Naples and made preparations for its conquest. But behind Frederick, the king of Naples, stood King Ferdinand of Aragon and Sicily who possessed some rights to the crown in case Frederick died. Louis asserted that the Neapolitan house had sprung from an illegitimate birth and that it was ruling Naples without legal right. Rather than go to war, Louis and Ferdinand agreed to partition the realm. The Treaty of Granada (November, 1500) gave the northern provinces to Louis and the southern to Ferdinand. This was a most immoral procedure but typical of the cynical disregard for justice in international affairs which pervaded Renaissance politics. The Neapolitan king could not maintain himself at the head of his kingdom when opposed by such a combination and accordingly abdicated in August, 1501. Ferdinand and Louis fought over their spoils, with the result that the French were expelled after the fall of Gaeta on New Year's Day of 1504.

Meanwhile Alexander prosecuted his design upon the Romagna. Fortified by the promise of Louis' friendship and assistance, Cesare Borgia attacked Imola and Forlì and secured them in January, 1500. Faenza was seized in April, 1501, and Alexander now made Cesare duke of the Romagna. In 1502 Fermo, Urbino, and Camerino fell before the duke's troops. He next moved to attack Bologna, but was thwarted by a conspiracy of the dispossessed rulers and others who were fearful that a like fate might befall them. Their plans were formulated at Magione, and a rebellion was promoted in Urbino. Confronted by this new danger, Cesare revealed masterful and unscrupulous resourcefulness. The story of how he slew the conspirators at Sinigaglia has been described by Machiavelli in one of his most interesting passages. This tale well illustrates that combination of power, craft, and success which Italians of the Renaissance called *virtù*.

[Cesare] dispersed his men throughout the Romagna, set out for Imola at the end of November [1502] together with his French men-at-arms; thence he went to Cesena, where he stayed some time to negotiate with the envoys of the Vitelli and Orsini, who had assembled with their men in the duchy of Urbino, as to the enterprise in which they should now take part; but nothing being concluded, Oliverotto da Fermo was sent to propose that if the duke wished to undertake an expedition against Tuscany they were ready; if he did not wish it, then they would besiege Sinigaglia. . . .

It happened that not long afterwards the town surrendered, but the fortress would not yield to them because the castellan would not give it up to anyone but the duke in person; therefore they exhorted him to come there. This appeared a good opportunity to the duke, as, being invited by them, and not going of his own will, he would awaken no suspicions. And the more to reassure them, he allowed all the French men-at-arms who were with him in Lombardy to depart, except the hundred lancers under Monsieur di Candales, his brother-in-law. He left Cesena about the middle of December, and went to Fano, and with the utmost cunning and cleverness he persuaded the Vitelli and Orsini to wait for him at Sinigaglia, pointing out to them that any lack of compliance would cast a doubt upon the sincerity and permanency of the reconciliation, and that he was a man who wished to make use of the arms and councils of his friends. But Vitellozzo Vitelli remained very stubborn, for the death of his brother warned him that he should not offend a prince and afterwards trust him; nevertheless, persuaded by Pagolo Orsini, whom the duke had corrupted with gifts and promises, he agreed to wait.

Upon this the duke, before his departure from Fano, which was to be on December 30, 1502, communicated his designs to eight of his most trusted followers . . . and he ordered that, as soon as Vitellozzo, Pagolo Orsini, Duke of Gravina, and Oliverotto da Fermo should arrive, his followers in pairs should take them one by one, entrusting certain men to certain pairs, who should entertain them until they reached Sinigaglia; nor should they be permitted to leave until they came to the duke's quarters, where they should be seized.

The duke afterwards ordered all his horsemen and infantry, of which there were more than two thousand cavalry and ten thousand footmen, to assemble by daybreak at the Metauro, a river five miles distant from Fano, and await him there. He found himself, therefore, on the last day of December at the Metauro with his men, and having sent a cavalcade of about two hundred horsemen before him, he then moved forward the infantry, whom he accompanied with the rest of the men-at-arms.

Fano and Sinigaglia are two cities of The Marches situated on the shore of the Adriatic Sea, fifteen miles distant from each other, so that he who goes toward Sinigaglia has the mountains on his right hand, the bases of which are touched by the sea in some places. The city of Sinigaglia is distant from the foot of the mountains a little more than a bow-shot and from the shore about a mile. On the side opposite to the city runs a little river which bathes that part of the walls looking toward Fano, facing the high road. Thus he who draws near to Sinigaglia comes for a good space by road along the mountains, and reaches the river which passes Sinigaglia. If he turn to his left hand along the bank of it, and goes for the distance of a bow-shot, he arrives at a bridge which crosses the river; he is then almost abreast of the gate that leads into Sinigaglia, not by a straight line, but transversely. Before this gate there stands a collection of houses with a square to which the bank of the river forms one side.

The Vitelli and Orsini having received orders to wait for the duke, and to honor him in person, sent away their men to several castles distant from Sinigaglia about six miles, so that room could be made for the men of the duke; and they left in Sinigaglia only Oliverotto and his band, which consisted of one thousand infantry and one hundred and fifty horsemen, who were quartered in the suburb mentioned above. Matters having been thus arranged, Cesare left for Sinigaglia and when the leaders of the cavalry reached the bridge they did not pass over, but having opened it, one portion wheeled toward the river and the other toward the country, and a way was left in the middle through which the infantry passed, without stopping, into the town.

Vitellozzo, Pagolo, and the Duke of Gravina on mules, accompanied by a few horsemen, went toward the duke; Vitellozzo unarmed and wearing a cape lined with green, appeared very dejected, as if conscious of his approaching death—a circumstance which, in view of the ability of the man and his former fortune, caused some amazement. And it is said that when he parted from his men before setting out for Sinigaglia to meet the duke he acted as if it were his last parting from them. He recommended his house and its fortunes to his captains and advised his nephews that it was not the fortune of their house but the virtues of their fathers that should be kept in mind. These three, therefore, came before the duke and saluted him respectfully, and were received by him with goodwill; they were at once placed between those who were commissioned to look after them.

But the duke, noticing that Oliverotto, who had remained with his band in Sinigaglia, was missing—for Oliverotto was waiting in the square before his quarters near the river, keeping his men in order and drilling them—signalled with his eye to Don Michele, to whom the care of Oliverotto had been committed, that he should take measures that Oliverotto should not escape. Therefore Don Michele rode off and joined Oliverotto, telling him that it was not right to keep his men out of their quarters, because these might be taken up by the men of the duke; and he advised him to send them at once to their quarters and to come himself to meet the duke. And Oliverotto, having taken this advice, came before the duke, who, when he saw him, called to him; and Oliverotto, having made his obeisance, joined the others.

So the whole party entered Sinigaglia, dismounted at the duke's quarters, and went with him into a secret chamber, where the duke made them prisoners; he then mounted on horseback, and issued orders that the men of Oliverotto and the Orsini should be stripped of their arms. Those of Oliverotto, being at hand, were quickly settled, but those of the Orsini and Vitelli, being at a distance, and having a presentiment of the destruction of their masters, had time to prepare themselves, and bearing in mind the valor and discipline of the Orsinian and Vitellescan houses, they stood together against the hostile forces of the country and saved themselves.

But the duke's soldiers, not being content with having pillaged the men of Oliverotto, began to sack Sinigaglia, and if the duke had not repressed this outrage by killing some of them, they would have completely sacked it. Night having come and the tumult being silenced, the duke prepared to kill Vitellozzo and Oliverotto; he led them into a room and caused them to be strangled. Neither of them used words in keeping with their past lives; Vitellozzo prayed that he might ask the Pope full pardon for his sins; Oliverotto cringed and laid the blame for all injuries against the duke on Vitellozzo. Pagolo and the Duke of Gravini Orsini were kept alive until the duke heard from Rome that the pope had taken the Cardinal Orsini, the Archbishop of

Florence, and Messer Jacopo da Santa Croce. After which news, on January 18, 1502, in the castle of Pieve, they also were strangled in the same way.[1]

THE PAPACY OF JULIUS II (1503–1513)

The death of Alexander VI in August, 1503, put an end to Cesare's successful course. Pius III, the next pope, ruled only a few months. Cardinal Giuliano della Rovere was thereupon elected and took as his name Julius II (1503–1513). He had been a candidate for the papal tiara in 1492 and was sorely disappointed in being passed by. As spiritual head of the Church he presents little that is interesting, but as temporal ruler he was one of the remarkable princes of the Renaissance. An outstanding example of the worldliness into which the papacy had fallen, he possessed in striking degree that quality which Italians admired and called *terribilità*—"spirit-quailing, awe-inspiring force," as it was defined by Symonds. Julius hated the Borgia family and found the means of getting rid of Cesare Borgia whose possessions he added to those of the papacy. He made a modern Renaissance state of the States of the Church.

The della Rovere family sprang from a village near Genoa. In common with most Genoese, it felt a strong hatred for Venice and her policies, for she had crowded others out of the lower Po valley by a method as persistent as it was cynically indifferent to the rights of neighbors. When Cesare Borgia fell, Venice seized Faenza, Cesena, and Rimini in order to fortify her southern border. At first Julius was not able to resist her and so awaited his time. He attacked Perugia and subjected it to the papal will. In 1506 he marched on Bologna which was forced to yield with little difficulty. Julius next turned his attention to Venice which, with serene indifference to the opinion of other Italians and to powers outside Italy, had kept her conquests in the Romagna. Julius resolved to drive the Venetians out. He found that the Emperor Maximilian was angry with them because they had seized Friuli, that King Louis of France wished to expand his Milanese territories at their expense, and that King Ferdinand of Naples resented their holding a number of towns in Naples on the Adriatic coast which had been given to Venice at the time of Charles VIII's invasion.

It was easy for these enemies of Venice to come to an agreement. The League of Cambrai, formed in December, 1508, at papal suggestion, aimed to divide the lands of Venice between Maximilian and Louis. The French king was to receive the investiture of the duchy of Milan from the

[1] Adapted from "Description of the Methods Adopted by the Duke Valentino . . .," in Machiavelli, *The Prince* (Everyman's Library).

emperor. The Venetians were defeated in the Battle of Agnadello in May, 1509, and all their possessions on the mainland were lost. They also lost their hold upon the Romagna. But the people living in Venetia resented the arrogance of their conquerors and remained loyal to Venice. In fact, hatred of foreigners was a strong force among Italians, and Julius himself keenly felt the disgrace of Italy being made the victim of foreign ambitions. He was the first native Italian prince to have such decided feelings, and Italians of his day approved of his attitude. He determined that the French should be driven out of Italy.

The Holy League, embracing Pope Julius, Ferdinand, and Venice, was formed in October, 1511, its object being the restoration of the lands lost by the Venetians, the return of Bologna to the papacy, and the further safeguarding of papal possessions. Although opposed by great odds, Louis determined to keep what he had won. His general Gaston de Foix, an able commander who moved with lightning rapidity, engaged Cardona, the general of the League, at Ravenna in a bloody battle on Easter Day of 1512. It was a Pyrrhic victory for the French whose losses were heavy. They were cordially hated by the people of the Po valley, and the morale of their troops was spoiled by the plunder of towns. The French position became grave when the Swiss poured down the Alps upon Milan. Maximilian also decided to move against the French, for he saw a chance of winning the duchy for himself. The French were forced to evacuate, leaving their conquests to their enemies.

The members of the league met at Mantua in September, 1512, resolved to uproot every vestige of French power in the peninsula. They demanded that Florence should drop her friendly policy toward France and permit the return of the exiled Medici. When the Florentines refused to abandon their internal policy begun in the days of Savonarola, Cardona attacked and sacked neighboring Prato. The Florentine constitution was changed and the Medici returned as private citizens. Milan was given to Maximilian Sforza, son of the ill-fated Ludovico. In February, 1513, shortly after these objects had been accomplished, Julius died. Italians grieved sincerely over the death of this great prince, for they understood his policy and saw that it harmonized with the best secular interests of Italy at a time when other princes aimed at personal or family advantage. On the other hand, the religious conscience of Christendom was not pleased with the pope's secularism—it was shocking to see Christ's vicar appear in an army, direct maneuvers, and plant cannon. According to medieval conceptions, however, the establishment of papal political power was necessary. Julius founded the modern States of the Church; this was his most significant work.

THE PAPACY OF THE TWO MEDICI: LEO X (1513–1521) AND CLEMENT VII (1523–1534)

Giovanni de' Medici succeeded Julius as Leo X (1513–1521). The cardinals did not wish to continue the ways of the vigorous Julius and desired quiet. Leo, a man of affable manners and conversation, and extremely ingratiating, desired peace above all things, for he had gained abundant experience of life while in exile after his family fled Florence in 1494. But the woes of Italy were not at an end. Louis died on the last day of 1515 and was succeeded as king of France by his youthful cousin Francis I. The new king was ambitious to reconquer what had been lost in Italy. Leo sought to win the favor of Francis and at the same time retain that of the king's Italian enemies. The French invaded the Milanese and in August, 1516, won a decisive battle at Marignano. Once more the wheel of fortune turned, and the French were in possession of what they had twice lost. Leo was a subtle diplomat and hastened to make terms with Francis. It was agreed that the Medici were to be supported in Florence. Furthermore, relations between the Church and crown in France were regulated by the Concordat of Bologna (August, 1516).

Politically, Adrian VI's brief pontificate (1522–1523) was of slight importance. Clement's passing in 1534 marked the end of the secularized Papacy of the High Renaissance. The change first came when Rome was sacked in 1527 by the Emperor Charles V in one of his wars—that of the League of Cambrai (1526–1529)—with Francis I of France. From this time forward Italian states, especially Naples and Milan, and also Sicily were drawn into the conflicts of the Balance of Power, warring on the side of Charles V against Francis I. For Italy, whose political fate now was settled by foreign troops fighting on her soil, this was an unfortunate period. But the Age of the High Renaissance was peculiarly disastrous for the cause of the Christian religion. Forces working for reform indeed were active within the Church, but the real beginning of reform had to wait until Paul III (1534–1549) mounted the papal throne and boldly faced the difficult task of reviving Catholicism, buried under Renaissance secularism and paganism, its very existence challenged by the Lutheran revolt.

ARTISTIC ENDEAVOR OF THE PAPACY OF THE HIGH RENAISSANCE

The "moral miseries of the reign of Alexander VI," as the historian Pastor calls them, were in a measure counterbalanced, however, by a splendid patronage of the arts. As vicar of Christ, it may be said that Alexander was a gross failure. Spiritual activities were neglected, to the great scandal of Christendom. Alexander devoted much attention to painting and architecture and beautified the region around the Vatican called the Borgo. A great street, the *Borgo Nuovo* of today, was laid out. The castle of Sant' Angelo was improved and assumed the appearance it still preserves. Many improvements were made in the Vatican. The Borgian Apartments (*Appartamenti Borgia*) were rebuilt and new rooms added. In one of the frescoes Pinturicchio, the artist who decorated them, gave the world a famous portrait of Alexander kneeling in adoration as he beholds the miracle of the Resurrection. Alexander also constructed the roof of Santa Maria Maggiore, and other churches were restored or repaired. Noble buildings were erected, such as the palace built for Cardinal Giuliano della Rovere by the architect Giuliano da San Gallo. Donato Bramante (d. 1514) built the important Tempietto in 1502, the first Roman church of the Renaissance to be constructed under classical inspiration.

Pope Julius was a far more significant patron, however. When one considers the enormous amount of political, diplomatic, military, and ecclesiastical labor which that pontiff undertook, one is astounded by the grandeur of his artistic projects, the variety of his interests, and the uniformly high quality of everything which was executed under his care. All of the world admires the genius of this man as revealed in his artistic interests; the moral obliquity of his pontificate is partly forgotten because of it. Rome became one of the most beautiful cities in Christendom, worthy to be the capital of the Church universal on earth.

Julius was especially interested in architecture. As pope he wished to build a new St. Peter's, a temple grander and more beautiful than any in Christendom, for the old basilica was so decrepit that it threatened to collapse. The greatness of Julius' mind is revealed by the magnificent scale of the new structure. His vigorous activity, his *terribilità*, brooked no delay. Now began the ruthless destruction of the old temple which for ages had been the goal of countless pilgrims. Only the tomb of St. Peter was left untouched—even Bramante and Pope Julius could not lay their destructive hands upon it. The new church was to be in the form of a Greek cross surmounted by a gigantic dome, with the four arms of the cross covered by smaller domes. The first stone was placed in April, 1506.

Bramante was also employed to construct a series of buildings north of the Vatican. Nicholas V had erected an open pavilion, called the Belvedere, which was now joined to the complex of structures just north of the buildings adjoining St. Peter's. The distance of more than 1000 feet was covered by two wings which were joined at their northern end by a structure called the *Nicchione*. The space between the two wings was divided into two parts. The northern was called the Giardino della Pigna or Garden of the Pine-cone, so named because of the enormous pine cone which is mounted in the *Nicchione*. The other yard is the Teatro, a space reserved for jousting and similar events. The great architect devoted much energy from 1505 to 1512 to the erection of these buildings.

During the first years of his pontificate Julius lived in the Borgian Apartments. But every time his eye fell on the frescoes in those rooms, he was reminded of Alexander whom he hated because he held him responsible for the disappointments and hardships to which he had been subjected. He determined to occupy the rooms immediately above them and at once prepared for their adequate decoration. Their walls had been decorated by excellent and even great artists, but Julius wanted the best of his own day, and the frescoes of the great masters of the *Quattrocento* were ruthlessly destroyed. Distinguished artists including Perugino and Sodoma were employed. Finally, Raphael of Urbino was given a commission in 1508 which kept him occupied until his death in 1520. The decision to entrust the task to this artist is a tribute to Julius' ability to appreciate truly great art, for all posterity has acclaimed the frescoes in these rooms as the very zenith of Renaissance painting.

Julius' pontificate is famed also because of his great interest in sculpture. The pope was interested in antique marbles and had long been an assiduous collector. He purchased the *Apollo Belvedere*, which had been discovered in the days of Innocent VIII. Justly proud of this famous possession, when he became pope he transferred it to the orange groves and fountains of the Belvedere. In 1506 the great *Laocoon* was discovered buried in the earth near the Baths of Titus. Julius made every effort to secure this treasure and it too was placed in the Belvedere. Other marbles were added, but the greatest of them was the colossal statue representing the River Tiber which was found in 1512 near the church of Santa Maria sopra Minerva.

There was nothing petty in the character of this great prince of the Church. Everything he did was conceived on a lofty plane and carried out with a mighty energy which astounded all observers. No one but Michelangelo could be entrusted with the task of constructing a great tomb, fitting receptable for his earthly remains, and one which would perpetuate for all time some conception of his mighty personality. We may

. . . represent to ourselves an isolated construction, accessible on all sides, measuring twenty-four feet in width, thirty-six in depth, and over thirty·

six feet in height. The base, thirteen feet high, and separated from the upper part by a massive and prominent entablature, presents on all four sides a continuous succession of immense niches flanked by enormous projecting pilasters: niches and pilasters proclaiming the mundane glory of Julius II— his glory as conqueror, and as patron of the arts. In each of the niches a winged Victory treads under foot a defeated and disarmed province; at each of the pilasters, an enchained athlete writhes, convulsed, shuddering, flinging to heaven a reproachful glance, or sinks exhausted and expiring. The two famous statues in the Louvre, so improperly called 'The Slaves,' were of this number. These unchained athletes personify the liberal arts, themselves become 'the prisoners of death' in the death of the Rovere; their great benefactor gone, they despair and perish! The upper part of the monument, which has a height of nine feet, lifts us toward a higher world, toward regions ideal and serene. In contrast with the Victories and athletes of the base, all represented standing and in attitudes heroic or pathetic, the eight principal statues above are either seated or stand in repose and solemn tranquility. We distinguish among them Moses, St. Paul, Active Life, Contemplative Life, perhaps also Prudence and some other allegorical Virtue. In the midst rises the great sarcophagus, destined to receive the mortal remains of the pope. At the very summit of the monument is seen Julius II himself 'held suspended' by two angels of contrasted aspect: the Genius of the Earth is sad, and weeps the loss which has just fallen upon this lower world; the Angel of Heaven rejoices, and is proud to introduce this new-comer into the abodes of the blessed. Two other angels stoop over the pontiff's feet.[2]

Many difficulties prevented the completion of this structure. The mighty Moses and a few figures in Paris and Florence, together with some drawings, are all that remain of the scheme. The pontiff had other tasks for the great master. Michelangelo was ordered to make a gigantic statue of the pope to celebrate fittingly the papal triumph over Bologna. This was placed over the doorway of the church of San Petronio in Bologna. It was the sculptor's only work in copper. Shortly after, the Bolognese pulled it down in their hatred of papal government and cast a large cannon of the metal. Julius next ordered Michelangelo to decorate the bare ceiling of the Sistine Chapel, a task which occupied him from 1508 to 1512. These frescoes are among the greatest creations ever conceived by the brain of man and are a fitting addition to those done in the days of Sixtus IV, already described.

Few patrons of the Renaissance dominated the spirit of art so vitally as did Julius. The Moses on his tomb expresses the fiery pontiff's *terribilità* and restless endeavor as ruler of the Church. Michelangelo's frescoes on the vault of the Sistine Chapel eloquently tell the story of the Christian

    [2] J. Klaczko, *Rome and the Renaissance* (New York, 1926), pp. 13–14.

drama of man's creation and fall. Raphael's frescoes in the Camera della Segnatura are an epic of civilization. The so-called *Disputa* is an eloquent pictorial statement of the Christian plan of salvation. In this, God in heaven appears above His Son at whose right is seated the Virgin in adoration and at whose left is John the Baptist pointing to the Redeemer. Christ is surrounded by the heavenly host of apostles and saints. The lower half is an earthly scene with an altar on which appears the Host, the object of adoration by popes, cardinals, bishops, and laymen. The Holy Spirit in form of a dove, placed midway between Christ and the Host, joins the two parts of the picture. Opposite this picture is the so-called *School of Athens*, epitomizing the Christian conception of secular culture as it was understood in the Middle Ages according to Thomas Aquinas. The great philosophers and scientists of antiquity whose intellectual efforts supplement the teaching of the Church are shown in their traditional capacities. Revelation and reason thus appear as harmonious parts of human knowledge.

In this room also appears the *Parnassus*. It portrays Apollo seated and surrounded by the Muses. Around them are gathered the great poets of antiquity from Homer to Horace. Dante and Petrarch also are represented. It reveals the kinship which men of the Renaissance felt for the great works of antiquity and the Middle Ages. Was it not fitting that Julius, Christ's vicar on earth and man's truest servant, should have these three pictures in his quarters? Even though this pontiff was chiefly occupied in the secular duties of the papacy, he did not forget his interests as priest. The *Mass of Bolsena,* which is in the room of Heliodorus, portrays a disbelieving priest at the altar gazing upon the Host which has begun to bleed and tinge the corporal. Facing him is the kneeling figure of Julius in pious reverence as Raphael no doubt often observed him. This portrait is one of the painter's masterpieces.

Leo X, as befitted this member of the Medici family, had been brought up in the lap of Renaissance luxury. He is the best example of the refined taste in art, manners, and social intercourse developed among the elite of *Quattrocento* bourgeois society. His kindly smile, well-modulated voice, and kingly bearing ingratiated him with all men. Humanists greeted his elevation with pleasure and were not disappointed in him as a patron. Literary men flocked to Rome and found favor at the curia. Pietro Bembo (1470–1547), a great master of Ciceronian style and noted for the excellence of his letters, became papal secretary. Although born in Venice, Pietro was educated in Florence and became acquainted with Lorenzo the Magnificent. He spent some time at the court of Ferrara. At Urbino he was associated with the brilliant coterie brought together by the duchess. Among his friends was Castiglione, and he figures in that author's *Courtier*. Jacopo Sadoleto (1477–1547) also was named papal secretary. Like Bembo, he cultivated a Ciceronian style, although he insisted less on absolute purity of form.

The curia now became the center of a vigorous literary life. All forms of writing were cultivated. Not only were ancient classical models closely followed, but Italian poetry also flourished. Some of the best minds were invited to accept posts at the University of Rome. The study of classical archaeology was stimulated when Raphael proposed to make a large map of ancient Rome based upon careful study of old structures and the ancient classics. Leo invited prominent Greek scholars to Rome and added books to the papal library. He was a munificent Maecenas who did not hesitate to spend any sum.

The Leonine Age, as this pontificate is often called, left a peculiar impress upon the history of art. Leo was very fond of Raphael and employed the great painter more than any of his competitors. The rooms in the Vatican were finished by Raphael and his assistants. In the room of Heliodorus is a famous fresco representing Leo I arresting the advance of the Huns under Attila. Leo I's face is a portrait of Leo X. Raphael also decorated the famous loggia on the third story of the Vatican which Bramante had built. These frescoes are peculiarly related to the Leonine age, for here are intermingled Christian and classical motives without any consciousness that they were hostile to each other. Raphael also prepared cartoons for tapestries which were to hang on the walls of the Sistine Chapel to supplement the frescoes which had been painted during the pontificate of Sixtus IV. These tapestries are a masterpiece of Renaissance art.

Leo also took Michelangelo into his employ. During the earlier years of this pontificate the sculptor was occupied with the tomb of Julius, but, when Leo proposed to provide a magnificent façade for the church of San Lorenzo in Florence, Michelangelo was awarded the contract. Two burdensome tasks now divided the sculptor's energies, and he made little progress with either. The plans for the façade were finally dropped, but soon Leo proposed to him another and greater project, the preparation of the monumental tombs for members of the Medici family in the Florentine church of San Lorenzo. The pope also employed the sculptor Andrea Sansovino to decorate the Holy House of Loreto. Sculpture did not play as prominent a role at the papal court as in the days of Julius. Architecture, however, was emphasized. Buildings were constructed according to the new style. Bramante was retained to carry on the construction of St. Peter's until his death in 1514, whereupon Raphael was appointed. The original plans of Bramante were modified, but little progress could be made owing to the lack of funds.

Adrian VI's pontificate (1522–1523) was but a brief interlude, for this pontiff was absorbed in the more arduous work of reform and the restoration of papal prestige. An old-fashioned man living an austere life, he could not play the part of a Maecenas. The Romans did not understand him, and disappointed humanists loosed many a shaft of ridicule at him. He was succeeded by Giulio de' Medici, a nephew of Leo X, who styled himself Clement VII (1523–1534). His pontificate also boasted artistic achievements. A genuine son of the Medici, he became a literary patron and formed a coterie of writers. Although the pope lacked money, the room of Constantine in the Vatican was finished by Giulio Romano (d. 1546), one of Raphael's pupils. Benvenuto Cellini received many commissions from the pope. Michelangelo was again employed to construct the new sacristy of San Lorenzo in Florence and finished the noble works which all the world admires. He also built the Laurentian Library in the cloisters of the same church. But before he could begin the *Last Judgment* in the Sistine Chapel upon which the pontiff's heart was set, Clement died.

Chapter 21

POLITICS DURING THE HIGH
RENAISSANCE

S TATES TENDED to become more definitely absolute during the Renaissance, marking the culmination of a long evolution which had begun
in the Middle Ages as far back as the year 1000. Revival of commerce and
industry, growth of towns, and increase in the use of coined money
produced an unprecedented amount of wealth. Kings and princes no
longer were forced to draw their incomes chiefly from manorial sources
but began to collect hard cash from their subjects. They built up a
bureaucratic government, maintained armies of mercenaries, and steadily
drew into their hands governmental functions which in former ages had
been controlled by feudal lords. They were especially jealous of the right
to dispense justice. Thus secular states, controlling purse and sword,
became more powerful than ever.

MATERIAL BASIS OF RENAISSANCE
POLITICAL ABSOLUTISM

The states of the Renaissance naturally took keen interest in economic
matters. They were in constant need of money for war and administration. They borrowed immense sums from private banking firms which had
been established by the wealthy bourgeoisie. For a long time princes had
followed a policy closely in harmony with the economic interests of the
towns. Ever since their first days towns had regulated their internal economic affairs with great minuteness, and they kept vigilant watch over
external relations as well. As governments became powerful and abandoned the manorial and feudal bases of their power they shaped their
policies to the wishes of townsmen. Economic and political practices of
towns were adopted by the governments. This was a characteristic
feature of Italian states during the *Quattrocento* and *Cinquecento*, and it
also became common among states north of the Alps and in the Spanish

peninsula. This new political policy toward economic matters in time came to be called mercantilism.[1] Public policy was no longer feudal but mercantile. The absolute state henceforth was to direct economic life.

A theory, and practice, of absolutism was developed during these centuries. Formerly the power of princes was tempered by the feudal organization of society and by the manorial character of economic life. Medieval princes taught that their authority proceeded directly from God who had established the state as a means of repressing man's evil passions. The emperor of the Holy Roman Empire was God's political representative on earth, and all men were subject to him. This theory of divine right underwent important changes during the last centuries of the Middle Ages. As kings and princes became more and more powerful, they too began to claim that they ruled as representatives of God. They frequently declared that they were "emperors in their own realms," owing allegiance to no one but God. The theory of divine right provided the basis of princely power in its dealings with feudal nobles, foreign powers, and the papacy. Divine right and mercantilism are two important aspects of the new absolutism of the Renaissance.

A parallel development is observable in military matters. Kings and princes developed mercenary armies; this was possible because they possessed well-filled war chests. The old feudal levies were obsolete in the face of the new power of the state and the new military arms and methods. Experience in the Middle Ages had shown that the common man when properly equipped and trained could hold his own against the cavalry of the feudal nobility—a lesson learned at Courtrai (1302), Crécy (1346), Poitiers (1356), and Agincourt (1415). The introduction of gunpowder also helped to reduce the importance of the nobility. Guns, large and small, were gradually perfected and became more effective weapons. With even imperfect firearms in hand the infantry was as important as the mounted nobility. Castles were no longer impregnable defenses. Furthermore, some of the greater princes developed an orderly army administration which made their troops far more effective than those of feudal nobles. This is one reason for the great victories of the English over the French in the Hundred Years' War, for not until the French king adopted some of these ideas was he able to cope with his

---

[1] For a discussion of the true significance of *mercantilism*, see R. Ehrenberg, *Capital and Finance in the Age of the Renaissance*, New York, 1929, pp. 21–22. The term *mercantilism* became popular after the appearance in 1776 of Adam Smith's *An Inquiry into the Nature and Causes of the Wealth of Nations*. The student should read especially the fourth book (Everyman's Library). Since the term is often misunderstood and usually interpreted too narrowly, the student would do well to read G. N. Clark, *The Seventeenth Century*, Oxford, 1929, chap. ii, especially pp. 21–29.

enemies. Furthermore, an army recruited from the common classes and paid by the king's treasury could be disciplined far better than the anarchic feudal soldiery. Hence the Swiss infantry, German *landsknechts*, and Spanish footmen were most effective in the wars of the Renaissance. The cavalry, usually recruited from the nobility, remained an important arm of the military. Rulers usually possessed an adequate artillery of heavy cannon, and they also built powerful forts. Finally, the king's treasury could pay for the costly new inventions.

New ideas and methods of diplomacy were developed during the Renaissance. In the earlier Middle Ages when society rested upon a manorial basis, relations between rulers were occasional and not continuous as in modern times. Diplomatic questions were discussed by special representatives appointed for the occasion. As princely power grew and relations between states became more numerous, it was necessary to use more permanent representatives. From the close of the thirteenth century the kings of Aragon had been in the habit of receiving reports from their agents abroad. But the sending of systematic observations was not begun until resident ambassadors were appointed at the end of the Middle Ages. Venetian agents were specially trained and were noted for their understanding of international relations. The reports to their home government, known as the *Venetian Relations*, constitute one of the most important collections of source materials for the political and economic history of the Renaissance. Contemporaries admired Venice's diplomatic service, and Italian diplomatic activity and ambassadorial customs exerted much influence upon the diplomatic service of other lands.

THE NEW HISTORY OF THE RENAISSANCE

The creation of the absolute state naturally brought on a change in the writing of history. Much of this literary activity had been excessively local in character, especially in the earlier Middle Ages. Monks wrote down the interesting events connected with their monasteries and recorded the deeds of petty dynasties or royal houses. Clerks and lay secretaries sometimes related the events which appeared significant in the life of some town. A few were able to raise themselves above localism, such as Otto of Freising (twelfth century) and Matthew Paris (thirteenth century). These writers were in the habit of recording interesting events without attempting to fuse the data together into a connected and logical treatise. They were annalists or chroniclers. But the development of the absolute state of the Renaissance created a new center of interest for the historian. The writing of history became political, but in Italy it also tended toward the lay and worldly, owing to the secularizing tendency of Renaissance life. When the Revival of Learning began and humanists eagerly perused such Greek and Latin historians as Livy, Sallust, Herodotus, Thucydides, and Tacitus, they learned to compose treatises which were logically constructed and artistically written. The custom of narrating events year by year was abandoned, and better literary productions were the result. Henceforth writers composed their historical treatises in splendid rhetoric.

The most remarkable historian to interpret the political life of the Renaissance was Francesco Guicciardini (1483–1540). Born of a noble family, he received a humanist education, became a lawyer, and in 1512 was named ambassador of Florence to King Ferdinand of Spain and Naples. In 1515 he entered the service of Pope Leo X and spent many years as governor of the papal lands of Reggio, Modena, Parma, the Romagna, and Bologna. Thus he had unique opportunity to acquaint himself with the tortuous and cynical diplomatic and political life of his day. His writings are characterized by an amplitude of vision which surpassed that of his contemporaries. In his *History of Florence,* which covers the years 1378–1509, he abandoned the old annalistic style and sought to give a complete analysis of political events. His *History of Italy,* which narrates the political and military fortunes of the peninsula from 1492–1534, may be regarded as his masterpiece. Guicciardini took pains to give some account of every aspect of political history during the struggles of the Balance of Power. He surveyed these catastrophic wars which ruined the prosperity of Italy as coldly and dispassionately as an anatomist dissecting a body. He aimed at accuracy and often sacrificed style to fullness. This prolixity has prevented his works from becoming as popular as they deserve.

Niccolò Machiavelli (1469–1527) ranks next to Guicciardini as Renaissance historian. Earlier in the *Quattrocento* Leonardo Bruni had written a *History of Florence* in twelve books which carried the narrative down to 1404. It recounted the many wars which had troubled Florence, but Machiavelli was dissatisfied with this account because he missed in it any consideration of the influence of these struggles upon the internal life of the state. Machiavelli was the first writer of the Renaissance to interest himself solely in the secular life of states, especially Florence. His *History of Florence* in eight books closes with the passing of Lorenzo the Magnificent in 1492. One central idea (and an erroneous one) dominates this work, namely, that the popes had ruined the unity of Italy by inviting the barbarians into the peninsula when the papacy was in danger of falling under the dictation of the Lombards. Such was the power of the popes that, according to Machiavelli, they successfully kept Italy divided in spite of the efforts of princes to establish central authority and bring to the troubled land the blessings of peace and prosperity. This book is written in a clear, crisp style which has given Machiavelli an exalted place among masters of Italian prose.

Machiavelli is particularly significant as an exponent of the political conceptions and practices of the Renaissance. He sprang from an old and petty noble family which possessed a modest patrimony in and near Florence. Little is known about his early years save that he received a humanist education. But his knowledge of Greek remained limited. He became acquainted with classical literature, especially that part of it which dealt with political affairs. He witnessed many stirring scenes during his earlier days such as the death of Lorenzo the Magnificent, the invasion by Charles VIII, the expulsion of Piero de' Medici, and the establishment of the Florentine republic. In 1498 he became secretary to the Ten, a division of the new government charged with war and internal affairs. His first important public duty was a mission to Catherine Sforza, ruler of Forlì. He did not acquit himself very creditably in this undertaking, for he was no match for the subtlety of this woman who successfully ruled her lands in the midst of plots and wars. Later he was sent to Louis XII and to Cesare Borgia when the latter was conquering the Romagna. These public duties gave him first-hand acquaintance with the political and diplomatic life of his day.

Thus Machiavelli learned that princes and states were guided by expediency and selfish interests without regard to moral principles. Politics was completely secularized during the Renaissance. The theory universally held during the Middle Ages that rulers of states must be instructed in moral and religious matters by the clergy was completely ignored. Even the pope as governor of the States of the Church acted simply as a secular prince without regard to traditional teachings. Machiavelli reflected long upon these facts and upon the wars which had brought so much woe to Italy. His reflections were written down in a number of books, the first of which was the *Discourses on the First Ten Books of Titus Livius*. He used the data recorded by Livy and other classical writers in formulating a philosophy of political life.

POLITICAL THOUGHT OF NICCOLÒ MACHIAVELLI

Machiavelli taught that states were founded by some powerful person like Romulus or Solon. Such a prince was all powerful and directed the life of the citizenry as suited his interest. The only standard by which public policy was to be judged was success. So important was the state that any successful political policy was a good policy. Morality had nothing to do with the matter. Having often observed the sudden changes in the fortunes of Italian principalities, Machiavelli developed a theory about the vicissitudes of states which may be summed up as follows: Men at first lived like animals, hostile to each other, but soon chose leaders for protection. A wise ruler or legislator was named, and, as he transmitted his power to his heirs, monarchies were established. Mankind, however, is selfish and certain to abuse its power, and the monarch degenerated into a tyrant. To save themselves, people expelled the tyrants. The patricians next attempted to govern the state, but this aristocratic government also abused its powers and became an oppressive oligarchy. The disgusted people rose against the oligarchy and created a democracy which because of its ineptitude soon fell under the power of demagogues. Thus the wheel of political fortune had turned completely around, and the state was ready to begin once more this evolution by putting a powerful prince or legislator at the head of affairs. Every state passed through this cycle over and over again.

It is not difficult to criticize this theory of the successive stages of governments and to show from history that so neat a scheme is pure fantasy. But men have usually believed in simple political philosophies. Hobbes' and Rousseau's theories of the origin of government by contract are equally unhistorical. The value of a political theory rests on the rational explanation it offers to contemporaries of the political and social situation in which they find themselves. It must be borne in mind that the state of the Renaissance was an absolute state. Theorists sought an acceptable explanation of the rights of despots who appeared in great numbers in Italy. The *Discourses* are a theoretical discussion of the advantages of an all-powerful legislator who guides the policy of the state and molds the character of its citizens. Machiavelli rationalized Renaissance despotism.

The *Prince* was written to show a ruler how to establish himself in a state, strengthen his power, and extend his territory. Machiavelli had witnessed the disastrous wars between France and Ferdinand of Aragon which brought ruin to Italy. His countrymen were certainly more than the equals of these foreigners, or barbarians as he calls them in imitation of the ancient Romans. He was an Italian patriot, like Dante before him and Mazzini 3 centuries later. The Medici had returned to Florence as rulers, Machiavelli dedicated the *Prince* to Duke Lorenzo de' Medici, intending that it should serve as a practical manual to show him how to unite all Italy against foreigners and drive them from the peninsula.

Machiavelli had studied methods employed by other princes, especially Cesare Borgia. He reduced his observations to some sort of system which was to guide the new prince in his effort to secure control of Italy. Success and expediency are to be the sole criteria of his actions. "A sagacious legislator of a republic, therefore, whose object is to promote the public good, and not his private interests, and who prefers his country to his own successors, should concentrate all authority in himself; and a wise mind will never censure anyone for having employed any extraordinary means for the purpose of establishing a kingdom or constituting a republic. It is well that, when the act accuses him, the result should excuse him; and when the result is good, as in the case of Romulus, it will always absolve him from blame." Such a prince exemplifies the Renaissance conceptions of *virtù* and *terribilità*.

THE PROBLEM OF MANAGEMENT OF STATES ACCORDING TO MACHIAVELLI'S *PRINCE*

The *Prince* opens with a statement that hereditary principalities are easy to control, but newly subjugated communities are likely to be unhappy and seek a chance to throw off the yoke of their prince and consequently he experiences difficulties in retaining them (Chap. 3). He is advised that there are only three courses open to him: "The first is to ruin them, the next is to reside there in person, the third is to permit them to live under their own laws, drawing a tribute, and establishing therein an oligarchy which will keep it friendly to you" (Chap. 5). It is difficult for princes who have suddenly risen to the control of a state to maintain themselves, as the author shows from the careers of Francesco Sforza and Cesare Borgia (Chap. 7). Often a prince must use "some wicked or nefarious ways" if he would secure territory. The career of Oliverotto who captured Fermo is related at length. Machiavelli learned from it that "in seizing a state, the usurper ought to examine closely into all those injuries which it is necessary to inflict and to do them all at one stroke so as not to have to repeat them daily; and thus by not unsettling men he will be able to reassure them and win them to himself by benefits" (Chap. 8).

Having established himself, the prince must consider the question of armies. Machiavelli knew from bitter experience that mercenary armies were dangerous because they might turn against the prince (Chap. 12). Each state should recruit its soldiery from its population, for such a fighting force will be loyal (Chap. 13). Princes ought to study warfare constantly and exclusively (Chap. 14). Beginning with the sixteenth chapter, the author discusses how a prince should act toward subjects. It is advisable to be liberal, but he must be careful not to spend his wealth or give away his property, for if he gives away all he will make himself hated because of his heavy taxation. It would be better to be regarded as mean; for a prince may be reproached for meanness, but he will be hated for his rapacity (Chap. 16). A prince should appear clement and not cruel in the eyes of subjects. ". . . A prince, so long as he keeps his subjects united and loyal, ought not to mind the reproach of cruelty; because with a few examples he will be more merciful than those who, through too much mercy, allow disorders to arise, from which follow murder or robbery; for these are wont to injure the whole people, whilst those executions which originate with a prince offend the individual only" (Chap. 17).

Should a prince keep faith? Machiavelli holds that it is laudable to do so. But conditions often make it impossible, for men as a rule are bad, laws are insufficient, and a prince must know how to treat his subjects as beasts as well as men. "He who has known best how to employ the fox has succeeded best." A prince, however, must disguise this fact. "Everyone sees what you are, and those few dare not oppose themselves to the opinion of the many, who have the majesty of the state to defend them; and in the actions of all men, and especially of princes, which it is not prudent to challenge, one judges by the result" (Chap. 18). A prince should avoid being hated and despised. Entrenched in the good will of his subjects, it is difficult for conspirators to overturn him (Chap. 19). Machiavelli believes that rulers should labor to gain fame through patronage, showing favor to guilds and similar groups, and giving entertainments (Chap. 21). They should take great care in choosing secretaries (Chap. 22). Although they must rely upon the advice of councilors, that of flatterers must be shunned (Chap. 23). Italian princes have lost their states because of their defective military, or because the nobility were hostile to them (Chap. 24). The twenty-sixth and final chapter contains a splendid appeal to Duke Lorenzo to act as liberator of Italy and drive the barbarians from the land.

The little treatise, *The Murder of Vitellozo Vitelli*, referred to above, describes the manner in which Cesare Borgia slew the conspirators who plotted to ruin him, and the methods employed by despots to secure control over territories. *Castruccio Castracani* is a short biographical sketch of the tyrant of Lucca who died in 1328. Its accuracy is open to criticism at almost every point, for the author arranged the facts to suit his ideas of how an ambitious tyrant should proceed. It is, however, a valuable account of methods employed by despots of the time. The *Art of War* is a dialogue in seven books, a treatise on military methods and warfare as it was waged under the direction of a Renaissance prince. In it

Machiavelli gives his objections to *condottieri* and mercenary soldiers. States should draw their fighting forces from their own population. The author was sceptical about firearms for which there was some little justification because of their mechanical imperfections in 1500.

From his day to our own Machiavelli's conceptions have been discussed diversely. None can deny the clarity of his thoughts and the lucidity of his exposition. His penetrating insight places him above other writers of his age. His objectivity is as great as that of Aristotle. Some have criticized him for his views on military weapons and fortifications and have ascribed his ideas to lack of experience in these matters. More serious is the complaint about his disregard of simple moral considerations. One instinctively disapproves of the idea that all political action is immoral and dictated solely by selfish interests. But it must be borne in mind that Machiavelli described political life as he saw it with his own eyes. To this there can be no objection. Valid criticism can be made, however, of his idea of lifting the ruthless despots of his day into models of statecraft valid in all ages. The conduct of a state must be elevated above simple expediency and practical interest which is oblivious to all moral considerations. But even at this point we must temper our criticism of Machiavelli's ideas by remembering that modern states are guided by self-interest and expediency in which questions of moral and abstract rights have had all too little place. To criticize Machiavelli is not merely to explain Italian politics of the day, but also to criticize much of modern statecraft.

PART X

Novel Creations of the High Renaissance

Chapter 22

NEW SOCIAL AND LITERARY FORMS

*T*HE CULTIVATION of the Greek and Latin classics and the striving for exquisite and significant form and its acquisition found all manner of expression in Italian social, artistic, and intellectual life. The humanist ideals invaded the vernacular Italian literature. In innumerable ways they contributed to the transformation of deeply entrenched ideals and institutions which had come into existence as far back as the eleventh century.

THE INTELLECTUAL POSITION OF RENAISSANCE WOMEN

The position of Italian woman changed markedly during the *Cinquecento*. Although she had been greatly exalted in the romances of the Middle Ages, one should not be misled by the idealized pictures of Guinevere and others. Women in feudal days were often treated with liberality but, as a rule, they remained subject to the limitations of their household tasks. Severity too often characterized the Middle Ages, and the weaker sex received more than its share of violence. Nevertheless it must be admitted that her position as wife, mother, and homemaker must have elevated her in the estimation of all.

The refined society of Renaissance Italy tended to make woman the equal of man, for the court life of the princes demanded that woman assume a leading role. Since woman should be educated in the same

347

manner as men, the schools of Vittorino da Feltre and Guarino da Verona were opened to both sexes. Some of the best pupils of those great masters were Elizabeth Gonzaga and Isabella and Beatrice of Este. They knew the Greek and Latin classics, were interested in the refined culture of humanism, and could hold their own with men. Nevertheless, it remained the fashion among humanists to regard women as inferiors and as useful drudges. This traditionalism is well revealed by Boccaccio in Griselda, a character in the Decameron, who illustrates patience and forbearance under impossible conditions. In describing an ideal woman, the writer did not forget the prejudices of his age.

This conservatism of writers ran counter to the facts of life, at least as far as the wealthier classes were concerned, for Florentine women played a prominent part in society. The daughters of the Albizzi family shared fully in the intellectual life of the time. Lucrezia Tornabuoni, the mother of Lorenzo the Magnificent, wrote poetry and inspired others to write—Lorenzo owed his interest in the mother tongue to her example. Isabella and Beatrice of Este have been mentioned above. Elizabeth Gonzaga, duchess of Urbino, was the central figure in the court life of Urbino. Probably the finest of all women of the Renaissance was Vittoria Colonna (1490–1547). She was well versed in Latin and Greek and wrote graceful Italian prose and verse. Her husband, the marquis of Pescara, was wounded in the Battle of Pavia (1525) and died in spite of her devoted care. "It seems to me," she said, "that the sun has lost the brightness of its rays, that the stars are paling, the trees losing their mantle of verdure, the fields their flowers, the waters their purity, the breeze its freshness, since the one I love has left me alone." She turned to the comforts of religion, becoming the friend of Juan Valdés, the religious reformer, and finally of Michelangelo. The great sculptor derived comfort from her sympathy and understanding, and her death made him a sad and lonely man.

Although the women of the Renaissance became emancipated, as it were, they did not become unwomanly, for their greatest influence was exerted in the court and in the home. The picture given by Boccaccio in his Decameron is misleading in this respect—Florentine women did not flee their homes and isolate themselves in country places, leaving their families to die of the plague. The Renaissance produced some women who took an active part in public affairs. The virago was an energetic and masterful type who displayed extraordinary virtù and won her meed of gloria. Such a person was Catherine Sforza, youngest daughter of Galeazzo Maria Sforza, born in 1462, who became countess of Forlì and Imola. Her husband was Girolamo Riario, a worthless and dissolute nephew of Pope Sixtus IV, whose tyranny so antagonized his subjects that they sought to assassinate him. The castle of Forlì was seized in 1487 while Catherine's husband was seriously ill, but she hurried to Forlì, seized the rebel leader, and on the next day gave birth to a child. Her husband was slain 7 years later, but she put down the uprising which had led to his death. Her second husband was assassinated at Forlì (1495), and Catherine once more was able to crush the rebels with a vigor and circumspection that would have done credit to any man.

The freedom of the Renaissance also affected women courtiers. There were a large number of these women who knew how to turn their beauty and charm to profit. Some of them were acquainted with music and literature and read the ancient classics. To win favor with the men of the time, it was necessary to employ the subtlest cunning. Most famous of such courtiers was Catherine of San Celso, or Imperia as she was popularly called, who was able to ingratiate herself with many of the prominent figures of the time. A poet wittily declared that "the gods have bestowed two great favors upon Rome: Mars gave her imperium over the world, but Venus gave Imperia to her!" She died in 1511. The popularity of such courtiers in Rome came to a close with the pontificate of Paul III (1534–1549) but continued to flourish in Venice. It assumed some interesting forms in that luxurious society which was becoming impoverished because of the decline of its commercial life. Carpaccio's picture, the *Two Courtesans*, which shows two of these women seated in a room, is an interesting study in costume and is to be viewed as a satire on the life of these people.

Family life in the upper classes of the Renaissance differed in many ways from that of the Middle Ages. The relations and life of a wealthy bourgeois family are illustrated in León Battista Alberti's remarkable treatise, *On the Family*, or *Della Famiglia*, in four books, written before 1434. The first book explains the relation of parents to their sons and daughters, and vice versa. The second deals with marriage, and the rearing and education of children. The role of the wife is discussed—she is the queen of the household, managing the servants and directing the family economy. The third book is devoted to finances. Thrift, the great virtue of the bourgeoisie, is to be inculcated, and every honorable means should be used to increase one's wealth. The last book is concerned with friendship which is discussed from the point of view of financial, moral, and intellectual advantage; a lofty moral tone pervades the discussion. Many bourgeois families governed themselves according to such rules. Daughters were treated with great rigidity and were kept in seclusion, especially in Venice, as is shown by the youthful experience of Bianca Capello (1548–1587), a daughter of the proud family of the Capelli, who eloped to Florence with an adventurous youth of that city and had an extraordinary career till the end of her life. But in Florence and elsewhere they were given more liberty.

THE REFINED MANNERS OF THE RENAISSANCE

Manners, at first dominated by the roughness of medieval conditions, became milder, for the wealth and leisure of bourgeois families, and of the nobility as well, made the continuance of crude practices impossible. Personal manners improved greatly. Many of the newer percepts were brought together by Giovanni della Casa (d. 1556) in his *Galateo of Manners and Behaviours.* In addition to listing many customs and mannerisms to be shunned, he also prescribed the correct manners in many situations:

> It is also an unmannerly part for a man to lay his nose upon the cup where another must drink; or upon the meat that another must eat, to the end to smell unto it; but rather I would wish he should not smell at all, no not to that which he himself should eat and drink because it might chance there might fall some drop from his nose. . . . Neither, by my advice, shalt thou reach to any man that cup of wine whereof thy self hast dronk and tasted, without he be more than a familiar friend unto thee. And much less must thou give any part of the pear or the fruit which thou hast bitten in thy mouth before.

The following advice about conversation well illustrates how the more cultivated folk of the Renaissance disliked the banalities of the common people of that day:

> When a man talketh with one, it is no good manner to come so near that he must needs breathe in his face, for there be many that can not abide to feel that air of another man's breath albeit there come no ill savour from him. These and like fashions be very unseemly and would be eschewed because their senses with whom we acquaint ourselves, cannot brook nor bear them.[1]

The *Courtier* by Baldassare Castiglione (1478–1529) is the greatest of all Renaissance books dealing with manners. Its purpose is to describe the ideal courtier, that is, the perfect gentleman of the Renaissance. Castiglione, born a count and educated in the humanist school of Mantua, combined what was best in chivalric tradition with humanist culture. He was made a knight while at the court of Duke Ludovico of Milan and later went on diplomatic missions. Becoming acquainted with Duke

[1] *A Renaissance Courtesy-Book: Galateo of Manners and Behaviours*, Boston, 1924, pp. 20, 25.

Guidobaldo of Urbino, he spent much time at his court over which the duchess, Elizabeth Gonzaga, and a number of other women presided. Here Castiglione began the composition of the *Courtier* in Italian in the form of a dialogue in which members of the court participate. The author believes that the perfect courtier should be of noble birth mainly because of the practical advantages he would gain in the society of the Renaissance which still accorded an important place to noblemen. But the true courtier is made by character and intellect rather than by birth. He must "have not only a wit and a comely person and countenance but also a certain grace and air that will make him at the first sight acceptable and loving unto who so beholdeth him." All sorts of personal manners and characteristics are discussed in this connection. The perfect courtier should speak and write well, especially in the native Italian. Knowledge of literature is regarded as a most important ornament, French noblemen being criticized for their neglect of it and their preference for knightly exercises. The perfect courtier should be skillful at arms and courageous in all situations. These ideas show how far the humanist society of Italy had moved away from the conceptions of the Middle Ages.

RENAISSANCE MUSIC AND DRAMA

Music naturally flourished in a society bent upon artistic refinement. By the opening of the sixteenth century remarkable progress had been made in Flanders from the Gregorian plain song, which was the common musical form of the Middle Ages. Flemish musicians, as we have seen, developed the use of the canon, a repetition of a melodic theme, and also counterpoint. The exclusive use of the plain song came to an end with the rise of polyphonic music which combined several voice parts. Flemish musicians became famous and were in great demand, and Duke Federigo of Urbino brought some of them to his court. Josquin des Prés (d. 1521), a native of Hainault, introduced Flemish methods into Italy when he became a member of the papal choir. Two other Flemish masters, Adrian Willaert (d. 1562) and Jacob Arcadelt (d. 1575), served as masters of the choir of St. Mark's in Venice.

The Italians of the Renaissance made their first contributions to music by developing new instruments and perfecting orchestral music. The simple rebec evolved into the violin, and the old clavichord was transformed into the spinet and harpsichord; wind instruments also were developed and improved. Venetians were especially fond of instrumental music which they considered a necessary part of their luxurious life. The pleasure which these people derived from music is revealed in pictures by

Venetian masters such as Giorgione's (or Titian's) *Music Lesson, Giorgione's Concert,* and many Venetian *Madonnas* accompanied by angels playing on instruments. Polyphonic music attained classic perfection at the hands of Giovanni da Palestrina (1520–1594), who was born near Rome and spent most of his years in the papal choir. Palestrina belonged to the age in which piety once more became capable of expressing itself in the highest art. His genuine religious sentiment was couched in the noblest devotional music, the *Mass of Pope Marcellus* being one of his great works. The next stage in the evolution of music was the presentation in 1594 of the first opera.

The drama was secularized during the Renaissance. The first step was taken in Florence when public festivals abandoned all direct connection with the Church. These were the *sacre reppresentazioni,* the first of which was entitled *Abraham and Isaac.* Lorenzo the Magnificent's *St. John and St. Paul* belongs to this class. The next step was taken by Poliziano in his *Orfeo* which was produced at the Mantuan court in 1471. It is the first play of a purely secular nature to be written in the vernacular. Furthermore, like Botticelli's paintings of the *Springtime* and the *Birth of Venus,* its theme was drawn from classical pagan sources. Next appeared the *Commedia del Arte,* the themes of which were taken from popular life and which resemble in many respects the stories told by such novelists as Bandello and Masuccio. The scenes are laid in the open squares of towns. The female parts were taken by married women, procuresses, and women of loose morals, for, as young Italian girls were carefully guarded and might not appear unchaperoned, they could not take part in these comedies. Male characters such as the resourceful servant, the parasite, the pander, and the helpless but conceited pedant became traditional. Thus was created the secular comedy of the Renaissance. Another form of this drama was the *Commedia Erudita,* or *Learned Comedy,* the motifs and characters of which were drawn from classical themes. Finally, the lyrical pastoral play was developed.

Theaters had disappeared during the decline of Roman civilization; even their use had been forgotten. Medieval plays had been performed in the streets or squares. But theaters were built again when the secular drama evolved, for the growth of the drama and the theatrical art necessitated more permanent places for the presentation of plays. The new playhouses borrowed much from their classic predecessors. The broad stage had walls on each side and at the back. Five openings led to it, three from the back, and one from each side. The theater of Vicenza, which was built according to the plans of the architect Andrea Palladio (d. 1580), is the oldest extant example of these Renaissance theaters.

EPIC POETRY DURING THE RENAISSANCE

Epic poetry likewise flourished. Pulci's *Morgante Maggiore* has been described as being a typical product of the Florentine bourgeoisie at the time of Lorenzo the Magnificent. The first knightly romance of the Renaissance, Boiardo's *Orlando Innamorato* (1486), written in the courtly society of Ferrara, was followed by Ariosto's *Orlando Furioso* in 1515. Ludovico Ariosto (d. 1533) was born in 1474 at Reggio in the Romagna. His father belonged to the nobility but lost the favor of his master, the duke of Ferrara. Reared and educated in Ferrara, Ludovico came under the chivalric influences which had fascinated Boiardo. Knighthood was still surrounded with a halo of glory in spite of the fact that the bourgeois culture of the Renaissance really had no place for it. Ariosto determined to write in Vergilian style an epic depicting the glorious perfection of chivalry:

> Of loves and ladies, knights, and arms, I sing,
> Of courtesies, and many a daring feat. . . .

Torquato Tasso (1544–1595) followed in his footsteps. But his poem, *Jerusalem Delivered*, had a special purpose, for the Turk was pressing hard upon Christendom, and it seemed that Italy might become the arena of his military endeavors. The reform of Catholicism was in full progress during Tasso's youth, and a more rigorous type of religious life was being developed among Italians. Charles V ruled over many lands which formed a vast Catholic empire. Small wonder that the younger men of these countries should conceive the idea of a universal Catholic culture in which Italian national aspirations were extinguished to further the political overlordship of Spain. The old knightly epics had met with little favor at the hands of Renaissance churchmen. Tasso spent some time at the court of Ferrara where chivalric themes were popular and finally, after many wanderings, in 1581 produced his epic of the Crusades. This masterpiece, which belongs to the age of Catholic Revival, deals with Christendom's struggles against heretic and infidel. The Church is exalted as the only bond to unite all nations:

> Well would it be, [if in harmonious peace
> The Christian powers should ere again unite,
> With steed and ship their ravished spoils to seize,
> And for his theft the savage Turk requite],
> That they to thee should yield, in wisdom's right,
> The rule by land, or if it have more charms,
> Of the high seas; meanwhile, let it delight

> To hear our verse ring with divine alarms;
> Rival to Godfrey, hear, and hearing, grasp thine arms.

Like Ariosto's great epic, so too Tasso's masterpiece opens with language and metric form inspired by Vergil's *Aeneid*:

> I sing the pious arms and Chief, who freed
> The Sepulchre of Christ from thrall profane:
> Much did he toil in thought, and much in deed;
> Much in the glorious enterprise sustain;
> And hell in vain opposed him; and in vain
> Africa and Asia to the rescue poured
> Their mingled tribes;—Heaven recompensed his pain,
> And from all fruitless sallies of the sword,
> True to the Red-Cross flag his wandering friends restored.[2]

THE CULTIVATION OF THE VERNACULAR IN RENAISSANCE LETTERS

Pastoral prose and poetry were a characteristic product of the High Renaissance. This type of literature sprang from many motives. Love for nature, a strong note of the Italian Renaissance, was shown in the desire to build country villas, in the paintings of Benozzo Gozzoli and in the poetry of Lorenzo the Magnificent. The humanist tone of this literature was born of the classical revival. Finally, the desire to live in an environment of ideal beauty and perfection became a passion. It was inevitable that writers should draw upon the poetic primitive purity and simplicity presented in Theocritus' *Idyls*, Vergil's *Eclogues*, and Ovid's *Metamorphoses*. Jacopo Sannazaro (1458–1530), who created this fashion, was born in Naples, lived in a villa at Mergellina just outside the city, and was a favorite at the Neapolitan court. He admired Petrarch and wrote Latin poems in Vergilian meter. His *Piscatory Eclogues*, which celebrated the life on the Neapolitan bay, won him instantaneous fame. His *Arcadia* was even more important. Written in elegant prose, it draws its inspiration from classical pastoral writings. Groves, nymphs, satyrs, fauns, shepherds, flocks, gods, maidens, and amorous swains fill the picture, reminding one of the pastoral idyls painted by Venetian masters.

Pietro Bembo (1470–1547) was perhaps the most brilliant of the humanists at the papal court under Pope Leo X. Born of aristocratic Venetian parentage, he became a senator and filled a number of important offices. While a mere lad he was taken by his father to Florence where he received a humanist education. Later he studied at the University of

[2] The *Jerusalem Delivered*, tr. by J. H. Wiffen, London, 1857, pp. 1–2.

Padua. Next he was a guest at the court of Catherine Cornaro, a Venetian lady who had become queen of Cyprus in 1468. Her husband died, and, in 1489 when Venice annexed her realm, she was given a pension and allowed to live in a castle at Asolo on the Venetian mainland. Here she kept a petty but brilliant court in Renaissance fashion, and Bembo became its most brilliant member. His sojourn at Asolo is immortalized by a treatise called *Gli Asolani* or *The People of Asolo,* consisting of some discourses on the subject of love. The theme is treated according to the ideas of Plato on an exalted poetic plane far removed from base human passions.

Bembo next entered the service of Duke Ercole of Ferrara to acquaint himself with diplomacy. A few years later, Ercole's son married Lucrezia Borgia (1502), who at once became a sincere friend of the courtly and polished scholar. This attachment continued after Bembo left Ferrara, and their correspondence forms a monument to Renaissance culture. Later, Bembo tarried at the court of Urbino and figures in the conversations recorded in Castiglione's *Courtier.* He became papal secretary under Leo X, at whose court he was a literary lion. During these years he carried on an extensive correspondence with most of the cultured ladies and gentlemen of the day. Upon Leo's death, Bembo retired to Padua where he lived like a humanist, studying the ancient classics, cultivating a pure Latinity, and corresponding with his many admirers. He collected a library and a museum and, until 1539 when called to Rome by Pope Paul III, enjoyed life in the country after the manner of Pliny and other ancient Roman gentlemen.

Although Bembo was eager to perfect himself in Latin, he was not blind to the beauty and practical value of the Italian mother tongue. He therefore disagreed with his humanist contemporaries who pedantically held that serious thought should be put forth only in Latin. His letters, written in graceful Italian to many of the most prominent personages of the day, constitute a noteworthy example of Renaissance culture. Bembo also wrote a treatise, *On the Mother Tongue (Della Volgar Lingua),* in which he extolled the use of the Tuscan vernacular. He studied Petrarch closely, and his sonnets are models of linguistic and poetic purity. His passion for beauty in language was characteristic of the Renaissance, but it is his advocacy of the native Italian tongue which gave him a special place among Italian humanists of the day.

The novelists expressed the rich and variegated life of the Renaissance better than any other group of writers. The tradition set by Boccaccio was continued by Francesco Sacchetti (1335–1410) whose tales, although far less artistically rendered than Boccaccio's, nevertheless are important for the student of *Quattrocento* culture. Masuccio Guardato (1420?–1475?) of Salerno enjoyed far greater fame than Sacchetti, but his witty tales are marred by a strong licentious note—to which, perhaps, they owed their popularity. Matteo Bandello (1480–1561), a member of the Dominican order who lived in Milan, wrote little novels which are important not only as pictures of morals and manners but also as sources for later writers.

Blackmail by means of lampoons and venomous pamphlets was an interesting feature of the High Renaissance. These lampoons were witty, personal, and malicious satires which flourished in a society particularly sensitive to the charm of literary style. They were called pasquinades after one Pasquino, a fault-finding schoolmaster of Rome during the previous century. His reputation grew after death and fired popular imagination. Soon his name was attached to a newly excavated statue which was set up in the Piazza Navona, and it became customary to affix to this statue lampoons attacking the acts of the government and famous personages. These verses and dialogues were elevated to the dignity of literary art by Pietro Aretino (1492–1556).

Like the novelists, Aretino was a characteristic product of life in Italian cities. Born in Arezzo of poor but honorable parents, he was forced to live by his wits. This he did by employing the new Renaissance skill in letters to win patrons and to extort favors. He resembled the modern yellow journalist; there was no limit to his scurrility and effrontery. In 1516 he entered the service of Agostino Chigi, a Roman banker who played a great financial role under Leo X. Aretino soon discovered his true vocation—writing lampoons with which to blackmail men of position and authority. Giulio de' Medici became his patron. The death of Leo X in December, 1521, gave him an opportunity to write furiously in behalf of his friend, but the Netherlander Adrian was elected in spite of all his efforts. Fearing the consequences of his malicious writings, he left Rome and went to Mantua where he found favor with the duke. He returned to Rome in 1523 when his protector Giulio de' Medici became Clement VII, but his methods made it unsafe for him to stay. He spent some time with Giovanni delle Bande Nere, a member of the cadet branch of the Medicean house and the most famous Italian military captain at the moment. In 1527 Aretino settled in Venice. He had so perfected his nefarious methods by this time that he met with easy success. He mingled with the best society, for everybody feared his terrible pen. People gave him food, money, and clothing. He received pensions from Charles V, Francis I, and Henry II, and Francis gave him a heavy chain of gold which he wears in the portrait painted by his friend Titian. He wrote verses, letters, and a number of satirical plays in a pungent style not unlike that of Rabelais. He won the name "Scourge of Princes."

FURTHER CULTURAL FEATURES OF THE RENAISSANCE

Academies, which were a typical feature of Renaissance intellectual life, were associations of humanists formed to discuss questions relating to classical lore. Such organizations had not existed during the Middle Ages, for the universities were too conservative to become leaders in the new humanist culture. To Cosimo de' Medici belongs the honor of forming the first of these academies, the Platonic Academy, and others were organized, among them the Neapolitan, Roman, and many of minor repute. These learned societies served as models for similar institutions in other lands.

Libraries, like academies, also were an indispensable part of the Renaissance scholarship. During the Middle Ages men had made collections of books, but these were mostly in monasteries and cathedrals and, needless to state, were designed to serve theological and religious interests. Some medieval princes also made collections of books. But the great age of book collecting opened with the revival of classical learning. The famous collections of Cosimo de' Medici and others have been described in previous chapters. These libraries catered to the intellectual needs of men interested in secular learning and for that reason were a peculiar feature of Renaissance life. There also were librarians; for example, Vespasiano da Bisticci (1421–1498), author of the famous *Lives of Illustrious Men of the XVth Century*, was employed by a number of princes to collect books for them. Museums and art galleries likewise became numerous during this age. Princes and wealthy townsmen collected fragments of classical art and the pictures and statuary of great contemporary masters. The *grotta* of Duchess Isabella of Mantua became famous in Italy, and the pictures of Gozzoli and Botticelli and the statues of Donatello and Verrocchio purchased by the Medici have since become the bases of the great art collections of Florence.

Religion naturally was deeply influenced by the great social changes of the age. The upper bourgeoisie strove for temporal pleasures and secular satisfaction. The traditional asceticism which had dominated their forefathers seemed antiquated and people became indifferent to religion. Pagan classical influences led many to adopt a purely secular view of life and morality. Poggio Bracciolini, Lorenzo Valla, Pomponio Leto, and other humanists cared nothing for the austere Christian morality practiced in former times by St. Francis. The cult of beauty and Platonic studies seemed to satisfy the deeper sentiments of the Medicean circles of Florence. But these influences did not permeate all classes, for since Renaissance culture was the culture of the well-to-do bourgeoisie and nobility and therefore was aristocratic, little of the paganism and secularity of the upper classes passed to the masses who remained faithful to the traditional teaching of their fathers. Some of the upper classes, like Savonarola, likewise maintained their loyalty to Christian principles.

Gardening attracted much interest during the Renaissance. In earlier ages monasteries and castles had their own gardens, and wealthy townsmen often constructed pleasure gardens adjoining their houses. But with the development of a more ample life during the Renaissance, people began to dream of better things. Love for the country led to the building of villas, and the construction of gardens became a matter of course. The Medici in Florence, the Este in Ferrara, and lesser persons shared in this enthusiasm.

The study of classical writings, especially those of Pliny, revived many ancient ideas, and architecture and gardening were thus peculiarly related during the Renaissance. León Battista Alberti was the first to apply ancient ideas to gardening. The Villa Quarrachi near Florence was adorned with a garden laid out, in part at least, by him. This significant example of the new art had three pergolas and a number of open paths with latticework on either side covered with vines and white roses. The garden was exposed to passers-by instead of being shut off by a stone wall as is often done in modern gardens. Its plan was geometrical and called for circles and semicircles made with laurel, citron, and yew with interwoven branches. There were porticoes, grottoes, pots with flowers, paths bordered with clipped box, streams, cascades, and cypress trees. Fruit trees were relegated to the family garden. Such villas and gardens were plentiful around Florence, at least until 1527 when the invading armies of Charles V destroyed many of them. The villa of the Este at Tivoli near Rome became especially famous. Botanical gardens also became common, the first one being laid out in 1545 at the University of Padua.

Increase in urban population and the general improvement of the artistic taste of despots and rulers demanded better city planning. Towns had grown up during the Middle Ages, usually without planning. A few constructed according to geometrical plan did exist in Italy, but they owed this feature to the fact that they had been founded during the Roman Empire or earlier. Thus Palermo and Syracuse had streets crossing each other at right angles. This was also true of the most ancient part of

Florence, a city which had begun as a Roman camp. But in most cases towns grew up around market places, near rivers, or along roads leading to bridges. Streets were crooked, narrow, crowded, often impassable, and the population was huddled into narrow quarters.

Italian cities of the Renaissance were noted for their beauty, for princes often sought to improve them by straightening and paving streets, laying out parks, and decorating squares with splendid buildings. Pius II beautified the great square of Corsignano with a series of magnificent early Renaissance buildings (about 1460) which give a good conception of what ambitious builders of the time sought to accomplish. Nicholas V and other popes embellished Rome by laying out new streets, clearing away slums, building bridges, and drawing up plans for beautifying the city around the Vatican. In general, new sections added to towns were more or less geometrical in arrangement, the streets were wider, and open squares more numerous. Many towns developed a body of sanitary regulations. Quarantines were established in Venice. This city also beautified its great square and removed unsightly structures and the public latrines. Toward the close of the *Quattrocento* the Venetian piazza had assumed the appearance which it has in Bellini's picture, *The Procession of Corpus Christi*, and still has.

Furniture evolved rapidly as the wealth of townsmen increased. The people of the earlier Middle Ages possessed few articles of furniture. The most important was the chest or coffer, a box-like affair made of heavy boards held in place by carapaces of ironwork. To keep the wood dry, it was customary to raise the chest from the floor by the addition of side-pieces. Development of the art of joinery and of the use of panels changed the character of these chests. They became lighter and stronger and were covered with carved decoration. Such chests were made in many sizes and were devoted to all sorts of purposes such as beds, wardrobes, repositories for manuscripts or for kitchen utensils. From this type of furniture developed many articles of Renaissance furniture, such as cupboards, credences, tables, buffets, and trunks, although tables were not common except for eating. Desks for reading and writing were developed. Very large heavy benches accommodating a number of people were placed along the wall. The medieval chair was a rough bench made of a heavy piece of wood with endpieces. The chair evolved out of the coffer. A small chest with raised sidepieces for arm rests and a higher backpiece was used as a chair and was the ancestor of a numerous progeny. Beds were rude affairs; they were covered with a canopy and surrounded by heavy draperies to keep out the cold in the drafty halls and houses of the Middle Ages.

The *cassoni,* or bridal chests, which were naturally popular, especially in Florence, were coffers which stood on the floor or were raised slightly by supports at the corners. The panels on some of them were painted or carved by some of the great masters of the Renaissance and decorated with scenes from sacred, secular, and sometimes classical literature. The *cassapanca* was a Florentine bench made from a chest. The principal chair of the house, reserved for the master at festive occasions, and called the *trono,* was a stately chair with a large backpiece. Credences, a variety of sideboard, came into general use. Those of Florence had two drawers, those of Siena three. Great cupboards were made. Clavichords and virginals or spinets were chests in which musical apparatus was placed. Mirrors were developed in Venice.

Ornament employed in Renaissance furniture differed greatly from its predecessor, for Gothic masters used straight edges or foliage, fruits, and flowers. However, these disappeared, and a variety of conventional and geometric designs were created, drawn for the most part from classical models. The most usual of these were the bead and pearl ornaments, the bay leaf garland, and various fret patterns. In moldings, the egg and dart, tongue and dart, and egg and leaf with its many variations were employed. Furniture makers were strongly influenced by architects, often copying façades of buildings. The Venetians, who borrowed ideas from the Levant and lands beyond, exerted much influence on ornament. Rich decoration was admired, especially gesso and *certosina* work. Marquetry and veneering were employed. Such inlaid work appealed to the luxurious taste of the time and consequently became popular.

Plain ceramic ware gave place to more artistic products. The word faïence is said to be derived from Faenza, a chief center of the manufacture of earthenware. Majolica ware, which appears to have originated in Romagna and adjacent parts, was made of clay with a white surface on which designs were painted. It became a genuine work of art at the opening of the *Cinquecento.* Lustered majolica also was produced. The high degree of excellence attained in the manufacture of this ware assured Italian makers a ready market for their products both in Italy and abroad.

Increase in luxury and improvement in taste are further illustrated by the increased use of forks in eating. It was customary in earlier medieval times to convey food to the mouth with the fingers, but during the *Cinquecento* forks with two and later three prongs came into general use, first in Venice and then in other Italian towns.

Chapter 23

SCIENTIFIC INVENTION AND THOUGHT

*A*LTHOUGH THE Age of the Renaissance made significant progress in science and technology, it must not be assumed, as has often been done, that this period uniquely marked the beginning of scientific and technological activity which in some way was effectuated by the "recovery" of ancient Greek and Latin codices. This idea must now be abandoned or, at least modified; for it appears certain that late medieval scientific practices in many respects equalled those of the later Greeks and Romans. This may be said to be the case also of medieval technological progress.

THE SIGNIFICANCE OF LEONARDO DA VINCI IN SCIENCE AND TECHNOLOGY

Humanists who devoted their energies to the study of classical authors were not able to make much progress in science, for their exclusive cultivation of literary studies often made them so pedantic that they believed the sum of learning consisted in aping the ancient classics and imitating the style of Cicero. Grammar, prosody, and syntax became ends in themselves. Thus humanists in their revolt against the scholasticism of the closing Middle Ages fell under the authority of the classics. They were unable to appreciate the need of a fresh study of nature, nor did they realize the significance of the geographical discoveries of Vasco da Gama and his successors. They did not approve of the new printing presses which made possible the mechanical multiplication of the texts of their beloved classical authors, but preferred the ancient and laborious method of making copies by hand.

Scientific progress in the Renaissance was, to a large extent, the work of practical men who were required to face the concrete facts of life. Original minds found opportunity to answer questions which demanded solution with increasing insistency. Thus artists were confronted with many problems when they sought to develop a scientific technique of painting. The greatness of Giotto lay in the fact that he clearly saw the problems confronting the artist who wanted to give reality to his creations. Corporeality demanded space which was a problem of mathematical perspective. Effective action depended upon correct anatomy and correct anatomy implied dissection. So painters were led into scientific studies pertaining to human expression. The artists of the *Trecento* copied the methods of Giotto. Those of the *Quattrocento,* beginning with Masaccio, struggled with the problem of inner harmony of action of groups. Paolo Uccello and Piero della Francesca made practical application of the theories of Brunelleschi and Alberti. Andrea del Castagno was interested in bony, vigorous forms, whereas Pollaiuolo made the study of muscular expression his specialty. Although from an artistic point of view these artists often exaggerated their anatomical interests, their scientific enthusiasm is significant.

Leonardo da Vinci, however, was the greatest of the artists who studied science. He knew little Latin or Greek, paid no heed to authority or tradition, but addressed himself to first-hand investigation of nature. His studies and experiments were conducted with the greatest virtuosity; the world probably has never produced a greater scientific mind. His anatomical drawings are models of excellence, combining scientific exactitude and artistic sense. He studied human anatomy in great detail, and his work in Milan on the equestrian statue of Francesco Sforza led him to make encyclopedic studies of the anatomy of horses. He studied plants with the utmost devotion to form and structure; delicate veins, curled petals, dried burrs, plants of all sorts were sketched over and over.

Leonardo yearned to know all things so that he might re-create them in art. His acute observations taught him that fossils were the remains of living organisms which had lived where these remains were found, wherefore he inferred that the sea once covered northern Italy, that mussels collected on the sea floor, that the sea receded, and that subsequent deposits of earth were scattered over the former sea bottom. His knowledge resulting from his wide experimentation was encyclopedic. He studied the structure of the eye in order to demonstrate the principles of optics. His investigations in mechanics and hydraulics introduced him to the great field of engineering, and he planned portable bridges, canals, sluices, roads, and flying machines. He had novel ideas about placing cannon to enhance their destructiveness, making rapid-firing bombards, constructing wagons armed with cannon with which to terrify the enemy, and creating new and effective machines with which to reduce fortresses.

He even studied domestic architecture and had original ideas on the arrangement of rooms, the construction of hearths and chimneys, the heating of buildings with hot air, the erection of public edifices, and the planning of cities with proper arrangement of streets and disposal of sewage.

POPULAR VOGUE OF ASTROLOGY AND ALCHEMY

Astrology, which teaches that the stars influence terrestrial affairs, is of ancient origin, either Chaldean or Egyptian. It was appropriated by the Greeks and Romans and became part of the speculations of Jews and Arabs in the Middle Ages. The Christian Church was opposed to astrological science because it seemed to contradict the principle of free will; nevertheless, astrology had devotees among Christians. During the closing Middle Ages, especially in the fourteenth century, it appears to have been accepted almost universally. The theory that stars exerted much power for good or ill was given a scientific basis by the Ptolemaic system of the universe then in vogue. The planets in their stately course around the immobile earth were moved by the elements which surrounded them. Obviously all earthly things came under the sovereignty of stars.

It became important to ascertain which stars were in the ascendant at the moment of birth. This was called judicial astrology and was closely akin to divination. A horoscope was drawn up consisting of a diagram of the heavens showing the position of the stars at the date of birth. The sky was divided into twelve sections called houses, each containing some fixed stars. These constituted the zodiac. Each house was designated by the name of some animal, except one which was called the scales. Each of these had a fancied influence upon human actions at the moment when it was in the ascendant. Thus the Ram exerted control over the head, the Bull over the neck, the Twins over the shoulders and arms, Cancer over the breast, Leo over the sides of the body, Virgo over the bladder, the Balance over the buttocks, the Scorpion over the genitals, Sagittarius over the thighs, Capricorn over the knees, Aquarius over the legs, and Pisces over the feet.

These influences were further complicated by the planet which happened to appear at the moment when any zodiacal sign was in the ascendant. The influence was not fixed, but varied according to the sign with which it happened to be associated. A complicated science was evolved in the effort to explain everything in human life from this point of view. Wars, famines, pestilences, revolutions, and deaths of monarchs could be predicted. This is the reason why medieval chroniclers usually noted meteors and eclipses in connection with catastrophes. Traits of human beings were influenced, it was believed, in the arrangement of stars at the moment of birth. Casting horoscopes became a profitable business. Princes often consulted the stars before undertaking any important matter of state. So popular was this science that students who had graduated from the universities made a professional practice of contemplating the stars for their clients. Astrology was based upon three things: ancient tradition, the authority of great masters like Pierre d'Ailly (1350–1420), and an assortment of erroneous facts. From any scientific point of view it was a hodgepodge of errors. Scholarship in those days needed the chastening discipline which only a close search for new facts can give.

Alchemy, like astrology, sprang from Babylonian, Egyptian, and Greek origins. It corresponded to our chemistry, but, as it was based upon erroneous theories and a scanty knowledge of facts, it was little better than astrology. Its basic conception was that the foundation of our material life was provided by a primal matter. This was always associated with some form in varying degree, thus producing the different elements with which we are familiar—air, earth, fire, and water. Human imagination, led by its innate inquisitiveness, asked why, if the material world was so constituted, one could not create some primal matter and then add to it the things necessary to make gold; this became the chief aim of alchemists. It was thought that this primal matter had to be treated with some substance called the philosopher's elixir or stone which consisted in the first principle of sulphur. When applied to primal matter, gold would result. Only in modern times under the influence of chemistry have these scientific fantasies been dispelled, but in our own time quacks still seek to exploit them.

THE STRUGGLE AGAINST WITCHCRAFT

Magic flourished mightily during the fifteenth century. It was inherited from the pre-Christian beliefs of Germans, Celts, Slavs, and classical peoples, and dates back to dim paleolithic times. The Church found it impossible to eradicate these primitive notions. This was natural because many priests came from homes where the truth of magic was firmly believed, and they could not completely free themselves from this environment. Even learned theologians and philosophers believed in the existence of evil spirits and in the ability of witches to employ them for nefarious purposes. Ignorant and conservative peasants were slow to give up these ideas; to this day their descendants continue to believe in spirits. The power of the Church to put down heretical teachings had greatly increased in the thirteenth and fourteenth centuries, partly because of the growing perfection of ecclesiastical organization and partly because secular states accepted canon law as the law of the land. But while the power to repress heresy and magic gained ground, the clergy did not increase in the effectiveness of their spiritual work. Many of them remained deficient in theological training, feeble in devotion to their priestly functions, and too concerned with worldly matters.

Such was the virility of the belief in witches that when lay influences began to dominate the life and thought of western Europe, a regular cult of witchcraft grew up. It was thought by many that God was the creator of all things beneficent, so the devil, His opposite, possessed a corresponding power over evil. Small wonder that the people called upon the devil to aid them against their enemies, real or fancied! The worship of the evil one was carried on in many communities by groups of witches or warlocks, called covens. Witches were active agents of the devil. They conducted meetings known as sabbats, to which they were said to fly through the air on broomsticks. In their ritual there were singing, dancing, and ceremonies in which the devil, as either a man or an animal, preferably a goat, was worshiped with disgusting rites. Witches possessed all sorts of power to do extraordinary things. They could cause rain or hail, blight fields or make them fertile, cause babes to be stillborn, and make invalids of children. Strange sexual irregularities occurred, such as the union of men with succubae and women with incubi. The offspring was half devil, half human. Pacts with the devil were commonly made, it was alleged.

These vulgar practices were opposed to the Catholic faith, and churchmen became frightened at the prevalence of this cult. Hence Church tribunals would condemn warlocks, and the secular arm would apply a fitting penalty. Pope Innocent VIII (1484–1492) issued his famous bull *Summis Desiderantes* in 1484, condemning the practice of witchcraft especially in Rhenish Germany and adjacent lands.

The pope and the medieval Church did not create the great witchcraft delusion as some books imply, nor is this bull a dogmatic statement about witchcraft. He merely moved to put an end to something which had existed a long time and was growing in intensity. Two Dominicans, Jacob Sprenger and Henry Kramer, were appointed inquisitors and produced a remarkable book about witchcraft called *The Witches' Hammer* (1487), the classic treatment on the subject and the source of many later works. It is a bulky compendium divided into three parts, the first dealing with the agents of witchcraft, the second showing the methods employed by witches in their nefarious work, and the third setting forth the judicial steps in combating the evil. Witchcraft was regarded as a crime by the state. To league with man's archenemy, the devil, deserved severe punishment. Torture was regularly invoked in continental Europe, and the rack was employed in England. Condemned witches were strangled, hanged, beheaded, and their bodies cast into the fire; often they were burned alive.

It is probable that more people were burned for alleged relations with the devil and his minions than for heresy. The theory and practice of witchcraft had been developed into a carefully organized doctrine, but its errors soon provoked criticism. Cornelius Agrippa of Nettesheim (1486–1554), a peculiar genius ready to test all things, adopted the occult thought of the day and in 1531 wrote an encyclopedic survey of it. Four years before this he had published another work in which he condemned all knowledge as worthless. He also was sceptical toward prevalent ideas about witchcraft and in 1519 hid a woman so that she could not be found by her accusers. The public was so incensed at his conduct that he had to retire from public office.

John Weyer (1515–1588), born in the duchy of Brabant, adopted the scepticism of his master Agrippa and developed an elaborate explanation of the phenomena of witchcraft. He taught that certain disorders primarily of a mental nature produced visions, illusions, and madness, and that people suffering from such maladies easily submitted to diabolical suggestion. Weyer's ideas are set forth in his *On the Illusions of Demons and on Incantations and Poisoners* (1563).

The physician, John Schenck (1530–1598), continued Weyer's work, arguing that the manifestations of witchcraft were hallucinations and that people possessed of demons were physically deranged. Finally, Frederick Von Spee (1591–1635), a Jesuit, took up these and similar arguments. But such new ideas ran counter to the fixed beliefs of lawyers, statesmen, and common people. Prosecution of witches continued throughout the sixteenth century and only died out at the close of the eighteenth.

SOME FAMOUS MEDICAL MEN OF THE RENAISSANCE

Ambroise Paré (1517–1590), a self-educated man, became famous in medicine. Born of poor parents, he received his first instruction from a barber-surgeon, later going to Paris where he spent 3 years in the Hotel-Dieu, a famous medieval hospital. Instruction in the traditional medical lore soon proved inadequate in his estimation. He was surgeon to the army of Francis I on the occasion of the latter's Third War (1536–1538) against Charles V. It was customary to cauterize wounds by pouring boiling oil into them, and Paré followed this practice with the wounded men at the capture of Turin:

> At last my oil ran short, and I was forced instead thereof to apply a digestive made of the yolk of eggs, oil of roses, and turpentine. In the night I could not sleep in quiet, fearing some default in not cauterizing, that I should find the wounded to whom I had not used the said oil dead from the poison of their wounds; which made me rise very early to visit them, where beyond my expectation I found that those to whom I had applied my digestive medicament had but little pain, and their wounds without inflammation or swelling, having rested fairly well that night; the others, to whom the boiling oil was used, I found feverish, with great pain and swelling about the edges of the wounds. Then I resolved never more to burn thus cruelly poor men with gunshot wounds.[1]

"See how I learned to treat gunshot wounds; not by books," were Paré's words. He wrote several treatises and invented a large number of medical instruments. He won fame as a successful surgeon, especially from his work with the wounded at the siege of Metz (1552). He had many enemies who, jealous of his successes, complained that he did not know Latin or Greek. His reply to these detractors was the publication of his remarkable *Journeys in Diverse Places*, written in French.

Paracelsus (1493–1541) also was a self-taught man whose services to medicine were of great importance. He was born near Zurich, learned medicine from his father, studied in Ferrara where he took a degree (1515), traveled far and wide, and accumulated a vast amount of knowledge. He spent some time in the establishments of the Fuggers in the Tyrol and learned much about diseases among miners. He had not the slightest respect for authority, and believed that first-hand study of phenomena was better than repeating the opinions of Galen and his successors. He paid no attention to traditional scientific literature and even neglected Latin so that he could not express himself in that language, an unpardonable defect in the eyes of his scientific contemporaries.

The time had come to break with traditional teachings which were woefully inadequate, and Paracelsus' tempestuous attacks on pedantic methods proved significant. Appointed professor of medicine at the University of Basel and physician to the city of Basel in 1527, he began to lecture from his own experience and not from the traditional authorities. On one occasion he publicly burned the books of Galen and other masters, to the great consternation of his competitors. His disrespect for

---

[1] A. Paré, *Journeys to Divers Places, 1537–1569* (Harvard Classics) XXXVII, 11.

authority and his disregard for the opinions and practices of others made his stay impossible, and in 1528 he again began his wanderings. The old-fashioned view that Paracelsus was a quack and of no account has been exploded. On the contrary, he was a skillful physician and surgeon, employing the best pharmaceutic and chemical knowledge of his day in his healing art, and thus laying the foundations of the important "iatro-chemical" school of medicine in the next century.

The study of botany received a strong impetus from its relation to medicine. Gardens of medicinal plants had been common during the Middle Ages, and lists of plants known as "herbals" were kept. Herbalists were the first botanists. The authority of such classical scholars as Theo-phrastus and Dioscorides exercised a dominating influence in this field during the closing Middle Ages. There were a number of important herbalists in Germany, such as Valerius Cordus (1515–1544) and Leonard Fuchs (1501–1566) who taught at the University of Erfurt. Dodonaeus, a Fleming born in Mechelen in 1517, was perhaps the most successful of all herbalists. Soon botanical gardens were established, the first at the University of Padua, the next two at Montpellier and Leiden.

Conrad Gesner (1515–1565), another self-made man, made many contributions to botany and zoology. Born in Zurich of poor parents, he was unable to secure much schooling. He drifted into the Lutheran ministry, but preferred medicine and science, and finally acquired a medical degree at Basel in 1541 and began practicing in Zurich. But he devoted much attention to plants and animals and insects, and wrote a number of books on botany and zoology. His accomplishments were made in the face of the greatest obstacles, but he overcame them all by his persistent industry.

Academic circles also produced their quota of scientific men. Tradition and authority were enthroned in many universities, but there were excep-tions. At Padua, for example, there was lively debate on the interpretation of Aristotle, and two schools developed. The first interpreted the doctrines of the great philosopher according to the thought of Averroës (d. 1198), a philosopher who had written commentaries on Aristotle. He taught that the soul was immortal but did not retain its personality because it was swallowed up in the greater reality of the world-soul. The opposing school, which interpreted Aristotle in accordance with earlier doctrines which had grown up in Alexandria, completely denied indi-vidual immortality. These Alexandrists, as they were called, were critical toward scholastic interpretations of Aristotle and were prone to study his works in the original language according to humanist methods. Pietro Pomponazzi (1462–1525), their chief protagonist, taught a materialist philosophy and held that the soul died with the dissolution of the body. Students of science at the University of Padua and such neighboring schools as Ferrara and Bologna thus became active in the criticism of traditional ideas about nature and immortality.

Girolamo Fracastoro (1478?–1553), born in Verona, was a product of the school of Alexandrists. Emphasizing the naturalism of Aristotle, he became an avowed experimenter and took deep interest in all scientific problems. He wrote *Syphilis sive de Morbo Gallico,* a poem describing the epidemic of syphilis which broke out in Naples during the sojourn of Charles VIII in 1494 and 1495. The origin of this disease is wrapped in mystery. Some contemporaries held that it had been introduced from America by the sailors of Columbus. Most likely, however, it was common throughout the Middle Ages, but suddenly became more virulent than ever. It spread rapidly in all levels of society and was variously called the "French disease," "the Neapolitan pox," or the "Italian disease." The word "syphilis," coined by Fracastoro, was adopted universally. Fracastoro also wrote a book on contagions which summed up knowledge on this subject and revealed the scientific lucidity of the author's thinking. He criticized the elaborate explanations of the movements of the planets by means of epicycles and eccentric circles, thus paving the way for the heliocentric theory. He also studied geography, and was the first scholar to use the word "pole."

VESALIUS' CONTRIBUTION TO ANATOMY

The publication of Andreas Vesalius' *Seven Books on the Structure of the Human Body* in 1543 laid the foundations of modern anatomy. Vesalius (1514–1564), a Fleming, was born in Brussels and studied at Louvain, Paris, and Padua. From the first he was keenly interested in anatomy and quite properly believed that the only way to understand the human body was to study at first hand the structure of its parts. This idea today is a commonplace, but in Vesalius' youth anatomy was not studied with the thoroughness which is necessary if it is to be the basis of medical therapy. Vesalius spent some time in the Venetian hospital of the Theatines and at the University of Padua, from which he received a degree in 1537 and was appointed to teach surgery. His book contained a large number of drawings, carefully made after original specimens and executed by the best technical skill of the day. When finished, the world possessed for the first time since antiquity a complete anatomical treatise illustrating minutely and accurately the human form. Its appearance marked a milestone in medical progress. The school of Padua continued to lead in medical science. Vesalius was succeeded by Fallopius (1523–1562) who won fame from his studies of the ovaries, vagina, placenta, and auditory and glossopharyngeal nerves. The Fallopian tubes were named after him. His pupil, Fabricius (1537–1619), made great progress in the study of the vasomotor system and was the teacher of William Harvey (1578–1657), the most significant medical authority of modern times next to Vesalius. His book, *On the Motion of the Heart and Blood* (1628), demonstrated the circulation of the blood.

COPERNICUS' REVOLUTION IN CELESTIAL MECHANICS

Ever since classical antiquity the people had believed that the sun revolved around the earth and that the earth was stationary. The eye appeared to confirm this idea. And Claudius Ptolemy of Alexandria in the second century A.D. had summed up Greek scholarship in astronomy and so determined the thought on this point of subsequent generations on mathematics, geography, and astronomy. His great treatise, an encyclopedia in thirteen books, was called the *Great Synthesis*.

Like Aristotle, Ptolemy accepted the theory of a "geocentric" rather than a "heliocentric" universe. He assumed that the seven bodies or planets—moon, Mercury, Venus, sun, Mars, Jupiter, and Saturn—move around the static rotund earth. But this homocentric theory could not explain why these bodies "wandered" now nearer, now farther away. Ptolemy proposed a theory to explain this phenomenon. He suggested, as had some earlier astronomers, that such planets might be moving in epicyclical paths. When this speculation failed to allow for the great divergences in the paths of the "wanderers" of planets, Ptolemy proposed the theory of "eccentric" circular paths, suggesting that planets traveled along the path of off-center circles, which might explain why at times they appeared nearer than at other times. Curiously, it never occurred to him or to any of his followers for over a thousand years to calculate planetary movements on the basis of an elliptical tract. This, the correct solution, was first offered by Johann Kepler (d. 1630).

Nicholas Copernicus (1473–1543) was born in Thorn and studied in Cracow, Bologna, and Padua. He entered the service of the Church but continued his work in science. He was sceptical about the geocentric system of the universe as taught in every school in Christendom and decided in favor of the heliocentric theory which had been advanced by Pythagoras but had been eclipsed by Ptolemy. Aquinas, however, preferred the Aristotelian theory. For a time Copernicus said little about his ideas and discoveries, but finally allowed his treatise, *On the Revolutions of Celestial Bodies,* to be published in 1543. In it Copernicus taught that the earth revolved on its axis and described a circular orbit around the sun, the immobile center of the system; the other planets also circled around the sun. Copernicus thus broke completely with current conceptions but not entirely with the old views, for he still clung to the idea of circular orbits in the new system. Nevertheless, it was an epoch-making discovery, for by disproving the theory that the planets move in circular orbits around the earth, Copernicus robbed astrology of its traditional foundations. His ideas were not accepted at first, however. Although Pope Paul III approved his theories, the Church, especially during the Catholic Revival, was suspicious of everything which seemed to contradict Biblical teaching. Most Protestant theologians, wedded to the idea that the Bible was verbally inspired in every phrase and word, refused to accept the theory, or ignored it.

AN AGE OF NEW INVENTIONS

Map-making made considerable progress at the hands of Gerhard Kremer or Mercator (1512–1594), a Fleming who devoted his life to the study of geography. Accurate maps of the world became a burning necessity, as knowledge about it expanded through the daring of explorers. The old *portolani* of Mediterranean sailors were inadequate and the methods employed in drawing them wholly inaccurate when applied to the newly discovered lands. Fracastoro suggested that the earth's crust could be accurately represented on a flat surface, and Mercator finally succeeded in doing this (1569). His map of the world was drawn on a cylinder on which were made lines of latitude parallel to the equator and lines of longitude at right angles to it. The greater accuracy attained by Mercator's method made possible the development of atlases which displayed the whole surface of the earth. During the closing years of his life Mercator prepared his monumental atlas which appeared in its completed form in 1595. Thus cartography began to catch up with explorations.

Inventions and scientific processes are of great moment in the history of mankind. Each revolutionary invention has produced profound changes in economic, social, political, and cultural life. Our modern culture is made possible by the bewildering array of inventions which we see at every hand. The age of the Renaissance boasts a number of such inventions and new scientific processes. Before 1400 mines were little more than pits like wells and were crudely worked. Soon, however, hoisting pumps were invented in order to drain water from the deeper wells; adits or lateral horizontal shafts were developed, and boring machines came into existence. Improved windlasses, composed of endless chains with buckets attached, were invented. Blast furnaces were built. Ere long someone produced the new amalgam process for reducing silver ore, an invention which made possible more effective exploitation of the Bolivian silver mines. Such new processes stimulated the mining industry of central Europe and poured great wealth into the coffers of the Fuggers and other capitalists. George Agricola (1494–1555), a practical man who was well acquainted with the mining industry of Germany, wrote a treatise on metallurgy entitled *On Metals*. He described the practice of subjecting cast iron to intense heat in the presence of some oxidizing substances and of frequent stirring in order to produce wrought iron. This process of "puddling" became important.

There also were many improvements in shipping, military weapons, clocks, and implements. But the most remarkable invention of the Renaissance was printing, which made possible the rapid and cheap multiplication of books. The new process of printing made it possible for a much larger number of the cultivated townsmen to secure the works of humanists. During the first half-century of the printing industry it is estimated that about 40,000 editions were produced. The appearance of so many books undermined the dominance of the universities and their traditional thought, and substituted for them the more vital ideas of writers who could not find expression in the schools. As the appeal of the new humanist culture was addressed to a wider public than in the Middle Ages, books in the vernacular became more numerous than ever and the sway of Latin as sole medium of thought ended. Pamphleteering increased in importance. New religious ideas were rapidly disseminated, thus contributing materially to the rise of Protestantism.

THE INVENTION OF PRINTING

The story of the invention of printing is a complicated one. Books had been written on parchment during the earlier Middle Ages, but paper, a cheaper medium, became common during the fourteenth century in the Mediterranean area whence it spread to other lands. Although parchment was sometimes used in printing, paper soon won great favor. Thus the history of the paper industry is closely bound up with that of printing. Little is known about the development of printers' ink. This is an important subject because ordinary writing ink cannot be used in printing. Great obscurity enshrouds the early history of printing, and many legends have sprung up such as the belief that the art was initiated by Lawrence

Coster of Haarlem (d. between 1435 and 1440). This story has been shown to be a myth. There also is much misunderstanding about the nature of Gutenberg's work.

The invention of printing was achieved by a gradual process of perfection until the famous Bibles with thirty-six and forty-two lines on a page were produced. The first step in this evolution perhaps is represented by the block prints which appeared early in the fifteenth century and which were simple pictures of saints with a few words added. Soon more elaborate pictures appeared. Several pages of block prints were put together to form such simple books as the *Mirror of Human Salvation* and the *Bible of the Poor* in which pictures supplemented with brief texts appeared. It was not long before printing from movable type was developed, but little is known in detail about the evolution of this process. It is certain that movable type was used at least as early as 1448. According to tradition John Gensfleisch, called Gutenberg, contributed much to it. Gradually the mechanical process was perfected and Gutenberg's Bible with pages of thirty-six lines and Peter Schöffer's and John Fust's with forty-two lines which appeared in 1546 mark the culmination of the invention. The city of Mainz has always been regarded as the home of printing, but it is possible that such centers as Strasbourg and Lyon may have contributed something to the development of this art. Whatever uncertainties may exist about the origin of printing, it is evident that this invention was the most important mechanical art yet produced for the diffusion of thought.

PHILOSOPHIC THOUGHT IN THE RENAISSANCE

There was a considerable body of philosophic thought in Italy during the Age of the Renaissance. The popularity of Aristotelian teaching in Europe, so noteworthy a feature of the thirteenth century, continued throughout the *Quattrocento* and the *Cinquecento*. Each of its three forms —Thomism, Ockhamism, and Scotism—were widely influential. Thomism was especially influential during the Catholic Revival in Spain. Thomas de Vio (1468–1534), or Cajetan, was a renowned commentator on the works of Thomas Aquinas of whose philosophy he possessed complete mastery. Ockhamism, which denied the existence of universals, also was influential, especially during the Reformation, and Scotism flourished in sixteenth-century Spain. Averroism had its devotees, especially at Padua who taught that there was but one immortal intellect in man. But there was another school of Aristotelianism in Padua—that which taught that there was no immortal intellect in man at all. Chief among those who held this doctrine was Pietro Pomponazzi (1462–1525), a Mantuan who exerted wide influence.

But there also were some humanists who opposed Aristotle, among them especially Lorenzo Valla (1407–1457) who may be regarded as a Renaissance radical. He disliked the subtle distinctions of Aristotelianism, and especially those of medieval Scholasticism, which he regarded as barbarous sophistry. He held that rhetoric was superior to logic and an instrument of deeper insight. Philosophically, he sympathized with the ideas of the Stoics and Epicureans. He expressed his literary humanist predilections in his *Elegances of the Latin Language,* his philosophic preferences in his *On Pleasure.* His sharply critical skill was demonstrated in his attack on the *Donation of Constantine,* which he showed to be a forgery.

Platonic, or rather Neoplatonic, philosophy had a long history during the Middle Ages. St. Augustine had shown his obligation to Platonic thought, and in this he was followed by such thinkers as John Scotus Erigena, Bonaventura, Roger Bacon, and to some extent Nicholas Cusanus (1401–1464) who also owes much of his thought to the followers of medieval Aristotelianism. His basic idea was that a great diversity of opposites existed, for example, matter and form, potentiality and actuality, motion and rest, essence and existence, all of which ultimately have their higher unity in God. We discover this unity by realizing that God, being infinite, is the object of our finite intellects. The things we predicate of God apply to Him in a manner that transcends our knowledge. To know Him we proceed negatively, ignorantly as it were; hence the title *Docta Ignorantia* of one of Cusanus' greatest books. Philosophically and in other respects he was a link between the thought of the Middle Ages and that of the new age we call the Renaissance.

Florentine humanists took an active interest in Neoplatonic thought. This was natural, for as early as 1396 Chrysoloras had begun to lecture on the Greek tongue in the University of Florence. Later, a kindred Greek spirit, John Argyropoulos (d. 1486) took his place. Cosimo de' Medici encouraged Greek studies by setting an ever active example. Under the inspiration of the noted Greek author, John Gemisthos Plethon (d. 1464), who advocated Platonic rather than Aristotelian or Scholastic thought, Cosimo established the Platonic Academy composed of men interested in discussing the problems of philosophy from a Platonic point of view. The Council of Florence (1438–1445), called to settle Church questions between the Latin and Greek Churches, also stimulated interest in Platonic thought. The Greek, John Bessarion (1395–1472), also a noteworthy scholar, came to take part in the proceedings. Before many years

Florence produced a Greek scholar of her own in the person of Marsiglio Ficino (1433–1499) who advocated a Platonic interpretation of Christianity rather than an Aristotelian (or Scholastic). Among Ficino's noted followers was John Pico della Mirandola (1463–1494) who knew Greek, Latin, and Hebrew and believed that Greek and Jewish thought could be combined in a system of Platonic Christianity. These ideas, although they exerted some influence, however, had little success as far as religion was concerned.

Besides these advocates of Platonic and Aristotelian thought, there were a number of other Italians who developed systems of naturalism, usually materialism. A Milanese physician and mathematician, Girolamo Cardano (d. 1576), was the first to lay down the principles of naturalism. He was followed by Bernardino Telesio (d. 1588) who developed an empirical method of investigating nature and taught that the universe sprang from three principles: matter, heat, and cold. Francesco Patrizzi of Dalmatia (d. 1597) imparted to this kind of thinking the metaphysics of pantheism. Giordano Bruno of Nola (1548–1600) developed a completely pantheistic system of the universe which he claimed to be infinite. As there could be no two infinites, he declared that God was identical with the universe, which was pantheistic. Later, Thomaso Campanello (d. 1639) followed in the footsteps of Telesio and his school. But, starting from the view that God is shown in nature as if in a mirror, he obviously was inspired by the Neoplatonic school. His naturalism like that of Bruno later was to find a link with the philosophic thought of the eighteenth century.

Chapter 24

ECONOMIC AND GEOGRAPHIC
REVOLUTION

*T*HE AGE of the Renaissance witnessed two great and sudden revolutions in geographical knowledge. The first of these was due to the opening by Vasco da Gama of the sea route around the Cape of Good Hope to India, and the second was the discovery of vast lands beyond the Atlantic Ocean. These two events which occurred in the last decade of the fifteenth century in the course of time entailed such extraordinary consequences in political, economic, and scientific activity that they may fittingly be regarded as marking the close of the Middle Ages and the opening of the Modern Age.

CONSTANTINOPLE AS A WORLD MART:
ITS ASIATIC HINTERLAND

Until the twelfth century Constantinople had been the great occidental terminus of commercial activity between the Mediterranean Sea, the Tigris and Euphrates valleys, India, and the Isles of Spice. The growth of trade and industry, the rise of cities, and the establishment of greater security throughout western Europe during and after the Crusades greatly extended these lanes of traffic. Bruges and Antwerp became the western termini of a busy commercial activity which extended to China and the Isles of Spice in the East. Lands lying outside this central commercial corridor were regarded more or less as economic provinces. Accurate geographical knowledge was restricted to this central area.

The founding of the Mongol empire by Genghis Khan (d. 1227) shortly after the opening of the thirteenth century greatly affected economic activities between East and West and increased geographical knowledge. The empire of the Mongols included all of southern Asia save Cochin-China, Siam, Hindustan, and Arabia; and it extended from the Japanese and Yellow Seas to the borders of Poland and Hungary, thus

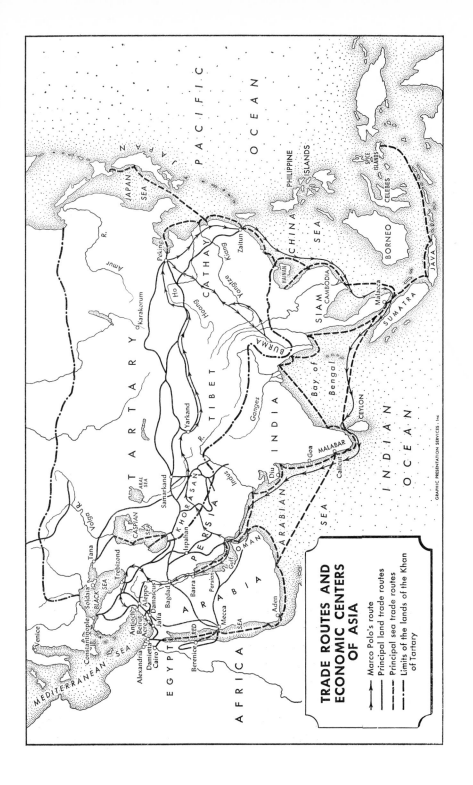

TRADE ROUTES AND
ECONOMIC CENTERS
OF ASIA

→ Marco Polo's route
— Principal land trade routes
--- Principal sea trade routes
-··- Limits of the lands of the Khan
of Tartary

GRAPHIC PRESENTATION SERVICES, Inc

embracing the broad lands of the Russian plain. The union of all these regions under the rule of one man produced greater security and therefore promoted commercial activity. From Kaffa on the Crimea and Tana at the mouth of the Don, trade routes extended eastward by way of Astrakhan, Samarkand, Yarkand, and Karakorum to Cambalec, the modern Peiping.

Europeans exhibited much interest in the work of Genghis Khan. The Mongols were a Ural-Altaic folk whose religion was shamanism. Their motley empire embraced peoples of Christian, Buddhist, Mohammedan, and other religions. Hulagu (d. 1265), grandson of Genghis Khan, was a Buddhist, and his wife was a Christian of the Nestorian sect. Believing that this was an excellent opportunity to bring about the conversion of the Mongols to Catholic Christianity, the pope in 1246 sent a Franciscan friar, John of Plano-Carpini, to Karakorum. On his return, a Flemish friar named William of Ruysbroeck was sent. He found a number of Europeans living at the court of the Great Khan, who appreciated their skill and knowledge. Next was sent John of Montecorvino who had been active in founding missions in Persia. On his way to the Orient he opened a mission in India and reached China in 1298. He mastered the Chinese language, established a school for the Christian education of young Chinese, and made converts. Such was his success that some hierarchic organization was needed, and Clement V created John archbishop of Cambalec. A number of Franciscans were sent as missionaries, and bishoprics were formed by 1312. Two years later these Franciscans had fifty converts in China. John of Montecorvino died in 1330 and was succeeded by his brother Nicholas who reached China in 1338. Missionaries were constantly sent out to help the young churches. Among these intrepid men was Oderic of Pordenone (d. 1331) who visited Tibet.

These efforts to Christianize Asia failed to attain the success which they promised in the beginning. Great wars broke out in China which led to the overthrow of the Mongol overlordship in 1368 by the ruler of the Ming dynasty. The missionaries were scattered, much of their work was undone, and some of the priests were slain. The condition of affairs in Europe also contributed to this failure. The papacy was crippled by the secular interests which overwhelmed it during its Avignonese residence. The rival pontiffs of the Great Schism were not in a position to support the struggling Church in China. And when the Mongols accepted Mohammedanism, Christianity became practically extinct in northern Asia.

Economic relations between East and West constantly grew in importance, as is illustrated by the travels of the Venetians Marco Polo (1254–1324), his father Niccolo, and his uncle Maffeo Polo. Being merchants, they traded in the Crimea, went to Sarai on the Volga, and traveled eastward to Cambalec by way of Karakorum. Kublai Khan received them graciously and sent them back as his envoys to the pope, requesting missionaries to instruct his subjects in the Christian faith and one hundred teachers to acquaint them with the studies of the liberal arts. On their return to Venice in 1269, they enlisted the help of Niccolo's son Marco and again set out for China, or Cathay as it was called then. Going by way of Kerman, Khorassan, the Pamir plateau, and Khotan, they reached the court of Kublai Khan in 1275. They tarried in China until about 1292, being detained by the Khan for diplomatic and other services. In 1292 they set out on their return voyage by way of Malacca and reached Venice in 1295. Marco Polo was captured soon after by the Genoese and while in prison composed the classic account of his romantic experiences.

The busy intercourse with the East by way of the trade routes from the Crimea, Trebizond, Acre, and Alexandria, and the constantly growing commercial and industrial activity of Italian, French, and Spanish towns greatly increased geographical lore. The use of the magnetic needle was imported from China where it had been employed since the second century. This needle, mounted on a straw or a piece of cork which rested in water, enabled sailors to ascertain direction even when it was too dark to see the stars. This device, in common use by the twelfth century, made navigation less hazardous than it had formerly been. Another instrument, the astrolabe, which was employed soon afterward, made possible the finding of latitude with greater exactness.

Sailors had long been in the habit of keeping notes about the coasts along which they plied their trade. Maps, called *portolani* or handy maps, came into existence and soon attained a surprising perfection, at least as far as the Mediterranean was concerned. The first extant map dates from 1300. Others followed, many of which showed greater accuracy and detail. The *Laurentian* or *Medicean Atlas* of 1351 shows the Mediterranean, Adriatic, Caspian, and Black Seas, the western coast of India, Africa with the Nile, and western and northern Europe from Spain to Scandinavia. Even the Azores are shown. The sailors of this period were the forerunners of the heroes of the great age of discovery which began with Columbus and Vasco da Gama, and the map making of these times laid the foundations for the extraordinary activity in cartography during the sixteenth century.

EXPLORATION OF AFRICA

Northern Africa, like Asia, also became better known to merchants of the Mediterranean, for Egypt, Tunis, Algeria, and Morocco were closely bound up with the economic life of this area. The antagonism of Christian and Mohammedan did not prevent trade between them. Such towns as Melilla, Oran, Algiers, and Tunis were the termini of caravan routes which traversed the desert of the Sahara to the valley of the Niger. Ivory was one of the articles exported from that region. Anselm Desalguier, a Frenchman from Toulouse, sailed along the African coast to Guinea, moved up the Niger River, and lived for 11 years among the colored natives of Nigeria. Little is known about him beyond these facts, except that he returned to his native land in 1417 accompanied by a colored wife, some half-caste children, and some colored attendants. Later, one Giovanni Malfante described the land and people of Nigeria whom he had visited in 1447. Italians showed great interest in Africa, which they knew to be a continent. At the opening of the fourteenth century a company of Genoese under Tedisio Doria and two brothers named Vivaldi sailed through the Strait of Gibraltar and proceeded southward in an attempt, it is said, to reach India by sea. At this time also, Venetians and Genoese merchants began sending their goods in ships by way of the Strait of Gibraltar to Flanders and Brabant, thus avoiding the tedious and more costly route over Alpine passes.

Meanwhile the discovery of new lands in the Atlantic and the exploration of the western coast of Africa had begun. The Canary Islands had been discovered by a Genoese sailor named Malocello. The Spaniards and Portuguese fought for their possession, and by 1495 it had passed to the Spaniards. The Portuguese were the first to tempt the fortunes of the Atlantic. Their country had struggled valiantly against the lordship of Mohammedans, and the chivalric crusading ardor burned in their breasts. Taught by Italian example, they too began exploration and expansion. Combining the work of crusaders and traders in this endeavor, King John captured Ceuta (1415), an Arab stronghold whose population had prevented Portuguese expansion along the African coast. Prince Henry (1394–1460), one of King John's sons known to history as Prince Henry the Navigator, was especially interested in exploration and expansion. He proposed to explore the coast south of Cape Bojador to Guinea, drive out the Arabs, and seize the trade of that region. Thus both religion and economic advantage would be served. The Madeira Islands were discovered (1418) and occupied. The Azores were taken in 1427 and

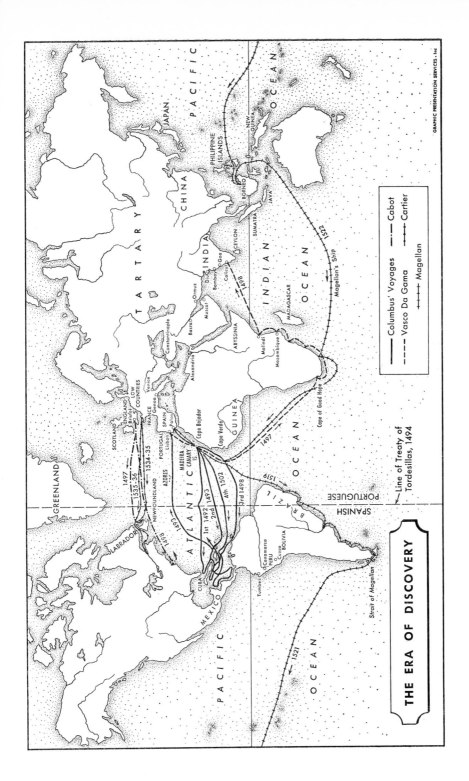

THE ERA OF DISCOVERY

populated by Flemings. Cape Bojador was rounded 7 years later, and Portuguese ships found their way to the River of Gold (Rio del Oro) and the Senegal River. The Cape Verde Islands were discovered. Colonies were established, fortifications erected, and trade was begun with the natives. This was the origin of traffic in slaves which later was to prove so important a factor in the economic development of the New World. Companies were chartered and authorized to exploit the new lands, organize defense, and further the work of exploration.

Route to India.   Finally, in 1486 Bartholomew Diaz reached the Cape of Good Hope and sailed beyond it to Algoa Bay. Meanwhile Pedro de Covilham and Alfonso de Paiva were sent to Egypt and to the lands of the Indian Ocean to gather information about routes in the Indian Ocean. Covilham visited Calicut in India and Solfala on the east coast of Africa. Vasco da Gama was commissioned to sail with three ships by way of southern Africa and open the sea route to India. He set out in June, 1497, and after 3 months reached the Bay of St. Helena. He sailed around the Cape of Good Hope in November, spent Christmas at Natal, missed Solfala, and stopped at Malindi where he secured a pilot. Boldly sailing directly across the Indian Ocean, Vasco da Gama reached Calicut on May 18, 1498. On his return to Portugal in 1499, the Portuguese feverishly began to exploit their discovery. Pedro Alvarez Cabral was sent with a squadron to secure concessions in India. The Malabar coast of India had long ago been cut up into a number of petty states which were too feeble to resist him. A factory, or trading post, was established at Calicut, and similar rights were forced from rulers of other places.

Francisco d'Almeida was appointed viceroy of India in 1505. It was his task to consolidate the work hitherto accomplished and to create permanent trading bases on the Malabar coast. These were momentous days, for Vasco da Gama's exploit is one of the turning points in European history. For centuries the Arabs had enjoyed a monopoly of the trade in the world's most prized articles between the East and West. Their preeminence in science and the arts of civilization during the Middle Ages was in large measure made possible by this fact. They instinctively realized that their monopoly was threatened the moment that Vasco da Gama appeared in the Indian Ocean, and every effort was made to trap the commander. The first Portuguese sailors to land at Calicut were greeted with the words: "May the devil take you! What brought you hither?" It was clear that the Arabs would make a determined effort to prevent the most lucrative trade of the world from falling into Christian hands. The ruler of Calicut, foremost in resisting the Portuguese, combined with the sultan of Egypt and other Arab potentates. Several naval battles were fought, but the struggle came to an end with Almeida's victory over a fleet ten times as large as his own in the Battle of Diu (1509), one of history's greatest engagements. The Mohammedan world lost to the Christians its favored economic position. The new lands about to be discovered in the Orient and the Occident were to be Christian and European. The Semitic races and Islam declined as their economic resources dried up; henceforth they played an inferior role in history.

The Portuguese now organized their colonial empire. Albuquerque completed (1509–1515) the heroic conquests begun by Vasco da Gama, Cabral, and Almeida. He established the seat of his viceroyalty at Goa, and seized Malacca on the Strait of Malacca and Ormuz on the Persian Gulf. A fleet was permanently employed to guard these places and the routes between them. While the viceroy at Goa supervised these newly won possessions, the Indian House (*Casa da India*) was created in Portugal to regulate the affairs of the factories.

DISCOVERY OF AMERICA

Meanwhile a remarkable feat of discovery occurred in the Atlantic when Christopher Columbus (b. 1446?–1506) in 1492 found a number of the Caribbean islands. This ocean for centuries had been an unexplored expanse. Sagas related how Scandinavians had sailed to Iceland and Greenland and even to lands still farther westward. The ancient legend of St. Brendan told of an island to the West. There were traditional tales as old as the Greeks and Romans of mysterious regions beyond the setting sun. There were rumors among sailors that lands existed somewhere in the silent West. Little did Europeans of that day dream what vast continents—North America, South America, and Australia, besides many islands—lay beyond the setting sun!

Columbus was born in Genoa in the midst of the seafaring and exploring activity of the western Mediterranean. He lived in Lisbon after his marriage, heard all about the exploits of the Portuguese, and is said to have voyaged to England and Iceland. He spent some years in Porto Santo on the Madeira Islands and visited the African coast.

Fired by the news shortly after 1480 that Portuguese seafarers had found land far beyond the Azores, Columbus determined to unlock the secrets of the Atlantic. After many difficulties three ships were prepared at the expense of Queen Isabella of Spain. One of them was commanded by Alonzo Pinzon, an able seaman who had had much practical experience in the seas off Africa, had studied *portolani,* and had carefully investigated the rumors about unknown lands to the west. It is not known just what Columbus had in mind. He hoped to find new lands, but it is also certain he knew that the east shores of Asia lay somewhere beyond the Atlantic. It was common knowledge throughout the Middle Ages that the earth was a sphere. By sailing westward one would ultimately reach the east.

Columbus' voyage was due to the spirit of adventure and a desire to find new lands, not primarily to a desire of sailing to Asia. It certainly was not caused by the Turkish capture of Constantinople in 1453 and the seizure of the lands through which lay the trade routes between East and West, for the Turks did not cut off the trade in articles of luxury, as is so often stated. Columbus' fleet of three ships and ninety sailors left the harbor of Palos on August 3, 1492. It tarried 4 weeks in the Canary Islands and after sailing west and southwest until October 12, land was found, probably one of the islands of the Bahamas. After cruising about, they discovered other islands including Cuba and Haiti. Columbus soon began his homeward voyage and arrived at Palos on March 15. His voyage was an epochal event. Though less hazardous than Vasco da Gama's famous voyage around Africa 6 years later and less significant in its immediate consequences, it was bound to be more important in its ultimate effects. Furthermore, it produced a revolution in geographical knowledge, for everyone, including Columbus, had believed that the world was much smaller than it is, and these ancient ideas were now suddenly disproved.

These discoveries aroused the animosity of the Portuguese who were fearful of Spanish intrusion. There was danger that the two nations might come to blows; consequently the pope by virtue of his recognized leadership in international affairs was asked to serve as arbiter. Alexander VI issued the Bull of Demarcation in May, 1493, which assigned to Spain all new lands west of the Azores and the Cape Verde Islands to a line from pole to pole one hundred leagues away, and to Portugal all new lands east of this line. Ferdinand and Isabella were not fully pleased with this division for they feared that their rights in the East Indies were not safeguarded, and finally in June, 1494, Alexander declared that the Spaniards were to have the new lands lying west of a line 370 leagues west of the Cape Verde Islands (Treaty of Tordesillas).

Columbus made three other voyages. The first (1493–1496), undertaken with seventeen ships and a large number of men, led to the discovery of Puerto Rico, Jamaica, and many smaller islands. On the second (1498–1500) he reached the coast of South America at the mouth of the Orinoco River. Complaints came to Ferdinand and Isabella about Columbus' conduct toward the natives, and a ship was sent to investigate.

The captain sent Columbus back to Spain in chains. The discoverer was exonerated, but was not restored to his dignity of governor of the new lands. He fitted out another expedition (1502–1504), sailed to Haiti, found the coast of Central America, and reached the Isthmus of Darien which he believed to be the coast of Malacca. Shipwrecked on the island of Jamaica, he fell ill, and after his return to Spain, robbed of his dignities and his rights ignored, died in 1506. Meanwhile Cabral, appointed to lead a fleet around Africa to the Indies, sailed far to the west, sighted the coast of Brazil in April, 1500, and claimed it for the king of Portugal.

Columbus' exploits roused in many a desire to imitate him. Balboa climbed the mountains of the Isthmus of Darien and was the first European to set foot on the Pacific coast (1513). Ferdinand Magellan, a Portuguese in the service of Spain (1520), sailed through the strait which today bears his name and reached the Pacific. Finally he arrived at a group of islands, later called the Philippines, where he became involved in some native feuds and was slain (1521). One of his vessels continued, and finally reached Europe. This voyage, the first around the world, gave men a more adequate conception of the size of the globe and revealed that America was a large continent and not an island. The Portuguese were perturbed, for Spaniards had appeared in the East Indies which they believed was their proper domain. As the Line of Demarcation of 1494 had been drawn with reference to contested spheres in the Atlantic, conflicts threatened to break out, but a serious war was avoided by the Treaty of 1529 whereby the Philippines were given to Spain and the Moluccas or Isles of Spice remained Portuguese. By this time the newly found lands were becoming known as America. Amerigo Vespucci, a Florentine who had made a number of journeys to the West, advanced claims of having discovered a vast region which he called the New World, whereupon some German professors suggested that the new lands be called America (1507).

The first settlements in the New World, Santo Domingo, Isabella, and a few minor places, were confined to the West Indies, no serious effort being made at first to explore or conquer the mainland. But the desire to find gold drove the Spaniards onward. Hernando Cortés (d. 1547) heard rumors of a wealthy and civilized people in Mexico, and in February, 1519, set out with a small number of men. He landed at Vera Cruz and advanced upon the city of Mexico, capital of the Aztecs. Their king, Montezuma, was impressed by the fair Spaniards, believing them to be envoys of the gods. This crippled their ability to resist the intruders who ensconced themselves in the city of Mexico. The Spaniards could not be driven out because of their superior arms, but finally in July, 1520, they retreated in the face of the bitterest hostility. Cortés received reinforcements and, supported by soldiers drawn from the Aztecs, returned to Mexico and laid siege to it. After a stubborn resistance the city fell (August, 1521). Cortés was named governor, and soon Yucatan, Honduras, Nicaragua, Guatemala, and finally also California were explored.

The success of Cortés, the first conquistador or conqueror, sharpened the appetites of other adventurers. Francisco Pizarro determined to seize the land to the south of Mexico which natives referred to as a land of gold. Landing at Tumbez in Ecuador in May, 1532, with but a handful of men, he advanced upon the Incas and their king, Atahualpa, at Caxamarca. Seizing Atahualpa, Pizarro managed to collect a fabulous amount of gold. Atahualpa was treacherously slain, and Pizarro set himself up as governor. An expedition was undertaken to the holy city of Cuzco, and Lima was founded in 1535 as the capital of these new possessions. Thus was begun the romantic *conquista* or conquest of Spanish America.

Meanwhile the Spaniards organized a system of colonial exploitation copied after that of the Portuguese India House whose fabulous success could not be ignored. The Spanish crown in 1492 named Juan de Fonseca, a priest attached to the cathedral of Seville, as agent of colonial affairs. His activities grew rapidly as exploration and conquest progressed. Soon emerged the *Casa de la Contratación*, or House of Trade, which regulated all manner of business, such as equipping vessels, furnishing licenses, and granting trading rights. Santo Domingo became the seat of the governor of the Indies who was bound by instructions from the colonial office in Seville. The governor was assisted by a staff of officials, priests, and soldiers. Relations with the natives soon became a difficult manner, for the Spaniards were hard taskmasters driven by thirst for gold. Unaccustomed to hard labor and cruel treatment, the natives perished in large numbers. When theologians declared that they had souls, the government sought to protect the natives with stern laws which, however, proved inadequate. Finally in 1512 a new system was introduced. Agents were placed in charge of the natives and directed to look after their religious, economic, and other interests. The grouping of villages of natives under such men proved ineffective in protecting the aborigines. Nevertheless, this system of *encomiendas*, as it was called, became a fixed method of Spanish colonial administration. Such was the exploitative zeal of the colonists on the Caribbean islands that the native populace soon became extinct, whereupon colored slaves were imported from Africa and a lucrative slave trade grew up.

Other nations attempted to follow the example of the Spaniards. John

Cabot, a Florentine, entered the service of Henry VII of England and made a voyage to the West in 1497, discovering some part of the North American coast. Verrazano, also a Florentine, made a voyage in 1524 in behalf of Francis I of France and visited the shores of Delaware, New Jersey, and New York. Ten years later a Frenchman named Jacques Cartier coasted along Labrador and entered the St. Lawrence River. The purpose of these expeditions was to discover a short route to China. These and other voyages, however, possessed for the moment little importance for European life.

Vasco da Gama's voyage laid the basis of Portugal's monopoly of supplying the European demand for Oriental goods. The cheapness of the sea route and its relative security after naval protection was organized made shipment along the ancient land routes unprofitable. This dealt a stunning blow to Italian mercantile supremacy. Venice and Genoa for centuries had enjoyed unquestioned monopoly of western European trade in spices and other articles of luxury, and the Mediterranean area during the Middle Ages had been the wealthiest and most significant of Europe. This ascendancy was brusquely cut short after Vasco da Gama's discovery. Italian industrial and commercial supremacy was sapped, and her cultural supremacy soon passed its height. Leadership now passed to the states situated on the Atlantic seaboard.

The discoveries of Columbus and his successors were of revolutionary importance to Europe. Quantities of precious metal were found in the New World after the conquest of Mexico and Peru. The sudden increase in the amount of these metals caused a rapid rise in the cost of all commodities and stimulated every human endeavor. An era of great progress ensued in northern Europe. Towns grew, population increased, and such lands along the Atlantic seaboard as England and the Low Countries soon became the leading states of Europe. The cities of southern Germany which had profited from the transit of goods from Venice, Milan, and Genoa northward to the Low Countries declined, whereas Antwerp became more important than ever.

This increase in the amount of coined money wrought important changes in conceptions of government. The medieval political experience that a well-filled treasury was better than the personal services of a host of feudal lieges was more fully substantiated than ever. Capital had become the basis of political life, a fact upon which Machiavelli and Guicciardini had commented. The stream of precious metal from the mines of Peru, Bolivia, and Mexico made Spain powerful. It was argued that the wealth of a country consisted in the quantity of gold and silver within its borders, and princes therefore supported the bourgeoisie in its endeavor to bring gold into the country, that is, to create wealth. This alliance between absolute princes and mercantile interests produced a policy which later was called mercantilism. It dominated war, statecraft, and colonization during the next centuries.

PART XI

Renaissance Art Outside Italy

Chapter 25

RENAISSANCE INFLUENCE ON NORTH EUROPEAN GOTHIC ART

*G*OTHIC ART in northern Europe began to succumb to the methods of Italian masters at the close of the fifteenth century. Painters, becoming aware of the superiority of the artists of the *Quattrocento* and the *Cinquecento*, tried to master the Italian treatment of space, arrangement of subjects, and portrayal of moods. The result was that the Gothic manner began to disappear. Furthermore, Italian humanism altered the point of view of these artists, for a decidedly secular tendency became observable, and painters displayed greater scientific knowledge. Art no longer sought solely to arouse sympathy with the pathetic ordeal of Christ on the cross or with the pathetic macabre.

LEADERSHIP OF ALBRECHT DÜRER AND THE TWO HOLBEINS

The first German master to turn from the traditional methods practiced north of the Alps and adopt the manner of Italians was Albrecht Dürer (1471–1528). Brought up in Nuremberg, he inherited all that was good in the school of painting which had developed there under local and Flemish influences. His father, a goldsmith, intended that Albrecht should

389

follow him in this craft, but the youth early evinced so decided a preference for painting that the father in 1486 apprenticed him to the painter Michael Wolgemut (1434–1519), who had successfully mastered the skill of the painters of Flanders. Although his work was faulty, Wolgemut stood head and shoulders above his contemporaries. For 3 years Dürer worked and studied in his shop. In 1490 he began his career as journeyman and shortly after went to Colmar to work in the shop of Martin Schongauer (1455–1491), an artist of some originality in spite of the fact that his works reveal strong Flemish mannerism. He exerted wide influence through his numerous engravings in which he showed an improved knowledge of anatomy and a keen sense of form. Dürer next proceeded to Italy and, it is believed, spent some time in Venice. Dürer probably gazed with intense interest upon the pictures of Mantegna and the Bellini, who at that moment were at the height of their popularity, and must have been impressed by their magnificent composition and delicate chiaroscuro. Later in 1506 he made a second visit to Venice.

In 1494 Dürer was back in Nuremberg, married, and beginning to make a living as a painter. It was difficult to make a living, for in spite of the considerable economic advance of the towns of the Rhenish area and of southern Germany, liberal patrons did not exist. Princes generally were too poor to employ artists as the Medici in Florence were doing. Municipal governments did not have the breadth of view or understanding to lend their support to a struggling artist, no matter how promising. The public was too closely wedded to traditional conceptions to appreciate new ideas. Most of them desired little pictures of the *Virgin*, the *Christ Child*, the *Nativity*, *St. Christopher*, and similar themes, and artists were forced to supply this demand. Engraving became popular, woodcuts and copperplates being made in great numbers. Copperplate engraving had been employed in Italy but soon attained high excellence in Germany, the Germans being especially successful in this mechanical art as in printing, clock making, and the production of weapons and tools for mining.

Four years later Dürer produced a series of sixteen woodcuts dealing with the *Revelation of St. John* in which the dreadful events attending mankind's last days are vividly shown. One of them portrays the fight between *St. Michael and the Dragon*; another, the ride of the *Four Horsemen*. These are medieval themes, but they were executed with the growing skill of a master who had profited from the study of the more mature art beyond the Alps. Some of Dürer's copper engravings illustrate his interest in such classical themes as Apollo, Diana, and Hercules, for obviously the vogue of classical studies was attracting the attention of others than a few professed humanists. Dürer's portraits, which are justly famous, reveal great skill in portraying passing modes of thought. Among the more noteworthy are the portraits of himself and those of *Emperor Maximilian, Wilibald Pirkheimer, Jerome Holzschuher,* and *Hans Imhoff.* Dürer ever remained interested in popular themes, as is shown by his scenes of peasant life. One of the finest of these is a copper engraving of a peasant couple engaged in a vigorous dance. His scenes of streets and squares and skylines combine skill in depicting details with artistic aspects.

Mantegna's influence is clearly perceptible in Dürer's *Adoration of the Magi,* for the treatment of space and the use of archaeological details such as fallen buildings reveal that Dürer studied the great master of Mantua. But he avoided Mantegna's hardness in the treatment of cloths, preferring to portray their soft texture, deep color, and rich embroideries as Giovanni Bellini had done. His *Trinity* is a magnificent rendering of a heavenly host adoring the Godhead. His *Crucified Christ* shows the body of the Savior stretched on the cross against a bleak and ominous sky. The lighted horizon, which reflects his study of the Italian treatment of distant prospects, added to the gloom. His *Four Apostles* are marvelous studies of realism, expressing his firm faith in Catholic Christianity at a moment when the old Church was rent by Lutheran teaching.

Dürer's nimble mind, like Leonardo's, was interested in all the concerns of man and the phenomena of nature, as is revealed by his drawings of plants, details of the human body and parts of animals, and his landscapes. His emphasis upon line was born of a wholesome respect for form. His engraving of *Melancholy* is thought to illustrate his scientific interests. A winged female figure is seated pondering restlessly upon the problems of life which appear insoluble. She holds a compass in her hand, and other instruments, including a saw, plane, scales, ladder, and hourglass, lie by her side.

In 1520 and 1521 Dürer made his famous tour of the Low Countries. He visited the great Flemish cities and admired their artistic treasures, and made a journey to Zierikzee in Zeeland to see a stranded whale. The journal which he kept of his experiences is a justly famous document illustrating the cultural life in northern Europe. Dürer was a German *uomo universale,* the greatest artistic genius of the German Renaissance. He broke with the Gothic traditions of his predecessors, appropriated the Italian manner, and thus changed the trends of German national art.

Other painters were seeking to give more mellow effects to their pictures and were attempting color and rhythmic movement. Mathias Grünewald (d. 1530), who worked at Mainz, though Gothic in inspiration as shown in Chap. 11, reflected the influence of Venetian masters in his attempt to introduce these qualities. His *Crucifixion* scene on the altarpiece of Isenheim combined color and rhythmic action with the stark realism traditional in German Gothic art. The ashen-hued body of the dead Christ twisted out of shape, the gruesome drops of blood on the body, the torn cloth around the loins, and the bent arms of the cross give a vivid conception of the Master's last agony. Hans Burgkmair of Augsburg (1473–1531), returning in 1508 from a visit to Italy, continued this tendency to look to the achievements of Venetian masters when he began to paint in a decided Italian manner; hence his pictures with classical details and his subjects with greater softness.

All these influences helped fashion the great Renaissance artist of Germany, Hans Holbein the Younger (1497–1543). His father, Hans Holbein the Elder (d. 1524), a prolific painter, was influenced by Flemish masters, but toward the end of his days began to temper the harshness of his work by imitation of Italian pictures. His son naturally followed in his footsteps and became the greatest painter of Renaissance Germany after Dürer's death. He went to Basel in 1515 in order to gain a living as illustrator for the printers in that city. Situated at the bend of the Rhine, Basel was a natural center for trade between Italy and the north, and justly renowned because of its printing industry, the shops of Froben and Amerbach being probably the most important. Young Holbein at once won the favor of Erasmus and drew the famous sketches for an edition of his *Praise of Folly*. He also produced the ornate initials and title page drawings for several editions of the Bible. He traveled in Switzerland and visited Italy. He was impressed by the treatment of space perfected by the masters of northern Italy and adopted some of the Venetian ideas about color.

One of Holbein's striking pictures represents *Christ in the Tomb*. The Lord's body lies in the rigor of death. His eyes and mouth are open— evidently it is the neglected body of a criminal. In this way Holbein emphasized the depth of the Master's degradation. It is an impressive picture but, thanks to the softening influence of Italian art, displays little of the traditional anatomy of the macabre. Holbein also painted pictures for the well-to-do townsmen of Basel. His portraits, which also reveal careful study of Italian work, combine the meticulous care which Germans bestowed upon their work with the broader and freer conceptions of Italian masters. The portraits of Boniface Amerbach, burgomaster Jacob Meyer and his wife, Froben, and Erasmus are justly famous. He also painted larger pieces such as, for example, the great altarpiece representing Jacob Meyer and his family kneeling at the feet of the Virgin.

During these years Basel became the scene of religious tumult. The

Reformation doctrines of Martin Luther were eagerly discussed, and the more radical conceptions of Oecolampadius and Zwingli were steadily winning ground. Holbein was drawn into this conflict. The altarpiece just referred to was painted for the burgomaster as an expression of his loyalty to the traditional faith. But Holbein also drew satirical pictures pillorying ecclesiastical abuses attacked by the reformers. The painter of the German Renaissance thus became an illustrator of the Reformation. The unsettled state of civic life and the bitter dogmatic debates ruined the demand for art and Holbein decided to move to England. He was introduced by Erasmus to Sir Thomas More through whom he became acquainted with other Englishmen (1526). He returned to Basel in 1528, but in 1532 settled in London.

Holbein now began to produce pictures for the aristocratic society of the English capital. His skill as portraitist attained classical perfection as is exemplified in his pictures of Archbishop William Warham of Canterbury, Bishop John Fisher of Rochester, and Henry VIII. Holbein produced a few larger pictures during this period, of which *The Ambassadors* is especially noteworthy. He also decorated the Steelyard for the Hanseatic merchants in London. From this time dates the admirable portrait of *George Gisze*, a young merchant shown seated behind a table and surrounded with the objects generally found in business offices of the time. This famous picture illustrates most of Holbein's characteristics: stern craftsmanship, sober treatment, harmonious design and coloring, and an honest and frank regard for the truth. Holbein was the first painter north of the Alps to belong entirely to the Renaissance.

LUCAS CRANACH: ARTIST OF THE REFORMATION

Lucas Cranach (1472–1553), born in southern Germany, acquired from native masters all his skill, even his knowledge of Italian art. In 1504 he settled in Wittenberg as painter to the elector of Saxony. His chief picture is the *Flight into Egypt*. The Holy Family has halted by a stream. In the background are a birch tree and an evergreen laden with moss. A group of angels is playfully hovering about the Virgin, and one of them offers the Christ Child some strawberries. St. Joseph is a plain and honest artisan. The colors are brilliant, almost too sharp. Cranach's work is eminently sincere without rising to the greatest heights. His popularity is due mainly to the fact that he was closely associated with Luther, Melanchthon, and other prominent personages in the Lutheran revolt. In fact, it was through his art that Germans knew what Luther looked like.

THE FLEMINGS ADOPT THE ITALIAN MANNER

Flemish painters for some time had admired the ampler skill of Italian masters. Roger Van der Weyden had visited Rome in 1450, but no trace of Italian influence can be detected in his pictures. Justus of Ghent was induced to go to the court of Duke Federigo of Montefeltro of Urbino who greatly admired Flemish painting and music. Justus combined the Flemish love for intimate details with the broader and more poetic methods of Italians. Although Memlinc never visited Italy, he was deeply impressed by Italian pictures. One of his Madonnas with the Christ Child shows the Virgin seated under a round arch decorated in the Italian manner. The columns at each side are drawn after classical originals, and above are festoons of fruit and flowers. These details suggest north Italian influences. For the rest, the picture is a typical example of Memlinc's Flemish art.

The first Flemish painter to break definitely with the traditions of the Low Countries was John Gossaert, or Mabuse (1478?–1535), so-called from the fact that he came from Maubeuge. After visiting Rome in 1508 he settled in Antwerp and received commissions from members of the ruling house of the Low Countries. His pictures show a keen sense of the beauty in the nude. He was lavish in decorating the backgrounds of his larger and more ambitious pictures with meaningless architectural detail. Bernard Van Orley (d. 1542), who visited Rome not later than 1514 and again in 1527, was important because he brought Italian taste and manner to Brussels, the capital of the Low Countries. His works reveal study of Raphael and Michelangelo. Van Orley was an able master who sought to retain Flemish love for truth and exactitude of detail in spite of his admiration for the Italian tendency to idealize. Henceforth Italian style dominated Netherlandish art.

John Scorel (1495–1562) trained under Gossaert, made a journey to Italy, visiting Rome during the pontificate of Adrian VI. He settled in Utrecht and exerted much influence upon the art of the Low Countries. He painted remarkable portraits which show an Italian influence combined with a strong note of sincerity and truthfulness which later were to characterize much of Dutch art. Lucas of Leiden (1494–1533) received his training exclusively in the shops of Low Country masters. But he showed keen sympathy for pictures painted under Italian influences, and he readily adopted the methods which were coming into favor. The advent of the Italian style did not create an era of originality. Instead, artists grasped eagerly at the subtleties which came from beyond the

Alps and allowed what was good in their native art to slip away. To be called a *Flemish Raphael* was the highest ambition of Flemish painters.

Antonio More (d. 1575) was a pupil of Scorel in Utrecht. He developed a strongly individualistic style in portraiture, being most successful in the treatment of eyes, mouth, and hands. This was necessary in an age which appreciated the psychological portraits of Leonardo da Vinci and other Italians. He received commissions from Philip II and painted portraits of personages prominent in Spanish and Netherlands political life. More was the ablest portraitist in the Low Countries before Rubens.

One artist refused to submit to Italian influence. Peter Brueghel (1528–1569) of Brabant was trained under native masters and did not visit Italy until 1551. He studied Italian art but never tried to imitate it, preferring to cling to traditional Flemish ideas and themes. Although he profited much from study of Italian form, he ever remained a Fleming. He loved the countryside of Brabant and Flanders and knew better than any other artist the simple life of peasants and other common folk. He loved to paint village fairs, pilgrimages, weddings, and witches' sabbats, and to illustrate proverbs. His powers as a satirist are shown in his *Blind Beggars* which illustrates a popular saying. A blind man leading five other blind men is falling into a ditch. The sightless faces are drawn with the utmost realism. Brueghel also criticized the Spanish regime in the Low Countries. In the *Massacre of the Innocents* he shows Spanish soldiers slaying Flemish children. Flemish parents are scurrying about along the main street of a Flemish village frantically seeking to escape with their infants. The ground and roofs are covered with snow, and the gloomy sky adds to the tragedy. The *Census at Bethlehem* also illustrates this tendency to criticize the policy of political superiors. Brueghel, the greatest artistic genius of Flanders in his day, thus clung close to his native soil and to his people, as did his contemporaries Rabelais and Shakespeare.

RENAISSANCE ART IN FRANCE

French painting remained peculiarly barren of noteworthy achievement during the age of the Renaissance. The expedition of Charles VIII into Italy in 1494 and 1495 aroused little interest in painting. The king and his soldiers were deeply impressed by the spacious architecture of Italian houses and public buildings and by the voluptuous character of Italian life, but they were too engaged in their military enterprise to note the magnificent achievements of Italian sculptors and painters. Louis XII possessed little appreciation for these things, although he did make an unsuccessful attempt to induce Leonardo da Vinci to come to France.

Francis I was a pleasure-loving monarch with a superficial understanding of the new art and learning. While he was able in a measure to stimulate the latter, his efforts to do something for painting were restricted to patronizing foreign, mostly Italian, artists. He invited the Florentine Andrea del Sarto (1486–1531) to come to France and rewarded him liberally. Il Rosso (1494–1541) and Francesco Primaticcio (1504–1570) were employed at the royal chateau of Fontainebleau. A school of artists grew up around these men, and thus the new art found its way into France. Leonardo da Vinci came to Amboise at the royal invitation. He painted the charming *Madonna and Child in the Lap of St. Anna* which illustrates the subtle craft of the great master. But Leonardo's health was declining, and he died in 1519 and was buried in Amboise. Portraiture flourished in the court and among the aristocracy, but little of its best work was due to French genius. The most noteworthy work was done by one John Clouet, of Brussels, and his son François. The father produced the portrait of Francis I. His son is noted for his pictures of Elizabeth of Austria, Diana of Poitiers, and Mary Stuart. These portraits are executed with a rare grace and delicacy and illustrate the Renaissance dissatisfaction with the social crudities of former times. The frank realism of the pictures of earlier years was abandoned in favor of humanist idealization.

Sculpture of the High Renaissance also had its devotees outside Italy, especially in France. Francis I handsomely rewarded the versatile Benvenuto Cellini who made a number of gold articles for the court. His saltcellar, dishes, ewers, and the bronze nymph for the palace at Fontainebleau revealed to Frenchmen some of the glories of Italian workmanship at the height of its perfection. Jean Goujon (d. 1565?), a Frenchman, produced the magnificent *Diana and the Deer*, now in the Louvre. Another of his famous creations is the set of sculptured water nymphs made for the fountain in the Place des Innocents in Paris. Their sinuous forms and the rhythmical arrangement of garments and body were inspired by classical conceptions. But Goujon was no slavish imitator, for he tried to combine foreign ideas with native French feeling for concreteness and reality.

Italian elegance and subtle forms now began to be seen in the old funereal sculpture which was so popular during the declining Middle Ages. The rigidity of Gothic figures disappears. The sarcophagi are placed in an open structure surrounded by columns or pilasters supporting a large marble slab. While the effigy of the departed lies recumbent upon the coffin, on the top of the sepulcher appears the same draped figure kneeling in prayer. In the niches and on the corners are seated figures representing the theological virtues or the prophets. This was the sort of tomb prepared for Louis XII and his queen, Anne of Brittany, by some Italian workers named Justi about whom little is known. This structure was placed in the ancient abbatial church of St. Denis and served as a model for the tomb of Francis I, which was designed in the form of a triumphal arch by Philibert Delorme (1515?–1570). Germain Pilon (1535–1590), who played an important role in the history of this funereal art, prepared the tomb of Henry II which also is in St. Denis. The forms of the departed, on the coffins, the praying figures of the royal couple, and the four virtues—Justice, Prudence, Temperance, and Faith— were executed by his hand. Pilon was not entirely overwhelmed by Italian love for the perfection of classical forms, for these figures possess strong realism. Old and native French feeling for truth and nature thus were chastened by the Italian cult of the ideally beautiful. This striking trait is observable in the portrait bust of Henry intended for the tomb. Pilon also prepared the monument for the hearts of the royal pair. Female figures representing the *Three Graces* or the *Three Virtues* support a receptacle for the hearts. Their superbly modeled forms are scantily dressed as if they are prepared for the dance. The work of Goujon and Pilon broke completely with the Middle Ages.

ENGLAND SLOWLY ADOPTS RENAISSANCE IDEAS IN PAINTING

England made practically no contributions to Renaissance painting. Her native talent remained backward, wherefore King Henry VIII, it is said, invited Raphael, Primaticcio, and even Titian to England. But it was impossible to entice any of the great Italians to a land which was still regarded as provincial. A few Italian artists, however, were employed by the court and the aristocracy. Meanwhile the works of Low Country artists appealed to Englishmen. Pictures by Massys and Gossaert were admired, and a number of minor Netherlands masters sought work in England. But Hans Holbein was the only significant artist who gladly spent his mature years there. The religious difficulties which began under Henry VIII and became a chief factor in national life under Edward VI, Mary Tudor, and Elizabeth were unfavorable to the development of native painting. Puritan bitterness toward most traditional medieval religious art destroyed the foundations of painting as they had been developed during the closing Middle Ages. Foreign masters, for the most part Netherlanders, continued to be imported, chief among these the excellent portraitist Antonio More of Utrecht.

SPANISH PAINTING OF THE RENAISSANCE

Painting in Spain and Portugal during the sixteenth century remained closely wedded to traditional methods and themes. The faith was more closely identified with national life in Spain than in any other land of Europe. Hostility toward Moor and Jew strengthened traditional medieval piety and retarded the tendency toward secularization of art. Native forces were dominated by Flemish methods introduced in the days of John van Eyck and Roger Van der Weyden, and by the increasing patriotic religiousness under Charles I and Philip II. While Italian ideas found their way into the peninsula, they generally fell on uncongenial soil. Among the more interesting Spanish painters of this period was Luis de Morales (1517–1586), generally called *The Divine*. His work is typical of the strongly primitive or late medieval conceptions which flourished without restriction in Spain. His Madonnas, Crucifixions, and Mater Dolorosas were very popular. Spain did not feel the full force of Italian superiority until the original and creative genius, El Greco (d. 1614), trained under Titian and other Venetians, began his work in Seville. Meanwhile Netherlands skill continued in demand. Antonio More of Utrecht became painter to Philip II and produced many fine portraits. He may be regarded as the originator of the Spanish school of psychological portraitists.

INFLUENCE OF RENAISSANCE SCULPTURE

Italian Renaissance sculpture was slow to influence European workmanship. The Low Countries, for example, contributed little to Renaissance sculpture. The sculptors of these lands adapted the new ideas to the old Gothic style which died a reluctant death. Choir stalls, baptismal fonts, furniture, rood screens, and tombs now began to be executed in a florid and somewhat heavy manner which characterized the art of the Netherlands from then on. The career of Giovanni Bologna (d. 1608) of Douai was especially important. He was inspired by his Netherlandish masters to study in Italy, whither he went about 1550. He fell completely under the influence of Michelangelo and developed the vicious mannerism which spoiled the work of so many of that master's followers. Vigorous and twisting forms were freely employed with no attempt to give them adequate psychological expression. The result was unfortunate, for it imparted to Low Country sculpture a heaviness and a labored quality which should have been avoided.

England created as little in sculpture as in painting. Flemish masters who had learned something about Italian form soon began to find favor in that country. Pietro Torrigiano (1472–1528) made the sepulchers of Henry VII and his mother, the Countess Margaret, which stand in King Henry's Chapel in Westminster Abbey.

Gothic sculpture in Germany began to succumb to Italian competition by the beginning of the sixteenth century. This was inevitable because of the frequent contact between southern Germany and Italy. Here as in other lands late Gothic and new Renaissance methods and motifs continued to exist side by side. Nuremberg became the chief center of sculptural activity because of the labors of Adam Krafft (d. 1509) and Veit Stoss (d. 1533?). But the great sculptor of the transition was Peter Vischer (1460–1529). He is responsible for a number of sepulchral works, of which the bronze tomb of St. Sebald in St. Sebald's Church in Nuremberg, made between 1507 and 1519, is the most famous. The old reliquary was placed in an open shrine, the details of which show an interesting mingling of Gothic and Renaissance forms. Three domes supported by eight piers bearing the twelve apostles constitute the upper part. On the lower section, the foundation upon which the reliquary rests, are sculptured scenes from the life of St. Sebald. The statues, which undoubtedly reveal the artist's greatest skill, betray careful study of Italian mastery of facial expression. bodily posture, and clothing.

Gradually Renaissance conceptions supplanted the traditional methods and ideas of Gothic masters. Alexander Colin (1529?–1612) brought the new ideas from Flanders to Innsbruck where he helped construct the great tomb for Emperor Maximilian. Hubert Gerhard, a Low Country sculptor who was greatly influenced by Giovanni Bologna, received many commissions, and it was through him that the Italian style definitely conquered the country. His chief work is the Augustus fountain erected in 1593 in front of the town hall of Augsburg.

Spanish sculpture, like painting, was strongly dominated by the political and religious characteristics of the Spanish people. Flemish ideas exercised an important influence, but less than in the fifteenth century. The Italian manner was first introduced by Alonso Berruguete (1480?–1561). From 1502 to 1520 he studied in Italy, becoming thoroughly acquainted with the work of Michelangelo and other artists, and on his return to Spain he was appointed painter and sculptor to King Charles. Berruguete combined love for concrete form with Spanish religious sentiment. His *San Sebastian* is the figure of a youth whose face reveals a deep longing to be freed from the fate which impends. Berruguete also brought Italian ideas about sepulchral architecture to Spain and had many imitators who dominated Spanish sculpture for the next generation.

EUROPEAN RENAISSANCE ARCHITECTURE

Italian Renaissance architecture first spread to France during the reign of Charles VIII. The king, admiring the spaciousness of the buildings which he saw along the route to Naples, brought back with him a group of Italian architects whom he supported liberally. The chief of these, Fra Giovanni Giocondo (1433?–1515), a pupil of Luca Signorelli, was a learned humanist as well as a practical architect. He and the other Italians lived at Amboise, one of the royal country residences which Charles was eager to transform into a magnificent chateau. The old castles which had been practical in the tumultuous feudal past were now antiquated. The power of the crown was no longer challenged by the feudality, peace reigned throughout the countryside, and the military residences in which the aristocracy were living were no longer necessary. More light, air, and space were desired. Greater aesthetic satisfaction was demanded. The Renaissance chateaux of France built under Charles VIII, Louis XII, and Francis I are therefore interesting monuments of the Renaissance.

The chateau of Amboise remained a Gothic structure in spite of the presence of Italian artists, although some of the decorations were derived from Italy. Building made little more progress under Louis XII who constructed a wing of the chateau at Blois along Gothic lines. But great changes were introduced by Francis I. That pleasure-loving prince needed greater room, and he built another wing which was decorated in the manner of the Renaissance. But even in this Gothic ideas were retained. The chateau of Chambord, however, which was one of Francis' favorites, contains a greater profusion of Renaissance decoration than any of the others. The chateau of Fontainebleau, begun in 1528, was also a great favorite with the king. The chateau at Azay-le-Rideau probably illustrates as well as any the perfect style of the period. The steep roof with its graceful dormer windows and the round corners of the structure give a pleasing effect. Francis also built the Louvre on the site of a medieval castle which dated as far back as the days of Philip Augustus. Its plans were drawn by Pierre Lescot (d. 1578), the greatest architect of the realm. Italian ideas were freely employed. Columns were used and windows alternated with pilasters. The decorations were carefully executed after Renaissance models. This impressive structure is worthy of a place beside the palaces of Rome or any other Italian city.

Spanish architecture also yielded to the charm of the Renaissance, but more stubbornly. The Moors of Spain possessed their own architecture characterized by an extraordinary profusion of ornamental detail. This style naturally influenced the flamboyant Gothic architecture of Spain. Churches were decorated with the utmost wealth of curious detail. Gradually Renaissance ideas made themselves felt, especially in Castile. The façade of the University of Alcalá, an early home of humanist learning in Spain, was clearly inspired by Italian ideas. The Escorial, built by Philip II between 1563 and 1584, is an immense royal dwelling revealing Renaissance influences in the gigantic Doric pilasters at the entrance and at many points in the interior.

Gothic architecture in northern Europe yielded slowly to the invasion of the Italian manner. Renaissance building naturally won a foothold in southern Germany in the lands situated near the Brenner, and such towns as Augsburg, Nuremberg, and Rothenburg began to erect buildings according to the newer ideas. Town halls, bourgeois dwellings, churches, and chapels were built. The first definitely Renaissance chapel to be constructed in Germany was that belonging to the Fugger family in Augsburg. German princes, particularly those of Bavaria, adopted the new ideas. This tendency became stronger during the days of the Catholic reaction. From Bavaria, chief citadel of the Catholic faith, Renaissance art flowed to other parts of Germany. Italian influences also penetrated into northern Germany and Scandinavia, but more slowly. The town hall of Cologne is an interesting monument dating from about 1570. The first Renaissance building in the Low Countries was a palace in Mechelen (1517), but the most significant building in all the Low Countries to be erected along Renaissance lines was the town hall of Antwerp, which was finished in 1565. Flemish architecture of this period exerted much influence upon Rhenish Germany. The new ideas about buildings penetrated more slowly into England.

LESSER RENAISSANCE ARTS IN EUROPE

Besides the major arts of painting, sculpture, and architecture a few of the lesser ought to be noted. The tapestry industry flourished in Brabant, Flanders, and Artois, commissions being received from Germany, Italy, France, England, and elsewhere for the magnificent product of the Low Country looms. The tapestries of the Sistine Chapel were executed on the looms of Brussels according to Raphael's cartoons, and Bernard Van Orley also made many designs for such tapestries. These articles of luxury were in great demand among the nobility and the bourgeoisie which was rapidly becoming more and more wealthy. All sorts of scenes, Biblical, classical, and medieval, were executed upon them. From the Low Countries this profitable industry was introduced into France by Francis I who established a factory at Fontainebleau, but it was not until the next century that the tapestry industry began to flourish in France.

Ceramics also made some progress in northern Europe. The bourgeoisie was tired of the rough dark-colored pottery and dishes which were in common use, if we may judge from the pictures of ordinary life by Peter Brueghel and his successors. Well-to-do folk were eager for better things and welcomed the beautiful majolica ware of Italy. Bernard Palissy (d. 1589?) of Saintonge, who greatly admired Italian ware and worked hard to learn the secret of its manufacture, experimented with glazes, and produced some beautiful results. His platters and other dishes are covered with leaves, plants, fishes, snakes, lizards, and all sorts of animals, and they became immensely popular. Some of this ware was intended purely for decorative purposes, for these pieces illustrated classical themes and pleased the humanist bourgeoisie as did the *Adages* of Erasmus.

PART XII

Northern Humanism from Erasmus to Shakespeare

Chapter 26

BEGINNINGS OF HUMANISM IN NORTHERN EUROPE

NORTHERN EUROPE gradually succumbed to the charm of the new Renaissance thought of Italy. In spite of the fact that north of the Alps commerce was expanding, cities were becoming more populous, great reserves of capital were forming, and powerful monarchical states were coming into being, the attitude toward problems of life generally had remained conservative. Education was dominated by the old ideals. Students were interested in theology, philosophy, medicine, and Roman law. Literature was concerned with the traditional themes of chivalry, piety, and religion. Intellectual progress had fallen behind the social and economic advance of the age. It bore the impress of the Middle Ages and had not yet begun to consider the problems of the new era. Readjustment was inevitable. Italian culture during the *Quattrocento* and the High Renaissance supplied a needed impetus in changing the old and everywhere exercised profound influence. In all branches of activity Europe became a province of Italian civilization. Many things were borrowed which enabled the new states to develop their national and secular cultures. Humanist ideals, pronouncedly patriotic in Italy, tended to stir the critical zeal of German students.

HUMANIST IDEALS PROPAGATED BY GERMAN
STUDENTS: THE PATRIOTIC MOTIF

Italian humanism had found its way into Germany as early as the days of Petrarch. This was inevitable because of the close political connections between Germany and Italy. Furthermore, merchants from the great cities of southern Germany carried on a busy traffic through the Brenner Pass with the cities of northern Italy. As Augsburg, Ulm, Munich, Strasbourg, Frankfort on the Main, Nuremberg, and Vienna became wealthy, their burghers could not help feeling the charm of the social, artistic, and intellectual life of the south. Students from the many universities of Germany went to Italian schools, especially at Padua which was situated near the southern end of the Brenner Pass. Impatient with the pedantry of German teachers who taught traditional things in traditional ways, some of them returned filled with the spirit of revolt.

One of the first of Germany's young men to lead the life of a roving apostle was Peter Luder (d. 1474?). Born about 1415, he early went to Rome as a cleric, wandered far and wide, and finally settled at the University of Padua where he found a congenial company of south German youths. One of them recommended Luder to the elector of the Palatinate who in 1444 appointed him as professor in classical languages and literature at the University of Heidelberg. His colleagues, disliking this innovation and fearful of the reception which the new studies might have, were ill disposed toward him, and sought to censor the manuscript of his introductory lecture and even to deny him access to the university library. He was an energetic protagonist of Latin studies and against the ancient accusation of immorality and paganism stoutly argued that the classics were capable of exerting an ennobling influence. He made many enemies because of this policy and because of his scant regard for religion. He was a spendthrift, always poor, and a hard drinker. In spite of his many talents he failed to exert an abiding influence on German humanism. Driven from Heidelberg by the plague in 1460, he returned to Padua to study medicine and subsequently taught at Basel and Vienna.

Conrad Celtes (1459–1508) was one of the most typical of the roving scholars who frequented the universities. Like other German youths, he wandered from school to school and went to Italy where he perfected his knowledge of Greek, collected manuscripts, and acquainted himself with the trends of humanist learning. On his return to Germany in 1487 he received the poet's crown in Nuremberg. Next he went to the Polish University of Cracow in order to study science, that is, mathematics and astronomy. It was then that he began his feverish career as a wandering humanist. Everywhere he became the center of those who admired humanist learning, or poetry as it was called. Old-fashioned professors distrusted him and tolerated him grudgingly, but the free spirits of the time listened to him. Finally, in 1497, he accepted a post in the University of Vienna where he became the leading force among the youths who were eager for humanist learning, and led in establishing the famous humanist club known as the Danubian Sodality. Grandiose schemes were hatched in his brain. He wanted to edit classical and medieval historical writings.

Being intensely patriotic, as was common among German humanists, Celtes conceived the idea of publishing a vast historical description of his native land. It was called *Germania Illustrata*, doubtlessly inspired by Flavio Biondo's similar works on Italy and Rome. However, Celtes never accomplished much, for his energies were expended in magnificent dreams, in stirring up students, and preaching a new cause. His poetry is a significant product of the new age, and in it he imitated to great perfection the verse and language of Horace. Like this great master of the days of Augustus Caesar, Celtes advocated a life of pleasure and enjoyment of secular things. His love of poetry often becomes erotic; his passion is not always uplifting. There were other humanists at the universities, but Luder and Celtes must suffice as examples.

HUMANISM AT THE COURTS OF GERMANY

Humanism found its way also into the court life of the century. Emperor Frederick III (1440–1492), however, felt no attraction for the new learning, preferring the study of astrology, alchemy, and chivalry, the care of his stables, and the practical concerns of his office. Aeneas Sylvius Piccolomini, later Pope Pius II (1458–1464), went to his court as ambassador of Pope Eugenius IV (1431–1447) in order to win imperial support against the Council of Basel. Piccolomini found Germany a very uncongenial place, for the nobility was interested in the customary chivalric ideals, and all life was dominated by medieval conceptions. Nevertheless, his sojourn from 1442 to 1445 was significant, for it gave Germans a glimpse of the broader intellectual life which was developing under Italian skies.

Emperor Maximilian (1493–1519) was especially significant as a humanist ruler. He was conscious of the greatness of the imperial dignity, a glory which extended back to the days of the Roman Caesars. He was a man of great personal charm, affable, and able to appreciate the new art and literature, and his restless activity captured the imagination of the

German people. He was able to divine the vague and subtle aspirations of the Germans. His success was due to these personal qualities and not to the resources of the imperial power. Although, owing to the rapid evolution of capitalism, royal power in other states was creating a new type of absolute state, the crown of Germany failed at this critical moment to subject the land to its autocratic will. The empire became a group of practically independent states and imperial cities. There was no imperial army, taxation, administration, or effective justice. Consequently Maximilian was unable to reduce the Swiss, oppose the French, maintain his rights in Lombardy, or retain the properties of his wife, Mary of Burgundy. In spite of his failures, Maximilian better than any other expressed the nationalist sentiments of the Germans.

His court became a center of humanist activity, for Maximilian burned to excel as a humanist. Poets and enthusiasts over classical letters hurried to his court and received gifts from the impecunious emperor, often being crowned by him. Maximilian loved to set the vogue of literary appreciation, and he caused to be written a tedious poetical allegory, the *Theuerdank*, relating to his courtship of Mary of Burgundy whom he married in 1477. The *Weisskunig*, or *The White King*, which was dictated by him, contains an account of his princely deeds. Although these works contained much that was medieval in spirit, they nevertheless reveal how the emperor had caught the ideal of princely leadership in culture which was common in Italy.

HUMANISM IN THE GERMAN CITIES

Humanism flourished in the more prosperous urban centers of southern Germany. Situated on the roads of traffic from Rhenish and other German lands to the Brenner Pass, Augsburg became a wealthy trading metropolis of immense importance and the German capital of fifteenth-century finance. The family of Fugger possessed banking establishments here and in many other European cities. This house rose from obscurity at the close of the fourteenth century and became identified with many phases of German economic life. Jacob Fugger (1459–1525), its most prominent representative, became very rich by investing money in trade in oriental articles which came by way of the Cape of Good Hope and Lisbon. He lent money to emperors, popes, and princes, and collected books, appreciated art, and built palaces. The Welser family, like the Fuggers, had long lived in Augsburg. In 1473 four brothers formed a banking house which carried on an active business with the needy rulers of the Hapsburg house and financed many businesses. Independent branches of the Welser

house opened offices in Ulm and Nuremberg. Hans Paumgartner, Sigismund Gossenbrot, and Ambrosius Hochstetter also were important finan-
ciers of Augsburg. All these firms maintained close relations with Emperor
Maximilian who constantly needed great sums of money with which to
finance his many wars and who repeatedly pledged his mining property
in Tyrol for them to exploit. These firms established branches in Antwerp
when that center became the northern mart for the articles of luxury
which were brought to Lisbon by Portuguese sailors who jealously controlled the new route to India.

These burghers of Augsburg were strongly attracted to the new secular
culture which was rising in Italy. Sigismund Gossenbrot (1417–1488?),
burgomaster of Nuremberg from 1458, championed the new learning and
in 1452 began a long polemic with an old-fashioned professor in the University of Vienna who bitterly opposed the growing prestige of such
humanist writers as Poggio Bracciolini and Lorenzo Valla. This contest
is an example of the bitter antagonism between men of the old order and
the younger generation who revolted against the aridity of traditional
thought and education. Conrad Peutinger (1465–1547) belonged to a
younger generation and was an even more fiery exponent of humanist
thought. He studied in Italy and in 1485 returned with a doctor's degree,
his mind steeped in the new learning. He at once entered political life and
served his native Augsburg in many ways. He repeatedly visited Italy
and became a confidential adviser of Emperor Maximilian who found it
necessary to keep on intimate terms with the moneyed aristocracy of
Augsburg.

Peutinger was an interesting example of the practical character of the
Renaissance in Germany. He did not devote his time exclusively to the
study of the classics; he remained an active man of affairs, never despising, or affecting to despise, simple bread-and-butter activities, as did some
Italian humanists. He was an enthusiastic collector of antiquities and his
house harbored coins, manuscripts, and other objects of the classical past.
He possessed an old map of the military roads of the western Roman
Empire dating from classical times. It was discovered by Conrad Celtes
and is known to this day as the *Tabula Peutingeriana*. But his zeal for
classical antiquity did not prevent him from being a patriotic German and
an enthusiastic collector of German chronicles. He also became the center
of a coterie of young humanists and acted as a sort of literary Maecenas.
His conservative character is shown by his great interest in theology, a
characteristic of nearly all German humanists, which differentiated them
sharply from Italian scholars.

Nuremberg became a noteworthy center of humanist culture, Wilibald

Pirckheimer (1470–1528) being its most prominent representative. His father John had long been a keen admirer of humanist thought, and it was due to him that the youth was sent to the universities of Padua and Pavia. Wilibald was supposed to study Roman civil law but, like so many of the more wide-awake youths of the day, preferred the classical languages and literature. His subsequent career was much like that of Peutinger. He became a councilor of the government of Nuremberg, was sent on numerous ambassadorial missions, and was intimate with Emperor Maximilian. He dearly loved the German fatherland and eagerly read its history, but he never wearied of poring over the ancient classics, and he made translations of Greek authors. He wrote much on politics, literature, and history. He was also an able pamphleteer and is supposed to have penned a biting satirical diatribe against John Eck, the opponent of Martin Luther. His sisters also were interested in the new ideas of the day —Charitas (d. 1532) read Latin classics and even conversed in the polished Latin of Cicero. She became abbess of a convent in Nuremberg and was one of the first German women to illustrate what humanism could accomplish for womankind.

HUMANISM AND PIETISM IN THE LOW COUNTRIES

Northern Germany also became a center of humanist culture, but here it did not originate in any princely court or among wealthy bourgeois families as in southern Germany. Following the death of Gerhard Groot of Deventer in 1384, the Brethren of the Common Life opened many schools in the towns of the Low Countries and adjacent parts of Germany. In those days the Low Countries were politically a part of the German empire, and, although culturally these lands bore some resemblance to Germany, they revealed many special features. The schools of the Brethren of the Common Life as a rule were excellently organized and very efficient, devoted to medieval conceptions of piety and morality. Thus they stood aloof from the secular ideals which characterized the schools of Italy. This conservatism, however, could not last, for, even before the middle of the fourteenth century, men of humanist learning appeared among the Brethren and began to introduce some of the newer learning. Wessel Gansfort (1419?–1489), for example, was one of their pupils. Brought up in the pious surroundings of the school in Zwolle, he early acquired that deep piety which characterized him ever after and became an important force among his contemporaries. His career will be outlined in a later chapter.

The school of the Brethren at Deventer early became famous. Its great teacher, Alexander Hegius (1433–1498), was conservative by nature, holding fast to the old while testing the new. During his office as rector the enrollment of the school grew so that more than 2200 youths received tuition under him. He was eminently pious, leading a devout life in accordance with the *devotio moderna* under which he had been brought up, and trying to practice charity as Christ had enjoined. But he also believed that his students should acquire a pure Latinity like that of Cicero. His zeal as a teacher led him to see many defects in the customary grammars and other textbooks, and he advocated thorough improvement in them. Under the influence of teachers like Hegius many youths received their first lessons in the improved learning of humanists, at the same time remaining attached to the old lessons of simple and devout piety inculcated by the *devotio moderna*.

Rudolf Agricola (1442–1485) was one of the most noteworthy pupils of the school at Deventer. Born near Groningen, he came under the influence of the Brethren, revealed special aptitude in classical languages, and developed a remarkably clear Latinity. He studied in Louvain where he obtained a master's degree, and then proceeded to Paris and Italy. He became acquainted with Reuchlin, it is said. Pedagogy was his prime interest, and he burned to bring to Germany the best methods of humanist teaching. Studying in Rome and Ferrara, he gained such proficiency in Greek that his fame spread throughout Italy. He returned to Germany in 1480 but, finding no congenial surroundings, felt like a stranger. He spent some time in the town of Groningen which finally sent him to the imperial court where he tarried for 6 months. In 1482 he was appointed to a post in the University of Heidelberg and enjoyed the cultivated environment of the elector's court. Agricola translated Greek classics into Latin and wrote pedagogical treatises which exerted wide influence and were often reprinted. His conceptions were those of the Italian humanists. He believed that Latin should be the basic language in education and that students should be carefully trained in it. Its mastery was to be acquired through industrious study, use of the memory, and constant exercise. Agricola also urged the study of Hebrew for he believed it indispensable to a correct understanding of Scripture.

Rudolf Von Langen, a pupil of the school in Deventer, reformed the cathedral school of Münster in 1500. The improvement which came from the teaching of the Brethren of the Common Life was effectively furthered by Von Langen's successor John Murmellius (1480–1517), a master who also had studied at Deventer. Another school was opened in Alsatian Schlettstadt in 1441. Its founder was Lewis Dringenberg (d. 1490), a native of Westphalia who had received some of his education at Deventer.

He served as rector of the school at Schlettstadt and was very influential, many remarkable pupils coming under his tuition.

John Wimpheling (1450–1528) was educated in the school of Schlettstadt and studied at the University of Heidelberg. He became a staunch advocate of reform in the Church which he believed was suffering from unworthy priests and unfaithful friars. Such was his zeal in this matter that he loudly opposed all who resisted the idea of cleansing the Church of vicious practices. His pamphlet, *De Integritate,* or *On Clerical Purity,* criticized the regular clergy who never forgave him his strictures upon their worldly lives. He also satirized the excessive subtleties of old-fashioned professors in the universities. Like Luther he complained of the mercenary methods employed by the Roman curia to collect vast sums of money from Germany. Intensely patriotic like most German humanists, in 1505 he wrote an *Epitome of German History.* Wimpheling also was an eager student of the classics, as well as one of Germany's greatest pedagogues. As became a humanist, he held that all classes of the population should be educated. A number of treatises appeared, designed to instill respect for learning among princely groups. He urged the common people to abandon their banal popular life, to become educated, to develop a mastery of the German tongue, and to cultivate religious knowledge. He also advocated the development of a choice Latinity and careful study of the Latin classics, and to this end opened a Latin school in Strasbourg. Wimpheling is an excellent example of the practical character of German humanists.

CRITICISM OF CURRENT ABUSES TOUCHING RELIGION AND LEARNING

Sebastian Brant (1457–1521), a close friend of Wimpheling, helped him in his polemics against old-fashioned men who opposed the study of classical authors. He ardently cultivated the Latin language and became a leading member of the coterie of humanists which lived in Strasbourg. His great reputation was won with the *Narren-schiff,* or *Ship of Fools,* a long poem in which he criticized and satirized the manners and morals of the day. Sin is represented as folly, and all sorts of fools are discussed. Of astrology, that outworn intellectual science, he had the following to say:

> A Christian true should never heed
> Base heathen arts of any creed:
> One can't by scanning planets say
> If this be our propitious day

> For business, war, or marrying
> For friendship or for anything.
> Whate'er we've done, where'er we've trod,
> Our conduct should rely on God
> He lacks a faith in God's creation
> Who trusts in any constellation. . . .

On Jack Sans Care who never reflected upon the vision of Death so common a theme in late medieval thought, Brant commented:

> His name is truly Jack Sans Care;
> Whom Death would grasp, let him beware,
> If he be young or fair or strong
> He'll take to leaping high and long,
> And this I call the leap of death,
> He'll sweat, freeze, writhe, and hold his breath
> And like a worm will twist and wiggle
> And finally will writhe and jiggle
> O Death, thy power is quite untold,
> Thou snatchest off the young and old,
> O Death, thy name is execration. . . .[1]

As compared with the refined verse of Pulci and Ariosto, the stanzas of Brant are decidedly inferior. Their significance lies in their earnest moral satire which was not lost on the people.

John Geiler of Kaisersberg (1445–1510), an intimate friend of Brant and Wimpheling, became famous as a penitential preacher in Strasbourg. He vigorously attacked abuses in Church and society and even drew texts for his sermons from Brant's *Ship of Fools*. Although he was interested in humanist learning, he remained wedded to the past, cautiously feeling his way. John Trithemius (1462–1516) also was a product of the pedagogical humanists of Deventer and Alsace. A precocious youth, he studied at Heidelberg, and became proficient in Greek and Hebrew, receiving instruction from Celtes and Reuchlin. In 1482 he entered the Benedictine monastery of Sponheim and soon became abbot. Like Reuchlin he was interested in cabalistic thought and wrote some treatises on it, some of which were none too orthodox. He shared in the belief in witchcraft which was general at the time, and some of his books are remarkable monuments of this folly. Although his views sometimes were traditional, he was a humanist; he was patriotic, was earnestly interested in history, and an eager student of chronicles. He also criticized the society of his

---

[1] *The Ship of Fools*, tr. by E. H. Zeydel, New York, 1944, pp. 217, 279. Quoted with permission of the publisher, Columbia University Press.

day, finding much fault with the nobility and even with the bourgeois capitalists whose importance he failed to understand.

Humanism also flourished in other centers. Cologne was centrally situated in the lower valley of the Rhine and wandering humanists often visited it. The University of Cologne was an old-fashioned place, adhering strictly to traditional ways. Its theological faculty was very conservative and hostile to new ideas, especially those of the humanists. Ortwin Gratius (1491–1542) was one of the better-known professors in the university. Educated by the Brethren of the Common Life, he was attracted to the new learning but remained conservative in all his views on life. He carried on a sharp polemic against a humanist who had been trained in Italy and who claimed that theologians so neglected the study of letters that they could not interpret Scripture adequately.

A group of humanists led by Conrad Mutianus Rufus (1471–1526) came into existence at Erfurt and Gotha, after Martin Luther left the University of Erfurt. Although brought up in the school at Deventer, Mutianus embraced the conceptions of Italian humanism when he studied in Italy. He accepted the mystical Platonic interpretation of the Christian faith which had become popular in Italy after the passing of Mirandola and Ficino. These highly speculative conceptions, he argued, could be understood by philosophers and humanists but remained a sealed book to the multitude; it was therefore necessary to teach them the facts of the Christian religion as it had evolved historically. His Platonism caused him to take an ethical view of religion; hence he rebuked the clergy for their unworthiness, criticized the crude ideas of the common people, and in general was opposed to formal and external acts of faith.

THE CRITICISM OF ULRICH VON HUTTEN

Mutianus inspired a number of young men, especially Ulrich von Hutten (1488–1523). Born into a noble family, von Hutten was brought up in the antiquated ideas of chivalry. He soon found his lessons irksome at the monastic school of Fulda and fled to Mutianus at Erfurt. He became acquainted with other humanists and found their thought as agreeable to his nature as the old-fashioned schooling in Fulda was distasteful. Rejected by his irate father when he fled Fulda, von Hutten began the restless wandering of a humanist, and, reduced to penury, he arrived at the University of Greifswald. Here he was mistrusted by one of the professors whose servants robbed him of his scanty clothes. Next he appeared in Rostock where he wrote a bitter diatribe upon the professor. His *Elegies*, Latin poems setting forth the thoughts which swarmed in his mind, were written during these trying days. He also penned a poem on versification. Like other humanists, he was patriotic, and, resenting the epithet, barbarians, which Italians were wont to hurl at people of his nationality, he wrote a poem to prove Germany's equality with other nations.

He tried to lecture at Vienna where this poem was written, but was prevented by the jealous professors "because he did not possess a degree." Next he appeared in Padua, poverty stricken, afflicted with the mortal Neapolitan disease and his legs covered with hideous sores. His indomitable will drove him ever onward, and he soon appeared in Bologna. This brief visit to Italy proved important, for von Hutten saw at first-hand the rivalry between France and the emperor in Lombardy. Hitherto he had been concerned primarily with the literary aspects of humanism, but now he became feverishly interested in politics. He poured out the vials of his wrath upon France:

> Why is he [France] flying away, comb bleeding and feathers dishevelled,
> He the proud cock and the valiant, the dread of the birds all around him?
> Why but because he preferred the din and the clamour of battle,
> Thinking to win o'er the eagle [Germany] a victory easy and sure.
> Little he measured his foe: he bore it awhile and was patient:
> But when his rage was aroused he defended himself with his talons.
> Truly, ill fares it with those who rashly dare to offend him.
> Better to make him a friend than be crushed by the might of his anger. . . .[2]

Von Hutten also attacked the pope, for he had seen Julius II carry on war like a secular prince and lay siege to the town of Mirandola in Lombardy. Angered by this debasement of the pope's high office, he did not hesitate to attack indulgences, mercenary issuance of bulls, and papal morals in general. By 1514 he was back in Germany, still rejected by his family and consorting with humanists. He carried on a typically chivalric feud with the duke of Württemberg from 1515–1517 which was begun by the murder of one of von Hutten's family. Thereupon followed his second visit to Italy (1516–1517), during which he studied in Bologna and Ferrara and visited Venice. He became more proficient in Greek and formed a deep appreciation for the satirist Lucian. This was important, for on his return to Germany he became that country's greatest satirist.

After 1517 Ulrich von Hutten continued his vagrant humanist life. He visited Augsburg in the summer of 1517, immediately after his second visit to Italy, and was crowned with the poet's laurel by Emperor Maximilian. In his patriotic frenzy he now attacked the pope. Soon he was attracted to Luther because of the latter's quarrel with Tetzel over indulgences.

---

[2] D. Straus, *Ulrich von Hutten, His Life and Times*, London, 1874, p. 51.

Von Hutten's later career will be discussed in connection with the Reformation.

JOHN REUCHLIN'S HUMANISM

Von Hutten at once was drawn into the bitter controversy between the theological professors of the University of Cologne and the humanist John Reuchlin (1455–1522). Born in Baden and educated at Heidelberg, Paris, and Basel, Reuchlin early became acquainted with humanist conceptions current among the students. His Latinity was superior to that of theologians and lawyers, and at the University of Basel he became proficient in Greek; he also studied law at Orléans. In 1482 and 1490 he visited Italy where he became acquainted with Mirandola and developed deep interest in the mystic teachings of the *Cabala.* He began studying Hebrew and soon knew more about that language than any other Christian. Throughout the Middle Ages scholars and theologians had only slightly interested themselves in the language of the people who had crucified Christ.

In 1496 Reuchlin became a pensioner of Archbishop John Dalberg of Worms (1445–1503), a man of strong humanist leanings who invited him to teach in the University of Heidelberg. Reuchlin became the center of an enthusiastic circle of humanist students, and his fame spread throughout Germany. He wrote two books, *On the Elements of Hebrew* (1506), and *On the Cabalists' Art* (1517). *Phoenix Germaniae,* or the German Phoenix, was the proud title which his countrymen gave him.

Reuchlin represented the Renaissance in one of its most important aspects, that of the study of language as a preparation for literature, secular as well as sacred. Although untrained as a theologian, he had not the slightest hesitation in discussing Biblical texts as simple literary works. All of Reuchlin's views were sharply challenged in his controversy with a Jew named Pfefferkorn. This man had renounced Judaism in 1506 and became an ardent proselytizer for the Christian faith. He wrote many pamphlets against the Jews, one of which was called the *Judenspiegel,* or *Jews' Mirror.* One of his contentions was that books written in Hebrew should be confiscated. Supported by the friars of Cologne, he approached the emperor, and in 1519 his proposal was set forth in an imperial decree commanding the Jews to surrender their books.

Empowered to carry out this law, Pfefferkorn set to work in the cities of the Rhineland, but his progress was blocked by the Archbishop of Mainz who did not share his fanaticism. This prelate demanded that some scholars should be asked to give their opinion on the advisability of destroying books written in Hebrew. Pfefferkorn agreed and rashly suggested Reuchlin, little thinking that the humanist did not share the old-fashioned views of the theologians. Reuchlin's opinion, given in 1520, was a humanist classic. Most Jewish books, he argued, were quite harmless and were even instructive to Christians. Since the *Talmud*, the *Cabala*, commentaries, and other literature were not directed against the Christian religion, he felt that they should not be destroyed.

Pfefferkorn, keenly disappointed and wrathful, attacked Reuchlin in a pamphlet called the *Handspiegel*, or *Hand mirror*, in which he stated that Reuchlin knew little Hebrew and was incompetent to render decision on so weighty a subject. Reuchlin was enraged at this impudence and put forth his *Augenspiegel*, or *Eyes' Mirror*, criticizing Pfefferkorn and justifying his own position. But the Jew had friends among the theological professors of Cologne who examined Reuchlin's book and drew from it a list of statements which they demanded he should recall. They were to some extent justified because Reuchlin's ideas drawn from the *Cabala* were not entirely consonant with Christian doctrine. Several universities condemned the *Augenspiegel*, and finally the inquisitor-general Hochstraten required Reuchlin to appear before him to answer for his heresies, as he termed them.

But Reuchlin's friends supported him, and Hochstraten appealed to Pope Leo X. The humanist curia of that day cared little for the notions of theologians and saw little that was heretical in Reuchlin's idea. Leo was slow to exonerate Reuchlin, however, because of the pleadings of Hochstraten. Frightened by Luther's revolt which began in 1517, the pope finally in 1520 pronounced the *Augenspiegel* a dangerous book. Reuchlin had published under the title *Clarorum Virorum Epistolae*, or *Letters of Famous Men*, some letters which he had received from men who felt as he did. It suggested a famous satire on his opponents, the *Epistolae Obscurorum Virorum*, or *Letters of Obscure Men*, written by stupid admirers to their equally stupid professors in Cologne. The first book appeared in 1516. Its authorship remains in doubt, but it is practically certain that most of the letters were written by Crotus Rubianus (1486–1539?), a member of the Erfurt circle of humanists who admired Mutianus. Ulrich von Hutten (d. 1523) also contributed some letters to the first book, and most, if not all, of the second book which appeared in 1517 came from his hand.

The *Letters of Obscure Men* is a classic in the satirical literature of the Renaissance. Theologians and professors of theology, wedded to the impossible methods of Biblical exegesis which had grown up during the Middle Ages, were loath to admit that humanists, or poets as they were called, who were untrained in theology could teach them anything about the interpretation of Scripture. Instead they sought to defend themselves by the Inquisition. The contest between Reuchlin and these theologians was one between free inquiry and authority, and, when simple argument failed, satire was employed by reformers like Sebastian Brant in his *Ship of Fools*. Admirers of the methods held sacred in the University of Cologne wrote letters to Ortwin Gratius under ridiculous names: Strauszfeder (Ostrich feather), Ziegenmelker (Goat milker), Ganseprediger (Goose preacher), Honiglecker (Honey licker), Glatzkopf (Baldpate), and Mistlader (Dung loader). They were a stupid lot, much perturbed that anyone should venture to question tradition; they conformed to accepted ideas and naïvely believed that the struggle for truth was finished. They were ridiculous because of their religiosity and their uncouth Latin, which often degenerates into doggerel. They were proud of their academic titles and were alarmed that Reuchlin and his crew of poets did not respect them.

Thus Heinrich Schafmaul (Sheep's mouth) wrote from Rome about a nice point in religion. He states that when he was dining with a friend in an inn, he found a chick in one of the eggs he was eating.

> This I showed to a comrade; whereupon quoth he to me, 'Eat it up speedily, before the taverner sees it, for if he mark it, you will have to pay a Carline or a Julius for a fowl.' . . . In a trice I gulped down the egg, chicken and all. And then I remembered that it was Friday! Whereupon I said to my crony, 'You have made me commit a mortal sin, in eating flesh on the sixth day of the week!' But he averred that it was not a mortal sin— nor even a venial one, seeing that such a chickling is accounted merely as an egg, until it is born. He told me, too, that it is just the same in the case of cheese in which there are sometimes grubs, as there are in cherries, peas, and new beans; yet all these may be eaten on Fridays, and even on apostolic vigils. But taverners are such rascals that they call them flesh to get more money.

But Schafmaul, troubled in conscience, begs Ortwin Gratius to settle whether the chick was flesh; and he adds,

> If you hold that the sin is mortal, I would fain get shrift here ere I return to Germany.

One Anton, doctor of medicine, wrote from Heidelberg about his interview with Erasmus. The works of Julius Caesar were mentioned which gave Anton his opportunity, and he writes:

> So soon as I heard this, I perceived my opportunity, for I had studied much, and learned much under you in the matter of poetry when I was in

Cologne, and I said, 'Forasmuch as you have begun to speak concerning poetry, I can therefore no longer hide my light under a bushel, and I roundly
aver that I believe not that Caesar wrote those *Commentaries,* and I will
prove my position with argument following, which runneth thus: Whosoever
hath business with arms and is occupied in labor unceasing cannot learn
Latin: but Caesar was ever at war and in labors manifold; therefore he
could not become lettered and get Latin. In truth, therefore, I believe that
it was none other than Suetonius who wrote those *Commentaries* for I have
met with none who hath a style liker to Caesar's than Suetonius.'

Amused by this ridiculous argument, Erasmus smiled and said nothing;
and Anton thought that he had defeated the great humanist.

HUMANISM IN SCANDINAVIA AND IN SLAVIC LANDS

German humanism was restricted chiefly to the Rhenish and Danubian
valleys. It also found its way into northern Germany, into the towns of
the Hanseatic League. These towns were hardly beginning to enjoy the
leisure which capital, accumulated from many business operations, made
possible. This was even truer of Scandinavia. Sweden and Norway were
an economic province of the Hanseatic League; the profits of their trade
went to swell the coffers of German merchants. Although Denmark also
was dominated by the Hanse, native merchants were able to share to
some extent in the business life of the realm. Humanism was cultivated
here and there, but did not become an active force until the beginning of
the Lutheran Reformation. Finland, a province of the Swedish crown, was
a backward country, and the new learning found no foothold in it, nor in
the lands of the Knights of the Sword and of the Teutonic Knights.

The situation in Poland was somewhat different. There the German
burgher and trader dominated the economic life of the land, the Slavic
peasant remaining sunken in the inertness of serfdom. The nobility, however, sent their young men to study in German universities and even to
the schools of Italy. Thus the culture of humanism was gradually brought
into Poland. Some of the nobility began to show interest in it during the
latter part of the reign of Casimir IV (1427–1492). The influence of the
crown proved more powerful. Sigismund I (1467–1548) took a bride
from the house of Sforza, Bona, daughter of Duke Gian Galeazzo of
Milan (d. 1494), and she stimulated interest in humanist culture. Italians
came to the Polish court, and Italian influences began to transform Polish
thought, manners, and letters.

Bohemia in the previous century had given some promise of humanist
culture, for Emperor Charles IV (1347–1378) was a friend of Petrarch

and was much interested in Italy. A number of Bohemians eagerly studied classical authors, but their influence on the course of humanism in Germany remained limited. Hungary, an agricultural land worked by serfs and ruled by nobles, offered no favorable home to it, and the Slavic lands to the south were hardly touched by it. Rumania, the Balkan peninsula, and the multitudes of Russians to the east escaped its influence almost entirely.

RENAISSANCE THOUGHT IN ENGLAND

Renaissance conceptions found their way into England later than into Germany. This was inevitable because of the more conservative economic development of the country. The towns were rapidly becoming important and were the chief source of the crown's power. London, the foremost urban center, led all others. Henry VII (1485–1509), however, was too busy setting his realm in order after the Wars of the Roses to play the part of a Maecenas. For some time Italian Renaissance culture had attracted the attention of Englishmen. Duke Humphrey of Gloucester (d. 1447), the most noteworthy, was deeply interested in classical letters and corresponded with the humanist Pier Candido Decembrio of Milan who dedicated an edition of Plato's *Republic* to him. Among the 300 or 400 books which he gave to the University of Oxford were copies of the works of Dante, Petrarch, and Boccaccio, and the recently rediscovered writings of ancient Latin authors. His example was not very fruitful, however, for the new learning was to acquire its most zealous and success-ful devotees from among the bourgeoisie and the scholars of Oxford. William Grocyn (1466?–1519) was educated in Magdalen College in Oxford. But learning in that venerable university was still of the tradi-tional variety and, attracted by the report of the great superiority of Italian thought, Grocyn went to Italy and visited Florence, Rome, and Padua. He studied Greek under such scholars as Chalcondyles and Poli-ziano, returned in 1491, and began lecturing in Greek in Exeter College, Oxford. William Latimer (1460?–1545), who became sufficiently pro-ficient in Greek to begin the translation of Aristotle, went to Italy with him. Thomas Linacre (1460?–1524) studied at Oxford and in 1485 went to Italy, visiting Bologna, Florence, Rome, Venice, Padua, and Vicenza. After receiving a degree in medicine, he returned to England in 1492 and began teaching Greek in Oxford. He brought to England the latest advances in medical science made in Italy, translated the works of Galen, and founded the London College of Physicians.

John Colet (1467?–1519), the son of a London merchant, was more important than any of these other men. After becoming Master of Arts at Oxford, he visited Italy to study Greek, law, and the Church fathers. Returning to Oxford in 1496, he began lecturing on the Pauline epistles— a bold step, for Colet had no degree in theology. He devoted much attention to the literal sense of the texts which others ignored in their zeal to consider the hidden and allegorical meaning, a method which so pleased people that his auditors rapidly increased. This was the beginning of a new method of studying Biblical literature in England, based upon the grammatical and literary ideas of the Renaissance rather than upon the antiquated methods employed by scholastics. Colet inherited his father's large fortune in 1508, and determined to use it in reëstablishing the school attached to St. Paul's Church in London. It was modeled after the new Renaissance schools of Italy, with control vested in the London Company of Mercers, a lay group, and not in the clergy. William Lilly, the first headmaster, taught Greek and Ciceronian Latin. This example of a successful institution of humanist learning proved contagious. Thus was developed a group of men known as the Oxford Reformers, the pioneers of a great literary and educational movement. Henry VIII (1497–1547) befriended Colet and other learned men and encouraged humanism, and the movement soon began to be felt also in Cambridge.

EARLY HUMANIST THOUGHT IN FRANCE

The Renaissance came to France before the memorable expedition of Charles VIII in 1494 and 1495, for Italian culture had attracted the attention of Frenchmen from time to time, and Italian humanists had visited the country and made the acquaintance of eager students. Little progress, however, was made between 1460 and 1500. Traditional conceptions reigned at the Sorbonne, the great theological faculty in the University of Paris which had so long dominated the orthodox thought of Europe. There was no desire to study classical literature or even to read the works of the Church fathers. Printing presses were set up in Paris, however, and one was installed in the Sorbonne itself, but it exercised little influence in behalf of humanism. A number of Italian masters, among them George Hieronymus and John Lascaris, taught in the university and stimulated some interest. Finally, Jacques Lefèvre of Étaples (1445–1537), or Stapulensis as he was called, went to Italy and became acquainted with Pico della Mirandola and Marsilio Ficino. He gained a deeper appreciation of humanist conceptions and became enamored of the Neoplatonic thought which throve in Florence. On his return to France he taught in the traditional manner, but his lectures contained the ferment of the new learning. French humanism had not yet appropriated that knowledge of the Greek language and literature which was regarded as the very source of all humanist conceptions. This shortcoming was remedied by a Frenchman named Francois Tissard who began teaching Greek in Paris after his return from Italy. Girolamo Aleandro (1480–1542), later known as Cardinal Aleandro, an Italian who knew Greek, Latin, and Hebrew, was even more important, large numbers flocking to his lectures which he began to give in 1508. Meanwhile a Netherlander from Ghent, Josse Badius Ascensius (1462–1537), began printing classical texts in Paris, the capital of the country, whereas hitherto all such books had to be imported from Italy, Germany, or the Low Countries.

Most important among early French humanists at this time was Guillaume Budé (1467–1540), who had been educated in the traditional manner and had studied law at Orléans. While studying subsequently in Paris he became acquainted with such humanists as Hieronymus and Lascaris. Greatly influenced by the scholarship of the latter, Budé undertook a translation of Plutarch. His fame soon spread to the court, and he was sent as royal envoy to Venice in 1501 and to Pope Julius II in 1505. Even Louis XII, who personally cared nothing for Greek or Latin scholarship, realized the importance of humanist learning for an ambassador to Italy. These missions gave Budé splendid opportunities to drink at the fresh fountains of humanist scholarship. He produced his *Annotationes, or Notes on the Pandects of Justinian,* in 1508. The method employed by him was novel in that a clear knowledge of the text was deemed necessary before one could begin the study of the law itself; he also believed that a thorough knowledge of Roman antiquities was indispensable. These ideas are accepted today without question, but at that time they were revolutionary. The study of Roman law henceforth became less banal and practical and more truly intellectual. In 1515 he published his *De Asse et Partibus ejus,* or *On the As and Its Parts,* which dealt with Roman coinage and gave the writer a chance to study more minutely than had yet been done. The book, like the paintings of the Italian artist Mantegna, illustrates the archaeological tendency of humanism so pronounced during the sixteenth century. His *De Philologia,* or *On Philology,* written in 1530, is a dialogue between King Francis I and himself, in which he advocates that every prince should be educated in classical literatures.

The noted scholar and printer, Robert Estienne (1503–1559), and his son Henry Estienne (1531–1598) must be mentioned, for so intimate was the relation between humanism and the printers that the establishment of a great press was an event of prime importance. Robert published the *Treasury of the Latin Language* in three folios in 1543, as well as important editions of Latin and Greek authors. His son published the *Treasury of the Greek Language* in 1572 in five folios. These lexicons, which were of great importance in furthering humanist studies, are a characteristic product of the later stage of humanism in which editing and archaeological and philological study occupied the attention of scholars.

Meanwhile the court under Francis I (1515–1547) greatly encouraged the cultivation of Renaissance learning. The king was an indolent man, luxurious, and superficially educated. But he appreciated the value of the new learning sufficiently to be eager to play the part of a Maecenas and encouraged the popularization of classical letters by means of translations. His sister Marguerite, duchess of Alençon and later queen of Navarre (1492–1549), played a significant part in the diffusion of the new ideas. Although not a beautiful woman, she possessed a gracious personality and attracted humanists to her court. She was abler than Francis, for whom she retained a deep affection to the last day of her life. She studied the Neoplatonic thought which had come to Florence under Mirandola. She was interested in religion; her study of Plato enabled her to criticize the crudity of current religious life. She was versed in Italian literature and wrote her *Heptameron* in imitation of Boccaccio's *Decameron*. This collection of seventy-two stories, however, does not borrow anything from the subject matter of Boccaccio's tales, but it marks an advance in the art of French story writing. Such tales as the *Cent Nouvelles Nouvelles*, or *Hundred New Tales*, written about 1450, are of a traditional character which had long been current, whereas Marguerite's stories are declared to be drawn from actual occurrences, thus differing from the tales of Boccaccio. The scene is laid at Cauterets, a small town in the Pyrenees, where a group of people are detained by a mountain flood. They improve their leisure by telling stories in which all sorts of themes, spiritual and lascivious, are commingled. Their language is fresh and the narrative sprightly. Marguerite's wit finds ample opportunity in the little discussions at the end of each story to criticize the conventions of society and religion, a favorite theme of the Renaissance.

Francis was not able at first to gratify his desires as a Renaissance prince, for his first two wars with Charles V from 1521–1525 and 1526–1529 engaged all his energies. Freed from these embarrassments by the Treaty of Cambrai (1529), Francis began what he had so long neglected. In 1530, in response to the earnest pleading of Budé, he appointed the royal lecturers who were to create a humanist college for the furtherance of classical and oriental studies. There were two lecturers in Greek, two in Hebrew, one in Latin, and one in mathematics. These lecturers were known as the College of Royal Lecturers, and, since the French Revolution, as the Collège de France. This humanist school was modeled after the College of the Three Languages which had been established a few years before in Louvain in the Low Countries. The conservative professors of the Sorbonne disliked the new learning of these humanists, fearing that their manner of studying literary texts and their refusal to be guided by the old-fashioned methods of theologians would damage their own positions. This hostility proved futile; the tide of humanism gained in strength and gradually the old ideas and methods were abandoned.

Chapter 27

RENAISSANCE LETTERS FROM ERASMUS
TO SHAKESPEARE

R ENAISSANCE THOUGHT of the sixteenth century was expressed in a great variety of forms by a group of literary geniuses of high order, of whom Desiderius Erasmus (1466–1536) was the most influential. In him were united the ethical and intellectual conceptions which that critical age of revolt brought forth. He was the first modern man of letters to rely almost entirely upon the printing press for the diffusion of his ideas, and he addressed his thoughts to all reading Europeans. Few men before or since have exerted so powerful an influence upon their contemporaries.

ERASMUS' YOUTH AND EARLY EDUCATION

Erasmus was born in October, 1466. His father was a priest, and Erasmus had an older brother named Peter. The pretty story later told in the preface to the *Familiar Colloquies* and made popular by Charles Reade's *Cloister and the Hearth* unfortunately is not correct. It recounts how the boy's father loved a girl whose parents objected to the match. Finding that marriage was out of the question, the young man left on a journey to Rome and became a priest. Much obscurity hangs over Erasmus' youth, and many points probably will never be cleared up. When about 4 years of age, he and his brother were sent to an elementary school in Gouda. Thence he went for a brief interim to the school of the Brethren of the Common Life in Deventer, and from 1475 to 1484 he served as choir boy in the cathedral of Utrecht. He returned to Deventer where he had some glimpses of the superior humanist education which the Brethren of the Common Life were introducing into their schools, Alexander Hegius being one of his teachers. Soon his father and mother died, and Erasmus and his brother were placed under the guardianship of three men who cared little for the boy's future and probably squandered the pittance which the father had left him. They placed the boys in the

Brethren school in 's Hertogenbosch, whose conceptions were of the traditional medieval variety untouched by the methods of humanism. Because of a plague the youths returned to Gouda. Their guardians sought to be rid of them, encouraging them to enter a monastery. The young men yielded, and Erasmus entered the order of Austin Canons who had a house at Stein near Gouda (1488).

Although Erasmus was a delicate lad and physically unfitted to lead a monastic life, he did not find his surroundings wholly uncongenial. He was free to study according to his inclination and to make friends with some of the friars who, like him, were interested in literary things and had caught more than a glimpse of humanist culture. For the moment he was content in his cloistered retreat and even wrote a treatise called *On the Contempt of the World*, which was thoroughly monastic in spirit.

Erasmus was religious, deeply affected by the practical piety of the *devotio moderna* which was so influential in Deventer, 's Hertogenbosch, and other places in which he spent his early days. In the convent near Gouda he read extensively in classical Latin literature and developed a lucid and effective Latinity. The spirit of humanism became steadily stronger in his breast and he longed to visit Italy, that paradise of culture toward which all humanist eyes were turned. He began to compose his *Book Against the Barbarians*. Written in the form of a dialogue, it expresses the thoughts of a person who is becoming a humanist, but its later version reveals the humanist's contempt for monasticism, the formal side of popular religious life as expressed in the veneration of saints and relics, and the supposed shortcomings of the Church. The opportunity of going to Italy seemed to present itself when he was offered a secretaryship by the bishop of Cambrai who was planning a journey to Rome. The post proved a disappointment, for it gave him no leisure to study, and the visit to the Eternal City did not take place. He soon left the bishop's service and went to Paris to secure a doctor's degree in theology (1495).

ERASMUS' EARLY HUMANIST ACTIVITY

The traditionalism which Erasmus found in the University of Paris displeased him. He lodged in the Collège de Montagu, an institution in which life was austere, the food bad, and the rooms uncomfortable; the delicate young man conceived an invincible hatred of this sort of life which clung to him to the last. He also learned to look with disgust upon the arid and formal instruction of the university. The stipend which the bishop of Cambrai had promised him failed, and Erasmus began to seek a chance to earn some money elsewhere. Some German and English youths engaged him as their teacher, and for them he wrote some pedagogical manuals. One of these contained vivacious dialogues which after repeated additions and revisions became the famous *Familiar Colloquies*. Other little books dealt with the art of writing and with courses of study. This was the beginning of Erasmus' long search for means to support himself in his studious life, for the cultivation of intellectual things requires leisure and wealth, and Erasmus possessed neither. Like many another humanist, he searched for a patron, and made the fortunate acquaintance of an English youth, William Blount, Lord Mountjoy, who was studying in Paris.

Erasmus' first sojourn in England from 1499–1500 was a noteworthy moment in the life of the humanist. As guest of Lord Mountjoy he became acquainted with Thomas More and John Colet, dean of St. Paul's. Association with these genial spirits meant much for a man of receptive mind, and Erasmus profited from their friendship and rapidly became more mature in his ideas. He met a number of the Oxford Reformers. Colet, More, and Linacre were very fond of him, and Erasmus ever after cherished the kindest sentiments toward England. Even the confiscation of his dearly won money by the customs officials at Dover according to an ancient law forbidding the export of coin from the realm did not chill the ardor of his affection for his English friends. Deprived of all funds, as soon as he reached Paris he set to work preparing the famous book of *Adages* (1500). It was a compilation of excerpts from classical authors intended to serve as models for students learning to write Latin and wishing to form an acquaintance with classical literature. Hitherto the classics had been studied almost exclusively by humanists, for, cheap as the works of ancient authors were, thanks to the printing presses which had been established, many people were still too poor to buy them. This little collection proved immensely popular; it was repeatedly revised and enlarged and reprinted.

Thus Erasmus became the chief teacher and disseminator of the new learning. His private correspondence was constantly increasing in volume. It is difficult in our age to form an adequate idea of the enthusiasm which men felt on receiving letters from him. These missives are a most important collection of sources for the study of the humanist world in Erasmus' day. Everywhere men bought and read his little books. One reason for his popularity was his mastery of Greek, for a knowledge of that language was still uncommon in northern Europe, and anyone possessing an acquaintance with it was certain to attract attention. Erasmus' translations of such Greek classics as Euripides' *Iphigenia* and *Hecuba* also attracted wide attention.

Like many humanists, Erasmus was a great traveler. Poor, and with university posts closed to him, he had to live by his wits, for his search for patrons was disappointing. In 1505 he again appeared in England where he renewed acquaintance with his old friends. He met some important churchmen and was even presented to the king who granted him a small living. Soon he grasped at a chance to visit Italy in company with an Italian, a physician to King Henry VII. Upon his arrival at Turin in 1506, Erasmus was at once given the doctorate in theology. Next he visited Bologna and soon entered into relations with the noted Venetian printer Aldus Manutius who now began publishing some of his writings. Together they worked over an enlarged edition of the *Adages* which was ready in 1508, and other editions of Seneca, Plautus, and Terence followed. News came that Henry VII had died and that Henry VIII, who knew Erasmus, had succeeded to the crown (1509). Believing that the new king might prove an eager patron and, encouraged by his friend Lord Mountjoy who also believed that the moment was auspicious, Erasmus hurried over the Alps down the Rhine to England.

ERASMUS' *PRAISE OF FOLLY* AND OTHER WORKS

This hasty journey will be forever memorable, for while passing through the Splügen Pass Erasmus evolved the plan of his *Praise of Folly*, a chief literary monument of the Renaissance. His ideas were written out after his arrival in London while staying in Sir Thomas More's house. The book is a long declamation delivered by a female figure named Folly, who embodies Erasmus' conception of human nature. The great humanist believed in the basic goodness of man and his natural impulses; human beings might do wrong, but it was only because of mistakes and misunderstanding. Men lived by their natural impulses and their instincts which keep the world moving. Folly, the personification of these human qualities, is an imperishable literary creation, possessing a "charming naïveté, the natural impulse of the child or of the unsophisticated man. Though her birth is derived from Pluto, she is no grim demon, but an amiable gossip, rather beneficent than malignant." This is a Renaissance conception of human nature. Emphasis upon the doctrine of man's depravity and insistence upon asceticism as the council of perfection were abandoned more and more in the Renaissance. Man's secular activities are good. To live well one should steer a middle course; one should be lenient, moderate in all things, and live according to his natural feelings without too much regard for the conventions of society. The book is a satire on human foibles and sometimes degenerates into the writer's characteristically strong denunciation of abuses in the Church, the schools of philosophy of the day, and the assumptions of the scientists of the time. In fact, Erasmus here criticizes almost every aspect of the society.

Erasmus did not stay in England, for, although he was fond of his friends in London, Oxford, and Cambridge, he was poor and had to make a living. He lectured on Greek and theology while in Cambridge and published a number of pedagogical works from the humanist press of Josse Badius Ascensius (1462–1535) in Paris. During 1514 he left England for Basel where he was planning to bring out his edition of the *New Testament*. There were many copies of the Bible in manuscript, and parts of the *New Testament* had been printed repeatedly. There also were collections of excerpts. But a cheap edition was needed to fill the wants of the educated bourgeoisie. His edition (1516) was less expensive than the great Polyglot Bible published at Alcala in 1520, and its appearance was an event of great importance in the intellectual history of the time.

Shortly afterward Erasmus produced the *Education of a Christian Prince* (1518), a little treatise written after he had been appointed councilor to Charles of Spain, who was soon to become emperor. In it the author held that princes should view their obligations to their subjects as moral and not merely from the standpoint of expediency. The end of government was the moral advancement of peoples; princes should therefore avoid selfish policies and not indulge in wars and unjust taxation. This was very different from the practical conceptions of Machiavelli and clashed with the actual political situation in the world of the day when peace hung precariously upon the system known as the Balance of Power.

Another important work was *The Ciceronian* (1528), a dialogue designed to show the futility of the slavish imitation of classical originals. Erasmus did not advocate the study of the classics in order to become enslaved to them. The treasures of classical antiquity, in his opinion, were valuable chiefly in elucidating the Christian religion and instilling a purer moral conception into the lives of people. Consequently he never aimed at complete purity of expression but preferred a terse and vigorous Latinity.

Erasmus also studied the texts of the Church fathers, applying to them the new philological science which had been developed in Italy. His edition of the writings of St. Jerome began to appear in 1516. Others followed, among which were the texts of St. Augustine, St. Ambrose, St. Cyprian, and Lactantius. He also published the texts of the Greek fathers of the Church. Bringing out the writings of the Greek and Latin Church fathers, according to Erasmus, was the best means of ridding the Church of its abuses.

Erasmus' *Familiar Colloquies Concerning Men, Manners, and Things* is one of the great classics of the Renaissance. This collection of seventy-two vivacious colloquies deals with all manner of social, religious, and moral matters. The vogue of making pilgrimages, the piety of a child, courtesy in saluting, imposture, marriage, fasting, and so forth, are treated with great fullness and in a facile manner. This work found much favor among Europe's upper bourgeoisie so that it was a force to be reckoned with in the Reformation following Martin Luther. Its trenchant criticisms, its sweeping statements, its frequently overdrawn denunciation of abuses in Church and society left a deep impression.

Erasmus' last years were spent for the most part in Basel where he worked in the printing shops of Froben and Amerbach. His share in the Lutheran revolt and in subsequent religious troubles is reserved for discussion in the chapters on the Reformation. His fame permeated into every corner of Europe. He possessed a subtle intellect, was fearless in asserting the truth, and to the very last persisted in his duty as he saw it. He was above all honest in his mental life, hating hypocrisy and pedantry. Frail in body, weak in health, timid to a degree, he nevertheless clung to his convictions until death. In 1529 he moved from Basel to Freiburg in Breisgau to escape the religious tumults which broke out. He returned to Basel in 1535, but his health soon failed. He died in July, 1536, and was buried in the cathedral where his tomb may still be seen.

FRANÇOIS RABELAIS' LIFE OF GARGANTUA

François Rabelais (1494–1553) was becoming the most famous French humanist just as Erasmus' life was drawing to an end. He was born near Chinon; his father was a lawyer who belonged to the provincial bourgeoisie and had inherited some property. He was an intelligent youth and in his ninth year was sent to school in a Benedictine convent, later to be transferred to the Franciscan house at Fonteray. In his seventh year he had received the tonsure; to all appearances he was destined to service in the Church. At Fonteray he continued his priestly studies and finally was admitted to holy orders. Humanist learning had found its way into the monastery, and Rabelais greedily appropriated every bit of it. A number of his fellow friars also were interested in the new learning. One of them had become proficient in Greek and corresponded with Guillaume Budé. But some of the other friars did not share Rabelais' enthusiasm for the classics, for there was much excitement in France over the question of religion, and the crown was inclined to take action against innovators. To avoid any evil consequences from fostering humanist studies, Rabelais and two friars were thrust into the conventual prison. The latter fled from their cells, but Rabelais received permission from Pope Clement VII to enter a Benedictine house.

Although his abbot was a humanist at heart and favored him, Rabelais found a monk's life uncongenial. However, he carried forward his studies with great industry and amassed an extraordinary amount of learning. The ferment of Renaissance ideas was working in him, and it is not surprising that he left the cloister and set out to Montpellier to study medicine, a science of extreme interest to him, since it apparently promised to unlock the secrets of life itself. He enrolled in 1530 and soon had appropriated all the medical knowledge of the day. Like Leonardo da Vinci, he was deeply interested in nature and paid little heed to authority or tradition, and, like many another humanist, was restless and had not the patience to study for the doctorate in medicine. He went to Lyons, a busy trading center where printing had become an active industry and whither scholars were flocking from all parts. He continued his work in medicine but was constantly drawn away from it to satisfy his thirst for learning. He began to love classical antiquity, read books voraciously, and became a follower of Erasmus. Unlike that great humanist, however, Rabelais never spurned his mother tongue and till the last wrote in French. He brought out almanacs filled with things which pleased humble folk. He wrote crude jokes and never tired of ridiculing quacks and astrologers. He became acquainted with the life of the people from whom he derived his astonishing knowledge of the crudities of popular life.

It is fortunate for literature that Rabelais turned to these things rather than to classical learning. In 1532 he produced a work which later became known as *The Inestimable Life of the Great Gargantua, Father of Pantagruel*. He did not regard it as a serious work and had it published with a mere bookseller instead of with a great publisher of serious literature. The book proved far more popular than any other work, including the Bible. The reason for this is plain. Gargantua was a well-known character of immense strength and gross appetites, and peasants never wearied of pointing to great tasks which he had done. The success of this work led Rabelais to revise it, and finally the first book on Gargantua and the second on Pantagruel were produced. A third was added in 1546, a fourth in 1548, and the last posthumously in 1562. The book was written in French in a style rough, vigorous, and difficult to understand because of its liberal use of popular expressions. Rabelais' thought was truly expressive of the Renaissance, for, hating hypocrisy, quackery, and tradition, he emphasized the physical and the secular side of everything. Hence his great interest in food, drink, and bodily activity.

Many of the incidents in the first book, which deals with Gargantua, are autobiographical. Chapters 14–24, a satire on traditional education, tell how a "great sophister-doctor" spent 5 years and 3 months in teaching Gargantua his ABC's so well that he could say them backward. Later the youthful giant was sent to Paris where his first achievement was to steal the great bells of the Cathedral of Notre Dame, in the thought that they might serve well to hang around his mare's neck. But a great hubbub arose, and a delegation from the university came to him to plead for the bells, the leader, Master Janotus de Bragmardo, delivering a stupid speech in which there was no sense and much bad grammar. The six chapters before the last one, devoted to Gargantua's founding of the abbey of Thélème, are a satire on the monasticism of the later Middle Ages and express the Renaissance antagonism to the ascetic ideals of the age. The abbatial rules in Thélème were the opposite of those of the established orders—its inmates were to be free, there was to be no clock or dial, and the women were to be young and pretty, for "a woman that is neither fair nor good, to what use serves she?" The inmates might leave the order at will and, if they desired, marry. "Do what thou wilt," the sole rule, was sufficient "because men that are free, well-born, well-bred, and conversant in honest companies, have naturally an instinct and spur that prompteth them unto virtuous actions, and withdraws them from vice, which is called honor." The structure was erected according to Renaissance architectural ideas and was furnished with libraries containing books in Greek, Latin, and Hebrew as well as in modern languages.

The second book deals with Gargantua's son Pantagruel and his mighty deeds, which are incidents from Rabelais' own life. A long genealogy satirizes the popular craze for genealogical tables. Pantagruel's early education is described in detail. He made great progress and soon set out to study in the universities of the realm, as was the custom of students, finally arriving in Orléans. But he learned only physical exercises. "As for breaking his head with over much study, he had an especial care not to do it in any case, for fear of spoiling his eyes. Which he the rather observed, for that it was told him by one of his teachers, there called regents, that the pain of the eyes was the most hurtful thing of any to the sight!" At last Pantagruel came to Paris where he made some progress in the liberal arts. He became acquainted with the library of the convent of St. Victor. The satirical catalogue of its books contains among others: *The Invention of the Holy Cross, Personated by Six Wily Priests; The Spectacles of Pilgrims Bound for Rome; The Ape's Paternoster,* and *The Hotchpotch or Gallimaufry of the Perpetually Begging Friars.* Chapter 8 contains a summary of Renaissance education and a statement as to why it was superior to the conventional variety. Chapters 10–13 satirize lawyers. The third book also is devoted to the deeds of Pantagruel.

The fourth book relates how Pantagruel visited the oracle of the Holy Bottle. The Renaissance was an age of expansion; the bounds of the world were suddenly and profoundly enlarged. This stirred the imagination of men, and the tales which came from the newly discovered lands soon found their way into literature. Rabelais, curious about everything, described a voyage westward and north of Canada, probably in imitation of the famous expedition by Jacques Cartier in 1534. The ship sailed past Sneaking Island "where Shrovetide reigned." Next the crew passed by Wild Island and spied a whale which Pantagruel caught by means of a harpoon. Rabelais' description of whale-catching is based upon careful observation, and this episode reminds the reader of French whaling off the Newfoundland coasts. Wild Island was inhabited by a people called Chitterlings who probably are Calvinists. Although Rabelais in the third book had shown himself favorable to Calvinists and Sacramentarians, in this book he seems to dislike the more zealous followers of John Calvin, for Pantagruel heartily enjoys the wholesale slaughter that was inflicted upon the natives when they treacherously attacked him and his following.

The fifth book, which remained unfinished, continued the tale of the journey to the oracle of the Holy Bottle. Soon they drew near Sounding Island and landed. The bells which were perpetually ringing on this island reminded Pantagruel of the regime of the Church, and he disliked it heartily. He found a large number of cages "spacious, costly, magnificent, and of an admirable architecture" which were filled with birds who lived like men but "stunk like devils." A hermit "called the males clerg-hawks, monk-hawks, abbot-hawks, bish-hawks, cardin-hawks, and one pope-hawk, who is a species by himself. He called the females clerg-kites, nun-kites, priest-kites, abbess-kites, bish-kites, cardin-kites, and pope-kites." They had been brought there by their parents without having been consulted themselves—an allusion to the practice common at that time of filling convents with children. Next the Island of Tools was visited, and the voyagers saw the trees laden with all manner of tools, their natural fruit, which fell into ready-made handles the moment the branches were shaken. Next came the Island of Sharping inhabited by cardsharps and vendors of fake relics and antiques. The Island of Sandals was inhabited by the order of Semiquaver Friars. Pantagruel could never sufficiently satisfy his desire to satirize friars.

Rabelais undoubtedly was the most significant writer of the Renaissance in France. His humanist ideas combined with the vigorous ferment which quickened the thought and life of the French bourgeoisie. The coarseness of his language, due to the medieval tradition which he did not abandon, made his satire and sarcasm peculiarly effective. His language, while dynamic and pungent, possessed little of that literary grace which Italians of the time were imparting to their works.

FRENCH LETTERS FROM CALVIN TO MONTAIGNE

John Calvin (1509–1564), a most significant Protestant reformer, rendered a noteworthy service to French Renaissance letters. Calvin was strongly influenced by humanist ideas and developed a clear and forceful Latinity. His French style was unsurpassed in clarity and simplicity. His numerous letters and his edition of the *Institutes of the Christian Religion* exerted a remarkable influence upon Frenchmen who did not adopt the style of Rabelais.

Imitation of classical models became more and more the fashion among the literary men of Europe. It marks the culmination of the Renaissance in art and literature and inaugurates a period of artistic stagnation. Something was gained, however, from the careful study of Vergilian and Ciceronian perfection. This quality was given to the French language by a group of writers known as the Pleiades whose original members were Pierre de Ronsard (1524–1585) and Joachim Du Bellay (1522–1560). These men, who chanced to meet in a hostel in Touraine and became firm friends, believed that the ideas about literary forms which had conquered in Italy should likewise be applied to French literature, and medieval forms of verse which were still very popular in France should be abandoned. Rhyme, indeed, was retained, but in other respects classical poems and classical themes—pastoral, mythological, and lyrical—were as eagerly appropriated by them as by Sannazaro in Italy. Thus began the long sway of classicism in French literature. Ronsard was the chief poet of this school. Du Bellay wrote a prose exposition, the *Defense and Illustration of the French Language* (1549), setting forth the theories of the Pleiades, in which he argued that the French tongue was the proper vehicle of thought. Writers were to be produced by careful study of Latin models, not by the spontaneous outburst of genius. Nourished by the form and substance of ancient books, the Pleiades rendered excellent service in creating a wholesome respect for artistic literary perfection.

The last significant French writer of the sixteenth century here to be considered is Michel de Montaigne (1533–1592). His father belonged to the bourgeoisie of Bordeaux and held several offices in the gift of the commune. The youth was brought up with every advantage of humanist education such as had been developed in Italy and was becoming common all over Europe. Next he studied law in preparation for public office and in 1554 received an appointment. These were troublous times in France, and Montaigne was not happy in the midst of religious and political turmoil. In his thirty-eighth year he began to withdraw from public affairs and rarely paid attention to them until he was elected mayor of Bordeaux in 1581. He retired to a rural castle where he collected books, conversed with friends, reflected upon the writings of classical authors, contemplated the ways of man, and wrote his famous essays. They are the compositions of a man of culture who has retired from the world but has not surrendered his interest in the problems of humanity. Montaigne was eminently rational, urbane, and polished. His essays on education contain many of the ideas which have dominated pedagogy to this day. His rationalism marks him as a forerunner of Voltaire and indicates the end of the Renaissance proper. The age of tumultuous interest in life and the desire to master all knowledge and art was over.

NOTEWORTHY SPANISH AND PORTUGUESE HUMANIST WRITINGS

The history of Renaissance letters in Spain is concerned to a large extent with the reformation of the Church and will be considered in the chapters dealing with Catholic Revival. Only two writers, Vives and Cervantes, can be considered in this section. Juan Luis Vives (d. 1540) was born in Valencia. He received a traditional education, but imbibed humanist ideas in his youth and subsequently studied in Paris and Louvain. While at the latter place, he wrote a commentary on St. Augustine's *City of God* which won him the approval of Erasmus and More. Vives lived many years in Bruges but spent some time at the English court where he enjoyed the favor of Queen Catherine. He was tutor to Princess Mary, later Queen Mary Tudor. Supporting Catherine's cause against Henry VIII, Vives was forced to leave England and returned to Bruges.

Vives enjoyed a wide reputation, and contemporaries linked his name with More and Erasmus. He wrote many treatises illustrating the social conceptions of humanists. In 1526 he produced *On the Help of the Poor* in which he advocated an advanced and novel system of charitable enterprise. Complaining that the clergy had failed in helping the poor, he held that governments of towns should assume the task of looking after the unfortunate. However, the poor should be cared for only if they were willing to work—hospices and hospitals were to be emptied of lazy people who refused to work. Even the blind were required to do something. Guilds were to take some youths as apprentices. Towns were to supervise the education of the poor in their charge and especially look after their religious welfare. Foundlings were to be reared at public expense. A list of the indigent was to be drawn up so that the officials might know exactly how many needed help, and towns should inquire into the private life of every such person. Physicians were to treat the worthy poor at town expense. Two persons in each parish were to be delegated by the government to visit the people and keep a careful watch over their activities. Vives' book, which was dedicated to the town of Bruges, was widely circulated and repeatedly translated, but it is not clear just what influence it exerted upon the legislation of Low Country towns concerning paupers. Ypres in the previous year had passed some remarkable legislation which illustrates many of Vives' views, and it is possible that the humanist may have had some influence upon it.

Profoundly impressed by the moral aspects of humanism, Vives was interested in all phases of education. He wrote a number of treatises, and his prestige was such that he has often been called a "second Quintilian." His *Causes of the Corruptions of the Arts* discusses the problem of study and criticizes the conventional methods of education. Vives followed in the footsteps of his classical Greek and Roman predecessors, and his doctrines are very like those of Vittorino da Feltre whose school in Mantua was the most significant of the Renaissance. Vives believed that Latin and Greek should be taught, but that the mother tongue should not be neglected; he regarded the skillful use of the native idiom as a splendid accomplishment. Students were to be given drill in grammar, syntax, and rhetoric. Religion was to be taught, the moral development of children being a primary concern. He believed that girls as well as boys should be instructed in these subjects. The end of education was not the amassing of mere erudition but the acquisition of knowledge which would make possible better living.

Miguel de Cervantes Saavedra (1547–1616), a late contemporary of Montaigne, represents some of the best characteristics of the Renaissance in Spain. His family belonged to the bourgeoisie. Little is known about his early education, but the youth shared fully in the intellectual ferment of the day. He served in the navy and was wounded at Lepanto in 1571. Captured by Algerian pirates, he was ransomed after heroic endeavors to escape. In spite of many difficulties experienced in gaining a livelihood, he persisted in writing. He was deeply impressed by the literary style which had been developed in Italy, and he produced some works in accordance with its rules, a pastoral romance named *Galatea* appearing in 1584. But his greatest work was *Don Quixote*, the first part of which he published in 1604. Like Rabelais' great work, it is a satire, written obviously to discredit the popularity which old chivalric romances and moral conceptions still possessed in Spain. The most solemn ideals of knighthood are made the subject of hearty burlesque. But it is difficult to tell whether the writer meant to attack anything else, although plausible arguments have been advanced to show that the butt of his ridicule was the government. Don Quixote is a nobleman whose mind is filled with traditional chivalric conceptions which are rendered ridiculous by his evident insanity. Sancho Panza, his squire, on the other hand, is a practical person interested in the more matter-of-fact conceptions of the common man, and his good sense throws the unbelievable follies of Don Quixote into bold relief.

The *Lusiad* is Portugal's greatest literary monument of the Renaissance. Its author, Luis Vaz de Camoëns (1525?–1580), it appears, was of noble blood and was born in Coimbra. He was deeply influenced by the achievements of Vasco da Gama and his successors who created the overseas empire of Portugal, and also by the story of the long struggles between Portugal and the Moors of Africa. His poem combines the fervor of the Crusader, the zeal of knights, and the daring of explorers. In form, the *Lusiad* is indebted to the classical standards developed in Italy, for it was written in imitation of Ariosto's *Orlando Furioso*. It deals with the adventures of Vasco da Gama, but the deeds of many other national figures also are woven into the narrative. For the most part the poem is good history, and it became the national epic of Portugal.

RENAISSANCE LETTERS IN ENGLAND: MORE TO SHAKESPEARE

The *Utopia*, or *The Land of Nowhere*, by Thomas More (1478–1535) was England's first significant contribution to the literature of the Renaissance. More was born in London and was sent to Oxford where he received the elements of a humanist education. He learned Greek from Linacre. In 1496 he began the study of law and during the next few years became acquainted with Erasmus. Although an eager student of law, More also studied theology and the classics and was especially fond of St. Augustine's *City of God*. He soon acquired the humanists' dislike for scholastic philosophy. For a while he was dominated by the popular ascetic ideals of the passing Middle Ages but finally yielded to the new humanist impulses which surged in his mind. His *Utopia*, published in 1516, is classed as a romance but, like Rabelais' *Gargantua and Pantagruel*, it is a masterpiece of humanist criticism of man and society. It was probably inspired by Plato's *Republic*, but it is impossible to discover much relationship between the two works. It is a description of a fabulous land called Utopia in which a fair city, Amaurote, was situated.

The first book serves as an introduction to the social perfection of Utopia and contains some discussion of glaring faults in English society and government, one of which was the severe punishment inflicted in connection with theft. The law demanded the death penalty for thieves, and as many as twenty of them sometimes were hanged on one gallows. The enclosure of open fields and the creation of immense sheep runs was criticized, for it robbed villagers of their ancient rights to common wood, meadow, and pasture. This social dislocation was held to be one of the causes of the growth of crime. The numerous wars between France and the empire were sharply criticized, for More, like Erasmus and Rabelais, was opposed to war.

The second book is a description of Utopia and of Amaurote, a model city of the Renaissance age. The houses had glass windows, gardens, and vineyards, and the roofs were made of a substance like plaster designed to prevent fire. The city possessed an excellent water supply. The streets were 20 feet wide. The markets were kept sanitary; impure foodstuffs were excluded, and cattle used for food were carefully cleaned. No filth was tolerated. There were splendid hospitals which provided service for the sick. The wars of Utopia were humane; noncombatants were not killed, cities were not ruthlessly plundered, and the countryside was not ravaged. While it was believed that there was but one true religion, dissenters were not prosecuted. They were forbidden to spread their doctrines among the common people but were encouraged to discuss their views with the better informed in the hope that finally they would see the light of truth. The *Utopia* soon became known throughout Europe.

More wrote his masterpiece in Latin to win a wider audience. This preference for a foreign idiom, however, was doomed to vanish during the course of the century, for townsmen, enriched by the economic revolution effected by the voyages of discovery and the influx of precious metals from America, did not readily learn Latin, no matter how much they might want to do so. It was inevitable that literature should voice the interests of this economically dominant class and use the native tongue more and more.

The highest expression of these forces in England is to be found in the drama of the days of Queen Elizabeth. The theater for generations had been intensely popular with the English people, and, as English culture and political life were less closely associated with the aristocracy than was the case on the Continent, England's greatest contribution to the Renaissance is to be found in her dramatic literature, culminating in the work of William Shakespeare.

Before considering this writer we must notice the work of a number of others who were active from the death of More in 1535 to the emergence of Shakespeare. Sir Thomas Wyatt (d. 1542) and Henry Howard, the Earl of Surrey (d. 1547), who wrote in English, adopted the Petrarchan sonnet. Roger Ascham (1515–1568) produced *The Schoolmaster*, a treatise setting forth the Renaissance ideal of education evolved in Italy. Sir Philip Sidney (1554–1586), a characteristic nobleman of the Renaissance, was devoted to literature and zealously studied the masterpieces of Italy. In 1580 he produced, in imitation of Sannazaro, a pastoral romance named *Arcadia* in which chivalric motifs abound. Its rare perfection of style was significant in the development of English prose, and its delightful imagery and delicate sentiment at once made the author famous. His lyrics, some of which were written for the *Arcadia*, and his sonnets have an abiding place in English letters.

Edmund Spenser (1552?–1599) marks the culmination of classical and humanist influences in England. His *Shepheard's Calendar* of 1579 was a pastoral poem in the tradition of Vergil and his Renaissance imitators. Spenser showed remarkable ability in using a number of poetic forms, thus revealing himself a devotee of the cult of significant form so striking a feature of the Renaissance. But Spenser is far more than a simple imitator. He was deeply interested in English life and became an ardent admirer of Chaucer, thus being able to engraft the Renaissance love for noble form upon the literature of his day. He also produced hymns, sonnets, and other works. His *Epithalamion* (1594) was written to perpetuate the memory of his own wedding day, and the scenes of that ceremonious occasion are recounted in magnificent stanzas which represent the poet's mature skill. But the greatest of all his productions was the *Faerie Queen*, an allegory which absorbed much of his best creative energy, and in which old and new are marvelously mingled. Each book sets forth an ideal moral virtue of the hero, Prince Arthur. The account is embroidered with pageants, tournaments, and encounters between dragons and giants. The poem, however, is far more than an Arthurian romance; like Tasso's *Jerusalem Delivered* and Camoëns' *Lusiad*, it is a masterpiece of the Renaissance, a poetic symphony almost without equal in any language. The passion for magnificent expression is apparent in every stanza. Classical learning adorns the poem throughout. Its variegated scenes have fittingly been compared with the magnificent tapestries made on the looms of the Low Countries. The poet also voiced the patriotic sentiments of Englishmen, for, deeply moved by the duel between Protestant Elizabeth and Catholic Spain, Spenser could not refrain from giving this theme a prominent place in his poem.

English drama now suddenly attained classic perfection. The old liturgical plays were still popular among the people, but important changes had been in progress for some time, for it was felt that the incongruities of the old plays could no longer be tolerated. The drama of the early Tudor period did not, however, rise to the highest art and much remained to be criticized. Thus Sir Philip Sidney complained:

> You shall have Asia of the one side, and Africa of the other, and so many other under-kingdoms, that the player, when he cometh in, must ever begin with telling where he is, or else the tale will not be conceived. Now ye shall have three ladies walk to gather flowers, and then we must believe the stage to be a garden. By and by we hear news of shipwreck in the same place, and then we are to blame if we accept it not for a rock. Upon the back of that comes out a hideous monster with fire and smoke, and then the miserable beholders are bound to take it for a cave. While in the mean time two armies fly in represented with four swords and bucklers, and then what hard heart will not receive it for a pitched battle.[1]

The doctrine that there should be unity of place, time, and action began to be emphasized. The influence of Terence and Plautus transformed comedy, and Seneca was frequently imitated, especially in tragedy. *Ralph Roister Doister* by Nicholas Udall (1505–1556) and *Gammer Gurton's Needle* by William Stevenson in 1575(?) are examples of native farces written in accordance with classical ideas. *Gorboduc or Ferrex and Porrex* (1561) by Thomas Sackville and Thomas Norton illustrates the influence of Seneca in tragedy.

But the drama of "the spacious times of great Elizabeth" was not to evolve from such classical predecessors, for classical influences were far less potent in England than on the Continent where the doctrine of the unities dominated all tragedy and comedy. English drama developed in its own way; dramatists took whatever suited them from their predecessors but used it in an independent manner. An important group of playwrights grew up under Elizabeth, including Thomas Kyd (d. 1594),

---

[1] P. Sidney, *The Defense of Poesy Otherwise Known as an Apology for Poetry*, Boston, 1896, p. 48.

author of *The Spanish Tragedy;* Christopher Marlow (d. 1593), who produced the *Jew of Malta, Tamburlaine, Tragical History of Doctor Faustus,* and others; and Robert Greene (d. 1592), author of *Friar Bacon and Friar Bungay* and *A Looking-Glass for London and England.* These writers and others of less repute would have given the age of Elizabeth undying glory even if William Shakespeare (1564–1616) had never appeared. But he cast all his contemporaries into the shadow, for more fully than any writer he represents the Renaissance in England.

Shakespeare was born in Stratford-on-Avon. His father was a well-to-do official who lost his fortune during the boy's early years. Shakespeare apparently received a good elementary education but could not continue his schooling owing to his father's misfortune. He grew up without discipline, married at 18, and was forced to flee from Stratford when his poaching activities were discovered. He went to London but nothing is known of his career between 1587 and 1592. A self-made man, he became well known as a playwright, and during the next 24 years dominated the London stage. He took an independent attitude toward tradition in the writing and production of plays, preferring to adhere to native developments rather than imitate foreign or ancient models. Untaught by classical tradition, he remained national and popular, and became the most resourceful playwright of the Renaissance. He possessed a ready pen, an amazing flow of words, and a keenly developed poetic sense, and he relied almost entirely upon his own instincts.

Shakespeare's historical plays expressed the patriotism surging in the breasts of Englishmen during the trying days of Queen Elizabeth. They deal with the careers of the English kings, John, Henry IV, Henry V, Henry VI, Henry VIII, Richard II, and Richard III, and were produced during his earlier years from 1592 to 1599 shortly after the Great Armada's defeat in 1588. Every Englishman was thrilled by the closing verses of *King John:*

> This England never did, nor never shall,
> Lie at the proud foot of a conqueror,
> But when it first did help to wound itself.
> Now these her princes are come home again,
> Come the three corners of the world in arms,
> And we shall shock them. Nought shall make us rue,
> If England to itself do rest but true.

Shakespeare's comedies appeared in an unending stream during his career, one of the first, *Comedy of Errors,* being produced in 1588(?) and the last, *The Tempest,* in 1611(?). He displayed the utmost freedom in adopting classical, Italian, and popular romantic themes. His knowledge of the thoughts and passions which surge in the human mind are revealed in his superb delineations, his women characters being especially interesting from this point of view. Feudal poetry pictured women as conforming to these types, hence the extreme self-denial and obedience of Griselda. But the new woman of the Renaissance was intellectually freer and knew how to assert herself in an environment all too dominated by the human male. Hence we have a group of magnificent living women, such as Beatrice, Rosalind, Julia, Desdemona, Lady Macbeth, and the incomparable Portia.

Shakespeare probably best displayed his matchless skill in his tragedies, the greatest of which are *Hamlet, Othello, King Lear,* and *Macbeth.* Other writers had produced excellent plays but none could approach him in portraying human passions in tragedy. The hesitant Hamlet who feels the urge of duty but cannot summon the resolution necessary to extract the last drop of revenge, the suspicious Othello crazed by the idea that his wife is unfaithful, the feeble Lear tossed about by his hostile daughters embittered by the favoritism he has shown to one of them, and the overly ambitious King Macbeth are supremely skillful portraits. It is well to compare the vivid concreteness of the Jew, Shylock, in *The Merchant of Venice* or Sir Andrew Aguecheek in *Twelfth Night* with the abstract characters of the older miracle plays. Shakespeare's satirical skill is nowhere better illustrated than in Touchstone's speech on a gentleman's code of honor. Shakespeare's lyricism is revealed by the songs which adorn his plays, and his sonnets are among the first in the English language. He expresses more fully than any other writer the nationalist tendencies of the Renaissance.

BOOK TWO

The Reformation and Catholic Revival

Introduction

WHAT ARE THE REFORMATION AND THE CATHOLIC REVIVAL?

THE TERM *Reformation,* as it is used in the following chapters, refers to the great religious crisis of the sixteenth century which shattered the centuries-old unity of the Christian faith of Western Europe.

Many a humanist of the *Quattrocento* criticized the religious life and thought of their day. Desiderius Erasmus, their most prominent spokesman, did likewise; in his Sermon on the Mount conception of the Christian faith he boldly found fault with Church and religious practice. Although he never broke with traditional Christian doctrines, his thought contributed to the upheaval of the Reformation. Martin Luther opposed this ethical conception of the Christian faith, taught that man, being totally evil, could be saved "by faith alone" and not by "good deeds," rejected the age-old doctrine of transubstantiation, repudiated five of the seven sacraments, and so tore from Rome the religious obedience of many Germans and of all Scandinavians. Sacramentarians—humanists of northern Europe who, like Zwingli, criticized morals, religious life, and the theological learning of the day—denied the Real Presence, teaching that the Lord's Supper was but a memorial. Their influence was immense. Ulrich Zwingli, sacramentarian in doctrine, opposed employment of painting and sculpture in the teaching and practice of the Christian faith and snatched many a Swiss canton from the traditional faith. The Anabaptists, of whom there were many groups, denied transubstantiation and the Real Presence, opposed infant baptism, taught that the Church was composed only of the regenerate, and added to the doctrinal confusion. In England, King Henry VIII, desiring to annul his marriage to his legitimate spouse, appealed to national sentiment in Parliament which declared the king head of the Church in England and broke her ancient ties with Rome. A state church arose, retaining much of the old doctrines, but soon accommodated itself to Lutheran, Zwinglian, and Calvinist influences within its fold. The doctrine of John Calvin, at once Biblical and assertive, infected

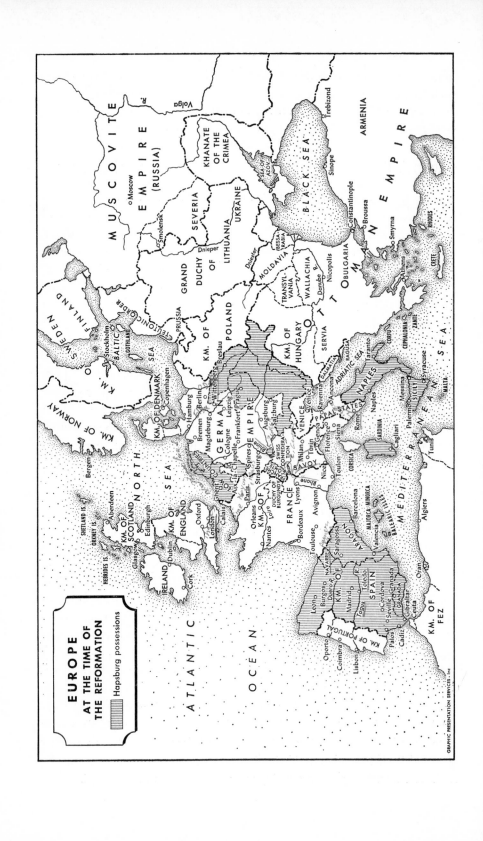

EUROPE
AT THE TIME OF
THE REFORMATION

||||||| Hapsburg possessions

GRAPHIC PRESENTATION SERVICES · Inc

large numbers in Switzerland, France, the Low Countries, and elsewhere. Socinians and other minor sects spread over Europe. Besides these groups there were influential individuals who broke with the Church—men like Sebastian Castellio who taught that religious minorities should be given full freedom in every state, and Michael Servetus who denied the Trinity, a cardinal teaching of traditional theology, Protestant as well as Catholic.

This surely was a violent crisis. For more than forty generations the Church by precept and example had taught the truths of the Christian faith. It was the most potent medium of higher culture, its ascetic ideals and churchly culture providing the chief formative principle of medieval life. Gothic architecture, sculpture, and painting are among the enduring creations of man, and scholastic philosophy and theology will ever constitute the greatest intellectual achievements of that age. A noteworthy scholar, an Anglican, trying to evaluate medieval Christianity, stated that it ". . . was the largest and most splendid fabric, and the most compelling influence that has ever risen among men. Its evangelical power converted men, and its Catholic power united them as nothing else could have done. And it was welcome. It was what they had waited for. The secular empires of the ancient world had been built up by conquest. Catholicism grew with the consent of its citizens."[1] This activity of the mother church of Rome impressed a certain unity upon medieval civilization which in spite of many changes the modern world has never quite abandoned. The Protestant revolt shattered the institutional religious unity of Europe and substituted for it a group of contending churches. No thoughtful student can fail to apprehend what this has meant to modern civilization.

To state the causes of events so varied and complex as those involved in the Reformation and the Catholic Revival is practically impossible. It is well, however, first to call attention to the far-reaching social, economic, and political transformation of European society during the centuries of the high Middle Ages (1000–1500). Life was becoming more and more mercantile, industries were growing, capital was accumulating, and towns were expanding rapidly. A new political edifice was erected upon these social and economic forces. Princes were able to govern in more routine manner. National states, powerful because of their ability to tax subjects, maintain armies, and organize staffs of officials, came into existence. The absolute monarch became more than ever the personification of the state. Many a prince in Reformation days strengthened his power by appropriating ecclesiastical properties. It is no exaggeration that this was a prominent aspect of the Reformation.

[1] S. C. Carpenter, *The Church in England, 1597–1688*, London, 1954, p. 164.

The Church also possessed vast privileges which it had received during the feudal days of the Middle Ages. Courts Christian clashed with the jurisdiction of state courts. Benefit of clergy exempted some individuals from secular tribunals. The Church endeavored to retain all ecclesiastical patronage, while secular princes wished to present candidates for clerical livings. The papacy sought to exempt ecclesiastical lands from taxation by princes, a claim which Philip the Fair of France had opposed. Papal tribunals called to Rome cases from Church courts in all parts of Christendom. Members of the Church hierarchy were closely bound to secular rulers. Archbishops, bishops, and abbots, and also many cathedral canons, owed their appointment directly or indirectly to secular princes. The power of such secular rulers was one of the prime evils in the life of the late medieval Church.

In spite of the Church's disciplinary care there was much superstition among the people, and witchcraft was common. Although the average man undoubtedly was sincerely Catholic, he clung to unchristian beliefs and practices. Excessive veneration of the saints all too often obscured the more fundamental aspects of the Christian religion. Too much faith was attached to the efficacy of pilgrimages and the power of relics. In short, the pure teachings of the Church were often contaminated by banal conceptions. That popular religious life often was crude cannot be surprising if one understands the social history of the Middle Ages. Although there were many zealous priests, genuine vocation was often lacking, for many men entered the clerical state for practical bread-and-butter reasons. Often they were uneducated, and this clerical ignorance lowered the efficiency of the priesthood.

It seemed impossible for the Church to adjust herself at once to the needs of the new age. The papacy had lately escaped destruction during the Great Schism (1378–1415) and the Age of the Councils (1409–1449). The bull *Execrabilis* (1460) forbade any appeal to a council save by the pope himself, and the papacy now became supreme in the Church. How could the hierarchy ever be induced to divest itself of privileges? Reform seemed impossible. A tense and dangerous state of mind was developed which might cause an explosion. Patriotism in the hearts of townsmen, the clash of papal and political interests, lay education, appeal to the masses through the newly invented printing press, the spectacle of a secularized papacy, impatience for reform, and ill-judged application of ecclesiastical penalties might produce revolts against the Catholic faith. But there were hidden forces in the Church, forces which were to set limits to the Protestant Revolt by setting her own house in order. This part of the religious movement of the sixteenth century we shall call the *Catholic Revival*.

PART I

Breakup of Religious Unity in Western Europe

Chapter 1

GENESIS OF LUTHER'S IDEAS

THE REFORMATION in Germany began under special circumstances. Emperors were elective, imperial power was becoming weaker, and princes were in large measure independent. Lay and ecclesiastical powers and imperial towns which dominated the diet usually pursued selfish interests. Absence of strong governmental organs made impossible any effective expression of German nationalist sentiment. Germany therefore was quite defenseless against the financial practices which had become so characteristic a feature of the Renaissance papacy. Ecclesiastical princes seldom restricted the activities of papal tax collectors. There was no parliamentary action as in England, or royal house as in France. There was sentiment against such ecclesiastical abuses as pluralism and absenteeism. People criticized laxity of morals and absence of genuine vocation among some of the clergy. They disliked current methods of obtaining money. The clergy often were so inadequately educated that they could not always command the respect of the more cultivated humanist laymen. Popular feeling, therefore, might easily be inflamed by the least untoward event. A public figure was needed, and such a person was Luther. The untoward event was the indulgence scandal of 1517.

MARTIN LUTHER'S EARLY YEARS

Martin Luther's parents were of peasant stock. Their ancestors lived in the Thuringian Forest in and around the little village of Möhra in the

447

county of Henneberg. They were sturdy freeholders who for generations had been able to wrest a scanty living from their meager holdings. Poverty was the lot of Hans Luther and his humble wife Margareta, and the memory of their hardships remained vivid to the very last in Martin's mind. Difficulty in making a living caused the couple to move to Eisleben

in the county of Mansfeld. There on November 10, 1483, a boy was born who, being baptized on the next day, the feast of St. Martin, received that saint's name. But again the father found no work, and the next year the family moved on and settled in the little town of Mansfeld.

This move was not merely an inconsequential event in the family history, for it revealed something of the temper of Hans Luther's mind. Mansfeld was the center of a considerable copper-mining industry. The counts were solicitous in promoting it, and people were moving thither to make their fortunes. The little town grew so rapidly that two new residential sections were added in a short time. In earlier ages peasants had found the few roads to advancement closed to them. Some indeed might become priests, but military careers were mostly reserved for the noble classes. Trade, industry, and towns in the later Middle Ages produced the bourgeoisie, and many a son of the peasantry found refuge in this new class. The expanding metal industry provided a new opportunity. Hans Luther, who had always possessed a certain hard-headed sense of realities, saw his chance and resolved to grasp it. He was successful. In 1491 he was member of a firm of copper miners, and 20 years later owned shares in at least six pits and two smelting houses. Thus he is an example of a peasant who through thrift, industry, and determination rose to become a petty capitalist.

Luther's childhood was spent in this peasant and bourgeois environment, from which he acquired many of the habits of mind which characterized him ever afterward. Belief in the multitude of spirits of farm, forest, and stream profoundly influenced him. The devil was a vigorous being who acted in a concrete manner. Nor did the boy escape the teachings about witchcraft which flourished everywhere. Besides these superstitious traditions which derived from the Pre-Christian past and which centuries of Christianity could not uproot, he acquired a blunt speech and uncouth language which sound indelicate and shocking to puritanical ears. He learned much from the primitive folkways of the people among whom he lived. He was genuinely *volkstümlich*, to borrow a telling word from the German language, and to the last day of his life he was proud of this trait. It was later to be the secret of his tremendous power to appeal to his countrymen, whether they were peasants or townsmen.

Luther's education was typical of the time. His stern parents were determined not to spare the rod and thus spoil their child. Thrashing was an important pedagogical device, and the boy never forgot the rigors of his early life. He was sent to the town school of Mansfeld in 1488, where he was introduced to the simplest rudiments of learning. He studied grammar, logic, rhetoric, reading, writing, arithmetic, singing, and a little Latin. He was subjected to religious influences of the traditional variety, but nothing especially significant can be discovered as far as his ideas are concerned. He undoubtedly received the sacraments and was taught the elements of the Catechism, the Confiteor, the Apostles' Creed, the Ten Commandments, and some prayers and songs.

At about 14 Luther was sent to a school in Magdeburg, probably the cathedral school in which instruction was given by the Brethren of the Common Life. During the year spent there he continued his elementary studies. The Brethren may have been important in implanting some of the sincere piety for which the order was famous in other places. They usually taught a simple practical religion of unquestioned orthodoxy and sought to inculcate a genuinely pious life. Whether they did this at Magdeburg is not known for certain. In any case this environment can have been no less religious than at Mansfeld. Magdeburg, a much larger urban center, was the seat of an archbishop, and religious life must have been especially rich. The sumptuous service, the numerous religious houses, and the busy coming and going of clerics must have stimulated the mind of a growing boy.

From 1498 to 1501 Luther was sent to school in Eisenach where his mother had relatives, and one of her aunts became interested in him. This too was a beginners' school, and his instruction was much like that at Magdeburg, but more advanced. He spent a great deal of time in composing Latin verses. He was also subjected to religious influences, for his great-aunt's husband was a sacristan. As Luther afterward regarded him with affection, he probably received favors from him. He continued the schoolboys' practice, so common at that time even if they were not paupers, of singing and begging in public. He was befriended by a family named Schalbe which provided him with food, and an obscure Frau Kotta seems to have given him lodging. From this grew a pretty tale of how the noble Frau Kotta took care of the poor boy when he was destitute and needed the watchful care of a pious woman.

LUTHER STUDIES AT ERFURT

Hans Luther next sent Martin to Erfurt to study in the university which had been founded in 1392. The city was the abode of a bishop and must have been a busy center of students and priests. The townsmen took vast pride in their university which enjoyed an excellent reputation among similar institutions of Germany. A narrow type of education dominated its curriculum; traditional methods still were sacred. Its philosophic and theological thought was of the school of Ockham, commonly called *modernist*. The works of the moderate realist, Thomas Aquinas, and others of the opposing school were scarcely read. Luther studied Aristotle and was especially skilled in dialectics and in scholastic philosophy. This training was later to exert profound influence upon his religious conceptions.

Although the official scholarship of Erfurt was decidedly traditional and conservative, humanist influences appeared, for some of the moderns evinced a tendency to welcome new ideas. Luther heard the humanist Emser of Ulm lecture at Erfurt in the summer of 1504, but even before this event he had acquired a love for the Latin classics which he read vigorously. But a humanist coterie did not exist at Erfurt in Luther's day. The circle of poets at nearby Gotha, composed of Crotus Rubeanus, Eobanus Hessus, Mutianus, and others, appeared only after Luther entered the monastery. Yet he acquired an abiding appreciation for classical writers and years after persisted in quoting passages from them. He did not become a humanist. His Latinity, never chastened by careful study of classical models, always remained brusque. Nor did he ever reach the point at which he could fully appreciate the humanists' zeal for what in that day was called poetry. Nevertheless, the scholarly equipment of humanism which he began to acquire at this time was to be of profound significance later when he began his Biblical studies.

After some review of his more elementary studies, the trivium and a further pursuit of the branches of the quadrivium, Luther received the degree of Bachelor of Arts in the autumn of 1502. In accordance with the methods in vogue in medieval schools, he then began to lecture while continuing his studies. In 1505 he received the degree of Master of Arts, standing second in a group of seventeen. It appears that he was an earnest, energetic student of excellent ability who applied himself diligently to his tasks. Hans Luther, who knew what it meant to earn one's living by the sweat of one's brow, had very definite ideas for his son's career. For centuries law had been the royal road to advancement for the sons of the bourgeoisie, and he planned that Martin too should go this way and rise in the world of practical affairs. His father had painfully climbed upward by slow degrees and was now recognized by the well-to-do bourgeois families of Mansfeld. A future bride from one of these was found for the young Master of Arts. The father was very proud of his son's achievement and addressed him no longer by the personal pronoun *du*, used among familiars, but by *Ihr*, the pronoun implying respect.

LUTHER ENTERS THE MONASTERY

But Luther was not to study law. He abruptly entered a monastery. This sudden change was most significant. What was the reason for it? As a student he had had his gayer moments and experienced the joy of life characteristic of students. Surely it could not be that the economic problem of life was too difficult for him to solve, now that he stood at the threshold of a successful career in practical affairs. Was it a question of religion? Earlier writers have usually passed over these events all too hastily. This is a mistake, for in those troubled days Luther took the first steps which reveal something of his mission in life. Here began a long evolution in his inner religious being which was finally to lead him into violent opposition to the hierarchy. Little is known of his religious life at the university. Without doubt it was plentifully stimulated by its conventional pious surroundings, and he probably adopted the concretely vivid conceptions of God generally held by the people. The last judgment and the rejection of the damned and their tortures in hell must have seemed very real in an age when artists were most ingenious in portraying them. Life seemed dramatic and filled with catastrophe. Death was ever a dread reality in an age of disease, famine, pest, war, burning of witches, and public execution of criminals.

It may well be that these things oppressed Luther. It is known that in May, 1502, he was wounded by a sword and that he was faint from loss of blood. The physician was a bungler and Luther, frightened, called upon the Virgin Mary and lost consciousness. A few days later the wound broke open and he again appealed to her. That he feared death is entirely possible, but that he suffered anxiety of soul at this time is by no means clear. The spring of 1505 arrived, and before the lectures in law began he had 3 months of leisure. Perhaps the death of a friend at this time troubled him. It is evident that Luther was overcome with fear and uncertainty, and terrified by the prospect of the last judgment and God's vengeance inflicted for sin.

Oppressed by these feelings, Luther began to attend the lectures in law on May 20, but apparently was dissatisfied. He went to Mansfeld in June to visit his parents, returned on June 30, and on July 2, when but a few miles from Erfurt, was overtaken by a thunderstorm near Stottern- heim. A bolt struck a tree near him, and he was thrown down by the electrical discharge. In imminent danger of death, he cried, "Help, St. Anna, I will become a monk!"

Many a person had taken such an oath under similar circumstances— indeed, it was the conventional thing to do. But the vow to God had been made. Since Catholics held that such promises had to be carried out unless a dispensation should be obtained, Luther apparently and mistakenly believed that he had no alternative but to enter a monastery. He bade his comrades farewell and on July 17 joined the Augustinian Eremites in Erfurt. His father, profoundly disgusted, almost disowned him; Luther's more gentle mother agreed with her husband. But the father, gravely troubled when two of his children were snatched away by the plague, yielded in his helpless grief to his son's wishes. This incident reveals young Luther as a religious character dominated by traditional concep- tions as shown by his resolve to carry out his vow. He was a genuine son of his time; nothing indicates that this was the beginning of a career which was to produce Protestantism.

Luther was received as a novice in September. After about one year spent in reflection, prayer, and the reading of religious works including the Scriptures, he took the vows of poverty, celibacy, and obedience. He studied theology and began to prepare himself for the priesthood. He read the works of the great scholar Gabriel Biel who followed the teaching of Ockham regarding universals. He successively became subdeacon, deacon, and priest, and, on May 2, 1508, celebrated his first Mass. He continued the study of theology according to the nominalistic conceptions of Ockham. His progress satisfied his superiors who suggested for him the temporary lectureship in philosophy in the recently founded university at Wittenberg, the capital of electoral Saxony. He entered upon his tasks in 1508 and at the same time continued the study of theology. He was back in Erfurt from 1509 to 1510 where he lectured on the *Sentences of Peter Lombard* and the works of St. Augustine.

BEGINNINGS OF LUTHER'S NOVEL RELIGIOUS IDEAS

The next important event in Luther's career was a visit to Rome, occasioned by the attempt to unite the Observantine branch of the Augustinian friars with the non-Observantine. This was the darling project of the vicar-general, John Staupitz, but seven Observantine houses, one of which was Luther's at Erfurt, refused to sanction the proposed step. Luther's zeal in behalf of these houses was such that they decided to send him with another brother to plead their cause at the curia. At Rome he went to see the places which pilgrims were wont to visit, worshiped in the chief churches of the Eternal City, and climbed the Sacred Stairs at the Lateran. He appears to have visited the catacombs of St. Sebastian, famed for the relics of saints. Without doubt he saw something of the corruption in Rome during the last days of Julius II. There is no truth in the oft repeated story of how, while climbing the Sacred Stairs, the thought rose in his mind that justification came by faith alone and that these acts availed nothing; whereupon he rose from his knees and slowly and sadly walked away. In the spring of 1511 he was back at Wittenberg. Soon after his return the projected union was abandoned. In May, 1512, he went to Cologne with Staupitz in the interest of his house. While there he was elected subprior of Wittenberg and was ordered to prepare for the doctorate in theology. He also visited the far-famed shrine of the Three Magi.

These facts indicate the esteem in which Luther was held by his colleagues. Had he been an uncongenial brother he certainly would not have enjoyed the fullest confidence of Staupitz, the vicar-general, nor would he have been appointed to these posts or sent on these missions. He now resumed the study of theology and on October 19 was promoted to the doctorate. Yet underneath the surface Luther was not contented, for he remained unsatisfied in the matter of salvation. He had gone into the monastery to win peace of soul and a sense of security by living the life of a religious. Whether he was constantly troubled by these difficulties from 1505 to 1512 is impossible to state, although later in his *Table Talk* he referred to these years as a period of profound unhappiness. Unfortunately he paid little heed to chronology and often interpreted the events of his career in the monastery in the light of later happenings. It is erroneous therefore to attach decisive importance to statements in that work. How Luther settled this problem of certitude about salvation is an event of central importance in modern history.

Impelled by the great fear which repeatedly came over him, Luther did the conventional thing; he tried to find relief in the sacraments, for in them, according to traditional conceptions, he should have found the solution to his problems. But it did not work thus. To win salvation it was necessary to do only what was holy. This was commanded in Scripture and by the teachings of the Church. His Ockhamist philosophic ideas appear to have exerted much influence in this connection. These represented God as a being who could not be shown by reason to have any existence. He could be known only through faith. He appeared as an arbitrary will, and this emphasized the problem of determinism. God's grace Luther of course understood, but he believed that this could be won only through merit on his own part. Herein lay a great difficulty, for, try as he might, he could never arrive at any inner assurance. He was frightened by the feeling that he fell short of being entitled to God's grace, and he continually contrasted God's sinlessness with his own corruption. The more he sought perfection the more he became aware of his inability to do any holy deed. The feeling that he was lost drove him to despair.

The troubled friar was aided by his superior, Staupitz, a mystic brought up in the practical religious ways for which the devout Brethren of the Common Life had become famous. He urged Luther to look upon the merits of Christ and consider their efficacy in forgiving the guilt of sin rather than to examine himself in order to discover defects from which he must purge himself before winning the grace of God. This simple expedient appears to have given Luther some peace of mind, and it also helped him in the grave difficulty presented by the doctrine of predestination. He felt that he was too deeply overwhelmed by sin to do anything that could be accounted good in God's sight. Yet in the Bible he was commanded to be perfect. Could he be certain of the divine grace necessary for salvation? In this Staupitz' practical mystical piety also helped greatly, for Staupitz insistently pointed to the promises that the merits of Christ would heal a soul of sin and urged that Luther should trustingly rely upon them. Reading works of German mystics such as Eckhart and the little classic *Theologia Germanica* also appears to have helped him.

Luther ever afterward retained a vivid memory of his way out of this impasse. It came to him one day in 1512 or 1513 while sitting in a tower in the monastery, reflecting upon the words of St. Paul's Epistle to the Romans (King James' Version, i, 17) : "For therein is the righteousness of God revealed from faith to faith: as it is written, The just shall live by faith." Suddenly he saw clearly what he had long been groping for. The believer is saved by his faith in the merits of Christ's sacrifice which washes away the stain of guilt. Of his own unaided self, corrupted by sin which assailed him and which he was powerless to control, he could do nothing to win that which these merits could give. Hence man is saved not by trying to be holy in the sight of God, but simply by believing in the merits of Christ's crucifixion. *Man is saved by faith alone and not by doing the works of the law*, that is, the commandments of God and the Church.

This is the famous Lutheran principle of justification by faith alone which was to exert vast influence in the religious thinking of the Reformation and succeeding centuries. Its revolutionary character lay in the fact that if salvation comes only through the believer's personal faith in the merits of Christ, a mediatory priesthood becomes unnecessary, for each man would become his own priest. The traditional institution of the Christian religion was thus robbed of its dogmatic foundations. It was a revolution of the first magnitude.

Luther continued to lecture on Biblical subjects. In 1513–1515 he treated the Psalms. In 1515–1516 he discussed the Epistle to the Galatians which was followed by the Epistle to the Hebrews, apparently in 1517–1518. Of all these the lectures on the Psalms and the Romans are without doubt the most important, for they came at a moment when his ideas about justification were becoming clarified; they mark an epoch in the history of the Reformation. Humanist influences which Luther had imbibed ever since he was a student at Erfurt now bore fruit. He took a very simple view of Biblical texts. Only the literal meaning in its historical setting interested him; he cared nothing for tedious allegories, far-fetched moral interpretation of texts, and bootless straining after impossible anagogical meanings. Grammatical studies now assumed unusual importance. His lectures greatly impressed his auditors, the students being especially fond of their professor's originality in handling Biblical texts, but none perhaps yet divined the revolutionary tendencies that lurked in them.

Luther had arrived at his characteristic conception of justification by 1513, if it is permissible to place his experience in the monastic tower so early. This precedes the indulgence controversy by as much as 4 years. Luther's chief concern was the question of salvation; neither he nor his colleagues were aware of the full dogmatic implications and practical consequences of his religious experiences. Only circumstances over which he had little control could bring out the heretical nature of his ideas. Meanwhile students took up his teaching, Bartholomew Bernhardi being the first to break a lance for Luther's views in a public discussion in September, 1516. His theses dealt with the capacity of human will in connection with divine grace and related themes. One of these theses stated that "man sins even when doing the best he can, for of himself he is unable either to will or to think."

Franz Gunther, another of Luther's pupils, next presented some theses in September, 1517, which followed Luther's theology at some length. "Man," he declared, "can will and do only what is evil," and "We do not become righteous by doing what is right, but only after we have become righteous do we perform what is right." Regarding Aristotelian thought he maintained that "without Aristotle no man can become a theologian. On the contrary, he is no theologian who does not become one without Aristotle." It is interesting to note that although these propositions echoed Luther they attracted little attention.

That Luther was no ordinary recluse, content to spend his day in the calm of his cloister, is shown by his mission to Rome and his activities as subprior of the house in Wittenberg. In May, 1515, he was chosen vicar of a group of Augustinian houses in Thuringia and Meissen. The new activities made him a busy man. He was keenly interested in reform, especially among the regular clergy, and his lectures on the Epistle to the Romans contained numerous references to the need of such reformation. He complained of abuses; in some sermons he attacked the avarice of the clergy in connection with indulgences. Heretics were to be suppressed. He spared neither bishops, cardinals, nor even the pope himself. Yet he apparently remained convinced of the necessity of maintaining the integrity of the institutions of the Church. He criticized princes for their unchristian conduct; in fact, he wanted to see a reform in state and society as well as in the Church. Soon all Germany was to resound with the clamor of the famous Indulgence Controversy.

Chapter **2**

RISE OF LUTHERANISM

BY THE AUTUMN of 1517 Martin Luther had advanced far in the religious development marked out by his experience in the tower of the monastery. His ideas were not compatible with the practices of many churchmen and they might readily become heretical. For the moment he was actively engaged in directing the affairs of his monasteries. The crisis arrived in 1517 when indulgences for the building of St. Peter's in Rome were preached in lands adjacent to electoral Saxony.

THE ELECTION OF ARCHBISHOP ALBERT OF MAINZ

Archbishop Albert, scion of the Hohenzollern house, which princely connection gave him many advantages, was only 23 years of age when in August, 1513, he was elected to the large and important province of Magdeburg. Very soon thereafter he was elected administrator of the see of Halberstadt. The province of Mainz now fell vacant. Vast political influence had been exerted in securing his nomination to this post, and after much maneuvering Albert was also given this province in March, 1514. His brother, the Elector Joachim of Brandenburg, was the chief political agent in securing these preferments. Holding more than one benefice was known in canon law as a cumulation and was illegal; furthermore, Albert was not of canonical age. Such irregularities could be permitted only by special dispensation from Rome.

Application to the curia was made forthwith by the archbishop, supported by Elector Joachim. Well might Leo X hesitate, for the prelate was little more than a youth, and to place such grave responsibilities upon immature shoulders seemed unwise. But the proposition nevertheless offered some advantages. It would guarantee for papal policy in Germany the support of two electors. This might prove a valuable advantage in the next imperial election which could not be far away because of Emperor Maximilian's advanced age. The money to be paid was also a strong argument, for Albert agreed to give 10,000 ducats for permission to hold two extra sees, and he paid 14,000 ducats for the confirmation. Consequently, in August, 1514, he was declared to be legally entitled to these dignities.

This transaction, sealed and ratified by the officials of the curia, illustrates how political considerations might influence the policy of granting dispensations. The whole affair was legal according to canon law, but it was not beyond criticism. The commercial aspect of the affair was an even more dubious matter. The archbishop-elect offered bond to the banking firm of the Fuggers of Augsburg which advanced 29,000 Rhenish florins to cover expenses. To discharge this very heavy debt, officials in the curia advised that the archbishop-elect should proclaim the extension of an indulgence for the construction of St. Peter's in Rome throughout the provinces of Mainz and Magdeburg and the see of Halberstadt. Arrangements were completed by March, 1515. Half of the income was to be given to the pope; the other half was to be kept by Albert to discharge his debt. This transaction was wholly reprehensible, for these terms were kept secret, the proclamation speaking only of the pious work of building St. Peter's.

INDULGENCES IN LATE MEDIEVAL TIMES

It is important to understand what is meant by the practice of indulgences. It may be difficult for some people in a peculiarly untheological age to grasp their nature, but, if the student seeks to look at them in their practical relationships, he will soon appreciate their true character. According to teaching laid down several centuries before, an indulgence was simply the remission of the whole or part of the penalty imposed for sin already forgiven. It was held that a sin first of all involved guilt (*culpa*) and that inevitably attached to this was the matter of penalty (*poena*) or punishment. Guilt was freely forgiven to a repentant sinner. The penalty, however, still had to be discharged. If the sinner was contrite, God would surely forgive the guilt, but the priest as representative of the Church would still insist upon a substantial penalty. If the penitent did not discharge this in life, he was required to do so in purgatory. From time immemorial indulgences had been granted by the Church, and by the end of the Middle Ages they had become an important feature in the moral, pious, social, economic, and cultural activities of the day.

While the theory of indulgences is quite simple, the practice is more difficult to understand. The early Church inflicted such drastic temporal punishments for sin that to render satisfaction for the gravest sins often required years of active effort. It happened from time to time that canonical penalties could not be paid at all. For example, a man who had lost a leg could not very well go on pilgrimage. Furthermore, the stern rigor of the early Church withheld absolution of guilt until satisfaction had been entirely made. It might happen that a truly repentant sinner might die before he could be absolved. This, of course, was not just, and so the Church adopted the custom of absolving the contrite from their guilt after imposing the satisfactions which were to be discharged in the future. A sense of equity also led to the idea of substituting penalties. A canonical satisfaction which would be impossible for a person to discharge might be commuted to an equivalent—going on pilgrimage might be changed to almsgiving. Finally in the tenth century, it was decided that the merits won by Christ, which were far in excess of the actual needs of men, formed a vast treasury, to which were added the merits of the Virgin Mary and those of the many saints who by holiness of life had won more than was necessary for their own salvation. This repository of merits was a most precious storehouse. The Church taught that she could draw upon this treasury of good works and apply the merits to extinguish canonical penalties. Such commutation was the essence of an indulgence.

Only under certain definite conditions could a valid indulgence be obtained. First, a person was required to be truly contrite. Next, he must confess his sins, whereupon satisfaction might be imposed and discharged later. Then followed absolution. An indulgence was effective in removing all or part of the penalty of sin. In addition, some good work was prescribed, for a contrite person was eager to do good works as evidence of true penitence. This natural impulse in religious life, when applied and directed, led to results of great social importance. It was to be the basis of much philanthropic activity. It is impossible to draw up an exhaustive list of the many charitable medieval foundations such as hospitals and almshouses which were built partly or entirely by indulgences.

TETZEL PREACHES THE INDULGENCE FOR THE BUILDING OF ST. PETER'S

Announcement of the extension of an indulgence for the building of St. Peter's, originally proclaimed by Julius II, was made in a bull of March 31, 1515. It named the Archbishop Albert chief commissary in his two provinces and the see of Halberstadt. The terms were liberal, being applicable to a large variety of cases. Contributors were allowed to choose their confessors and were assured full remission after proper contrition and due confession. Benefits from grants of money were declared to be equivalent to those gained from pilgrimage to Rome or Compostella. The indulgence was to run for 8 years, and for each of the first 3 Emperor Maximilian was to receive 1000 Rhenish guilders to be applied to building a church in Innsbruck.

Johann Tetzel, a Dominican prior in Leipzig, was designated sub-commissary in the province of Magdeburg and the see of Halberstadt. He issued instructions to the parish clergy and the preaching of the indulgence began. In January, 1517, he was at Eisleben, Jüterbogk, Zerbst, and other places in ducal Saxony near the confines of electoral Saxony within whose boundaries no preaching of the indulgence was permitted by the government. People from Wittenberg nevertheless met the indulgence preachers at these places, and through them as well as through general report Luther became acquainted with what was happening.

Just what Tetzel preached is difficult to state. Much has been written for and against him. It is certain that the charges of Tetzel's evil living were unfounded. Neither was he ignorant of the teaching of the Church regarding indulgences; the fact that he was a Dominican would preclude it. He probably even preached the official doctrine. But it is most certain that he did it in a popular manner, by using exaggerated language and urging his hearers to give liberally. He probably did not make clear to the simple folk the exact value of these indulgences. Indeed, it was easy for them to be confused by the variety. There were indulgences for the living which have just been described. There were indulgences for the dead also, for it was widely thought, and taught by the Church, that a pious offering in behalf of a dead friend or relative would certainly be of great advantage to his soul in purgatory. The Church held that the pope as Christ's vicar could intercede in behalf of the departed. Some indeed taught that he could apply the merits of Christ and the saints to souls in purgatory in virtue of his power to bind and loose. Tetzel undoubtedly taught this as true doctrine in spite of the fact that the Church never advocated it and that it had been rejected by the theological professors in Paris. Probably the grant of confession letters contributed to the misunderstanding. Such letters were given on payment of money and were of limited application. These documents merely gave the holder, when in imminent danger of death, the right to choose a confessor and obtain absolution from certain cases reserved to the pope. They presupposed contrition before absolution. In such circumstances it was inevitable that ordinary folk might misunderstand, especially when Tetzel, using colorful language in order to stimulate the flow of gifts, dwelt so eloquently on the value of indulgences, particularly those for the dead. He luridly described the pains of purgatory and pathetically pictured to his hearers the souls of their dead relatives crying to them for help. Would they callously abandon them to the torments of the flames, when for a mere trifle they might deliver them?

LUTHER POSTS HIS INDULGENCE THESES

Luther had long been opposed to the emphasis placed upon good works, for he thought that man was so corrupted by sin that his good works could avail nothing in the sight of a righteous God. Only by faith could one be saved, not by his deeds. The conduct of Tetzel angered him. Furthermore, he had ample opportunity to see with his own eyes the consequences of such gross mercenariness. He drew up a series of theses in Latin setting forth his doubts about the practice of indulgences, affixing them to the door of the castle church on the Sunday before All Saints' Day (October 31, 1517). According to the ways of academic life he proposed to defend these theses against all comers, and he also wrote to Archbishop Albert begging him to withdraw his instructions to Tetzel.

The *Ninety-Five Theses* have always been accorded an important place in the history of the Reformation, but it is certain that Luther's religious development between 1512 and 1517 was of greater moment theologically. During these years he arrived at his characteristic doctrine of justification by faith alone. Although he himself did not at first see the bearing of this doctrine, events such as the indulgence controversy brought out its doctrinal tendencies. Many of his theses were not heretical; some were even without much point, but throughout there was a typically Lutheran dislike of a mediatory priesthood. This is the root of the statement in the sixth thesis: "The pope cannot remit any guilt (*culpa*), except by declaring that it had been remitted by God and by assenting to God's remission. . . ." However, according to traditional teaching the pope possessed the power of the keys, the authority to bind and loose. Most of the theses sharply criticized current practices relating to indulgences, and in some Luther protested that formal, mercenary expedients avail naught in so spiritual a thing as religion.

The theses at first attracted little attention and the disputation did not come to pass. But their author, curious to know what friends thought of them, sent a few written copies on November 11 to the houses of the Augustinian order in Erfurt and Nuremberg. Someone betrayed his confidence and handed them to a printer, and by the close of the month printed copies were circulating in Leipzig and Magdeburg. In December a German translation appeared, and by March, 1518, the theses were known generally throughout Germany. They produced a sensation. Chagrined at being halted in the midst of his preaching, Tetzel replied to the theses by issuing 106 theses of his own in January, 1518, completely denying Luther's position. Tetzel boasted that within 3 weeks Luther would meet a heretic's death. Other Dominicans followed Tetzel and attacked Luther.

OFFICIAL REACTION TO LUTHER'S *THESES*

Archbishop Albert sent a copy of Luther's theses to Pope Leo X who referred them to Cardinal Cajetan, a theological light of the day. Early in December this churchman reported his opinion. He was acquainted with the abuses attending the preaching of indulgences and the theories about the efficacy of indulgences for the dead, but he did not yet realize the immense consequences which Tetzel's activities had among Germans. Neither did Leo, the child of the Renaissance culture of Florence and Rome. "A drunken German wrote these things, but as soon as he is sober he will talk differently," he declared with some of the contempt of Italians for the barbarians of the north. It was this spirit, in part at least, that lay at the root of German resentment of the papacy. Leo soon took a more serious view of the commotion in Germany and besought Gabriele della Volta, general of the Augustinian order, to induce Luther to keep silence. There was a meeting of German Augustinians at Heidelberg in April to discuss Luther's position and induce him to retract. He, however, sustained his theses well and to the satisfaction of many of his fellow friars.

It was determined that Luther should send to the curia a statement of his views. This he did in his *Resolutions*, addressed to Leo, accompanied by a letter to Staupitz in which he sketched the events that had led to the publication of the *Theses*. He also recounted the abuses of indulgence preachers, protesting that the theses were intended only for academic purposes, not to set forth dogma. "Now what shall I do?" he wrote. "I cannot recant them: and yet I see that marvelous enmity is enflamed against me because of their dissemination." He was willing to defer to papal wisdom. "I cast myself at the feet of Your Holiness, with all that I have and all that I am. Quicken, kill, call, recall, approve, reprove, as you will." He still believed in the necessity of priests, yet insisted on the supereminent function of faith, for through faith alone came salvation. In the *Theses* Luther had protested against current practices in preaching pardons, but now he progressed farther toward the inevitable goal, the sufficiency of man's faith without the mediation of a priest to win the boon of salvation.

Luther's enemies at the curia persisted in their hostility. The papal censor Prierias, asked to study his writings, condemned Luther's statements about indulgences, relying upon the principle of authority, whereby the bishop of Rome, the head of the Church universal who could not err, had full authority in faith and interpretation of Scripture. Anyone who would not be instructed by him was a heretic. Luther answered in characteristic fashion. Formerly he had protested against the emphasis traditionally placed upon good works, holding that faith only could justify in the sight of God, and that the priest's mediation was less important than a man's faith. Now he went a step farther. The Church universal was the body of the faithful in Christ, and Christ was its head. Supreme authority was to be found only in a council representing it—an audacious opinion, for it denied papal headship.

The citation which followed was not, however, to bring Luther to Rome. The Saxon elector Frederick the Wise stood staunchly by Luther, for he was proud of the prestige which the University of Wittenberg conferred on his lands, and as German prince he was jealous of his authority. Furthermore, Emperor Maximilian was advanced in age, and in the forthcoming imperial election the elector's vote might prove important. Maximilian wished to secure the succession to his grandson Charles. Frederick received the emperor's suggestions coolly and his attitude seemed doubtful. For a while Luther thought that Maximilian would prevent his extradition to Rome, but in this he was mistaken, for the emperor wrote in strong terms about him to the pope. The imperial diet met at Augsburg in the summer of 1518, and Leo sent Cajetan to represent him. Knowing that the emperor was opposed to Luther, the legate first thought to induce the secular arm to strike the heretic down. This summary method appeared attractive to him, and seemingly the emperor stood ready to aid him.

Politics, however, influenced Cajetan's conduct. The curia was not sympathetic to Charles' candidacy. He was king of Naples and might use his power to harm the papacy. Furthermore, were he elected emperor, he could claim the duchy of Milan as an imperial fief, which would place northern as well as southern Italy at his mercy. Frederick also opposed Charles and favored a subsidy to help the pope in a crusade against the Turks, whereupon the curia showed favor to the elector by conferring upon him the Golden Rose. Luther's citation was soon changed, however, and he was required to appear before Cajetan in Augsburg. The elector supported him, but Luther entertained fears. Finally, on October 7, he arrived in Augsburg, and 4 days later received the imperial letter of safe conduct. Cajetan knew that Luther's complaint against the preachers of indulgences was well founded. He would overlook much, but one thing he could not let pass unnoticed, for certain heresy must needs be corrected. He required (October 12) that Luther recant unconditionally and without discussion, but his language and bearing were fatherly and conciliatory.

Luther, not the person to yield meekly, asked to be instructed wherein his error lay. Cajetan pointed to certain of the *Ninety-Five Theses* which were contrary to the accepted teaching regarding penance and the treasury of merits, and also to statements in the *Resolutions*. But Luther insisted that the teaching about the treasury was not well supported in Scripture. Cajetan contended that the pope was final authority in faith and morals and in interpretation of Biblical texts. Luther denied this supremacy.

More serious was the next point in the discussion, when Luther insisted that the ministrations of the priest were of no avail apart from the faith of the participant. Cajetan insisted on the traditional teaching. They were poles apart. Luther recapitulated his points in a statement on October 14 in which he held that popes had erred and would err, and that infallible authority rested only in Scripture whence the believer could draw the pure doctrine of salvation. A stormy altercation began. "Revoke or be gone" was the cardinal's command. On the eighteenth Luther appealed from the ill-informed pope to one better informed, thus rejecting the finality of Leo's opinion. Two days later, under cover of night and fearing some hostile move, he departed for Saxony.

LUTHER'S DEBATE WITH DR. JOHN ECK AT LEIPZIG

The true character of Luther's theological views became clearer under pressure of circumstances. The next important step was the famous debate at Leipzig with Dr. John Eck, professor of theology in the University of Ingolstadt, a keen theologian, devout son of the Church, and to the end a determined enemy of Luther. He burned to distinguish himself, rushed into the lists, and circulated an attack on the *Theses* in which he accused Luther of holding Husite views. These observations which at first appeared in manuscript began a controversy with Andrew Karlstadt, Luther's colleague at Wittenberg. By the close of 1518 preliminary arrangements for the debate had been made. Eck also attacked Luther in the theses aimed at Karlstadt, singling out the supremacy of the pope which Luther impugned. The latter welcomed a public disputation. He knew little about the historic position of the bishop of Rome in the life of the Church and even stated that it was little more than 400 years old. He also held that it was contrary to Scripture and to the decrees of the Council of Nicaea.

Leipzig was situated in ducal Saxony. Duke George was a loyal son of the Church but, like many princes, objected to the excessive power, as he regarded it, of the clergy. When the bishop sought to prevent a debate, the duke insisted that it be held. Many people flocked thither, attracted by the promise of a lively discussion on a burning question. For 4 days Karlstadt and Eck battled about freedom of the will and efficacy of good works apart from grace. It was an unequal encounter. Eck was far superior in debate, but had great difficulty in meeting his opponent's arguments without resorting to subtleties which humanists, trained in the literary methods of the Renaissance, despised. Luther was next pitted against him. Eck based his arguments upon the traditional teaching of theologians, that the Church formed one body with one head, Peter, who had been named by Christ to be His vicar on earth, and whose successors ever since had possessed the power of the keys to bind and loose. To parry this argument for the infallible authority of the papacy, Luther held that the head of the Church was Christ alone. The word rock in Matt XVI: 18, he declared, referred to the whole Church, not merely to that founded by St. Peter. Papal headship rested only upon human foundations, and its development could be traced historically.

Eck labored to discredit his opponent in the minds of the hearers by accusing Luther of entertaining the heretical opinions of Marsiglio of Padua, John Wycliffe, and the Bohemian John Hus, all of whom had been condemned by the Church. Nationalist feeling against the Bohemians was especially keen in ducal Saxony which adjoined Bohemia, and the University of Leipzig had been founded in 1409 by a secession of German masters and students from the University of Prague. But Luther did not hesitate. He boldly declared that some of Hus' positions were not heretical, for they could be proved true by Scripture. Duke George was visibly disturbed by this turn in the discussion. Luther argued, when forced to it, that even councils could err. Only Scripture possessed final authority, and popes and councils were to be obeyed if their acts and decrees were in harmony with it. In the discussions regarding indulgences Luther was pleased to see that Eck had little to criticize, for the latter was fully cognizant of the evils that accompanied their use.

The debate proved an important event in the history of the Reformation. Luther had now wandered far from the official position. Appealing to the historical evolution of papal supremacy and placing it on a purely human basis was a dangerous thrust which was to exert much influence. The debate settled nothing; it merely accentuated the differences in point of view. It now remained to cast Luther and his followers out of the fold.

Luther's enemies continued their efforts with increased vigor. Eck pressed the curia for action against so manifest a heretic, and others in the papal camp wrote books and pamphlets. But Luther also had his supporters, for the most part humanists. They had for years shot many a satirical dart at Church officials who were especially vulnerable because they often wrote bad Latin, possessed no real appreciation for classical literature, and preferred the logic and philosophy of the schools to a fresh study of Latin and Greek letters. Was not Luther merely another Erasmus? Humanists thought so, at least until the moment came when they realized that his conception of salvation by faith without works was little to their taste. The more serious of them were inclined to make an ethical matter of religion and so were really nearer the Catholic than the Lutheran position. This is the reason Erasmus and others finally abandoned Luther. For the moment, however, they followed him.

LUTHER BREAKS WITH ROME

Younger Germans led by patriotic sentiments gathered around Luther in opposition to the Roman hierarchy. Ulrich von Hutten was vociferous in supporting him and published an edition of Lorenzo Valla's study of the *Donation of Constantine*. Luther read it in February, 1520, and was amazed at the exposure. The papal bull *Exsurge Domine*, which was finally drawn up by June 15, 1520, did more than any other document to focus the attention of people upon Luther. It described the gravity of his heresies and condemned them, and ordered the faithful, under threat of excommunication and loss of benefices, to shun him. Luther was given 60 days in which to cease from his course, after which, should he fail to comply, he was to be severed from the body of the faithful and to be seized by Church or secular authorities. Such communities as would not listen to this order were to incur sentence of interdict. It was due to Eck's activity in Rome that this bull was drawn up, and Eck now appeared in Germany to see that all authorities were properly informed of the text.

Meanwhile Luther continued his studies. He resolved to pen an appeal to the people of Germany. The three great Reformation tracts which now appeared (1520) marked his complete rupture with the papacy. The first of these was *An Open Letter to the Christian Nobility of the German Nation Concerning the Reform of the Christian State* (June–August, 1520), addressed to the emperor, the head of the German people. The argument is as follows: The champions of papal supremacy have built three walls behind which they are intrenched: (1) spiritual authority is superior to temporal authority, (2) the authority to interpret Scripture resides in the pope, and (3) the pope alone can convoke councils. Luther replied to this in short fashion: the first wall falls, since all believers are priests. There is no distinction therefore between clerical and secular estate. A priest exists simply because of the principle of division of labor! "A priest in Christendom is nothing else than an officeholder. While he is in office, he has precedence; when deposed, he is a peasant or a townsman like the rest." The second wall has no secure basis. "If we are all priests, . . . and all have one faith, one Gospel, one sacrament, why should we not also have the power to test and judge what is correct or incorrect in matters of faith?" And "the third wall falls of itself when the first two are down. For when the pope acts contrary to Scripture, it is our duty to stand by Scripture, to reprove him, and to constrain him, according to the word of Christ in Matt. XVIII: 15."

Having thus destroyed the theoretical bases of papal supremacy in the Church, Luther next described the abuses which should be discussed in councils. These included the wealth of pope and cardinals, the system of taxation, and administrative abuses. The last section of this remarkable pamphlet listed certain proposals for reform. Among them were abolition of annates, the whole complicated system of making appointments to benefices which fell vacant when their holders died in Rome, the control of local churches by the curia, ecclesiastical justice, secular authority in Naples and the States of the Church, reform of the mendicant orders, marriage of the clergy, abolition of mortuaries, interdict, saints' days, pilgrimages, and many other topics. This tract, written in German, made a tremendous national appeal.

Far more damaging was *The Babylonian Captivity of the Church*, written at the close of August, which struck a vigorous blow at the sacramental system. The pamphlet, being written in Latin, was not intended for the general public. It declared that only two of the seven sacraments were valid, the Lord's Supper and baptism, and possibly also penance. Luther thought that no scriptural texts could be adduced in support of the others. *A Treatise on Christian Liberty* appeared in November, a letter to Pope Leo being added as a preface. The book was milder in tone than its two predecessors and appears to have been composed before them in response to the papal envoy Miltitz, with whom Luther had had a conference in October of the previous year. In it he elucidated his doctrine of the priesthood of all believers, and explained why good works had no power to save and why faith in the merits of Christ won by His sacrifice could alone bring salvation.

Fifteen years had now elapsed since Luther entered the monastery in quest of salvation. Why he could not find full comfort in Catholic conceptions will probably never be explained; it is the everlasting and insoluble mystery of human personality. Through much groping Luther had sought to discover the truth. His dogged tenacity was accompanied by a peculiar conservatism which made it difficult to break with the faith of his fathers. Gradually his ideas took form. External events usually forced him to clarify his thoughts and commit them to writing. The three Reformation tracts capped the climax. The bull *Exsurge Domine* definitely pronounced the position of the Church in regard to his heresies. A dramatic ceremony on December 10 closed this chapter of the Reformation, for on that day Luther burned the papal bull, a copy of the canon law, and some other writings outside a gate of Wittenberg, an enthusiastic crowd of students and townsmen applauding him. He was now the cynosure of all eyes—the simple monk had become religious reformer and national leader.

PART II

Lutheranism Ascendant

Chapter 3

TRIUMPH OF LUTHERANISM
IN GERMANY

E VENTS IN GERMANY moved swiftly during the closing months of 1520. The pope had issued the bull *Exsurge Domine* which Luther burned. On January 3, 1521, Leo X issued the bull of excommunication. The breach between Luther and the curia now was complete. What would be the next step? All eyes turned to the emperor and to the coming meeting of the German diet at Worms.

LUTHER AND HIS SUPPORTERS, 1520

The youthful Charles V had been crowned at Aix-la-Chapelle on October 23, 1520, just after Luther had launched his famous tracts. Charles was bound, according to medieval conceptions of the relations between empire and papacy, to extirpate the tares of heresy. Would he do it? The federal nature of the empire made very difficult any effort to control the internal policies of states. Elector Frederick of Saxony, who stood between Luther and the emperor, was loath to allow any imperial interference in his lands. Though born in Flanders, Charles' views of the relations of Church and civil authority were formed by what he saw in Spain. He was truly orthodox, but preferred to manage ecclesiastical affairs himself by means of national councils. The curia wanted him to suppress the new heresy, and Leo appointed two nuncios to prepare the imperial mind to this end and to manage the negotiations. Aleander and

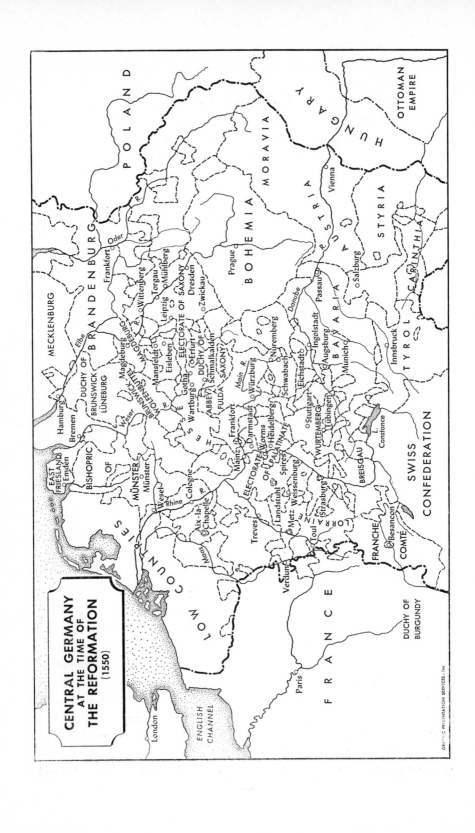

CENTRAL GERMANY
AT THE TIME OF
THE REFORMATION
(1550)

Caraccioli, the nuncios, were both humanists well versed in the ways of men and acquainted with the methods of Renaissance diplomacy.

It was their view that Luther should forthwith be silenced by the empire. He had been condemned and excommunicated, and it only remained for Charles to put the bulls into execution. Elector Frederick of Saxony urged that Luther should first be tried by capable and impartial judges. Charles promised this at a meeting in Cologne on November 1, to the chagrin of the nuncios who wanted to see Luther condemned without trial or deliberation by the diet. The emperor had to consider the political aspects of the situation. He was on the brink of war with Francis I of France and needed papal support, especially in Italy. Nor could he afford to antagonize the Germans from whom he expected military aid.

Public sentiment in Germany was clearly on Luther's side. Aleander was distressed to find that most of the people were for Luther. Even if the rest cared little for him, they were bitter toward the papacy and insisted that a council should be called to air the grievances of the realm and apply correction. People even threatened violence to Aleander's person. Luther's books were hawked about everywhere, and heretical ideas seemed to infect everybody. Erasmus as usual issued bitter jibes at the shortcomings of the hierarchy. Ulrich von Hutten (1488–1523) made a great impression, his patriotic and humanist sentiments appealing to all classes of Germans. Since the debate at Leipzig he had entertained great respect for Luther and had greeted his writings with enthusiasm. His acrid spirit was bent on castigating the papacy and exalting Germany. In 1520 he issued his *Vadiscus* in which the clergy were mercilessly satirized. His violent criticism made it unsafe for him to stay in the country and he sought shelter with Franz von Sickingen in his castle at Ebernburg.

Von Hutten was of knightly origin and retained the prejudices of his class. He possessed patriotic feelings toward the emperor, opposed the papacy, and hated friars and other clergy alike. He supported Luther because he was momentarily the national hero of Germany, but he cared little for the deeper religious questions involved in the struggle. During all his career he had written in Latin, but the astonishing success of Luther's tracts of 1520 led von Hutten to address the public in German. In December he published the *Complaint and Exhortation against the Overweening and Unchristian Power of the Pope in Rome and of his Unspiritual Clergy*. Ensconced in Ebernburg, he published the most vitriolic attacks. His patriotic sense overcame the prejudices of his knightly origin. He believed that knights, princes, towns, and emperor should join in common service to the fatherland against the papacy, hoping thus to effect a revolution. It is certain that he wanted to seize the nuncios. He criticized

the prelates assembled at the diet at Worms, but a few miles from Ebernburg. He launched invective and satire against Charles, but overshot the
mark. His language was indeed bold, but he did not have the material
resources with which to start a revolution; furthermore, his plans were
never well formulated. The castle became a rendezvous of fugitive clerics
who embraced the teaching of Luther. The latter, however, refused to
join them.

LUTHER BEFORE THE GERMAN DIET

The diet opened at Worms in January, 1521, amid manifestations of
admiration for Luther and open declarations of hostility toward the curia.
Aleander, addressing it on the thirteenth, demanded that, since the heretic
was already condemned, it was the manifest duty of the emperor and the
estates to suppress Lutheran books. Indeed, no time was to be lost, for
Germany was afire. But the electors feared popular opposition, and refused to sanction any decree ordering the burning of Lutheran books.
They insisted that Luther be summoned to Worms under imperial safe-
conduct to be questioned by a committee about the authorship of his
books. There was to be no discussion about doctrines. Charles agreed to
this, notwithstanding Aleander's disapproval. On March 6 a safe-conduct
was sent to Luther, together with citation to appear in Worms. Elector
Frederick also gave him a similar letter, and on April 2 Luther set out on
a journey fraught with danger.

Luther everywhere received the enthusiastic ovation of the public. Some
of his admirers warned him that the fate which befell Hus might also
come to him, for under certain circumstances solemn promises might not
be binding when they concerned heretics. On April 16 he entered Worms
and at once made preparations for the hearing. Late the following after-
noon he was ushered into the presence of the emperor, electors, and
princes of the realm. He was addressed by the official of the see of Mainz
who asked whether he had written the books whose titles had been read,
and whether he intended to defend their contents. To the first question
Luther answered in the affirmative; but the second he declared was so
weighty that he wished to consider prayerfully before replying. It was
agreed that he should have 24 hours in which to formulate an answer.
When Luther appeared before the emperor the second time, he stated
that some of the books were directed against abuses, some were written
against his enemies, and others merely retailed the teachings of Scripture
and were written for purposes of edification.

But he would not recant one word of any of these three kinds of books unless he were convinced of error in a disputation and by the authority of the Old and New Testament only.

"Martin," continued the official, "if your wrong opinions and heresies were new and invented by you, perhaps his Imperial Majesty would request the Holy Father to have them examined by pious and learned men, so that no wrong should be done you. But your errors are those of the ancient heretics, the Waldenses, Beghards, Adamites, Poor Men of Lyons, Wycliffe, and Hus, and have all been long ago condemned by holy councils, popes and the usage of the Church, and therefore ought no more to be discussed and brought into question contrary to divine and human law." Then the official added the question, which especially concerned the German nation, whether he would not recant what he had written against the holy Council of Constance, which had been attended by all nations and was recognized by the whole world. He refused, and would submit to the decrees of the council only in so far as they were founded on the authority of Scripture, for, he said, councils had erred and contradicted one another.[1]

In these words Aleander reported the proceedings on April 17 and 18. They eloquently set forth Luther's doctrines. Popes could and did err; so did councils contradict each other. The truth lay in Scripture alone which would enlighten the zealous seeker for truth about things divine. Thus Luther denied the bases upon which rested the whole fabric of the traditional Church. It was a clear and final assertion of rebellion. What was to be done? Aleander would gladly have had Charles break his safe-conduct, but this was impossible, for Frederick and other electors would surely oppose this step. There was also the surging tide of German patriotic and nationalist sentiment to be taken into account, for threats of a popular rising were becoming more audible. Much as the orthodox Charles regretted it, he was not free to act. He could not move to suppress the new teaching. The estates insisted on a further hearing before a committee which should seek to secure submission from Luther. If he should refuse to yield, they would support the emperor in his desire to uproot Lutheranism, provided the safe-conduct were respected.

The committee met with Luther on the twenty-fourth, but failed, as might have been expected. When nothing could be gained, Charles ordered Luther to return to Saxony, whither he set out on the twenty-sixth. Meanwhile Aleander drafted an edict placing Luther under the ban. Many of the members of the diet had gone home, and a greatly reduced number accepted the document on the twenty-sixth. It placed Luther under the ban of the empire, forbade all subjects to give him aid and

[1] *Luther's Correspondence and Other Contemporary Letters*, tr. and ed. by Preserved Smith, Philadelphia, 1913, I, 529–530.

comfort, ordered his arrest and that of his abettors and protectors, enjoined confiscation of their property, forbade anyone to read or own any of Luther's books, ordered that they should be burned, and provided that publication and censorship of books should be more carefully controlled in the future.

Luther now was declared an outlaw. But it was a different matter to get action against him in a state constituted as was Germany. Elector Frederick sought to quiet the uproar and gave orders to place Luther in safe-keeping. When the latter was on the way back to Wittenberg and passing through the country of his childhood days, he was suddenly seized and carried to the old castle of the Wartburg (May 4). The secret was well kept; even the elector knew nothing of Luther's whereabouts. For nearly 10 months he stayed there occupied in writing letters and brochures. Chief of them was the important tract, *On Monastic Vows*, which maintained that, being saved by faith alone, man could not profit from a religious life. Monasticism was not in harmony with Scripture, and celibacy he thought to be invalid. Since in practice it was said to be often violated, it would be better to allow the religious to marry. The simple secular life of Christians outside monastic walls was the true Christian life.

Especially important is Luther's translation of the New Testament made at this time. Other translations into the German had been made from the Vulgate. His vast knowledge of the Bible aided him in this gigantic task, for he had laboriously studied its pages ever since he went into the monastery. In an incredibly short time he finished the work, which became a great literary landmark in the history of the German language and literature. It set the standard of speech and attained great popularity among the people. The translation appeared in September, 1522, and was called the *September Testament*. In this way too Luther was closely associated with the great outburst of nationalist sentiment.

THEOLOGICAL RADICALISM IN WITTENBERG

While Luther was hiding in the Wartburg, the new freedom in religion produced some interesting results in Wittenberg. One of Luther's colleagues at the university, Andrew Bodenstein von Karlstadt (d. 1541), was especially zealous in carrying out in detail what was implied in the principle of justification by faith. He celebrated the Lord's Supper by giving both elements to the people. He opposed the idea of a propitiatory sacrifice in the Mass; removed altars, pictures, and images; thought that vows of celibacy whether by priests, monks, or nuns were invalid;

and taught that all things should be tested by Scripture. He laid aside his clerical vestments, and wore the ordinary dress of a layman while conducting services. He distributed Holy Communion in evangelical fashion. Modifying the liturgy to suit his ideas, he placed the bread in the hands of communicants and put the cup in their hands.

Gabriel Zwilling, an Augustinian friar, proved an able assistant, and violently assailed the traditional conception of the Mass. His words stirred the people to action which sometimes bordered on riot. Karlstadt's innovations were followed by his own marriage, an example adopted by other clergy. The Augustinians now removed the altars from their chapel, took down images, and destroyed pictures of saints. Monks left their houses and became handicraftsmen. With the abolition of the Mass and the introduction of many novelties it was felt that an ordinance governing public religious exercises should be drafted. Karlstadt urged this and secured the adoption of a document by the council of Wittenberg in January, 1522. It provided for a common fund for the support of the poor, into which were to be deposited incomes from religious foundations. Religious services were to be conducted according to conceptions advanced by Karlstadt; and altars, pictures, and similar objects were to be removed in all convents. This ordinance, based partly upon a measure for the relief of the poor which had emanated from Luther in 1520, was typical of the policy of medieval towns regarding the control and regulation of religious service and its social aspects.

Wittenberg was still more disturbed by the arrival of three prophets from Zwickau, followers of one Thomas Münzer, a man who was to attract much notice in the Peasants' War a few years later. Two of them, Nicholas Storch and an unnamed friend, were cloth-makers and quite illiterate. The third, Mark Stübner, was a student. They had a mission from God to preach; they prophesied and foretold the future. They rejected infant baptism which, they asserted, was contrary to the spirit of Luther's teaching. Since Zwickau was situated within the confines of Bohemia, Husite notions may well have influenced them. The influence of these agitators was but a passing event. This episode is nevertheless interesting because it shows what crude theological concepts untutored folk were likely to form in days of storm and stress.

At first Luther sympathized with the course of events at Wittenberg. He approved Karlstadt's marriage. But his innate conservatism soon led him to take a different attitude. Even though the innovations were logically a consequence of his own teaching, he opposed precipitate action. Political considerations certainly should be weighed. Karlstadt and Zwilling were impatient of such matters. Luther's friends begged him to return, and on March 6, 1522, the reformer was back in Wittenberg. He at once began a series of sermons designed to quiet the agitated public. Moderation was the burden of his discourse. He agreed that Mass should be discontinued and that it should not be obligatory to keep vows of celibacy, retain pictures and images in churches, or continue the practice of fasting. He held that the wine should be given the laity in communion. Confession he would keep as a pious and laudable practice. He also addressed the excited folk in other towns of electoral Saxony. An expedient conservatism was now injected into the Reformation, and elector Frederick was pleased by this turn of events.

TRIUMPH OF LUTHERANISM

Lutheran doctrines continued to win adherents everywhere. Nationalist sentiment, dissatisfaction with religious practices, and antagonism toward Rome all combined to fan the excitement. Pamphlets continued to flow from the press. Monks and nuns broke their vows and left their houses in large numbers, and most Augustinians followed Luther's example. Some of the more noteworthy preachers of the new doctrines came from monasteries, among them the Dominican Martin Butzer (Bucer) and the Franciscan Oswald Myconius. Laymen repeatedly assumed direction in preaching the new doctrines. Townsmen were especially interested, and meetings were often held in market places. In southern Germany the important towns of Strasbourg, Ulm, Nördlingen, Constance, Augsburg, and Nuremberg, to name but a few, resounded with Luther's teaching. Bremen, Magdeburg, and Hamburg in the north also received it eagerly. Some of the German princes showed strong interest in the new doctrines, and some of the lesser nobility were inclined to favor Luther. Elector Frederick of Saxony still held aloof, chiefly for political reasons, it appears.

To comply with the Edict of Worms proved impossible under such circumstances. Princes, loath to enforce it, simply ignored it, and in the towns the opposition was usually great. It was evident that the edict was a dead letter as so many before had been. Duke George of Saxony and elector Joachim of Brandenburg were the most important princes to oppose Lutheranism. But even in states where princes were loyal to the old Church there was little effective effort to suppress the heresy. This matter came up for discussion in a meeting of the diet at Nuremberg in session from November, 1522, to March, 1523. Pope Adrian VI (1522–1523), who had succeeded Leo X, sent his nuncio Francesco Chieregati, bishop of Tiramo, to demand that the edict be enforced. At the same time he frankly admitted the evil practices of the curia and promised that they would be rectified as soon as possible.

The diet was loath to accede to this demand for enforcement of the edict, pointing to the evident fact that Lutheranism was far too popular to be repressed, especially when the hierarchy was open to much criticism. Reform of course was necessary, and the diet insisted on a council in which laity as well as clergy were to take part which should convene within the borders of Germany within one year. Meanwhile preachers were to teach the truth as contained in Scripture. This response was a defeat for Chieregati, for it practically suspended the Edict of Worms. Nor was the next meeting of the diet from January to April, 1524, more favorable to the cause of the papacy. Pope Clement VII (1523–1534) sent Campeggio to demand the execution of the edict. The diet insisted on a German council to consider reform. Before it should meet, a national German assembly was to ascertain what was heretical in Luther's teaching. Until such action there should be no interference in the preaching of Scripture. But the emperor sided with the nuncio and ordered that the edict should be put into immediate execution. This could not be done, however, for Lutheranism was rapidly gaining adherents whom the emperor could not afford to antagonize while he was at war with Francis I of France.[2]

LUTHER AND THE GERMAN KNIGHTS

Meanwhile Germany was drifting toward revolution. Luther had sensed this as he rode homeward from Worms. He reflected upon the news which came to him in the solitude of the Wartburg. There were riots in Erfurt against the clergy. A multitude of accumulated grievances cried aloud for redress. There was much maladjustment in German society which at any moment might lead to violence. Masters of guilds formed hereditary corporations which kept out newcomers. Apprentices and journeymen found the road to advancement closed to them; it was their lot to labor forever at unrequited toil under unfavorable conditions. The lower nobility, or knights, were bitter against the great princes of the empire. They belonged to a bygone age and keenly resented the fact that the great days of their class were past. They continued their antiquated ways. Their castles were built on hilltops. From these strongholds they

---

[2] Charles V fought four wars with Francis I of France which seriously affected the course of Lutheran reform: (1) 1521–1526 (Treaty of Madrid, Jan. 14); (2) 1527–1529 (Peace of Cambrai, Aug. 3); (3) 1536–1538 (Truce of Nice, June 18); and (4) 1542–1544 (Treaty of Crespi, Sept. 18).

rode out to plunder and slay merchants, and to them they retreated when danger threatened. They were a curse upon the land.

Franz von Sickingen now appeared as a possible leader of revolution. He well understood the advantage which the new military weapons, guns and powder, gave an army. His prejudices and dislikes derived from the antiquated ideas of his class. He as well as other German knights were dissatisfied because towns and urban economy were making vast gains at the expense of this class who supported themselves more or less on a manorial economy which was obsolescent. Von Sickingen possessed in supreme degree the great vice of knights, the right of private warfare. For many years he had done as he pleased. He even thought of selling his services to Francis I, for such was the moral decline into which this class had fallen that its notions of loyalty were distorted.

Von Sickingen had never heard of Luther until the reformer began to be discussed in connection with revolution. The knight cared naught for religion. When Hutten appeared in the Ebernburg he too began to talk against priests and prelates. But von Sickingen was not the man to lead a revolution. Instead, he planned a war on his personal enemy, the archbishop of Trier, and other knights who cherished similar sentiments chose him as their captain in 1522. Von Sickingen talked loudly and pretended to be an ally of Luther—the time had come to strike a blow! He moved upon the archbishop, but the walls of the city of Trier and its cannon compelled him to withdraw. Thereupon the Council of Regency placed him under the ban as an outlaw. He retired to his stronghold at Landstuhl where he was besieged and mortally wounded. His death (May 7, 1523) was a significant event, for it marked the final defeat of the knightly class which had become politically and economically obsolete. Germany was saved from a great war upon the clergy. Von Hutten fled to Basel where he was rejected by Erasmus. Thereupon he went to Zurich, near which place in 1523 he died in bitter disappointment.

LUTHER AND THE INFLAMMABLE ECONOMIC SITUATION

The unsatisfactory economic position of the peasantry made it equally ready for some kind of blind revolt. It is impossible to give a correct picture of these conditions because they varied greatly from place to place, and, furthermore, the sources fail to give adequate statements. The agricultural population lived in the many degrees of dependency characteristic of the Middle Ages. A few free peasants possessed land without servile obligations, but most peasants were constrained to rent parcels of land from lords. The status of many was midway between that of free-man and serf. Serfs in the lowest degree of dependency were not to be found in many communities. Relations of peasants with their landlords often were unhappy. Peasants were deprived of the right to wood and pasture which had been theirs from time immemorial, and in some places they were robbed of the right to hunt in the forests and fish in the streams. The lords usually were inclined to increase their burdens as much as possible.

The strain and stress of this unequal position were constantly increas-ing under the transformation of German society. The material standard of living was rising rapidly, for nobles no less than bourgeois were eager to gratify their appetites for luxuries. The petty nobility had no income other than what they could extract from their peasants. They constantly sought to increase it and therefore extended old manorial rights wherever possible. In their pride and haughtiness this obsolete class extolled the ancient virtues of knights. It was their privilege to indulge in private warfare. Wealthier nobles were confronted by the same conditions. They too found that they could not increase their income to keep pace with the steadily mounting cost of living, and they sought to put the burden on the shoulders of the peasants. Ecclesiastical princes acted in the same manner, for they also subsisted on manorial incomes.

The situation was aggravated by the fact that in southwestern Germany feudal and manorial holdings were smaller than in the north and east, and the burden of supporting so large a class was thus much greater there than elsewhere. Nor could the peasants look to the state for help, for its federal character made the central government too weak to take notice of their misfortunes. Social disturbances accordingly had often marred the peace of these regions. Peasants had sought justice by direct action, especially after 1493, adopting as their emblem a peasant's shoe with a long string attached.

This Bundschuh standard, as it was called, was often raised. Leaders insisted upon simple justice in their economic relations with landlords, whether laymen or priests. They usually demanded that streams, forests, and pasture lands should be free, and insisted on reduction in tithes. The people remained deeply religious in all these movements; in fact, priests who had risen from the lower classes and understood their problems often joined them. Peasants usually were strongly opposed to the wealthy clergy and monastic foundations, and townsmen, especially the lower element, repeatedly sympathized with and sometimes joined them. The authorities wiped out such risings without mercy and savagely hunted down their victims as if they were beasts.

Strange doctrines were readily accepted by the unfortunates, and it is not impossible that Husite ideas of equality influenced them. Religion usually figured strongly in their acts. Especially interesting is the case of Hans Böhm of Niklashausen who in 1476 suddenly turned from his worldly life, saw visions, taught that the chapel of Our Lady of Niklashausen was the holiest spot in Christendom, railed against priests and the papacy, declared that all taxes were unlawful, and became famous far and wide. He planned an appeal to arms but was seized by the bishop of Würzburg, imprisoned, and finally burned as a heretic. His last words were a simple hymn to the Blessed Virgin. Böhm's movement was an interesting compound of religious ideas and agrarian and social doctrines, while the Bundschuh revolts were primarily concerned with the relations of peasants and their lords. The simple peasant was ever prone to appeal to the basic ethical ideas of Christianity when he sought fairer economic treatment. Taking religion literally and seriously often led to social and political radicalism in the eyes of both Church and state.

LUTHER AND THE PEASANTS' REVOLT

To these complicated social problems was added the ferment of Lutheran ideas. The great leader himself had taught the priesthood of all believers, a doctrine which appealed to the oppressed because of its apparent insistence on the essential equality of men. Luther has often been erroneously accused of causing the revolt. It may have been stimulated by his teaching, but it was due to old and deep-seated causes. Luther was of peasant origin and sympathized with the peasants' difficulties. But he also was conservative and hated violence, and he was frightened by the rumblings of the gathering storm. When in the Wartburg, he wrote *A Faithful Exhortation to Christians to Keep Themselves from Riot and Revolution*, in which he maintained that reform was necessary. It should, however, be initiated by the princes and by the state. Simple folk, no matter what their burdens and injustices, might not take the initiative. All revolt was wrong; it was the devil's way of hurting the teaching of Scripture. These ideas reveal Luther's intense loyalty toward constituted authority, the princes of Germany, a loyalty so strong that it led him to contradict a basic principle of his teaching, that of the equality of all believers before God. He held that it did not apply to secular matters. It was a point fraught with the gravest consequences.

Between 1522 and 1524 occurred the rising and defeat of the knights under Franz von Sickingen. A serious crisis thus passed, but it was followed by another far more dangerous. The peasants rose at Stühlingen in the Black Forest in June, 1524. They were goaded into this by the exasperating insistence of the countess of Lüpfen upon petty services which prevented them from harvesting their crops. At least this was their pretext; in reality they nursed many other grievances. The movement spread rapidly. The men of the Kletgau and the Hegau rose in August and drew up some articles setting forth the social inequalities which burdened them. The movement spread during the winter into northern Swabia and Württemberg and eastward as far as Memmingen. By the spring of 1525 it had gone northward into Franconia, Hesse, Thuringia, and even into Brunswick; westward into Alsace, Trier, and Lorraine; and southward into Tyrol, Salzburg, and neighboring lands.

The peasants drew up numerous documents setting forth their grievances. Especially important were the *Twelve Articles* drawn up at Memmingen in 1525. Lutheran agitation in behalf of Scripture had appealed to them, and they repeatedly insisted that the Bible should be the norm of social relations. Biblical texts were plentifully used to buttress their demands. Most of the *Twelve Articles* concerned manorial dues and obligations. Tithes were to be dropped, except the chief grain tithe which they thought had Biblical sanction, peasants were to be allowed to hunt and fish, water rights were to be left to the community, in certain cases woods were to revert to the people, burdensome services were to be removed, only ancient manorial customs were to be respected, a fair price was to be paid for labor, rents were to be just, and death dues were to cease. Clauses dealing with religion declared that the peasants wanted no revolution but the simple justice of Christian teaching.

Unfortunately, moderate counsels did not prevail among the nobility who were inclined to look to their rights and who possessed the attitudes characteristic of their class toward social inferiors. Moderation as exhibited in the *Twelve Articles* could not be maintained toward the peasants. As the spring of 1525 wore on, violence increased. Property of ecclesiastical lords was pillaged, monasteries were sacked, and even churches were plundered. Images and relics were destroyed, vestments torn, and the Host profaned. The peasants had justly criticized churchmen who were so closely associated with feudal and manorial institutions that they became simply tools of the propertied classes. Resentment toward a property-holding clergy was common. Many roving bands engaged in desultory fighting, and it was impossible to prevent plundering. Nevertheless, moderation was the dominant note of the revolt. The peasants sometimes even accepted nobles to lead them and present their demands. Indeed, many nobles, knights, princes, and ecclesiastical lords had for centuries set the peasants a splendid example in this respect.

Soon after the battle of Pavia (February 24, 1525) professional troops of the emperor's army began to return to Germany, and princes were now able to collect armies with which to put down the malcontents. Philip of Hesse defeated a force of peasants which had been brought together by Münzer, who had announced the coming of a communist age. All mankind was to form a community like that of the children of Israel. Only princes and the upper classes were to be excluded and put to the sword. This band was defeated at Frankenhausen (May 15, 1525) and Thuringia was freed from the rebels. Princes now began to slaughter the unfortunates, it being related that the duke of Lorraine put 17,000 to the sword. Others with equal inhumanity hacked down the simple folk. Many broke promises with impunity the moment they thought themselves strong enough to do so, the electors of Trier and the Palatinate, the bishop of Würzburg, and even the Swabian League was guilty of this execrable conduct. By the autumn of 1525 the Peasants' Revolt, which had promised to be successful at the opening of the year, was stamped out in blood and death.

What was Luther's attitude toward these events? He had not been displeased with the demands of the peasants when the *Twelve Articles* appeared. He wrote a pamphlet, *An Exhortation to Peace in Reply to the Twelve Articles of the Swabian Peasants* (April, 1525), in which he declared against tyrannous princes whom he held responsible for much of the discontent. Indeed, they deserved to be overthrown. But, he told the peasants, there was something more important than temporal justice. This was righteousness. Violence was never allowable; only false teachers held that revolution was permitted. Rather it was the teaching of the Gospel that Christians must suffer. Obedience was a prime virtue, as St. Paul taught, and therefore no show of force could ever be lawful. Luther would not recognize the truth taught in scholastic philosophy that all men were justified in defending their natural rights. He declared, "Suffering, suffering, cross, cross; this is a Christian's only right!"

This appeal to princes to be just and to peasants to commit no violence could not but fail, for princes of the Middle Ages were not compounded of mercy and justice, especially where the peasantry was concerned. Bitterness increased, and the peasants were guilty of excesses which greatly disturbed Luther. He thought that insubordination was stirred up by the devil himself, and he hastily penned a pamphlet, *Against Robbing and Murdering Peasant Bands* (May, 1525), couched in brutal and intolerant language. Luther now sided with the princes. Rebellion was a grievous sin, and the peasants should be put down with force for they attacked the Roman powers instituted by God. In a lamentable burst of passion he wrote: "Therefore let every one who can, strike, strangle, stab secretly or in public, and let him remember that nothing can be more poisonous, harmful, or devilish than a man in rebellion."

This change in point of view is a blot on Luther's name. It was typical of Luther's attitude toward the sanctity of temporal authority which would make redress of grievances, whether political, economic, or even religious, entirely impossible if the legally constituted authorities should refuse to sanction any change. The peasants pondered sullenly over Luther's teaching and concluded that he was a false prophet. They would have no more of him and henceforth sought solace in the faith of their fathers. On the other hand, princes accused him of fomenting revolt even after he issued his terrible pamphlet. Thus much of southern Germany was saved for Catholicism. Luther kept his movement from destruction by repudiating radical social revolution, and he won the support of princes in the north. At Worms in 1521 Luther had stood as spokesman of Germany; after the Peasants' Revolt he led a faction. His marriage to Catherine von Bora, a renegade nun, in 1525 seemed scandalous to many, and further impaired his prestige with the faithful.

Meanwhile the rapid growth of Lutheranism produced serious problems in Church organization. Luther's doctrine of justification by faith alone originally implied that the religious community should be managed in a democratic manner. He now held that preaching and celebration of the sacraments required special training. For this reason and for the preservation of order a ministry should be appointed. He justified it solely on the principle of division of labor. But the clergy were not to be separated from the laity by any special sacramental character, as was the case with Catholic priests. Luther could not, however, accept a purely popular church organization. The Peasants' War made him a conservative; henceforth he leaned heavily on the power of princes. He argued that political authority was instituted by God and was therefore sacred, and he believed that this divinely created secular government possessed the right to manage ecclesiastical affairs. This meant that Lutheran churches would become state churches, managed by princes much like secular branches of the state government. This was a great revolution in religion because Catholics had always taught that the Church was self-sufficient and could not admit any princely control. Church and state according to Catholic conceptions were parallel institutions, each independent in its sphere, but the Church possessed the right to instruct the state in moral and religious matters.

In Lutheran churches the episcopal function was shorn of its sacramental powers, and bishops remained as overseers or superintendents appointed by princes. The basis of this new arrangement was laid by the Saxon Visitation conducted from 1526 to 1528. A committee of lawyers and theologians was sent into every parish to inquire into the state of religion. When their investigations were finished, they drew up instructions for the guidance of churches. These served, with minor modifications, as a model for the religious organizations of Prussia, Brandenburg, Brunswick, Mansfeld, and Schleswig-Holstein, as well as for many cities.

LUTHER: CHARACTER OF THE MAN

The epochal character of Luther's work was finished by 1525. Although the reformer continued to live in the public eye until his death on February 18, 1546, his activities were limited chiefly to teaching, preaching, pamphleteering, organizing the new worship, and giving advice on innumerable topics. Luther remained the unquestioned leader of the evangelical party, receiving homage from all classes in many parts of Germany. Students flocked to Wittenberg to listen to his lectures, and many poor pupils received financial help from him in preparing themselves for the ministry, some of them even living in his house. His hospitality was well known, and many a student, theologian, or curious visitor was welcomed to his table where he entertained them with that curious conversation which has been preserved in his *Table Talk*. This work, which has become one of the great biographical classics, contains the reformer's spontaneous reactions to all sorts of questions. From its pages we learn to know Luther better than from his more serious and polemical works or the pictures which Lucas Cranach the Younger (1515–1586) painted of him.

Luther's character was a remarkable combination of diverse qualities. His attitude toward the physical world was naïve. He believed in the reality of that unseen body of spirits to which witches ministered. Popular tradition dominated his mind. In religion he boldly assailed the headship of the pope yet insisted upon the truth of the Real Presence. He taught the doctrine of the priesthood of all believers which rested upon the principle that justification came through faith alone, yet turned against the people when they sought to translate this equality of all men into the field of politics. This combination of radicalism and conservatism made possible his successful appeal to the people of his age.

Luther was a man of deep sentiment. His piety was real and profound. The questions which he raised about salvation disclosed a spirit delicately sensitive to religious values. This confused all who took refuge in traditional views without plumbing them to the depth. The reformer's keen spiritual sense is revealed in his hymns, many of them are veritable gems of inspiration which have comforted generations of men and women. His love for music seems to have sprung from the same spiritual source. His family life was remarkable for its simplicity, and he bestowed a husband's solicitous care upon his wife, Catherine von Bora. He made the following remark about marriage:

He who takes a wife ought to be a good man, but Hans Metzsch is not worthy of this divine gift, for a good woman deserves a good husband. To have peace and love in marriage is a gift which is next to the knowledge of the Gospel. There are heartless wretches who love neither their children nor their wives; such things are not human. The greatest blessing is to have a wife to whom you may entrust your affairs and by whom you may have children.

Luther was fond of his children, to one of whom he said:

You are our Lord's little fool. Grace and remission of sins are yours and you fear nothing from the law. Whatever you do is uncorrupted; you are in a state of grace and you have remission of sins, whatever happens.

If Luther was gentle toward his loved ones, he could be rude toward opponents. He frequently indulged in the most unmeasured language when referring to the Catholic clergy, his speech sometimes too indecent to be translated. The following is an undignified sally:

Franciscans are our Lord God's lice which the devil has put on His skin. Dominicans are fleas which the devil has put in our Lord God's shirt.

Of the papacy he said:

The world is unwilling to accept God as the true God, and the devil as the real devil, therefore it is compelled to endure their representative, namely the pope, who is the false vicar of God and the true vicar of the devil. The papacy is a government by which the wicked and those who despise God deserve to be ruled, for it is fitting that those who are unwilling to obey God of their own accord should be forced to obey a scoundrel.[3]

Luther was a child of his age and did not rise above it. He showed less of the refinement one discovers in Calvin. But Luther's coarseness springs from the uncouthness of peasants, not from sensuality. The reformer was in the habit of making exaggerated statements in a blunt manner, and his enemies were easily misled by them. Luther possessed a vigorous physique

[3] P. Smith and Ballinger, *Conversations with Luther*, Boston, 1915, pp. 45–46, 47, 151, 138.

and ate and drank heartily. He was no Puritan in these matters. But the closing Middle Ages were not noted for their abstemiousness, and Luther was no worse in this respect than the average person of his day.

PHILIPP MELANCHTHON: LUTHER'S ADVOCATE AND COLLABORATOR

Luther, a busy man, had many collaborators. Chief of these was Philipp Melanchthon (d. 1560) who exerted profound influence upon the development of Lutheran intellectual life and theological thought. Born in 1497 at Bretten in Baden, he studied at Tübingen and Heidelberg and became a humanist scholar of rare repute, probably the best in Germany. Such was his reputation that he was given the flattering epithet of *Preceptor Germaniae*. In 1518 he was named professor at the new university in Wittenberg. Two years later, in 1520 and 1521, he published his classic *Loci Communes Rerum Theologicarum, or Theological Common Places*. This book was a topical outline of Lutheran theology, widely read by the Lutheran clergy and educated laity. Among the topics discussed in it were the Trinity, Man, Sin, the Law, the Gospel, Fruits of Grace, Faith, Sacraments, the Magistracy, Church Government, Damnation, Predestination, and Original Sin. The Reformation produced few books as influential as the *Theological Common Places* of Melanchthon.

Melanchthon's influence as a humanist is nowhere so strikingly to be seen as in his teaching regarding the difficult problem of the freedom of the human will. From the beginning he had embraced Luther's teaching that the will was corrupt and that natural man, incapable of righteousness, could be saved only through divine choice or predestination. (We have seen that Luther taught that man is saved by righteousness *imputed* and not *earned*.) Free will seemed out of the question. Humanists, particularly Erasmus, since they held to free will, might have opposed Luther on this ground; but, if they approved of Luther, they usually did so because of his trenchant criticism of medieval culture and not so much because they approved of his doctrine of justification by an imputed faith and not by good deeds even if such good deeds sprang from a spirit of charity. But humanists could not amicably live with Lutheran theologians whenever the fundamental question of free will came up, and this was nearly constantly. So Erasmus attacked Luther in his *On Free Will* (1524) to which Luther replied in his *On the Will Unfree* in 1525. A solution of the problem was needed in Lutheran theology, and it was supplied by Melanchthon. It was known as *Synergism*. This taught that

God calls. His Spirit works through His Word, the will moves under the influence of divine grace and divine truth. The human will accepts the proffer of grace and salvation. The will then accepts or rejects. There is no self-moved activity in things of the spirit. So the human will coöperates —works with—the divine. This is the famous Melanchthonian *Synergism*.

Chapter 4

LUTHERANISM IN SCANDINAVIAN
AND OTHER COUNTRIES

VIEWED FROM the standpoint of its economic progress, Scandinavia at the close of the Middle Ages was for the most part an undeveloped country. Its foodstuffs and raw materials were coveted objects of trade, and merchants of the Hanseatic League possessed practically a monopoly of its commercial activity. Many Germans had settled in the interest of commerce in such urban centers as Copenhagen, Bergen, Stockholm, and Wisby. The influence of Wittenberg readily filtered into these towns almost as soon as Luther broke with Rome. The rupture of the Scandinavian peoples with the faith of their fathers was everywhere influenced by special social, economic, and political factors.

THE CROWN INITIATES THE REFORMATION
IN DENMARK

Church reform in Denmark was due initially to the personal policy of the crown and the ambitions of the nobility. The peasantry and townsmen were everywhere sincerely attached to the old faith. Although there was some criticism of the moral laxity and flabby spirituality of the clergy, nevertheless the common man without questioning sought comfort in appealing to saints and receiving the sacraments. The pilgrimages to the Virgin's chapel at Karup in Denmark testify to the genuineness of the popular faith. The nobility was powerful; a council of nobles was able to keep the king subservient in political matters and thus prevent the crown from becoming hereditary. The higher clergy, as in other lands, were drawn from the nobility. Both groups possessed much land; they controlled the realm economically and politically.

King Christian II (1513–1523) was a characteristic prince of the Renaissance. He wished to free the crown from dictation by clergy and nobility and sought to make himself absolute as other rulers had suc-

SCANDINAVIA
AT THE TIME OF
THE REFORMATION

ARCTIC OCEAN

ATLANTIC

OCEAN

WHITE
SEA

NORWAY

Trondhjem

JAEMTLAND

HEREDAL

EIDSIVIATHINGSLAG

GULATHINGSLAG

Bergen

DALECARLIA

RANRIKE

SWEDEN

FINLAND

Westeras

Upsala

Stockholm

Strengnas

Venern

Stavanger

Vadstena

Linkoping

BALTIC

Jonkoping

Vettern

Wisby

GOTHLAND

Kalmar

Viborg

JUTLAND

DENMARK

SKANE

BLEKINGE

SEA

SLESWIG

Roeskilde

Copenhagen

SEELAND

Lund

Odense

HOLSTEIN

BORNHOLM

Danzig

Lubeck

Hamburg

Bremen

ceeded in doing. Able, vigorous, and unscrupulous, he brought about the ruin of his adversaries. In his early days he served as regent of Norway, and at Bergen became enamored of a girl named Duiveke (Dutch for *little dove*) who became his mistress. Her mother, Sigbrit Willems, an innkeeper of Bergen, was one of the many foreigners who had settled in that important commercial center. She was a native of Amsterdam, at that time the most important Netherland center of trade with the Scandinavian north. Her point of view, as one would expect, was that of a member of an advanced bourgeois community. She was well acquainted with the medical science and practice of the day and was interested in alchemy.

Sigbrit Willems through Duiveke gained control over Christian. She was a woman of ability, possessed sound sense about finance, government, trade, and the duty of princes. When Christian mounted the throne in 1513, she became in effect his chief minister of state and guided the royal policy in most matters. Such was her influence over the monarch that she even became the royal midwife. This petticoat rule was resented by the nobility and their allies, the higher clergy. They forced the king at his accession to accept a document in which he promised to be governed by their instructions. The fact that Christian, at the counsel of Sigbrit, sought to strengthen himself against them by an alliance with the nonnoble classes aroused their hostility.

Christian finally took as his legitimate wife Isabella, sister of Charles of Hapsburg, who was soon to mount the thrones of Spain and Germany, and who was already ruler of most of the states in the Low Countries. The political import of this alliance with the chief economic center of northern Europe is a clear indication of the king's new policy. Duiveke continued to hold the royal affections, Sigbrit guided the royal policy, and the nobles viewed her power with intense bitterness. In 1517 Duiveke died of poison, it was said, suspicion pointing to the royal agent of Copenhagen, one Torben Oxe, as the guilty man. Christian tried him before a jury of peasants, without regard for established procedure which required that noblemen should be judged by their peers, and ordered him to be beheaded. This marked an abrupt change in the king's policy. He now flouted the nobility and surrendered to Sigbrit's advice.

It was inevitable that the clergy, opposed to the crown quite as much as was the nobility, should be the first to feel the royal displeasure. Christian, however, did not adopt a consistent policy toward the Church. If it suited his interests he would side with it; if not, he would follow an independent course. This is shown by his treatment of the nuncio Giovanni Arcimboldo (d. 1555), sent by Leo X to collect alms for the construction of St. Peter's by preaching indulgences in Scandinavia. Christian hoped to enlist Giovanni's aid in securing control of Sweden whose subjects steadfastly refused to accept him as king, although he enjoyed the support of Archbishop Gustavus Trolle (d. 1535) of Upsala. But Arcimboldo betrayed the royal confidence and revealed all he knew of Christian's plans. Arcimboldo's secretary Slageck divulged this betrayal to the monarch and ingratiated himself to such an extent that he became Christian's confidant. The irate king confiscated the money which the nuncio had collected. Meanwhile Trolle had been deposed from his archiepiscopal office by the Swedes who knew him to be a tool of the Danish king. Christian and Slageck made vigorous complaint to Rome about this action, and Leo X replied by putting the Swedish viceroy, Sten Sture, under the ban of the Church.

In Denmark King Christian sought to set up a state Church which would fall under royal control. Led by Sigbrit, he prepared a code of law which should regulate both crown and Church. This *Secular and Ecclesiastical Code,* promulgated in 1521 and 1522, set up a court of secular judges who were to settle ecclesiastical as well as secular cases under the royal will. Judicial relations between Rome and the Church in Denmark were broken, and courts Christian were robbed of jurisdiction in questions relating to property. Some salutary provisions were included: non-residence of clergy was forbidden, only such persons as had studied at a university and could expound Scripture in the Danish tongue might be admitted to the priesthood, the clergy were forbidden to acquire real property, and monasteries were required to submit to regular visitation by bishops.

Provisions regarding the nobility were equally interesting, for, conceived in the interests of bourgeoisie and peasantry, they sought to destroy the chief competitor of royal authority. The right to flotsam and jetsam which the nobles long had exercised was abrogated. Serfdom was abolished. Most interesting is the royal order that products of the realm were to be sold to Danish dealers in Copenhagen and not to foreign merchants of the Hanseatic League. It was evident that Christian proposed to build a powerful monarchical state by ruining the nobility and clergy and by strengthening the bourgeoisie and peasantry.

In his personal opinions Christian was influenced mainly by humanism. He was acquainted with Erasmus and, like him, believed in tolerance, and he also believed that the Church should be cleansed of crude practices and abuses. The spirit of humanism clearly permeates his ordinances, for humanist propaganda was busy in Denmark as everywhere else in Europe. Chief of the Danish humanists was Paulus Eliae, a Carmelite who inveighed against shortcomings in the Church, and whom Christian appointed to lecture on theology in the University of Copenhagen. He also imported scholars from Wittenberg (1519) who began Lutheran propaganda in Denmark.

Christian was deposed by the clergy and nobility in 1523. He had not only aroused them to bitter hatred but also had antagonized his relative, Duke Frederick of Schleswig and Holstein. The duke, who was supported by the Hanseatic League, was invited to Denmark and elected king. But peasantry and bourgeoisie stood loyally by Christian who, had he displayed his former energy and decision, might have beaten his opponents. However, Christian and his family embarked in April for the Low Countries, whereupon Frederick became master of the realm. But in the Empire and the Netherlands Christian was recognized as lawful king of Denmark and was the source of much trouble for that country.

Frederick I (1523–1533) had promised at his accession to suppress Lutheran agitation and to favor the old Church, but he was inclined toward the new doctrines. Hans Tausen (1494–1561), a Benedictine who had studied in Louvain and Wittenberg, returned at the order of his prior who, alarmed by his heresy, sought to make him harmless by placing him in a monastery in Viborg. But Tausen was able to influence so many that he became the center of a reform movement. At Malmö there was vigorous preaching of Luther's ideas. Christian Pedersen (d. 1554) translated the Bible into Danish, and many copies were circulated among the people. The bishops were eager to employ force in order to suppress heretical teaching, but they could do nothing because the king, who owed his election in part to the powerful nobility, was forced to allow the latter to seize some of the lands of the clergy. In Denmark therefore the Reformation was made possible by the cupidity of nobles. The king followed his own Lutheran wishes, and the nobles enriched themselves at the expense of the Church.

Influenced by the success of the Reformation in other lands, Frederick became a Lutheran and set up a national Church. Frederick was also influenced by the religious policy of Duke Christian, for the latter had introduced Lutheran preachers from Germany into Schleswig and Holstein, suppressed Anabaptism, and imposed Lutheran forms of worship upon the unwilling clergy and laity. Frederick followed his example and appointed Hans Tausen his chaplain to preach Lutheran doctrine, thus placing Tausen beyond the power of the clergy. The Danish bishops were disturbed and sought to check him and other preachers, but they were powerless; they sought redress in the diet of Odense (August, 1527). But the king was resolved to maintain freedom of preaching, and the nobles were loath to agree with the clergy in their demands. The result was that the *Ordinance* drawn up was a compromise: (1) there was to be freedom of conscience for both Catholics and Lutherans, (2) the king was to protect Lutherans as well as Catholics, (3) the clergy were to be free to marry, and (4) the clergy might no longer seek the pallium from Rome but were to be confirmed by the crown after election by their chapters. From this time forth progress of Lutheranism was rapid.

Frederick I died in 1533, and civil war followed until 1536. Lutherans wanted Duke Christian to succeed him, but Catholics preferred Christian II. His friends and the peasants seized Jutland, the towns supported him, and the Catholic clergy backed him. The city of Lübeck also aided the pretender. But the nobles enlisted the services of King Gustavus I of Sweden, and Christian showed utter lack of leadership in emergency. Finally the tide turned completely; Copenhagen yielded to the duke of Schleswig and Holstein, and Christian II surrendered. This was the famous Counts' War. Peasantry, bourgeoisie, and Catholicism had supported Christian II; Lutheranism and the nobility aided the duke who became Christian III (1536–1559). Catholicism was doomed, and the lower classes were ruined. The newly established monarchy was controlled by the Lutheran nobility who enriched themselves at the expense of the Church.

Christian III at once reorganized the Danish Church. Its property was confiscated for the crown, its temporal authority came to an end, and an assembly held in Copenhagen (1536) transformed it into a national Danish Church. The king next received the help of John Bugenhagen, the reformer of Pomerania and a personal friend of Luther, who reorganized the Church according to Lutheran ideas. Shortly after this the *Augsburg Confession* was adopted, and the Bible was translated into Danish. A rigid suppression of Catholics and Protestant dissenters (Anabaptists) was instituted.

THE DANISH KING ESTABLISHES THE
REFORMATION IN NORWAY

In Norway, the Reformation was almost entirely the work of the king, Frederick I of Denmark. The masses were loyal to Catholicism and, living in remote parishes, were little influenced by heretical propaganda. Not so the towns, however, for foreigners, especially Hanseatic traders, frequented them. Lutheranism was introduced very early into Bergen, and this city soon became an active center of iconoclasm and violence against the old Church. Even in Trondhjem, the ancient religious capital of

Norway, there was violence. Archbishop Olaf Engelbrektsson had allied himself with Christian II, but the defeat of his cause meant the ruin of Catholicism in Norway as in Denmark. Confusion followed, and Christian III sought to establish himself as king. Archbishop Olaf resisted in behalf of Catholicism, but his flight to Brabant in 1537 left the way open to Christian.

The Reformation was now speedily established, and Norway was declared to be an integral part of the crown of Denmark. The king appointed Lutheran bishops whose rule in the cities usually did not deeply influence the religious life of the country parishes. The ministry, recruited largely from Denmark, could not work effectively because they were strangers to the ways of the people in their secluded parishes and could understand their language only with difficulty. Many of the imported clergy were unworthy men. In many places Catholic priests continued at their tasks so that vestiges of the old faith long persisted. Such was the scarcity of Lutheran ministers and such the royal neglect that, when old Catholic priests died, their places were often left vacant for years, to the detriment of the religious welfare of the people.

Iceland belonged to Norway which became an integral part of Denmark under King Christian III (1536–1559). It was the policy of the crown to force the Lutheran faith and organization upon the Icelanders, but at first the Reformation enjoyed little support among the populace who resented forced change. The two Catholic bishops of the island had long lived in feud, but, when Lutheranism began to show itself, being imported through the country's commercial connections with Bergen, they buried their differences. Many Lutheran tracts circulated among the people, and in 1540 the New Testament appeared in the old Norse tongue. Finally, in 1548, opposition broke out in revolt against the king's authority, and the bishop of Holar was seized and executed as a traitor. Only gradually was order restored, and in 1554 the Reformation was established by royal decree.

THE SWEDISH CROWN ESTABLISHES THE NATIONAL LUTHERAN CHURCH

In Sweden, the Reformation grew out of the difficult problems confronting the new king, Gustavus I, in establishing royal authority. The power of the bishops was extensive since they possessed vast property and judicial authority. The nobles were haughty and independent, and the free peasantry of the interior would brook no restraint. The result was that the king had neither army, navy, officials, nor income. Furthermore, Sweden like Norway had been united to Denmark in the Union of Kalmar (1397), but the Danish kings had always neglected Sweden, and their rule was cordially disliked. Denmark also possessed the southern tip of the Swedish peninsula which separated Sweden from the Sound and the Kattegat. A Swedish bourgeoisie could hardly be said to exist because foreign commerce was almost entirely in the hands of the Hanseatic League. Thus it seemed impossible to create a modern monarchy out of such a country. Nevertheless, this was accomplished by the king at the expense of the Church within a few years.

When Christian II became king of Denmark in 1513, the Swedes were loath to accept him because of their national antipathy to the Danes. Sten Sture was viceroy of Sweden, a man of great ability who wished to free his country from its Danish bondage. Gustavus Trolle, newly appointed archbishop of Upsala, also was ambitious for power. These two men for some time had lived in feud, and Trolle now turned to Christian in order to further his schemes. We have already seen how the Danish king sought to make use of the papal nuncio Arcimbaldo in order to insinuate his way into Sweden, and how Arcimbaldo revealed all of Christian's plans to Sten Sture, thus compromising Trolle. Such was the nationalist hatred loosed upon the prelate at this time that he has come to be known as the Swedish Judas Iscariot. He began actively to urge a Danish invasion, with the result that a national diet deposed him in 1517.

Meantime Sten Sture defeated the invading Christian II in 1516 and 1517. But the viceroy was soon placed under the ban by Leo X, and Christian as temporal prince of the realm proceeded to execute it. By thus placing itself on the side of the national enemy, the Roman curia made a capital mistake, for the Swedes began to regard the pope as a dangerous meddler. Christian invaded the land a third time and inflicted a bloody defeat (January, 1520) upon Sten Sture on the ice of Asunden Lake. Sture died from his wounds, and his widow, Christina Gyllenstierna, won undying fame from the stubborn defense she offered against the invader at Stockholm. A fierce battle was fought between the invaders and the Swedish peasantry near Upsala, in which the Danes were victorious. A great number of Swedes lay dead upon the field. Their bodies were left exposed to the elements for the traitorous Trolle refused to let them have Christian burial because they were under the ban and hence were regarded as heretics.

This battle was followed by one of the most execrable deeds in all history. Stockholm surrendered on November 7, 1520, after Christina exacted a promise of amnesty, and Christian was crowned king in the cathedral of Stockholm before the high altar and invested with the

insignia of his exalted office. Trolle urged the monarch to punish all who
had had anything to do with his deposition from the see of Upsala. The
notables of the realm who were in Stockholm were seized and more than
ninety were summarily executed in the market place. Thus was Trolle
avenged and the wrath of Christian sated. The king's hypocrisy was
especially reprehensible, for, although he despised the Catholic Church,
he did not hesitate to act as punitive agent in executing the ban in order
to further his own interest. It ruined his cause and incidentally filled
Swedes with hatred toward the Church.

A national revolt broke out under Gustavus Vasa, a kinsman of the
late Sten Sture. His undisciplined hosts, drawn from the embittered
peasantry, were not able to reduce the fortresses occupied by Danish
troops, but they inflicted defeat upon an invading army in April, 1521,
at Västerås. Finally, however, the garrisons were reduced, but Stockholm
held out until June, 1523. Meanwhile Gustavus was proclaimed king at
Strangnas. The war of independence proved a success, and Christian,
confronted by rebellious nobles at home, could do no more to gain his
crown in Sweden and soon even abandoned Denmark. Frederick I of
Denmark was not able to establish himself in Sweden. Gustavus, nevertheless, found the burdens of government heavy. The nobility were not
able to resist his will, as most of them had perished in the massacre, but
the free peasants were loath to give him the necessary money with which
to manage the country and fight the Danes. The king was heavily indebted to the men of Lübeck for their fleet which they had sent to help
in the reduction of Stockholm. They also obtained extensive trading
privileges for themselves and other Hanseatic towns, and soon began to
press for payment.

Gustavus wished to appropriate some of the Church properties in
order to pay his debts, for he as well as other Swedes resented the support
which Leo X had given their national enemy. Pope Adrian VI sent a
nuncio, a Swede named John Magnus, to settle differences with the
crown. The king and his council insisted that Trolle should be deposed
and that only Swedes of upright life should be elected to Swedish sees,
for until this was done it would be impossible to uproot Lutheran propaganda. The chapters now elected bishops, and at their head appeared
John Magnus in the place of the deposed Trolle. This list was sent to
Rome, and approval was requested. The king was secretly inclined toward
Lutheranism and was loath to listen to Magnus' plea that the Lutheran
agitation should be suppressed. Pope Clement VII now made the great
error of insisting that Trolle should be accepted, and also at about this
time he named an Italian to the see of Skara.

These events caused Gustavus to put aside his mask, and henceforth Lutheranism received official favor. For some time Olaus Petri (1493–1552), who had studied in Wittenberg, had been busy disseminating the new ideas. On his return to Sweden in 1519, he became acquainted with Lars Andersson (1470–1552), archdeacon and canon of Upsala cathedral, a capable theologian who had seen much of the world. Andersson was a man of daring; he was resolved to cleanse the Church of the corruption which he had witnessed when he visited the Eternal City on three occasions. Furthermore, he was opposed to the power which popes, cardinals, and bishops were able to exercise in political as well as in religious matters. Gustavus consulted with him and came to believe that a break with the ancient faith was necessary for reasons of state. Although the king at first was personally not opposed to Catholicism, it seemed to him as to so many princes of the age that political exigencies dictated a change—a striking example of how secular concerns were crowding religious interests into the background. Lars Andersson became the king's private secretary, and Olaus Petri also entered the royal service. Petri, an intrepid preacher, defined the conventional rules of the Church and married. He translated the New Testament and published it in 1526, Erasmus' and Luther's example having inspired him to undertake this work for the Swedish people. Petri now became an active writer and exerted wide influence by popularizing Luther's teaching among the people. The old ideal of ascetic life began to vanish, and it seemed that a new vigorous activity and interest in political and economic life sprang up. Lutheranism and Swedish nationality were closely related.

A decisive step was taken at the diet of Vasteras in 1527. Gustavus needed money and had sought to extract some from the reluctant free peasantry. Twice they revolted against his financial policy, wishing to restrain the man they had elevated to the kingly dignity. The cost of maintaining the government was more than twice the income of the crown. The monarch presented a financial statement to the representatives at the diet, but nobles and churchmen, influenced by the old but vigorous Catholic, Bishop Brask of Linköping, were inclined to reject it. It was evident to all that the crown proposed secularization of clerical property and confiscation of incomes. The king, bitter, left their presence and proposed to abdicate. The peasants were alarmed by this threat and soon were insisting that the king should have his way.

The king's demands were granted in what is known as the Västerås Recess. Surplus revenues of ecclesiastical foundations and properties were confiscated for the royal chest, and nobles were able to recover such of their properties as had been granted to the Church since 1454. The royal courts alone were to have authority over the clergy when involved in causes of a temporal nature. The Ordinances of Västerås still further defined the relations between crown and Church. Its twenty-two provisions forced a reform in the life and work of priests and in their financial activities. But it should be noted that nothing was said about basic dogmas. The Church in Sweden steadily became Lutheran under the influence of the crown and zealous preachers of the new doctrine, but no formal doctrinal statement was made until toward the close of the century.

Finland was a possession of the Swedish crown, and hence Gustavus' policy was applied to that country. Lutheranism was introduced first by Peter Sarkilahti who returned in 1524 from a student's career in Wittenberg. Michel Agricola (1508–1557), also a student at Wittenberg, later continued Peter's labors by publishing a number of devotional works. He translated the New Testament, which he had begun in Wittenberg under Luther's influence, the first edition being printed at Stockholm in 1548. As in Germany, Denmark, Iceland, and Sweden, the Bible became a book of the people.

THE TEUTONIC KNIGHTS AND KNIGHTS OF THE CROSS BECOME LUTHERAN

The lands of the Teutonic Knights now also were converted to Lutheranism. Grand Master Albert seemed a most unlikely person to break with the old faith since the Hohenzollern family to which he belonged remained a staunch bulwark of Catholicism. But the new ideas about celibacy and the validity of religious orders, promulgated by Luther's tracts in 1520, influenced him. He became better acquainted with the Lutheran position while attending the diet at Nuremberg in 1522 and 1523. Secretly won to the new doctrines, he began to invite Lutheran preachers to Königsberg and other places in East Prussia. Like Luther, he came to believe that the exercise of temporal authority by churchmen was not justified. He married Dorothy, daughter of Frederick I of Denmark, and thus founded a dynasty which was to rule over the secularized land of the Teutonic Knights. In 1525 he came to an agreement with Sigismund I of Poland (1506–1548) whereby the lands of the Knights were to be erected into a duchy, subject to the overlordship of Poland. Soon Albert, now duke of Prussia, publicly declared himself a Lutheran, and in the work of reform he had the support of the bishop of Samland. Synodal decrees and episcopal visitations followed, and everywhere Lutheranism was established. The common people could do nothing but acquiesce in these changes.

North of Poland lay the lands of the Knights of the Cross, comprising Estonia, Livonia, Courland, and Semgallia, and since 1237 affiliated with the Teutonic Order. Here as in East Prussia German traders had built towns and laid the basis of such culture as the region possessed. Lutheran ideas found their way into Reval and Riga as early as 1521. Progress was slow, however, until 1539, when William of Brandenburg, brother of Duke Albert, became archbishop of Riga. He was ambitious to do for himself what his brother had done in East Prussia. In order to make certain the work of secularization he began by filling his chapter with clergymen sympathetic to Lutheranism. But to erect a temporal state out of the possessions of the Order was a difficult matter, for this involved the conflicting national interest of neighboring powers, Russia, Poland, and Sweden. Gotthard von Kettler, the last grand master of the Order, did not possess the strength necessary to repel his ambitious neighbors, and in 1561 Sweden annexed Estonia, Denmark seized the island of Ösel, and Poland received Livonia. Courland was erected into a vassal duchy of Poland.

LUTHERANISM IN POLAND AND BOHEMIA

The Reformation in Poland was peculiarly dependent upon the political conditions of the country. By the opening of the sixteenth century the government was controlled by its numerous gentry (*szlachta*) who had encroached upon the crown. They also were opposed to the ascendancy which the higher clergy enjoyed, for the bishops possessed vast wealth and had been successful in securing for themselves extensive influence in secular matters. Recruited from the upper nobility and appointed for the most part by the crown, they were usually place-seekers who possessed little of the priestly calling. Their worldly and unspiritual lives gave offense to the gentry who resented being disciplined by episcopal courts. For these reasons the people were prone to criticize them and were likely to adopt heretical teachings.

The townsmen of Poland also were an important class. Many of them were Germans whose ancestors had settled in the newly founded urban centers and had become well-to-do as the wealth of the country increased This was true especially in such centers at Danzig, Posen, and other places in Great Poland. In many towns the native Polish element spoke German and adopted the culture of the merchants who came from the West. Among these people, as among the bourgeoisie in other lands of western Europe, there was a strong current of hostility toward the upper clergy whose unapostolic character has already been referred to. It can cause no surprise, therefore, that Lutheranism was readily accepted by people of this class.

But the peasantry, purely Slavic in blood and speech, continued to live in the stolidity typical of that class in the Middle Ages. They were sincerely loyal to the traditional faith, and remained faithful to Catholicism, no matter what heresy was brought into the land. The priesthood of the countryside, ignorant and poorly trained as they were, also clung to the ancient dogmas. Conditions were somewhat better in the towns, but there humanism and heresy led the people out of the Catholic Church. In Lithuania there were many adherents to the Greek Orthodox faith. This diversity of class and of social and racial elements, the feebleness of the crown, and the flabby spiritual character of the higher clergy made possible a variety of heretical movements. But the staunch devotion of the peasantry to Rome at length succeeded in keeping Poland Catholic.

Many a Polish nobleman's son studied in Italy or elsewhere and returned filled with humanist ideas. Erasmus' writings were widely read. Dissatisfaction with the corruption of the upper clergy and aversion to their great wealth and secular authority now induced many to go to Wittenberg and listen to Luther's denunciations. Polish townsmen for centuries had looked to Germany in business matters and cultural life, and, when Luther's ideas spread among the German burghers, it was inevitable that these doctrines should also find their way into the towns of Great Poland. John Seklucyan began preaching in Posen (1521) the necessity of a reform of the clergy. It should be noted that the grand master of the Teutonic Order was faltering in his loyalty to the old Church (1522–1523) and that the bishop of Samland was not far behind. Meanwhile a priest of Danzig renounced celibacy and boldly married, to the dismay of the archbishop who vainly sought to halt the threatened defection. The priest's example was approved by many people, and the Lutherans were soon strong enough to seize control of the city's government, but Sigismund I, who felt that he could use force after his treaty with Duke Albert of Prussia, overthrew the Protestant government of the town.

Lutheranism steadily advanced into Great Poland in spite of the efforts of the hierarchy and King Sigismund. He resorted to decrees which, however, accomplished nothing. He ordered that no one might import German books into the realm, and in 1523 came the decree condemning everyone preaching Lutheran doctrines to be burnt at the stake. In 1534 all students were forbidden to study at Wittenberg. However, the royal power could not punish heretics because the gentry would tolerate no interference, nor would they permit the archbishops and bishops to cite them before their inquisitorial tribunals. Lutheranism therefore spread without restraint but never appealed to the peasantry and the Slavic bourgeoisie of Little Poland, and it never won the allegiance of more than a minority of the population.

That Lutheranism should spread into Bohemia was inevitable, for a large part of the population was German in race and speech. From neighboring Saxony and Franconia the new doctrines passed into the valley of the Eger. Joachimstal became an important center of Lutheran influence because of the preaching of John Mathesius. The Czech population also received the new teaching. The Bohemian Brethren, the more conservative wing of the Husites, kept aloof for a while because they had some doubts about the truth of Lutheran teaching, especially in respect to the Lord's Supper. Some of the more youthful brethren, however, who went to Wittenberg and became enthusiastic advocates of the new doctrines, wished to renounce Wycliffite asceticism and adopt Luther's ideas about the justifiability of appropriating and enjoying the things of this world. Even some of the nobility joined this group. Many Utraquists, those who held that the cup as well as the bread should be extended to the laity, also accepted Lutheranism, Prague being the chief center of their activities. Luther's teaching also penetrated into Moravia. German settlers at Iglau, a town which had become famous because of its mining, eagerly embraced the new doctrines and passed them on to the Slovaks.

LUTHERANISM IN CARINTHIA AND HUNGARY

Luther's influence also spread among the South Slavs of Carinthia, Styria, and Carniola. For centuries their lands, ruled by the dukes of Austria, had been subjected to German cultural influences, and it was inevitable that the new doctrines should speedily find their way thither. John Ungnad of Sonnegk fled to Württemberg where he set up a printing press which brought forth many translations of Lutheran tracts in the Slovene tongue. Primus Truber (d. 1586), a Carinthian and a most important agent in advancing the cause of Protestantism, was forced to flee and settled in Württemberg where he associated himself with Ungnad and translated the Bible into the Slovene language. This achievement marked the beginnings of literary culture among Slovenes.

Lutheranism also was received among the Magyars. Hungary owed much of its cultural life to the Germanic lands which marched with its western border. Sons of the Magyar nobility were wont to study in German universities and thus brought the new ideas back with them. At first the government and the bishops sought to repress the movement by force, but the death of the king and most of the Catholic prelates in the slaughter at Mohácz in 1526 gave Protestants much freedom. Matthew Devay, one of the most active of Lutheran propagandists, studied in Cracow where he became a priest and entered an order. He was a humanist and for some time a devoted servant of the traditional Church. In 1529 he attended the University of Wittenberg. On his return 2 years later, he began his vigorous ministry at Budapest and other places. He was thrown into prison but on his release found protection among the powerful nobility. He published a number of religious works and a Hungarian grammar in the Magyar language. At this time another Magyar named Erdosi translated the New Testament, under the influential example of Luther. The works of Erdosi and Devay laid the foundations of Hungarian literary culture.

The Saxon population in Transylvania reacted sympathetically to the writings of Luther which came into the country as early as 1519. Hermannstadt was an important center of reform. John Honter, who received a humanist education in various German universities and in Cracow, settled in Kronstadt where he began an active career as priest, teacher, and printer; and his devotion to Lutheranism exerted wide influence. As in Saxony and other Lutheran lands, schools were opened with the funds from confiscated convents and clerical lands. A new Lutheran university was opened at Kronstadt.

PART III

Novel Protestant Teaching

Chapter 5

HUMANIST AND SACRAMENTARIAN ENDEAVORS AT REFORM

$\mathcal{J}$T IS A common error to suppose that Luther, Zwingli, Calvin, and their followers were about the only men of their day who sought to destroy the authority of the Roman Church. So decisive, indeed, were their endeavors and so violent was their onslaught that large sections of Germany, Switzerland, and other lands were forever torn from the Catholic fold, and consequently it was natural that their activities should have first claim upon the attention of students. The reforming efforts of humanists have not therefore been sufficiently emphasized, nor have the sacramentarians been accorded an adequate place in the history of the Reformation. Let us first direct our attention to those humanists who were interested in reforming the Church and purging religious life of its cruder pious practices.

SIGNIFICANCE OF NORTHERN HUMANISTS AS REFORMERS

When the humanism of Italy moved northward over the Alps, it frequently underwent noteworthy changes. It indeed perpetuated the cult of classical letters, but definitely took deeper interest in religion. Scholastic philosophy, older social conceptions, and the traditional faith were as deeply entrenched among the better classes of the north as in Italy.

This is well illustrated by the *devotio moderna* which exerted much influence in the more populous parts of north Europe such as the Low Countries, the Rhineland, northern Germany, and northeastern France. Its followers were first of all laymen whose deep practical piety called for constant reflection upon the sacrifice of Christ. This led them to deny the things of this world and to follow the example of Christ as set forth by Thomas à Kempis in his *Imitation of Christ*. The *devotio moderna* spread into all parts of society, dominated monastic houses, permeated the schools, and filled the life of many a pious burgher. Scholars who had been brought up under its influence carried some of this piety over into humanism, and this is one reason why humanists of northern Europe so often exhibited keen interest in things religious. Whereas Italian humanism was interested primarily in aesthetic things without much concern for religion, that of northern Europe was essentially moral and aimed at religious reform.

The piety of northern humanists led them to study the original texts of Christian literature rather than those of pagan classic antiquity exclusively. Besides the Old and New Testament, they studied the great fathers of the Church such as St. Jerome, St. Ambrose, St. John Chrysostom, and St. Augustine. Philological science had made great progress in Italy, revolutionizing the study of Greek and Latin texts, and it now became the means of a more accurate study of the Bible. The fact that humanist methods of studying profane letters were applied to the books of Scripture led to practical results, for the humanists began comparing popular religious practices of the day with the teachings of the Gospels and the Epistles of the New Testament.

There was much to criticize in the religious life of the people as well as in the practices of curia and hierarchy, but, although these men might adopt a very independent attitude toward the Church, they usually remained loyal to her, for to them Catholic theology seemed preferable to the theologies of Protestant reformers. These humanists objected to the doctrines of predestination and total depravity. Being interested in practical ethical religion, they did not sympathize with the Lutheran, Zwinglian, and Calvinist teaching that men were saved not by becoming holy but by having the perfection of Christ imputed to them through faith in His sacrifice on Calvary. The influence of these men, in spite of the diversity of their opinions, was very great. It would be a simple matter to draw up a long list of names, but only a few need be given as examples: Jacob Wimpheling and Sebastian Brant in Germany; John Colet, Thomas More, and Thomas Wolsey in England; Guillaume Briçonnet and Faber Stapulensis in France; Juan Valdés and his brother

Alfonso in Spain; Cardinal Sadoleto and Bishop Gian Ghiberti of Verona; and the prince of them all, Desiderius Erasmus of the Low Countries.

BIBLICAL HUMANISTS OF THE NORTH

In northern Europe, especially in the Low Countries, there was a group of these men who had received the name of Biblical humanists,[1] since they were interested mainly in Biblical studies and ethical conduct founded upon the Sermon on the Mount. Often they were guided by a mystical love of Christ and a desire to pattern their lives after His example. One of the first of these humanists was a Netherlander, Wessel Gansfort, born in Groningen in 1419, the son of a baker. In 1432 he was sent to a school of the Brethern of the Common Life in Zwolle where he came under the influence of the *devotio moderna*. He became a warm friend of Thomas à Kempis who was living in a monastery at Mount St. Agnes near Zwolle. Later, at the University of Cologne, he found opportunity to acquire sufficient knowledge of Greek to read some of its classics in the original tongue, and he also learned some Hebrew. It is remarkable that he should know the three important languages—Latin, Greek, and Hebrew—long before Erasmus and Reuchlin were eagerly propagating their study. He also studied at Paris and subsequently visited Rome, Florence, and Venice. He retired to the abbey of Aduard in the Low Countries where he spent the last years of his life from 1482 to 1488. He died in Groningen in 1489.

Gansfort was above all things interested in Scripture, which he believed to be the source of all religious knowledge and in point of authority superior to popes and councils. He did not value very highly the medieval conception of the Church as an organ of salvation, for an individual's own faith and a somewhat mystical love and communion with God crowded the priest into the background. He accepted the official teaching of the Real Presence—the transubstantiation of the bread and wine into the body and blood of Christ.

At the same time, however, he insisted that whenever a person thought piously of Christ, the Saviour was at once present corporeally, wherefore the priesthood was not an indispensable mediating agent between God and man. All persons truly sorry for their sins were fully absolved even before entering the confessional; indeed, confession was not absolutely necessary. He held that salvation came through one's deep mystical love for the Saviour whose example was to be followed in everyday life.

---

[1] This apt phrase is borrowed from J. Lindeboom, *Het Bijbelsch Humanisme in Nederland*, Leiden, 1913.

Gansfort is an important man in the religious history of the fifteenth century in that his mysticism led him to minimize the usefulness of the priesthood, to exalt the Bible, and to criticize some of the popular practices of the hierarchy.

John Pupper of Goch (d. 1475) was, like Gansfort, a pupil of the Brethren of the Common Life through whose influence he became acquainted with the *devotio moderna*. Little is known of his early career beyond the fact that he was born in Cleves. In 1454 he went to study in the University of Cologne, and soon after he became rector of a house of Augustinian Canons Regularesses in Mechelen (Malines). Like Gansfort he insisted on an intense love of God as the sole norm of religious life, and he emphasized the great significance of Scripture without placing it unequivocally above the dictates of popes or Church. He never arrived at full clarity on this point, but it is certain that traditional conceptions about the priesthood did not win support from him. Much that he wrote was basically hostile to Catholicism, although it usually was couched in cautious language. His *De Libertate Christiana* (*On Christian Liberty*), written about 1474 and reprinted repeatedly, was destined to play an important role in the age of the Reformation.

ERASMUS' THOUGHT AND INFLUENCE

It would not be difficult to extend the list of noteworthy men who received inspiration from the Brethren of the Common Life and the *devotio moderna*. Some exerted much influence, others less; but of all these none are worthy of greater honor than Desiderius Erasmus of Rotterdam. He never wholly abandoned the pious inspiration of his youth, but, as the years passed, he identified himself more and more with the humanist movement north of the Alps, becoming the outstanding spokesman of humanist conceptions about religious life, social practices, political activities, and intellectual labors. Of all the humanists, none so completely identified himself with the revolt against the superstitions, ignorance, and social crudities of contemporary life. He exerted a mighty influence upon the religious thought of the Reformation. Occupying a middle-of-the-road position, he cared little for the obscurantism of old-fashioned Catholic theologians, nor did he like the violence of Luther and Zwingli or the radicalism of the Anabaptists. He therefore kept aloof, adhering to the even tenor of his peaceful way, criticizing the crassness of current religious life, and advocating his own conceptions of reform. His wit and skill in language made him a dangerous opponent or a powerful supporter. Let us examine his ideas briefly.

Erasmus thought that religion was a guide to right living rather than a correct doctrine about salvation as Luther and Zwingli taught. In other words, it was ethical and not primarily confessional. The Bible was the only source of theology and therefore occupied a central position in his thought. It was also the guide of Christian living, but as such the Old Testament was less important than the New, for in the Gospels and Epistles was set forth the Christian conception of life, their teaching being immeasurably superior to the philosophic abstractions of Aquinas or Scotus. Christ was the great divine teacher of the truth, and His finest thoughts are to be found in His Sermon on the Mount. Erasmus' emphasis upon conduct had important consequences, for he was at great pains to express his views on social, political, and religious matters. His Biblical humanism led him to contrast everyday practices in religion with the admonitions of Christ and the apostles.

A man of this temper is hard to classify, for labels are misleading. In the background of his personal piety lay the heritage of the traditional faith, but as the years passed much of this faded. He also believed— without much fervor, however—in Christ as the Saviour because of His sacrifice on Calvary. He really could give no support to the position of the pope in the Church. Although he believed the papacy was based purely on historical factors and not instituted by Christ as officially interpreted from Matt. XVI: 16–19, it was a practical necessity to have such a head and hierarchy to give form and direction to the Church. In short, Erasmus cared little for the supernatural element in religion, the mystery and efficacy of the sacraments, or the Church as the unique institution of salvation. In the matter of the reformation of the Church, in which he believed most emphatically, he sharply opposed the reformers, for he wished it to be cleansed first among the upper clergy and next among the lower, peacefully and gradually, and preferably by means of councils.

Since Christianity was an ethical code, Erasmus thought that it would be possible to prepare for Christian life by some method of training or education. The Christian faith was a code of ethics, and not, as with Luther, a simple trust in the belief that Christ would snatch man out of the depth of his degradation, no matter how unworthy he might be:

> We will enforce to give certain rules, as they were certain points of wres-
> tling, by whose guiding and conveyance, as it were by the guiding of the
> thread of Dedalus, men may easily plunge up out of the blind errors of this
> world, as out of Labirinthus, which is a certain cumbrous maze, and come
> into the pure and clear light of spiritual living. None other science is there
> which hath not her rules. And shall the craft of blessed living only be with-

out the help of all manner of precepts? There is without fail a certain craft of virtuous living and a discipline, in which whosoever exercise themselves manfully, them shall favor that Holy Spirit, which is the promoter and bringer forward of all Holy enforcement and godly purposes.

The craft of Christian living—how simple it sounds! But something stood in the way of practicing that craft, for even though baptism removed the guilt of original sin, the soul bore evidences of the original stain:

These be blindness, the flesh, and infirmity or weakness. Blindness with the mist of ignorance dimmeth the judgment of reason. For partly the sin of our first progenitors hath not a little dusked that so pure a light of the countenance, resemblance, or similitude of God, which our creator hath shewed upon us. And much more corrupt bringing up, lewd company, forward affections, darkness of vices, custom of sin hath so cankered it, that of the law graven in us of God scarce any signs or tokens doth appear. Then as I began, blindness causeth that we in the election of things be as good as half blinded and deceived with error, in the stead of the best, following the worst, preferring things of less value before things of greater price. The flesh troubleth the affection so much, that even though we know what is best, yet love we the contrary. Infirmity and weakness maketh us that we being overcome either with tediousness or with temptation, forsake the virtue which we had once gotten and attained. Blindness hurteth the judgment, the flesh corrupteth the will, infirmity weakeneth constancy.

Certain rules should be observed by the soul so weakened and maimed:

The first point therefore is that thou canst discern things to be refused from things to be accepted: and therefore blindness must be taken away lest we stumble or stagger in the election of things. The next is, that you hate the evil as soon as it is once known, and love that which is honest and good: and in this thing the flesh must be overcome, lest contrary to the judgment of the mind we should love sweet and delectable things in the stead of wholesome things. The third is, that we continue in these things which we began well: and therefore the weakness must be underset, lest we forsake the way of virtue with greater shame than if we had never been about to walk or enter therein.

An exhortation typical of Erasmus follows:

Ignorance must be remedied, that thou mayst see which way to go. The flesh must be tamed, lest she lead thee aside out of the highway, once known, into bypaths. Weakness must be comforted, lest when thou hast entered into the strait way thou shouldst either faint or stop or turn back again, or lest after thou hast once set thy hand to the plough shouldst look backward, but shouldst rejoice as a strong giant to haste the way, ever stretching forth thyself to those things which be afore thee, without remembrance of those things which be behind thee, until thou mayst lay hand on the reward appointed and on the crown promised to them that continue into these three things: therefore we shall apply certain rules according to our little power.[2]

Erasmus was critical toward monks and friars about whom he wrote many a caustic squib:

> And next . . . come those that commonly call themselves the religious and monks; and most false in both titles, when both a great part of them are farthest from religion, and no men swarm thicker in all places than they. . . . For whereas all men detest them to that height, that they take it for ill luck to meet one of them by chance, yet such is their happiness that they flatter themselves. For first, they reckon it one of the main points of piety if they are so illiterate that they can't so much as read.

He made bitter comments on the formalism of monks without, however, making it clear that there were many among them who were sincere in conduct and anything but enslaved by routine:

> And then when they run over their offices, which they carry about them, rather by rote than understanding, they believe that God is more than ordinarily pleased with their braying. And some there are among them that put off their trumperies at vast rates, yet rove up and down for the bread they eat; nay, there is scarce an inn, wagon, or ship into which they intrude not, to the no small damage of the commonwealth of beggars. . . . Yet what is more pleasant than that they do all things by rule and, as it were, a kind of mathematics, the best swerving from which were a crime beyond forgiveness:—as how many knots their shoes must be tied with, of what color everything is, what distinction of habits, of what stuff made, how many straws broad their girdles and of what fashion, how many bushels wide their cowl, how many fingers long their hair, and how many hours sleep. . . . And amongst these there are some so rigidly religious that their upper garment is hair-cloth, their inner of the finest linen; and on the contrary, others wear linen without, and hair next to their skin. Others, again, are as afraid to touch money as poison, and yet neither forbear wine nor dallying with women.

At the popes he hurled many a bitter gibe:

> And for popes, that supply the place of Christ, if they should endeavor to imitate his life, to wit poverty, labor, doctrine, cross, and contempt of life, or should they consider what the name pope, that is father, or holiness, imports, who would live more disconsolate than themselves? Or who would

[2] *Enchiridion Militis Christiani,* Oxford, 1905, pp. 112–114.

purchase that chair with all his substance or defend it so purchased with swords, poisons, and all force imaginable?[3]

The popular cult of the saints also received his sarcastic attention, for he held that people often cared for the holy ones of the Church not because of their saintly lives but because of some property which might aid them when in need:

> How many are there, who put more trust in the safeguard of the Virgin Mary, or St. Christopher, than Christ Himself? They worship (!) the mother with images, candles, and songs; and offend Christ heinously by their impious living. A mariner when in a storm is more ready to invoke the mother of Christ or St. Christopher, or some one or other of the saints, than Christ Himself. And they think they have made the Virgin their friend by singing her in the evening the little song *Salve Regina,* though they don't know what it is they do sing; when they have more reason to be afraid, that the Virgin should think they jeer her by their so singing, when the whole day, and great part of the night is spent in obscene discourse, drunkenness, and such doings as are not fit to be mentioned.[4]

And ceremonies! Laudable customs as they might be, many people were placing an improper emphasis upon them:

> Again I both hear and see many who place religion in places, garments, meats, fasts, gestures, and songs, and for the sake of these things judge their neighbor contrary to the precept of the Gospel. From whence it comes to pass, that whereas faith and charity constitute the Christian religion, they are both extinguished by those superstitions. For he is far from the faith of the Gospel who depends upon these acts; and he is far from Christian charity, who for the sake of meat or drink, which a person may lawfully use, exasperates his brother, for whose liberty Christ died.[5]

Relics also received due attention at the hands of Erasmus, for popular religious practices persisted among the unlettered folk of the day. This is nicely illustrated in his dialogue, *The Religious Pilgrimage,* in which the relics of the church in Walsingham, England, are described:

> Ogygius: From thence we return to the choir. On the north side they open a private place. It is incredible what a world of bones they brought out of it, skulls, chins, teeth, hands, fingers, whole arms, all which we having first adored, kissed; nor had there been any end of it, had it not been for one

---

[3] *The Praise of Folly,* Oxford, 1913, pp. 126–128, 145.

[4] *The Colloquies of Desiderius Erasmus Concerning Men, Manners, and Times,* II, 309–310.

[5] *Enchiridion Militis Christiani,* p. 114.

of my fellow-travelers, who indiscreetly interrupted the officer that was shewing them.

Erasmus had no sympathy for the exhibition of relics of whose genuineness he entertained profound doubts, and of whose efficacy he was not at all convinced. At best they could not take the place of doing good—following Christ's example—and so he closed this dialogue with these words:

> *Ogygius:*   But hark ye, haven't I set you agog to go on pilgrimages?
> *Menedemus:*   Perhaps you may, by that time you have finished your relation; but as I find myself at present, I have enough to do to travel my Roman stations.
> *Ogygius:*   Roman ones, you who never saw Rome?
> *Menedemus:*   I'll tell you! After that manner I walk about my house, I go to my study, and take care of my daughter's safety; thence I go into my shop and see what my servants are doing; then into the kitchen, and see if any thing be amiss there; and so from one place to another, to observe what my wife, and what my children are doing, taking care that every one be at his business. These are my Roman stations.
> *Ogygius:*   But St. James would take care of these things for you.
> *Menedemus:*   Holy Scripture enjoins me to look after them myself, but I do not find any text to leave them to the saints.[6]

This emphasis upon the practical and the ethical in religion dominated much of Erasmus' career as a writer. His *Handbook of a Christian Soldier* (1503), which passed through many editions, was intended as a *vademecum* to instruct people in the gospel. Especially important was his edition of the *New Testament* in Greek (1516). Erasmus endeavored to present a better text by consulting many manuscripts without, however, knowing the best method of using such materials. The cheapness of the volume made it significant, for the bourgeoisie, already enthusiastically embracing humanist ideas, could secure copies in large numbers. An edition of St. Jerome (1514) was important for the same reason. At this time also appeared his *Paraphrases* in Latin (1516) intended to guide laymen in the study of Scripture, for Erasmus believed that the laity should know the texts of Christianity and insisted on a mastery of the three tongues in which they were written.

Besides these works on religion Erasmus also published a number dealing with more practical matters. The *Praise of Folly* (1509) was a most successful satire on life and its foibles; in it the clergy, monks, and friars in particular are exposed to criticism. His *Correspondence* is a most

---

[6] *The Colloquies of Desiderius Erasmus*, II, 236, 246–247.

important literary monument of the age, for, from the letters which he received and sent, the student can form a splendid conception of the issues of the age of the Reformation. The *Education of a Christian Prince* (1518) forms an interesting contrast to the more famous work by Machiavelli and sets forth a conception of the ruler quite characteristic of the author's ideas: "The prince, then, instructed in Christ's commandments, and fortified by wisdom, will hold nothing so dear as the happiness of his people, all of whom, as one body, he must love and cherish. He will devote every thought and effort to such an administration of the kingdom entrusted to him as will be approved by Christ when he demands an account, and leave his memory most honored by all men."[7] The ruler was to be a Christian and the policy of state was to be guided by Christian precepts. How different this was from Machiavelli's doctrine that expediency and not moral or religious precept should be the prince's directing motive!

Erasmus did not want to subject life to any hard and fast creed, as was shown in his struggle with Luther. The latter emphasized the corruption of human will and held that its efforts to do good were valueless in the sight of God. To Erasmus the idea that the human will was shackled by sin and vitiated by total depravity was shocking. Freedom was necessary if men were to lead truly Christian lives. Indeed, humanists generally felt this way about religion. For a while, especially after the debate between Eck and Luther at Leipzig in 1519, they were pleased to applaud the latter's attack upon Rome, but in a few years the incompatibility of Luther's ideas and the doctrines of humanism became apparent. Erasmus at first approved Luther's views, but his ardor soon cooled. He hated Luther's conception of human depravity, and he did not want to be linked to any party or school, especially when its methods were violent and demagogic. Consequently in 1524 he issued his *Treatise on Free Will*, the *De Libero Arbitrio Diatribe*, which Luther answered in October, 1525, in his book on the *Servitude of the Will*, the *De Servo Arbitrio*. The contest was significant, for it was a struggle between two conceptions of life which could not well exist together.

Erasmus thus stood aloof from all religious parties, and to the end of his life preferred to stay in the Catholic fold. People usually overlook his great influence, although his middle position on theology, his common sense, his refusal to bind the spirit of man by hard and fast dogmatic bonds made him the father of middle positions in all groups, Lutheran, Calvinist, Anglican, and Catholic. Hence his influence was to prove an abiding factor in religious and intellectual history in succeeding centuries.

[7] *Institutio Principis Christiani*, London, 1921, p. 53.

BEGINNINGS OF SACRAMENTARIANISM

Although Biblical or Christian humanists often were hostile to the traditional faith they usually did not, however, become open heretics. But during the years when Luther began his attacks on the Church of Rome a definitely heretical movement began to take form among some of them. For lack of a better term these heretical humanists may be called *sacramentarians,* a name employed at that time because they denied the validity of the Lord's Supper in the hands of unworthy priests. They were the spiritual spawn of Erasmus and other humanists and were especially numerous in the Low Countries, as the heretics in the county of Holland and the lands of the bishop of Utrecht were nearly all sacramentarians. A reforming group developed independent of Luther and Zwingli and exerted such widespread influence that it cannot be ignored. Its members protested against the sacraments when administered by unworthy priests and even denied the real presence. Often they insisted on a more spiritual faith and less reliance upon indulgences, good works, pilgrimages, and similar practices, much in the manner of Erasmus.

This spirit appears to have been quite common. The more or less aristocratic chambers of rhetoric (literary clubs) often criticized popular religious practices. Especially famous are the productions of the meeting of nineteen chambers from towns in Flanders and Brabant held at Ghent in 1539, which were written to answer the question, "What is man's chief comfort when dying?" It is instructive to note that most of the chambers opposed good works such as fasting, prayers, pilgrimages, burning of candles in memory of saints, and keeping fast days. The chamber of Antwerp insisted that the resurrection was man's chief comfort; that of Ypres, the Gospel of Christ; that of Thielt, only the merits of Christ; that of Bruges, only trust in Christ's love. The chamber of Courtrai insisted that good works availed naught; only true inward sorrow could please God. The chamber of Middelburg presented a composition in the same year called *The Tree of Scripture* which insisted upon zealous searching of the Bible. Priests were most sharply criticized as blind leaders and rapacious wolves and were described as "standard bearers of Lucifer who deceive the public with false teaching."

Other manifestations should be noted. There was much pietistic and mystical literature of a practical nature, such as hymns, edifying treatises in the spirit of the *Imitation of Christ,* sermons in the vernacular, and Dutch or Flemish versions of parts of the New Testament. It cannot cause surprise that in this environment, made rich by commerce and industry and advanced beyond all other parts of northern Europe in social and economic development, heretical movements should flourish. Several years before Luther began teaching, a Dominican of Utrecht named Walter began to preach against abuses in the Church. He was forced to recall his words, but, when Luther openly broke with Rome, he cast aside his habit and imparted his ideas to the townsmen of the county of Holland, especially at Delft. The fact that his followers soon became sacramentarians clearly reveals the nature of his teachings. Friar Walter was forced to flee and soon after died in Strasbourg.

It is difficult to determine how many people shared these sacramentarian views or what social groups welcomed them. Certain it is that among the better classes many seem to have entertained heretical thoughts about the Real Presence. Most documents which could throw some light upon this problem have been lost, but in the case of Leiden, a typical large town in the county of Holland, some facts are known. In 1530 large numbers of sacramentarians were in the habit of meeting in secluded places outside the gates of the town where they would be reasonably free from disturbance. In these conventicles they read and interpreted passages from Scripture and delivered sermons. There was no singing. There were similar meetings in Antwerp and undoubtedly in other towns also.

One of the members of the group at Delft, Cornelis Hoen, a man at law attached to the government of Holland, should be noted. He read the writings of Wessel Gansfort and, especially impressed by his novel conception of the sacrament, drew up a statement of the matter. Hinne Rode, rector of St. Jerome's school in Utrecht, brought it to the attention of Oecolampadius and Zwingli apparently as early as 1523, and it is certain that Luther saw it in 1521. Of course Luther could not be pleased with the view that the elements represented Christ only in a figurative sense. Zwingli, however, was impressed by this argument and appears to owe his idea of the Lord's Supper to it. It is important to note also that Hinne Rode went to Strasbourg and visited Butzer who was leading the Reformation in that city. Butzer, like Zwingli, agreed with Hoen's dissertation that the words *This is My Body* mean *This represents My body*.[8]

This conception of the Lord's Supper, to which was joined the belief that adoration of the elements was idolatrous, exerted much influence on the Reformation. It separated the reformers of Switzerland and southern Germany from the Lutherans, and it also reveals the basic difference between reform in the Low Countries and Germany. Lutheranism cer-

[8] For the facts here mentioned, see A. Eekhoff, *De Avondmaalsbrief van Cornelis Hoen (1525) in Facsimile uitgegeven*, The Hague, 1917.

tainly influenced religious ideas in the Netherlands, but never could win the support of a large part of the population. The first revolt there against the old cult took the form of a protest against the sacrament of the altar. Sacramentarian ideas also influenced religious thinkers in France. Anabaptists in Germany and Switzerland adopted this teaching of the Lord's Supper as one of their chief tenets.

Among the more important of the sacramentarians was Johannes Sartorius of Amsterdam, who had the advantage of a humanist education and was early associated with Biblical humanists, especially Friar Walter and the group at Delft. He published a tract *On the Holy Eucharist* (1525) in which he denied the Real Presence. Far more important was William Gnapheus of The Hague (1493–1568), who also received a humanist education and was acquainted with Hoen and the Delft group. Both he and Sartorius were prosecuted and thrown into prison for their teachings. Gnapheus' religious ideas were derived in part from Erasmus. He held that love of God sprang from faith and insisted upon a simple trust in God and constant thankfulness toward Him. Good works as prescribed by the Church were of little value in comparison. He denied the Real Presence. The believer should place no trust in outward ceremonies, for the kingdom of heaven lay within the heart, and the Christian should live a happy and peaceful life in ardent love of God.

Johannes Pistorius of Woerden, a pupil of Hinne Rode, is especially to be noted. He believed Scripture to be the only authority in matters of faith, denied the Real Presence and the legitimacy of celibacy for the priesthood. Although a priest, he took a wife "in the sight of God," and refused to admit that he did wrong in acting thus against the official teaching of the Church. He was tried by the inquisitors in 1525, and condemned to be burned in The Hague on September 15.

Other martyrs also sealed their faith with death, among whom was Wendelmoet of Monnikendam. She was seized in 1525, and accused of a number of sacramentarian teachings. She cared nothing for crucifixes or holy oil, and denied the sacrament, affirming that there was no change in the elements. She was condemned by the secular authorities to be burned to dust in The Hague on November 20, 1527. Her death was a heartrending spectacle. A popular ballad perpetuated the feeling of the people toward this execution:

> The hangsman drew near to strangle her,
> Then closed she her eyes so beautiful,
> She cherished hidden within her heart
> A Comforter; she had no cause to fear,
> She longed to go to her heavenly home,

Thus sweetly did she yield her spirit,
This Wendelmoet, into the hands of the Lord.
But friars and priests with mouths agape
For Christian blood will ne'er be satiate.[9]

[9] Adapted from *Een Liedekin van Weynken Claes Dochter*, in *Bibliotheca Reformatoria Neerlandica*, The Hague, 1904, II, 429.

Chapter 6

REFORMATION IN SOUTHWESTERN GERMANY

*W*HILE LUTHERANISM was leading Germans out of the Church of their fathers, in Switzerland Ulrich Zwingli was tearing whole cantons from the traditional faith. In Alsatian Strasbourg Martin Butzer (Bucer) and some others created new doctrines and conceptions of the Church which not only destroyed the unity of the medieval Church but also further split the ranks of the Protestants.

ZWINGLI'S EARLY MENTAL FORMATION

Conditions in Switzerland were very different from those in Germany. The Swiss Confederation in theory was still a part of the German empire, but as a matter of fact, it was practically independent. This league of cantons found that the Hapsburg princes who had long ago been driven out had not dropped their enmity toward them, and, when princes of that house mounted the German throne, trouble ensued. Finally Emperor Maximilian with the aid of the Swabian League attacked them and was defeated by the Swiss soldiers in a number of encounters. By the terms of the Peace of Basel (1499) all disputes with Maximilian were left to arbitration, and all cases before the Imperial Court of Appeals were to be dropped. Nothing was stated about the relations of the cantons with the empire, but in the years following no effort was made to subject them to any imperial legislation. Thus the Swiss Confederation became a free state within the empire. The course of the Reformation in these cantons was to be independent of that of northern Germany and was to have a character all its own.

Ulrich Zwingli, the hero of the Swiss Reformation, was born on January 1, 1484, at Wildhaus, a small village in the upper Toggenburg, a valley in the canton of St. Gall. Alpine mountains surrounded his home on all sides. His father was an official of this little democratic mountain community, and the boy's life and surroundings gave him a democratic attitude toward life and a love for freedom which he never forgot. It is instructive to compare him in this respect with Luther who was never much interested in the problem of secular liberty and whose attitude was always influenced by his peasant origin.

Zwingli went to school at Wesen on the Wallensee, an uncle taking charge of him while he studied music and the subjects of the trivium. At ten he went to a humanist school in Basel, and continued his studies under a famous humanist pedagogue in Berne. Here Zwingli attracted some attention because of his musical talent. It appears that the Dominicans hoped to secure him for their order, but his parents were opposed and transferred him to the University of Vienna (1498) where Conrad Celtes and others were teaching in the new humanist manner. For some unknown reason he was excluded in the following year.

He next went to Paris, if we may credit tradition. On his return he studied at Basel from 1502 to 1506, interesting himself in the quadrivium, which in Basel was dominated by the doctrines of Aquinas or, as they were called, the *via antiqua.* Nevertheless, humanist conceptions had found their way into this university. Zwingli did not, however, begin to take an interest in them until toward the close of his studies, nor did he pay much attention to theology. After receiving a bachelor's and a master's degree he became pastor (1506) in Glarus, a small town in the valley of the river Linth which flowed from the peaks of the Glarner Alps.

This pastorate marked an important stage in Zwingli's career. He industriously studied theology according to humanist conceptions and corresponded with prominent advocates of the new ideas. He studied the Church fathers and the classics of antiquity. Erasmus' conceptions influenced him profoundly. Zwingli's theology at this time was a simple ethical code of Christianity much like that of the great humanist and drawn mainly from the Sermon on the Mount. His patriotism and public spirit led him to oppose the policy of forming alliances with foreign powers and of receiving pensions from them, and he disapproved the practice of allowing France to hire mercenaries in the canton of Glarus. He criticized this in his brochure, *The Ox and the Other Beasts* (1515), a product of his first-hand knowledge of the evils of foreign service, but he was much criticized therefor, especially when the canton of Glarus allied itself with Francis I of France.

In 1516 Zwingli moved to Einsiedeln in the canton of Schwyz. He already knew Greek, was studying Erasmus' edition of the New Testament, and had just begun to acquire Hebrew. The monastery nearby possessed a collection of books which aided him materially, and there also was a statue of the Virgin which attracted a large number of pilgrims. Zwingli's humanist ideas were opposed to such pilgrimages, and he was led to criticize them in his sermons, thus gaining some reputation as a preacher. He complained of other practices in the Church and advocated reforms to be initiated by the upper clergy and extended by them to all parts of the Church. In December, 1518, he was elected to a vacancy in the great church of Zurich, but there was some objection to the appointment because of his irregular life. However, his frank admission that it was not a model of morality apparently did not stand in the way. This well portrays the decline of discipline among the clergy of that day and incidentally reveals a condition not uncommon among humanists themselves.

REFORM IN ZURICH

Zwingli began preaching in Zurich on New Year's Day in 1519. As befitted a man of humanist training, he based his discourses entirely on Scripture, paying no attention to the customary methods of preachers. Nor did he limit himself to mere texts; he preferred to study the entire historical setting of Christ's mission and the activities of the disciples. In this manner he systematically covered the New Testament by 1525 and at once began the Old Testament. He criticized the abuses current among priests, such as excessive devotion shown to saints, and many other pious practices.

He also continued his political interests. As a humanist he was a genuine pacifist. He opposed all manner of professional military activities for the Swiss and continued to oppose foreign service and acceptance of pensions. So effective was his preaching that Zurich refused to form an alliance with Francis I. Many Swiss were slain on the field of Bicocca (1522), and the people of Schwyz were disconsolate. To them he addressed his *Godly Exhortation*, whereupon the canton passed a resolution not to entertain any further connection with foreign powers. Unfortunately this decision was revoked within 6 months.

Zwingli began his religious career as a Biblical humanist and so emphasized conduct and morality. But in 1519 he passed through a deep religious experience, for he was stricken by the pest which raged in Zurich from August until the following April. Henceforth he viewed life from a very different angle. His theological ideas also underwent change in that they approached the Lutheran conception of grace and redemption. But his humanist training could not be blotted out entirely; hence he always exhibited an intellectual clarity which was lacking in Luther. He taught that man's original sin had not bequeathed a fatal heritage of guilt as Luther maintained, and he therefore believed that man was not thoroughly debased. He insisted more vigorously on predestination but at the same time taught that Christ had caused the great truth of His redemption to be known even among pagans—Socrates, Aristides, and others like them would surely be saved. Nor could he agree with Luther to the presence of Christ's body and blood in the Eucharist, for to him the sacrament was merely a memorial and a pledge that Christ's merits would prove efficacious in saving sinners.[1]

Zwingli's censure of the traditional faith soon bore fruit. In 1522 he refused to observe the customary abstinence during Lent, and his example was followed by the printer Froschauer and other prominent citizens. The town council discussed the matter and decided that although there was no Biblical foundation for it, the practice should be retained in order to prevent trouble. The bishop's commissioners argued that it was well grounded in ancient customs of the Church and therefore should be obeyed. The question of celibacy also arose, for in July ten priests presented a memorial to the bishop of Constance requesting that priests be allowed to marry and that the preaching of Scripture should be unimpeded. Zwingli, supporting their petition, asserted that Scripture was the sole guide of all action and challenged the bishop of Constance to a disputation upon the unbiblical or antibiblical nature of Catholic teaching. Zwingli's innovations were resented by Zurich's neighboring cantons, and they induced the diet of the confederation to demand that these novel doctrines be suppressed immediately.

On January 3, 1523, the government of Zurich issued a circular notifying priests that a disputation would be held in the town hall on the twenty-ninth. This step was characteristic of Zwingli's conceptions, for to him the Church was a lay and democratic body holding the faith of Christ. It was an invisible Church which possessed one head; Christ and Scripture was its only law. Therefore, each church community could decide questions of faith for itself. It was a congregational conception, quite contrary to the territorial conception of Catholics and Lutherans. It should be noted, however, that the reformer did not hold fast to this conception to the end, for he resorted to state action to secure the triumph of his ideas. And, when his dogmas were not accepted by the Anabaptists, he urged the state to reduce them to submission and even inflict

[1] The reader's attention is here called to the theory, for which there is considerable basis, that Zwingli, in forming his doctrine of the Lord's Supper, was influenced by the sacramentarians of the Low Countries.

the penalty of death. Zwingli's ideas fitted nicely with political conditions in the Swiss cantons. The result of the disputation was a foregone conclusion—the burgomaster, council, and great council ordered that preaching from Scripture as Zwingli had hitherto done should be continued. The clergy were to teach only those things that could be proved from Scripture, and no one was to indulge in injurious language. The disputation was conducted in the local German vernacular, the civil officials of Zurich constituting themselves the arbiters of religious differences.

Zwingli himself had taken a wife in 1522, although he did not legally marry her until 2 years later, and many priests now abandoned their celibate lives. The burgomaster and councils of Zurich took another weighty step on September 29, when they declared against the practice of exacting fees for baptism, the Eucharist, and burial. The clergy were ordered to preach only from Scripture. The canons attached to the great Church were to be reduced gradually in number by leaving unfilled posts which became vacant through death. Furthermore, there was to be public reading of the Bible in the original Hebrew and Greek languages. From October 26–28 graver steps were taken when images were forbidden because they were thought contrary to Scripture. Thus the outlines of Zwingli's reformation became clearer. Only what was in accord with Scripture was to be permitted; everything else was to be swept away. More revolutionary still was the decision denying the basic conception of the traditional faith, which declared that the Mass possessed no sacrificial character and denounced it because of the many abuses that were said to accompany its celebration.

During 1524 and 1525 the rupture with the old faith was completed, and the basic conceptions of Zwingli's teachings were carried out in detail. In January, 1524, the canons of the great Church who still clung to the old faith and sought to defend it were ordered to accept the new teachings without further opposition or else to leave Zurich. During the next spring and summer many of the old pious practices were discontinued. The great procession to the Virgin of Einsiedeln was abandoned by decree of the councilors, and relics were removed from reliquaries and buried. Zwingli's conviction that organs had no place in worship was now put into practice, and they were removed. Bells were no longer rung during storms, nor were they tolled at funerals. Pictures, images, and statues were removed. Saints no longer received the veneration of the public, processions ceased, and the use of candles and holy water was abandoned. In short, all practices not ordained in the Bible were discontinued.

Although Mass had been divested of its sacrificial character, it was still celebrated. However, Zwingli felt that the meaning of this sacrament was so obscured by superstitious practices that he determined to purify it as soon as he thought it safe to do so. He argued the matter before the council on April 11, 1525, insisting that a simple ceremony should be substituted. After some opposition his proposal was agreed to, and 2 days later communion was celebrated for the first time according to what was to become the reformed rite. A long table covered with spotless linen was placed in front of the altar in the transept, and the bread was dispensed on wooden platters and the wine in wooden cups. The Latin service of the Mass was translated into the German spoken in Zurich, but all references to the sacrificial nature of the ceremony were studiously omitted. Deacons passed the bread and wine among the recipients, men and women being separated by an aisle between them. No music accompanied the service. Thereby was accomplished a doctrinal revolution as well as liturgical.

THE SPREAD OF ZWINGLIAN DOCTRINE

At the opening of the Reformation Basel promised to become a more important center of reform than any other part of the confederation. Humanist ideas had conquered the university; Erasmus lived there and was the center of a coterie of like-minded men, and Froben won renown as a printer of the books of Erasmus and other writers. But, while humanists might undermine traditional conceptions with their witty diatribes and their insidious propaganda, they were not men of action—they usually stopped short of revolution. The arrival of the reformer John Oecolampadius (d. 1531) was an important event. Born in 1482 in Württemberg, he was deeply influenced by Erasmus' teachings, became a follower of Luther, and for a time sought refuge with Sickingen at the Ebernburg, but finally settled in Basel (1522) where, shifting his ground, he speedily adopted Zwinglian ideas. He became a teacher of Biblical literature in the university. The old-fashioned professors, wedded to antiquated methods of scholarship, unsuccessfully sought to have him ejected. There was much antagonism between the town and the bishop of Basel whose feudal rights were resented by the burghers. On the other hand, conservative elements of the population were opposed to any change. But people listened to Zwinglian propaganda, and in 1529 the gathering storm at last burst forth in a violent breaking of statues and pictures.

There was similar agitation in other cantons. In Schaffhausen a Franciscan friar, Sebastian Hofmeister, labored for the new doctrines, but in

1525 fled in the face of opposition. This was only a temporary setback, because 5 years later the canton definitely accepted Zwinglianism. In Appenzell an assembly went so far as to decide that people should be free to do as they wished about images and the Mass. In St. Gall propaganda was conducted through secret Bible readings. Zwingli's ideas also spread into Glarus and the Grisons. On the other hand, the forest cantons of Uri, Schwyz, Unterwalden, Zug, and Lucerne remained staunchly loyal to the old faith and formed the center of a vigorous opposition to the Reformation, even organizing a special league in 1524 to eradicate all heretical teaching.

The spectacle of a successful reformation in Zurich exerted much influence upon Berne which occupied an important position in western Switzerland. It was a large canton, an outpost of those in which German was spoken. Lutherans had been active for some time in the town of Berne, and Berthold Haller propagated Zwinglian ideas among a public inclined to be critical of current practices in religious life. Nevertheless, aristocratic townsmen would fain have expelled these dissidents, but the great council on October 23, 1523, refused to accede to their requests. Thus reforming ideas were allowed to undermine the old faith.

From Berne agitation for reform soon began to permeate the French cantons to the west, as will be shown later. The orthodox cantons realized its important strategic position and sought to keep it faithful to the old doctrines, and their delegations to Berne (1526) insisted that no religious changes should be tolerated and received promise that their wishes would be respected. They even went so far as to threaten to foment revolution among the discontented elements of the canton. But this was more than a proud commune could tolerate, and the authorities arranged for a public disputation in the vernacular, which was held in January, 1528, and lasted about 3 weeks. So powerful was Zwingli's preaching that the clergy attached to the great Church of St. Vincent, who were for the most part Dominicans, agreed to receive the reformed tenets. The clergy of the canton followed suit. Only in the uplands to the south, the Oberland, was there much opposition. A decree went forth on February 7, 1528, which ordered reformation everywhere in the typical Zwinglian manner.

By the opening of 1529, Zwinglian ideas had made noteworthy strides. Basel, Biel, St. Gall, Glarus, Appenzell, Mühlhausen, the Grisons, and Berne had definitely cast their lot with that of Zurich. Other communities such as Solothurn were overrun by propaganda in behalf of the new ideas. The five cantons, Uri, Schwyz, Unterwalden, Zug, and Lucerne, remained faithful to Catholicism, as did Fribourg. The confederation was thus divided into two factions. The situation was dangerous, for at this moment Emperor Charles was defeating Francis of France and the pope who had joined him in the League of Cognac (1526). Charles now seemed about ready to settle the religious disputes which rent Germany and to aid the Catholic cantons against those who adhered to Zwinglian teaching. This was particularly likely, since he was eager to resume old Hapsburg rights in Switzerland.

The tension was aggravated by Zwingli's policy in southern Germany. His doctrines had been accepted in Ulm, Strasbourg, Augsburg, Lindau, Memmingen, Frankfort, Constance, and many smaller places, especially in the duchy of Württemberg. Leagues were formed for protection. Zurich allied with Constance in 1527, and St. Gall joined them in 1528, to be followed in 1529 by Biel, Basel, and Mühlhausen. All this show of energy seemed dangerous in the eyes of Catholics, and the five Catholic cantons, supported by Fribourg and the Valais, approached Ferdinand of Austria for support in April, 1529. They formed an alliance with him and the duke of Savoy, and the cantons of Aurich, Berne, St. Gall, and Mühlhausen organized a counter league.

Meanwhile relations between Zurich and the Catholic cantons became strained over the question of jurisdiction in certain lands adjacent to the canton. Zurich possessed all sovereign rights in them save that of justice in life and limb which belonged to the cantons collectively. Naturally Zurich supported the movement for reform in these lands and this proved a fertile source of friction. War broke out over the burning of Kaiser by the canton of Schwyz. Kaiser was a preacher of Zwinglian doctrine, and the authorities had caught him while he was busy in one of the territories ruled by Zurich and the cantons collectively. The Catholic cantons were apt at any moment to receive help from Ferdinand, and it was therefore better to strike at once while he was busy with the Turks who were making ready to advance on Vienna. In June, 1529, the Zwinglian cantons completely surprised the Catholics at Kappel, a small village on the confines of Zug. They were forced to accept the Peace of Kappel, in which Zurich dictated that in territories ruled by Zurich and the cantons collectively the inhabitants should be free to choose the faith they wished. It even insisted on complete freedom of religion in the five cantons, which were also to abandon their alliance with Ferdinand, pay the costs of the war, and indemnify the family of Kaiser.

Soon the Peace of Cambrai (August 5, 1529) was signed between Charles and Francis, and the pope and the emperor were in accord. The final decree of the second Diet of Speier, which had met in February, was a severe thrust against the Lutheran princes. To oppose the emperor in his designs against the Protestants a close union between Lutherans and Zwinglians was desirable. Landgrave Philip of Hesse was especially active in promoting it, for he possessed greater political vision than any of the other Lutheran princes, and he especially feared a renaissance of Hapsburg power which might jeopardize his own hopes. Since 1527, he had sheltered the fugitive Duke Ulrich of Württemberg through whom he was led to accept some Zwinglian views.

Luther was bitter toward Zwingli. He could not well be otherwise, for the two men were cast in different molds, and Zwinglianism was markedly at variance with Lutheranism. The greatest point of difference was that of the Eucharist, Luther insisting on the Real Presence and Zwingli denying it. Eck and others had done their utmost to emphasize the differences between them. Thus the movement of reform was hopelessly rent asunder. Undismayed, Landgrave Philip determined to seek an understanding, and he invited the theologians of both camps to meet at Marburg on the Lahn to discuss their differences. The colloquy was held in his castle in October. Luther at once attacked the main problem. Writing on the table before him the words "This is My body" in Latin, he insisted that the word *is* meant *is* and not *represents*. In vain did Zwingli argue that where Christ referred to Himself as a vine or a door He was to be taken figuratively because it seemed impossible to interpret such expressions literally. After much discussion, in which Zwingli and his supporters were forced to yield nearly everything, the fifteen *Marburg Articles* were drawn up (October, 1529). But no harmony could be reached about the Eucharist. Luther tersely stated the problem when at the close of the Marburg Colloquy he rejected Zwingli's proposal of brotherhood with the words, "Your spirit is different from ours."

The implacable demands of dogma thus made a political settlement impossible just when union among all Protestants was so highly necessary. The Diet of Augsburg met in June, 1530, but its action was hostile to Lutherans. Strasbourg, Constance, Memmingen, and Lindau refused to accept the *Augsburg Confession* because of the tenth article which treated of the Eucharist. Instead they presented the *Confessio Tetrapolitana* which emphasized the central doctrines of Zwingli. The rupture between the two groups was definitive.

Relations between the Catholic cantons and the adherents of Zwingli became more acute during 1531, the former again approaching King Ferdinand. Conflict appeared imminent, and Zurich placed an embargo upon foodstuffs going to the five cantons. This precipitated hostile measures, and the cantons sent a force against Zurich. The burgomaster and councils of Zurich hurriedly sent forth a body of troops accompanied by Zwingli as chaplain, but the soldiers of her allies could not come up in time to help in the battle which ensued on October 11 at Kappel. Zwingli was slain and with him a large number of Zurich's best sons. Another defeat was inflicted upon Zurich, Basel, and Schaffhausen (October 24), and a second Peace of Kappel was effected on November 16. The same spirit which had made Swiss political institutions so virile and lasting breathed through its clauses. Each canton was to be free to settle its own faith without external interference, and all alliances with foreign powers were declared null and void. The death of Zwingli closed the first chapter of the Reformation in German Switzerland; the next began with the arrival of Guillaume Farel and John Calvin in the French cantons.

MARTIN BUTZER AND REFORM AT STRASBOURG

Strasbourg, situated in the center of Alsace, occupied a prominent position in southwest Germany. France lay to the west, Switzerland to the south, and Lutheran Germany to the north and east. This central political position gave Strasbourg a splendid opportunity of becoming the mediator between Zwinglian, Lutheran, and French ideas. This was to become the role of Martin Butzer who was born in the Alsatian town of Schlettstadt in 1496. When but a youth, he had been placed in the Dominican Order by his parents against his wishes. He early was attracted to humanism and became especially fond of Erasmus' *Praise of Folly*. When Luther began his work, he was attracted to him and met the reformer when he appeared before a meeting of his order at Heidelberg in April, 1518, whereupon a close friendship followed. Butzer forsook his order, married, and settled at Weissenburg in Alsace. He was forced to flee for preaching Lutheran doctrine without restraint. He settled in Strasbourg and began preaching the new ideas (1523).

Religious refugees poured into Strasbourg from many quarters. Butzer showed himself eager to listen to all views. Indeed, all people were welcome, although Anabaptists were not greeted with cordiality. Butzer became pastor of St. Aurelia's church and soon accepted Zwinglian doctrine. Images were removed from his church, and the miracle-working grave of St. Aurelia was closed to visitors (October, 1524). This new change was due most likely to the visit of Hinne Rode, a Netherlander, who brought with him Cornelius Hoen's sacramentarian treatise on the Eucharist. Zwingli was greatly impressed by it and to it he probably owed his radical view of the sacrament of the altar. Butzer henceforth assumed a mediating position between Zwingli and Luther. He was able to influence Landgrave Philip of Hesse and the towns of South Germany, and he took part in the discussions between Luther and Zwingli at the castle of Marburg (October, 1529). In this same year the Mass was abolished in Strasbourg, whereupon the city definitely became Protestant. Butzer also helped in drawing up the *Confessio Tetrapolitana* at the Diet of Augsburg in 1530.

During the next few years Butzer remained active in establishing harmony between Lutherans and Zwinglians. He visited Luther, discussed bases of understanding with the more complaisant Melanchthon, and even sought to bring the Waldensians into fraternal union with the Protestants. The death (1531) of Zwingli and Oecolampadius made him a leader of Protestantism in southwestern Germany, but by 1538 he had gone so far in his zeal to accommodate Luther's insistence upon the Real Presence that he alienated the Zwinglians.

By this time Butzer was able to influence Calvinism which had become important in French lands. Strasbourg had attracted attention among Frenchmen, and when the group at Meaux was attacked by the Parlement of Paris, Stapulensis, Roussel, and Farel sought refuge within its walls. Sacramentarian ideas were disseminated from Strasbourg among Frenchmen. These influences were very important. Thus Calvin was led to revise the Zwinglian conception of the Lord's Supper somewhat in accordance with Luther's teaching. Butzer agreed with Zwingli that the body of Christ was not appropriated through manducation, but he rejected that reformer's idea that it was purely and simply a memorial of His sacrifice.

Butzer came to hold that Christ was spiritually present in the sacrament, an idea which, it is believed, later guided Calvin in forming his view of the sacrament. Butzer's order of worship, including congregational singing in the vernacular, also appears to have inspired Calvin's singing of the psalms. All of this activity made Butzer a marked man. When exiled in 1549, he found refuge in England where his liturgical ideas influenced the drawing up of the Anglican service.

Chapter 7

THE ANABAPTIST REVOLT

*J*HE TERM Anabaptism as used in this book applies to the religious movement which began in Switzerland under the leadership of Conrad Grebel and Felix Manz and continued in a great variety of manifestations until the advent of Menno Simons (1496–1561). After Menno's death Anabaptists became generally known as Mennonites.

Origins of religious movements often are difficult to trace, and this is especially true of the Anabaptists. One must consider first of all the basic religious experience which gave rise to this group. Next should be studied the peculiar social, economic, and political conditions out of which it rose. But at the outset one is confronted with questions which have engaged the attention of many scholars, and most of which cannot be solved because documents are lacking. It has been argued that Anabaptists trace their origin back to the Taborites of Bohemia, the Waldensians, and other sects who continued to live unnoticed in sullen insubordination to the traditional Church. Direct connection with these medieval sectaries cannot be proved. More and more it is recognized that the movement really began with the doctrines advanced by Felix Manz and Conrad Grebel and their supporters in Zurich against the teachings of Zwingli.

DIVERSITY OF RELIGIOUS AGITATION

Considerable difficulty confronts the student of Anabaptist history of the diversity of the movement. Lutheranism and Zwinglianism owe their being largely to the activities of two remarkable personalities, the biographical element in each group providing a central thread which makes it possible to trace its progress with comparative ease. But it is different with Anabaptism. In Switzerland many leaders besides Conrad Grebel and Felix Manz revolted against Zwingli and spread their doctrines throughout the cantons. In Germany Hubmaier, Denck, Schwenckfeld, and Hoffmann, to mention only a few, were responsible for the propagation of new ideas. In Moravia and Austria Hut, Wiedemann, Huter, and a few others exerted much influence, and in the Low Countries there was a large number of active agents. Indeed, Anabaptism spread over all lands in which German influence was powerful, and even into England, France, Sweden, and Denmark. This geographical diversity alone renders it impossible to trace its history in simple outlines.

Doctrinal differences were so numerous among these people that it sometimes is difficult to decide whether a group may be correctly classed with Anabaptists. From the beginning Swiss Anabaptists taught that union of Church and state was unchristian. They held that the Church was a company of the regenerate, and that the sign of such regeneration was to be expressed in the rite of baptism. Because baptism followed conversion and was a sign of it, they held that infant baptism at the hands of Catholic priests and Lutheran and Zwinglian ministers was not valid. Their opponents therefore called them Anabaptists (rebaptizers). They also rejected the idea that the state possessed the right to control people in their faith, to inflict punishment in life and limb because of their religious beliefs. They were opposed to all violence, and held that military service was wicked and that payment of taxes to the state which engaged in war was sinful. Often they refused to recognize the state in any way, community of goods being advocated by some groups.

Their Biblical literalism prompted many to put forth strange doctrines. Some taught that the millennium was imminent; others held that it should be ushered in by the use of the sword. Besides these, there were some who seem to have descended spiritually from the mystics of the Middle Ages. Some believed in visions, direct revelations of the truth, or special illumination from God which would interpret for them the letter of Scripture. But most of them lived simple lives without ostentation, trying to apply the precepts of Christ to every act of life.

At this time three prophets from Saxon Zwickau came to Wittenberg —Nicholas Storch and an unnamed friend, weavers, and a former student of Melanchthon named Stübner. It is possible that Taborite conceptions influenced them. Storch prophesied God's speedy judgment upon the world—the end would come in 5 or 7 years; all the unrighteous would be slain, and only those professing the true faith and who had been rebaptized would be left. Stübner argued against the baptism of infants.

Thomas Münzer (d. 1525), priest at Zwickau, also was to exert much influence. He admired Storch whom he thought inspired by the Holy Spirit, therefore he knew more about things divine than any priest; for Münzer believed that a special inner voice taught man how to interpret the Bible and that whatever was so taught had binding value over every dictum of the Church and her theologians. He held that this inner voice subjected the body in such manner that it would faithfully proclaim its message. Man must look for signs sent by God to test his faith. Münzer thought that visions and dreams were important, but he inveighed against priests, altars, pictures, images, and the use of Latin in the service. German was used in his services. He claimed to hold special commission from God to found a new kingdom in which, following the example of apostolic days, equality of social status and community of goods were to be established. If this new realm could not be instituted peacefully, it was to be done by force—one of the elect guided by God could strangle 1000 enemies, two could slay 10,000! Münzer's teaching became popular. He settled as a pastor in Alstedt in Thuringia and married a fugitive nun. He was killed at Frankenhausen on May 15, 1525, during the Peasants' War, when trying to command his disorderly followers.

BEGINNINGS OF ANABAPTISM IN ZURICH

For a while Zwingli's teaching in Zurich was acceptable to all, and his appeal that the Bible was the sole standard of faith and religious practice was readily received. Soon, however, there was difficulty, for some wanted a complete application of Biblical teaching, and Zwingli was loath to go to such lengths. The zealots held conventicles which for a time the reformer attended. In 1522 a number of enthusiasts from Basel joined them, as did Conrad Grebel and Felix Manz. This gave the dissenters great strength because these men were well educated according to the humanist conceptions of the day, Manz being a splendid scholar in Hebrew literature. They held that Church and state should be completely separated. The Church was to be spotless as it had been in apostolic days, and people of dubious life should be excluded. Zwingli, a man of practical political insight, felt that such an organization was impractical and rejected their plea.

A disputation was held in October, 1523. To their argument that conditions obtaining in apostolic days should be revived, Zwingli sought to make crushing rebuttal by showing that the clothes of those times and the practice of washing feet had nothing to do with religion. But Manz and Grebel offered bitter opposition. They continued their meetings at which they expounded the Bible, and they went so far as to sunder themselves entirely from Zwingli and his supporters in all social matters. Other sympathizers came to Zurich at this time, among whom were Louis Hetzer who knew Hebrew and the classics, and George Blaurock, a runaway Premonstratensian monk. The latter was held to be possessed of the Holy Spirit and to be a second Paul.

The group appears to have grown rapidly. In 1524 its leaders began to discuss the validity of pictures, images, and the Mass. They questioned the lawfulness of paying tithes to the established Church and the practice of infant baptism. It appears that Münzer's influence brought about this latter agitation, although Karlstadt's writings about the rite also became known at this time. The group now came to believe that baptism was a sign of regeneration and that infant baptism was a device of the devil. A disputation was held in January, 1525, and a decree followed, ordering that all unbaptized children should forthwith be baptized under pain of banishment of the parents. Conventicles were now also forbidden, and a number of zealots were ordered out of the jurisdiction of Zurich.

These steps to repress the movement only provoked greater resistance, which was led by Grebel. At Zollikon on Lake Zurich a meeting was held at which Grebel baptized Blaurock, a man who was to display a zeal characteristic of neophytes. He at once administered the rite to fifteen more. Baptism of those old enough to understand the step which they were taking and a simple table of the Lord as a memorial of Christ's sacrifice were adopted as the chief tenets. Soon they also rejected predestination, adopted the doctrine of free will, and insisted on moral character and practical Christian conduct. Thus they were opposed to the idea of total human depravity. Their denial of any connection between Church and state seemed like treason to Zwingli, and he wrote such tracts on baptism as *Refutation of the Tricks of the Baptists*, and *Concerning Baptism, Rebaptism, and the Baptism of Children*. The officials of Zurich were alarmed. In March, 1526, drowning was made the penalty for holding Anabaptist ideas, and in January, 1527, Manz was drowned in the Limmat, the river on which Zurich is situated. The Anabaptists dispersed. Now began their long and painful martyrdom, one of the saddest on the page of history.

SOME EARLY ANABAPTIST LEADERS

Balthasar Hubmaier came forward at this time as chief leader of these persecuted folk. He was of bourgeois parentage, born about 1481 in Augsburg, and educated at the University of Ingolstadt under John Eck. He was a humanist and was acquainted with the great scholars of the day. He became pastor at Waldshut just over the Rhine in Germany where he soon abandoned the old faith and accepted Lutheran and Zwinglian doctrines. He left for Schaffhausen because of the design of the Austrian government to seize him. In 1524 he wrote a tract, *Concerning Heretics and Those Who Burn Them,* which was a noble plea against the execution of people for their faith. He was much interested in the progress of the Reformation in Zurich and, after his return to Waldshut, became convinced that baptism of children was contrary to Scripture. Swiss Anabaptists visited him in 1524, and one named Roubli baptized him. On Easter Day Hubmaier baptized more than 300 persons. Water for this purpose was conveyed in a plain pail, and the font, so long used in baptizing the children of Waldshut, was unceremoniously cast into the Rhine. He also inaugurated the simple rite of the Lord's Supper and, in literal application of Scripture, instituted the washing of feet. Hubmaier now became one of the more important Anabaptist leaders. But the Catholics of Waldshut were opposed to him, and the Austrian government was unceasing in its hostility. He and his wife fled to Zurich; he was seized, subjected to torture, found guilty, and banished from the town.

Quite different in many ways was Hans Denck (d. 1527). He was educated as a humanist and was acquainted with many famous men of learning. He was appointed rector of St. Sebald's School in Nuremberg. Soon he abandoned his Lutheranism and began to accept the teachings of Münzer but not his radical revolutionary doctrines. He was also influenced by Karlstadt and owed much to the German mystics of the Middle Ages such as Tauler, Eckhart, and the author of the *Theologia Germanica.* In 1525 he began to teach about the inner voice which he claimed came from God. He held that all external rules, rites, and practices were of no value. God's love was universal, His voice spoke to the soul, and there was no total depravity. Men might not resist violence. Salvation came only by participating in God's love, as did Jesus. Denck was expelled from the town by its Lutheran officials, wandered from place to place, and finally died of the pest in Basel.

Nicolsberg in Moravia became a haven of refuge for Anabaptists. The seigniors of Liechtenstein tolerated them and even accepted their doctrines. Hubmaier was the first of the persuasion to settle in this community, which became famous far and wide. Thither trekked many of the persecuted brethren, and a vigorous propaganda went forth from it. Sectarian factions arose. Hans Hut, a follower of Thomas Münzer, had been captured in the fight at Frankenhausen, but he escaped execution and continued expounding his master's ideas. He taught that the righteous should use the sword to exterminate the wicked and should set up God's kingdom with ruthless might. He knew little of the Bible, but had conned well the texts which he believed supported his notions. He preached that the day of the wicked was nearly over; he himself had been sent by God to announce their speedy overthrow. Indeed, it was to happen on May 15, 1527. Then would God's seed rise and, like the Israelites of old, smite their enemies. He became, until his death at the close of 1527, a leader of the extreme left wing of the Anabaptists.

Jacob Wiedemann taught community of goods which he held to be a prime doctrine in Scripture and the rule of apostolic society. No Christian might use force or violence under any circumstance. Taxes were sinful because the state used the money thus gotten for war. Finally some of Wiedemann's followers united with those of Hut. Hubmaier was a practical man and disapproved of these extreme views. He liked none of their chief tenets, especially their prophetic visions which foretold the advent of Christ's kingdom on earth. The seigniors of Liechtenstein also opposed this radicalism. Hubmaier now defended the institution of the state in his tract, *On the Sword*, in which he argued that rulers might use compulsion in all matters hostile to the established order. Meantime, after the Battle of Mohácz (1526), Ferdinand of Austria became margrave of Moravia. His orthodox conscience and his conception of government prevented toleration, and on August 28, 1527, he ordered that the Edict of Worms be enforced in Moravia without delay.

Officials soon began to ferret out people who denied the real presence. Hubmaier and his wife were brought to Vienna, and Hubmaier was tortured, tried, and finally burned on March 10, 1528. Three days later his wife was thrown into the Danube with a large stone tied to her neck. The Anabaptists fled, and Wiedemann settled at Austerlitz where his followers practiced community of goods. An even stricter faction separated from them under the leadership of Jacob Huter. Ferdinand insisted on their expulsion when an Anabaptist kingdom was set up in Münster, and persecution began in 1535. These poor people, simple, ignorant, morally austere and upright, who only sought to live according to the precepts of Scripture as they understood them, were hunted down like savage beasts and dragged forth from their hiding places in forests and mountains. Huter was burned at the stake in Innsbruck in 1536.

Of the numerous itinerant Anabaptist preachers and teachers, only few can be mentioned here. Melchior Hoffmann (d. 1543), a furrier's apprentice born in Swabia, never received a formal education. He fabricated his own system of theology. At first he was a Lutheran, but soon fell under Anabaptist influence. He pondered long and earnestly over the advent of Christ and the last judgment, prayerfully studying the Bible for answer to all his questions about these themes. Soon he believed that he was a prophet of God, a tool in His hands. He led a wandering life, preaching in Livonia, Sweden, northern Germany, and Holstein. He clashed with Karlstadt, fled to East Friesland, and finally arrived in Strasbourg. The Zwinglians in that center refused to accept him, and he went over to the Anabaptists. He taught that the advent of Christ was imminent, foretold it in the most fantastic manner, completely rejected all violence, and denounced baptism of infants. Later he preached that Strasbourg would become the center of God's new kingdom in 1533. He returned to East Friesland and at Embden formed a large group of Anabaptists. Expelled from the country, he went to Holland, but soon returned to Strasbourg. He was cast into prison, terribly abused and tortured, and finally died in 1543.

A mystical tendency among some of the Anabaptists remains to be noted. Sebastian Franck (1499–1543) of Donauwörth opposed formalism in religion and worship of the letter of the text of Scripture, preferring instead a church composed of folk ruled directly by the spirit of God. Since the Bible was to be understood only in a spiritual manner, Franck opposed all groups, even many Anabaptists to whom he showed kinship. Casper Schwenkfeld (1489–1561) advocated an inner and spiritual divine voice which should lead men to God. He denied Lutheran, Zwinglian, and Catholic conceptions of the Lord's Supper, and taught that the bread and wine were simply spiritual food and drink.

By 1530 Anabaptism had become common in many parts of Germany. This was a period of grave religious unrest. Luther and Zwingli were the first to break with Catholicism, but, when they drew back from their own demand that religious practices must be justified by Scripture, the common man often insisted on continuing to the logical end. Like Zwingli, Luther also was opposed to Anabaptists, but at first he preferred to have them banished rather than executed since he believed that the simple itinerant preachers were emissaries of the devil. Soon he was alarmed and urged summary methods. Even the more gentle Melanchthon thought that the death penalty was justifiable. Butzer, the theologian of Strasbourg, likewise opposed Anabaptist teaching and urged the government to proceed against the sectaries with force. A decree was issued against them by the officials of Strasbourg in July, 1527. Butzer believed also that the authorities should punish Anabaptists in life and limb. Indeed, the reformers generally looked to the state to establish the reformed cult. The Church in effect became a branch of the state; heresy was to be repressed by secular law, and Anabaptists, because of their refusal to have anything to do with the state, were treated as rebels as well as heretics. In short, princes and reformers generally believed in repression. Prosecution by sword, fagot, drowning, mutilation, and burial alive was the order of the day.

All things conspired to force a fanatical outburst. The fires of persecution burned brightly. The more moderate of the Anabaptists soon perished, the doctrine of nonresistance gaining them no mercy. Extremists became more prominent and assumed leadership. After the Peasants' War ended in defeat, disappointed folk fondly dreamed of Christ's coming and the dawn of His kingdom in which only righteousness would reign. Economic difficulties, social dislocation, and hard times also contributed their share. These conditions make it possible to understand the motives which led to the founding of an Anabaptist kingdom in Münster, an episode which has attracted undue attention simply because of its extraordinary character. It is an error to assume that all or even most Anabaptists were revolutionaries.

Anabaptism in the Low Countries centered around Amsterdam where John Trypmaker, a pupil of Melchior Hoffmann, carried on active propaganda. The more moderate and really typical Anabaptist teaching of the Swiss brethren occurred in Cleves, Juliers, and Berg where Henry Roll introduced it from southern Germany. But the more radical Melchiorite propaganda was to have great success in the county of Holland. Times were hard in that land after 1525. Trade with Scandinavia and the Baltic area was nearly at a standstill because of the struggle over the Danish succession. Christian II of Denmark was a brother-in-law of Emperor Charles and sought to use the Low Countries as a base of operations. Poverty and hunger stalked the land, and the authorities feared violence. Anabaptism appeared in Rotterdam, and David Joris (George) of Bruges (1501–1556) began to teach his doctrine in Delft. Its adherents were also plentiful in Friesland and Groningen.

INGATHERING OF THE SAINTS AT MÜNSTER

Melchior Hoffmann appeared in Amsterdam in 1531 with many of his followers who had come with him from Embden. Secret meetings were held, and propaganda was spread rapidly among people of low degree in town and country. In a state of religious ecstasy, these simple people hoped for a new order which would correct all the ills under which they lived, if not in this world at least in the next. Hoffmann wished no violence, but he could not restrain his more ardent followers, especially after he returned to Strasbourg in 1533. John Matthyszoon, a baker from Haarlem and a fanatic without conscience, now assumed leadership.

He had given the officials of Haarlem some trouble because of the laxity of his private morals. This apostle of wrath asserted that he had received a revelation from God in which he was commissioned to use the sword. The Anabaptists were no longer to be led to the shambles like sheep! Christ was surely coming, and His servants should prepare the way for Him; Münster in Westphalia was the place!

Towns and cities in northern Germany had in recent years witnessed great religious changes, often accompanied by social disturbances. Catholicism was displaced by Lutheranism, but in most cases Anabaptism exerted some influence. Münster was the seat of a bishopric. Since 1529 Bernhard Rothmann, a canon, had been preaching in an Erasmian vein, criticizing abuses in the Church and emphasizing the futility of such practices as pilgrimages, indulgences, and veneration of saints. In 1531 he returned from a visit to Wittenberg determined to effect a Lutheran revolution. The council refused to entertain any such move, but the common folk, led by Rothmann and Bernhard Knipperdollinck, persisted. Knipperdollinck was a member of the upper classes who a few years before had consorted with Anabaptists. Thus the aristocratic element was opposed to a change while the handicraftsmen insisted upon a thorough reformation. The council could not expel Rothmann for fear of violence. On June 1, 1532, a new bishop was named—Franz von Waldeck, a man who boasted connections among the Westphalian nobility. Finally in the face of growing agitation the council yielded to the Lutheran preachers who on August 10 occupied a number of pulpits.

Emperor Charles ordered the bishop in July, 1532, to drive out Rothmann and uproot the heretical nest, but this only resulted in more determined opposition, whereupon the bishop began to collect troops. Finally, at the intervention of Landgrave Philip of Hesse, the town was permitted to adopt the new faith and to enter the Schmalkalden League (February, 1533). The better class of townsmen remained true to Lutheranism whereas Anabaptist propaganda won adherents among the lower groups. Meanwhile Rothmann progressed in his beliefs and became a radical Zwinglian. In 1532 he fell under the influence of Henry Roll of Juliers and embraced Anabaptist doctrines. By the end of 1533, Rothmann and other clergymen refused to baptize infants. They began to talk about the necessity of obeying God rather than man and sought to put into practice such Anabaptist ideas as selling all and giving to the poor. The authority of the town council waned visibly.

At this juncture arrived emissaries of John Matthyszoon, among them his agent John Beukelszoon of Leiden, a tailor 25 years of age whom he had baptized the previous year. John of Leiden had a wife in Leiden who managed a hostel of shady repute, and he himself was polygamous before he entered upon his strange career in Münster. He was courageous, eloquent, and handsome, and he easily won the confidence of people, especially women. He was received into Knipperdollinck's house and married his daughter Clara. He and his host became the center of vigorous propaganda. There was a demonstration on January 28, 1534, but it was put down with little trouble. Some townsmen thereupon attacked a convent of nuns, and the inmates renounced their vows.

One day John and Knipperdollinck rushed out of the house into the streets, their eyes fixed heavenward. They cried, "Penance, penance, woe, woe, woe, do penance, and convert yourselves that you may not draw upon you the wrath of your heavenly Father!" Some people had visions —one man, a simple tailer, saw God in His glory in the skies with Christ beside Him bearing a banner in His right hand. Knipperdollinck's daughter began to prophesy and preach to excited crowds. Many fled the town, convinced that it was dangerous to remain. A climax was reached on February 25, when the Anabaptists secured control of the council and the reign of saints began.

Just before the council fell, Matthyszoon arrived in Münster, bringing with him the radiant beauty Divara, a fugitive nun from one of the convents of Haarlem. He at once acquired much influence, and his fanaticism led to violence. On February 27 the godless who refused rebaptism, whether men, women, or children, were ejected from the town. Around the walls were gathered the troops of the bishop and his allies. But it was necessary to increase the number of able-bodied men to help defend the new Zion, and Matthyszoon issued an appeal to all coreligionists in Cleves, Holland, and elsewhere to come to the defense. They were to meet in Guelders near the town of Hasselt on March 24, whence they were to proceed up the Yssel valley toward Münster. Boats loaded with men, women, and children came from Zeeland, Leiden, Haarlem, Amsterdam, and many other places. About 3000 deluded folk, for the most part unarmed, carrying with them some scanty possessions and money received from the sale of their property, were seized by agents of the government. There is some comfort in the fact that only their leaders were put to death.

Matthyszoon's career came to an end on April 5, 1534. He announced that God had chosen him to be His prophet—another Gideon. With twenty men he would drive off the besieging troops! As he and his band sallied forth on Easter Day, they were set upon and hacked to pieces.

KING JOHN OF LEIDEN RULES THE SAINTS

John of Leiden now assumed leadership. This man was without doubt a great religious quack, ignorant, able, without conscience, and violent. It is not certain whether he really believed in his divine mission. He now married his friend's widow Divara. What followed is a most amazing chapter in the history of the Reformation. The organization of the town was remodeled to make it conform somewhat to Old Testament ideas, and twelve elders were appointed. All marriages hitherto contracted were dissolved. Polygamy was introduced after the example of the patriarchs, the leaders taking several new wives each. John eventually permitted himself the luxury of as many as sixteen wives besides Divara.

For the moment the cause of the saints flourished. Internal opposition was extinguished in blood, and an assault by the besiegers in May was repulsed—victories which still further stirred the ecstasy of the populace. Another reorganization of government took place, and John became king in the New Jerusalem and imitated the regalia of the kings of the Holy Roman Empire. Aldegrever has left a splendid engraving of the man decked with the imperial insignia, wielding a scepter of gold studded with costly stones, and bearing an orb emblematic of the Christian world with two swords crossed through it to indicate his high jurisdiction. A royal and an imperial crown were made, each set with jewels. Divara was named queen, his other wives becoming her handmaidens. There was much pomp and ceremony—all for the exaltation of God whose unworthy agent John claimed to be.

Similar strange manifestations took place in other towns. When men and women began to set out for Münster in March, 1534, there was much excitement in Amsterdam, and on March 23, five Anabaptists rushed through the streets, brandishing swords and shouting something about God's blessing and curse upon the people. Chiliastic propaganda grew apace because the rule of the saints in Münster seemed successful. The government of the county of Holland was uneasy—it was a dangerous sign that many officials were loath to proceed against the poor fanatics. In October, King John of Münster sent out twenty-seven apostles to carry his message to the world. They left all their wives at home in Münster. Four of the prophets appeared in Amsterdam carrying handbills exhorting the faithful to unsheath the sword against the ungodly. God, they stated, would surely come, but not until the wicked had been exterminated. These emissaries were to plant a banner in each of four places—Juliers, Limburg, Amsterdam, and Groningen.

Fortunately many Anabaptists refused to listen to this counsel, and thus wholesale risings were prevented, but nevertheless there was much agitation. On February 11, 1535, four men and seven women rushed naked through the streets of Amsterdam crying, "Woe, woe is come over the world and over the godless." They were executed soon after capture. In another town a man ran through the streets shouting in prophetic strains, "Strike dead, strike dead all monks and priests, destroy all government of the world, especially ours!" On May 10 a group of excited men seized the open space before the town hall of Amsterdam but were put down on the following day.

Meanwhile, hunger and famine stalked in the streets of Münster. Treachery delivered the city into the hands of the bishop and his allies on June 25, 1535, Rothmann falling in the fighting which followed. After 4 days of frightful carnage and plunder, a judicial court was set up. Divara refused to recant and was beheaded, and all men who had played a conspicuous role were treated in like fashion. On January 22, 1536, King John, Knipperdollinck, and their partner Krechting were done to death in the most cruel manner of that cruel age. Afterwards their bodies were placed in an iron cage and hoisted high up to the tower of St. Lambert's church. Their remains were not removed until 1881.

The saints of Münster have always been condemned by Anabaptists for their violence and are not to be regarded as typical of the group. Even when the wildest ecstasy and chiliastic prophesying swept numbers off their feet, many more adhered faithfully to the saner view that violence was wrong. The failure in Münster discredited forever the extremist faction. John van Batenburg sought to restore King John's fallen realm. He also advocated polygamy and claimed to be the prophet Elias. But his propaganda found little acceptance in Holland, and he was executed in 1538. David Joris, another fanatic, also claimed to be a Messiah and exerted much influence upon the people. He favored polygamy, marriage according to him being an outworn institution which should not bind the regenerate. Fleeing prosecution, he finally settled in Basel where he lived until 1556 on the money he had collected from his followers. Henry Nicholas taught doctrines much like those of David Joris. Love, according to him, drew the faithful close to God, and believers were to retire from the world as much as possible. His organization, Family of Love, became a famous institution.

MENNO SIMONS REFORMER

Soon after the tragedy of Münster, Menno Simons (1496–1561) began to preach among the scattered and persecuted brethren. Born at Witmarsum in Friesland, he became a priest but abandoned the traditional faith in 1536, after he had come to doubt transubstantiation, the Real Presence, and the validity of infant baptism. Soon after he fled to East Friesland and began the career of an active itinerant preacher. Opposed to the doctrines of the brethren of Münster, he published pamphlets and treatises, engaged in disputations, and was eminently pious, humble, and devoted to the ministry.

The greatness of Menno Simons lay in his heroic devotion to the Anabaptist cause. He succeeded in weaning the sympathizers of the Münsterites from their doctrines of violence and bringing them back to the original teachings of Anabaptist leaders. He held that the Church was the communion of the faithful, the chosen of God set aside by act of baptism, the sign of conversion, and cannot be applied to infants. The Lord's Supper is in both kinds. Justification is by faith only. Denying predestination, they held to free will; perfectionism was the object of the Christian's life, and there were no new revelations. Menno was in part responsible for the institutions peculiar among his followers, known as the ban and its attending practice, avoidance. They were liberally employed even to separate husband and wife or parents and children, and to prevent marriage between parties who would not submit to discipline. His great service lay in quieting the excited brethren. His missionary activity was spent in the Low Countries and adjacent lands of northern Germany.

Menno's life was one of great difficulties; the government at every hand was against him. After 18 years of labor among his people, Menno wrote the following about his difficult life:

> For eighteen years now I, my poor feeble wife and little children have endured extreme anxiety, oppression, affliction, misery, and persecution; and at the peril of my life have been compelled everywhere to live in fear and seclusion; yea, while the state ministers repose on beds of ease and of soft pillows we generally have to hide ourselves in secluded corners; while they appear at weddings and banquets with great pomp, with pipe and lute, we must be on guard when the dogs bark lest the captors be on hand. Whilst they are saluted as doctors, lords, and teachers on every hand, we have to hear that we are Anabaptists, hedge preachers, deceivers and heretics, and must be saluted in the name of the devil. In short, while they are gloriously rewarded for their services with large incomes and easy times, our recompense and portion must be fire, sword, and death.

It would be hard to find a story sadder than that of the Anabaptists. Because they denied the teachings of Luther and Zwingli as well as of Catholicism they invited prosecution. But their denial of any connection between Church and state, and their refusal to have anything to do with the state led secular authorities to view them as insurrectionists. As the world of that day was constituted, separation of Church and state was unthinkable, and in affirming this doctrine they deliberately chose the bloody path of martyrs, their martyrology thus being a most impressive monument of the Reformation. They sacrificed themselves for a principle which could not yet be accepted. Not until later in the century—in the United Netherlands under William of Orange—did they win for the first time legal rights in any land.

Anabaptist hymns are worthy of study. Written in the vernacular, composed often in halting meter, they nevertheless possess the spirit of hymnology. They usually deal with martyrdom, and in reading them one gets glimpses of the dreadful ordeals through which these people were forced to pass. Anabaptism was a crime for which outraged majesty demanded the extreme penalty. Many of these stirring martyrdoms are preserved in the great martyrologies. The following from Schiemer's *Martyr's Hymn* is a fair sample:

> Thine holy city they destroyed,
> Thine altar overthrew they,
> Thy servants have they put to death,
> Where they could apprehend them.
> Of us alone, thy little flock,
> But few are still remaining.
> Throughout the land, in shameful flight,
> Disgraced, they have expelled us.
> Scattered are we like flocks of sheep
> Without a shepherd near us;
> Abandoned stand our home and hearth
> And like the owl or birds of night
> Seek shelter we in caverns.
> In clefts, on crags, in rocky wilds
> We make our home—still they pursue;
> Like birds or fowl we're hunted.

Anabaptists were usually workmen possessing little learning. They studied the Bible long and earnestly, and as a rule their leaders knew but this one book. Their aversion to secular learning, government, and industry made it impossible for them to become anything but farmers, a mode of life which enabled them to form a society composed of men and women who cherished these simple world-denying ideas. In this capacity they were successful wherever they settled. Their influence can be traced in many subsequent religious movements whose adherents sought asylum in distant places in Russia and along the American frontier.

PART IV

Protestant Movements in England, Spain, and Italy

Chapter 8

THE ANGLICAN REVOLT

$\mathcal{T}$ HE REFORMATION in England was determined mainly by the secular interests of the Tudor crown. The English king willed the separation from Rome, whereas in Germany the revolt against the papacy arose with the people and was encouraged by humanists. In Switzerland popular agitation was aroused until the governments of the cantons were forced to take action. The absence of a strong central government in both countries made possible radical Anabaptism among the people in town and open country. But in England it was otherwise; there the entire land was led by the royal power away from the faith of its fathers, and the Anglican Church, differing in many respects from the Lutheran, Zwinglian, or Anabaptist communions, was established.

RESOURCES OF THE TUDOR CROWN

It is important to grasp the basic economic and social forces from which the masterful English crown drew its power. The days had long passed when England was a land of peasants and graziers. Towns were expanding rapidly and manufactures were flourishing. The townsmen were becoming the most powerful class in the realm. They, and not the nobility alone, determined the public policy of the country.

By the side of the townsmen now appeared the owners of sheep ranges who soon found that it paid to put an end to the ancient method of

543

dividing land into strips held by tenants who lived in villages and tilled their holdings by an equally antiquated method of agriculture. They inclosed these open strips, thus making large fields in which to pasture their flocks.

These two classes, landowners and townsmen, were closely related: the one produced the wool from which the other made cloth, and both waxed wealthy. Thus a group of *nouveaux riches* came into existence who transformed the social aspect of the country. The old nobility with its purely manorial economy receded into the background, and a new nobility came forward—that of the more successful members of the new groups who demanded and could command recognition. These ambitious and aggressive folk cast covetous glances at the broad estates of the Church which they did not scruple to despoil. As often happens in times of profound social transformation, much suffering was caused. The peasants, deprived of their ancient holdings, were forced to seek new means of sustenance. Poverty thus increased greatly among one class while another became inordinately wealthy. More's *Utopia* referred to these conditions in a few striking passages:

> Your sheep that were wont to be so meek and tame and so small eaters, now, as I hear say, become so great devourers and so wild, that they eat up and swallow down the very men themselves. They consume, destroy, and devour whole fields, houses, and cities. . . . For one shepherd or herds-man is enough to eat up that ground with cattle, to the occupying whereof about husbandry many hands were requisite.[1]

The strength of the new Tudor monarchy was drawn from the groups made wealthy by these economic transformations. Henry VII (1485–1509) was descended through three generations from the union of Catharine Swynford and John of Gaunt (d. 1397), son of Edward III. Margaret Beaufort, great-granddaughter of John of Gaunt, had married Edmund Tudor and by him became the mother of Henry, earl of Richmond, later Henry VII. Thus his title, derived through females and from a line none too firmly established legally, was doubtful. He came to the throne after the tumultuous Wars of the Roses (1455–1485), a contest among members of the Plantagenet royal family for the crown. The great victory at Bosworth (1485) marked the definitive end of this anarchic feudal strife. The old nobility was discredited. The future control of the government was to rest in new hands—the bourgeoisie whose patriotic support laid the sure foundations of Tudor authority.

With unerring sense of statesmanship Henry VII sought the support of

[1] *Utopia* (Everyman's Library), pp. 23–24.

the newer groups. Discontented members of the old families who plotted to unseat him were frustrated. The king endeavored to destroy the outworn customs of nobles who insisted upon retaining their privileges, including the right of waging private feuds. The vogue of supporting retainers who wore the livery of noble families was obnoxious to the peace of the realm, for townsmen had little liking for these feuds. In 1487 Henry established the Court of Star Chamber to try persons who violated the law against livery and maintenance. Great nobles could no longer engage in feud or rebellion with impunity, each rising being crushed in decisive manner. Small wonder that ere long no one dreamed of resisting Henry's authority or questioning his right to rule.

Thus dawned a new age in England's history. The towns of the east and southeast under the direction of London, and a few in the west including Bristol, now assumed leadership in the life of the nation. Tudor rule was popular among townsmen; indeed, a splendid proof of the popularity of Henry's autocratic tendencies is furnished by the fact that, while reducing the nobility, he did not create a strong army or call Parliament frequently. On the other hand, he encouraged trade and peace with foreign princes. The rulers of the Burgundian-Hapsburg house in the Low Countries had often given aid to the old factions which disturbed the peace of the realm, and consequently trade had sadly declined. But in 1496 the *Magnus Intercursus* (the Great Intercourse) reopened trading relations with the Low Countries to the great profit of English townsmen. Further advantages were won in 1506, when a treaty was secured which Netherlanders thought disadvantageous to themselves, calling it in derision the *Malus Intercursus* (the Bad Intercourse). A new orientation was thus imparted to the foreign policy of the realm.

The Low Countries were now also drawn into a wider political combination. The union of Castile, León, and Aragon in 1474 had made their rulers, Ferdinand and Isabella, more effectively dangerous to France, for sooner or later Spain would draw closer to other enemies of France—the Hapsburg rulers of the Empire and of the Low Countries who inherited the old Burgundian hatred of their Valois cousins. Traditional rivalry of France and England in Scotland, English economic interests in the Low Countries, and the memory of old antagonisms dating from the Hundred Years' War kept green by the English possession of Calais, made it natural for the crown to seek alliance with Spain. Philip the Fair (d. 1506), son of Maximilian of Austria and Mary of Burgundy who ruled in the Low Countries, was to marry Joanna, a younger daughter of Ferdinand and Isabella, and negotiations were begun to secure a similar union between England and Spain. After 5 years of correspondence the marriage of Catherine of Aragon and Henry VII's eldest son Arthur was arranged. This union which coördinated Spanish dynastic and political dreams and Netherlands commercial and industrial interests satisfied the interests of the English crown as well as the bourgeoisie.

CHURCH AND RELIGION UNDER THE EARLY TUDORS

To a monarchy so strongly entrenched in the affections of the people and supported by the new wealthy classes of the land, the Church could offer no effective opposition. Its world-wide organization ran counter to the strong national prejudices of which the crown was the spokesman. The king exerted vast influence in the appointment of archbishops, bishops, and abbots; in fact, the hierarchy in England appeared to be little more than a group of royal functionaries. Popular sentiment against the papacy was also a force to be taken into account, the statutes of *Praemunire* and *Provisors* having been passed by Parliament in the fourteenth century in obedience to it. Criticism of current practices was frequent. Thomas Gascoigne (d. 1485) complained of abuses and laxity of life in his *Loci e Libro Veritatum*. Embers of Wycliffe's heresy were yet warm, especially among lower classes in the towns—perhaps there was some lingering memory of Marsiglio of Padua's notions. Anticlericalism as expressed by the poet Langland, far from dying, grew stronger early in the reign of Henry VIII (1509–1547), and benefit of clergy and right of sanctuary became the butt of attack. In 1512, Parliament took away from criminous clerks not in holy orders the privilege of benefit of clergy in all cases where people had been murdered in their own homes, in hallowed places, or while on the highway which was under the protection of the crown. This is but one example of the feeling of the laity toward the clergy, with its many categories and privileges.

Heresy was not common, however, for it would seem that Englishmen were well enough satisfied with the traditional faith as far as its teachings were concerned. Nevertheless, there were some cases of avowed heresy, Foxe's *Acts and Monuments* reporting about forty cases from 1510–1522 for the diocese of London alone. The case of Elizabeth Sampson is interesting. She criticized certain practices and held novel ideas about the sacrament of the altar, but was required to recall her words. James Brewster, a carpenter of Colchester, spoke against misuse of pious practices and also argued against the sacrament of the altar, and William Sweeting also held the same ideas. They were burned at Smithfield. They remind one of the sacramentarians who at this time were common in the nearby Low Countries.

English humanists also criticized religious practices; a group known as the Oxford Reformers were eager to renovate the spirit of devotion and purify the Church of abuses. Among these men were John Colet, since 1505 dean of St. Paul's (d. 1519), and Sir Thomas More (d. 1535). Colet had gained a new vision from Thomas Grocyn at Oxford. Like many a humanist of the more serious type, he studied the texts of the Christian faith whereby he hoped to cleanse the Church of many of its ills. He refused to study Scripture in the customary manner, with the result that the texts took on a fresher and deeper meaning. In 1512 he preached a strong sermon before the clergy of the province of Canterbury, denouncing in forceful words the laxity of the clergy who only too often pursued worldly interests. Venal practices were common also, and these were the reasons why heresy seemed to be rising. No better antidote to this condition could be found, he argued, than to foster a clergy sincerely devoted to its duties. This discourse produced a profound impression.

More believed, like Colet, that reform in the Church was needed and that the faith and practices of apostolic days should be restored. He did not rebuke the clergy for its immorality in the forceful terms employed by Colet, but criticized the abuses of state, society, and religion of the day in his description of an ideal commonwealth, the *Utopia* (1515–1516). More studied law at the Inns of Court in London, was admitted to the bar, and became a member of the House of Commons. As a man of practical affairs he had full knowledge of the ills of English society. He aired many of his views in his masterpiece. Much of what he says on religion, which is discussed in the second part of the book, must be accepted as an oblique criticism of religious conditions of which all readers were aware. And there were other advocates of mild reform which was to be carried out by the hierarchy itself and not by external forces or by violent measures. Cardinal Wolsey, archbishop of York and chancellor of the realm, was one of these.

A variety of conditions, political, social, economic, and ecclesiastic, all coöperated to create a crisis in the English Church. It was not heresy, however, that was to sweep away the foundations of the religious edifice, for Henry VIII was staunchly orthodox. When Luther issued his devastating tracts in 1520, the king felt called to reply and penned his *Defense of the Seven Sacraments* (1521), whereupon the pope, to whom a magnificent copy was presented, conferred upon him the title of Defender of the Faith. Luther's books found their way into the realm as early as 1520, and many copies were burned by the authorities. Heretical ideas appear to have been disseminated vigorously, especially at Cambridge where one Robert Barnes was prior of a house of Austin Canons. He preached a sermon in 1525 against popular practices in the Church, but recanted when brought before his superiors. Heresy, however, did not make much progress; it was the king's desire for an annulment of his marriage to Queen Catherine that was to bring the matter to a climax.

HENRY VIII. ANNULMENT OF MARRIAGE
TO QUEEN CATHERINE

Henry VIII had succeeded to the crown in 1509, his brother Arthur having died in 1502 shortly after his marriage to Catherine of Aragon. So important was the alliance with Spain in his father's eyes that it was deemed wise for Henry to marry Catherine. According to canon law the union of a man with his sister-in-law was forbidden, but Julius II granted a dispensation in December, 1503, on the ground that Arthur and his bride had never lived together. Catherine and Henry were married in 1509, shortly after the opening of the reign. Catherine appears to have been a faithful and dutiful wife, but in spite of that Henry grew weary of her, for she was his senior by 5 years and had probably aged rapidly. They had a number of children, but all died in infancy save Mary (b. 1516), and the need of a male heir weighed heavily upon Henry. Only 35 years ago the Tudor family had been established on the throne, and, since the dangers of a debated succession were vividly in the minds of people, a male heir was considered necessary for reasons of state and dynasty.

Meanwhile Henry had succumbed to the charms of Anne Boleyn, a pretty and vivacious attendant in the queen's suite who had spent some time at the French court and appears to have become acquainted with its slippery morals. Her sister Mary was no better, for the king had had improper relations with her. Henry conferred many favors upon Anne's ambitious father Sir Thomas, and on his brother-in-law, the duke of Norfolk, who formed a party at the court opposed to the ascendancy of Cardinal Wolsey, for the latter, as chancellor of the realm, was all-powerful with the monarch, directing the foreign as well as the internal policy of the kingdom. The enamored king determined to put away his legitimate queen and marry Anne Boleyn, and Anne herself eagerly aspired to the exalted dignity of queen.

Two difficulties stood in the way of securing the coveted annulment. The first was the law of the Church, for marriage was a sacrament and not to be dissolved, although it might be annulled if the union was invalid at the beginning. But here was a difficult obstacle that could hardly be overcome. Henry and Catherine had lived together for at least seventeen years and had been considered as married in the eyes of the Church. But Henry claimed that his conscience troubled him, for he feared that this union with his deceased brother's wife was against the will of God who had shown His displeasure by withholding from him the blessing of a male heir. He thought that Julius II's dispensation should be revoked, wherefore the union with Catherine could in consequence be declared annulled.

A second impediment was the peculiar situation in international affairs. Clement VII had joined the League of Cognac in May, 1526. With Francis I of France, and Florence, Milan, and Venice he hoped to drive the Spaniards out of Italy, to put an end to Charles' extraordinary power in that peninsula, and to rearrange the political map as it had been in 1494. Wolsey had persuaded Henry to join Francis in the war on Charles. As far as the political situation was concerned it appeared possible for the pope to grant the coveted annulment. But in May, 1527, when Henry was considering an appeal to the pope, Charles' Spanish and German troops sacked Rome. The pope was in the emperor's power, and Charles, a nephew of Catherine, would have little interest in the demands of the English king. The pope was hardly free to grant the dispensation, since he had fallen into the Spaniard's hands. Furthermore, Clement could not grant the annulment because of obstacles presented by canon law. The papacy had indeed sunk deep into the secular mire, but to yield to the king's suggestions was impossible. At first Henry sanguinely expected to be freed from his ties to Catherine, for it was undeniable that on a number of occassions prior to this declarations of nullity had been granted, but not in exactly parallel instances.

Clement adopted a temporizing policy and appointed a Decretal Commission in April, 1528. Campeggio as papal legate was to act with Wolsey. This wily Italian was well versed in the circuitous methods of Italian diplomacy. He traveled slowly, being conveniently delayed by the gout, and did not arrive in England until the spring of 1529. Catherine was obdurate in claiming her rights; she would listen to no argument. Supported by popular sentiment in England, she denied the right of the special court to try the case and finally appealed to the pope. Clement now advoked the case to Rome. Charles' power in Italy was still in the ascendancy, and Clement was unable to act against Charles' wishes even if he had wanted to. Campeggio departed from England in the fall, and the royal wrath now turned against Wolsey who was finally charged with treason. Death, however, cheated the monarch of his victim, for Wolsey died while on his journey to London (November, 1530). "I am come to leave my bones among you," he said to the monks as he stopped at the abbey of Leicester.

Henry's subjects turned against Rome the moment the case was called to the papal court, for their patriotic sentiments were aroused. Nothing did more to alienate men's minds from the papacy. Henry would never have been able to obtain his divorce on its merits as they appeared to the people. But now the divorce became closely interwoven with another and a wider question, the papal jurisdiction in England; and on that question Henry carried with him the good wishes of the vast bulk of the laity. The new Parliament, summoned to meet in November, 1529, was destined to give sure expression to such national sentiment. When it convened "it consistently displayed three characteristics: it was anti-papal and anti-clerical; it endorsed the royal will; but it refused dictation where its pocket was concerned." This Parliament was to exalt the royal power of England in a most extraordinary manner.

HENRY VIII'S REFORMATION PARLIAMENT, 1529–1536

By this time Thomas Cromwell was firmly entrenched in the royal favor. This man of humble origin had risen while in Wolsey's service and now the king found him a most useful servant.

> He saw life through plain glass, spurned ethics and sentiment, and set the *Prince* of Machiavelli above the *Republic* of Plato. Sly, cruel, greedy, yet not without the witty and agreeable converse of a man of the world, he drove straight to his end, settling the will and steadying the course of his royal master. . . . In the power and privileges of the Catholic Church he saw a series of obstacles to absolute monarchy; in Catholic culture he discerned a form of obscurantism injurious to the intellectual freedom with which Italy had acquainted him. He was a new man, and men of his class were drifting into Lutheranism, a creed which had hitherto escaped the patronage of the aristocracy.[2]

He was a fit instrument to forge the royal despotism.

The first session of the Parliament of 1529 proceeded to attack certain palpable abuses in the ordinary relations of the clergy with the people. Burial dues, fees for probating wills, pluralities, and absenteeism were regulated by the *Mortuaries Act*, the *Probate Act*, and the *Pluralities Act*, the king being on safe ground in directing the attack against them. Burial

---

[2] H. A. L. Fisher, *The History of England from the Accession of Henry VII to the Death of Henry VIII*, London, 1906, p. 296.

dues seem to have been exacted generally, and the practice apparently was growing. It was bitter irony that priests would let a small sum of money stand in the way of comforting a poor soul with the blessing of the last rites. Such abuses were not of course basically a part of Catholicism, but they did help to turn the affections of many a pious man and woman away from the old Church, and the same can be said of other abuses. Renovation was indeed needed, and the king at the moment of his quarrel with Rome found that he could command the patriotic support of his subjects.

At the same time Henry continued his pressure on the hierarchy. He declared that the clergy had violated the statute of *Praemunire* because they had recognized Wolsey's jurisdiction as papal legate. They were obliged to purchase their pardon by granting a large subvention and were compelled to recognize the king as "their singular protector, only and supreme lord, and, as the law of Christ allows, even Supreme Head." In other ways it was clear that Henry was planning radical procedure against the papacy, especially if his demand for an annulment should be rejected. Clement forbade (January 5, 1531) any tribunal to decide the matter of Henry's marriage since it properly belonged to the Holy See.

Under such circumstances Parliament met in its second session in January, 1532, and the attack upon clerical privilege, begun in the previous session, was resumed. Benefit of clergy was regulated, and the *Mortmain Act* restricted the right of the clergy to hold property. Another act reduced the amount of money to be paid as annates. These excessive dues were a patent abuse, and this measure which would cut off much papal revenue was a grave threat against Rome. Especially interesting as indicating which way the political wind was blowing was the *Supplication against the Ordinaries*, which set forth the royal grievance regarding legislation by churchmen in their assemblies or, as they were called in England, convocations. It also complained about the manner in which the courts Christian were conducted and the burdensome fees which were charged in them. This was no doubt in response to popular sentiment; it shows how well the king kept his finger on the pulse of popular anticlerical opinion.

In the Middle Ages monarchs grew powerful by subjecting to their will the nobility of the realm. In England and elsewhere the special privileges of the Church also seemed to stand in the way of that which all princes were determined sooner or later to achieve, full control of political functions within the borders of their state. The clergy struggled to avoid the destruction which lurked in the *Supplication*, but they were compelled to yield, and in May, 1532, they assented to the *Submission of the*

Clergy. They agreed that they would not make any new laws without royal approbation and that all laws previously made were to be submitted to the scrutiny of a royal committee composed of men from the Lords and Commons for amendment, rejection, or approval. This was a most serious step. Whereas throughout the Middle Ages secular and ecclesiastical jurisdiction had been established side by side and independent of each other, at least in theory, this novel measure meant that the secular authority henceforth would control the ecclesiastical, a step quite typical of the new age.

Henry met with no success at the curia during these months. Pope Clement issued a statement that, if Henry did not receive Catherine as his lawful wife, he would be excommunicated. Since it was clear now that a declaration of nullity could not be obtained from Rome, Parliament therefore passed the *Restraint of Appeals* in April, 1533, declaring that:

> This realm of England is an empire, and so hath been accepted in the world, governed by one supreme head and king, having the dignity and royal estate of the imperial crown of the same, unto whom—people divided in terms and by names of spirituality and temporarily, be bounden and ought to bear, next to God, a natural and humble obedience: he being also institute and furnished, by the goodness and sufferance of Almighty God, with plenary, whole, and entire power, preeminence, authority, prerogative, and jurisdiction, to render and yield justice, and final determination to all manner of folk. . . .[3]

The act merely restated a principle laid down in previous legislation, but it was a spirited asseveration of the superiority of the prince in his realm. It amounted to a repudiation of papal authority in England.

It was no longer possible to continue the old connections with Rome. When the see of Canterbury fell vacant in 1533, Henry appointed to the post Thomas Cranmer, a university doctor at Cambridge. Cranmer had shown himself zealous in Henry's cause, declaring that the royal power was supreme in the realm, even in the matter of divorce. When he became archbishop, he held a court, summoned Catherine before him, pronounced her guilty of contumacy when she did not obey, and forthwith declared her marriage to Henry null and void from the beginning. The breach with Rome was now practically complete. The pope at once declared Cranmer's judgment illegal. The *Act of Supremacy* (1534) soon completed the rupture with the see of Rome by declaring that the king should be recognized as the supreme head of the Church in England.

---

[3] H. Gee and W. Hardy, *Documents Illustrative of English Church History*, London 1914, p. 187.

Meanwhile Henry had secretly married Anne. An *Act of Succession* was passed (1534) which declared Mary ineligible to succeed to the throne and named Elizabeth, Henry's daughter by Anne Boleyn, as successor. This act carried the requirement that subjects should swear to support it. Sir Thomas More and Bishop John Fisher of Rochester refused to swear to the nullity of Catherine's marriage, although they were entirely willing to admit the king's right to determine the succession, and in 1535 they were executed as traitors. Others to suffer death were the monks of the Charterhouse in London. The unfortunate Catherine did not long outlive the unkind fate that was hers; she died in January, 1536, and Anne, accused of improper relations with some courtiers, outlived her but a few months. Truth is that the king, grown weary of her partly because she had given him no male heir, had transferred his affections to Jane Seymour, a lady of Catherine's former suite. Anne was beheaded on May 19, 1536, and Henry married Jane. Elizabeth was at once declared illegitimate.

The spoliation of the monasteries was the next great step. Cromwell, appointed vicar-general of the king in ecclesiastical affairs, dispatched commissioners to investigate all monastic foundations in the realm. This led to the suppression of all houses which possessed an income under 200 pounds a year (1536), their goods being declared forfeit to the king. It was a serious step, for many people who gained their living by working for the monks were now deprived of a livelihood and cast adrift. This led to a rebellion, the Pilgrimage of Grace (1536). The leaders, however, disbanded, having been persuaded to abandon their appeal to force. But in the next few years riots occurred and Henry set up a new court, the Council of the North, to take care of such cases. By 1539 all monastic houses were in the royal hand. Their property was diverted to secular uses, but much of it was squandered.

PROTESTANTISM IN ENGLAND UNDER HENRY VIII

Henry had led his people out of the church of their fathers for political and personal reasons. But in matters of doctrine Henry was staunchly Catholic and would not tolerate any change in the ancient beliefs. However, once he had cut England loose from Rome, it was difficult to maintain unity in matters of faith, for Lutheran teaching was spreading over the realm. At Cambridge especially there was much interest in the German innovations, and since 1520 a group of Lutheran sympathizers had been meeting in a local tavern. It is interesting to note that this propaganda bore fruit, for many of the leaders of the revolt came from Cambridge, among them Barnes, Tyndale, Cranmer, and Coverdale. William Tyndale was moved by the example of Luther to publish the New Testament in translation for the education of the English. It was smuggled into England and first appeared in 1527. The authorities sought out every possible copy and consigned them to the flames. Lutheran doctrine also appeared in Oxford.

Zwingli's doctrines also won some adherents. John Frith, for example, stoutly maintained them in 1533, and suffered a heretic's death by burning on July 4 in Smithfield. Two years later two Dutch Anabaptists met a like fate, and other examples can be added. Thus Henry sought to destroy Lutherans, Zwinglians, Anabaptists, and such Catholics as refused to admit his authority in religious matters, but he was adamant in asserting his orthodoxy and was determined that his people should remain orthodox. In 1536 he caused to be issued the *Ten Articles* which were intended to calm excited spirits. These articles admitted nothing new in the matter of dogma, but they asserted that pious and laudable practices which were not necessary were to be kept in a category separate from the great basic dogmas. The possibility of dropping them was entertained.

More important were the *Six Articles* of 1539, which held that transubstantiation and Real Presence were basic dogmas, priests should remain celibate, auricular confession was to be retained, and the laity were to receive only the bread in communion. The penal clauses which are especially interesting, provided that persons denying the Real Presence were to suffer death by fire and forfeit their goods to the crown. The royal solicitude to depart not a jot from the old doctrines is made plain by the savage punishments designed to make the penalty fit the crime. It was a serious measure, for many people were soon thrust into prison. It seemed that there would be no change in dogma. Until Henry's death in 1547, many men and women suffered at the stake or languished in prison.

GROWTH OF PROTESTANTISM UNDER EDWARD VI
(1547–1553)

A great change in Church matters came about in Edward VI's reign (1547–1553). This son of Jane Seymour was a frail youth of 10 years, and Henry VIII had taken care to ensure the proper functioning of the government during the boy's minority. He appointed a council of regency composed of sixteen nobles in which opponents of the new policies in religion and enemies of the old faith were evenly balanced. But the council named the duke of Somerset Lord Protector, and he was given almost regal powers which he used to gratify his desire to extend the Reformation. Archbishop Cranmer, who by this time had become an avowed Protestant, had caused much stained glass to be destroyed, images taken down, and altars removed. Thus many fine objects of religious art were lost forever, which makes it impossible for scholars to reconstruct the history of English art at the close of the Middle Ages. Henry's *Six Articles* were repealed by Parliament. Finally, in 1549, the *First Prayer Book* of Edward VI was made compulsory by the *First Act of Uniformity.* Cranmer had prepared it by translating the old Latin service into English. The marriage of priests was legalized and many abandoned their vows of celibacy. But the Lord Protector proved an incapable ruler, for he failed in Scotland, lost Boulogne, and could not alleviate the discontent of the people who burst into rebellion in Norfolk. In 1549 the government fell into the hands of the earl of Warwick, or the duke of Northumberland as he soon came to be called. He was an ambitious man without principle or ability, a zealous Protestant but only for reasons of policy.

The desire of the earl of Warwick to lead the English Church away from Rome was helped by the arrival of a number of theologians from the Continent. Germany was no longer a safe country after 1546, when Emperor Charles V began aggressive action against Protestants, and many of the more radical reformers fled into England. The sacramentarian Martin Butzer left Strasbourg to become a professor of theology in Cambridge. The Italian Pietro Martire Vermigli accepted a similar post in Oxford. Bernardino Ochino, also an Italian, was made a canon in Canterbury. Two other significant refugees were John Utenhove, a Fleming, and John à Lasco, a Pole, who exerted much influence through the newly founded Dutch Church in London. The result was that the more radical conceptions of the Lord's Supper and Church government advanced by Zwingli and Calvin were introduced into the realm. The *Second Prayer Book* was made compulsory in 1552, and was followed in the next year by the *Forty-two Articles.* These innovations more definitely separated the English Church from the Roman fold, a move encouraged by the earl of Warwick because it made possible the confiscation of Church properties which were distributed among himself and his friends. Many people became wealthy at the Church's expense, and the people so enriched, even though they were Catholics by conviction, became sturdy supporters of the new arrangement. As in other lands the Reformation often depended on the spoliation of Church lands. Thus by the time of Edward VI's death in 1553, a new Church had been founded in England. It expressed the spirit of the times, in that, dominated by the crown, it was subservient to the political government.

Chapter 9

FAILURE OF REFORMATION MOVEMENTS IN SPAIN AND ITALY

The reformation in Spain and Portugal, except for a small number of remarkable persons who spoke up in behalf of Protestantism, is interesting chiefly because of the reasons for its failure. For centuries the princes of these lands had identified themselves with their subjects in their long struggle with the Moor in behalf of the Catholic faith. Hence there was little chance of any wide acceptance of Protestant doctrine. Nor could Protestant teaching win many adherents in Italy where the lower classes were devoted to the traditional faith and humanists generally opposed to Lutheran, Zwinglian, and Calvinistic championing of pre-destination and denial of free will. And Italian princes, worldly in their outlook upon life, also had slight sympathy with Protestantism.

THE APPEAL OF HUMANISM

Humanism won adherents in Spain, but the force of much of its criticism of Church and contemporary religious life was broken by the patriotic sentiment of the people and by the fact that under Queen Isabella a vigorous reformation of abuses had been effected. Rigid discipline had been injected into every member of the ecclesiastical organization, and much of the obvious corruption which humanists attacked had been removed. It was thus impossible for Spanish humanism to lead to universal heresy and initiate reform movements as was so often the case in France and Germany. Nevertheless, Erasmus' influence at first promised to become as profound in Spain as elsewhere, and many Spaniards corresponded with him. His *Enchiridion Militis Christiani*, or *Handbook of the Christian Soldier*, was translated into Spanish and was widely read, and the *Familiar Colloquies* enjoyed an extensive circulation, many humanists greeting these works in the spirit characteristic of international humanism. But devout Spaniards disapproved of these writings because of the freedom with which they discussed religion and the flippant tone in which they criticized the popular religious life of the day. Two schools developed, one favoring Erasmus and the other opposing him. The first party was victorious for a time but in the fourth decade of the century the Inquisition began to ferret out Erasmian opinions, disciplining people who accepted them, and confiscating humanist books wherever possible. The result of these efforts was that Erasmian ideas, unable to make progress, disappeared from Spain during the course of the century.

After Erasmus came Luther, publishing his fiery tracts against the papacy. These were translated into Spanish, and copies were smuggled into the peninsula, especially by merchants who had offices in Antwerp. Luther's commentary on St. Paul's *Epistle to the Galatians* which discussed whether salvation was gained through faith or works was also translated into Spanish. Often Lutheran opinions were printed in books with false titles or in footnotes of books which otherwise were perfectly orthodox. A translation of Calvin's *Institutes* found many readers. The Inquisition never relaxed its vigilance in hunting for such books in private and public libraries and in prying into private homes. Nothing could withstand the all too meddlesome inquisitors armed with authority to inflict excommunication upon those unwilling to cooperate with them. Englishmen, Germans, Frenchmen, and Netherlanders who came into the realm for the purpose of trade were often taken into custody, tried, and, if found guilty, burned at the stake.

Two of the more noted heretics who adopted Erasmus' views were Francisco de Enzinas (d. 1570) and his brother Jaime (d. 1546), born in Burgos. Francisco was sent to Antwerp to live with some relatives, but his parents, fearful lest he should come in contact with heresy, recalled him. Later he returned to the Low Countries, studied at Louvain, proceeded to Wittenberg in 1541, and translated the New Testament into Spanish. Returning to the Low Countries in order to see his translation through the press, he was imprisoned, but after a year escaped. Francisco also became personally acquainted with Butzer and Calvin. His brother Jaime also visited the Low Countries and drew up a confession of faith in Spanish, but he was seized and burned at the stake in Rome, the first Protestant martyr to die in Italy (1547).

Another interesting Protestant was Juan Diaz of Cuenca who traveled to Geneva, being attracted thither by Calvin's teaching. He visited many cities in Germany, to the disgust and anger of his parents. His brother, resolving to remove the blot from the family honor, proceeded to Germany and slew him. Francisco de San Roman, a merchant who had business relations with Antwerp, visited Bremen where he came in contact with Protestants and became a fiery Lutheran. He was imprisoned, brought to Spain, tried, and burned at the stake (1524). Protestants were numerous in Seville, but they seem to have followed the teaching of Calvin rather than that of Luther. Many of them fled to Switzerland in the sixth decade of the century, and a congregation of Spaniards was formed at Geneva. There was also a group of Protestants in Valladolid, which appears to have owed its inspiration to the ideas of Juan de Valdés.

An *auto de fé* was held in 1559, and every trace of heresy was effectively wiped out. Protestantism could not succeed under such conditions, for it was an exotic manifestation. Spain remained Catholic, as did Portugal. Damiao de Goes (d. 1573), the most significant heretic of Portugal, adopted Lutheran tenets while in the Low Countries and, in spite of the pursuit of the Inquisition, escaped its clutches. Aside from foreigners who came into Portugal to trade, there were few dissidents. The Inquisition was established as a state tribunal in 1532. The king's desire for such an institution is explained by the income it produced from the confiscated properties of Jews who had been baptized but were guilty of apostasy.

THOUGHT AND WORK OF JUAN AND ALFONSO DE VALDÉS

Juan de Valdés (d. 1541) was the one Spanish reformer who exerted much influence outside the borders of Spain. He and his twin brother Alfonso (d. 1534) were born at the close of the previous century, the sons of a royal official at Cuenca. They grew up under humanist influences and became disciples of Erasmus. When Lutheran doctrines began to be disseminated, Juan was impressed by them, and his ideas changed remarkably. Only faith in Christ's sacrifice could save man; external forms such as veneration of the saints, burning of candles, pilgrimages and indulgences possessed little value in comparison; the Bible was the sole source of religious teaching. These ideas were grafted upon humanist doctrines, and the result was that in Valdés' beliefs a practical ethical teaching was tinged by Lutheran thought. But there was more in his doctrine than humanism and Lutheranism, for a mystical note is evident in his writings, derived without doubt from the rich heritage of mysticism which is so striking a feature of Spanish thought in the sixteenth century.

His brother Alfonso was almost exclusively a humanist and without doubt had a hand in composing the works commonly attributed to Juan. Together they produced a *Dialogue of Mercury and Charon* in imitation of the *Familiar Colloquies* by Erasmus. Mercury was stationed by the murky Styx, and Charon stood ready to convey across the flood such souls as death had released. Princes, prelates, preachers, and those occupying humble positions came, the authors employing these characters to present their own ideas about conduct.

The book contains much satire. One of the most interesting souls is that of a good woman, the account of her being filled with the moralisms of a devout humanist:

> *Mercury:*   O soul . . . are you willing to tell us how you lived when upon earth?
>
> *Soul:*   Yes, most willingly. That which my parents left me of greatest value was the ability to read, and some little knowledge of Latin. Such pleasure did I feel in reading sacred Scripture, that I learnt much of it by heart; and not satisfied with the mere knowledge of it, I endeavored to conform my life and conduct to it, losing no opportunity of instructing those of my female friends and companions who conversed with me in what God had taught me. . . . And because silence in women, and especially in young women, is becoming and praiseworthy, as excessive talkativeness is unbecoming and disreputable, I ever strove that my actions should speak louder than my tongue. Thus I lived many years, without the desire to become a nun, or to marry; contemplating one style of life as most alien to my condition, and the dangers of labors incident to the other. My great fear was, lest they should give me a husband so estranged from my views that he should pervert me from my own line of duty, or that I might have to lead a weary life with him. For this cause I determined not to marry; but, at last, everything having been well weighed, and recalling all the advantages of which I had read in connection with marriage . . . I held it to be safer for me to marry. . . . At length they gave me a husband, with whom God only knows what I suffered at the beginning; nevertheless, I suffered patiently, trusting in the goodness of God that I should rather lead him to adopt my views than he lead me to adopt his. And I availed myself of opportunity so carefully, countermining his vices by virtues, his pride by meekness, his rudeness by caresses, his extravagance by moderation, his diversions and luxuries by my chaste and holy exercises, and his anger by patience; ever regulating myself with profound and perfect humility in all my relations with him; at times dissimulating certain things, at times tolerating and permitting others, and at times softly reprehending those things which appeared to me to be clearly deserving of rebuke; that by degrees I tamed him. In this manner I led him to lay aside all his vicious and evil habits, and embrace virtue with such earnestness, that within a short interval I learned of him what I had taught him. And thus getting used to each other's ways, and striving to please each other, we lived in such peace

love, and concord that all marvelled at seeing him so altered, and at the change that I had wrought in him, as also at our mutual sympathy.

Charon: Let her go Mercury; and remember that it is late.[1]

Juan de Valdés wrote the *Dialogue between Lactancio and an Archdeacon* in the summer of 1527. The writer was shocked by the horrible sack of Rome in which nothing sacred was spared; the first part of this work sharply criticizes the worldly policy of the pope which Valdés thought was responsible for the event. In the second part he contends that the misfortunes were the simple operation of God's vengeance upon a wicked city. This part also criticizes the character of organized religion in Rome, papal finance, the charging of fees in the chancery, political machinations, improper use of indulgences, and false relics all being discussed with the utmost candor and disapprobation.[2]

The greatest of Valdés' works is the *Hundred and Ten Considerations,* an exposition of his theology. It emphasizes inner spiritual understanding which is to be gained by experience and prayerful reflection rather than by much reading:

> Oftentimes have I studied to understand in what that image and likeness of God properly consists of which sacred Scripture speaks, when it declares that man was created in the image and likeness of God. So long as I strove to understand it by consulting authors, I made no advance toward its apprehension, because I was led by reading, at one time to entertain one opinion, and at another time another; until gaining the conception of it by reflection, it appeared to me that I apprehended it, or at least that I began to do so; and I feel certain that the same God who has given me the knowledge I possess, will give me that which I still want.[3]

Juan de Valdés spent some time in Rome after 1531, but soon settled in Naples where he died 10 years later. His work in Naples is discussed later in this chapter. His great significance as a reformer is shown by his influence upon Italians, although in Spain he exerted a restricted influence.

THE CAREER OF MICHAEL SERVETUS 1511–1553

Before turning to Italy it remains to notice Michael Servetus (1511–1553) who played a sad and lonely role in the Reformation. He was born in Vallanova, studied law in Spain and in Toulouse, and began theology, reading Protestant works of all kinds. Soon he went to Germany and

---

[1] B. B. Wiffen, *Life and Writings of Juan de Valdés, otherwise Valdesso, Spanish Reformer in the Sixteenth Century,* London, 1865, pp. 7–9.

[2] *Ibid.,* pp. 61–75.

[3] *Ibid.,* p. 207.

when in Strasbourg published his monumental *On the Errors of the Trinity* (1531). Its denial of the Trinity, the basic dogma of Christianity, scandalized Butzer and the other reformers. Next he went to Paris where he studied medicine and received the doctorate (1538). His insatiably curious mind led him to continue his theological study, and he came to the conclusion that the vast body of Christian teaching as it had developed since ancient times was a tangled growth of errors. With complete disregard for the historical past he proposed to restore the Christian faith to its primitive purity. The result was his *Restoration of Christianity* which was published in 1553. A strange book filled with radical heresies, it "aimed to refute the Nicene conception of the Trinity, which he called 'a sort of three-headed Cerberus,' and to substitute an essentially pantheistic conception of God, with a denial of the preexistence of Jesus. He also rejected predestination, denied the efficacy of infant baptism, and was in advance of his times in the principles of Biblical criticism in that he interpreted Old Testament prophesies as referring primarily to contemporary events."

The book scandalized everybody. By means of a third party Calvin denounced Servetus to the inquisitors in Lyons who promptly arrested the heretic. But he escaped from their prison and tried to make his way into Italy through Geneva which he rashly visited. He was caught one Sunday after listening to a sermon by Calvin and cast into prison. A long trial ensued in which Servetus had every disadvantage, and finally he was condemned to die at the stake on October 27, 1553. He met the frightful ordeal bravely. His fate is typical of many others in that century when desertion of an established faith was regarded as the worst of crimes by all officials. Responsibility for the burning of Servetus rests mainly upon Calvin, who, however, thought that he was doing a meritorious service in ridding the earth of so revolutionary a teacher.

ITALY OFFERED LITTLE FAVORABLE OPPORTUNITY TO PROTESTANTISM

As in Spain, conditions in Italy were also unfavorable to the reception of Protestantism. The peasantry and lower classes in the towns were whole-heartedly attached to the old faith, and the upper bourgeoisie were dominated by the secular conceptions of the Renaissance. The more serious of these people, and there were not a few, might sympathize with Erasmus and Valdés, but Lutheran or even Calvinist doctrine could not appeal to many. Humanism always implied that man being born free could rise in the scale of morality and that virtuous social and political life was eminently good. People brought up under these influences could not favor the doctrines of total depravity and rigid foreordination. Furthermore, it should be borne in mind that the papacy was a prized national possession of Italians who were reluctant to see it destroyed.

Lutheran ideas and writings appeared early in Venice, as was inevitable because of the commercial relations which that city enjoyed with Germany, and it appears that many people accepted the new doctrines. There were also some Anabaptists in Venice. As the mightiest trading center in Europe, its government was inclined not to look closely into the religion of its subjects or the visitors who thronged its streets. Translations of Lutheran and Zwinglian works appeared, and Melanchthon's works circulated among the people. In 1532 appeared Antonio Bruccioli's translation of the Bible into Italian, another of the evidences of Luther's mighty influence. But the antipathy of zealous Catholics was aroused, especially that of Bishop Caraffa of Chieti who now began his energetic career of uprooting heresy. A number of men were imprisoned and the movement of reform in Venice, which Luther for a time believed would be successful, failed.

Sacramentarian and Calvinist teachings appeared in Ferrara under Duchess Renata, a daughter of Louis XII, whose contact with France made it possible for French heretical ideas to filter into the duchy. John Calvin visited Ferrara in 1536 in the hope that it might become a center of reformed ideas, but in this he was disappointed, for the political situation and the new zeal which the papacy began to exhibit against Protestantism made any progress impossible. However, the university in Ferrara stimulated free inquiry and was responsible for some of the heresy which grew up. Furthermore, Duke Ercole II (1534–1559) was tolerant in religious matters as became a prince of the Renaissance, and his lands were a haven of refuge for students and wandering teachers. But the prompt action of the Inquisition and the increasing influence of the papacy compelled Ercole to frown upon teachers of new doctrine.

There was a coterie of reformers at Modena where the tolerant policy of Duke Ercole, who was also duke of Modena, was enjoyed. One of the many academies formed during the Renaissance flourished here, and to it belonged a number of spirits, one of whom was the famed anatomist Gabriele Fallopio (1523–1562). The interest of this group readily turned from humanism to theological topics. Many a townsman not belonging to the academy discussed all manner of theological points. Heretical books were published, and a renegade Franciscan friar named Paolo Ricci assailed the Church of Rome and expounded Scripture before the people.

But Duke Ercole dispersed this group of heretics, and the Inquisition began to remove every vestige of Protestantism. A youth from Faenza named Fanini was seized and taken to Ferrara where he became the first martyr of Italian Protestantism (1550).

These reformers were destined to play no lasting part because they were isolated in a society which was becoming acutely hostile to revolutionary religious ideas.

JUAN DE VALDÉS IN NAPLES

But the role of the Spanish Juan de Valdés and his followers in Naples was more significant. Among the most devoted of these was Giulia Gonzaga, countess of Fondi (1499–1566). A woman of rare beauty, purest character, lofty intellect, and one of the noblest figures of the Renaissance, she was at once attracted to Valdés because of his fine character and elevation of spirit. He drew up for her instruction a statement of the Christian faith in his famous *Christian Alphabet*. It was a practical manual such as were plentiful in those days, and the idea is explained in his prefatory letter: ". . . that you make use of this dialogue as children use a grammar when they learn Latin, in the manner of a Christian alphabet, in which you may learn the rudiments of Christian perfection, making it your aim, the elements being attained, to leave the alphabet and apply your soul to things more important, more excellent, more divine."

Valdés' practical mysticism is shown in his advice to her: "I wish you, signora, to act. Turn within yourself, open the ears of your soul, so that you may hear the voice of God, and think as a true Christian, that in this life you can have no other real contentment and rest, than what will come to you by means of the knowledge of God, through the faith and love of God. Settle your mind in this consideration; most earnestly putting aside all those things that are transitory and cannot endure."[4]

Among Valdés' other writings are commentaries with translations from the Greek of St. Paul's Epistles to the Romans and the Corinthians (the first) and a translation of the Psalms. The author's knowledge of the original Greek was adequate for an intelligent study of the text. His commentaries are couched in a simple straightforward style such as one would expect from a humanist of Erasmus' school.

In the environs of Naples at Chiaia, Valdés conversed long and earnestly with kindred spirits. Most of them belonged to the nobility and

[4] *Ibid.*, pp. 118–122.

the official class who were trained as humanists, and the movement was therefore aristocratic in tone. In their walks along the Neapolitan Bay they discussed such lofty themes as man's highest good, the love of God, and the futility of all external acts of contrition as compared with an intimate and mystic communion with God. Valdés, as became a humanist, did not wish a radical reorganization of state or society, nor did he want to set up a new church. He simply wished to renovate popular religion, cleanse the hierarchy of its worldly practices, and regenerate mankind by means of a simple, mystic faith in Christ which would be reflected in proper living and noble character. His noble mind drew persons of exalted thought to him, Vittoria Colonna (1490–1547) also belonging to Valdés' circle. Among noteworthy men in this group was a Florentine, Pietro Carnesecchi (d. 1567). A humanist, he became a priest, associated with zealous churchmen who yearned to purge religion of its popular crudities, and became papal secretary under Clement VII. In 1531 he became acquainted with Valdés who was papal chamberlain. The Neapolitan coterie of reformers profoundly influenced this man of quiet manner and deep reflection.

The *Benefit of Christ's Death*, a little book containing the marrow of Valdés' doctrine, was one of the most important of all Italian works on the Reformation. Its authorship has long been the subject of dispute, but it has practically been decided that it is from the pen of Benedetto of Mantua, a Benedictine monk who lived in Sicily on the slopes of Mount Etna. Marcantonio Flaminio, a celebrated poet and a disciple of Valdés in Naples, prepared it for publication in 1540. It achieved great popularity, many copies were printed, and it became the chief organ of the Reformation in Italy.

SOME PROMINENT FOLLOWERS OF
JUAN DE VALDÉS

The most prominent follower of Juan de Valdés was Bernardino Ochino (1487–1565), born in Siena. He entered the Franciscan order which he soon abandoned, however, to join the more rigid Capuchins. Trained as a humanist, he discarded conventional methods of Biblical study and became a penitential preacher whose influence resembled that of Savonarola. Ochino preached in Naples and was impressed by Valdés' ideas, but the fiery Caraffa detected the heretical tendency of his preaching. In 1538 he was elected vicar-general of the Capuchin order but declined reelection in 1541. He continued his zealous preaching, especially in Venice, and gave public expression to a desire to preach without restraint. Summoned in 1542 to appear in Rome before the newly organized Inquisition, Ochino hesitated. Well might he do so, for the teaching that salvation came through faith alone could never be acceptable to the Church of Rome. But he obeyed and set out on his journey.

At Florence Ochino met Vermigli who had just been cited before the chapter of his order. Ochino decided to follow Vermigli's example and flee, and, in spite of broken health and advancing years, he hurried to Switzerland, tarrying some time in Basel, Zurich, and Geneva. In 1547 he set out for England where Cranmer offered him a canonry in Canterbury, and became the pastor of a group of refugee Italians. The accession of Mary Tudor to the English throne in 1553 again compelled him to flee and he settled at Zurich in 1555 as pastor of an Italian congregation. Another noteworthy fugitive was Galeazzo Caraccioli (1517–1586), a Neapolitan nobleman who was charmed by the teaching and personality of Valdés. This nephew of Caraffa was an eager disciple of Vermigli. Feeling that he ought not to dissemble and practice idolatry, as he termed the ancient worship, he fled and settled in Geneva (1553).

Another eminent follower of Valdés was Pietro Martire Vermigli (1500–1562). He was born in Florence, enjoyed a humanist education, became an Augustinian friar, and in 1533 was appointed prior of a convent in Naples. By this time he had become acquainted with the writings of Butzer and Zwingli, and he now fell under the influence of Valdés. In 1541 he became abbot of San Frediano in Lucca where he at once assumed leadership in disseminating the new doctrines. Vermigli held a Calvinist view of the Lord's Supper. A regular academy was formed to which were brought noteworthy scholars, and much interest was aroused in dogmatic points, even the common people of Lucca beginning to dispute about theological dogmas and to read the Bible. The authorities could not countenance this agitation, and Vermigli was cited to appear before a capitular meeting of his order in Genoa. Fearing for his life, he determined to flee and settled in Strasbourg as a lecturer on the Old Testament. In 1547 he was invited to England by Cranmer to become professor of theology at the University of Cambridge. He was imprisoned during Queen Mary's reign but escaped to the Continent in 1553, returned to Strasbourg, and ultimately became professor of Hebrew in Zurich.

Such reformers as were courageous enough to stay in Italy were apprehended one by one and brought before the tribunal. Aonio Paleario, a humanist born in Roman Campania and influenced by Valdés' ideas, was condemned to be hanged and burned, this sentence being executed in Rome in 1570. Pietro Carnesecchi was condemned as contumacious when he failed to hearken to a citation to appear in Rome, but Venice, where he had sought refuge, did not surrender him to the Inquisition until 1566. He was subjected to torture, and every effort was made to force from his lips evidence which might incriminate his many friends and acquaintances, but he steadfastly remained true to them and little was divulged. He was executed, and his body was burned (1567). Such was the zeal of the holy office that everyone who had belonged to Valdés' circle, or had been zealous in the work of purifying the Church was suspect and likely to be subjected to torture. The severity with which the inquisitors worked is explained by the fact that these suspected persons were members of the aristocracy or of the official groups, and hence influential. The existence of heretical malcontents was undesirable. Caraffa thought that extreme rigor was necessary to keep the Reformation from gaining a foothold in the peninsula, and he did not scruple to betray those members of the Oratory of Divine Love whom he had known years ago and with whom he had exchanged thoughts about corruption in the Church and the need of reform.

The reformation and restoration of the Catholic Church made the success of Valdés' ideas impossible. Pope Paul III (1534–1549) began the arduous task of renovation. The Roman Inquisition was established in 1542 and soon began its work, continuing under Julius III (1550–1555). But it was under Caraffa, Paul IV (1555–1559), that its acts may properly be described as pitiless, for this pontiff tracked down every heretic. Followers of Valdés fled, and Italian reformers found safety in Switzerland. As a consequence, their chief influence upon religious ideas of the Reformation was exerted outside of Italy.

RISE OF SOCINIANISM

It remains to consider the work of Lelio Sozzini (1525–1562) and his nephew Fausto Sozzini (1539–1604). Their followers, known as Socinians, constituted the most radical branch of Protestantism in the age of the Reformation. They denied the dogma of the Trinity, the very corner stone of Christian theology, and offered a divergent view of the Atonement. Lelio was born of a noble family in Siena and belonged to the humanist elite of that city. He studied law and was led to extend his studies to the Bible. He visited Venice where he became acquainted with Lutheran and Anabaptist thought, and he came also under the influence of mystics. Next he visited northern Europe where he made the acquaintance of Melanchthon and other Protestant divines. Deeply moved by the execution of Servetus, he began to investigate the dogma of the Trinity, and at Zurich took an active part in Swiss theological speculation. Calvin disapproved of Lelio's subtle thinking and believed that he was a secret heretic. In 1551 Lelio visited Poland where he exerted slight influence. Upon his death he left some manuscripts to his nephew. It is usually stated that Fausto owed his theology to him, but this appears to be an exaggeration.

Fausto Sozzini was suspected of Lutheran sentiments and fled from Italy to Switzerland. He settled in Basel where from 1574–1578 he studied theology and developed unique and radical interpretations. Meanwhile Poland seemed to offer a favorable soil for heretical ideas because of the feebleness of the central government and the hostility of the nobility toward the Catholic hierarchy. A number of refugee Italian Protestants had found a welcome there, chief among whom was Giorgio Biandrata (1515–1588). He had in his earlier days fallen under the influence of Anabaptists in Venice who adopted antitrinitarian views. Like other Italians, Biandrata fled to Switzerland. He had difficulties with Calvin and in 1558 went to Poland where he labored with Ochino and Giovanni Gentile, attacking the trinitarian teachings of Catholics, Lutherans, and Calvinists alike. Such was the progress of Unitarian teaching in Poland that in the Synod of Wengrow (1565) a Unitarian church was organized.

Biandrata went to Transylvania in 1563, becoming court physician to King John Sigismund. The Calvinist bishop, Francis David (d. 1579), adopted Unitarian doctrine, and in 1568 the Unitarian Church was officially constituted. Fausto Sozzini visited Transylvania in 1579 and at once proceeded to Poland where he remained active until his death. He wrote many tracts and exerted much influence, especially in introducing Anabaptist ideas about baptism into the Unitarian Churches. Socinianism, which was influential in developing liberalism in the next century, was characterized by a remarkable combination of supernaturalism, derived from the scholastic philosophy of Scotus, and Erasmian ethical conceptions, to which were added elements derived from other sources such as the Anabaptists.

PART V

The Peace of Augsburg: An Epoch in Protestantism

Chapter 10

LUTHERANISM AND BALANCE OF POWER: THE PEACE OF AUGSBURG, 1555

THE PERENNIAL STRUGGLE between Emperor Charles V (1519–1555) and Francis I of France (1515–1547) engrossed the attention of all Europe. Their four wars between 1522 and 1546 involved in one way or another the political interests of every nation on the continent. These interests are summed up in the Renaissance conception of the Balance of Power. Even the voyage of Vasco da Gama to India and the discovery of America attracted less attention. This great contest for the control of Europe profoundly influenced the course of the Reformation and the fortunes of Lutheranism.

RESOURCES OF CHARLES V AND FRANCIS I

Charles ruled over numerous lands. As king of Castile and Aragon he dominated Spain, a land of little shipping. This country possessed no cavalry, but it produced a splendid infantry which was to bring success to Spanish arms on many a field of battle. The crown of Sicily gave Charles control over the wheat supply of the Mediterranean world. That of Naples made him an Italian prince, although the fact that he owed homage to the pope placed him in a peculiar position. In the Low Countries Charles possessed a most important group of lands. Brabant was rich in trade and industry. Flanders was still the wealthiest of all the Netherlands, and Holland was the great agent of trade with northeastern Europe. The central position of these lands between England, France, and Germany gave him great political advantages. The county of Burgundy (Franche-Comté) provided a convenient corridor between the Low Countries and Savoy in northern Italy. Germany was a large state but too weak to aid him in his numerous problems. However, it provided large numbers of mercenaries useful for his wars in Italy. The imperial dignity gave him the illusion of great power. It made him overlord of the duchy of Milan, the key to Italy. Besides all these lands he claimed both North and South America, the islands of the Caribbean Sea, and the Philippines.

Francis' possessions, on the other hand, were very different from Charles' far-flung empire. France was a compact state. It was surrounded on all sides by Charles' territories, but this central position gave the French king unique advantages, for he could always fight from inner lines while his opponent would have to dissipate his energies in many quarters. Furthermore, France was economically self-sufficing and hence invulnerable. She possessed a splendid cavalry which gave French arms unique advantages on many battlefields. Because Francis' lands were much smaller than the emperor's, people erroneously supposed that the French king was in a weaker position. He had held Milan unlawfully since the Battle of Marignano (1515) and thus dominated northern Italy. He also controlled Genoa whose position gave him access to the peninsula and whose fleet might prove an important aid in a war with his rival.

Rarely has history told of a prince apparently so fortunate as was Charles at the moment when he succeeded to the government of his lands. In him converged the hopes, interests, and aspirations of three great lines of rulers. He was Hapsburg, Spaniard, and Netherlander (or Burgundian) all in one. From his grandparents, Ferdinand (d. 1516) and Isabella (d. 1504), he inherited Spain, Sicily, Naples, and the Americas. This Spanish descent gave him his peculiar attitude toward the Church and heresy and was responsible for his policy in Italy. From his grandmother Mary of Burgundy (d. 1482) and his father Philip the Fair (d. 1506) he received an important Netherlandish bias—all the Burgundian passion against France burned in him. From his grandfather, Emperor Maximilian, he received the lands of the Hapsburgs in the Danubian valley. And when the emperor died on January 12, 1519, the question of the imperial crown was raised. Francis also sought it, but, after much expenditure of treasure by him, his rival finally secured the election (June 18). Not bribery alone but a sense of German national interests placed the crown in Charles' hands.

FIRST TWO WARS BETWEEN CHARLES V AND FRANCIS I, 1521–1529

Francis was alarmed to see one prince, and that person none other than Charles of Spain and the Low Countries, ruling over most of the territories along the French border. It was a dangerous matter; both sides felt that war was inevitable. Charles hurriedly wound up his affairs in Spain, and in May, 1520, sailed for the Low Countries. He interviewed Henry VIII (1509–1547) at Sandwich and made sure of the attitude of Henry and his minister Wolsey in the event of war with France. In October he was crowned in Aix-la-Chapelle, and in January, 1521, met the representatives of Germany in the diet at Worms. Besides the war with Francis for which he wanted the support of his German subjects, he was called upon to settle certain questions about the government of the empire. It was decided that a Council of Regency (*Reichsregiment*) should direct foreign as well as certain internal affairs, subject to the royal will. The Imperial Court of Appeals (*Reichskammergericht*) was somewhat altered, and an army of 20,000 infantry and 4,000 cavalry was provided.

But religion proved a most thorny question. Pope Leo X had favored the candidacy of Francis when negotiations for the imperial election were in progress. He disliked seeing Spanish Charles rule in Naples and also in the empire, for as king of Lombardy Charles would be tempted to interfere in Italian affairs. Papal policy had always been opposed to the concentration in Italy of so much power in the hands of one man, yet it was the emperor's peculiar duty to stand by the vicar of Christ and stamp out heresy. The pope's political interests and religious functions thus clashed. To serve both he must needs play politics, and in doing this he descended to the tortuous intrigue and diplomatic chicanery practiced by princes of the Renaissance. Charles wanted to be sure of Leo's help, but he thought twice about condemning Luther unheard. Since he needed money and troops from Germany, he yielded to the demands of the Germans that Luther should be heard at Worms. Personally he hated the heretic and would gladly have seen him burned. Finally the Edict of Worms was issued, and Leo now realized that it was to his interest to join Charles against Francis.

Henry VIII of England joined Charles and the pope against France.

But war had hardly begun when Leo died. He was succeeded in January, 1522, by the emperor's former tutor who became Adrian VI (1522–1523). The new pope did not relish imperial domination in Italy, preferring that the powers of Christendom should unite in a crusade against the Turk. For a moment it seemed that a quarrel might develop. Indeed, the supporters of Francis began to collect forces against the imperialists. But at Bicocca in April, 1522, the emperor's forces defeated the French who yielded the Milanese except for the citadel in Milan. Soon also they lost Genoa. Adrian died on September 14, 1523, and was succeeded by Clement VII (1523–1534), a typical son of the Medici who wanted to balance Charles' influence against that of Francis and thus save the States of the Church. The French king invaded Italy but was defeated and taken prisoner at Pavia in February, 1525. Charles forced his royal prisoner to accept the Treaty of Madrid (January, 1526) which gave to the emperor the duchy of Burgundy and sovereignty over Artois and Flanders. Thus ended the First War (1521–1526).

Charles was not able to take up the question of heresy and Church reform after the Treaty of Madrid. This document had been extorted by force; hence Francis repudiated it as soon as he was safely back in France. Disliking imperial ascendancy in Italy and elsewhere, the pope and other powers formed the League of Cognac (May, 1526), Clement absolving Francis from his oath to uphold the treaty. The dreaded Turk, Suliman the Magnificent, appeared in the East. His attack on Hungary resulted in the Battle of Mohácz in August, 1526, in which King Louis II was slain and his monarchy destroyed. The French king now opened negotiations with the Turk in order to wrest diplomatic advantages from his traditional enemy.

The emperor thus was threatened with a Second War (1526–1529). His enemies moved slowly, however. Charles' German and Spanish troops marched upon Rome and seized the Eternal City after a brief siege. The Germans showed their scant respect for the Church by plundering its possessions but were outdone in cruelty and rapacity by the Spaniards. This sack of Rome on May 6, 1527, was a great shock to the people of that day. A French army arrived in Italy too late to help Clement, and it pushed on to Naples where it might have been successful had not Francis by his folly forced the Genoese to abandon him and place their fleet at Charles' disposal. The French cause was ruined, and Francis was compelled to leave Italy. By the Peace of Cambrai which followed on August 3, 1529, closing the Second War, Francis retained Burgundy but yielded all claims in Italy, Artois, and Flanders.

FATE OF EDICT OF WORMS

How did the Lutheran movement fare during these years? The vivid nationalist sentiments of the German and French enmity to the emperor combined to make the Lutheran movement a success. Obviously Charles was not able to suppress it so long as he needed troops and money from the very principalities which had embraced the new doctrines. The Council of Regency therefore could not enforce the Edict of Worms (1521). So compromised was Charles by these factors that he could not ally himself with the zealous German princes who had become more prominent during 1524, and who sought to suppress Lutheranism in their territories. The nuncio Campeggio met them at Ratisbon in June, 1524. At this assemblage the Catholic princes formed a league on August 7, which decided that reform of abuses in the Church was urgently needed. Lutheran books were to be seized, and students were forbidden to leave their states to study in Wittenberg. This congress of Catholic princes was significant, for it was the beginning of an AntiLutheran faction. Charles repeatedly denounced Luther and ordered the Edict of Worms to be enforced, and at the same time tried to frighten the pope into supporting him by urging a national German council. Meanwhile the Peasants' Revolt occurred in 1525 and 1526, and effectively kept Lutheranism from conquering central and southern Germany.

When news of the Treaty of Madrid arrived in Germany, Lutherans feared that Charles' efforts to put the Edict of Worms into effect might prove successful. Landgrave Philip of Hesse was able to organize a league of Lutheran princes which by June, 1526, embraced the elector of Saxony, the count of Mansfeld, a number of dukes, and others. Lutherans were in control at the Diet of Speier in June, 1526, owing to the absence of several Catholic princes, and they spoke their minds without restraint, pointing to the abuses in the hierarchy and demanding reform. They suggested among other things that the clergy should be allowed to marry, that the German tongue should be used in baptism and communion, and that private Masses be abolished. But Charles felt strong enough to reject these propositions. The diet, however, insisted on a national council, and that, until it could meet, each state should be free to act as it wished about the Edict of Worms.

The net result of the Diet of Speier in 1526 was that the princes who were inclined toward Lutheranism established it in their lands, while zealous Catholics endeavored to suppress it. This is an interesting fact in the history of political theory. Throughout the Middle Ages every community in Germany embraced the faith universal, the emperor holding that it was his task to establish it everywhere. The federal principle in the empire, however, did not for a long time militate against unity of religion. But with the appearance of Lutheranism a novel principle was injected into politics. Each prince adopted such action as he deemed right, and for this he was to be answerable to God. It was the beginning of the policy expressed in the famous formula, *cuius regio eius religio*. Formerly religion had been a self-sufficient matter elevated above all political concerns. Now it was to be subjected to the control of secular states.

Meanwhile relations between Lutheran and Catholic princes became more bitter. The former continued to secularize ecclesiastical lands and forcibly suppress the traditional worship within their borders, while the latter sought to uproot heretical worship as much as possible. Suspicions were rife. And when the duke of Saxony, the elector of Brandenburg, and Archduke Ferdinand of Austria, the emperor's brother, held a meeting at Breslau in 1527, some of the reforming princes believed that a coalition of Catholic princes was being formed to wage war on them. An official in the government of the duke of Saxony, one Otto von Pack, forged a letter (1528) purporting to set forth an agreement whereby the Catholic princes were to attack the elector of Saxony and the landgrave of Hesse. This fraud netted him the handsome sum of 4000 florins. Plans were made to attack the supposed plotters by invading their lands. The elector of Saxony and the landgrave went so far as to collect troops. It was not discovered that the letter was a forgery until these princes were seriously compromised. These acts increased the bitter feelings.

As long as his second war with Francis I (1526–1529) lasted, Charles was not in a position to enforce the Edict of Worms. The Treaty of Cambrai (1529) gave him for the first time since he assumed the crown of Germany the coveted opportunity to uproot heresy. The estates of Germany were convened at Speier in March, 1529, and he instructed his agents to secure a cancellation of the decisions made in the preceding diet at Speier. It was a serious moment for the reforming party. They were discredited by the rash conduct of the landgrave of Hesse and Otto von Pack toward the duke of Saxony. Furthermore, they were weakened by the rise of Anabaptism in many towns of Germany and by the progress of Zwinglian ideas in Switzerland and southern Germany. Catholic princes were determined not to retreat one inch and, outnumbering their foes, were confident of victory.

The Diet of Speier of 1529 therefore reflected Catholic interests. It advised that in all localities where the Edict of Worms was being enforced it should continue to be upheld, but no further innovations were to be permitted in Lutheran states until a council could meet and settle all questions. If such council could not be had, a national German council should take its place. It was specified that Catholics were to have full liberty to attend Mass everywhere and under all circumstances. This was important because Catholic agitation was to be unchecked in Lutheran lands, while Lutheran propaganda in Catholic lands would be sternly interdicted. Lutheran princes and fourteen south German towns presented a reply in which they stated that inasmuch as each person must give account to God in all matters regarding salvation they were determined to follow their conscience rather than the dictation of the emperor. They could not permit Mass to be said in their lands, nor would they acquiesce in the enforcement of the Edict of Worms even in lands ruled by Catholic princes.

The Catholic majority in the diet was not moved by this statement. The reforming princes thereupon presented their famous *Protestation* declaring that the present diet could not undo any measure of a previous diet without their consent. The protesters, or *Protestants* as they were henceforth called, included the elector of Saxony, the dukes of Lüneburg, the margrave of Brandenburg, the landgrave of Hesse, the prince of Anhalt, and fourteen cities of southern Germany. The Protestant cause was in great danger, and a secret agreement was made by Philip of Hesse, the elector of Saxony, and the towns of Ulm, Strasbourg, and Nuremberg to defend each other.

For the moment Charles seemed to triumph, but again the imperial wish was to be frustrated. The Turkish menace had become greater than ever. After the battle of Mohácz (1526) the Magyars had elevated John Zapolya to the Hungarian kingship. In earlier treaties it had been stipulated that Charles' brother, Archduke Ferdinand, should be king, but Magyar nationalist sentiment prevented this from being carried out. Ferdinand, however, did secure possession of the eastern parts of Hungary, Bohemia, Moravia, Silesia, and Lusatia electing him king in 1526 after the death of Louis II of Hungary. Ferdinand coveted the entire realm over which his brother-in-law Louis had ruled, and thus was extremely hostile to Zapolya, behind whom stood his Turkish overlord Suliman, who was eager to settle scores with the Hapsburgs. Both Zapolya and Suliman were in close diplomatic relations with Francis who wanted to multiply trouble for the Hapsburg house in the East. A Turkish host moved on Vienna and besieged it from September 26 to October 15, 1529. The garrison resisted with determination, and, when his troops began to suffer from the frosts of autumn, Suliman gave the order to retreat.

Protestant princes patriotically rallied to defend the empire in spite of the hostile action threatened by the decrees of the Diet of Speier. Luther himself had urged full support of military preparations against the Turk. An imperial army was collected at Linz, but Suliman withdrew. However, Charles and all Germany knew that the Turk would soon return and that preparations would have to be made against him, wherefore once more the emperor would have to postpone his plans to suppress heretics.

THE AUGSBURG CONFESSION, 1530

Charles V, having with apparent success concluded the war with Francis I, now seemed to be in a position to settle the question of religion in Germany and summoned the Lutheran party to a parley at the coming diet at Augsburg. The Elector John of Saxony summoned the theologians of the Wittenberg faculty to Torgau in March, 1530. They drew up a declaration, the *Torgau Articles*, which firmly set forth the new doctrines. In June the sessions of the diet began. The party held that Lutheranism had long ago been condemned and that it was the emperor's duty to proceed with its extermination. On the other hand, Protestant princes, with secularized Church property and Church government in their hands, were determined not to yield. However, feeling their weakness before their ruler who was now the political arbiter of Europe, they sought to appear conciliatory. One reason for their disunion was their inability to tolerate the peculiar conception of the Lord's Supper held by the Zwinglians, for Luther had sternly refused to extend a fraternal hand to any who denied the Real Presence. Melanchthon drew up the *Augsburg Confession* (1530) which set forth the essential doctrines of Lutheranism and aimed to refute the assertion of Catholic opponents that they were heretical. Differences between the two were minimized. Dogmatic points were presented without rancor, but abuses of the old Church were strongly emphasized. While thus seeking to court the favor of Catholics, the document magnified the points on which Lutherans differed from the followers of Zwingli and the Anabaptists.

Charles would have accepted the *Confession* in spite of its uncatholic character, but the orthodox princes, supported by the papal legate Campeggio and the theologians Eck and Faber, refused. These men prepared a refutation of the *Confession*. Of course agreement could not be reached. Charles announced that he was satisfied with the rebuttal and declared that he intended to enforce the decision of the diet as he was the divinely instituted custodian of the true faith. A deadlock ensued, and it appeared that nothing could be accomplished. Philip of Hesse hastened away. But Charles, fearing the Turks, begged the Lutherans to tarry. Even threats did not shake their determination. Charles finally issued a statement announcing that the *Confession* had been shown to be contrary to Catholic faith. Six months (until April 15, 1531) were given the princes in which to adjust themselves and their affairs. During this time there was to be no further propaganda in favor of Lutheranism, and the points on which no agreement had been reached were to be accepted as true until the meeting of a general council. The emperor, determined to proceed against the Lutherans, instructed the Imperial Court of Appeals to institute suits against all parties who had appropriated ecclesiastical property. Lutheranism was to be stamped out by force after April 15, 1531.

Lutheran princes and delegates from the towns met in Thuringian Schmalkalden at the close of 1530, and the League of Schmalkalden was the Protestant answer to the emperor's policy. They promised to aid one another if attacked for religious reasons. Ever since the Peasants' War, Luther had taught the sanctity of secular princes and the duty of obedience. But the princes now argued that the emperor was elected and not absolute, and ruled with their coöperation, wherefore he had no right to impose his will upon them if they objected. Luther finally allowed himself to be won over by this reasoning and the league was formed (March 29, 1531) to last 6 years. It arranged to hire troops and appointed jurists to defend accused members before the Imperial Court of Appeals. Many cities of northern Germany joined the league, and by the close of the year a constitution was adopted and an army of about 12,000 was enrolled. A Protestant league now confronted the Catholic majority.

THE RELIGIOUS PEACE OF AUGSBURG, 1555

But, as in former crises ever since the Diet of Worms in 1521, Charles was in no position to enforce the Edict of Worms. The continued enmity of France alone was almost sufficient to deter him. Against Francis I Charles fought his Third War (1536–1538), concluded by the Treaty of Nice; and his Fourth War (1542–1544), closed by the Treaty of Crespy. Meanwhile the Turk was moving up the Danube against Vienna and Austria. So confronted by the Schmalkalden League, Charles arranged the Truce of Nuremberg (July, 1532). No hostilities were to be undertaken against the Lutheran princes before the meeting of the council for which Pope Clement VII was making plans. Cases in the Imperial Court of

Appeals also were to rest until then. Once more political circumstances forced Charles from the path of duty as he conceived it.

After the Peace of Crespy there was a lull in international strife. Francis died in 1547. Charles now turned his attention to the question of Lutheranism. He met his subjects in the Diet of Ratisbon and flatly refused to renew the Peace of Nuremberg which had suspended the imperial decrees made in 1530. He declared the princes of the Schmalkalden League outside the pale of the law and prepared to move against them. The league was in no condition to resist the emperor. Elector John Frederick of Saxony was a mediocrity, and Philip of Hesse revealed little leadership.

Meanwhile Charles had found an ally in the fold of Protestantism. Duke Maurice of Saxony (1541–1553) was eager to snatch the electoral crown of Saxony from his distant kinsman. Maurice was an ambitious and unscrupulous man and, although a determined Protestant, did not hesitate to make capital out of the misfortunes of his coreligionists. To win his support Charles granted him the electoral title as well as the administration of the sees of Magdeburg and Halberstadt which Maurice was ambitious to annex. When Charles moved with his army against the Schmalkalden League, Maurice suddenly invaded electoral Saxony while John Frederick was vainly seeking to check the emperor's victorious advance. But Maurice was defeated by the elector and his army scattered. Wittenberg fell on May 19. The emperor visited the tomb of Luther who had died the year before. With him were his councilors Granvelle and Alva who later were to win notoriety in the Low Countries. They besought him to tear open the tomb and drag forth the bones of the archheretic, but Charles refused. "He has met his Judge," he declared. "I wage war upon the living, not upon the dead."

Philip of Hesse also surrendered. With the two most prominent leaders of the Schmalkalden League in his power, Charles met the Diet at Augsburg in September, 1547. The avowed purpose of this meeting was to settle definitely the matter of religion in the empire. A document known as the *Augsburg Interim* was drawn up (June, 1548). Many Lutheran princes were absent, and those present were so discomfited that they accepted it. It was a curious instrument. The fundamental tenets of the Catholic faith were kept, but the language employed was vague, calculated to accommodate opposite views. Justification by faith apparently was granted, the pope was referred to as chief bishop, but communion under both kinds and clerical marriage were to be settled in a future council. It is evident that this was no settlement; Lutherans and Catholics were too far apart to be brought together by so flimsy a formula.

Charles' success gave him little strength. Germans resented being treated as Spaniards, and princes feared for their independence—it was the eternal question of the relations between the emperor and his nobles. Maurice of Saxony, now decked with the electoral title, disliked Charles and decided to abandon him, for, having won his reward, he hoped to obtain freedom from imperial control. Furthermore, Henry II of France was uneasy because he feared Charles' increased power. Maurice, now leader of the Protestants, approached Henry. This was the first great act in that long suicidal drama in which German princes joined with the French king in order to devise some solution of their petty problems at the expense of their fatherland. The result was the Treaty of Friedwald (February, 1552) which stipulated that Henry should pay them a goodly sum in support of their struggle with Charles. In return he was to occupy as "vicar of the empire" the lands belonging to the sees of Toul, Metz, and Verdun. War began when Henry renewed his dynastic claims upon Milan, Naples, and Flanders, which his father had renounced in the Peace of Crespy.

Meanwhile Elector Maurice moved against Charles who had stationed himself at Innsbruck, and the emperor was forced to flee over the mountains into Carinthia. An agreement was made between the Lutherans and Charles' brother Ferdinand, by which the question of religion was to be settled in the imperial diet. This reveals how low the emperor's fortune had sunk, for Charles always wished to solve the country's religious ills in a council which he could control and not in a parliamentary assembly which would give expression to the secular ambitions of German princes. He opposed this procedure but was forced to yield. This settlement is known as the Peace of Passau (August 2, 1552).

Charles returned to Germany. Sorely chagrined because the three sees were occupied by Henry II, he doggedly resolved to give an exhibition of imperial power by driving the French out of Metz. Eighty thousand Germans marched to besiege it, but the French defended it so skillfully that Charles failed. The cold of winter set in, and with it came the horrors of camp life characteristic of an age in which sanitary science had not yet come into existence. On December 26 the emperor raised the siege, leaving behind him the maimed and the dying, men half frozen and incurably sick. The siege of Metz has become famous because of Paré's noteworthy surgical work with the wrecks of humanity he found in the emperor's deserted camp.

The imperial diet after many delays finally met at Augsburg in February, 1555. The outcome was the Religious Peace of Augsburg, promulgated on September 26, which was really a treaty between Catholic and

Lutheran princes of Germany. Its most significant provisions were in substance as follows: (1) Lutherans were not to war upon Catholics, or vice versa. It was left to each prince to determine the faith of his subjects. (2) Adherents of doctrines other than Catholic and Lutheran were not to be tolerated. This applied especially to Anabaptists and Calvinists. (3) Ecclesiastical property secularized before the Peace of Passau (August 2, 1552) was to remain secularized, but no further secularization was to take place. If in the future any ecclesiastical prince should become a Protestant, he would be required to relinquish his titles, which were to remain the property of the Catholic Church. In this way new and orthodox officials could be elected so that the old religious life would continue in its wonted course.

This meeting of the Diet in Augsburg was destined to become one of the most significant parliamentary assemblages in history, for it wrote into the public law of Germany a novel conception of the relationship of religion and politics. The time-hallowed parallelism of the Middle Ages in which the Church of divine foundation taught the true faith for the state to establish was abandoned. Religion henceforth was held to be the peculiar concern of princes; they were divinely ordained powers who were to dispose of ecclesiastical as well as secular matters. This is the famous principle of *cuius regio eius religio*. It was a revolution of the first magnitude.

The new settlement was significant also for its bearing on the political power of princes. Luther's teaching on the sanctity of the ruler's authority marked the plenitude of princely absolutism and provided the theoretical basis for monarchy by divine right. In this respect Luther was surely one of the founders of the modern state, but not of political or religious liberty, for these ideas imply that people should be unmolested in the exercise of religion. This was impossible under the provisions of the Peace of Augsburg. Rather it should be said that the peace, in subjecting religion to state control, created the idea of state-established religion which was to remain practically unquestioned until the outbreak of the French Revolution.

PART VI

The Calvinist Revolt

Chapter 11

CHURCH AND DISSENT IN FRANCE: THE REIGN OF FRANCIS I

*T*O UNDERSTAND the course of reform in France it is necessary to know the social conditions of that country. The crown played a significant role. The king had inherited traditions of the sanctity of royal power developed ever since the days of Pippin (d. 768). In the Middle Ages the Church coöperated in raising the prestige of rulers by anointing each successor to the kingly dignity. The teachings of Roman law and the theory of feudal law which held that in the last analysis the king was head of the realm also aided in extending the ruler's authority over all political functions of the state. When the Hundred Years' War came to a close in 1453, an era of unusual prosperity began which enabled French kings to concentrate still more power in their hands. Thus the French crown was becoming absolute at the time of the Reformation. Humanists rose among the class which had grown wealthy from the new economic activity. They enthusiastically told how the rulers of France were descended from Homeric characters, just as Vergil once traced for the Romans their descent from Aeneas who had fled burning Troy.

CONTROL OF THE CLERGY BY THE FRENCH CROWN

Since 1438 relations between the Church in France and the Holy See had been regulated by the Pragmatic Sanction of Bourges. This document, which grew out of an attempt to free the French Church from control by Rome, set forth some of the decrees of the Council of Basel. The Church was spared the pressure of papal tax collectors but tended to fall under royal control, for more and more the king was able to secure the appointment of officials who would coöperate with his plans. Finally the Concordat of Bologna (1516), arranged between Pope Leo X and Francis I (1515–1547), relinquished control into the hands of the king. Popes were to receive annates; but the crown was to name candidates to archiepiscopal, episcopal, and abbatial vacancies, subject to papal confirmation which, as the future was to show, was granted as a matter of course. Thus the French hierarchy was composed of royal appointees and became a solid support of the crown and its policies. The king could now control the resources of the Church to favor his friends, an arrangement which had an important bearing upon the Reformation; it was not necessary for the crown to inaugurate a policy of secularization, for it already could dispose of Church property by way of patronage. In short, political and economic interests, aside from purely religious reasons, dictated that the crown should remain Catholic.

Next to the crown stood the concordatary or upper clergy. The king controlled appointments to 10 archbishoprics, 82 bishoprics, 527 abbacies, and a large number of priories and canonries. Thus the higher clergy of France, appointed by the crown from motives of political expediency, were certain to carry out the king's wishes as well as the behests of the Church. Many of the clergy had been useful to the crown in some political or diplomatic capacity, but all were certain to be loyal servants of state as well as Church. Many of them were humanists who might believe in reforming the hierarchy and Church life by first renovating the upper clergy, after which the entire lower priesthood was to be improved, but they could hardly be induced to toy with heresy.

The lower clergy, on the other hand, were little dominated by considerations of policy. Recruited from the lower classes of the population, they took from them their social views. Some of this class had studied at the universities, and many of them were poor. When agitation about religion became acute after 1520, members of this group were loud in their criticism of corruption and worldliness in the Church and fomented discontent.

Next to be considered is the nobility. Toward the close of the Middle Ages its position in French society declined relatively to that of the bourgeoisie, for it was steadily being sapped by the inexorable growth of commerce and industry. Yet it remained most important by reason of tradition, landed property, and vested interest. Unlike the English custom, all children of the French nobility were nobles, but the principle of

FRANCE
IN THE RENAISSANCE
AND THE REFORMATION

primogeniture which gave paternal property to elder sons impoverished
the younger ones. These accordingly became a restless element and were
prone to disturb the public peace. Furthermore, the nobility still cherished
memories of their quondam greatness which they had lost to the crown.
Could they recover their vanished fortunes? The turmoil occasioned by
religious differences in the second half of the sixteenth century would give
them a chance. Many a noble became Protestant, some from conviction
and some from policy because of their hostility to the Catholic crown.

The fourth group was the upper or aristocratic bourgeoisie, composed
of people who had grown rich from trade or industry and had become
definitely capitalist. A good example was Jacques Coeur of Bourges who
at the time of Charles VII (1422–1461) won fame because of his wealth.
Economically secure and socially stable, this class was satisfied with the

old faith and was opposed to any violent change. Their sons might enter the royal service, receive important livings in the Church, or enter the profession of law—they might even receive patents of nobility. Many became humanists since they possessed the leisure necessary to study Greek and Latin classics. They often evinced a desire for reform in the Church; but such reform was usually to be initiated by the upper clergy who would extend it to their inferiors without disturbing established organs or doctrines. This upper bourgeoisie controlled the towns and excluded its lesser brethren from power and economic prosperity. This latter class of hard-working handicraftsmen, shopkeepers, and manufacturers often took to reading the Bible, for religion lifted them out of the deadly monotony of life and its straitened circumstances.

The fifth and last group to be discussed is the population of town and country. The peasantry who owned their lands in fee simple or worked them on terms were well satisfied and opposed any change in religion which might bring social upheaval in its wake. Scandalized by the patent immorality of some of the clergy and the mercenary character of their activities, day laborers who at best could earn but a precarious livelihood often were led to criticize the wealth and pomp of the established cult, and their brethren in the towns were likewise often inclined toward heretical ideas, for growth of wealth among the upper bourgeoisie usually entailed the progressive impoverishment of this group. Small wonder that the lower bourgeoisie were not satisfied! This hard-working, practical, and virtuous people became the backbone of the Huguenot movement.

FRENCH HUMANISTS SEEK TO REFORM RELIGIOUS LIFE: THE GROUP AT MEAUX

In France as in other lands humanists evinced a keen desire to reform the Church, most important of them being Jacques Lefèbre of Étaples, or Faber Stapulensis as the name was rendered into Latin according to humanist fashion. Born about 1455, he studied in the University of Paris and became Master of Arts. He traveled in Italy, studied under Argyropoulos (1416–1486) and thus drank at the fountainhead of humanist culture. Returning to France, he became a professor of mathematics in the University of Paris and published many books. He studied Scripture in its original tongues and learned to prefer the Greek text to the Vulgate. He became the inspiring genius of a coterie of choice spirits such as Vatable the Hebraist, Postel the orientalist, Budé the great master of classical letters, Guillaume Farel, and Guillaume Briçonnet. The latter became abbot of St. Germain-des-Prés in 1507 and brought his master Stapulensis thither in order that he might be free to study in its cloistered quiet.

While in this abbey, Stapulensis published his edition of the Psalter (1509) in which the text was presented in several languages. Three years later he issued his edition of the Pauline Epistles with commentary in which the text of the Vulgate was improved by study of the Greek original. However, it is a mistake to regard him as a herald of Protestantism. He indeed believed in the supremely important role of Scripture in the life of Christians and emphasized justification by faith which to him was more important than good works. A mystical love of Christ was the chief note in his life, and he believed that this love should guide Christians to do good and become righteous. He taught that man should learn to know God through love and raise himself up to Him through humility, finding all his satisfactions in His divine personality alone. Although he attached little value to confession, pilgrimages, indulgences, relics, and other practices in the Church, he never even drew near the Lutheran position. He insisted on freedom of the will and the efficacy of good works and thought that great moral lights of pagan times, such as Socrates and Plato, would be saved. He desired purification of religious practices and a moderate reform in the Church, and he was also opposed to the traditional scholasticism which dominated theological and other studies.

When Briçonnet became bishop of Meaux in 1516, he embarked upon a remarkable policy of reform. It is important to note that this movement was independent of Luther. Briçonnet, who desired an ordered reform, collected a group of choice spirits—among them Stapulensis, Farel, Roussel, and others—who soon won fame because of the innovations which they introduced into the religious life of the diocese. Stapulensis translated the New Testament into French (1523) for the instruction of the people and became vicar-general in spiritual matters. Bible reading became a habit among the people of Meaux, and the humanist manner of criticizing the religious life of the day soon produced results. The bishop insisted that priests should not absent themselves from their parishes. Eager orators were appointed to preach Biblical sermons which were to lead the people to a better life. More effective episcopal supervision was to reform the parish clergy. The Franciscans, dominated by traditionalism, were excluded from the pulpits. "Bishops," said Briçonnet, "are angels sent by Christ to bring his message to the people, to carry out the tasks of angels in purging, enlightening, and making perfect the souls of men."

Briçonnet was supported in his work of reform by King Francis I. Although he did not possess profound religious convictions and did not lead an exemplary life, this monarch was nevertheless keenly interested in reform. His sister Marguerite of Angoulême was still more zealous, for she had imbibed some of the Neoplatonic mysticism current in Italy and was influenced by the Christian tinge which Stapulensis imparted to it. An apt pupil of Briçonnet, by whom she had been much impressed when he was abbot, Marguerite was led to appreciate the supreme importance of Scripture in religious life, and she became critical of the many crudities of this life. Her *Heptameron* complained that the friars usually were ignorant of the Bible, and she expressed preference for Biblical religion in her *The Mirror of a Sinful Soul,* a striking example of the mystical yet evangelical faith of contemporary humanists.

THE SUPPRESSION OF RELIGIOUS CRITICISM

Meanwhile Lutheran teaching began to interest Frenchmen, for the great reformer's pamphlets against the papacy poured into France from Strasbourg, Switzerland, and the Low Countries. Many people read them, and bookstores enjoyed a thriving business. Some of the more violent tracts were translated into French. Small wonder that the theological faculty of the Sorbonne were frightened! In April, 1521, they condemned over one hundred propositions drawn from Luther's books, especially from his revolutionary *Babylonian Captivity*. This learned and ancient body considered themselves the protectors of Catholicism and resolved to resist the spread of heretical doctrines. They appealed to the Parlement of Paris, the greatest judicial body of the realm, which in August ordered that Lutheran books should be surrendered under penalty of heavy fine or imprisonment. This command proved ineffective, and forbidden books became more common than ever. They were sold in provincial towns and by colporteurs who were active in Normandy.

The reformers of Meaux could not escape criticism and hostility. Fearful that the Church would be destroyed, theologians of the Sorbonne, headed by Noel Bédier (d. 1536), proceeded against them in spite of the royal support which Briçonnet enjoyed. Bédier belonged to the old school, cared naught for the free investigation of the classics, and feared the harmful consequences which study of Scripture and the Church fathers might have. He thought that the liberal arts should serve only as preparation for scholastic theology and that textual and historical study was useless. He believed that there was ample reason for so thinking. When in 1517 Stapulensis published a dissertation showing that Mary the sister of Lazarus, Mary Magdalene, and the woman described in Luke, VII:37–38, were not, as was currently believed, one and the same, but three distinct persons, the theologians of the Sorbonne were wroth, for they thought that this criticism touched the offices of the Church. Such freedom they deemed dangerous and they went so far as to declare that any such teaching was heretical.

Nor did they like Stapulensis' translation of the New Testament. This work at once found its way into the hands of the people who evinced interest in its teachings. The theologians thought that as Lutheran influences were active it was dangerous to add to the public uneasiness, and they ordered that copies of the Bible be seized and burned. At the suggestion of Marguerite, Francis I took Stapulensis under his special protection. But trouble began after news came that the king had been defeated and taken prisoner at the Battle of Pavia in February, 1525.

The example of the wool-carder Jean Leclerc was fresh in the minds of officials and theologians. This man, objecting to an indulgence offered and to the fasting and prayers which it commanded, had torn down from the Church doors in Meaux Clement VII's bull regarding the coming jubilee. In its place he posted a placard which declared the pope to be Antichrist. He was caught, branded with the fervent iron, and banished from the realm. But he tarried at Metz, made no secret of his religious ideas, and was so rash as to cast down images in a place to which a pilgrimage was to be made the next day. He was seized and burned at Metz in July, 1525, after submitting to the frightful mutilation so commonly practiced upon heretics in that day.

The Parlement of Paris now proceeded against the group at Meaux, and Briçonnet was summoned to appear before it. He had issued a synodal decree in October, 1523, against the reading and possession of Lutheran tracts, and now he yielded to authority and allowed Parlement to proceed in stamping out heresy (1525). Thus ended the activities of the group of Meaux. Stapulensis fled to Strasbourg, accompanied by Roussel. A number of victims were executed, chief of these being the wool-carder Jacques Pauvin of Meaux who perished at the stake on the *Place de Grève* in Paris (1526).

Francis I returned from prison in Madrid in the middle of March and at once gave orders to suspend persecution. Stapulensis was recalled from Strasbourg and became the king's librarian at Blois. The aged Stapulensis soon retired to Marguerite's court at Nérac where she had lived since 1527, when she became the wife of the king of Navarre. He soon died in 1535. In spite of the burning of a few heretics the reformers hoped that the king would tolerate their activities. They were soon disillusioned, however, by the unfortunate desecration in 1528 of an image of the Virgin Mary at a street corner in Paris. This act of sacrilege caused much excitement. Francis, it is said, was so irate that he wept, and the population of the city burst forth in unwonted energy. Expiatory processions were held, all of them to the spot where the desecration had occurred, the king himself taking part in them. Finally, the mutilated statue began to work miracles and was said to have raised two children from the dead.

Francis now permitted persecution of heretics to proceed without restraint. Louis de Berquin was seized because of his heretical record which made him an object of suspicion. He admired the teachings of Luther and Erasmus, but he neglected to follow their admonitions to act in such a manner that he would not be caught by the executioner. Francis had twice interfered in his behalf, but he now yielded to the importunate prayers of the excited clergy and people not to let this heretic escape a third time. Even Marguerite could not prevent his death which was inflicted on the *Place de Grève* in Paris (April 17, 1529).

Thus came to an end the efforts of the group at Meaux to lead reform in Church and religious life. Thus far humanists had also been reformers, but the fires of persecution soon caused them to cease these activities. Reformers interested themselves more and more in dogma. Heresy continued to grow among the proletariat and middle classes in the towns, and handicraftsmen at Beauvais, Cambrai, Rouen, La Rochelle, Nîmes, and numerous other places were infected. Many of the heretics appear to have belonged to the crafts which manufactured cloths. "When religious persecutions threaten, the working classes emigrate. Nothing binds them to the land. A few tools and his two arms constitute all the capital of the workman; he carries them into countries where he can worship God in his own way and in his own speech. The ruin of French industries in the second half of the century is, for the most part, to be thus explained."

Heresy did not spread among the wealthier peasantry, for great changes in economic life profoundly affected the folk of the countryside. Increase in the quantity of hard cash was steadily sapping manorial institutions and the chivalric life founded upon it. Wealthy peasants were able to buy land and thus rise in the social scale. In this respect the rural situation was very different from that of southern and central Germany—no Peasants' War was possible in France. Nor did the well-to-do peasantry manifest much desire to embrace novel doctrines. This class remained tenaciously loyal to the traditional faith, for they were satisfied with the ministrations of the priests in their parish churches. These priests had cast their lot with them, knew them well, understood their problems. It is evident that humanism, sacramentarianism, and Lutheranism could find little support among this group.

It was different with rural laborers who possessed nothing but their hands with which to gain a livelihood. Like their unfortunate brethren in Germany, many of them became heretical, for these itinerant workers had little to lose. Heresy can be traced among them in most parts of France after 1525. In Normandy one community received the name of "little Germany." These humble laborers obstinately clung to the country in which they had been born while their urban brethren emigated to strange lands. "If Protestantism did not completely succeed in taking root in France, the reason may be that in the sixteenth century, owing to the social state of the time, it won more adherents among the workmen, a travelling and migratory class, than among the peasantry, which was the stable and permanent element of the nation."[1]

FRANCIS I, CHARLES V, AND SUPPRESSION OF RELIGIOUS DISSENT

That Francis' policy toward religion should be influenced by his relations with Charles V causes no surprise. Although he was a humanist and desired some reform both in church and education, his first war with his imperial adversary from 1521–1525 engaged all his attention and finally ended in his captivity. For a while his mother, Louise of Savoy, supported the zeal of the Sorbonne and the Parlement of Paris against the group at Meaux. She wished to court the favor of the pope because she hoped to enlist his help against the emperor.

On his return Francis plunged into his second war with Charles which lasted from 1526–1529, and political expediency now dominated royal policy. The mutilation of the statue of the Virgin in Paris in 1528 opened a brief period of persecution and repression. But after the Peace of Cambrai (1529) it soon became apparent that war with Charles would begin again. Francis turned to the Turkish sultan Suliman, and also opened negotiations with the Protestants of Germany who had formed the Schmalkalden League after the emperor sought to exterminate Lutheranism (1531).

Francis first assured himself of the pope's support. An agreement was formed at Marseilles by the king and Clement VII whereby they would support each other in Italy; Francis' second son Charles was to marry Catherine de' Medici, the pope's niece, and Francis was to crush heresy. In spite of this last clause the king with characteristic Machiavellian policy

[1] H. Hauser, "The French Reformation and the French People in the Sixteenth Century," in *The American Historical Review*, IV (1899), 223, 227.

approached the Schmalkalden League, and in February, 1534, formed a treaty with Landgrave Philip of Hesse. He furnished a large sum of money to help Duke Ulrich of Württemberg regain his lands which were held by King Ferdinand of Germany, brother of Emperor Charles. This was successfully accomplished and a severe blow was inflicted upon Hapsburg power in Germany. For a moment it was thought that a common agreement about reform could be reached, and Francis sent Bishop du Bellay of Paris to discuss the matter with Melanchthon who as usual was pliant and willing to sacrifice several points. But the hope of reformation by means of a council, as was suggested, was doomed to failure. The placards of October 18, 1534, brusquely put an end to these schemes.

The placards in question were written by some reformers in Paris but printed in Switzerland, a man named Feret undertaking the dangerous task of bringing the placards back. They were entitled *True Articles about the Horrible Abuse of the Papal Mass* and were found early one morning posted about Paris upon the walls of buildings. A copy was affixed to the door of the royal bedchamber in Amboise couched in the most violent imaginable. There was much confusion among the people, and the king was incensed. What was to be done? Clement VII, who had just died, was succeeded by Paul III (1534–1549), and it was necessary to win the new pope's favor. Again there were expiatory processions. Arrests were made, and victims were soon led to the stake. Gibbets testified to the zeal of the king's officials. Large numbers of "Lutherans" now hurried out of the realm; Clément Marot, poet and humanist, found refuge at the court of Duchess Renata in Ferrara.

But the royal decree of January 29, 1535, ordering complete extirpation of heretics could not be carried out, for Francis found that it alienated the Germans whose sympathy he would surely need in his struggles with Charles. Accordingly on July 16 was issued the Edict of Coucy which freed prisoners held for heresy and permitted fugitives to return provided they would forswear their heretical ideas within 6 months. Only relapsed heretics and sacramentarians were excluded from its provisions. In the future no one might publish or teach any doctrine contrary to the traditional cult.

Finally on May 31, 1536, the Edict of Lyons extended amnesty even to sacramentarians, but this policy could not last. From 1536–1538 Francis was engaged in his third war with Charles. When the Truce of Nice left him isolated, with only the Turkish sultan as ally, he resolved to take up once more the task of upholding the old cult. His meetings with the pope at Aigues-Mortes and Nice changed the character of his reign, for repression now became the royal watchword. In December, 1538, the Edict of Coucy was revoked. The Edict of Fontainebleau of June 1, 1540, provided a complete law to care for all heretics, and the king appointed Matthew Ory, a friar, as inquisitor for the realm.

This reaction bore heavily upon the harmless Waldensians who were living in a number of villages in the valley of the Durance. These people had long lived in great simplicity, and their orthodox neighbors had nothing but good words for their purity of life and uprightness in their dealings with all men. The only criticism made was that they persisted in their peculiar Waldensian ideas about the Mass, impropriety of images, use of the cross and pictures, and other pious Catholic practices. While they could scarcely be regarded as obnoxious heretics, public excitement was such that the authorities could not overlook them. The Parlement of Aix condemned nineteen Waldensians to be burned alive and the village of Mérindol to be destroyed. This decree was not enforced because Francis' approval could not be obtained, and Bishop du Bellay of Paris succeeded in getting the order revoked.

Francis met with nothing but reverses in his fourth war with Charles (1542–1544), and the Treaty of Crespy forced him to listen to the behests of politics. He lost interest in the innocence of the unfortunate Waldensians and listened to the misrepresentations sedulously propagated about them. When Cardinal Tournon told the king that the Waldensians were in revolt and opposing his sovereign government, he revoked his refusal to deal harshly with them. The cardinal had no pity in his breast; he hurried away, and, after fixing a seal upon the document himself and fabricating a military order, launched the soldiery upon the innocent villages. One reason for this dastardly act was the ambition of the Baron d'Oppède to possess the fertile lands which the Waldensians during six generations of toil had transformed into a blooming garden. The result was that Mérindol, Cabrières d'Aigues, and twenty-two other villages were denuded of their population with revolting barbarism (1545). The official conscience knew that it was one of the worst crimes in all history, and Francis commanded his heir, Henry II, to bring the guilty ones to justice, but all except one were exculpated.

There remains to be noted the execution of Étienne Dolet and the fourteen of Meaux. Dolet, a man of pure life and of a singular spirituality, was found guilty of the crime of printing books written by Stapulensis, Erasmus, and Clément Marot and was burned to death in the Place Maubert in Paris on April 3, 1546. Meanwhile at Meaux conventicles were increasing, and on one occasion Pierre Leclerc, whose brother had suffered at the stake in 1526, was seized while ministering to a group of about sixty persons. Fourteen of them were condemned to die at the stake on the market place of Meaux (1546). Thus closed the reign of Francis I in a holocaust of simple people, sacrificed to intolerance and momentary political advantage.

Chapter 12

BEGINNINGS OF CALVINISM: RELIGIOUS MOVEMENTS IN FRENCH SWITZERLAND

PROTESTANTS IN France were passing through a most trying time after Louis de Berquin was burned in 1528, for they had no adequate leader, one who by superiority of intellect and strength of character could assume command and direct people sorely troubled about religion. Guillaume Farel, a man of fiery temper who counted not the cost of teaching the Gospel, attracted most attention, but he did not possess the intellect requisite to guide the theological questionings of Protestants. He was a most ardent propagandist of the new ideas, but could not play the part of a conserving leader. This need was filled by Calvin.

JOHN CALVIN: ORIGINS AND EDUCATION

John Calvin was born in 1509 in Noyon, a town in Picardy in northeastern France. His father, Gérard Calvin, was a notary and was so successful that he became a respected and solid citizen of Noyon. This is an important fact in the early education of John Calvin, for the boy thus had an opportunity to become acquainted with the world and the ways of man. Luther's father was a peasant and can be said to have become a burgher only when Martin was getting ready for his university studies. Thus while Luther's attitude toward life ever remained that of a peasant, Calvin's tastes, manner, and conceptions were always bourgeois.

Calvin's father was able, through his influence with the bishop of Noyon, to secure for the youth a petty benefice (without cure of souls) in the Church of Noyon while he was attending the best school in the town. Finally, when he had finished his preparatory studies, John was sent to Paris in his fourteenth year to study in the university. He became a member of the Collège de la Marche where he came under the tuition of the remarkable master of humanist methods of instruction, Mathurin Cordier, from whom he received the best ideals of the new learning. Humanism, tinged with Erasmian conceptions, became a most important formative influence in his life. Soon, however, he was transferred to the Collège de Montagu. Here Noel Bédier was the chief influence, and instruction was of the narrow scholastic type, hoary with age, inferior to that of the humanists, which the choicer spirits of the new age were assaulting with relentless sarcasm.

Nevertheless, the youth made much progress. He gained facility in Latin and soon passed on to more advanced subjects such as philosophy which really marked his entrance into university studies. He formed the acquaintance of the humanist Guillaume Cop who boasted of a friendship with Reuchlin and Erasmus. When his study of the liberal arts was nearly finished, Calvin's father insisted that he should study law as a preparation for a practical career. Like Luther, he was to travel along the road by which many a youth in the Middle Ages arrived at important posts in secular and ecclesiastical life.

Accordingly, Calvin went to Orléans, for law was not studied in the Parisian schools. He began his lessons under Pierre de l'Estoile, an old-fashioned pedagogue thoroughly wedded to the time-honored methods of instruction in law. Calvin also continued his humanist interests at Orléans. He formed the acquaintance of Melchior Wolmar, a great master of Greek from Germany, from whom he acquired some knowledge of Greek letters. Thus he was enabled to carry to completion his studies, the foundations of which he had laid when under Cordier.

In 1529 Calvin went to the University of Bourges in order to profit from the novel humanist methods of instruction in law introduced by Alciato of Milan. This master was wont to inquire into the historical setting of law and to employ his knowledge of literature in elucidating it. Wolmar also moved to Bourges and Calvin resumed his connection with him. Meanwhile his father died while in difficulties with the Church in Noyon. He had been excommunicated, probably because of his heretical tendencies, and he had also fallen into financial difficulties with the cathedral chapter. It is thought that this episode influenced Calvin's attitude toward the Church. At about this time he returned to Orléans and received a degree in law.

In 1532 Calvin was back in Paris, free to do as he wished. He listened to lectures by the royal lecturers appointed by Francis I, humanists who were hated by the doctors of the Sorbonne and opposed by them. Calvin profited much from the remarks of Vatable, the famous Hebrew scholar, Budé, the great light in classical literature, and Danes, a remarkable master of Greek. He now finished his commentary on Seneca's De Clementia, in which the youthful author sought to find basic connections between the philosophy of stoicism as set forth by Seneca and the teachings of Christ in the Gospel. This work, which was published in April, 1532, reveals Calvin as a humanist, the influence of Erasmus being evident throughout. It is not surprising that this great humanist's ethical conceptions should be adopted by Calvin.

CALVIN'S CONVERSION AND THEOLOGICAL THOUGHT

The conversion of Calvin is a difficult theme. It occurred apparently between the publication of the commentary and the close of 1533. He had begun with a humanist's interest in a simple moral religion. Perhaps his father's death shocked him. Perhaps he was influenced by his friend and relation, Pierre Olivetan, who already was tainted by heresy when Calvin was with him in Orléans. Many people were questioning the validity of practices in the Church and some of the teachings of the old faith, and an inquiring mind such as Calvin's naturally came in contact with them. Indeed, these questions could hardly escape him, for the doctors of the Sorbonne were waging bitter war on the new humanist methods which, they thought, led to heresy. They even went so far as to seek to suppress Queen Marguerite's *Mirror of a Sinful Soul*. These influences may well have impressed Calvin, although his conversion is described as having come suddenly.

These were important years for Calvin. A mind as sensitive and intelligent as his would inevitably be moved by the pressing problems of religion. His first overtly heretical tendency is revealed when he collaborated with Nicholas Cop, rector of the university, in the preparation of the latter's address which was given on November 1, 1533. Much of it clearly was borrowed from Erasmus, and it opened with a discussion of that humanist's philosophy of Christ. But it also seems to have drawn something from Luther. Thus the speaker dwelt upon the Gospel as opposed to the law and in consequence declared in favor of salvation through faith in the grace of God and not through the performance of good deeds. It is evident that Calvin at this moment was essentially an Erasmian tinged with Luther's ideas. He still had a long way to go before arriving at the doctrines which he was to express in 1536.

The effect of this discourse upon the conservative professors can well be imagined. The Parlement of Paris, with Francis I on its side, proceeded against Cop, who fled. A number of arrests were made. Calvin went into hiding at Chaillot near Paris, and later in Saintonge, a little town not far from Angoulême. Next he went to Nérac to see the aging Stapulensis whose advice to pursue a moderate course did not impress him as being feasible. He now broke definitely with the humanists and adopted a purely evangelical conception of religion. Swiss and other sacramentarian influences were operating in France, the ideas of Oecolampadius were known, and Butzer of Strasbourg also was exerting considerable influence. Calvin, meditating whether he should break with the traditional faith, decided to do so and surrendered his Church income at Noyon in May, 1534. During a visit to his native city he was imprisoned, probably because of some manifestation against the old faith. When released, he returned to Orléans where he wrote a polemic against Anabaptists. On October 18 were discovered the placards on the walls of buildings of Paris, violently denouncing the Mass, and, as we have seen, the king determined to destroy the heretics. It was a dangerous moment, and Calvin fled to Basel where he arrived about the opening of 1535.

Calvin found Basel, where the Reformation had triumphed in 1529, a congenial environment. He had been meditating on a systematic treatise on the Christian faith and was now in a position to finish it. This was the _Institutes of the Christian Religion,_ published at Basel in March, 1536. Although the author's theological ideas had not yet arrived at their full development, his system was essentially complete. It is perhaps the greatest work on systematic theology produced by the Protestants of the Reformation, and its immediate service was to provide French Protestants with a theological guide which their early leaders had not been able to produce. The edition of 1541 was a masterpiece of prose and exerted much influence in the development of an artistic and brilliant prose style in French letters. The definitive edition of 1559 contained his mature views.

That the author aimed to help the persecuted of France he himself states in his famous preface to the _Institutes,_ addressed to Francis I:

> When I first engaged in this work, nothing was farther from my thoughts than to write what should afterwards be presented to your majesty. My intention was only to furnish a kind of rudiments, by which those who feel some interest in religion might be trained to true godliness. And I toiled at the task chiefly for the sake of my countrymen the French, multitudes of whom I perceived to be hungering and thirsting after Christ, while very few seemed to have been duly imbued with even a slender knowledge of Him.

Calvin urged Francis to accept the new doctrines and abandon Catholicism, stating that, if he rejected the teaching of the Gospel, he would meet with adversity.

> Your duty, most serene prince, is not to shut either your ears or mind against a cause involving such mighty interests as these: how the story of God is to be maintained on the earth inviolate, how the truth of God is to preserve its dignity, how the kingdom of Christ is to continue amongst us compact and secure. The cause is worthy of your ear, worthy of your investigation, worthy of your throne. The characteristic of a true sovereign is to acknowledge that, in the administration of his kingdom, he is a minister of God. He who does not make his reign subservient to the divine glory, acts the part not of a king, but a robber. He, moreover, deceives himself who anticipates long prosperity to any kingdom which is not ruled by the sceptre of God, that is, by His divine word. For the heavenly oracle is infallible which has declared that where there is no vision the people perish.

The following is a typically Calvinist note:

> Let not a contemptuous idea of our insignificance dissuade you from the investigation of this cause. We, indeed, are perfectly conscious how poor and abject we are; in the presence of God we are miserable sinners, and in the sight of men most despised—we are, if you will, the mere dregs and offscourings of the world, or worse, if worse can be named: so that before God there remains nothing of which we can glory save only His mercy, in which, without any merit of our own, we are admitted to the hope of eternal salvation: and before men not even this much remains, since we can glory only in our infirmity, a thing which, in the estimation of men, it is the greatest ignominy even tacitly to confess. But our doctrine must stand sublime above all the glory of the world, and invincible by all its power, because it is not ours, but that of the living God and His anointed whom the Father has appointed king, that He may rule from sea to sea, and from rivers even to the ends of the earth; and so rule as to smite the whole earth and its strength of iron and brass, its splendor of gold and silver, with the mere rod of his mouth, and break them in pieces like a potter's vessel; according to the magnificent predictions of the prophets respecting His kingdom.[1]

This introduction is a noble piece of exposition. It is refreshing to read these pages in which princes were told the truth which they should accept. Princes were not, as Luther thought, rulers to be obeyed in all matters, secular and ecclesiastical. But Calvin's appeal to Francis was in vain, for that monarch would never leave the established Church, the buttress of French kingship.

[1] *Dedication of the Institutes of the Christian Religion*, 1536, tr. by J. Allen (The Harvard Classics, XXXIX).

GUILLAUME FAREL AND THE CONVERSION OF THE FRENCH CANTONS

It is now necessary to relate in what way the ground had been pre-pared for Calvin in the French-speaking cantons of Switzerland. Zwing-lianism had been accepted by most German cantons; only the five cantons of Uri, Schwyz, Unterwalden, Zug, and Lucerne adhered to the old worship. Berne was the western outpost of Protestantism, and from it the conquering impulse, which had seemed to cease upon the death of Zwingli in 1531, proceeded to win to the Protestant fold the cantons of Valais, Geneva, Vaud, and Neuchâtel. Of the French cantons, only Fribourg remained staunchly loyal to Catholicism.

Guillaume Farel, the first reformer to labor in the French cantons, was born near Gap in Dauphiné in 1489. His family, like Calvin's, belonged to the bourgeoisie and had intimate connections with the Church. Farel went to Paris to study, soon fell under the influence of Stapulensis, and was thus led to study the Scriptures in the manner of humanists. He saw that there was a glaring contrast between religious practices of his day and the statements of Christ and the apostles. He followed Briçonnet to Meaux in 1521, and soon accepted Luther's idea that salvation came only through faith. He was a most energetic man who moved directly toward his objective without considering the obstacles which stood in the way. Apparently he failed to work in harmony with Briçonnet and in 1523, when the group at Meaux was being attacked by conservatives who wished to suppress them, he fled to Basel.

Now began Farel's tumultuous apostolate. He at once attacked Catho-lics and extended his hostility to Erasmus because of the latter's Laodi-cean sentiments as he called them. Expelled from Basel, Farel went to Montbéliard, to Metz, and finally to Strasbourg. He spent several months preaching in Alsace and appeared in Berne in the fall of 1526. He settled in Aigle, a town on the Rhone above Lake Geneva. He began charac-teristically as a schoolmaster, and this gave him a chance to insinuate his way into the confidence of his hearers and thus spread his ideas about the Gospel. At all times he could rely upon the protection of Berne. In 1529 he was sent by Berne into those parts of the Vaud which were under the joint government of Berne and Fribourg. Wherever Berne's authority was uppermost, Farel denounced the traditional cult with the greatest violence and audacity. Pierre Viret and Antoine Froment assisted him in Orbe, Grandson, and Morat which became centers of propaganda.

In 1529 Farel appeared in Neuchâtel which had abandoned Catholicism in 1530, Orbe and Grandson following in 1531. Froment was sent into Geneva in November, 1532, to disseminate the new doctrines under the guise of teaching languages. Geneva was profoundly influenced by its external political relations. Situated at the foot of Lake Geneva and surrounded by territory of the king of France, its citizens feared the loss of their independence. Hence they had formed an alliance with Berne and Fribourg.

The situation was further complicated by the ancient ambition of the dukes of Savoy to control the city, members of that house often being elected to the see of Geneva. And as the dukes of Savoy usually were allied with the emperor of the Holy Roman Empire, the political position of Geneva was much disturbed by the ever recurring wars between Charles V and Francis I. Also, there were divisions within the city. The clergy and zealous Catholics supported the bishop and were willing to seek the aid of the dukes of Savoy in combating heresy. Many citizens, however, wished to perpetuate their independence and opposed the bishops and Savoy. It was a field favorable for the spread of heresy.

Froment's teaching at once won a large following in Geneva. The ardent reformer was so bold as to address his listeners on the Place du Molard which drew upon him the wrath of the bishop's officers, and he was forced to leave the city. Many Catholics in Geneva were angry because the council of Geneva did not act against the heretics who were supported by Berne, but no action could be undertaken against that powerful canton. On May 4, 1533, a riot occurred in Geneva in which a canon, a native of Fribourg, was slain while brandishing a weapon against the Protestants. This was a turning point. Fribourg demanded justice and the immediate suppression of heresy, while Berne insisted with equal emphasis upon freedom of preaching. Vacillation was dangerous for the Catholics, for the excitement caused the reformers to proceed with greater audacity; Farel who had fled returned with Viret and began preaching to the excited public. A disputation was held before the council on January 29 and 30, 1534. When it was apparent that it would bring no practical result, Farel and his followers seized a Franciscan chapel on March 1.

These events displeased Fribourg which withdrew from the alliance with Geneva. This was unfortunate, for Geneva was thus abandoned to Savoy and Berne. The council was forced to listen to the wishes of Berne more than ever and could not act against Farel even had it wished to do so. The bishop thereupon sought support among his relatives in Savoy and soon began to make war on the people of Geneva, even ordering the townsmen to quit the city. Finally, on May 30, 1535, a great disputation was held before the council in which the fiery Farel won an easy victory. Still the council refused to act, and on August 8 the reforming party began to destroy images, pictures, and other objects in the cathedral church of St. Peter. Two days later Farel appeared before the council insisting on the immediate destruction of the old cult. The bishop had forbidden the secular priests to enter into any discussion about religion, and consequently there was no one to defend the Catholic faith by argument. Thus Farel won the battle. The populace rejected Catholicism, the clergy fled, and the bishop, aided by Savoy, besieged the city.

Communal independence, opposition to Savoy, and Protestantism now dictated the policy of Geneva. The situation was especially dangerous, for at this moment Charles V and Francis I were about to begin the third of their wars (1536–1538). The city's independence was placed in great jeopardy. Berne feared that the bishop of Geneva and his party of Savoyards might secure the support of the emperor, thus bringing the war into Switzerland, which she wanted to avoid if possible. This indeed was precisely what Charles proposed to do. Neither did Berne overlook the fact that the five Catholic cantons might join Charles, the bishop, and Savoy in order to call a halt to the triumphant advance of Protestantism. Berne finally decided to act when news came that Francis had definitely proposed to support Geneva if she would accept his sovereignty, and on January 16, 1536, Berne declared war on Savoy.

Berne's army advanced toward Geneva. On the way it had to pass through the Vaud, the region between Berne and Fribourg on the east, Lake Neuchâtel on the west, and Lake Geneva on the south. The energetic action of the troops, supported by levies from Neuchâtel and other places sympathetic to the cause, induced the towns of the Vaud to surrender. The troops of the duke of Savoy were surprised and outmaneuvered, and early in February the Bernese entered Geneva to be hailed as liberators.

Now also came the settlement of accounts with the bishop of Lausanne who, like his colleague in Geneva, had favored and even abetted the Savoyards. Accordingly on April 1 the troops of Berne seized all the episcopal property in the diocese. Thus did Swiss national sentiment triumph over French, Savoyard, and imperial ambitions. And incidentally Protestantism was established as the legal faith everywhere in western Switzerland save in Fribourg which has adhered most tenaciously to the traditional Catholic faith down to our own day.

It remained to establish the reformed cult in Geneva and Lausanne. On May 21, 1536, the people of Geneva, assembled by sound of bell and trumpet, swore to live according to the Gospel, which meant that all traditional Catholic practices were to be abandoned. They also approved a measure which provided for the establishment of a school, the hiring of a master and teachers, and the offer of free education for the poor. All citizens were required to send their children to this school. The Reformation in Lausanne was accomplished in the following October. A great disputation had been arranged in which Farel and Viret assumed the leading roles. The emperor had forbidden the debate in a letter to Berne early in July, but it was not obeyed. The clergy were not in a position to resist the arguments of their opponents, for they had been bidden to keep silence; and the bishop's vicar, as might be expected, was so poorly versed in Scripture that he could not defend the Catholic position. It is instructive to note that the defense was left to a man named Blancherose, a layman who was eager to uphold the old faith. The edict of December 24 established the reformed faith everywhere in Vaud. Ecclesiastical property was appropriated for schools, hospitals, and similar uses. Viret was established as minister, and out of his lectureship grew the University of Lausanne.

CALVIN BEGINS HIS APOSTOLATE IN GENEVA

Meanwhile Calvin had returned to Switzerland. After publishing his *Institutes* in 1536, he left Basel apparently to escape attention, directing his steps to Ferrara where Duchess Renata, a daughter of Louis XII of France, was known to be sympathetic to reformers. At her court had gathered a number of them, including the poet Clément Marot. It is not known why Calvin went to Ferrara. Probably it was to propagate his ideas, perhaps to gratify desires natural in the breast of one who had been brought up as a humanist, or to see Italy. His sojourn was brief evidently because it was too dangerous to stay in this place upon which persecution descended even while he was staying there. Accordingly he recrossed the Alps and, passing through Basel, proceeded to Paris. He left soon after, bringing with him a brother and sister. But his design of going to Strasbourg was interrupted by the hostilities between Charles V and Francis I, for he was forced to make a detour by way of Geneva where he was destined to spend the rest of his life.

Calvin had intended to spend but one night in Geneva. He was loath to engage upon active work, preferring the quiet of his study in order to write theological treatises for the guidance of Protestants. Farel addressed him with characteristic impetuosity, declaring that God would never give him His blessing if he should refuse to enter upon the path of manifest duty. Calvin, frightened, capitulated and agreed to stay. He made a hurried visit to Basel for business reasons, returned in August, 1536, and took up his work in the city which during the next 28 years he was to organize into a theocratic commonwealth framed according to Scripture as he interpreted it.

Chapter 13

CALVINISM IN GENEVA

ALVIN'S THEOLOGICAL SYSTEM was the most elaborate and scientific body of dogma produced in the Protestant camp. Luther was a powerful revolutionary with deep intuitive religious feeling which, however, never could be reduced to system. Melanchthon was a follower and never blazed new theological trails. Zwingli was the product of diverse influences and acted under the impulse of specific events only; he was not a systematic theologian. The Anabaptists wrote much edifying literature and some acutely reasoned works, but they also failed to create a masterpiece of theological thought which could assume basic importance in the religious life of the Protestant world. Since this task was peculiarly the achievement of Calvin, it is advisable at this time to outline the main points of his theological system.

It must not be forgotten that the reformer was deeply indebted to his early teachers and friends. He had learned much from Erasmus and other humanists who were interested in the Bible. Like Zwingli, he had received from Luther a deeper conception of grace from which he derived his doctrine of justification by faith alone. From Zwingli and the sacramentarians of Strasbourg and elsewhere he had drawn his ideas about an incorporeal presence in the Eucharist which, however, he modified by teaching that Christ was spiritually present. From his early humanist training he acquired a lucid Latinity and a thorough knowledge of the classics and the Church fathers, both Latin and Greek. The study of law without doubt added logical precision to a mind natively endowed with clarity. These forces were all combined in this master whose systematic exposition of Protestant theology was destined to exert great influence.

Calvin's logical reasoning began with a well-conceived doctrine about God, the sovereignty of God being the corner stone of Calvin's great system. God was a being without limitation of time or place; He was omnipotent and omnipresent. Out of the depths of His wisdom and for reasons sufficient to Him, which were beyond human ability to understand, He had fashioned the world and all things in it. Man was created in His image, sinless and immortal. The first parents, Adam and Eve, lived in the Garden of Eden in close fellowship with God, utterly unconscious of the effects of sin. The injection of sin into this fair creation, due to the rebellion of Satan, changed this blissful state. Man fell through disobedience to God's command, and his progeny fell with him. His total depravity resulted, for so spotless was God's purity that any stain of sin, no matter how slight, was sufficient to corrupt man's moral nature completely. Man did indeed possess a knowledge of God drawn from the resources of his intellect, but this could not save him; it was insufficient because man was smitten with sin. A much fuller knowledge of God was offered in Scripture which contained His unique revelation whereby man might discover the way of salvation.

God's sovereign will in the universe necessitated a doctrine regarding man's relations to Him, and Calvin's logical mind did not hesitate to draw the inevitable consequences. He taught a rigid foreordination of some to eternal glory and eternal damnation for many more. Justification, as with Luther, came from faith or trust in God's promises to save through the sacrifice of Christ. Predestination was a mystery inscrutable from man's point of view, because a corrupt nature could not form any but perverse views of God's righteousness. This doctrine often aroused rebellious sentiments among Calvin's followers, a fact which in numerous instances caused later theologians to soften its rigor.

God's plan for salvation was set forth in Scripture. This was an inspired book written by certain people who acted as simple secretaries of God and faithfully and authentically recorded His revelation. Calvin held that every phrase and sentence was infallible, which led to a remarkable bibliolatry among his followers. The Old Testament was as important as the New, each of its books being regarded as a part of God's law and revelation. When Castellio suggested that the *Song of Solomon* was merely love poetry, Calvin was horrified, for such tinkering with God's inspired word was impious and presumptuous.

There were but two sacraments: baptism and the Lord's Supper. The former was a rite whereby a person was made a member of the community of the Christian Church, and it possessed none of the far-reaching power which the Catholic Church ascribed to it—that of removing the guilt of original sin. The second was a spiritual feast at which the believer received the spiritual body of Christ. These sacraments were established by God and were simple external symbols, like seals attached to an authentic document. The seals attested to its authenticity, but without them the validity of the document was not impaired. Therefore without the sacraments a believer's faith was truly able to save, the sacraments being merely external confirmatory signs of such saving faith.

The Church was a visible and an invisible company composed of the elect, living and departed. Its visible section comprised all who participated in the Lord's Supper, listened to the preaching of the Gospel, and regulated their acts according to its precepts. It was to be organized according to the model given by God to man in the New Testament. Ministers were appointed by the congregation to interpret the Word of God as contained in Scripture. They were God's agents and were entrusted with the keys of salvation. Yet it must not be thought that they possessed sole right of interpreting dogma or Scripture, for such final authority reposed in the whole body of the faithful guided by the Holy Spirit. The Bible, "the Word of God," was the supreme source of trust, and all were required to submit to its teaching. Teachers were appointed to aid in instructing the people in religion, and elders and deacons were chosen from among the members who possessed genuine inclination toward religion and who had received the approval of the congregation. A community thus established possessed the right to discipline or to excommunicate any person for heresy or improper conduct.

Calvin and his followers held that the Church could inflict no punishment beyond driving offenders out of its fold, it being the duty of the officials of a secular state to proceed against them at the bar of justice. This relationship was very like that of the Church and the state in the Middle Ages. In general the Calvinist clergy claimed authority to instruct the state as to its moral and religious duty. It was the duty of the state to purge its citizenry of erroneous dogmas. Heresy was treason against God, and in the case of the most obstinate assertion of heresy the death penalty was justified, as in the case of Servetus. Denial of the dogma of the Trinity was a grave affront to the Christian community, and the death penalty was not too severe for any person holding such radical conceptions.

This right of the clergy to instruct in faith and morals laid the basis for a rigid regulation of private conduct, dress, arrangement of the hair, jewelry, sports, and diversions. The rigidity of Calvinist dogma and the lynx-eyed moral supervision of ministers made the laws of Geneva particularly efficacious in all these private concerns. Calvin was determined to put an end to all violations of morality, especially adultery, an offense which merited the death penalty according to the twenty-second chapter of Deuteronomy. Observance of the Sabbath was compulsory. Calvin also believed that card playing should be shunned because it consumed precious time which might be better employed in serving God.

Dancing was regarded as bad because it invited immorality. A similar objection was raised against the theater, but, though the drama was not entirely forbidden, it was to be censored by the clergy. Many of the laws of Geneva which regulated moral, social, and religious conduct in accordance with these concepts may be traced back to the medieval communal acts of the city. Much of the severity with which they were enforced was due, however, to the zeal of a clergy schooled in a theology which interdicted many of life's simple pleasures and charms.

Blasphemy, regarded as a horrible sin, was given a wide meaning. God's name was so holy that it should not be used irreverently or contemptuously, and no slighting remark was to be made about Him. It was the attitude of mind which determined whether an utterance was blasphemous.

> The name of God is vulgarized and vilified when used in oaths, which, though true, are superfluous. This too, is to take His name in vain. Wherefore, it is not sufficient to abstain from perjury, unless we, at the same time, remember that an oath is not appointed or allowed for passion or pleasure, but for necessity; and that, therefore, a licentious use is made of it by him who uses it on any other than necessary occasions. Moreover, no case of necessity can be pretended, unless where some purpose of religion or charity is to be served. In this matter, great sin is committed in the present day— sin the more intolerable in this, that its frequency has made it cease to be regarded as a fault, though it certainly is not accounted trivial before the judgment-seat of God. The name of God is everywhere profaned by introducing it indiscriminately in frivolous discourse; and the evil is disregarded, because it has been long and audaciously persisted in with impunity. . . . Another form of violation is exhibited, when, with manifest impiety, we, in our oaths, substitute the holy servants of God for God Himself, thus conferring upon them the glory of His Godhead. It is not without cause that the Lord has, by a special commandment, required us to swear by His name, and, by a special prohibition, forbidden us to swear by other gods.[1]

Idolatry also was a grave offense and was likewise given wide interpretation. Not only did it refer to worship of idols, but also included the reverence shown by Catholics toward images of Christ, Mary, and the saints, and to the sacrament, the Mass being regarded as the extreme of idolatry. Calvin and his followers never scrupled to denounce these traditional Catholic practices. This temper of mind made Calvinists especially bitter toward relics, and Calvin wrote a remarkable treatise against them in which he satirized their use. It was not difficult to do this,

---

[1] *Institutes of the Christian Religion*, tr. by H. Beveridge, Edinburgh, 1845, pp. 455–456.

for a credulous age had rarely questioned the authenticity of the remains of saints. The following is a fair sample:

> The inquisitive genius of the monks has set them to rummaging in the Virgin's drawers and toilet-boxes; the thieves have brought off considerable plunder. At Charroi they have one of her chemises; another is at Aix-la-Chapelle. The apostles and other pious men of old were not sufficiently sensible of their blessings to care aught for Mary's wardrobe. Out of curiosity, however, let us examine the cut of this chemise. That at Aix is frequently carried about in pomp, stuck upon the end of a long pole, and it resembles what is called the sacerdotal alb. Now if Mary had sprung from the loins of an antediluvian giant, she could not have worn a chemise of such dimension as that of Aix-la-Chapelle.[2]

Calvin soon began to revise the religious life of the city. Farel had started this work before him, but now the task was continued in earnest. The two men presented propositions to the council which were promulgated in the *Ordonnance* of January 16, 1537. The Lord's Supper should be celebrated four times a year, discipline was to be maintained through excommunication, a catechism was to be prepared for children, congregational singing should be inaugurated, and regulations were to be made for the observance of Sunday. The catechism was introduced soon after. The council commanded the officials of each of the twenty-six districts of Geneva to order the inhabitants to appear at a specified time at the cathedral church of St. Peter to listen to the reading of the catechism and give their promise to receive it as the sole and true doctrine. There was much opposition to this procedure, but the government threatened to banish those who failed to comply.

Calvin and Farel soon learned that they had enemies. Citizens whose families had long been established in Geneva were loath to suffer the domination of the ministers. They had shaken off the bishop and the house of Savoy, and they did not relish another and more annoying tyranny. The elections to the town councils in February, 1537, had proved favorable to the ministers, but in the following year a hostile group was chosen, and Calvin and Farel were powerless to oppose them. When it was voted to accept the method of serving the Lord's Supper followed in Berne, trouble ensued, Calvin strenuously refusing to admit that the state had any authority in dictating religious policy. On Easter Sunday, 1538, he and Farel refused to administer the Lord's Supper with unleavened bread. Calvin's enemies, eager to put a limit to his influence, tried to assert the right of the secular community in purely Church ques-

---

[2] *On Romish Relics; Being an Inventory of Saints' Relics*, New York, 1844, p. 29.

tions. The government thereupon exiled Calvin and Farel on April 23, ordering them to depart within 3 days. Farel went to Neuchâtel, and Calvin proceeded to Strasbourg at the invitation of Butzer.

Calvin lectured on theology for which he received a small honorarium from the city, and he also became a pastor of the French refugees. He was free to develop an order of worship, subject to the general policy of the authorities of Strasbourg. Thus was created the liturgy adopted wherever Calvinist influences were able to establish churches. The order of worship was as follows: invocation, prayer, confession, absolution to all who were truly repentant, singing of the Table of the Law, reading from the Bible, sermon, psalm or hymn, and benediction. Psalms were drawn from the Book of Psalms. Clément Marot translated some of them, and Calvin set others to rhyme. To this day in Reformed and Presbyterian churches psalms are preferred to hymns.

Meanwhile the internal affairs of Geneva were much troubled. One group still hoped that the Catholic worship might be brought back. Another, called *Guillermins* from Guillaume Farel, supported the reformers, and a third wanted to accept the leadership of Berne with which Geneva had made an accord. Because of this action they were nicknamed *Artichauds* (from the word *articles*). The strife caused by these factions gave Catholics hope that Genevans might be induced to return to the Church, and in 1539 Bishop Jacopo Sadoleto of Carpentras penned an appeal to the officials of the city. The town of Berne, preferring to keep Geneva Protestant, invited Calvin to answer it. The reply was printed and put on sale. In it Calvin reiterated his position regarding the true nature of the Church and his opposition to Catholicism. This response had an important effect. The magistrates and council of Geneva were weary of contentions and desired above all things some person who could establish peace. Only Calvin, it was thought, could quiet the turmoil, and they invited him to return.

At once, upon his arrival in Geneva in September, 1541, Calvin set about to revise the religious organization of the community in such manner as to make the city a model of Christian government. The *Ordonnances Ecclésiastiques* were promulgated on November 20. Originally drawn up by Calvin, they were changed at many points by the council and finally accepted by the townsmen. They established: (1) An association of ministers, known in Genevan history as the *Vénérable Compagnie des Pasteurs,* was to have charge of discipline in a large number of cases. (2) A second order, that of the teachers, was to teach pure doctrine. (3) The third group constituted the famous *consistory,* composed of twelve elders who were to be chosen by the city councils. They were charged to look into the conduct and opinions of the people, each elder to have supervision over a district. (4) The last group were the deacons who were appointed to look after the poor, disburse alms, care for the sick, and regulate the hospitals. These four orders were held to be instituted by Christ for the governance of His Church.

It was difficult at first for the pastors to subject all public and private life to their regime, for there was much opposition and criticism. But Calvin was not the man to retreat before it, and he relentlessly crushed every sign of insubordination. To his imperious nature, conscious of a calling from God, it seemed that no mercy should be shown to anyone who questioned what was believed to be the teaching of Scripture. Sebastian Castellio (1515–1563), who was born in a village near Geneva, was a thorn in his side. In spite of the poverty of his parents, he managed to acquire a humanist education. He became acquainted with Calvin in Strasbourg in 1540 and was led to abandon his thoroughgoing humanism for the religious views of Calvin. But not entirely, for soon after he became rector of the academy in Geneva he advanced the startling idea that the *Song of Songs* was purely amorous poetry which had no place in the "Word of God." He was called before the council and, when he persisted in his views, was constrained to leave Geneva (1543). He settled in Basel where he led a life of great poverty.

Calvin's rigid doctrine of predestination to eternal damnation as well as to eternal glory provoked criticism most sharply uttered by an ex-Carmelite named Jerome Bolsec. Bolsec became interested in Reformed ideas, fled France, found refuge at the court of the Duchess Renata of Ferrara, and finally settled near Geneva. His eagerness for debate led him into difficulties with the ministers. When he attacked predestination, a very central proposition of Calvin's system, a disputation was held in 1551, and Bolsec was cast into prison for opposing a doctrine officially established in Geneva. His accusation that Calvin did not understand the Bible galled the reformer. He was tried and banished from the city. He settled at Thonon nearby and accused Calvin of teaching that God was the author of sin.

Severe punishment was meted out to others, for a section of the population remained indifferent to Calvin's doctrines. One Jacques Gruet was suspected of having posted a placard in the pulpit of St. Peter's which threatened revenge for the tyranny which the people had endured. He had written some bitter brochures against Calvin's regime but did not publish them, and they were discovered in his house after he was arrested. He was subjected to dreadful tortures, and the magistrates decreed that, as his ideas were a deadly insult against God's law, he should be executed

(1547). This severe policy proved successful in dealing with such people, and Calvin's authority was undisputed. He ruled as no pope had ever ruled in Rome. Such was the rigor of this regime that it has been computed that between 1542 and 1546 fifty-eight persons were executed and seventy-six sent into exile. Among those who lost their lives were thirty-four accused of the crime of witchcraft, which the people as well as Calvin believed was the cause of the plague of 1545.

The execution of Servetus in 1553, described in a former chapter, greatly aroused Calvin. Castellio produced a pamphlet denying the right of secular governments to punish dissenters in life and limb. It was published under the assumed name of Martin Bellius and bore as title, *Concerning Heretics and Whether They Should Be Punished*. Castellio held that there were two kinds of heretics. Those who acted against the moral precepts of Scripture should be punished, but those who misunderstood the Bible should not be so treated, for it was unjust to prosecute them because the teaching of the Bible was not clear. The humanist author thought that this earth could be made better only if every person would carry out Christ's precepts in his daily life. Rigid adherence to official dogma was not so important as moral conduct. In a bold passage he asked the question, "If, O Christ, Thou art the author of these things or if Thou hast given order to cause them to be done, what is left for the devil to do?"

Théodore de Bèze, Calvin's staunch follower, undertook to answer this audacious book in 1554 with a treatise entitled *Heretics Are to Be Punished by the Civil Magistrate*, which undoubtedly voiced the sentiments of Calvin. Human society had as its chief object the establishment of God's glory. Civil magistrates, who were required to promote it as much as possible, had the right to restrain rebels against God's authority. Capital punishment was legitimate because heretics impugned God's majesty, a more serious offense than opposing secular authority which demanded a rebel's life. Why should obstinate heretics therefore not be deprived of life?[3] The Protestant world very generally approved the punishment meted out to so manifest a heretic as Servetus, even Melanchthon believing that he deserved his punishment.

A government organized and managed by such ideas could not appeal to the easygoing citizenry of Geneva. Many of them opposed excommunication and were prone to make caustic statements about the pastors whom they delighted to annoy in many ways. But the frightful example of Servetus' death silenced all opponents, and the elections of 1555 were

[3] H. M. Baird, *Theodore Beza: The Counsellor of the French Reformation*, New York, 1899, pp. 52–70.

favorable to Calvin's cause. The *Libertines,* as these latitudinarians were called, were reduced in strength, and a riot caused the magistrates to execute a number of them. A large number of the old families now left Geneva, thus reducing the formidable character of the opposition. Meanwhile the city more and more became a haven of refuge for those of the Reformed faith who fled persecution in France, England, the Low Countries, and elsewhere.

Calvin will long be regarded as one of the world's great men. Although frail in body, he preached each day during every alternate week and attended weekly meetings of the consistory. He was an energetic writer, his literary remains filling fifty-seven large volumes in the *Corpus Reformatorum. The Institutes of the Christian Religion* is his greatest work. He repeatedly revised it until he produced a definitive edition in 1559, which is still used in some quarters as an authoritative guide to theology. His *On Romish Relics* is worth reading as an example of pure literature. He also wrote long commentaries on the books of the Bible which served as handbooks for ministers and students of theology. In addition, Calvin carried on a voluminous correspondence with the great lights of the Protestant world of the time. These literary products, Latin as well as French, are marked by great clarity of thought and incisive diction which won for him leadership among Protestants and lasting reputation as a writer of French Renaissance prose. His enormous labors sapped his strength and brought on a painful illness to which he succumbed in 1564.

Calvin's labors as an energetic organizer are no less remarkable. He sought to make Geneva a model of government for other states. Besides organizing the Reformed Church, he rendered vast services to education in that city. The academy, which later became the University of Geneva, was founded in 1559. As one would expect, its instruction was guided by humanist conceptions, Théodore de Bèze becoming the rector. Calvin also assisted in organizing the Reformed worship in foreign countries, France, the Low Countries, Poland, Germany, Hungary, Scotland, and England, to which a constant stream of zealous and well-prepared preachers was sent forth. Large numbers of young men went to Geneva to drink at the original fountain of Reformed theology. The Reformed Church, thus organized in many lands, provided a most effective bulwark against Catholicism. Calvin's systematic theology became the best intellectual provender to nourish struggling Protestant churches everywhere, and it alone of all the rival systems produced by the Protestants may be called universal.

PART VII

Leadership of Calvinist Thought in Protestantism

Chapter 14

SPREAD OF CALVINISM: LOW COUNTRIES AND CENTRAL EUROPE

*T*HE PASSING of Martin Luther in 1546 and of Ulrich Zwingli in 1531, as we have noted, marked the apogee of their reforming ideas. Henceforth Calvin's thought and doctrine were in the ascendancy. Beginning in 1536—the year in which the *Institutes of the Christian Religion* were first published—Calvinism was a force to be reckoned with, especially in the Low Countries, in the Palatinate, in the states along the periphery of the Empire, and in Switzerland.

THE EMPEROR CHARLES' RESOURCES IN THE LOW COUNTRIES

The establishment of a Protestant state in the Low Countries was an event of capital importance, for when the seven northern provinces embraced the teaching of Calvin they became a center of vigorous Protestant influence which was felt in all neighboring lands. This revolt against Catholicism should not be separated from the revolt against the political domination of Europe by Spain. The success of the United Provinces ruined Spanish hopes of employing the commercial and industrial resources and the geographically strategic position of the Low Countries to

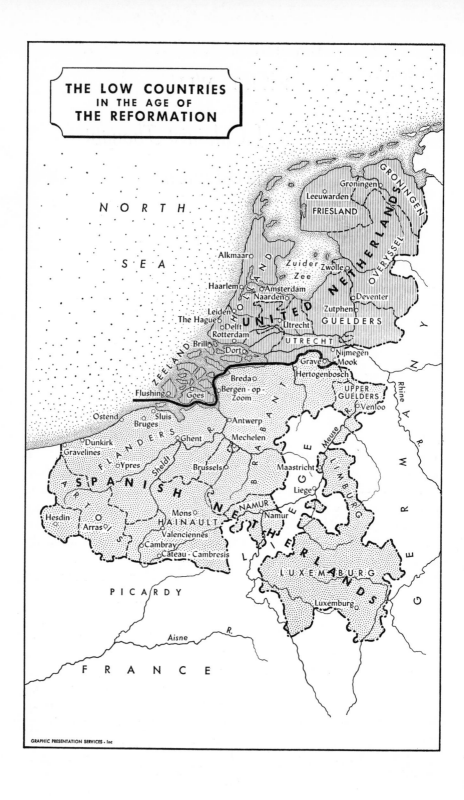

THE LOW COUNTRIES
IN THE AGE OF
THE REFORMATION

NORTH

SEA

Groningen
Leeuwarden
FRIESLAND
GRONINGEN

Alkmaar
Zuider
Zee
Zwolle
OVERYSSEL

Haarlem
Amsterdam
Naarden
Deventer

Leiden
Zutphen
The Hague
Delft
Utrecht
GUELDERS

Rotterdam
Brill
UTRECHT

HOLLAND
UNITED NETHERLAND

Nijmegen
Dort
Grave
Mook

Breda
Hertogenbosch

Flushing
Goes
Bergen - op -
Zoom

UPPER
GUELDERS

ZEELAND
Venloo

Ostend
Sluis

Bruges
Antwerp

Dunkirk
Ghent
Mechelen

Gravelines

Ypres
Brussels
Maastricht

FLANDERS
Scheldt
Liege

SPANISH
Namur
LIMBURG

Hesdin
Mons
Namur

ARTOIS
Arras
HAINAULT

Valenciennes

Cambray
Cateau - Cambresis

LUXEMBURG

PICARDY
Luxemburg

Aisne
R.

FRANCE

NETHERLANDS
BRABANT
LIEGE

Rhine
R.
Meuse
R.
NAVARRE
GERMANY

GRAPHIC PRESENTATION SERVICES - Inc

perpetuate and extend Spanish international power. The failure of this ambitious policy also made impossible King Philip II's scheme of reëstablishing Catholicism in northern Europe. The views of Calvin's followers about the right to rebel against princes played a peculiar part in this struggle.

Charles of Spain, grandson of Ferdinand and Isabella, succeeded to the governance of the Low Countries in 1515 and was crowned emperor in 1520. It soon was apparent that he held the political ideas characteristic of the day. He wished to consolidate political authority in the states over which he ruled, and he was determined to conquer certain lands whose possession was necessary to complete his control of the Low Countries. Thus he annexed Tournai and its subject territories in 1522, the principality of Friesland in 1524, the secularized properties of the bishop of Utrecht with the subject land of Overyssel in 1528, the territories of Groningen and Drenthe in 1536, and, finally, the large duchy of Guelders in 1543. When Charles abdicated in October, 1555, he gave to his son Philip seventeen provinces which constituted the Low Countries save the lands dependent upon the bishop of Liége.

Rulers of the Burgundian house, which came to an end with the death of Charles the Bold in 1477, had found it difficult to manage the common affairs of these lands. Each state cherished a strong spirit of independence and preferred to manage its own affairs, since everywhere there was suspicion of the Estates General. Emperor Charles sought to break down this provincialism. In 1531 he established three central councils, the Council of State, the Privy Council, and the Council of Flanders, which gave him more effective control of the problems common to all the provinces. Councils of Justice had been appointed in several provinces by Charles' predecessors, and their number was extended and their functions perfected. Chambers of Accounts to take care of financial matters were created at Brussels, The Hague, and Lille. Lieutenants, or stadholders, were appointed in the various provinces to represent the prince in the management of public affairs.

Charles also developed his military resources. Princes of the Renaissance were confronted with serious problems. Abroad they were constantly called upon to resist other rulers who like themselves were consolidating all political and financial power and making it subservient to a new state policy. At home nobles and towns which boasted rights and privileges usually dating far back into the Middle Ages were likely to resist. It was therefore important to develop an army. Charles inherited the military organization developed by his Burgundian forbears, and toward the end of his reign he had fifteen companies of 3000 horses each.

Drawn from the lesser nobility, commanded by the more important seigniors of the land, and placed under the control of the prince who could dispose of them freely without dictation by the Estates General, they became an effective means of establishing central authority.

While Charles was thus laying the political and military foundations of a Netherland state, his foreign policy was designed to give the Low Countries greater homogeneity and independence. He fought a series of wars with Francis I (1515–1547) and Henry II (1547–1559) of France. By the Treaty of Madrid (1526) at the close of the first war, the king of France as feudal lord yielded all claim upon Flanders. This cession became definitive in the Treaty of Crespy (1544) at the close of the fourth war. Thus the independence of the Low Countries, which had been subject to political and military encroachment of French kings, seemed established. Charles also severed the old bonds with Germany where he bore the imperial title and ruled with his brother King Ferdinand. He organized his Netherlands seventeen provinces into the "Circle of Burgundy" (1548), thus making them independent of the empire in administration and justice.

REFORMATION IN THE LOW COUNTRIES

In few lands is the course of the Reformation so interesting as in the Low Countries. No other region outside Italy had made such remarkable advance in economic and social life, and in this most highly developed bourgeois environment there appeared a remarkable level of culture. Humanist conceptions took deep root even among townsmen of moderate circumstances. Erasmus appears to be, in part at least, a product of these surroundings, and his teachings exerted a deeper influence in the Low Countries than elsewhere. Sacramentarians, especially numerous in the county of Holland, owed much to this humanist culture. Their opinions, however, could not win the multitudes as Calvinism did later, for they were popular mainly among the well-to-do and intelligent elite in the towns.

Nor did Lutheranism win many adherents, for national antipathy to Rome was not nearly so pronounced here as in Germany.[1] Humanists, of

[1] It is an error repeated in nearly all books on the Reformation that the earliest reformers in the Low Countries were Lutheran. Luther's influence certainly reached into these lands, but most of the dissatisfied were sacramentarians. Thus the three Augustinian friars who perished in Brussels (Henry Vos, John van Essen, and a third whose name is not given in the documents) denied the Real Presence and insisted that in the elements Christ was present only spiritually. This surely is not Lutheran, for Lutherans rigidly insisted that Christ was present in the elements of the Lord's Supper. Fur-

whom Erasmus was typical, might be moved by Luther's protests, but they were slow to join him. Sacramentarian and Lutheran teaching could not go together, since the former denied the doctrine of transubstantiation and owed much of its clarity to the thought of the Renaissance, whereas the latter developed the doctrine of "consubstantiation" which was as displeasing to sacramentarians as Catholic transubstantiation. Futhermore, Luther abandoned the political implications of his democratic idea of justification by faith alone, for he was alarmed by the Peasants' War in 1524 and 1525. Henceforth authority and respect for rights of princes dominated his teaching—a spirit alien to the temper of Netherlanders. Later when the revolt against Philip II took place, Lutheranism had no possible chance to win adherents, for it taught the necessity of obeying legitimate princes in all things secular as well as religious, no matter how tyrannical rulers might become.

Anabaptism, which was closely related to sacramentarianism and humanism, was much more important in the Low Countries than Lutheranism, spreading among the bourgeoisie and peasants. Pinched by hard times, these humble people often were eager to try force and so adopted Melchiorite doctrines about a heavenly Zion on earth. It is obvious that this group could never win support from the bulk of the population, for the socially stable and economically secure section of the population refused to countenance violence. It was an age of growing complexity in economic life. Simple conceptions of the untutored lower classes could not please hard-headed townsmen who held practical ideas about state and society. This class would never exchange the reality of economic prosperity and solidarity for the visionary prognostications of Anabaptists and the fulminations of radical Melchiorites about a coming Utopia wherein saints would reign in peace and justice over a renovated society.

The government of the Low Countries, as elsewhere, sought to repress heresy. Charles was orthodox, for no Spanish king or Holy Roman emperor could be otherwise. He believed it his duty to compel men to live according to the truth taught by the universal shepherd, the bishop of Rome, a policy in which the hierarchy and zealous laymen supported him. In an age of commerce, industry, and increasing use of coined money

---

thermore, they would not affirm the existence of purgatory which Luther did not attack until 1525. For the best exposition of the matter, see L. Knappert's *Het Ontstaan en de Vestiging van het Protestantisme in de Nederlanden*, Utrecht, 1924, chaps. iv and v; and *De Opkomst van het Protestantisme in eene Noord-Nederlandsche Stad: Geschiedenis van de Hervorming binnen Leiden*, Leiden, 1908, chap. i. The best work on Lutheranism in these lands is J. W. Pont's *Geschiedenis van het Lutheranisme in de Nederlanden tot 1618*, Haarlem, 1911, vol. xvii of *Verhandelingen rakende den Natuurlijken en geopenbaarden Godsdienst Uitgegeven door Teyler's Godgeleerd Genootschap*.

it required vigilance to check unauthorized opinion. The townsmen had grown rich. They were numerous, and many of them were enlightened, having been brought up under the novel opinions of humanists. The printing press was pouring forth tracts on religion, orthodox as well as heretical. Governmental restrictions proved ineffective; they merely succeeded in making printing of forbidden works more profitable.

Charles resolved to introduce into the Low Countries the Inquisition as it had developed in Spain, a step which his Netherland councilors vigorously opposed. He nevertheless appointed Francis Van der Hulst, a member of the Council of Brabant, to investigate all people charged with heresy and to inflict proper punishment (April, 1522). Van der Hulst was given extensive authority and, although only a political official, he received a papal appointment in the following year. Pope Adrian VI had been Charles' tutor, and a close understanding existed between them. Another arrangement was effected in June, 1524, when three ecclesiastics were named inquisitors under state direction. But this organ could not check heresy, for the people as a rule did not share the emperor's zeal. Some of the towns, especially those of the county of Holland, declared that their own officials were sufficiently capable of taking care of religious dissenters.

Obviously greater rigor was necessary; hence the placard or ordinance of October 14, 1529, which declared that all laymen who discussed questions about faith, failed to report heretics, or made insulting remarks about images of God, the Virgin, or the saints should pay with their lives. But Anabaptism was rising everywhere, especially in Holland, Friesland, and neighboring parts. A strange pantheistic sect appeared in Lille and Hainault, and another unusual sect, the Loists, became numerous in Antwerp. The latter revived some ancient Manichean notions about the evil nature of matter. Small wonder that the government was concerned! Still more severe was the edict issued on October 7, 1531, under which all property of the accused was to be confiscated. Melchiorites were shown no mercy, and no Anabaptist, even though he merely believed in or practised rebaptism, suffered any kindlier treatment.

When Münster fell and the Melchiorites were discomfited, the government seemed to feel that a dangerous crisis was past. But repression was clearly a failure. The presses of Antwerp were printing forbidden books. Subversive literature poured into the land from East Friesland, the town of Embden being an important center of heretical agitation. Books by heretics were smuggled all over the land in merchandise and sold covertly. False titles were common, and the most skillful deception was practised. Officials sought to control printers by requiring from each a license and a promise under penalty to publish only approved books. Schools were subjected to rigid supervision, and no references were to be made in the popular miracle and morality plays either to the Bible or the sacraments.

Still heresy grew. Accordingly a new placard in September, 1540, announced that heretics henceforth could not devise any property, and that people who offered petitions in favor of the accused would be treated as their accomplices. The same treatment was to be accorded people who neglected to report heretics. Officials prone to treat suspects with leniency —and this is eloquent of their sympathy with the unfortunate—were threatened with fitting punishment for neglect of duty. Humanists and sacramentarians usually knew how to conduct themselves without being caught in the clutches of the law, but simple Anabaptists suffered most. No list of these victims is complete, nor will such a catalogue ever be made. One collection names 877, of whom 717 were Anabaptists. Charles executed 223 of these; the rest were destroyed after 1555 by Philip whose policy was more drastic. New regulations were drawn up making possible better coöperation between state officials and inquisitors, and special agents were appointed in a number of the provinces. Several additional placards designed to perfect the organization for repressing heresy were issued by Charles in 1550.

Heretics who attracted notice during the last 20 years of Charles' reign are especially worthy of study. They were men of independent views and cannot be classed as Lutherans, Zwinglians, Anabaptists, or Calvinists. Chief among these was Angelus Merula (1482–1557) who may best be considered a sacramentarian. He must be regarded as one of the original minds common in the Low Countries who never joined the greater movements of the day and who therefore cannot be readily classified. He read all theologians, orthodox as well as heretical. He denied transubstantiation, yet believed that the Mass was an important institution. He opposed veneration of saints and the Virgin; only God and Christ should be addressed in prayer. Faith in Christ saved souls; works were necessary, but they were dead and profitless unless they proceeded from love. He believed it wrong to leave the Church in spite of the manifest corruptions of clerical life. Merula was condemned to be burned, but, as the executioners were binding him to the stake, he suddenly died from natural causes.

Anastasius Veluanus also should be noted. He early embraced heretical opinions and was sentenced (1553) to study at Louvain in order to correct his erroneous notions. He wrote *The Layman's Guide* which was printed in Strasbourg in 1554, and he subsequently served several German congregations in the Rhineland. Although he admired Luther, he never became a Lutheran. He taught that it was more godly to confess sins to a pious layman than to a wicked priest, and that the Roman Church was so corrupt that it was useless to stay in her fold. He denied predestination and championed free will. Salvation could not be earned by man's unaided efforts, for it consisted in improving oneself morally after the example of Christ. Many more names of persons who held similar beliefs could be added. These dissenters lacked organization; this was given them by the disciples of Calvin.

Repression was part and parcel of Spanish and Hapsburg political policy. Charles was staunchly Catholic; in Spain the hierarchy was practically a part of the government, and the maintenance of Catholicism was a national concern. By reason of their central geographical position and their extraordinary economic resources, the Low Countries were a most important element in the Hapsburg political combination. They would prove useful in any conflict with France, and such was their economic importance for England that Hapsburg princes could confidently hope to influence the foreign policy of English kings. Possession of the Low Countries also helped Charles to steady his power in Germany. Since the Hapsburgs controlled the Low Countries, they were able to assert their interests everywhere in northern Europe. And as Hapsburg policy meant the preservation of the Catholic cult, heresy in the Low Countries would have to be stamped out at all cost.

RISING FEELING AGAINST PHILIP II.
GROWTH OF CALVINISM

Philip II of Spain (1555–1598) succeeded his father Charles who abdicated in Brussels on October 25, 1555. The new prince was typical of the age, absolutism being the guiding principle of his government. The ancient constitutional privileges of the towns and the provinces were ignored, the army was directed solely by the ruler, and the severe placards against heresy were to be enforced in the Low Countries without question, as were royal decrees in Spain. The Estates General which represented each of the provinces was to be relegated to the background. Thus all political activity was subordinated to his will and to the interests of his dynasty as Philip thought that traditional rights and liberties of town and countryside which had grown up in the Middle Ages could safely be overridden.

The history of Spanish domination of the Low Countries is the story of Philip's efforts to keep under the yoke a land which would help him to assume the role required of the head of the Hapsburg family as well as to acquit himself of his duty as the champion of Catholicism. The Low Countries were to be sacrificed for projects which did not concern them. Would Philip succeed? In this connection, it should be noted that he could draw little from Spain beyond a splendid infantry, and Naples added little to his vital strength. Milan was important, commercially and industrially, but was steadily being eclipsed in these respects by the Low Countries. Mexico, Peru, and Bolivia gave him much wealth. But of these lands the Low Countries were the most important, for they possessed a society which we may call modern. It was industrial and commercial and provided with the foundations necessary for a struggle against tyrannical absolutism.

Philip proceeded to put his ideas into effect, Margaret of Parma, his natural sister, being made regent to represent him in the Low Countries during his absence. She was assisted by a council framed after Spanish models and composed of three men, chief of whom was Cardinal Granvelle, bishop of Arras, and president of the Council of State. The other two members, Berlaymont and Viglius, were heads of the Council of Finance and the Privy Council, respectively. In reality this council of three transacted all business of importance, much to the disgust of the nobles who had always been consulted in the past and who therefore heartily hated Granvelle. Born in the Franche-Comté, Granvelle had risen in the service of the king because of his ability of making himself useful —he was a perfect tool of princely despotism. He did not understand the people of the Low Countries, nor did he speak Flemish.

William of Orange, chief and ablest of the nobles who now began to oppose Granvelle, was born in 1533 of the German house of Nassau which had long ago settled in the Netherlands. This family acquired vast wealth and also a princely title from the marriage of one of its members with an heiress of the little principality of Orange in southern France, and William's forbears had served the Burgundian house well ever since the days of Charles the Bold (d. 1477). As was characteristic of the times, William lived the easy life of prodigal noblemen. His experience in state affairs gave him keen insight into political problems. He learned to be Machiavellian. In religion he was Catholic, but in earliest youth had been a Lutheran. He believed that the repose and prosperity of the country should not be jeopardized by forcibly maintaining any legally established faith, and he was thus the first important prince to oppose religious persecution, a remarkable exception to the universal intolerance among princes of the time.

At the opening of Philip's rule William of Orange was stadholder of the counties of Holland and Zeeland—his position, wealth, superior qualities of mind, and affability making him a powerful personage in state and society. The count of Egmond, stadholder of Flanders and Artois, and the count of Hoorne became leaders with him in a determined opposition to Philip's methods. They were all latitudinarian in the matter of religion and, although Catholic, inclined to oppose the rigor of Philip which called for severity in the enforcement of decrees and greater activity by the Inquisition. Many a noble had been instructed in his youth by humanists whose admiration for Erasmus had inculcated repugnance to extremes in religion. A break between the nobles and Philip was inevitable. They insisted on a meeting of the Estates General for redress of grievances and removal of the Spanish soldiers who had been brought into the country by Charles during his last war with France and kept there by Philip for the same purpose. The Treaty of Cateau-Cambrésis (1559) now made an army superfluous. Charles' policy had been expensive, and princes as well as common people desired to have the soldiers withdrawn.

Philip left the Low Countries in 1559 and sailed to Spain, never to return, and Granvelle became the real head of government. His influence was increased by the reorganization of the Church, a step which Charles had repeatedly sought but had failed to achieve. During Charles' rule heresy had increased rapidly, and to save the faith it was necessary to revise its organization. The old divisions were obsolete, for they had been instituted in the earliest Middle Ages when the population was sparse, long before the growth of trade and industry began to dot the country with towns. This reorganization was effected by papal bull of May 12, 1559. Henceforth there were to be fifteen bishoprics and three archbishoprics, Mechelen, Cambrai, and Utrecht. Each diocese was to contain on the average about 160,000 souls, and appointments were to be made by the king and the pope. This change was made possible by new ideas about reform within the Church which began, as we shall see, to attain success as the result of the Council of Trent.

The discontent roused by this measure was intense. The nobles had not been consulted, and they were embittered by what they believed to be a new extension of despotism. Henceforth they would not be able to appoint members of their families to episcopal and other ecclesiastical posts since the king would nominate only those who would support him. The common people did not like it because they feared that the decrees against heresy would become effective. Abbots opposed it because some of the abbeys were now joined to the episcopal establishments in order to provide the necessary economic support for the new episcopal organization. Many of the laxer clergy were alarmed because they feared stringent enforcement of canonical regulations and inquiry into their worldly lives.

The result was that the nobles concentrated even greater hatred upon Granvelle who, they erroneously thought, was solely responsible for the novel measure.

Religious discontent aggravated the tension. Calvin's teachings now were vigorously propagated; they satisfied the temper of the day, for a system of dogma such as his, founded upon the "Word of God," gave clarity and definition to religion. Its semidemocratic character appealed where aristocratic Lutheranism failed. Calvinism was sacramentarian (but with a big difference), bore some impress of humanism, and therefore appealed to the more intellectual groups. In a time of tension this faith could unify where Melchioritism merely produced an explosion.

It is a mistake to suppose that Calvin's teaching was introduced into the Low Countries from Geneva directly by way of France alone. That the Huguenots were responsible for some of the propaganda is undoubtedly true, but some Netherlanders went directly to Geneva and Lausanne in order to draw their doctrine from the very source. Calvinist ideas first found foothold at Tournai when Pierre Brully began to preach. He was Calvin's successor in the French congregation in Strasbourg after the great reformer's departure for Geneva, and in 1544 he was active in the Low Countries whither he had been sent by Butzer in response to a petition. A martyr's death awaited him in 1545. Another Calvinist, Guido de Bray of Mons, who had published *The Rod of Christian Faith* in 1555, established a congregation in Lille in 1556. Soon Calvin's works were very generally known, and Geneva became the Wittenberg of Netherlanders.

England was likewise a channel for the dissemination of Calvinism. Persecuted Flemings and other Netherlanders had fled their native country during Charles' rule. Henry VIII had welcomed to England these industrious and skilled workers of cloth who could contribute to the economic upbuilding of his realm. They founded churches at Sandwich, Norwich, Colchester, and London. The last-named congregation was organized in 1544 and was given the chapel of the Augustinian Friars in Threadneedle Street as a place of worship. This church exerted much influence upon religious developments in the Low Countries, its Calvinist doctrine and organization being directed by John à Lasco (or Laski), a Polish nobleman who had become a disciple of Calvin, and by John Utenhove, a Flemish nobleman. Important influences also went forth from Embden in Friesland where à Lasco produced a catechism which was used by the London congregation. As tension increased under Philip's rule, other congregations were formed at Friderikstad in Denmark, and at Wesel, Frankfort on the Main, and elsewhere in Germany.

Agitation increased markedly when the First Huguenot War (1562–1563) broke out in France, many refugees fleeing to the Low Countries for safety. Philip's officials found it increasingly difficult to enforce the placards, and the inquisitor Titelman was followed in Flanders by menacing crowds of angry men. Revolution was probably averted by the royal French Edict of Amboise in 1563 which quieted the agitation in France as well as in the Low Countries, but only for a while. Calvinist preachers continued to address numbers of auditors in deserted places outside the walls of towns, and Bible reading increased in spite of inquisitors. Granvelle's enemies formed a league, with William of Orange as its spokesman and guiding spirit. Philip disregarded their requests, and bitterness became intense. Finally, Philip yielded (1564) when the regent joined Orange and Egmond in demanding Granvelle's removal.

Calvinism now made rapid progress. Many noblemen sympathized with it, and they formed the League of Breda (November, 1565) which presented a petition requesting that the Inquisition and laws against heretics be suspended. When they produced the document, one of Margaret's councilors referred to them as beggars, and this became the watchword of a movement which to Philip looked like rebellion. Times were hard, trade was at a standstill, and hunger threatened many a home. During August there were tumults in the towns of Flanders and Brabant. Churches and monasteries were plundered, pictures and images destroyed, and costly vessels and vestments stolen. Taught by Calvinist doctrine to regard the Mass as idolatry, the rabble profaned the Host. In 3 days 400 churches and chapels were treated in this manner. The movement next broke out in Holland and Zeeland (August, 1566).

Philip, deeply moved by the report of this desecration, appointed the duke of Alva to be regent in the Low Countries. His rule (1567–1573) was fatal to his master's schemes and proved a crucial moment in the history of the Low Countries. Alva instituted in all its severity a special tribunal modeled after those that had developed in Spain. It was popularly called the Council of Blood. If violence and tyranny can ever be successful, they should have triumphed in these lands. A Spaniard named Vargas, who understood neither laws, language, privileges, nor feelings of the people, acted as the directing genius of the tribunal. The tribunal was illegal, but Vargas was pleased to listen only to his master. To the protests of the towns that his acts violated their ancient privileges he replied contemptuously: "We do not care for your privileges!"

Meanwhile a rebellion led by Orange broke out in 1568. Alva's Spanish foot soldiers, more than a match for Orange's hastily collected troops, dispersed and defeated them, and Orange sought refuge among his kinsfolk in Germany to await a happier moment when he could come forward once more to oppose Alva. Hoorne and Egmond were executed by Alva on the Great Square in Brussels on June 5, 1568, a deed which caused Netherlanders to curse the king and his lieutenant. Alva now demanded from the Estates General a tax, copied after Castilian models, of one percent on all property, another of 5 percent on each sale of real property, and one of 10 percent on sales of movables.

Suddenly came the report that the beggars had seized Brielle, a seaport in Holland, on April 1, 1572. These men, because of the hard times, could no longer make a living by honest trade and were forced to a life of robbery on the high seas. They plundered the ships of all people, but especially those of Catholics and the hated Spaniards. Holland, Zeeland, Guelders, Friesland, and Utrecht now rose in rebellion. Since 1570 Gaspard de Coligny, the leader of the Huguenots, had swayed the mind of the French king Charles IX, who dreamed of an international offensive against Catholicism. Orange was to coöperate in this movement and was to receive help from French Huguenots with which he hoped to eject Alva and the Spaniards. However, the death of Coligny in the Massacre on the eve of St. Bartholomew's Day (August 24, 1572) in Paris made this coöperation impossible. Orange's invasion proved a failure, and he was forced once more to withdraw to Germany.

Freed from the necessity of facing Orange, Alva turned his attention to the reduction of Mons which also had risen. Zutfen next yielded to him without opposition, and he allowed his soldiers to massacre a large part of the population which was mostly Catholic. The same procedure was followed at Naarden (December 1, 1572). Haarlem's turn came next, although it held out stubbornly for 7 months, the inhabitants in desperation determining to die of hunger rather than surrender, which meant certain massacre. Exhausted by their desperate defense, they were, however, forced to yield. Many of the townsmen had died during the siege, but most of those who remained were summarily executed or tied back to back and drowned in the River Sparne. The next attack was made on Alkmaar, but it failed because the natives opened the dikes and flooded the countryside thereby forcing the Spaniards to retreat. This marked the turning point in the national resistance. "At Alkmaar began the victory," became a famous saying. The enemy next invested Leiden (1574–1575) but, thanks to the energy of Orange and the resolution of the townsmen, was unsuccessful, for the land around the town had been flooded, and the besiegers were forced to flee.

These heroic efforts from 1572–1575 form one of the thrilling themes in history, for they mark the beginning of independence for what was soon to become known as the United Provinces. But in the history of continental Europe they meant much more; they signified the defeat of Spanish Hapsburg dynastic ambitions, absolutism, and disregard for national interests. Philip hoped to advance Catholicism which in turn would serve as a buttress of his power. The national revolt of the Dutch also implied a religious revolt. Orange now accepted Calvinism as his faith and threw his lot in with that of the revolting provinces. A great synod was convened at Dordrecht in 1574. It adopted the Heidelberg Catechism and made Calvinism the official creed of the land.

CALVINISM IN THE PALATINATE, IN OTHER GERMAN LANDS, AND IN GERMAN SWITZERLAND

Calvin's teaching also won ground in Germany, especially in the lands along the Rhine. Elector Frederick III of the Palatinate (1559–1576) was much concerned over the rancor which had arisen among his subjects over Melanchthon and Luther, and, in order to satisfy himself as to the questions at issue, plunged into theological study. Gradually abandoning the Lutheran teaching, in 1561 he decided in favor of Calvin's doctrine about the Lord's Supper, and invited Calvinist professors to teach in the University of Heidelberg. His electorate now adopted the Reformed faith, and Catholic forms and practices which Lutheranism had left intact were swept away. Nevertheless, the milder theology of Melanchthon, especially in the matter of predestination, was not to be entirely overthrown. The Heidelberg Cathechism, drawn up in 1563, made no mention of it. This catechism became authoritative for the Reformed in other parts of Germany and either was adopted by or exerted much influence in Nassau, Hesse, Lippe, Bremen, Baden-Durlach, and electoral Saxony.

German Switzerland clung to Zwingli's teaching after the death of that reformer on the field of Kappel in 1531. Henry Bullinger (1504–1575), who succeeded to Zwingli's position, was born in the Aargau and educated in the University of Cologne, the chief center of old scholastic theology in Germany and a stubborn opponent of rising humanist studies. Nevertheless, Bullinger was estranged from the old faith even as a student. On his return to Switzerland he became a teacher in the monastic school at Kappel where he lectured on Melanchthon's *Loci Communes*. He was attracted to Zwingli and his teaching and in 1529 became pastor in Bremgarten, the place of his birth. After Zwingli's death his position became insecure because of the powerful Catholic reaction, and he fled to Zurich, where he was elected to Zwingli's post.

Bullinger became an important figure in the religious life of German

Switzerland. While many of the cantons accepted Zwingli's doctrines, they were not agreed about certain practices. The desire of Bullinger and Calvin for harmony led to the *Zurich Agreement* (*Consensus Tigurinus*) of 1549. Zwinglian ministers had sought before this to win the Lutherans of Germany to their views, but in vain. They now decided to abandon the Zwinglian teaching that the Lord's Supper was but a memorial, substituting instead Calvin's doctrine that Christ was present only in a spiritual sense, but many Swiss Protestants failed to accept Calvin's doctrine. A confession of faith, the *Second Helvetic Confession*, Calvinist in thought, was accepted in 1566 by all but Basel which did not yield until the next century.

CALVIN'S TEACHING IN POLAND AND HUNGARY

Calvinism won a temporary foothold in Poland. Luther's teaching had made a strong impression upon the nobility and the bourgeoisie of Great Poland where many Germans were living. But Lutheranism was an importation from Germany and thus did not satisfy Polish feelings. For this reason it found slight favor in Little Poland and other places where the Slavic element predominated. Calvin's doctrine proved more popular with these people, men who had enjoyed the advantages of a humanist education being especially pleased with it. Poland, it should be remembered, was an aristocratic republic managed more and more by the gentry, or *szlachta*. Members of this class were jealous of their privileges, did not care for a strong central monarchy, and preferred Calvin's conception of Church management by both clergy and laity to Luther's which allowed laymen no such influence, but placed ecclesiastical authority in the hands of princes. Furthermore, the teaching elaborated by Calvin's followers, that people had a right to resist rulers who governed contrary to the "Word of God," suited the nobility in their aspiration for independence. The *Institutes of the Christian Religion* became a popular book.

Queen Bona Sforza, wife of Sigismund I (1506–1548), was much interested in Calvinism. Her confessor, the Italian Lismanini, corresponded with Calvin, and the reformer dedicated one of his *Commentaries* to King Sigismund. The next king, Sigismund II Augustus, was a Catholic, but his wife Barbara, daughter of Nicholas Radziwill, chancellor of Lithuania, was a devoted follower of Calvin. She labored to spread the Reformed faith and translated the Bible, the result being that many priests became Calvinists and a large part of the nobility followed their example. So numerous were the Calvinists in the Diet of Piotrkow (1552) that they secured suspension of penalties inflicted in Church courts. It is instructive to find that even Catholic nobles supported them in their opposition to Catholic clerical jurisdiction. The result was that Calvinist nobles, more powerful than ever, so completely dominated the diet that the policy of repression was completely abandoned.

The Reformed faith also spread among the bourgeoisie of Little Poland where German immigrants were far less numerous. The movement was stimulated by the expulsion of the Bohemian Brethren at the order of King Ferdinand of Germany in 1548 and after. These followers of Hus were more closely in sympathy with Calvin's doctrines than with Luther's. They preferred, for example, the teaching that Christ was spiritually present in the elements of the Host. This was more in harmony with the view of Wycliffe. At the Synod of Kozminek in 1555 a union of both groups was effected. Calvinism, however, remained the faith of only a minority. The peasantry was staunchly Catholic, and the strong Lutheran element in the towns remained hostile. Hence it was impossible to establish a national Polish church. A condition of religious anarchy ensued in which each person chose what pleased him—Lutheranism, Calvinism, Socinianism, or Catholicism. Protestantism spread to such an extent that in the Diet of Warsaw (1556) it was decided that any member of the gentry might choose whatever faith he deemed best.

John à Lasco (1499–1560) was an interesting product of the Polish Reformation. Like many another noble, he was early introduced to humanism and became an enthusiastic follower of Erasmus. He spent some time in the great humanist's home in Basel and also became acquainted with the ideas of the Swiss reformers, Zwingli and Oecolampadius. From 1525 to 1537 he traveled about western Europe. On his return to Poland he found that he could not bring about a reformation according to Erasmian conceptions and so again started on his wanderings. His activities now became important. In his religious conceptions he was an eclectic, for while influenced by Luther in matters of dogma, he was Zwinglian in ritual and Calvinist in Church government, but his conceptions, which were essentially Erasmian, colored all his acts. He was tolerant of divergent opinions and exerted much influence at Embden, London, Frankfort on the Main, Wesel, Basel, Strasbourg, and elsewhere. He played an important part in bringing into England the Reformed or Presbyterian conceptions of Church and ecclesiastical government in the reign of Edward VI.

In 1556 à Lasco returned to Poland where he began an impossible task. It was hoped that his tolerance, numerous connections, and wide sympathies with all reforming groups might enable him to bring unity out of the Protestant chaos, but he died 4 years later, having accomplished little.

The idea of a Polish national church could not be realized, for Protestantism spent its strength in party strife while the peasantry and nobility of Lithuania and eastern Poland remained loyal to Catholicism. When the ancient faith became aggressive, Calvinism put forth no more effective resistance than Lutheranism.

Calvinism offered considerable appeal to the Magyars of Hungary. Lutheranism made some progress among them before 1540, but it was never cordially received because of its German origin. Magyar nobles were a haughty people, jealous of their privileges, and impossible to discipline. They did not like Germans and were opposed to the ambitions of German kings—it should not be forgotten that after the Battle of Mohácz in 1526 King Ferdinand of Germany claimed the Hungarian crown. To accept Lutheranism implied an extension of German influence, and here as in Poland nationalist antipathies prevented that faith from winning a large following among the non-German population.

The Turkish government was indifferent to the faith of the subject Hungarians, official repression being abandoned after the Battle of Mohácz. Nobles, who were given a great deal of freedom in things touching religion, did not care to help Ferdinand secure the crown, for that would lead to the establishment of Catholicism which, it was feared, would in turn support the dynasty. Nor did they like Lutheranism because it taught that princes must be obeyed in all things, and anything that promised to establish absolutism was distasteful to them.

It appears that Matthew Devay (d. 1546) was the first Magyar to accept Zwinglianism, but he soon adopted Calvin's teaching about the Lord's Supper. After 1550 Calvinism spread rapidly. Young men studied in Strasbourg and Geneva, and Calvin's and Beza's works were eagerly read. Kasper Karoli (1529–1592), one of the most energetic of Magyar preachers, translated the entire Bible into the Magyar tongue, and this book did for the Magyars what Luther's translation accomplished for Germans. Since all Reformed services were conducted in the native tongue, the new faith was never hampered by the fact that its literature and services were in German. The first organization of the new churches was effected in 1562 and 1563. The greatest reformer of Hungary was Peter Melius (1536–1572), to whom, more than to any other person, was due the fact that many Magyars became Calvinists. At the Synod of Debrecen in 1567 a definitive organization was adopted; but, while Magyars in some number became Protestant, the vast majority remained loyal to the ancient faith.

Chapter 15

SPREAD OF CALVINISM: FRANCE AND SCOTLAND

*A*FTER THE publication of the *Institutes of the Christian Religion* in 1536, advocates of reform in France had generally embraced Calvinism. The more cautious humanists made their peace with the Church but found that they could effect little among a group of officials whose concern was to protect the established order simply by destroying dissenters and silencing critics. The more pronounced this spirit of repression became, the more fiery were the reformers in denouncing the corruptions of the Church. Wealthy merchants and men of moderate means joined the movement, and many a student at the universities accepted the new doctrines. Even priests and monks cast their lot with the Calvinists, as the reformers were now called.

Quite different was the situation in Scotland, for there the Calvinist Reformation was a national affair, while in France it was regarded by many as something merely hostile to French interests.

THE FRENCH CROWN AND BEGINNINGS
OF CALVINISM

Calvin directed an incessant and vigorous propaganda in behalf of the "Word of God." Numerous pamphlets were published at Geneva, Lausanne, Neuchâtel, and Strasbourg, and were disseminated in all parts of France by daring colporteurs. Many a brochure on burning questions about religion was printed covertly on the presses of Lyons. Calvin carried on an enormous correspondence with Frenchmen encouraging them to cling to the faith and labor for the "Word of God." His French followers sent large sums of money to Switzerland. Young men zealous in propagating their newly found truths went to receive the pure doctrine at the very source from Calvin, Theodore Beza, Pierre Viret, and others. Returning as fervid ministers who preached the gospel with the greatest intrepidity, they addressed their followers in cellars, abandoned houses, fields, woods, and along little-frequented roads. Teachers carried on a bold propaganda among the young. Prosecution could not dampen their ardor, for those seized by the king's officials were replaced by others equally zealous.

These fervent preachers in many instances profited from the better humanist education of the day. Their sermons were concrete, to the point, and devoid of formal logic such as characterized the discourses of their opponents who possessed neither their zeal nor their learning. The upper clergy were to all intents and purposes political appointees. The hierarchy was a buttress of the throne. It can cause no wonder, therefore, that the bishops could not oppose the preachers successfully. It was their task to guard the Church, but their ideas drew biting sarcasms from men like Rabelais. There were exceptions, such as Bishop Jean du Bellay of Paris, but they formed only a minority. The professors in the universities, especially those who taught theology, were no better. Instead of reforming the Church and revising their methods of study, they sought to employ the old instruments of repression which had once worked so well. This dangerous expedient could not succeed now, for townsmen had become wealthy and numerous. Their lay humanist culture was more than a match for the superannuated methods of the old schools, and their Calvinist theology stiffened their opposition.

Francis I died in 1547 and was succeeded by his son, Henry II (1547–1559). The new king was sluggish in intellect but loved an active life. Henry was orthodox as far as he possessed any personal convictions, and from the point of view of political expediency he felt called upon to stamp out dissent because he feared that any damage to the Church would react unfavorably upon the throne. The chief influence at court was the Guise family of Lorraine. The old Duke Claude died in 1550, leaving three ambitious sons, Francis, who succeeded him as duke, and Charles and Louis, both cardinals. They were determined opponents of dissenters and eager to win for themselves important posts in Church and state. Their sister Mary had married James V of Scotland (1513–1542), and the young daughter of this union, the famous Mary Stuart, was betrothed in 1548 to the French king's son and heir apparent, Francis. Calvinists therefore could expect little leniency from the government.

Just before his death Francis I established a special tribunal at Rouen to take care of the great number of dissenters in Normandy. By royal ordonnance Henry formed a similar tribunal in the Parlement of Paris, the severity of its provisions causing the people to call it the Burning Chamber (Chambre Ardente). The Edict of Fontainebleau of December 11, 1547, forbade printers to print any books about Scripture or to publish any books brought into the land from abroad, especially from Geneva or Germany, or to offer them for sale unless first approved by the theological faculty of the University of Paris. Violators of this rule were threatened with imprisonment and confiscation of goods. Nor might printers and booksellers offer for sale copies of the Scriptures unless the printer's name and that of the person who had provided the notes and comments, with a statement of domicile, appeared on the title pages. The books might be exhibited for sale only in printers' or dealers' shops, and not clandestinely.

None of these acts had the desired result, and in spite of prosecution and capital punishment Calvinism kept on spreading. Accordingly, in November, 1549, another edict was issued, in the preamble to which were reviewed the efforts begun by Francis I to eradicate dissent. The degree of the royal disappointment is shown by the length to which the king was willing to go in coöperating with ecclesiastical tribunals. Officials were required to present persons to the judges appointed by the Church to take care of dissent, and these judges were given complete jurisdiction in all cases of dissent which did not arise from pernicious willfulness. In cases which were accompanied by some public disturbance or act of rebellion royal judges were to coöperate with the representatives of the Church when called upon. In the execution of these rules the officers of churchly justice could make arrests without permission from the royal officials and, in case of necessity, call upon them for assistance.

Since these provisions did not produce the desired result, a new decree was issued in June, 1551, the Edict of Chateaubriand. Its preamble once more recited the efforts which had been put forth to purge the realm of dissenters; its forty-six articles were an extension of the provisions of former edicts and revealed the care which the king and his councilors had bestowed upon the matter. Henceforth initiative in bringing to justice people who were guilty of sedition or other crimes accompanying dissent was to be taken by special royal judges (*juges présidiaux*) from whose decision no appeal could be taken. The royal exasperation is revealed by the provision that henceforth no books of any character whatever might be read if printed in Geneva or any other places which had forsaken the Roman Church. Penalty for violation of this rule was confiscation of property and corporal punishment. Other articles laid down rules for royal officials on many new points. Booksellers everywhere were required to keep a list of books approved by the theological faculties, and they were not to sell any books not listed. No one might write disparagingly of the saints or paint disrespectful pictures of them.

But these and other severe regulations were without result. Unlawful books were printed, foreign heretical works were hawked about by bold colporteurs, preachers persisted in addressing eager auditors, and large numbers sold their goods and betook themselves and their families to Switzerland or to Germany. Nor did prosecution stop the spread of dissent. Especially interesting is the case of five ministers who came from Lausanne, where they had studied with Pierre Viret and Théodore de Bèze, and who proposed to preach the "Word of God" to Frenchmen. They were apprehended before they had said a word about their mission, but according to Article 38 of the Edict of Chateaubriand they were guilty of a serious offense. The Swiss cantons put forth their best efforts to save them from the stake, but in vain, for they were burned to death in May, 1553. Such stirring martyrdoms became a popular theme. Accounts of them were collected by Jean Crespin in his *Acts and Monuments*, one of the more remarkable martyrologies of the Reformation. But all this show of energy was unavailing; still the heresy spread. In September, 1555, the first Reformed Church was founded in Paris. Its minister was Jean de Macon or La Rivière, a dauntless youth of rare ability, and elders and deacons were named to constitute the consistory.

It is a remarkable fact that these terrible laws often caused the judges to show sympathy toward the unfortunates. The king was greatly disturbed by their leniency and accordingly in July, 1557, issued the Edict of Compiègne. All preachers and others who had taken any part in public meetings or in conventicles, and those who were found to be sacramentarians—that is, Calvinists—who had dishonored the Virgin, the saints, or images, and others who had led people astray or had sold unlawful books or had visited Geneva, were to receive the death penalty. Judges were not to change these rulings in any way. Thus a secular tribunal was to dispose of purely religious offenders. So zealous was Henry against dissenters that he even thought of establishing the Inquisition in the realm, and would have done so had not the Parlement of Paris opposed it.

All these repressive endeavors proved a complete failure. In Paris, under the very eyes of the Parlement itself, meetings were held in the Rue St. Jacques. In September, 1557, the royal officers raided this meeting house, and a large number were seized and sent to the stake. It was useless to attempt to suppress heresy among people who coveted the crown of martyrdom. Most remarkable was the effect which this relentless policy produced upon the judges of Parlement. Charles of Guise, Cardinal of Lorraine, declared that their sympathy was in large part the cause of the rapid growth of heretical doctrine, and special sessions of Parlement were held (1559) to test the opinion of the judges. When asked what methods should be adopted to bring people in the realm back to the old cult, some of the judges made bold suggestions. Relying upon the dignity of their office, some of them demanded a council to settle the legality of heresy and requested that the edicts should be suspended in the meantime. Anne du Bourg was so bold as to insist upon this point, and warned that it was a serious matter to burn to death people of exemplary life who called upon Christ while writhing in the flames. This speech cost him his life.

The Reformed Churches of France adopted their national synodal organization in 1559. The Calvinists of Paris had formed their Church in 1555, and their bold example was followed in many parts of France. A closer organization was felt to be necessary. Divergent views about predestination had risen in Poitiers in 1558. A number of ministers and elders met covertly in May, 1559, in a house in the suburb of St. Germain, a Parisian minister named de Morel presiding. They represented the Churches of Paris and a number of other towns whose names are not all known. The synod drew up a *Confession of Faith* and several articles about discipline. The Confession was a digest of Calvin's theology, and the discipline was drawn from the Churches of Geneva and Strasbourg. Each Church was to have a minister, elders, and deacons who constituted the consistory. Ministers were to be chosen by the elders, deacons, and congregation; and elders and deacons were to be elected by the congregation. Churches were to be grouped into provincial synods which in turn were to be organized into general synods, and a national synod was to represent the entire Church.

FIRST BEGINNINGS OF REFORM IN SCOTLAND

The Reformation in Scotland was peculiarly the product of local conditions. The country possessed a primitive social organization. Tribal life still flourished in the Highlands and heads of the clans lived in blood feud. Unrestrained by the royal will, the baronage dominated the Lowlands. The Scottish Parliament was merely an assemblage of greater barons who exercised inordinate influence in public life. Because of this condition and the absence of taxable wealth, the crown's authority remained elementary. Aside from Edinburgh, Dundee, and Perth, the towns were but hamlets, for commerce and industry which had contributed so much elsewhere in Europe to the destruction of tribal, manorial, and feudal conditions had as yet exerted little influence in Scotland.

Under these circumstances the Church, which owned a large share of the land, became an appanage of powerful families, important livings being held or controlled by sons of the baronage. Furthermore, churchmen in Scotland often were ignorant, uncouth, and incompetent. But social conditions were changing. Commerce was growing, and towns were becoming more active, and the quickened economic life helped produce new conceptions.

Foreign relations exercised a decisive influence upon religion. For centuries English kings had sought to win the Scottish crown, and to prevent this, the Scots had enlisted the aid of France. Scottish politics therefore were dominated by the age-old rivalry of England and France. James IV (1488–1513) had married Margaret Tudor, daughter of Henry VII of England, Henry hoping thereby to strengthen English ties with Scotland and thus prepare the ground for an ultimate union of the two crowns. But in 1513, James joined France in the war upon England and was defeated on Flodden Field (September, 1513). This humiliation at the hands of the ancient enemy perpetuated among the Scots the popularity of the French alliance, and, when Henry VIII broke with Rome, an additional reason for hostility was created.

James V (1528–1542) married Mary of Guise, or Mary of Lorraine as she was known in Scotland. She was a daughter of Duke Claude of Guise, head of the powerful Lotharingian family which was to play a prominent role in the French Wars of Religion. The Scottish royal house was thus bound to the Catholic cause. Thus the crown, Catholicism, hostility toward England, and the foreign connection with France were all linked together. Relations between Henry VIII and his nephew James, which were anything but cordial, finally led to an invasion by the English. James' troops were defeated at Solway Moss in 1542, and the king died soon after, heartbroken because of the disaster.

James left his realm to an infant daughter, Mary Stuart, born soon after the defeat, his wife Mary of Lorraine acting as regent until her death in 1560. Henry VIII desired to unite Mary Stuart in marriage with his son Edward, and a treaty was drawn up in 1543 arranging the terms. But the violence in the English invasion of the Lothians so inflamed the Scots that national hatred again flared up with all its ancient intensity. The Scots sought support from France, and the Scottish Parliament agreed to the betrothal of the infant heiress to Francis, son of the French king Henry II. Under Edward VI (1547–1553), another invasion was planned by the duke of Somerset who was in authority in England. The Scots were again defeated (1547), and the southern counties were sadly pillaged. In their wrath the Scots determined upon Mary's speedy marriage and sent her to France. Thus the conduct of these invasions kept the two crowns apart.

Meanwhile religious dissent was growing. There had been Lollards in the realm, but they appear to have become extinct by the opening of the Reformation. Lutheran books and pamphlets spread over the land, and in

1525 Parliament forbade their importation. The first Scottish Protestant martyr, Patrick Hamilton, was a Lutheran. He showed interest in the new ideas, visited Wittenberg where he became acquainted with Luther and Melanchthon, and studied at Marburg. On his return to Scotland in 1527 he began to teach at the University of St. Andrews. He publicly expressed belief in justification by faith only and asserted that the pope was Antichrist, whereupon the bishop of St. Andrews seized and tried him. He was found guilty and sentenced to a heretic's death. Although he was tied to the stake at noon, so unskillful were the executioners that he lived until six. He showed rare constancy in this dreadful ordeal, asking his accusers standing around him to prove their faith "by putting a little finger into the fire with which I am burning with my whole body."

George Wishart, another important martyr, was more deeply interested than Hamilton in humanism. Returning from a visit to Switzerland in 1543, Wishart began preaching, was seized by Bishop Beaton of St. Andrews, tried, and burned to death in 1546. He taught Reformed doctrines and exerted much influence upon John Knox (1513–1572), the chief figure of the Scottish Reformation. Born near Edinburgh, the son of peasants, Knox like Luther displayed many of the characteristics of that humble class. "Knox was the true flower of this vigorous Lowland thistle. Throughout life he not only 'spoke what he would,' but uttered 'the truth' in such a tone as to make it unlikely that his 'message' should be accepted by opponents. Like Carlyle, however, he had a heart rich in affection; no breach in friendship, he says, ever began on his side. . . ." He was educated in St. Andrews and became a priest in 1540, but he fell under Wishart's influence 5 years later and henceforth was an advocate of Reformed doctrine.

Meanwhile dissent made rapid progress, although the government suppressed new doctrines whenever possible. Ballads were composed satirizing priests and friars, and English Bibles circulated in great numbers. Later when Mary Tudor ruled in England (1553–1558), many Englishmen fled to Scotland in order to avoid prosecution.

Bishop Beaton was hated for his share in the death of Wishart, and less than 3 months after the burning was surprised in his castle by the sea and hanged without ceremony (May, 1546). The murderers ensconced themselves in the episcopal castle, where they were joined by Knox, who thus seemed to approve the murder. The regent of Scotland besieged them and with French help took the castle. Knox began a 19 months' career as a galley slave in a French man-of-war (1548–1549). When freed, he became the minister of a church at Berwick, was promoted to another post in Newcastle, and was offered the see of Rochester during the reign of

Edward VI. When Mary Tudor ascended the English throne Knox hurried to the continent and went to Geneva where he formed a close friendship with Calvin. For a brief time he served a group of English exiles at Frankfort on the Main but was forced to leave because he was so bold as to compare Emperor Charles V with the persecutor Nero. He returned to Geneva to preach to the English congregation there. Meanwhile he watched closely the situation in Scotland and in 1555 concluded that the moment had arrived for a vigorous attack on the established faith.

Knox was not mistaken in holding this view, for agitation was more and more pronounced, and humble Scottish folk were becoming deeply concerned in religious questions. Pious ballads circulated among them, some of these songs expressing complete trust in Christ's crucifixion.

> I call on Thee, Lord Jesu Christ,
> I have no other help but Thee,
> My heart is never set at rest,
> Till Thy sweet word comforteth me.
> A steadfast faith grant me therefor
> To hold by Thy word evermore
> Above all things never resisting,
> But to increase in faith more and more.

This evangelical sentiment produced criticism of the cult of saints:

> To pray to Peter, James, or John,
> Our souls to save, power have they none,
> For that belongeth to Christ alone,
> He died therefor, He died therefor.

Some of the songs were directed against the Catholic clergy:

> Priests, Christ believe,
> And only trust in to His blood,
> And not in to your works good,
> As plainly Paul can prove.
> Priests, learn to preach
> And put away your ignorance,
> Praise only God, His work advance
> And Christ's people teach. . . .
> Priests, mend your life
> And leave your foul sensuality
> And vile stinking chastity,
> Let each one wed one wife.
> Priests, pray no more
> To St. Anthony, to save thy sow,

> Nor to St. Bride, to keep thy cow,
> That grieveth God full sore.

The pope also received his share of criticism:

> The pope, that pagan full of pride,
> He has us blinded long,
> For where the blind the blind doth guide,
> No wonder both go wrong;
> Like prince and king, he led the reign,
> Of all iniquity,
> Hay trix, tryme go trix, under the greenwood tree.[1]

The rest of the stanzas express criticism of clerical morality.

These songs reveal the fact that the old Church as ark of salvation had lost its appeal to many people. In its place had come the teaching that salvation was gained only through faith in the merits of Christ whose role as Savior was set forth in "God's Word." Calvinist theological thought ruled the minds of these folk, hence their hatred of idolatry.

SCOTLAND BECOMES CALVINIST

Upon his return to Scotland in the fall of 1555, Knox found that the Reformation had indeed gone forward. He preached in Edinburgh and other places and finally was summoned to appear before the courts for violation of the laws against heresy, but so many supporters crowded about him that the government dropped the matter. Knox soon returned to Geneva but left a determined group of followers to extend his teaching, which they did with success. Meanwhile opposition to Mary of Lorraine, who had become regent in 1554, and her foreign and Catholic policy grew rapidly.

The next step to be taken was one in harmony with Scottish political tradition. Often in the past groups of nobles and others had banded together for some special purpose, and this was to be the practical method of bringing about the Reformation. A faction of nobles met in Edinburgh on December 3, 1557. These Lords of the Congregation, as they were called, vowed that they would use their life and property in establishing the "Word of God." They assailed the idolatry of the Catholic Church and denounced the Church as the "Congregation of Satan," this language without doubt being inspired by the vigorous exhortations of Knox. What caused the lords to take so determined a step was the fear that if Mary

---

[1] Adapted from *A Compendious Book of Godly and Spiritual Songs* (The Scottish Text Society), Edinburgh, 1879, pp. 65, 67, 195–197.

Stuart became queen of France she would subordinate Scottish national interests to French policy. Negotiations for her marriage to the Dauphin Francis were already in progress, and the ceremony took place on April 24 of the next year. Thus Protestantism and Scottish national interests seemed arrayed against Catholicism and the French alliance.

Knox returned from Geneva in May, 1559, a thundering prophet of "God's Word" who feared neither noble nor sovereign. He met a zealous group of Protestants at Dundee and on May 11 preached a sermon in St. John's Church in Perth in which he denounced the "idolatry of the Mass." After the sermon the people began breaking images in this and other churches in the town. A remarkable pamphlet, *The Beggars' Summons*, had appeared addressed to the friars who were accused of having "stolen" from the people the hospitals committed to their care, and advising them to go to work, and "steal" no more. Whitsunday was the day set when the friars were to be ousted. This fiery composition expressed the tense feeling in the hearts of the people against clerical property, for Church holdings were very extensive, some estimates running as high as one half of the land of the realm.

Reformation had begun. The Lords of the Congregation were actively opposed to Mary of Lorraine who possessed a decided superiority over them, for she had brought into the country a large force of French soldiers who were superior to the untrained levies of the lords. Meanwhile Mary Stuart became queen of France, for Henry II died unexpectedly in July, 1559, and her Guise uncles encouraged her to assume a more active policy in suppressing heresy. When a new force of French soldiers was introduced into the country, the reformers, feeling that help was necessary, appealed to Queen Elizabeth of England who had succeeded Mary Tudor in 1558. Elizabeth, a Protestant and daughter of Anne Boleyn, was a heretic and illegitimate in the eyes of Catholics, and therefore unfit to rule.

As granddaughter of Margaret Tudor, Mary Stuart claimed a better title than Elizabeth and many Catholics agreed with her. In fact, it was Mary's hope some day to mount the throne of England. Hence Knox and the Lords of the Congregation were led to seek support from Elizabeth against the regent, Mary of Lorraine. The Reformation was a national revolt against the ancient French connection, substituting for it a policy of friendship with Protestant England. Elizabeth was loath to assist the Scots, for she did not approve rebellion nor did she like the outspoken Knox who rarely tempered his words with caution. He had issued a violent pamphlet, the famous *First Blast against the Monstrous Regiment of Women* (1556), directed against Mary of Lorraine and Mary Tudor. Knox had the hardihood to write that "to promote a woman to bear rule above any realm is repugnant to nature, contumely to God, a thing most contrarious to His revealed will and approved ordinance; and finally it is the subversion of good order, of all equity and justice." Elizabeth disliked this work and never could forgive the author; and this ill feeling at first prevented cordial relations between the queen and the Scots.

But Elizabeth did not permit her resentment of the reformer to dictate her policy, for she perceived clearly that her safety demanded the removal of French troops from Scotland. Therefore she listened to suggestions from the Lords of the Congregation, and sent money and a fleet in 1560. These united forces began a siege of Edinburgh, but this proved an impossible task. Mary of Lorraine died on June 10, and one great obstacle to a settlement was removed, for her Guise supporters were not in a position to protect Mary Stuart's interests because of difficulties in France.

The Treaty of Edinburgh, arranged on July 6, provided that only a handful of French soldiers was to remain in the realm, and Mary Stuart and her husband Francis II of France were not to employ force against England, nor were Frenchmen to hold office in Scotland. Not a word was said about religion but, as the future was to reveal, the Lords of the Congregation, being in power, were to have their way. This treaty was a revolution in the history of Scotland in that it changed her foreign policy, made possible the future union with England, prepared the way for Presbyterian doctrine, and marked the arrival to power of the smaller baronage and the bourgeoisie who had never played a part in national affairs.

The defeat of Mary's French policy was greeted with enthusiasm, solemn thanks being offered in St. Giles Cathedral. Soon another step was taken. Parliament met as had been provided for in the treaty, but instead of limiting attendance to those who had been in the habit of coming, many new members were admitted. Persons concerned about religious questions found their way into the assembly, among them townsmen, petty nobles, and preachers of the Gospel. In former times rarely more than twenty nobles had attended; now there were over a hundred who took an active interest in matters of state. The session began on August 3, and its policy was a foregone conclusion. This most important Parliament in Scottish history completely broke with the old faith, its members asking the ministers to draw up a *Confession*. Knox took direction of this work, and the strictly Calvinist statement which resulted was accepted by an overwhelming majority. Opposition to these proceedings was limited almost entirely to the few mitered members bold enough to attend.

Three acts were passed on August 24. Under the first, all authority of the pope in the Scottish Church was declared at an end, and temporal and spiritual jurisdiction was taken from the prelates. The second act repealed every statute against heresy, and the third declared the Mass to be illegal. Penalty for celebrating Mass or attending such celebration was provided—imprisonment and confiscation of goods for the first offense, banishment for the second, and nothing less than death for the third.

Parliament took another important step when it ordered the ministers to prepare an organization for the new Church. *The First Book of Discipline* was laid before the new Parliament in January, 1561, Calvin's ideas being closely followed. The Churches were organized in presbyteries which were grouped into a general assembly. The *Confession* was to be the rule of faith, and a system of national education was sketched; care of the poor was also provided for. But difficulties arose in disposing of the property of the ancient Church, for Knox held that it all should pass to the new Kirk; but many a nobleman had enriched himself with Church lands during the recent disturbances, and it was futile to hope that they would give them up.

Mary Stuart set foot in Scotland on August 19, 1561. An extremely beautiful woman, she possessed a refined intellect, and wherever she went she won the enthusiastic admiration of men. But she did not have the subtle craft which made Elizabeth so successful. Mary was great as a woman, but Elizabeth was great as a Machiavellian politician. Mary, devoutly Catholic, was eager to restore Catholicism but found it impossible to bend the ministers to her will. Dour and outspoken, Knox never yielded to her blandishments. His interviews with her are famous, the following being the report of one of them:

> "Well then I perceive that my subjects shall obey you and not me; and shall do what they list and not what I command: and so I must be subject to them and not they to me."
>
> "God forbid," answered Knox, "that ever I take upon me to command any to obey me, or yet to set subjects at liberty to do what pleases them. But my travail is, that both princes and subjects obey God. And think not that wrong is done unto you, when you are willed to be subject unto God, for it is He that subjects the people under princes, and causes obedience to be given unto them; your God craves of kings that they be, as it were foster-fathers to His kirk, and commands queens to be nurses unto His people. And this subjection unto God and His troubled kirk, is the greatest dignity that flesh can get upon the face of the earth, for it shall carry them to everlasting glory.
>
> "Yea, but ye are not the kirk that I will nurse. I will defend the kirk of Rome, for it is, I think, the true kirk of God. . . . My conscience is not so.

"Conscience, madam, requires knowledge; I fear that right knowledge you have none."[2]

The queen's policy failed chiefly because of certain defects in her character. Feminine sentiments dominated her activities and led to her undoing. She sought to win the crown of England, and the Catholic world generally agreed that she should have it rather than Henry VIII's illegitimate daughter Elizabeth.

Mary married her cousin Lord Darnley who next to herself possessed title to the English crown. This would have been a politic move if Darnley had proved a worthy husband, but Mary had fallen in love with him because of his handsome exterior, failing to note that he was incapable of any intelligent conduct which might help her. Inordinately vain and jealous, he murdered Mary's secretary, the Italian, David Rizzio. The queen thereupon conceived the greatest loathing for Darnley and fell under the influence of the earl of Bothwell, an able and dashing soldier but a man of evil ways and unscrupulous withal. Mary fell in love with him, and the result was that Darnley was killed when the house in Edinburgh in which he was staying was blown up with gunpowder. The queen was said to be privy to this murder, and the public openly accused her of complicity.

What made matters worse was Mary's immediate marriage to Bothwell. The queen's enemies thought to depose her and raise in her stead her infant son by Darnley, the future James VI, born after the murder of his father. Finally Parliament, in spite of her resistance, forced her to abdicate under threat of prosecution. It was during these days that the famous Casket Letters, written by Mary to Bothwell, were brought to light. The originals have been lost, and only copies are extant. As they were produced by the queen's enemies, many have questioned their authenticity. If they are genuine, they prove beyond a shadow of doubt her complicity in the fate of Darnley. The question of their genuineness, however, is a difficult problem which challenges the critical ability of scholars.

Mary planned to regain the crown and escaped from Lochleven Castle where Parliament had placed her. She raised some troops, but her forces were not equal to those of her opponents and in a skirmish at Langside they were worsted. Mary fled across the Solway and threw herself upon Elizabeth's mercy (1569). Her further fortunes were mingled almost entirely with those of the great political Catholic reaction and will be traced under that heading. Whatever chance Mary had of saving some-

[2] Adapted from A. Innes, *A Source Book of English History*, Cambridge, 1902, I, 326–327.

thing for Catholicism in Scotland was ruined by her folly, and her flight put an end to any possibility of Catholic reaction in Scotland. Her son James VI, who became a pedantic theologian and a convinced Protestant, ruled in harmony with the wishes of the Scottish Kirk and soon became practically the head of the religious establishment.

The Reformation, a decisive event in Scottish history, was far more than a religious movement. It was a period made memorable by the rise of the lower nobility to power in state and society. Nationalist sentiment, which the historian encounters so often in the turmoil of the sixteenth century, aimed at effective direction of the state by its monarch. Mary Stuart failed lamentably, for she proposed to use Scotland as an element in the international Catholic reaction, to the detriment of national welfare. Catholicism and nationalist sentiment were opposed to each other, and Catholicism therefore was defeated by the national will. It was but another example showing how secular concerns proved more powerful than religious doctrine. Furthermore, on the ruins of the old order her son James VI was able to construct a royal absolutism such as Scotland had always lacked. The Reformation helped make Scotland a modern state.

PART VIII

Catholic Reform

Chapter 16

THE FOUNDATIONS OF THE
CATHOLIC REVIVAL

*T*O OBSERVERS in 1540 it seemed that Catholicism had reached the moment of dissolution. Scandinavia was Lutheran. Northern and central Germany had abandoned the old faith. Lutheran propaganda was active in Hapsburg and Bavarian lands. Lithuania, Poland, and Hungary were inclined to welcome heresy. Swiss cantons for the most part had embraced the doctrines of Zwingli or Calvin. England had established her own national Church. In France Calvinism was gaining ground. The Low Countries were filled with hostile teaching. Revolutionary Anabaptism had indeed been put down at Münster only a few years before, but another outbreak was feared; and many princes, states, and cities were sternly repressing people who practiced rebaptism. Protestantism was active sporadically even in Spain and Italy. Would the tide ever turn?

THE ROOTS OF CATHOLIC SURVIVAL

Forty years later in 1580, the situation was quite different. Catholic reform was triumphant in Italy, southern Germany, Spain, and the southern Low Countries; and even in France it was evident that Calvin's doctrine could not win the people. What was the cause of this change? It has often been said that reform of Catholicism was due to the rise of Protestantism which insisted on purification in the Church. This undoubtedly was a factor, but scarcely more. Reform was due to the fol-

645

lowing conditions: (1) persistence of traditional piety among the lower classes, (2) zeal of the Spanish rulers and other princely families, (3) ardor of cultivated Italians, the finest intellectual product of the Renaissance, (4) rise of new religious orders, (5) reforming efforts of the papacy which were stimulated by the rise of Protestantism and which began with the accession of Paul III in 1534, and (6) the Council of Trent (1545–1563).

Let us first review the social conditions from which Catholic reform drew its strength. The countryside everywhere remained the stronghold of the old cult. Peasants clung to their priests and reluctantly obeyed their princes when commanded by them to embrace new doctrines. Often it proved impossible to force them to forsake Catholicism. In Poland, for example, they remained staunchly loyal to Rome while townsmen and nobility coquetted with the doctrines of Luther, Calvin, or the Sozzini. Italian peasants never changed their faith, and even in Brabant and Flanders heresy was essentially a bourgeois movement. The unchanging countryside with its conservative population saw no reason to abandon the old cult in which generations had lived and died.

The Renaissance has been shown in previous chapters to be mainly a bourgeois movement which did not affect the rural population to any extent. Its critical spirit, sardonic wit, and sarcastic literature did much to sap the old faith, and clamant abuses and corruptions caused many to hate the Church or to ignore it. But the cultivation of humanist learning required leisure and wealth, which were possessed only by the upper bourgeoisie. The lower classes among the townsmen usually shared but scantily in the new culture; they too remained conservative in outlook. The proletariat might experiment with radicalism, as was illustrated at Münster, but, when it failed, they were likely to return to the old cult. It was to such people that Savonarola made effective appeal.

It is a common error to assume that all humanists abandoned Catholicism. It should be remembered that humanism arose in Italy in a Catholic environment, and its devotees, formally at least, remained faithful to the Church. They believed in the perfectibility of man and advocated the full development of his powers. Since they thought that secular excellence was good and noble, they could not agree with Luther and Calvin that all such activity was totally worthless in meriting salvation. Therefore humanists generally rejected their teaching that the will was totally enslaved. Herein lay the significance of Erasmus' contest with Luther. Nor could they sympathize with the other-worldly and unintellectual views of most Anabaptists. Humanists saw little reason for abandoning the old faith, especially before the rigid reforms of Pope Paul IV (1555–1559) began.

First, we should review some of the more important reforming humanists of Italy. The Oratory of Divine Love was a society of priests and laymen who fervently desired renovation in religion and who proposed to begin the work of reform by dedicating their lives to all kinds of religious activities. The Oratory in Rome was founded during the pontificate of Leo X, and its members were wont to meet in the little church of St. Silvester and St. Dorothy on the right bank of the Tiber. Other Oratories had previously been founded in Genoa and Milan. A fervent love of God and fellow man, born, in part at least, of the great zeal for platonic teaching during the Renaissance, characterized their religious life. Gaetano da Thiene of Vicenza (d. 1547), known also as St. Cajetan, was an illustrious member of the order. Born in 1480, he led a devout life amid the secularity of the Renaissance, laboring zealously in serving the poor and alleviating the suffering in hospitals. The example of his work in Rome, Vicenza, Verona, and Venice proved contagious. It is interesting to note that although extremely devout he did not enter the priesthood until 1516.

Gian Pietro Caraffa, another member of the Oratory, was born of Neapolitan parents in 1476, studied theology, and was rapidly promoted at the papal court under Alexander VI and Julius II. It is remarkable that he escaped the corruptions of this environment and lived all these years in the brilliant High Renaissance of which Rome was the center without ever giving up his austere morality and his medieval philosophy and conception of life. He was a man of much physical and mental vigor, recalling in this respect the *virtù* of great characters of the Renaissance. The see of Chieti was entrusted to him in 1504, and he soon began the toilsome task of reforming his diocese. So successful was he that by 1513 he felt that he had accomplished this work. As a member of the Oratory of Divine Love, he associated with other spirits who like himself were convinced of the necessity of reform in the Church and of purification in official religious life. Out of these ideas grew the Order of the Theatines which demanded a thorough reform of the secular and regular clergy.

Gian Matteo Ghiberti was born in Palermo in 1495, rose in the service of Leo X, Adrian VI, and Clement VII, and became bishop of Verona in 1524. A man of noble life unsullied by the worldliness of the time, he profited much from intercourse with noble personages in Rome. He knew Caraffa and associated with members of the Oratory of Divine Love. After the sack of Rome in 1527 he went to his see and began active reform of the clergy and the religious life of the laity. He carefully investigated every priest, suspended all who disgraced the clerical cloth, vetoed non-residence, insisted on preaching and administering the sacraments, and zealously discharged his visitorial duties. He supported the charitable institutions of the diocese and applied relief wherever necessary. He emphasized the study of Scripture in a humanist but orthodox manner.

Ghiberti's example stimulated other bishops. Cardinal Ercole Gonzaga (1505–1563) reformed the see of Mantua which he ruled with the utmost moral rigor. Gasparo Contarini (1483–1542), born of a Venetian patrician family, was originally a member of the Maggior Consiglio of Venice, thus gathering much practical diplomatic experience. He was a man of pure life and sincere piety and as a humanist was the center of a coterie of noble spirits who loved books and discussion on exalted themes. Although a layman, he was well versed in patristic literature. In his younger days he wrote a book about the duties of bishops. He helped in the reformation of the sees of Mantua and Verona and, after becoming bishop of Belluno in 1536, vigorously put an end to many abuses. Gregorio Cortese (1489–1548), abbot of San Giorgio Maggiore in Venice, was a reformer of monasteries and also a humanist who became the center of an important group.

The Church laid claim to a very high calling as an institute of salvation, and she should have kept herself without spot or wrinkle in the eyes of the world. But it proved difficult to keep the Church uncontaminated throughout the Middle Ages; secularism and indifference triumphed during the Renaissance, and the papacy all too often appeared indistinguishable from secular government. The cry for reform had been raised repeatedly but was hushed with the failure of the Council of Basel (1431–1449). Protestants criticized the Church unsparingly, and Catholics like Eck, Campeggio, and Cajetan also felt the imperative need of renovation. The significance of the newer type of prelates lies in the fact that they addressed themselves to concrete abuses and corruptions. They worked with the people and the clergy and themselves set an example of what the clergy should be. This appeal met with ready response. Indeed, the success of Catholic reform was in large measure due to this very thing.

Many a humanist layman, devoutly attached to the old faith but longing for reform, criticized the Church. Michelangelo, who had abundant opportunity to witness the worldly character of the papacy under Julius II, expressed his feelings in this sonnet:

> Here helms and swords are made of chalices:
> The blood of Christ is sold so much the quart:

His cross and thorns are spear and shields; and short
    Must be the time ere even His patience cease.
Nay let him come no more to raise the fees
    Of this foul sacrilege beyond report!
    For Rome still plays and sells Him at the court,
    Where paths are closed to virtue's fair increase.
Now were fit time for me to scrape a treasure!
    Seeing what work and gain are gone; while he
    Who wears the robe, is my Medusa still.
God welcomes poverty perchance with pleasure:
    But of that better life what pope have we,
    When the blessed banner leads to nought but ill?[1]

Humanism produced no nobler person than Vittoria Colonna (1490–1547), a woman who combined in her religious devotion the piety of the old faith with inspiration from the Oratory of Divine Love. None of her sonnets expresses this better than the following:

From joy to joy, from one to other hand.
    Of such and gentle thoughts, supernal Love
    From the hard winter and the cold thereof
    Guides me to springtide's warm and verdant land.
Haply the Lord—since He beholds me stand
    With breast like wax whereon the eternal seal
    Hath deeply cut a faith profound and real,
    Moulding my inmost beneath His hand—
Wills not with bitter cross and steep ascent,
    But with the easy yoke and burden light,
    To lead me into port by some smooth road.
Or it may be this little peace is lent
    By the wise goodness from my Father and God
    To arm and fit me for a weary fight.[2]

SPAIN—THE WELLSPRING OF REFORM

Catholic reform first actively began in Spain. For centuries Spaniards had fought the Moors. The *Song of Roland* (eleventh century) gave a vivid conception of the crusading ardor of warrior pilgrims who followed the long road from France to Galicia to worship at the shrine of St. James of Compostella. The Cid Campeador became a national hero because of

---

[1] *The Sonnets of Michael Angelo Buonarroti*, tr. by J. A. Symonds, London, 1912, p. 5.

[2] M. Jerrold, *Vittoria Colonna with Some Account of her Friends and her Times*, London, 1906, p. 286.

his fame won in combat with the infidel. Many a great event in Spanish history is associated with the struggle against the invading infidel—we need think only of the Battle of Las Navas de Tolosa (1212) and the military orders such as Calatrave, Alcantara, and St. James of Compostella. In no other land was Christian mysticism so deeply entrenched. Among the greater mystics were Francesco de Osuna (d. 1540), San Pedro de Alcántara (1499–1562), both Franciscans; Juan de Avila (1500–1569), St. John of the Cross (1542–1591), and Luis de León (1528–1591). The mysticism of these men was of an intensely practical kind, for they accepted the teachings of the Church as unquestioned truths and sought to arrive at religious satisfaction by the route of purgation, illumination, and unity with God. Out of this environment came Loyola and St. Teresa.

Isabella began her rule in Castile and León in 1474. The soul of this great woman was intensely pious, and she glowed with the zeal of Spanish mystics and the inspiration of heroes who had won fame in the fight against the Moors. She became the wife of Ferdinand of Aragon in 1469, and together they gave Spain more effective government than it ever enjoyed in the Middle Ages. Their absolutism was made possible by the support of a loyal bourgeoisie, for town and crown united in restricting the nobility whose ideals were so contrary to the aims of the new monarchy. Thus began a new era in the peninsula. Loyalty toward Catholicism became a chief element in Spanish nationalism, for Spaniards were resolved to destroy the Moors and to put down the Jews. The former stood in the way of national unity and safety; the latter were hated because of their suspected sympathy for the Moors. The Spanish Inquisition, founded in 1480, was an ecclesiastical organ in the hands of the rulers, designed to exterminate heretics hated equally by Church and crown. The zealous Thomas Torquemada, the first inquisitor-general, organized its activities and procedure; and in the 18 years until his death in 1498 he is said to have burned about 2000 people. His severity has given odium to the practice of compelling people to accept an established faith under threat of death.

The conquest of Granada was achieved in January, 1492. National ambition to bring all parts of the peninsula under the royal sway had led the Catholic sovereigns to attack this last stronghold of Moorish power. The defeated Moors were given considerable privileges. They were to retain the use of their language and be free both in the practice of their faith and in the education of their children. They were guaranteed personal freedom, were to live under Moorish law, and in all litigation were to be tried by their own judges. This liberal policy, inspired by the queen's gentle confessor, Archbishop Talavera of Granada (1428?–1507), contrasts vividly with the vigor applied to the Jews, who in March, 1492, were given 4 months to leave the realm or accept Catholicism.

Isabella's zealous devotion to the faith was directed by the fiery Ximenes de Cisneros (1436–1517). In 1492 he became her confessor and was named provincial of the Franciscans in Castile, and 3 years later was appointed archbishop of Toledo. A man of deep piety and austere morals, he was eager to reform the Church and insisted that members of his order should live in complete Franciscan poverty. He also extended his efforts at renovation to the other regular clergy and to the secular clergy of his province. Being interested in education, he secured the appointment of men of learning to canonries. The new Renaissance culture met with little favor among the average churchmen who were trained in the methods of medieval schools, possessed no vital learning, and had been named to their posts through special influence.

Ximenes was a man of lowly birth and, like many a youth of that class, was educated in canon and civil law. The promotion of such a man was a significant event in the history of the Spanish Church, for all important posts until this time had been occupied by members of the nobility. Ximenes was one of that class of lowly subjects who eagerly supported monarchs against a lawless nobility. He owed nothing to the nobles and so was ready to oppose them. Nor was he wedded to old intellectual conceptions, for he appreciated the new learning at its true worth. His great importance lies in the fact that he made it a useful servant of Catholic culture. In Italy humanism often acted as a disintegrating force, but in Spain it became a bulwark of the old faith. The example thus established was followed by Jesuits, reforming popes, bishops, and universities.

Urged by Ximenes' desire for severity, Talavera's mild policy toward the Moors came to an end. Although the Moors had loyally accepted the conditions imposed after the fall of Granada, these promises were speedily broken, and revolts broke out in 1501. Isabella now ordered that all Moors should abandon their faith or leave the realm under pain of death. Their copies of the Koran and other religious writings were seized and cast into the flames. Peace was restored after much fighting, and the Moors were forced to choose either death or baptism. Ximenes assumed control of the Inquisition as grand inquisitor. He also led a crusade against the Moors on the African coast opposite Spain in which Oran was seized and Algiers was blockaded, for the Spanish government feared that the African Moors would help their brethren in Spain. This crusade was Isabella's darling project, but Ximenes was not able to accomplish much because the queen's treasury was exhausted. Ximenes was made a cardinal in 1507.

Ximenes wished to revive the study of Scripture which had fallen into decay because of the methods employed during the late Middle Ages. This work was undertaken at the University of Alcalá, founded shortly after the opening of the sixteenth century, and Ximenes brought to its faculties learned men from Paris, Salamanca, Bologna, and other places. One of the most remarkable contributions made by the scholars of Alcalá was the famous edition of the Scripture, the *Complutensian Polyglot*, in whose preparation the new philological knowledge produced by the Italian Renaissance was employed. The work, which embraced six large volumes, was finished in 1517 and was published with the sanction of Leo X in 1520. The leading feature of this work, the most scientific book on Scripture in the sixteenth century, was the reproduction of the text of the Bible in all original languages, as well as in the Vulgate version.

THE PAPACY OF THE RENAISSANCE

From this survey of the social situation in Spain it is clear that there still was much vigor in the traditional cult. Many humble folk, humanists, and some princes evinced a fervid desire to purify the Church; and even in the darkest days of its degradation there was not entirely lacking, even in the papacy, some feeling that reform should be undertaken. The worldly pontiff Alexander VI (1492–1503) named a commission which reported that sales of benefices and the practice of pluralities should be curtailed. But the pope was immersed in the political concerns of the States of the Church and nothing could be accomplished. Nor was Julius II (1503–1513) better able to take in hand the task of reformation, for it was a cardinal point in his policy to drive foreign powers, especially France, out of Italy, and this absorbed all his energies. Angered by the pope's policy, Louis XII of France (1498–1515) retaliated by attacking him in his spiritual rights, a step which threatened to start an avalanche of criticism against the papacy. Louis called a synod of the French clergy at Tours in September, 1510. This body, which was Gallican and national in sentiment, declared that French kings possessed the right to defend their realm and crown against the bishop of Rome even to the extent of withdrawing from his obedience. Louis went so far as to appeal to a general council against the pope and revive the decrees of the Council of Basel. The prelates insisted on a council in which Julius' conduct and character should be discussed freely. Meanwhile there was revolt in the curia itself, and in 1511 Cardinal Carvajal, who personally desired reform, and a small number of other cardinals supported by Louis, called a general council to be held at Pisa on September 1, 1512.

The schismatic meeting at Pisa would possess no authority in the eyes of Christendom, and Julius II met this move of the cardinals by summoning a council to meet in the Church of the Lateran in Rome in April, 1512. The purpose of this Lateran Council was to reform the Church, prepare for a crusade against the Turks, and put an end to schism. Emperor Maximilian was inclined to oppose the pope, but Germans desired reform in the financial and judicial relations between their country and the curia which had been demanded repeatedly since 1457 in the *gravamina* or complaints drawn up by the German diets. They were opposed to the drastic step contemplated by Louis and did not send envoys to Pisa. Julius II died shortly after the fifth session of the Lateran Council, and Leo X succeeded him. The council had begun in May, 1512, but accomplished nothing save declaring the council at Pisa illegal.

Discussions were held about reformation of the Church, and a committee was appointed. Little could be accomplished because the papacy of the Renaissance throve all too much on the financial abuses and malpractices which corrupted it, and reform measures therefore could not strike at the root of the problem. A number of decrees were issued, but they concerned such minor problems as certain types of exemptions from episcopal jurisdiction, visiting convents exempt from such control, and supervision of printing presses. As on former occasions, papacy and prelates feared that reform would hurt their interests and so were loath to put their hands to the task. Because of this hostility ecclesiastical authorities succeeded in evading all serious consideration of reform, and the council came to an end in May, 1517.

When Leo X died in December, 1521, it appeared for a moment that the Renaissance papacy had also come to an end. Adrian VI, a Netherlander, was elected to succeed him in January, 1522. Adrian of Utrecht was pious, virtuous, austere, and filled with a desire to reform the Church. Educated by the Brethren of the Common Life, he had studied theology and philosophy at Louvain, taught as a professor in that university, and became tutor of Charles, son of Ferdinand and Isabella. Adrian was a friend of Cardinal Ximenes, was appointed bishop of Tortosa, and in 1518 became inquisitor-general of Castile and León. He was named Charles' viceroy in May, 1520, and he finally became pope, due to his master's influence, but he was not exalted by this honor. "To God only is it easy thus suddenly to uplift the lowly. This honor brings me no gladness, and I dread taking upon me such a burden. I would much rather serve God in my provostship at Utrecht than as bishop, cardinal, or pope. But who am I to withstand the call of the Lord?"

A man of such temper would be a lonely stranger in the Rome of the Renaissance. It would be impossible for him to work with the cardinals and officials who had been appointed by Alexander VI, Julius II, and Leo X, for they did not relish his ideas about reform and were not interested in a crusade against the Turk. They viewed him as an ascetic barbarian from the north, unschooled in the refinements of Renaissance society, and cared little for the piety of the *Imitation of Christ*. Adrian was criticized because he was slow in bestowing canonries and other posts in his gift, nor did the Romans like his Netherland servants. The courtiers were disappointed by his empty treasury; his economies caused resentment. Nevertheless, he went ahead with his tasks. He withdrew all permission given to princes since Innocent III to present candidates for benefices, for he wanted to fill all posts in the future with good men.

Adrian was much concerned over corruption in the Church. Leo X had done nothing to eradicate it and had not properly appreciated the gravity of the Lutheran revolt until it was too late. Adrian sent his nuncio Francesco Chieregati (1479–1539), an able diplomat and a man of pure life, to the Diet of Nuremberg to present the papal ideas about heresy and reform, with instructions to make a frank statement about corruption in curia and hierarchy. Adrian declared his determination to proceed at once with reform in the Holy See itself, thus setting an example to the world. Chieregati delivered this message in January, 1523. It was a most remarkable declaration, but it did not make Lutherans eager to return to the Church; rather it steeled them in their convictions, for now they could point to the admissions of the supreme pontiff himself to prove that the Church was honeycombed with corruption.

Adrian was supported in his zeal for reform by the views of Dr. John Eck who visited the Vatican in the spring of 1523. Eck painted a sad picture of the rampant abuses which destroyed the piety of the people. Flagrant misuse of indulgences, venality of benefice hunting, taxes imposed for dispensations, and the system of taxation practiced by the curia were cited as causes. Eck argued that in these circumstances it was futile to issue bulls against heretical teachings and that reform should be initiated at once. A general council could not be successful because at that moment Europe was so divided politically between France and the Hapsburg powers that no harmony would be possible. Honest reform should begin in the curia. Special attention should be paid to the clergy of Germany in the matter of preaching, management of dioceses, teaching, and personal conduct of the clergy. Eck also presented some concrete proposals for reform such as appointment of visitors for each archdiocese, suspension of the University of Wittenberg, and frequent provincial and diocesan synods. But the time for a successful comprehensive program had not yet arrived.

Adrian VI died in September, 1523. His pontificate was too brief to accomplish much, but it was important. "If Adrian is judged only by the standard of success, no just verdict will be given. The significance of his career lay not in his achievements, but in his aims. In this respect it is to his undying credit that he not only courageously laid bare the scandals in the Church and showed an honest purpose of amending them, but also with clear understanding suggested the right means to be employed, and with prompt determination began reform at the head."[3] The politically minded son of the Renaissance, Clement VII (1523–1534), succeeded him and any serious thought of reform had to wait until the elevation of Paul III in 1534. However, an event occurred during Clement's pontificate which sobered many minds—the terrible devastation of the peninsula during the second war (1526–1529) between Charles V and Francis I which culminated in the horrible sack of Rome in 1527. This date, which virtually marks the end of the High Renaissance, was also a turning point in the history of the papacy, for vigorous reform was to be undertaken within a few years.

[3] L. von Pastor, *The History of the Popes from the Close of the Middle Ages*, IX, 125–126.

Chapter 17

NEW RELIGIOUS ORDERS

CATHOLICISM DREW enormous strength from its monastic institutions during the Protestant revolt. Man as a religious being does not live in a vacuum but in a complicated and intensely practical environment, and religion therefore becomes a social force of the greatest importance. In the age of Catholic reform the Church witnessed a remarkable revival of the ascetic spirit which had played so significant a part during the Middle Ages.

The new orders which now arose proved that religious and ascetic impulses in the old Church were far from extinct. These bodies sought to translate once more into action the social conceptions inherent in Catholic teaching, and they thus are worthy continuators of the Benedictines, Premonstratensians, Franciscans, Dominicans, Augustinians, Beguines, Alexians, and the Brethren of the Common Life. Some of the new orders were formed to remedy specific social evils; others were created to combat Protestant beliefs.

NEW ITALIAN RELIGIOUS ORDERS

First of the new orders to be considered is that of the Sommaschi. The second war between Charles V and Francis I (1526–1529), which reached its climax in the sack of Rome in 1527, had wrought great havoc in Italy. Contending armies harried the land in accordance with the custom of the age. Especially tragic was the misery inflicted upon Venetia and the Milanese, the most populous parts of the peninsula. Spanish and other troops lived on the country and converted it into a barren waste. The inhabitants were reduced to starvation, homeless waifs wandered about the countryside, and unburied bodies lay along the roads and streets.

Girolamo Miano (d. 1537) or St. Jerome Emilian, the founder of the order of the Sommaschi, was born in 1481. He became a soldier, was

656

taken prisoner, and passed through a religious experience which led 'him to adopt an ascetic view of life and devote his energies to good works. His labors among unfortunates during and after 1528 entitle him to be remembered as long as men live, for he helped the needy, buried neglected bodies, and collected, educated, and fed waifs. He founded orphanages in Brescia and Bergamo. He associated with himself such devoted priests and laymen as he could find. Although their activities embraced many parts of Venetia and Milanese, the little village of Sommasca was the center of their organization whence they received the name Sommaschi. Gian Pietro Caraffa of the Theatines befriended them, and a hospital for incurables founded by this order at Venice was turned over to the Sommaschi.

The order of the Barnabites, who were very much like the Sommaschi, was founded by a nobleman named Antonio Zaccaria (1502–1539). He and a number of like-minded men, in an effort to counteract the hideous ravages caused by the second war between Charles V and Francis I, organized a society of clerks regular which in 1533 was changed into an order. The center of their organization was the monastery of St. Barnabas in Milan, for which reason they were called Barnabites. The Barnabites were active in caring for destitute children and in teaching religion among the lower classes. They took pains to stir the feelings of the ruder sort of people by open-air missions and public exercises of penance; they were to be seen, crucifix in hand, preaching in the most crowded thoroughfares; some carried heavy crosses, others confessed their sins aloud. They were organized after the model of the Theatines (see below), and like them also were interested in stimulating the zeal of priests, some of their reforms being adopted later by Archbishop Borromeo of Milan. The Angelice, a sisterhood with the same object, was established by Luigia Torelli.

The Ursulines were founded by Angela Merici (1469–1540). Left an orphan while young, she turned to religion for comfort and became a member of the Third Order of St. Francis. She brought together a number of young girls who thought like herself, and their activities centered in Desenzano on Lake Garda. Later she resolved to form a religious community to teach children and care for the sick, dedicating herself to this ideal in 1535. St. Ursula became the patron of the community, and their organization spread among the towns and villages around Brescia. The Ursulines were supported by Borromeo, and such was their popularity that they were welcomed in most Catholic lands. Paul III approved their society.

The Theatines were founded by Gaetano de Tiene or St. Cajetan (1480–1547) and Giovanni Pietro Caraffa (1476–1559). These members of the Oratory of Divine Love desired a stronger association to infuse fresh vigor into religious life, and the new order was to be composed of priests wholly devoted to preaching and administering the sacraments. Organized as clerks regular, they did not dissipate their energies in striving for wealth, a thing which had brought reproach upon many secular priests. Absolute poverty was not a popular ideal in the Renaissance, but Pope Clement nevertheless issued a letter favoring their petition (1524). The associates took the three vows of poverty, celibacy, and obedience, surrendered their benefices, and began living a common life on the Pincian Hill in Rome. Caraffa was chosen superior.

The group lived in great austerity, preaching in public, administering the sacraments, caring for the sick and destitute pilgrims who thronged Rome, and tending the dying in the hospitals. The hospital for incurables founded by them in Venice has been mentioned above. The order spread rapidly throughout Italy. Pope Paul III chose Caraffa to help him in the work of reform, making him a cardinal in 1537, and henceforth Theatine ideas led in the reformation of Church and religious life. Gaetano's work in Naples proved important, and St. Paul's church in that city became an influential center. The service was made more dignified, and greater decorum was insisted upon, a procedure especially needed among the lax Neapolitans. Gaetano revived the practice, popular even today, of reproducing the holy manger at Christmas time. Although Franciscans had been fond of this custom, it had apparently fallen into disuse. The example of these vigorous and zealous Theatines proved a mighty influence in papacy, Church, and popular religious life.

The Capuchins formed a striking contrast to the Theatines, for many of the latter were nobles and the order long retained an aristocratic air. The Capuchins, however, were Franciscans and perpetuated the popular sympathies of their founder. The Franciscans were divided into two groups: Conventuals who did not follow the rule of St. Francis in all its severity, and Observants who aimed to carry it out to the letter. But even the Observants were not strict enough for some members, for example, Matteo da Bascio (1495–1552). He had the robustness of the healthy peasant whose forebears had been inured to hard labor in the fields, and that natural refinement of character sometimes found among those who have tilled the soil they live upon, a spiritual quality gained in intimate communion with nature's mysteries. Matteo was much perplexed and finally thought that he heard a voice saying, "Observe the rule to the letter." He had heard that even the habit was not the same as it had been in the days of St. Francis, wherefore he adopted the pointed hood which was to become typical of the Capuchins. His views brought him into conflict with the Observants.

One night Matteo slipped out of the convent at Montefalcone near Fermo, resolved to go to Rome to lay the matter before the pope and implore his permission to live according to the original rule of St. Francis, a request which Clement VII readily granted. Retracing his steps, Matteo passed through Assisi where he renewed his vows at the tomb of St. Francis and then returned to his Umbrian convent. Since he had sprung from peasants and knew what pains and troubles oppressed humble folk, he worked unselfishly among the plague-stricken people of Camerino in 1523. He began preaching against sin, and, as he entered towns, was wont to cry, "To hell, to hell! ye usurers; to hell ye adulterers; to hell ye blasphemers!" Austere in morality and severe in denunciation as this prophet was, the people nevertheless loved him as one of themselves.

Clement VII commanded Matteo to present himself once a year to his minister provincial in token of obedience. This he did, but was received in an unfriendly manner. One year he was put into the prison of the friary, but was freed, however, upon the imperious request of the duchess of Camerino who had not forgotten the friar's service among her dying subjects a few years before. Matteo resumed preaching. His ideas were discussed far and wide by friars who believed that the rigid rule of St. Francis should be followed in all its details. Some of them, intent on following the rule closely, left their Observant brethren. Appeal was made to Clement who declared that the runaway friars were apostates, and included even Matteo among them. An effort was made to bring them back, first by force, then by persuasion, but the duchess of Camerino protected them, and they were allowed to live as they wished. They rendered noteworthy service to the poor during the terrible year of 1527, feeding and nursing the sick, comforting them as they lay dying, and burying the dead.

The Observants did not relax their efforts against the apostate brethren. But the duchess of Camerino interceded for her friars before the pope at Viterbo, whither he had gone after the sack of Rome in 1527, placing before him a petition for permission to follow the primitive Franciscan rule, preach to the people, and live under the protection of the Conventuals but to be governed by a superior of their own choice. Clement accepted their petition and on July 3, 1528, issued the bull *Religionis Zelus*. The new fraternity soon became known as the Order of Friars Minor Capuchin from the peculiar hood they wore. In accordance with their popular character, their constitution was drawn up in Italian, not in Latin. The house at Camerino, built in 1531, became the center of the order which did much to improve religious life among the lower classes of Italy. In 1538 women were permitted to live according to the Capuchin rule, and these Capuchinesses also rendered noble service among the destitute and lowly.

The Oratorians were founded by St. Philip Neri (1515–1595), who had received his first religious lessons from the Dominicans of San Marco in Florence. He went to Rome in 1532 and, although a layman, worked among the destitute and sick. He paid many a visit to the churches and the catacombs in order to pray. He began home mission work, the distinguishing characteristic of his life; he traversed the city, seizing opportunities of entering into conversations with persons of all ranks and of leading them on with searching questions, with words of wise and kindly counsel, to consider the topics he desired to set before them. He founded a confraternity whose task was to aid destitute pilgrims. He and his associates met for prayer at the church of St. Girolamo in Rome, and from these meetings arose the order of Oratorians, their object being prayer, preaching, and the celebration of the sacraments. Their preaching was especially successful, for their sermons were simple, direct, and free from the scholastic verbiage in which old-fashioned friars and priests were wont to address their auditors. They dealt with the lives of saints, passages from Scripture, themes in Church history, and practical topics. Gregory XIII approved the Congregation of the Oratory in 1575. It always remained an association of secular priests bound by no vows but living according to a rule. The Oratorians exerted much influence upon the people, especially in their emphasis on learning. Caesar Baronius (1538–1607), author of the *Ecclesiastical Annals* which contains a vast number of documents relating to Church history, belonged to their fraternity. The musician, Palestrina, one of their penitent followers, composed many of their lauds.

St. Camillus de Lellis (1550–1614) founded the order of the Fathers of a Good Death. Although in his earlier days a soldier, a gambler, and a spendthrift, he became a priest and brought together a number of devoted spirits to care for the sick in their homes and in hospitals. The order was confirmed by Clement VIII in 1592. St. John of God (1495–1550), a Spaniard, organized the Brothers Hospitallers of St. John of God, or the Brothers of Mercy, their duty being to serve the afflicted. Their first hospital was organized in Granada. Paolo Giustiniani founded a new congregation of eremites among the Camaldolese. They retired to inaccessible fastnesses in the mountains. Monte Corona was their chief center from which they received the name, the Congregation of Monte Corona (1522).

THE CARMELITE ORDER

Among fervent and influential Catholics none was more interesting than St. Teresa (d. 1582). Born at Avila in Spain in 1515, she early lost her mother. She became pious even in her earliest youth—at seven she and her brother planned to become martyrs. "With this brother," she wrote, "I used to discuss how it might be accomplished. We decided to go to the country of the Moors, begging our way 'for the love of God,' and to be beheaded there. And I think the Lord had given us courage enough even at so tender an age, if we had seen any way of accomplishing this. Only the greatest obstacle seemed to be our parents." Teresa and her brother actually set out on their journey, but an uncle led them back to their home, and Teresa entered the Carmelite convent in Avila where she spent many years in mystic contemplation. Her writings became famous. Her soul smitten by the fact that the Order of Carmel had greatly declined in the rigor of its religious life, she founded the house of barefooted Carmelites at Avila in 1562, its members devoting themselves to contemplation and prayer. In this way she reformed the nuns of Carmel. The monks of Carmel followed this example, St. John of the Cross (1542–1591) receiving his spiritual guidance from St. Teresa. He wanted to join the Carthusians because of their strictness but finally was persuaded by her to become a Carmelite. In spite of some opposition he successfully introduced his reforming ideas into the whole Carmelite order.

The chief characteristics of the spirituality inculcated in the Carmelite order were the supreme importance of God, man's nothingness, and the striving for complete detachment from creatures in order to arrive, under divine grace if it is given, at a state of contemplation. Carmelite spirituality, in spite of the limited numbers of monks and nuns in the order, exerted extensive influence far beyond the cloisters.

THE JESUIT ORDER AND ITS CONTRIBUTION

Important as these orders were in the service of the Church, that of the Jesuits overshadowed them all. The founder of the Jesuits, St. Ignatius Loyola, was born in the kingdom of Navarre in 1491. His family belonged to the petty nobility, and it was natural that Ignatius should dream of a soldier's life. He wished to acquire the graces of chivalric intercourse and hoped to cut a pleasing figure among noble ladies. His father sent him to a nobleman's home to be brought up as a page, and ultimately he planned to go to court.

Wounded at the siege of Pamplona in the first war between Charles V and Francis I, he was carried to a hospital where his leg had to be broken because it had been improperly set. He submitted to the ordeal in characteristic fashion—he said nothing, not a groan escaped him; he merely clenched his fists. When the leg was healing, it was discovered that he would ever after be deformed, for part of the bone protruded, and this would prevent him from wearing gracefully the trunk hose then in fashion. He submitted to an operation in which the flesh was cut away and the bone sawed off; but the leg now was found to be shorter than the other. He could never be a knightly figure, for he would always be lame! The surgeons stretched his leg in an iron frame, and he became very ill; fever racked his body. But in all this agony he was fortified by the chivalric idea indicative of an iron will. He called for knightly romances, but as none could be found he was given some lives of saints and a life of Christ.

The conversion of Ignatius Loyola is one of the most interesting in the history of religion. He was charmed by the tales of the saints whom he admired in chivalric fashion—for them and the Virgin he would break a lance; he would defend them with all his might. He began to regret his misspent youth and yearned to exceed even the greatest saints in the service of the Virgin. So ill was he that it seemed he would die, whereupon he received the last sacrament, but in a vision St. Peter promised that he would recover.

As soon as Ignatius was well enough, he set out, his leg still unhealed, on pilgrimage to the monastery of Montserrat near Barcelona. Clad in the garb of a penitent, he began his austerities.

> With *Amadis de Gaul* still in his head, he resolved to 'watch his arms' at the church of Our Lady of Montserrat. Here, then, on the eve of the Annunciation, March 24, 1522, you have our Ignatius seeking a beggar on whom he bestows his fine clothes; then girding himself in the sackcloth gown which symbolized his armor of poverty, he hangs up sword and dagger by Our Lady's statue, and watches through the night before the altar—now kneeling, now from much weakness leaning on his staff. Never religious order had such chivalric birth. For on that night, one may say was born (though yet its founder dreamed not it) the Company of Jesus, the Free-Lances of the Church.[1]

Ignatius' religious experiences in the cave of Manresa near Montserrat, the goal of his pilgrimage, have been preserved in his *Spiritual Exercises*. This book is but one example of a vast literature on the ascetic life which

---

[1] F. Thompson, *St. Ignatius Loyola*, London, 1910, pp. 17–18.

Christians had developed ever since the early Middle Ages, and in it Loyola set forth the object of such exercises in these simple words:

> Man is created to praise, reverence and serve God our Lord, and by this means to save his soul; and the other things on the face of the earth are created for man, and to help him in the pursuit of the end for which he is created. Whence it follows that man ought to use them in so far as they help him to this end, and to rid himself of them in so far as they hinder him from attaining it. For which purpose it is necessary to make ourselves indifferent to all created things, in all that is allowed to the freedom of our free choice and is not forbidden it; in such sort that we do not desire on our part health rather than poverty, honor rather than dishonor, a long life rather than a short one, and so of all the rest, only desiring and choosing that which better leads us to the end for which we are created.

This is the foundation of his ascetic psychology.

The *Exercises* are divided into 4 parts, or weeks. The first week contains exercises intended to show the hideousness of sin, the second the incarnation and Christ's mission as Savior, the third His sacrifice on Calvary, and the fourth His resurrection and ascension. This was the typical procedure of mystics, who taught that a person advances through four steps: didactive, in which he is taught the facts; purgative, in which the process of purifying the soul of all extraneous desires is achieved by contemplating the earthly mission of Christ; illuminative, in which the soul acquires the mystical truth through spiritual eyes; and unitive, in which the soul learns to feel with a calm joy the presence of God.

A striking feature of Ignatius' method is its concreteness, as vivid as that of Flemish primitives, the five senses providing, as it were, the material basis for the imagination. The second contemplation of the second week may be chosen as typical:

> *First Point.* The first point is to see the persons. That is to say, to see Our Lady, and Joseph, and the maidservant, and the infant Jesus after His birth, making myself a poor little creature and unworthy little slave, considering them, contemplating them, and serving them in their necessities as though I found myself present, with all deference and reverence possible; and afterwards to reflect within myself in order to draw some profit.
>
> *Second Point.* The second: to consider, to notice and to contemplate what they say, and reflecting within myself, to draw some profit.
>
> *Third Point.* The third: to observe and to consider what they are doing, for example, how the journey and toil are in order that the Lord may be born in extreme poverty; and in order that at the end of so many hardships, of hunger, of thirst, of heat and of cold; and all this for me. He may die on

the cross; and all this for me. Afterwards reflecting to draw some spiritual profit.[2]

Many readers find the *Exercises* difficult to follow. This is inevitable, for Ignatius did not give a complete exposition. He merely set down the essential points to guide the person leading the devotions; all directions must be followed implicitly, step by step, for about 4 weeks. They are skillfully arranged and charged with so much practical pedagogical insight that the result is tremendous, for by focusing the mind's attention upon the concrete facts of the drama of Christ's sacrifice, the soul finally arrives at a state of exaltation. Ignatius used this book in recruiting his followers, and many a layman was helped by it to rededicate his life. As a master-piece of religious literature it ranks with anything that Luther or Calvin wrote, and it became the textbook of militant Catholicism.

At Manresa, Ignatius attracted some followers. He devoted much energy to saving souls, and from the beginning showed keen interest in preaching and teaching among the destitute and neglected; this later became a prime concern among Jesuits. In 1523 Ignatius resolved to go to Jerusalem to fulfill his vow made when he was ill. He sailed from Barcelona to Gaeta, and from Gaeta he went afoot by way of Rome to Venice, where he begged food and slept in the Piazza of San Marco. He took ship for Jaffa and finally reached Jerusalem. He could not preach, for the Benedictine abbot who possessed authority in this matter deemed it impolitic as it was likely to stir the Mohammedans to opposition. Eagerly he visited the spots hallowed by association with Christ's life, and he sadly turned back to Venice whence he proceeded to Genoa, finally arriving in Barcelona in 1524.

Ignatius had learned much, and it was clear to him that his resolve to preach and teach could not succeed in the sophisticated world of the Renaissance and in a society teeming with heresy. Therefore, he would go to school and acquire learning. Ignatius went to study with boys in a beginners' school in Barcelona. He had been trained in the manner approved for gentlemen in the Middle Ages, in chivalric excellence but not in things of the intellect. To learn Latin and Greek is a difficult task for a person over thirty, but Ignatius persevered, believing it the devil's work whenever his mind wandered away from the declensions and conjugations. As soon as he could follow higher studies he went to the University of Alcalá. There he persisted in converting souls with such vigor that he was suspected of heresy. Indeed, he was thrice arraigned before the

[2] *The Spiritual Exercises of St. Ignatius*, ed. by C. Latty, London, 1928, pp 13, 54–55.

Inquisition, but such were his devotion and patience that he was acquitted.

In 1528 he went to the University of Paris and entered the College de Montaigu where Erasmus and Calvin had studied. He attracted a number of zealous spirits whom he won to his plans. Led by Ignatius, this little group of six—Lefèvre, Xavier, Laýnez, Salmerón, Rodriguez, and Bobadilla—finally after ripe deliberation went to the little chapel of St. Denis on the slopes of Montmartre north of Paris in August, 1534. Lefèvre celebrated Mass and, facing his companions with the Host in his hands, received from each the vows of poverty and celibacy, whereupon Lefèvre also pronounced the vows for himself. They proposed to take no fees after they should become priests and vowed to go to the Holy Land and work for the conversion of infidels. If this should prove impossible, they were to place themselves at the disposal of the pope. In January, 1537, they all met at Venice to carry out their vows, and here they refused the invitation of Caraffa to join the Theatines. They devoted much time to teaching and serving in hospitals until they could proceed to Rome to obtain papal approval. There were now ten in their company, for Broet, Codure, and Le Jay had joined them.

Meanwhile Ignatius was admitted to the priesthood, having spent a whole year in solitude to prepare himself so that he could take in his hands so holy a thing as the consecrated Host, the substance of Christ's body. Since Venice was at war with the Turks, it was impossible to go to the Holy Land; and consequently in 1538 Ignatius and two companions went to Rome determined to place themselves at the disposal of Pope Paul III. Meanwhile they continued teaching the people and serving the poor and needy, especially in hospitals. Cardinal Contarini was sympathetic to their plan, and the Company of Jesus was officially recognized, their constitution being ratified in the bull *Regimini Militantis Ecclesiae* (September 27, 1540). Thus came into existence the greatest agency created by Catholicism to stimulate the faith of the common people, bring back into the fold many whose minds were tainted with hostile teaching, and through persuasion and argument check the advance of Protestantism.

The novitiate in the Jesuit order began with the *Spiritual Exercises*, and at the end of 2 years novices of ability took the vows of poverty, celibacy, and obedience, and were called scholastici; those of slight ability were to become secular coadjutors. The scholastici were required to study theology, science, and the humanities in the colleges of the order, and after about 12 years they were ordained priests. If they succeeded in fulfilling all tests and took the fourth vow of absolute obedience to the pontiff, they were admitted to the professed who formed the central element of the order. A general congregation chose a leader who held office for life, and also heads of provinces and rectors who were to manage the houses of the order. Each official was to be absolute within his circumscription but was watched by agents chosen by the general congregation. Ignatius was chosen by his comrades to be their first general.

The Jesuits addressed their efforts to the humble and destitute, the great mass of common folk who composed the bulk of the Church, and whom these devoted priests sought to purge of heresy. Everywhere they introduced rigid discipline, and education was a most important instrument of reform. They appropriated the humanist pedagogical ideals developed in the Italian Renaissance which had so often been used, as in the case of Erasmus, to the detriment of the faith; but these ideas now became a means of strengthening the Church. Theologians of the order fought for the faith at the Council of Trent and wrote polemical treatises, and science and literature were cultivated which won universal respect for the Jesuits. As confessors to rulers and princes, they were able to save whole regions for the faith.

Chapter 18

REFORM IN THE PAPACY

one thing on each of popes

$\mathcal{T}$HE YEAR 1534 is an important date in the history of the papacy, for then it was that Alexander Farnese became Pope Paul III. Ever since the pontificate of Sixtus IV (1471–1484) popes had been guided by secular interests. The incumbency of Adrian VI (1522–1523) was but a brief interlude, and his efforts at reform seemed fruitless, for they were followed by the pontificate of the worldly-minded Clement VII (1523–1534). Alexander Farnese, or Paul III, as he was subsequently called, now ascended the chair of Peter and began a renovation of the papacy which was so successful that he may be regarded as one of the greatest of popes.

PAUL III (1534–1549) AT THE TURNING POINT OF REFORM

Alexander Farnese was born in 1468 at the time when humanists were beginning to play a part in the cultural life of the papal court. Alexander himself was a pupil of Pomponio Leto and, like Michelangelo and many another Florentine humanist, studied in the household of Lorenzo the Magnificent. He entered the papal service under Innocent VIII and rose steadily, Julius II being especially gracious to him. Alexander had three illegitimate sons, in spite of the fact that he had been a cardinal since 1493. It should be noted, however, that he was not yet a priest and that in 1513 he broke with the laxness which he had acquired under the wordly Alexander VI. Due to the improvement in his moral life and his seriousness of purpose, his past was gradually forgotten. He built the Farnese Palace which still stands in Rome. A man of ability, he became the most important force in the curia during the latter days of Clement VII. At the moment of his elevation to the papacy he was respected universally for his moral uprightness and his zeal for reform. The people of Rome were pleased by the choice, and the best spirits in the Church approved the election of so sagacious a man.

667

Paul III has been accused of worldliness. It is true that he showed himself as keenly interested in political concerns as any of his predecessors; he was prone to nepotism and to favor the political fortunes of his son Pier Luigi. But it should cause no surprise that this son of the Renaissance did not completely abandon all the characteristics of that age. Rather one should emphasize the great moral change in his life after 1513 and his successful insistence that the papacy was a spiritual institution and that it had some right to be heard in the secular affairs of man. To Paul III more than any other pope is to be ascribed the beginning of a new age in the history of the papacy.

As soon as he mounted the chair of Peter, Paul announced that the work of reform would begin at once with the curia. To the great consternation of older cardinals, he insisted that no renovation was possible without a change of life in the curia. He appointed commissions to investigate the delicate matter of clerical morals, but this action was a little too precipitate. Accordingly as soon as the first new cardinals were created another commission was named to initiate reforms in the curia and the government of Rome and was given unlimited powers to remedy both secular and religious matters whenever necessary.

REFORM IN CURIA AND EPISCOPACY

At first it appeared that the pontiff would not emancipate himself from the vice of nepotism which had brought discredit upon the papacy. The promotion to the cardinalate of his nephews Guido and Alexander (December, 1534) created a bad impression, but the appointments of the following May were significant in that they included such men as Simonetta and Ghinucci of Siena, Gasparo Contarini of Venice, and John du Bellay of Paris. Many people were pleased at the advancement of worthy men, and the disappointment caused by the promotion of the pope's nephews was soon forgotten. The appointments of December, 1536, also were important. No better choice could have been made than Caraffa, who was one of the number. Reginald Pole of England also was appointed, as was Jacopo Sadoleto (1477–1547), bishop of Carpentras, one of the finest products of humanism and a noble light of the Church. Two years later others were admitted to the Sacred College, chief of whom was Pietro Bembo. His elevation provoked much comment, for, a typical son of the Renaissance, his earlier life had not been pure; but like Paul himself he had definitely abandoned the ways of his younger days and the prestige of his learning proved a valuable asset to the papacy. Others were added in 1539, three of whom were bishops: Federigo

Fregoso, Uberto Gambara, and Ascanio Parisani, all of whom were zealous for reform.

Paul disregarded the wishes of the older cardinals who, relishing no change, naturally expressed disapproval of the pope's choice of new cardinals. Paul understood the character of these men who had been appointed in the worldly days of Leo X and Clement VII. Furthermore, he had seen how the zeal of the Netherlander Adrian VI failed when it deserved better success, simply because the pope was a foreigner to Italy and did not understand the ways of Renaissance men. Consequently, instead of seeking to impose a rigid regime upon the cardinals, Paul wisely began laying the sure foundation for success by promoting the right kind of men. He showed additional wisdom by appointing French and Spanish prelates in 1535 and 1538, thus giving the Sacred College a more international character which he hoped would enable him to pursue a policy of neutrality toward Charles V and Francis I. It is to Paul's credit that his efforts in this difficult task were crowned with success.

At the same time the pope contemplated the proper steps toward other reforms. The appointment of Contarini was acclaimed by all those interested in cleansing the Church, and his influence was an important factor in the formation of the new papal policy. A commission of nine cardinals was appointed, and it submitted to the pope a *Report of the Cardinals and Other Prelates on the Reform of the Church* (March, 1537). Frank in tone yet respectful and devout throughout, it is one of the most remarkable documents of the Reformation.

The preface sets forth in the noble Latin of the Renaissance that the great ills of the Church have come upon it because former pontiffs all too readily had accepted the teachings of canonists and flattering courtiers that the papal power was absolute, and that they therefore had assumed full authority to dispose of all goods and rights of the Church which they had often exercised in a reckless manner with evil consequences. Then follow twenty-six sections discussing evils that needed reform—worldly bishops and priests had been appointed, benefices had been bestowed without regard to the worthiness of incumbents, an evil traffic in benefices had sprung up under the influence of canonists who were able to discover devious ways to circumvent canonical rules, and many cardinals absented themselves from the curia and did not discharge the duties of their office.

The memorial also complained that bishops were hindered in their work because culprits whom they wished to punish often obtained remission of canonical penalties at the pontifical court through the payment of money. Schools required careful supervision, for children received many impressions hostile to religion. They were permitted, for example, to read the *Familiar Colloquies* of Erasmus. Attempt was made to stop malpractices of indulgence preachers who did not hesitate to deceive, and the lavish use of dispensations, granting of confession letters, and other abuses were criticized. Few churchmen had spoken with such candor and determination. A copy of this document, obtained in some illegitimate manner and printed in Milan and Rome, was greeted by the Lutherans as proof of the strictures they had been making for two decades. Luther made its appearance an excuse for vitriolic comments upon the pope as Antichrist.

Contarini, a member of the commission of nine, and as candid as ever, urged a complete renovation of the curia. He declared that disgrace had been brought upon the Holy See by financial practices resulting from the unrestrained right of patronage in papal hands, and he complained against the pope's absolute power out of which flowed these evil practices which alienated so many men.

> The law of Christ is a law of freedom, and forbids a servitude so abject that the Lutherans were entirely justified in comparing it with the Babylonish captivity. But, furthermore, can that be called a government of which the rule is the will of one man, by nature prone to evil, and liable to the influence of caprices and affections innumerable? . . . The authority of the pope is equally with others a dominion of reason. God has conferred this rule on St Peter and his successors, that they might lead the flocks confided to their care into everlasting blessedness. A pope should know that those over whom he exercises this rule are free men; not according to his own pleasure must he command, or forbid, or dispense, but in obedience to the rule of reason, of God's command, and to the law of love, referring everything to God, and doing all in consideration of the common good only. For positive laws are not to be imposed by mere will, they must be ever in unison with natural rights, with the commandments of God, and with the requirements of circumstances. Nor can they be altered or abrogated, except in conformity with this guidance and with the imperative demands of things. . . . Be it the care of your holiness never to depart from this rule; be not guided by the impotence of the will which makes choice of evil; submit not to the servitude which ministers to sin.[1]

Paul, taking these remarks in good part, decided to hasten the reform of the offices of the curia, and for this purpose a commission of eight, under the direction of Contarini, was named. In April, 1540, Paul ordered that all proposed reform should forthwith be put into effect, in spite of the

[1] L. von Ranke, *History of the Popes: Their Church and State*, New York, 1901, I, 102.

opposition of many of the other cardinals, and the work so well begun was given every encouragement. There was much discussion about the reform of preaching, for the pulpit was in sad decline at the close of the Middle Ages, few secular priests delivering sermons. It was unfortunate that so much of this activity was left to friars. It was also especially dangerous for the traditional faith at this time, inasmuch as many Protestant ministers had been brought up on humanist ideas and, as preachers, in this respect were superior to the rank and file of friars and priests.

Residence of bishops cried loudly for reform. As chief shepherds of the flocks entrusted to them, bishops should have lived in their dioceses, but many of them delegated their cares to others. Paul, resolved to put an end to this abuse, summoned more than eighty bishops before him and required that they return to their flocks. This was an important step, for in many places the Church had suffered a great loss of prestige because of ignorant and careless bishops whose continued absence permitted Protestant ideas to meet with friendly reception in their dioceses. Henceforth all benefices to which the cure of souls was attached would necessitate residence. Much was accomplished by Paul III, but much more remained to be done. The significance of his efforts lies in the fact that they inspired the actions of the Council of Trent. To eradicate all vicious practices would have been too drastic; Paul's statesmanship consisted in the singularly happy combination of moderation, determination, and ability to choose the right men who could be trusted to carry on the work of reform.

POLITICAL AND OTHER OBJECTIONS TO CALLING A COUNCIL

We have noted above that the calling of a general council was beset with all sorts of objections. Protestant princes and preachers as a rule objected to any council called by the pope and directed by him. On the other hand, popes were unwilling to allow lay persons to manage a council. Of the baneful effects of lay influences in the councils of Constance and Basel, popes had seen enough, and Paul III naturally opposed calling a council if it would be controlled by princes and laymen.

Paul believed that the Church organization ought to be reformed by means of a general council and began to express this conviction immediately after his elevation to the chair of Peter. Some of the cardinals, however, were opposed to a council because they feared that a general renovation of the Church initiated by a council would curtail their power. Nevertheless, the pope sent representatives to the emperor and the king of France. Cardinal Pietro Paolo Vergerio (d. 1565), who was negotiating with Germany during 1535, discovered that the new policy of the curia was winning friends among Catholic princes, even Lutheran cities and princes showing themselves courteous. With strong hopes that reconciliation would be possible, he visited the electors of Brandenburg and Saxony and had a meeting with Luther. The reformer, however, bluntly declared that Protestants did not need a council, but he thought one might be useful in cleansing the Catholic Church of its "errors," which, of course, were doctrinal.

Vergerio appeared before the Schmalkalden League at the close of 1535. Hitherto Lutheran princes had received him favorably, had repeatedly insisted on the necessity of calling a council, and had loudly demanded reforms as recently as the Diet of Augsburg (1530). Since that date, however, the situation had changed materially. The Schmalkalden League had been formed, and many more princes and cities had become Lutheran. The princes, who were now powerful, did not wish to take part in a council, for to reform the Catholic Church would strengthen the Holy Roman Emperor. They had become strong by secularizing the property of the Church, taking over the justice of its courts, and managing in Lutheran fashion the affairs of the new territorial churches. In their answer, so framed that it amounted to a refusal, they insisted that the council should be composed of persons of all ranks chosen by the princes and that it should be held in Germany, thus showing their opposition to any papal direction of it.

Such a council, however, could never be a true council. Furthermore, the theologians at Wittenberg, with Luther as chief author, had drawn up the Articles of Schmalkalden in December, 1536, in answer to the elector's request for a statement about the conditions on which Lutherans could take part in a council. The Articles asserted that a council was not necessary and that they could have nothing to do with the pope, who was "Antichrist."

Meanwhile Charles' Third War (1536–1538) with Francis I broke out, and the proposed council was impossible, whereupon its meeting was postponed until May, 1538. In the meantime Paul III negotiated the 10 years' Peace of Nice between Charles and Francis (June, 1538), and both princes declared themselves willing to second the pope's project. But Francis was not in earnest and raised difficulties about the place of meeting. As nothing could be accomplished, the council was once more postponed until Easter, 1539.

Because of the war which finally broke out between him and the Sultan Suliman in 1540, Charles now changed his policy and no longer supported Paul's wish for a council. He needed the aid of Lutherans and therefore abandoned hostile measures against them, but he went so far as to welcome any proposal which promised to establish harmony between Lutherans and Catholics. Elector Joachim of Brandenburg, one of the Lutheran princes most influenced by Erasmus' middle-of-the-road conceptions, thought that an agreement might be reached between Lutherans and Catholics if the latter would only grant the cup to the laity and permit priests to marry.

Charles grasped at this uncatholic idea and began discussions with the Lutheran princes at a diet in Frankfort in April, 1539, at which it was agreed that a group of theologians and laymen should draw up an agreement about religion. This looked very much like a national German council, for the papacy could not admit the legitimacy of permitting laymen to discuss, on an equal basis with theologians, questions touching the faith.

In May Charles informed the pope of his new views, for as far as he was concerned a council was out of the question for the moment. The Diet at Spires in May, 1540, which was transferred to Hagenau because of the plague, accomplished nothing, the Lutherans remaining obdurate in their insistence on the *Augsburg Confession*. The diet was reopened at Worms in October, and here Lutherans and Catholics agreed to a statement about the Trinity, but they could reach no understanding as to original sin.

Charles appeared before the next meeting of the Diet at Ratisbon in April, 1541, to request the pope to send the diplomatic and conciliatory Contarini as nuncio in the hope that he might make concessions to the Protestants. Political considerations outweighed questions of dogma with Charles, and he was eager for compromise. Lutherans were determined not to abate their claims in the least, for they wanted to preserve their political gains as well as their religious convictions. This diet considered the twenty-three articles drawn up at Worms in the previous year which professed to contain the substance of doctrine acceptable to Catholics and Lutherans.

Dr. John Eck appeared as defender of the Catholic position. Although it was easy enough to agree on certain topics, trouble arose about the question of justification, but even this difficulty was smoothed away. Transubstantiation and the character of the sacraments, however, proved insurmountable obstacles, for it was the conviction of Contarini, the papal nuncio, that compromise was impossible on these points. Discussions on other articles, however, continued because the princes and the emperor viewed the matter from a political point of view.

Accordingly it was decided that the articles upon which agreement had been reached were to be accepted by all subjects of the empire and the other points were to remain in abeyance until the meeting of a council. Meantime toleration was to be accorded to dissenters. In this way Charles received the support of his Lutheran subjects in his foreign difficulties with the French and the Turk. But Contarini and the curia were displeased that the emperor, whose traditional duty it was to stand by the Church, should presume to settle matters of religion.

Charles' role as Christian emperor made it impossible to act as national ruler of Germany. Medieval universalism foundered on the rocks of the new absolutist power of princes. His duty as custodian of the faith universal drove princes into political opposition, wherefore it was to their interest to embrace Lutheranism and oppose Catholicism. In other words, the new autocratic power of princes exalted localism in politics to such a pitch that the principle of universalism, one of the great ideals of the Middle Ages, was overthrown.

And as Charles desperately needed the support of the princes, he took more and more a political view of the matter, which explains why he was eager for compromise. But in making compromises he was acting contrary to the medieval conception of the emperor's duty toward the Church. Lutheranism thus ruined not only the universality of the medieval faith, but also put an end to the universality of the medieval empire. It exalted the power of princes by producing a theology which gave a theoretical and divine basis to their absolutism.

Catholicism suffered severe reverses in 1541. Staunchly Catholic Duke George of Saxony died and was succeeded by his brother Henry who made Lutheranism the faith of his subjects, and Elector Joachim II of Brandenburg followed his example. Other defections followed. Archbishop Albrecht of Mainz was forced by his estates to permit the Reformation to be established in Halberstadt and Magdeburg; the bishop of Schwerin, the abbot of Fulda, and the town of Hildesheim became Lutheran.

The archbishop of Cologne and the bishops of Münster, Minden, and Osnabrück seemed on the point of renouncing Catholicism, secularizing the lands of the Church, and establishing their houses as new dynasties. Brunswick also embraced Lutheranism. By 1542 all Germany from the Baltic to the Rhine had become Lutheran or appeared to be in the process of breaking with the old faith. Lutheranism was also spreading into Bohemia and Hungary and even into Austria and among the south Slavs.

After much discussion Paul, such was the urgency, decided to summon a council. As the Germans were opposed to an Italian city because they distrusted papal influence, and as the curia did not want to go to some city in the center of Germany where hostile feelings would surely defeat their efforts, Trent in the Tyrol on the confines of Italy and Germany was chosen. Francis I, who professed to be displeased at the choice, was now allied with Suliman, and his Fourth War (1542–1544) with Charles broke out. Not until the Treaty of Crespy was it possible to secure a measure of coöperation from Francis. Freed from the embarrassments of war, Charles could now pursue his policy of reducing the Lutherans. The latter refused to appear in Trent, and Luther wrote a violent polemic entitled *Against the Roman Papacy Founded by the Devil.* Its purpose was to justify the Protestants' refusal to accept Charles' invitation to attend the council, and in it Luther denounced the pope in an abusive manner.

The council of Trent opened its sessions in December, 1545. Charles and the pope could not agree, for the former insisted on reform for political reasons, while the latter wanted clarification of dogma in order to proceed more effectively against heresy. The result was that both matters were discussed simultaneously by separate committees and were presented alternately before the fathers. The acts of the council were promulgated in sessions, each of which dealt with dogma and reform. Ten of these were held before adjournment in September, 1547. In the spring of 1547 a plague broke out in Trent, and it was decided to transfer the council to Bologna. Charles was strongly opposed to this step, and the Germans would not go to Bologna. Even the Spanish members of the council were loath to go there. They did not want the pope's power to increase and so supported their king, Charles, who remained in Trent while the curial party went to Bologna. It appeared that the quarrel might lead to a schism, but in September Paul suspended all further sessions, and the work of reform was for the time halted.

Chapter 19

THE PAPACY RENOVATED
AND ASSERTIVE

*T*HE SECULARIZED papacy of the Renaissance had definitely come to an end by the time Paul III died in November, 1549, and the spiritual nature of the institution again began to dominate its life. The reform decrees of the late pope and his cardinals, the decisions of the Council of Trent, the vigorous administration of the pontiff, and the example of austerity and purity of life set by him and by the recently appointed cardinals exerted a profound effect. Bishops zealous in reforming their sees made sure that the work of renovation would continue, and the pontiffs who followed Paul III successfully carried forward the work of restoration.

PAPAL REFORM UNDER JULIUS III, 1550–1555

Julius III (d. 1555) was raised to the chair of Peter in February, 1550. The conclave began soon after the death of Paul III, but French and Spanish rivalry made prompt election impossible. This external manipulation was a feature of the Renaissance papacy which Julius was determined to make impossible. As cardinal he was known to be interested in reform, and to it and the abolition of heresy he pledged himself during the conclave. Yet certain features of the age remained to hamper the efficacy of any program. Furthermore, Julius was weak enough to appoint his nephew, a man notoriously scandalous in his private life, as cardinal. The pope's own morals were beyond reproach in spite of insinuations which never were substantiated.

Julius appointed a commission to discuss the reformation of such abuses as had not been considered in the recent session of the Council of Trent, work which the pope was determined to direct himself. Statutes were issued regulating the clergy, both regular and secular, and there were also to be new regulations regarding conclaves. His own election had made it clear that this was necessary, and he felt that no outside scheming should determine the choice of popes. Cardinals were to act as councilors of the pope. They were to possess only one benefice each and conduct their visitorial duties regularly, nor were they to hold benefices with cure of souls without doing the necessary pastoral work. Julius also vigorously pressed for reform in papal governmental bureaus. This was a bold step, for a large part of the papal income was derived from these offices.

The pope began to consider the task of reconvening the Council of Trent, and a bull calling the council was issued in November, 1550. The second period of the Council of Trent lasted from May 1, 1551, to April 28, 1552. Its decrees were published in six sessions, the ninth to the fourteenth inclusive, the thirteenth and fourteenth of which defined the Eucharist and penance. The Spanish prelates were inclined to minimize the authority of the pope in the affairs of the Church, but Julius was adamant and prevented any diminution of papal authority. Emperor Charles' attitude was favorable to the Roman Church at this moment— he had vigorously pursued the Lutherans in Germany and had defeated them in battle at Mühlberg (1547). Now he found that Henry II of France had joined the Protestants in the war against him (1552); hence he desired the pope's friendship. Under these circumstances it was impossible for the prelates to tarry in Trent, and, as it became evident that further progress was blocked, the pope decided to suspend the council. So troubled was the peace of Europe during Charles' remaining years that its speedy reconvening was out of the question.

Julius also supported the agencies established by his predecessor Paul III to extirpate heresy. In a series of bulls he reconfirmed and extended the privileges already granted to the Jesuits who, rapidly gaining in strength, brought many back to the faith. The Roman Inquisition was reconfirmed by the bull of February, 1550, and continued the example set in Paul III's days. Protestant books were common in Catholic lands, especially in Italy, for hitherto it had been thought that reading books written by apostates might counteract the growth of heresy. Julius revoked such permission to the lay and clergy alike and ordered that heretical writings should be handed over to the inquisitors. But death overtook the pope in March, 1555, before he could summarize his reforming activity in a comprehensive bull.

The pontificate of Marcellus II (April 10 to May 1, 1555) was extremely brief. Marcellus II, a man of pure life, was eager for reform, learned in the writings of the Church fathers, and interested in the

Vatican Library. His pontificate was too short to accomplish anything for reform.

VIGOROUS REFORMS OF PAUL IV, 1555–1559

Gian Pietro Caraffa, prominent member of the Oratory of Divine Love, succeeded Marcellus II, took as his papal name Paul IV, and reigned until 1559. In spite of his advanced age he was a man of vigor who had lost none of the fiery enthusiasm which had characterized his earlier days. He belonged to the Middle Ages rather than to the Renaissance, and his ideas were formed by careful study of St. Thomas Aquinas, not by the master-pieces of humanism. Not only did the new pope propose to reform the Church, strengthen ecclesiastical discipline, and rid the Church of heresy, but also he was resolved to free it wherever possible from the political control which princes everywhere sought to exercise.

Paul was also determined to liberate the papacy and Italy from Spanish domination for, being a Neapolitan, he knew better than anyone else the baneful political influence which Spain exercised over the peninsula. So long as it owned Naples and Sicily in the south and Milan in the heart of Lombardy, papal freedom could not exist, for smaller states such as Florence tended to become satellites of Spain. Paul accordingly sought support from France. King Henry II seemed on the point of accepting the Truce of Vaucelles (February, 1556), and the war with the emperor and Spain was about to end. Duke Francis of Guise, who was influential at the French court, had designs upon the crown of Naples, ostensibly to advance the interests of the French king but really for himself.

A treaty was made in December, 1555, in which Henry and the pope agreed to attack the Spaniards. The republic of Florence was to be re-established, and Duke Cosimo of Tuscany, a vassal prince of Spain, was to be expelled. Thus, notwithstanding the Truce of Vaucelles, war began anew. Devotion to the Church caused Philip II of Spain (1556–1598) to consult his theologians about the justifiability of resisting the pope with arms, but finally the duke of Alva was ordered to attack the States of the Church. He invaded Campania and moved upon Rome, and the duke of Guise's forces failed to give Paul any support. For a moment the pope feared a repetition of the dreadful sack of 1527, but Alva displayed the greatest deference. A treaty was made in September, 1557, on the basis of the *status quo ante* except for a few points, and Paul's chief venture into politics thus proved signally miscalculated.[1]

---

[1] For the connection of Pope Paul IV's war with the Hapsburg-French conflict prior to the Treaty of Cateau-Cambrésis (1559), see pp. 695–696.

These events strangely recalled the days of Julius II whose policy it was to drive the Spaniards out of Italy, and it seemed that the secular interests of the papacy would again become dominant. In another way it appeared that the habits of the Renaissance papacy still continued. Paul was guilty of nepotism, advancing his nephews Carlo and Giovanni Caraffa to the cardinalate and making Carlo his chief agent in secular matters. This was an unfortunate choice, for Carlo was unworthy; but Paul was totally blind to his nephew's notorious life, even when it became common knowledge.

Although Paul's zeal made it impossible for him to work with a council —which explains why none was convened during his pontificate—he issued orders putting into execution the decrees enacted by the earlier council. Scarcely a day passed without some important order designed to remove unworthy priests, educate the people in the faith, or purge the Church of abuses. New cardinals announced in December, 1555, were chosen with the sole idea of helping him put these orders into execution. A thorough reformation in all branches of the curia was carried out with energy.

The Inquisition received special attention. Hitherto its penal action had been comparatively mild, but Paul, who as head of the Theatines had never shown any clemency toward dissenters, was resolved to uproot heresy ruthlessly. The sphere of activity of this tribunal was made to include serious breaches of immorality and simoniacal use of the sacraments, that is, dispensing sacraments and granting orders for money. Henceforth the Holy Office became a vastly more effective tribunal. It proceeded with the greatest vigor, subjecting the accused to torture and condemning heretics to the stake. Protestantism in Italy rapidly retreated before this triumphant activity.

So zealous was the pope in the restoration of clerical morals that he did not even spare his nephews. Forcing one of the cardinals to tell him the truth about their evil ways of life, he banished them from Rome, a step which practically marked the end of nepotism which had wrought so much damage to papal prestige since the days of Calixtus III (1455–1458). Mortified by the discovery that his nephews had abused his confidence, the aged pontiff resolved to devote himself to the task of reform more assiduously than ever, and a strenuous regime was introduced into the city of Rome. Henceforth public life lost some of its gaiety.

The struggle to keep the faith uncontaminated was aided by the publication in 1557 of an *Index* of forbidden books, and heretical productions were cast into the flames. The zeal of inquisitors, fortified by the imperious commands of Pope Paul, made their tribunal a terror to the populace; insinuation, calumny, and canard often led to citation before the dreaded officials. With a zeal which amounted almost to ferocity the pontiff turned against his former friends in the Oratory of Divine Love, and they as well as the followers of Juan de Valdés were forced to appear before the dread tribunal or flee Italy. Cardinal Giovanni di Morone (d. 1578) had advocated a mild policy toward Protestants, but Paul would have nothing of gentleness toward apostates. Morone was cited before the tribunal but defended himself successfully. Nevertheless, he was kept in confinement until after Paul's death. The fierce old pontiff also caused Reginald Pole to be summoned, for he had roused the papal ire because he yielded title to monastic lands secularized in the reign of Henry VIII. Pole, in England at the moment, prepared to obey but died before he arrived in Rome. Thus the pope carried on his energetic policy until his death in August, 1559. His pontificate marks the beginning of the successful rejuvenation of the Church.

CONTINUATION OF THE REFORM UNDER PIUS IV

As soon as Paul IV was dead the cardinals, resolved to elect a successor who would be less masterful, chose the gentle Giovanni Angelo de' Medici who took as his name Pius IV (1559–1565). No one questioned his devotion to reform which he sought to carry out in irenic fashion. He was determined to reconvene the Council of Trent. The political situation was favorable, for Ferdinand of Germany and Philip of Spain were eager to help in upbuilding the Church, and the French court was willing to coöperate but loath to support a meeting in German lands. Pius issued a bull in November, 1561, directing that the council be opened at Easter of the following year, but again it proved impossible to secure the attendance of Protestants. The decrees of the council, which came to an end in December, 1563, were drawn up in nine sessions. The council decided a large number of questions regarding discipline and dogma and provided an authoritative statement on many points which Protestant reformers questioned. Papal authority emerged triumphant in spite of the fact that the Spanish bishops desired to subject it to the council. Papal ascendancy in the Church, interpretation of Catholic dogma according to St. Thomas Aquinas and other scholastic authorities, regeneration of clerical morals, emphasis upon the education of laymen and clergy, and no concessions to Protestantism—such were the chief characteristics of Catholic reform as planned at Trent.

The Council of Trent, one of the most significant events in the age of the Reformation, led to a renaissance of Catholicism. A purified papacy possessed of the most devoted and self-effacing agencies to propagate the truth now stood ready to assume the offensive. The year 1563 therefore constitutes an important date in the history of Catholicism. "Convulsed to its center, endangered in the very groundwork of its being, it [Catholicism] had not only maintained itself but found means of renewed force. In the two southern peninsulas all influences hostile to its ascendancy had been promptly expelled, all the elements of thought and action had been once more gathered to itself and pervaded its own spirit. It now conceived the idea of subduing the revolted in all other parts of the world. Rome once more became a conquering power, projects were formed and enterprises engaged in, recalling those proceeding from the Seven Hills in ancient times and during the Middle Ages."[2]

Pius was careful to prevent unworthy relatives from exerting influence, but one of his most important acts, however, was the elevation to the cardinalate of his nephew, Charles Borromeo (1538–1584). In this case the favor shown to a nephew by a pontiff was amply justified. Borromeo, a Milanese, early received the tonsure, made good progress in learning, and because of his character and ability was called to Rome by the pope who made him a cardinal and entrusted important tasks to him. As papal secretary he rendered much service in reform, carrying on an enormous correspondence with the papal legates at the reconvened Council of Trent. He also corresponded with the crowned heads of Europe and so played a significant part in Catholic reform. Borromeo became a priest and soon was made archbishop of Milan. He appointed a zealous priest to administer the see. Visitations were held, irregularities were checked, abuses suppressed, and unworthiness among priests came to an end. Preaching became important, Church ceremonies were made more impressive, education of children was emphasized, and monastic discipline was tightened. Much of this was accomplished while Borromeo was at the papal court, for he insisted that the clergy themselves should begin reform, himself setting the example which all were to follow.

REFORM EMPHASIZED UNDER PIUS V (1566–1572) AND GREGORY XIII (1572–1585)

The death of Pius IV in December, 1565, required Borromeo's presence in Rome, but after the election of Pius V (1566–1572) he returned to Milan and vigorously took up the work of reform. He created a model administration by appointing learned, zealous, and worthy men. He was especially interested in the catechetical instruction of children, and pious

[2] L. von Ranke, *History of the Popes: Their Church and State,* I, 4.

foundations constantly looked to him as a friend, for during the Middle Ages there had been all too little formal systematic religious instruction. The famine of 1571 was a serious crisis in the thickly populated Milanese, and Borromeo directed the work of relief, taking care of more than 3000 at his own expense for 3 months. During the great plague of 1576 and 1577, which was even more serious, Borromeo comforted the sufferers in their sore straits, and when the plague left built a church in honor of St. Sebastian, chief of the plague saints.

Pius V was a man of piety and austere life. He was a Dominican, had served as inquisitor-general, and while a cardinal, when he was known as Michele Ghislieri, he had given splendid evidence of zeal for reform under Paul IV. Unalterably opposed to the practice of nepotism, as pope he definitely broke with it by issuing his bull *Admonet Nos* in 1567. The *Tridentine Catechism (Catechism of Trent)*, drawn up in 1566, was widely used in Catholic teaching. Two years later appeared an improved breviary and a new missal. By this time the papal name was once more respected in Italy and other parts of the Catholic world. The decrees of Trent were fully applied in Italy, and Rome became a city of monks and priests.

Gregory XIII (1572–1585) now succeeded to the papal chair. In his younger days, when he was known as Ugo Buoncompagni, he was not worthy of the priestly vocation. But like Paul III, he changed his ways, became a man of holy life, and followed in the footsteps of his predecessor by refusing to alienate Church property for the benefit of his relatives. Determined to abolish abuses and evil practices, he appointed a committee for this purpose. Gregory, especially interested in education which was to play so noteworthy a part in the regeneration of Catholicism, gave the German College in Rome all necessary financial support. A college for the schismatic Greeks was founded in 1577, another for the English in 1579, and a third for the Maronites in 1584. He built quarters for the Jesuit Roman College which henceforth became known as the Gregorian University. Other seminaries were established outside Italy, of which the one at Douai was especially famous. Gregory is also noted for the support which he gave to the reform of the Julian calendar, the new Gregorian calendar being introduced into most Catholic lands in 1578.

ACME OF REFORM IN THE PAPACY AND HIERARCHY UNDER SIXTUS V (1585–1590)

Sixtus V (1585–1590) was one of the most remarkable rulers that ever occupied the papal chair. He entered the Franciscan order at the age of twelve and became a successful preacher. Believing that the banditry and lawlessness rampant in the States of the Church were incompatible with the dignity of the apostolic see, he resolved to uproot these evils. "No day passed without an execution. Over all parts of the country, in wood and field, stakes were erected, on each of which stood the head of an outlaw. The pope awarded praises only to those among his legates and governors who supplied him largely with these terrible trophies; his demand was ever for heads: there is a sort of oriental barbarism in this mode of administering justice."[3] This method of terrorism proved effective.

Sixtus exhibited boundless energy in reorganizing the papal finances and collecting treasure, and he instituted the most rigid economy but spent much money on the Lateran Palace and other buildings. His imperious will is known to all the world by the restored columns of Trajan and Antoninus Pius upon which this prince of the Church, in token of the conquest of Christianity over the classical Renaissance, placed statues of St. Peter and St. Paul. Eager to beautify the Eternal City, he constructed noble streets, built the Via Felice and the Borgo Felice, laid the foundations of the Piazza di Spagna, erected the Egyptian obelisks in the squares before St. Peter's, Santa Maria Maggiore, the Lateran, and Santa Maria del Popolo; finished the dome of St. Peter's planned by Michelangelo, except for its covering of lead, and built the great aqueduct, the Aqua Felice, which provided water for twenty-seven fountains.

The reorganization of papal government was also undertaken. The number of cardinals was limited to seventy by the bull *Postquam Verus Ille* of 1586, and fifteen permanent congregations were created to take care of all spiritual and temporal business, final authority being reserved to the pope. This change was effected by the bull *Immensa Aeterni Dei* of 1588. Thus the old papacy of the Renaissance changed in still another respect, for hitherto affairs had been managed by the pope and his cardinals in consistory. These permanent bureaus made possible more rapid and effective dispatch of business. Sixtus appointed excellent cardinals. In 1588 there was issued a new edition of the Septuagint prepared from the manuscripts in the Vatican and printed on the presses set up by the pope.

SUCCESSFUL MISSIONARY ENTERPRISE

By 1590 the papacy may be said to have cleansed itself, and new life was pulsing in the old Church which had so long taught the people of Europe. The Church successfully assumed the aggressive, first in the

[3] Von Ranke, *op. cit.*, p. 311.

territories where its teachings were not strongly challenged; next in the borderlands where Lutheran, Calvin, Anabaptist, and other teachings battled Catholicism, and finally in the very strongholds of Protestantism. The Jesuit order was a most effective agent in this great task, for the Jesuits turned their attention to the people who had never received a thorough doctrinal grounding in the faith through catechetical instruction, and they labored long and hard to teach young and old the fundamentals of Catholic doctrine. They also became popular as preachers. People were in the habit of hearing friars give sermons, but their parish priests did little to instill a more accurate knowledge of the faith. Consequently zealous and well-trained Jesuits were welcomed by the laymen.

The numerous schools founded by the Jesuits were especially successful, for these schools emancipated themselves from the older methods of study and teaching which had grown up in the Middle Ages. Their curriculum was based upon the pedagogical ideas developed in the *Quattrocento*, careful instruction being given in Latin and Greek classics, logic, mathematics, and natural philosophy. The devotees of humanism, which had often been closely associated with the rise of Protestantism, had criticized unceasingly the out-of-date method of the old teachers and their ignorance of the classics, but henceforth such strictures were impossible. Indeed, the vigor of the organization which characterized the Jesuit order made its success so striking that it was soon more than a match for its rivals. Ignatius had founded the German College and the Roman College in 1540 and 1541, respectively. Under the generalship of Laýnez (1555–1565) and Francis Borgia (1565–1572) many more were founded in Italy, Spain, Portugal, Switzerland, and especially in Germany, for the land which had brought forth Luther and Zwingli was to be the battleground for the faith. The first colleges in this country were established in Cologne, Munich, Mainz, Trier, Augsburg, Dilengen, and Würzburg, centers which had remained true to Catholicism.

Success in checking Protestantism in Germany was due to St. Peter Canisius more than to anyone else. He was born in Nijmegen in 1521, studied at Louvain and Cologne, and was admitted to the Jesuit order in 1543. His first great task was to combat Protestantism in Cologne where Archbishop Herman von Wied was thinking of abandoning Catholicism and establishing himself as a political prince in the secularized lands of his province. Here Canisius founded a Jesuit college. In 1547 he attended the Council of Trent. His next great task was to save Bavaria, thus preparing this land for its great role in the history of Catholic reform. Duke William IV (1508–1545) had asked Paul III to send Jesuit professors to teach in the University of Ingolstadt. Canisius, Le Jay, and Salmerón were chosen for this task, and so effective was their work that in 1564 Duke Albrecht V (1550–1579) finally felt that he could inaugurate a vigorous policy in behalf of Catholicism. Protestants were excluded from the country, heretical books were forbidden and burned wherever found, and Jesuits were placed in charge of education.

Canisius became rector of Ingolstadt in 1550, but 2 years later was ordered by Loyola to go to the new college in Vienna. Here he preached in the great church of St. Stephen and before the court of King Ferdinand. The lands of the Hapsburgs were filled with Protestant propaganda and seemed ready to abandon the old faith entirely. Canisius traveled far and wide in these parts, visiting parishes where Catholic worship had been practically abandoned. His devotion and zeal in celebrating the sacraments impressed everybody, and he was able to drive Lutheranism from the court of Vienna; but he steadfastly refused the see of Vienna which would have limited his sphere of activity. He became superior of the Jesuit province of Upper Germany, was active as adviser to the emperor, and succeeded in smoothing away misunderstandings between him and the curia during the final sessions of the Council of Trent. Finally, Pius IV sent him to Germany as nuncio charged with securing the adoption of the Tridentine decrees.

This vigorous pastoral and diplomatic activity did not exhaust all of Canisius' efforts, however, for with untiring zeal this Jesuit apostle to Germany also served the Church with his ready pen. He wrote much devotional literature, urged the establishment of Catholic presses, and did what he could to stimulate scholarship. He made an important compilation of Catholic doctrine for the instruction of the youth, and issued two briefer forms of this work, the shortest being intended for children. Printed in German as well as Latin, they were used extensively. At length Canisius was relieved of the arduous labors which had occupied him as provincial since 1566, and he retired to Fribourg in Switzerland where he took up the work begun by Borromeo who had established the Helvetian College in Milan. A Jesuit college was founded at Lucerne and another at Fribourg of which Canisius assumed direction until his death in 1597.

Thus a great work was accomplished, for even in northern Germany bishops took courage and began to work zealously for the faith. Great changes took place in the sees of Cologne, Mainz, Münster, Paderborn, and Osnabrück, and in the abbatial lands of Fulda. Bishop Otto Truchsess of Augsburg (1514–1573) was one of many who had zeal for the old faith. The Jesuits also proved successful in Poland where Protestants were split into groups: Lutherans, Calvinists, and Socinians. The Catholics were numerically the most powerful, and were better organized.

Canisius visited Poland soon after the Diet of Piotrkow (1558) and again in 1566, and Jesuit colleges were opened. The Protestants, fearful of their future, formed the Union of Sandomir (1570), but they were no match for the highly trained Jesuits who possessed a superior organization and enjoyed the confidence of the peasantry and many of the lower bourgeoisie in Great and Little Poland.

The success of the Jesuits in Poland is one of the most noteworthy achievements of Catholic reform. They supported King Stephen Batory (1574–1586) whom they pleased with their teaching about royal absolutism. The theory that a prince was instituted by God's sanction and that, according to Scripture, an unlimited monarchy was the best form of government appealed to a prince engaged in a determined struggle against the disintegrating political power of nobility and bourgeoisie. Batory therefore showed the Church many favors, although he remained tolerant toward his Protestant subjects. In France, however, the Jesuits found it difficult to secure a foothold, for the Sorbonne did not like them as competitors, and the crown feared their great devotion to the curia and thought that they could not be so easily managed as the concordatary clergy of the realm. Their cause was defended by the cardinal of Lorraine who founded the college at Pont-à-Mousson in 1574, and others also supported them; but for many years there was opposition to their activities.

Spain, the home of St. Ignatius Loyola, welcomed the Jesuits; here they founded a large number of colleges. Most of the Jesuits who joined the order in the first decades of its existence were Spaniards, and, so numerous were they, that wherever the order went Spaniards usually assumed a leading part. The order was even more successful in Portugal. But the provincial Simon Rodriguez did not entirely fit into the scheme of Jesuit organization, pursuing instead an independent policy. Ignatius, dissatisfied with this, deposed Rodriguez in 1552. In the Low Countries it was impossible at first for the Jesuits to secure permission to open colleges. Philip of Spain, however, was favorable, but his subjects, even though loyal Catholics, labored hard against the Jesuits. He finally overrode this opposition and by a decree of August 20, 1556, gave the society the necessary civil rights and instructed them to proceed with their work.

While thus resuscitating the wounded Church in Europe, the Jesuits were also active as missionaries in Asia and the newly found lands of South America, although Franciscans, Dominicans, and Augustinians had preceded them in America. In 1549 six Jesuits under Emanuel de Nobriga arrived at St. Vincent in Brazil and began their missionary activity which was crowned with much success. The resourcefulness of the order is illustrated by the development of the *Reductions,* whereby the natives were induced to abandon their roving life and settle on large estates under the direction of Jesuit fathers. This order was a most effective agency in the spiritual conquest of the country, one reason for their success being their desire to defend the aborigines against the rigors of slavery and unconscionable exploitation by greedy whites.

Interesting also was the effort to Christianize Asia. St. Francis Xavier (1506–1552), one of the devoted followers of St. Ignatius, was, like the latter, born of the fighting nobility of Navarre, and attracted to Ignatius through the *Spiritual Exercises.* John III of Portugal (1521–1557), desiring to plant the Christian faith in his oriental possessions, begged for the help of the Jesuits. Xavier was named apostolic nuncio and, provided with letters of recommendation from King John and Paul III, he sailed with two companions from Lisbon in 1541, arriving in Goa, a Portuguese trading center in India, in the following year. The Portuguese who lived there were not noble examples for the natives, and Xavier set to work to improve their life. He journeyed through southern India teaching people the Lord's Prayer and the *Ave Maria* and baptizing entire villages. From 1542 to 1547 he labored at Malacca, Amboina, the Moluccas, and Ternate, working with the greatest devotion and without the least fear. New churches were established, and converts gathered around him, attracted by his asceticism.

Xavier was induced to visit Japan by a Japanese convert named Yajiro. They arrived in Kagoshima in August, 1549, and Xavier worked zealously for more than 2 years in bringing the faith to the natives. The first Catholic church was erected at Yamaguchi, and many Japanese became Christians. But Xavier yearned to visit the vast empire of the Chinese who jealously kept out all foreigners and whose country was the original home of the cults of Japan. He believed that the conversion of China would be followed by that of Japan. Converts and missionaries in Japan made great progress after his departure in November, 1551, and Nagasaki, a newly founded city, and the island of Kyushu became largely Christian. Xavier never entered China for he died before the close of 1552 on the island of Changchuen off Macao. His work begun in India continued to go forward; Goa became the seat of an archbishopric of which Malacca and Cochin were suffragan sees. Franciscans, Dominicans, and Capuchins supported these labors of the Jesuits, and their successes in a measure compensated the Church for her losses in Europe.

PART IX

Catholic Political Reaction

Chapter 20

THE CATHOLIC CAUSE IN SPAIN AND SCOTLAND

T HE PRECEDING chapters have shown that the restoration of Catholicism was due largely to an inner vitality in the traditional faith of the people. So powerful was this movement which arose in the humbler levels of the population that by 1580 the faith which had dominated Europe ever since the decline of the Roman Empire and which threatened to succumb under the blows of Lutheran and kindred teachings again stood forth revivified and capable of making progress against its enemies. After about 1555 a new phase of the movement set in, namely, the political. During this period Spain occupied the central position among nations in Europe, and under Philip II (1556–1598) that country, with its satellite states in Europe and its possessions in the New World, marshaled its resources to establish the Catholic faith which the king and his people believed to be the very foundation of Spanish security and greatness.

THE POSITION OF SPAIN IN THE CATHOLIC POLITICAL REACTION REIGN OF CHARLES I

Save for Portugal, the Spanish peninsula was ruled by one king. Beyond the broad seas lay the Americas whence the crown drew fabulous quantities of precious metal which greatly impressed Europeans, both friendly and hostile. Philip was also king of Naples and Sicily, his supremacy in the Mediterranean depending upon the cities of Barcelona, Palermo,

Messina, and Naples. In the duchy of Milan he possessed the rights which the vicar of the Holy Roman Empire formerly exercised, and the strategic position, military resources, and financial power of Milan enabled Philip to control northern Italy. The republic of Genoa became a submissive agent of Spanish policy, its capital serving as an Italian water gate for Spain which was eager to maintain communication with Milan. Florence, Mantua, Ferrara, Savoy, Urbino, and the States of the Church became auxiliary powers of Spanish imperialism.

Corresponding to these Italian states which securely established Spanish ascendancy in the Mediterranean area were the numerous provinces of the Low Countries in northern Europe. Situated at the confluence of the Scheldt, Meuse, and Rhine, equidistant between Spain and Scandinavia, Scotland, and Italy, and wedged between the greatest powers of western Europe, these lands seemed to make it possible for Philip to dominate England and France. Italy was joined to the Low Countries by a corridor, the Franche-Comté, which promised to become useful as a means of communication with Italy. The Holy Roman Empire had been assigned to Emperor Charles' younger brother Ferdinand who since 1531 had borne the title of King of the Romans. This close relationship, it was fondly hoped, would produce a unified regime in religion and politics in the lands which had fallen into Hapsburg hands by the marriages of Maximilian of Austria to Mary of Burgundy, and of their son Philip the Handsome to Joanna of Castile.

Charles I of Spain (1516–1556)—as emperor known as Charles V— continued the policy of his illustrious grandparents, Ferdinand and Isabella. Born in Ghent, he spoke only Flemish and French and was a total stranger to Spain. At the outset his rule in Spain was challenged by a revolt of the Castilian communes, for when he arrived in 1519 he instilled resentment in the hearts of the proud Castilians by his favors to Flemish courtiers. But the widespread revolt was put down in the Battle of Villalar (April, 1521), the net result of this rising being that the royal power became stronger than ever. Political absolutism, more highly perfected in Spain than in other European states, became a chief characteristic of Spanish life. A second feature, the most loyal devotion of Spaniards to Catholicism, is to be explained largely by the political, social, and economic exigencies of the nation.

In his religious policy also Charles followed in the footsteps of Ferdinand and Isabella. The rebellion in Valencia, which accompanied the rising of the Castilian communes but was independent of it, carried forward the policy of extirpating infidels. Tradesmen and handicraftsmen in the towns of Valencia formed an association, known as the Germania, which rose against the nobility who had long dominated the government to the disadvantage of the bourgeoisie. The Moors, who for the most part belonged to the agricultural section of the population, remained loyal to their nobles, in nearly every instance opposing the rebellious Germania. But the fanaticism of some of its members turned the association against these inoffensive people, and the bourgeoisie forcefully subjected many of them to baptism. This rite made them proper subjects of the Inquisition which vigorously began stamping out Mohammedanism in Valencia as it had done in Granada.

The Inquisition was also the means of purging the realm of humanists and Protestants whose ideas were regarded as incompatible with Spanish citizenship. They were hunted down wherever they appeared, and even the followers of mild Erasmus were suspected and proceeded against. This zeal in tracking down heretics did not imply, however, that Charles took orders politically from the pope in Rome, for the king made it a cardinal point of his policy to subject the Church of Spain entirely to his will. This explains why he could use all his resources in Germany, the Low Countries, and other lands to ferret out Protestants, and at the same time oppose the pope in Italy and Germany. Spanish delegates to the Council of Trent, supported by the logic of their theologians, resisted every proposition which promised to exalt the papacy.

CHARACTER AND POLICIES OF PHILIP II

Charles' son, Philip II of Spain, likewise proposed to employ the economic, political, geographic, and military resources of his widely scattered territories in order to establish his control of Europe. Catholicism, identified with Spanish patriotism, was to rise on the ruins of Protestantism. His ideals of government, religion, and society were planted by his father, Emperor Charles. The latter had gradually identified himself with Spain, making it the center of his vast empire; but in Philip the identification was complete from the beginning. Born in 1527 in Valladolid, Philip spoke only Spanish, and his view of life, religion, and politics was thoroughly Spanish. His personal character is an interesting study. Castilian pride and conservatism dominated him. He was reserved in speech; and while he might solicit the opinion of men he rarely expressed his own mind. He was saturnine, unimaginative, and endowed with an infinite capacity for work—probably never in all history has a more industrious monarch reigned. His orthodoxy was never questioned.

That Catholicism and Spanish citizenship should go hand in hand was a fixed idea in Philip's mind, and, upon his return to Spain from Flanders in 1559, he inaugurated a determined policy of exterminating dissenters. The Inquisition was to be the principal tool to accomplish this end, and he therefore strengthened that tribunal. He gave public expression to his policy by appearing at the *auto de fé* held in the open square before the church of St. Martin in Valladolid in October, 1559. A crowd assembled from all parts to see twelve unfortunate wretches executed. One of them, a nobleman, as he passed Philip, asked the king why he was condemned to suffer such a horrible death. The gloomy king gave a characteristic response: "Had I a son as obstinate as you I would eagerly carry fagots to burn him."

The Spanish Inquisition, a religious tribunal actively supported and directed by the crown, was composed of a supreme council, at the head of which stood the grand-inquisitor appointed by Philip himself, and its members were for the most part Dominicans. No appeal from their decisions could be taken to the pope. There were many subordinate tribunals. People were urged to make accusations against all and sundry. There was no confrontation of accuser and accused, for trials were secret and subtle casuistry was employed by skilled theologians to trap the unwary. Every device of torture which the age could think of was employed to wring confessions from lips quivering with pain. This most successful organ was readily used even against churchmen. Ignatius Loyola was brought before it to be questioned, and St. Teresa, as Catholic a woman as ever lived, was pursued by it. Archbishop Carranza of Toledo (d. 1576), a learned theologian and delegate to the Council of Trent, a man of pure life whose greatest offense was a leaning toward Erasmian convictions, was tried for 7 long years, after which he was sent to Rome for further interrogation. The emphatically political character of this tribunal is shown by the fact that it was also employed against purely political offenders.

This singular union of Spanish interests and Catholicism led Philip to assume the burden of active war upon the Turk and the extirpation of the converted Moors (or Moriscos) living in Granada. Although formally compelled to become Christians, many of them clung secretly to their ancient faith and practices. A series of drastic edicts was issued against them from 1560–1567, some of which were most tyrannical, as the one which decreed that their houses should be open on wedding days so that officials might ascertain whether any ancient customs were observed. A revolt broke out in 1568, and a determined resistance was made in the Alpujarra Mountains. The war was conducted with great ferocity, many towns and villages being put to the sack and their inhabitants massacred without regard for age or sex. The revolt was finally put down by Philip's natural brother Don Juan; and by the decree of October, 1570, the Moriscos were ordered to settle among the Christian peoples of the north, in Castile and León.

The destruction of the Moors, demanded as a national patriotic measure, was inspired by the Turkish attempt to seize Malta, for the conquest of Malta would seriously jeopardize Spanish ascendancy in the western Mediterranean and expose Christian lands to piratical raids. The Knights of St. John were holding this island as a shielding bulwark against the Mohammedan world. Suliman the Great (1520–1566) and his vassal, the Barbary prince of Tripoli, attacked it in 1565. The knights put forth an heroic resistance, one of the most famous in history, and finally, after great efforts, the Spanish viceroy of Naples was able to drive off the assailants. This, however, did not put an end to Turkish ambitions of conquest, for in 1569 the new sultan, Selim II (1566–1574), attacked Cyprus, a Venetian outpost.

A league between Philip, Venice, and the pope was formed to oppose Selim, and a great crusading fleet under the command of Don Juan was prepared by Spain. Fortified by the prayers of all Spain, and with blessed banners floating from the masts, it sailed forth to do battle. In the Bay of Lepanto it met the Turkish fleet which outnumbered it greatly in both ships and men, and a terrible struggle ensued on October 7, 1571, ending in complete defeat for the Turks. The Battle of Lepanto marks the high point of Turkish expansion in the Mediterranean.

Absolutism by divine right was as much a feature of Philip's government as the maintenance of Catholicism. Philip ruled by means of as many as thirteen councils, each of which was entrusted with a carefully delimited field of activity. They were consultative bodies with no freedom to initiate action. The king reserved the right to direct all public policy and regulate every governmental affair. His was the personal government of a monarch who deemed himself God's agent to carry out His holy will. His subjects enveloped him with special sanctity because he was the divinely appointed protector of Spain and Catholicism; St. Teresa called him "our holy king." To carry out the multitude of duties which such ideas entailed greatly increased the formal task of ruling, and Philip has become the model of the hard-working despot who must originate everything, pass upon everything, and direct everything. He labored long hours writing letters to his officials, and carried on a vast correspondence. The archives at Simancas contain an extraordinary number of these missives, all carefully annotated by this conscientious king.

But this absolutism imposed an impossible task upon a man of Philip's limitations, for, though industrious and solicitous for the welfare of his subjects, Philip was deficient in understanding. Conservative Castilian that he was, he could not comprehend the mighty forces of economic life which were remaking European life, society, and politics. He sacrificed Spain for an ideal increasingly impossible to realize, freely wasting the public wealth in a vain endeavor to establish Spanish dominion everywhere by force. When his father surrendered the Spanish crown to him in 1556, the realm was in a relatively prosperous condition, for colonization of the Americas had produced a demand for manufactured goods which stimulated industries. Production of cloth throve, especially at Medina del Campo. The fairs of Valladolid, Toledo, and Segovia became busy marts of trade, and quantities of gleaming gold and silver came into the realm from Mexico and Peru. Wool production was thriving, and agriculture, especially in southern Spain, was not far behind.

But Philip with all his zeal and labor could not direct the national economy to higher levels, for neither he nor the many advisers who surrounded him knew anything about economic laws. Medieval traditional methods and devices of all sorts were employed. Prices were rising because of the influx of precious metal from America. To combat dearth, restrictive laws were made regulating manufacturing, price of food stuffs, and exports and imports. These were often very arbitrary, such as, for example, the law forbidding export to the Americas of iron, leather, and cloth in order to increase the supply of these commodities for Spanish consumers and thus lower their cost. A more fatal policy could hardly be conceived; as a result, commerce and industry could not thrive. His far-reaching schemes consumed every ounce of the gold and silver from the New World. Because this flow of wealth fell into the hands of foreign, especially Genoese, bankers, it failed completely to build up Spanish economic power. The *alcabala* (a ten percent tax on sales) worked with devastating effect upon trade and manufactures and ruined many an enterprise. The result of this policy even in Philip's reign was economic decline at home, bankruptcy of the treasury, and finally the collapse of Spanish policy in Europe.

Having thus described the character of King Philip of Spain and stated the nature of his rule, we shall next relate the story of Spain's efforts to maintain Catholicism in lands where it was in danger of being overthrown. To do so it will be necessary to outline the general situation in Europe as it concerned the fortunes of Catholicism during the last years of Emperor Charles, father of Philip II. This can be done only at the risk of some repetition, but the complicated character of Philip's far-flung activities makes this necessary.

MARY TUDOR AND PHILIP II OF SPAIN

Although Charles had fought four exhausting wars with Francis I of France from 1522 to 1544, and since 1552 had been involved in another war with Henry II of France (1547–1559), he still hoped to win a great victory for Catholicism in northern Europe. England had set up a national schismatic church, but Edward VI (1547–1553) was fatally ill and likely to die in the near future. The English crown would in that case devolve according to the will of Henry VIII (1509–1547) upon Edward's sister Mary Tudor (1553–1558), daughter of Catherine of Aragon, Philip's aunt.

Mary, devoted to Catholicism, was eager to redress the wrongs inflicted upon her faith and wanted to bring England back into the Roman fold. It was hoped that she would accept her cousin Philip's hand in marriage, whereby English resources would then be enlisted in support of Spain and Catholicism. With English help Philip would be able successfully to oppose France from the Low Countries. In October, 1553, the new queen publicly avowed her intention to marry Philip. Englishmen were likely to resent foreign meddling in their affairs and so, by the marriage articles of January, 1554, Philip was excluded from the English throne in case Mary should have no children by him. Furthermore, any children born of this union should rule in England and succeed to Philip's titles in the Low Countries. And, finally, Philip pledged that English resources should not be employed by his father Charles in his wars on the Continent.

Meanwhile the war which had broken out in 1552 between France and the emperor continued. Charles grew more and more weary under his unequal burdens. Racked by rheumatic pains and disappointed because he could not realize his high mission, he abdicated the crown of the Low Countries in 1555, and that of Spain and of Germany in 1556. To make the first years of Philip's rule as easy as possible, he negotiated with France the Truce of Vaucelles in February, 1556, under which hostilities were to cease for 5 years. It failed because, as was related above, Pope Paul IV (1555–1559) enlisted French aid in an attempt to drive the Spanish from Italy.

This contest also dragged England into the fray, for the French opposed Mary Tudor and favored Mary Stuart, queen of Scotland, who as granddaughter of Margaret Tudor, a sister of Henry VIII, stood close to the succession. A number of refugee Englishmen in France planned a rebellion and actually invaded Yorkshire. Sentiment in England had been decidedly adverse to helping Spain in her struggles, but the invasion produced such keen resentment against France, which had encouraged these rebels, that Mary Tudor declared war. The result was that Calais fell into French hands (1558). But the French were completely defeated in Italy, and they lost the famous Battle of St. Quentin (July, 1559) fought on the borders of the Low Countries. Both sides, exhausted, agreed to the Treaty of Cateau-Cambrésis (April, 1559), by which France retained the bishoprics of Toul, Metz, and Verdun, and abandoned all claims to Milan and Naples. England was forced to allow France to keep Calais. As Mary Tudor had recently died, a marriage was arranged between Philip and Elizabeth of Valois, a daughter of Henry II and Catherine de' Medici. One of the motives for ending the war at this time and arranging this matrimonial alliance was to unite the two Catholic nations so that they might pool their resources in combating Protestantism.

It is necessary to understand these events in order to grasp the motives which underlay the Reformation in England during the reigns of Mary and Elizabeth Tudor. Two points are to be noted in connection with Mary Tudor's reign (1553–1558), the first of which is the typically English resentment at Spanish influence in English affairs. Mary's marriage to Philip of Spain became intensely unpopular, and her participation in the war against France which ended in the loss of Calais (an English possession dating back to the Hundred Years' War) did not improve national sentiment. The second point is the policy of repression which she initiated in her endeavor to make England a Catholic nation, for during her brief reign about 300 unfortunates suffered death for their faith. The people probably would have acquiesced in the queen's intention of undoing as much as possible the work of Henry VIII and Edward VI if only she had not embarked upon the Spanish marriage and the relentless persecution of her subjects. These turned her subjects against the queen, Spain, and Catholicism, so that, rightly or wrongly, for many a generation she has been represented as "Bloody Mary" who suffered England to be sacrificed to the cause of Spain.

Almost immediately after her accession, Mary requested her subjects to return to the faith of their fathers. Everyone knew that she purposed to repress Protestantism by force, and some of her subjects fled to the Continent. These Marian exiles, of whom there were at least several hundred, settled at various centers, such as Frankfort on the Main, Wesel, Strasbourg, Geneva, Basel, and Zurich. Here they were schooled more thoroughly in the ideas of John Calvin, and expressed greater horror than ever before of every form of idolatry, as they termed it, in the Catholic Church.

It was the Spanish marriage, however, that aroused the most intense opposition, for it led to a revolt in the Midlands, another in Devonshire, and a third and more serious one in Kent. In the autumn of 1554, shortly after the queen's marriage, Cardinal Reginald Pole arrived as papal legate, and in November Parliament petitioned him for a full reconciliation of the English Church with Rome, a step made possible only when the legate agreed not to insist upon the return of ecclesiastical lands.

ELIZABETH TUDOR, MARY STUART, AND PHILIP II OF SPAIN

Elizabeth (d. 1603), who stood next in order of succession according to the will of Henry VIII, became queen upon her half-sister Mary's death in November, 1558. Rarely a monarch ascended a throne amid such trying difficulties. First of all was the claim of Mary Stuart. As wife of Francis, son of King Henry II of France (1547–1559), she would become queen of that realm upon the death of Henry, and on the death of her mother, Mary of Guise, she would become queen of Scotland. She was a staunch Catholic, and many English Catholics were inclined to prefer her as queen to Elizabeth. Furthermore, behind Mary Stuart stood France and Scotland, bound together by ancient alliance. If Mary should mount the English throne, she might sooner or later unite in alliance with England, Scotland, and France, which would be a source of strength for France in any contest with Spain, her national enemy. On the other hand, Philip feared that Elizabeth would steer England into the wake of French politics. Accordingly he proposed to marry her, for this, he hoped, would array English resources on the side of Spain against France. In these circumstances it behooved Elizabeth to be wary. Gifted with a keen sense of realities and cautious to a degree, she usually chose the safest course. She knew that her subjects would not rebel against her because that would throw the realm into the arms of France, its ancient enemy, and she also knew that Philip would not harm her because he feared that if her power were weakened she might come under French control.

These problems profoundly influenced the religious settlement which had to be made in 1558. Englishmen were heartily weary of Mary Tudor's forceful attempt to restore Catholicism. Moderation dictated by political expediency was the result, and a position midway between Rome and extreme Protestantism was chosen, thus satisfying the patriotic and religious sentiments of the great majority of Englishmen. Parliament early in 1559 enacted the new Act of Supremacy in which the queen was most diplomatically described as "supreme governor." The *Prayer Book* was revised, the last book prepared under Edward VI being used as its basis. Some definitely Protestant passages were altered so as not to offend Catholic feelings, and many ceremonial customs and Church ornaments were retained. An *Act of Uniformity* (1559) made the acceptance of the new *Prayer Book* obligatory upon all the queen's subjects. Many people, however, could not approve of this settlement.

A large number of Marian exiles returned to England as soon as Elizabeth became queen; and, indoctrinated by Calvin during their sojourn on the Continent, they assumed leadership of many zealous persons who had stayed in England but who were opposed to practices in the Church which they described as "idolatrous," "papistical," and even "satanic." They attacked the custom of using vestments, and they also demanded that the ancient episcopal organization of the Church be changed so that it would resemble a Presbyterian organization. The chief exponent of these views was Thomas Cartwright, a professor of divinity in the University of Cambridge.

From their demand that the Church be "purified" of its ancient Catholic practices these people were called Puritans. Nearly all of them stayed in the Church, protesting constantly and vigorously that a complete renovation should be made. Some there were, however, who abandoned it and formed conventicles, associations which can be traced back to the days of Queen Mary Tudor. Since these people severed all connection with the Church, they were called Separatists or Nonconformists. The origins of the movement are obscure, but it appears certain that they owed little or nothing to the Anabaptists as is often alleged. Groups of them lived in London and other towns in the southeast. Chief among their leaders was one Robert Browne (d. 1633?), but much more extreme in his demand for reformation of the English Church was Henry Barrows (d. 1593), after whom the Barrowists were named. Although these Puritans and Separatists troubled the quiet of religious life in Elizabeth's day, they did not play a great role until the next century.

Until 1587 Elizabeth's chief concern was the activity of Mary Stuart, who, upon the death of her husband King Francis II of France in December, 1560, had returned to Scotland. Just before this the Scots under John Knox had abandoned Catholicism and made Scotland a Presbyterian country modeled upon the Reformation in Geneva. Mary Stuart purposed to reëstablish Catholicism if possible, and also to secure the crown of England, alleging that her claim was superior to that of Elizabeth. Englishmen, however, Catholic as well as Protestant, rallied around their queen because they would not tolerate French and Scottish intrigues in their land. Although his proposal of marriage was rejected, Philip during these years was forced to be friendly to Elizabeth, outwardly at least, for he thought that a union of England, Scotland, and France would be most deleterious to the Spanish cause.

Mary Stuart soon placed herself at the head of a Catholic party in Scotland. She might have been successful in her design of restoring Catholicism had she been a little wiser in her loves and more circumspect in her dealings with the Scottish baronage, but she was finally forced to flee and threw herself upon the mercy of her cousin Elizabeth (1568) — a rash step, for Mary had become the head of a Catholic party in England. Elizabeth thought that it would be unsafe to leave her at liberty and so kept her in honorable confinement. Most English Catholics supported their queen in this matter, but there was a small number who preferred to help Mary. The Jesuits, who were active in missionary work, supported the English Catholics, and some Catholics repeatedly sought to help the imprisoned queen. The pope adopted a hostile policy toward Elizabeth, and Parliament in turn initiated repressive legislation against Catholics who opposed Elizabeth's religious policies.

All these plots came to a climax in 1570 when Pius V excommunicated Elizabeth. This fiery pontiff was convinced that England was the chief bulwark of heresy, and in February of that year he issued his ill-counseled bull deposing her. Its net result was that most Catholics, being hostile to foreign meddling in domestic affairs, loyally turned to the queen's support. Parliament declared it high treason to call Elizabeth a heretic and issued stringent laws against Catholics. Meanwhile plots were laid to depose Elizabeth and put Mary in her place. The last one, Babington's Plot, aimed to assassinate the queen; but every move of the schemers was known to the government, and, when the evidence was more than complete, they were seized. Mary, who apparently knew nothing of the plot, was tried, found guilty, and beheaded in February, 1587, for from the point of view of English political interests her death had become a political necessity.

Chapter 21

FRENCH CATHOLICISM AND LOW
COUNTRY CALVINISM

CATHOLIC REACTION in continental Europe met with two significant checks between 1560 and 1598. The first of these was the establishment of the United Provinces as a Protestant state on the basis of a revolutionary act which repudiated a prince who ruled by divine right. The second was the long series of religious wars in France which nearly ruined the monarchy and finally, in 1598, culminated in the Edict of Nantes, a document which provided a new solution of the vexing problem of religious minorities by conceding to Protestants a measure of religious and political freedom. These two groups of events, in addition to England's struggle with Spain, proved to be the most important factors in setting a limit to the Catholic revival under Spanish leadership.

GUISES, HUGUENOTS, AND THE POLITIQUES.
FIRST RELIGIOUS WARS IN FRANCE

When Henry II of France died in 1559, a troublous period opened in the history of French Protestantism, for a series of eight dreary civil wars, fought between 1562 and 1588, damaged the peace and well-being of the land. Francis II (1559–1560) succeeded his father, but as he was only a youth, he could not give much direction to the government. His wife was the famous Mary Stuart, daughter of James V of Scotland and Mary of Guise, the latter being the daughter of Duke Claude of Guise. The Guises were ambitious, militant, capable, and above all zealously orthodox. Two of Mary's brothers, Charles and Louis, were cardinals, and her elder brother Francis was the famous duke of Guise (d. 1563), a soldier who had won renown in the late war between Henry II and Philip II of Spain. His son Henry (d. 1588) was destined to play a prominent part in the religious wars. The Guises, all-powerful at the court, were most determined protectors of Catholicism and did not hesitate to use foreign power in order to safeguard the old faith. Now that Mary Stuart was queen of France it seemed that the moment had arrived when they could gratify their aspiration to control the royal council.

Catherine de' Medici now began her tortuous policy. As mother of three short-lived kings—Francis II (1559–1560), Charles IX (1560–1574), and Henry II (1574–1589)—she exerted a peculiar influence upon public life until her death in 1589. She became the wife of Henry II in 1533, but her husband showed her neither favor nor deference because of his blind infatuation for the notorious Diana of Poitiers. Kept in the background, she was wrapped up in the welfare and future of her weakling sons upon whom she lavished a mother's tenderest solicitude. Interest, not principle, guided her policy. In this respect she was a typical product of the Renaissance, a true child of the house of Medici. Formally a Catholic, she possessed little conviction about religion. Ever since the Concordat of Bologna in 1516, the Church in France had been a powerful support of the throne, wherefore she always remained true to Catholicism as the national faith, for the future of her children demanded this. On the other hand, she was determined to free herself from the control of factions, whether Catholic Guise or Protestant Bourbon; and in doing this she revealed herself adept in Machiavellian statecraft.

The house of Bourbon, which proved the chief obstacle to the ambitions of the Guises, was headed by Anthony of Bourbon, duke of Vendôme, whose wife was Jeanne d'Albret, daughter of Marguerite of Angoulême and Henry II of Navarre, a petty principality in southern France. Reformed doctrine had been brought to the court at Nérac in 1560 by Beza who undertook a hazardous journey from Switzerland in order to persuade the royal Bourbon family to accept the "Word of God." Henceforth Anthony appeared as the head of a Protestant group among the nobles. Furthermore, he stood close to the throne and appeared likely to ascend it some day, for all Catherine's children were weak and seemed incapable of long life. He and his group resented the overweening ambition of the Guises whom they regarded as interlopers and to whom they showed intense hostility. Anthony's brother, Louis of Condé (d. 1569), had married a relative of Gaspard de Coligny, an avowed Huguenot (or French Protestant) whose sons, Gaspard the Admiral and Francis d'Andelot, were to play prominent parts in the wars which followed. These men became the center of a powerful group which opposed the Guises, and many a Calvinist nobleman, whether from material interest or religious conviction, joined them. In this way the reform which hitherto had been purely religious became more political.

When Francis II succeeded to the throne, the Guises were in a position to dominate the government, and Catherine was thrust into the background. Far-reaching schemes were entertained by them. Since they hoped that Mary Stuart ultimately would supplant Elizabeth on the throne of England, they accordingly supported Mary of Guise, regent of Scotland, against her Protestant enemies. All power and influence which this family could command was to be used to uproot their political opponents and Protestantism.

Naturally the Bourbons did not approve their schemes, and a plot was formed to rid the court of the foreigners, as the Guises were called because they came from Lorraine. Louis of Condé was privy to it according to rumor. The young king was to be seized at Blois, and control of the government was to pass to the Bourbons who had a better right to it than the Guises. The secret was revealed to Duke Francis who hurriedly took the king away from Blois to Amboise. When the plotters tardily arrived in groups they were easily captured; many of them were hanged from the crenelated walls of a castle (1560). The Guises yielded to the wishes of their opponents and agreed to the appointment of Michel de l'Hôpital, a man of moderate views, as chancellor and to the convocation of the Estates General at Orléans. The supporters of the Bourbons remained in prison, and Condé was condemned to die.

At this juncture Francis II died, and Charles IX succeeded him. Catherine became regent and, eager to be freed from the ambitious Guises, drew closer to the Bourbon faction, Anthony of Bourbon assuming control of the royal policy. Louis of Condé was freed from the charge of treason and set at liberty, and the Guises were forced to withdraw with Mary Stuart to their estates in Lorraine. The Edict of St. Germain, issued in January, 1562, gave the Huguenots liberty of worship outside the cities, provided they taught only what was found in Scripture and the decrees of the Council of Nicaea. They were also required to observe Catholic feast days and to secure royal authorization to hold synods. This edict of toleration marked an important step in the progress of the prosecuted faith. Numerous congregations were founded—about 2150, according to an estimate by Théodore de Bèze, Calvin's trusted supporter in Geneva.

During the following years there grew up a party of patriots in France called Politiques who adopted a novel view about relations between the state and religion. During the Middle Ages it was held that secular government should establish the true faith as taught by the Church and labor to guard it and extend its influence. The first significant departure from this conception was the rule adopted by the Lutheran princes of Germany, who held that each ruler in the empire should decide for himself and his people whether the faith of his subjects should be Lutheran or Catholic. The Anabaptists were deemed by nearly all men to be impossibly radical because they held that the state could take no cognizance of religion, but they were never able to write their ideas into the public law of any state. Calvin and his followers, on the other hand, insisted that the Church was a body independent of the political action of the state, which was a noteworthy point of difference between them and Lutherans.

The Politiques placed the common weal above questions of religion, for they did not believe in sacrificing the material well-being of the state in order to create unity in religious belief. They were Catholics who loved king and country and lamented the destruction of national prosperity. Trained in the humanist thought of the Renaissance which emphasized the things of this life, they were loath to place religious unity in the state above peace and prosperity. The Politiques have been cleverly described as men "who preferred the repose of the kingdom or their own homes to the salvation of their souls; who would rather that the kingdom remained at peace without God, than at war for Him." The ideas of the Politiques are symptomatic of a basic change in attitude toward this question, and they herald the coming toleration which was later to be accorded to religious dissenters.

THE HUGUENOT WARS AND ST. BARTHOLOMEW'S MASSACRE, AUGUST 24, 1572

But the Guises plotted to destroy the new faith and began negotiations with Philip II of Spain. They won over the inconstant Anthony of Bourbon by a promise that Philip would return to him Spanish Navarre or make an equivalent compensation. The First Huguenot War (1562–1563) broke out after the massacre at Vassy in which a large number of Protestants who had come together in a barn for religious services were slain. Religion and control of the crown became burning questions in this and the following wars. The people of Paris, being orthodox, sympathized with Duke Francis of Guise who displaced Anthony of Bourbon in the royal confidence. Duke Francis received support from Catholic Spain; the Huguenots, from Protestant England. Anthony of Bourbon was slain, and Duke Francis was assassinated in 1563. The Peace of Amboise followed, under which Calvinism was to continue wherever it had been established, except in Paris.

The Second War (1567–1568) followed because the Huguenots were suspicious of the friendliness of the court toward the Spanish government whose agent, the duke of Alva, had just assumed his task in the Low

Countries. In a battle at St. Denis the Catholics were defeated, and their leader Montmorency was slain. To avoid interference by foreigners Catherine proclaimed the Peace of Longjumeau which renewed the Peace of Amboise. The Peace was soon violated, for the Guises remained in control and continued to enjoy the moral support of Philip II and Alva. De l'Hôpital was dismissed, and an effort was made to seize Condé and Coligny, but they escaped.

In the Third War (1568–1570), which now began, the Huguenots received money and military aid from Elizabeth, and the Guises accepted help from Spain. Condé was shot in a battle at Jarnac in 1569, whereupon his son Henry of Condé, together with King Henry of Navarre, came forward to lead the Huguenots. The Peace of St. Germain, which brought the struggle to an end, reconfirmed the privileges accorded to the Huguenots in the Peace of Amboise and granted them certain cities of refuge and equal treatment with Catholics in appointment to governmental posts.

It seemed that the Huguenots were in a fortunate position, for King Charles was inclined to favor them, and their enemies were discredited, for the moment at least. French royal sentiments were dictated by an apprehension of Spain's growing power. Don Juan had won the Battle of Lepanto in 1571, and the duke of Alva appeared to be successful in reducing rebellious Netherlanders. In England there was some chance that Mary Stuart might replace Elizabeth. If so, that country might be drawn into a great Catholic coalition surrounding France on all sides and most dangerous to French safety. Therefore, any further favor to the Guises, who supported Mary Stuart and looked to Spain for assistance, was out of the question. Charles felt that a better understanding with the Huguenots should be cultivated, for French nationalist sentiment should at all costs, even at the expense of religion, resist the strivings of Spain to dominate Europe. A considerable number of the Catholic Politiques sympathized with this policy.

Catherine, not wanting to fall under the thralldom of the Huguenots and determined not to be thrust into the background again, opposed this policy. The Guises of course did likewise, preferring to champion Catholicism even if it meant the surrender of the nation into Spanish hands, for they did not care to support French national interests which were always opposed to those of Spain if it meant the advancement of Calvinism. The people of Paris were staunchly true to the old faith and zealously repressed dissenters. In 1572 while Catherine was secretly drawing closer to the Guises against the Huguenots, important festivities were arranged in Paris to celebrate the marriage of Catherine's daughter Marguerite of

Valois to Henry of Navarre, leader of the Huguenots. King Charles appeared to be in full harmony with his new Huguenot friends and brother-in-law. A large number of Huguenots came to Paris to celebrate the event.

Coligny, who now seemed to control everything, had far-reaching plans for an international offensive of Protestant forces against Spain, and was relying upon the Prince of Orange to overthrow Spanish control in the Low Countries. Catherine's resentment at Coligny's influence grew apace, and she prevented a declaration of war upon Spain, a proposal advocated by Coligny. Out of the tension created by these circumstances came the infamous Massacre of St. Bartholomew (August 24, 1572). On August 22, an assassin hired by Duke Henry of Guise with the queen's knowledge, aimed a shot at Coligny from the window of a house occupied by a supporter of the Guises. Charles, shocked by this attempt at assassination, expressed his sorrow to Coligny. But Catherine and the Guises, who needed little to encourage them, took a different view of the matter, for they felt that the Huguenots were a menace to the state and that it was best to exterminate them while so many of them were in Paris for the royal marriage.

Charles was weak enough to be persuaded that the Huguenots were not loyal to him, and he yielded to his mother and the Guises, apparently expressing some desire to be rid of the traitors. This was only a momentary impulse which he soon regretted, but it was too late, for in the early morning of August 24 the bells of St. Germain l'Auxerrois began ringing—the signal for the rising. Coligny was murdered. Houses in which Huguenots were staying were broken into, and many an unfortunate was slain in his bed; others who sought safety in flight were cut down in the streets. The troops of the Guises took a leading part in the massacre, and the guard of Paris joined them. Responsibility lay first of all with Catherine because she had allowed the Guises, who nourished in their hearts a long-standing feud with the Huguenots, to have their way. Next it rested upon the king, and here the only plea is that he was incompetent. The Fourth Huguenot War (1572–1573) broke out, to be followed by three brief wars in tiresome succession (1575–1576, 1577, and 1586–1588).

THE DUTCH REVOLT FROM 1574.
SPAIN'S TRIBULATION

Meantime the revolt in the Low Countries more than engrossed the talent and resources of Philip II.[1] The violent policy of the duke of Alva

[1] For the earlier years of the revolt in the Low Countries from 1566 to 1575, see pp. 615–626.

having failed to reduce the rebels, Philip recalled him in 1573, and his successor Louis Requesens, who was there from 1574–1576, also failed. The siege of Leiden ended in a brilliant triumph for the Netherlanders, and, as was noted previously, Calvin's doctrines were accepted as the state faith in Holland and Zeeland. Surrounded by the waters and stagnant pools of the delta formed by the Scheldt, Meuse, and Rhine, these provinces defied their Spanish ruler, every effort to reduce them proving unavailing. The Spanish military was hopelessly bankrupt, Philip's credit was at a low ebb, and Requesens' troops had not been paid for a long time. They finally rose in revolt, chose a leader whom they called an *eletto*, and sacked Antwerp. This event, which became famous as the Spanish Fury (November 4, 1575), filled the hearts of Netherlanders with loathing for the Spaniards and aroused them to more determined opposition.

Terrified by this catastrophe which might be repeated in any one of the many other towns of the Low Countries, the Netherlanders sent envoys to Ghent in order to discuss the situation with William of Orange, and on November 8, 1576, a treaty called the *Pacification of Ghent* was arranged. The provinces bound themselves to secure the departure of the Spanish soldiery and to follow in both secular and religious matters the decisions of the Estates General. The illegal methods adopted by Alva to uproot heresy were to be dropped. Requesens, who died in 1576, wearied by the impossible task which Philip had placed upon him, was succeeded by Philip's natural brother Don Juan, dashing and brilliant hero of Lepanto. But Don Juan could accomplish nothing, for his mind was filled with wonderful schemes. He hoped to free Mary Stuart from the confinement into which Elizabeth had put her, marry her, place her upon the throne of England, and thus win a signal victory for Catholicism as well as glory for himself. He died in 1578 without accomplishing any of his dreams and was succeeded by Alexander Farnese, duke of Parma, who ruled from 1578 to 1592.

Parma, one of the ablest men of his age, was well schooled in the Machiavellian statecraft of Italy and had won fame as a general. Philip's fortunes in the Low Countries began to mend, for Parma sought to insinuate his way into the confidence of the southern Low Countries, and by promises and show of force won many towns and whole provinces to his side. The reason for this defection to the side of the Spaniard is to be sought in the question of heresy—was it to be tolerated? William of Orange was one of the first among Protestants to insist upon tolerance for religious minorities, Protestant as well as Catholic. But a policy so liberal could not be adopted by the rank and file of the people in an age peculiarly hostile to religious dissent. Provinces in which Catholicism predominated endeavored to suppress Protestants, whereas in Calvinist Holland and Zeeland William found it almost impossible to secure liberty for Catholics. It was inevitable therefore that the southern provinces whose population remained loyal to the traditional faith should separate from the northern in which Calvinism was gaining the upper hand.

The *Union of Arras* (January 6, 1579), logical outcome of these circumstances, comprised the provinces of Hainault and Artois, and the communities of Lille, Douai, and Orchies. They proposed to adhere to the terms set forth in the *Pacification of Ghent*, but declared that such was the confusion in religious and political life that reconciliation with the king was necessary. This action by a group of Catholic communities in the Walloon sections of the southern Low Countries meant that a center of resistance was forming against the policy of toleration advocated by the Prince of Orange and the Estates General, for if possible, they would prevent the spread of Calvinist ideas which would result under such a policy.

Meanwhile an opposite tendency was manifest among the northern Low Countries, for these people wished to maintain the Pacification of Ghent, especially in connection with toleration of Calvinism. To protect themselves, the deputies of Holland and Zeeland met with those of Guelders, Utrecht, and Groningen, and on January 23, shortly after the signing of the *Union of Arras*, affixed their signatures to the *Union of Utrecht*. Besides regulating military matters and taxation, this agreement provided that each province could decide the question of religion as seemed best which, of course, meant that the doctrines of Calvin would be established. There were now three Unions in the Low Countries. The first, the Pacification of Ghent, was destined to perish because the principle of toleration in the interest of peace, so dear to the heart of William of Orange, was too idealistic a conception for the age. The *Union of Arras* and the *Union of Utrecht* were each to be the germ of a state, the Spanish Low Countries which remained faithful to Catholicism, and the United Provinces, a Calvinist republic.

FAILURE OF PHILIP'S DESIGNS

The next several years were to prove a sore trial to Philip, for his plans and purposes met with virtual defeat on every hand. The great burden which his political ambition and his religious policy placed upon Spain proved too onerous and ended in national bankruptcy. Destructive methods of taxation, throttling of industry by regulation of prices, ruin of trade by restrictive export provisions, borrowing money at excessive interest, placing financial activities of the state in the hands of a consortium of Genoese bankers provided a most inadequate foundation for Philip's ambitious schemes. By 1598 Spain was defeated in her designs against England, France, and the Low Countries, and internally she had squandered her resources and mortgaged her future for years to come.

For a moment, however, Philip appeared successful. In 1580 he added the crown of Portugal to his many possessions. King Sebastian, who had died in 1578 in battle with the sultan of Morocco, was succeeded by a great-uncle, Cardinal Henry, who died in 1580. Philip now claimed the crown because his mother Mary was a daughter of King John III of Portugal (1521–1557), and dispatched to Portugal an army under the duke of Alva who reduced the country and seized Lisbon. The crown of Portugal was a desirable acquisition, for it completed the policy, undertaken by Ferdinand and Isabella, of bringing the entire peninsula under the rule of the king of Castile and Aragon, and, furthermore, the best possessions of the Portuguese king in the East Indies and Brazil now were added to the Spanish empire. Philip appeared richer and more successful than ever.

But Philip was in danger of losing all his power in the Low Countries where William of Orange continued to be the soul of the revolt. But William felt that the protection of some princely house would strengthen the cause of Holland and Zeeland. All efforts to secure the support of Elizabeth of England failed, for that queen held aloof because she wished to remain neutral and was able to do so as long as she possessed so excellent a hostage as Mary Stuart. Furthermore, since she also disapproved of rebellion against legitimate authority, she could never quite approve the rebellious action of the Netherlanders even if it was dictated by sore necessity. Under these circumstances Orange again turned toward France, from whom since the beginning he had sought help. In 1568 and 1572 the well-planned coöperation of French troops had failed. Charles IX died in 1574 and was succeeded by his brother Henry III, a young man incapable as a ruler, who frittered away his time in useless schemes and idle pleasures. Orange turned to Henry's brother, Duke Francis of Anjou (d. 1584), who in 1576 was offered the title of count of Holland and Zeeland. These negotiations proved successful, for at the close of 1580 Francis accepted the dignity of prince of the northern Low Countries.

The royal house of France thus was enlisted by the Netherlanders in their struggle against Spain—a new example of the inveterate hostility of France toward Spain. The grant of sovereignty to Anjou was an act of rebellion, and it was followed by a still more remarkable step, the formal abjuration of Philip's sovereignty on July 26, 1581. The audacity of this declaration of independence becomes apparent when one reflects that the sixteenth century was an age of absolutism sanctioned by divine right. The theory upon which this revolutionary action was based is that of natural rights, an idea repeatedly expressed in the great pamphlets on political theory produced in the storm and stress of religious wars in France. Hotman's *Francogallia* and the *Vindiciae Contra Tyrannos* undoubtedly influenced the men who drew up this act of abjuration.[2]

A theological justification for the renunciation of Philip's sovereignty was advanced in addition to the casuistry of political theorists. Ample use was made of Calvin's doctrines, for that reformer had taught that obedience to temporal rulers was necessary; indeed, it was enjoined in the "Word of God." He did not subscribe to Luther's views of the sanctity of temporal power, but held that resistance to legally constituted authority was permitted as a last resort if princes ruled contrary to the ordinances of God as set forth in the Bible, especially if they prevented people from worshiping God. Such revolt was to be initiated only by the nobility, for Calvin distrusted democratic action. The rising of the Dutch may have begun more or less in harmony with his theories, but it was the more radical writings of French publicists which moved the rebels against Spain. Philip was regarded as a public enemy who contravened the laws of the land, sacrificed the public welfare, and proceeded against man's highest obligation, the worship of God. In such circumstances revolution became a duty.

The abjuration of Philip by the Dutch was a most significant event in the history of the age. Lutheranism was too servile toward princes and Anabaptism too indifferent toward government and the legitimate claims of property and business to steel the hearts of people in rebellion against their princes. Calvin's teaching provided the needed theoretical basis for a national revolt. Indeed, the spread of his doctrines among Netherlanders is to be explained in part by the great national trials through which the Low Countries were passing. Reformed (Calvinistic) doctrines, established in 1574 as the faith of Holland and Zeeland, spread throughout the north. Sacramentarian, Anabaptist, and humanist ideas were brought into

---

[2] François Hotman (1524–1590), the author of the *Francogallia*, taught in this treatise that the people were permitted to rebel if their prince ruled contrary to law. The *Vindiciae Contra Tyrannos* was written by "Brutus," but the identity of its author has never been settled. Among the names suggested is that of Hubert Languet (1518–1581) and Philip du Plessis Mornay (1549–1623), both of whom, like Hotman, were influential Huguenots. According to the *Vindiciae Contra Tyrannos*, when all other means have been exhausted, it is only proper to rebel.

the Calvinist fold under the pressure of national patriotism, but these ideas survived, however, later to produce a harvest of theological and political disputes.[3]

Duke Francis of Anjou possessed none of the qualifications needed for leadership in such trying times. He entertained extravagant hopes of bringing England into the conflict, and even of marrying Elizabeth, driving out the Spaniards with her help, and establishing himself as sovereign prince in the Low Countries. He could not work under limitations, and his vain spirit was nettled by the restrictions which the Netherlanders sought to place upon him. He attempted a *coup d'état* in January, 1583, by seizing Antwerp, but was repulsed. Discredited, he returned to France and died the next year. William of Orange died at an assassin's hand in 1584, and the duke of Parma began to make successful inroads upon the United Provinces. Elizabeth feared that Philip would establish himself on the banks of the Scheldt, Meuse, and Rhine, whence he could readily assail England in behalf of Catholicism and the imprisoned Mary Stuart.

In France also events seemed to be shaping themselves to the detriment of Protestantism. Henry III had no children, and it appeared that he would have none. Since his brother the duke of Anjou was dead, the crown of France would devolve upon the nearest male heir who derived his title through male descent—none other than King Henry of Navarre who had married Marguerite of Valois at the time of the St. Bartholomew Massacre. But Henry was a Huguenot, and many Frenchmen could not bear the idea of a Protestant mounting the throne of France. Ever since the first wars of religion Catholic nobles had tended to form associations, and a Catholic League came into existence, the leader of which was Duke Henry of Guise, a man who possessed in abundance all the virtues which a nobleman should have. He was affable, courteous, and extremely free in spending money. If the next king must be a Catholic he thought that no one had a better chance than himself. Indeed, as early as 1576 he began to entertain the hope of succeeding Henry III.

The Catholic League feared that Henry of Navarre would establish a Protestant state after the pattern of Henry VIII. Philip also was alarmed because a Protestant France would be likely to coöperate with the rebellious United Provinces and ruin all possibility of his reconquering them.

---

[3] It is well to emphasize at this point that religion was not necessarily the primary cause of the Dutch revolt, for many devoted Catholics joined in the national resistance to Spain. In fact, it has lately been ascertained that the Calvinist party in the province (or county) of Holland in 1587 numbered no more than 10 percent of the population. For a modern account which rectifies many of Motley's views and statements, see P. Geyl, *The Revolt in the Netherlands, 1555–1609*, London, 1932.

As long as France was in confusion, Spain had little reason to fear any hostility in that quarter. Furthermore, Philip, a fervent Catholic, earnestly hoped, for the sake of his faith, that no heretic confessing the doctrine of Calvin would sully the throne. He accordingly decided to assist the League. This organization possessed local units and spread like a network over all France. An important branch was established in Paris, whose inhabitants had at all times shown antipathy toward Calvinism and the Huguenots.

Philip made a treaty with the Guises at Joinville in January, 1585, whereby the latter promised to purge France of heresy and prevent the accession of a Protestant prince, in return for which they were to receive a large subvention. Thus for the sake of the purity of the faith the Guises of France were willing to perpetuate civil war to the detriment of the realm, a policy contrary to the ideas of the Politiques. It was precisely this alliance with the national enemy of France which ruined the League's cause and made inevitable the triumph of Henry of Navarre.

Elizabeth now assumed a more aggressive policy, for she believed the moment had come for her to take a decided stand against the machinations of Philip and the plans of the League. The duke of Parma invested Antwerp, the last of the towns south of the Scheldt to remain in opposition to Philip, and its surrender in August, 1585, was a severe blow to the United Provinces. The United Provinces had extended an invitation to King Henry III to accept their sovereignty, but he in accordance with his preferences for Catholicism favored the League and declined. Next they approached Elizabeth, but that cautious ruler likewise refused the proffer of sovereignty. However, she believed it absolutely necessary to undertake some action for the safety of her realm, and she finally consented to send a force of men and horses to the Low Countries under the earl of Leicester as commander; but this incompetent man aroused so much opposition that after 2 years he was recalled (December, 1587).

This English support of his rebellious subjects determined Philip to strike a blow against Elizabeth, and he planned a large fleet which would coöperate with the duke of Parma and transport his troops from the Low Countries to England. The Catholics of England were to rise and depose Elizabeth whose place was to be taken by Mary Stuart who was still languishing in prison. At this juncture occurred the Babington Plot (1586) which has already been discussed. Elizabeth's government believed in the complicity of Mary Stuart who, as a result, was beheaded in 1587. The failure of this plot momentarily deranged the schemes of Philip, and his descent upon England was delayed until 1588.

Finally the Spanish Armada sailed on its mission of avenging the death of Mary Stuart and of punishing the power that had thwarted Philip's plans. The story of this enterprise is one of the most romantic in all history. The coöperation of the duke of Parma with the fleet proved impossible, for the Netherlanders impressed boats and infested every inlet and stream along the coast of the southern Low Countries, thus preventing the transportation of Spanish troops to England. English ships boldly attacked their adversaries in the Channel, and storms and treacherous seas did the rest, a sorry remnant finally returning to Spain. A ghastly fiasco, it meant that England was safe from any Spanish designs; it implied that the United Provinces had a better chance of beating back their enemy along their southern border, and it also was a victory for Protestantism and hence a defeat for the militant international Catholicism under Philip.

Meanwhile stirring events were taking place in France, for Henry III weakly joined the League in spite of the fact that Henry of Guise had designs upon his crown. He revoked the decrees of toleration which had been issued on previous occasions, whereupon the War of the Henries followed from 1586–1588. It was a dull struggle in which the duke of Guise assumed such lofty airs that Henry III decided to be rid of him. The incompetent king could think of no better way than assassination, a plan which was carried out in December, 1588. Catherine died 2 months later. The king was a sorry figure; he appeared to have lost the respect of all men, and the members of the League hated him. Rejected by the Catholics, he was forced to seek help from Henry of Navarre, and the two Henries now moved upon Paris, stronghold of the League. But the alliance between Henry and the Huguenot king of Navarre exasperated many, and tyrannicide was freely discussed. It was argued that a prince who ruled contrary to the welfare of the Catholic Church and who had murdered the duke of Guise ought to be removed, and that no sin would attach to the hands of the man who slew him. These inflammatory sentiments bore fruit, for on August 2, 1589, a demented friar stabbed the king to death.

1598: HENRY IV, THE CATHOLIC FAITH, AND THE EDICT OF NANTES

Henry IV (1589–1610), as the king of Navarre now began to be called, retired to Normandy because the League was powerful enough to keep him out of Paris. He relied upon Elizabeth's favor, even receiving reinforcements from England, and he steadily gained supporters in spite of his Protestantism. He fought a battle at Ivry in March, 1590, in which he defeated the forces of the League, and soon after he appeared before Paris but could not enter because of the spirited defense offered by the League. Early in September, when starving Paris seemed in his grasp, he withdrew into Normandy before the advance of the duke of Parma who led a splendidly equipped army from the Spanish Low Countries. Meanwhile the League was becoming more and more unpatriotic in its subserviency to Philip. Some of its members were openly saying that he should become king of France. In 1592 Henry won a signal advantage over his opponents and began the siege of Rouen which Elizabeth had urged, for she wished to see Henry's enemies driven out of northern France so that her own communications with him would not be interrupted. Again the duke of Parma appeared with an army of veterans seasoned in the long wars against the Dutch, but he was wounded in an engagement at Caudebec and died in December. He was the ablest general of his day, and his passing weakened the ability of Spain to stir up trouble.

By this time Henry IV had decided to cut the Gordian knot by becoming Catholic, for Frenchmen who were loyal to Rome and who believed that the king of France must be a Catholic were loath to give their support as long as he remained a Protestant. By renouncing the teaching of Calvin, Henry knew that he would win many members of the League. As for himself, he was not a man of deep conviction; the austere doctrines of the Genevan reformer never dominated his thought. His attitude toward religion was much like that of the Politiques, in that he placed national welfare above the faith in which he had been reared. As a patriot his duty was plain. His becoming a Catholic would ruin the League, and France would be his. Accordingly, after proper instruction he was received into the Catholic faith on July 25, 1593, in the magnificent Gothic church of St. Denis. On February 27 of the next year he was anointed and crowned king in the cathedral at Chartres. The ceremony could not take place in Rheims which was held by forces of the League, for the League maintained that a man who had been a heretic could not receive the crown of France.

Henry correctly estimated the effect of his conversion and coronation, for many Frenchmen who had opposed him now saw that the nearest male heir, a Catholic, anointed and crowned king, was actually ruling. They began to consider their own interests and patriotic duties and concluded that obedience was advisable, and soon only a remnant of extremists protested against Henry. On March 22, 1594, the king entered Paris and offered solemn thanks in the cathedral of Notre Dame. The old feeling of hatred of Spain flared up, for more and more it was felt that Philip's real concern was to dismember France. But the League obstinately persisted in its alliance with Spain, and therefore steadily lost prestige. Finally, in February, 1595, France declared war on Philip, and the discomfiture of the League was complete.

One further step remained to be taken—reconciliation with the pope. But Clement VIII was slow to act, for he was too closely associated with Philip to do otherwise. Meanwhile the old quarrel blazed forth between the Gallicans, who championed the freedom of the Church in France from papal control, and the ultramontanes who backed traditional papal policies toward the Church in France. The Gallicans hated the Jesuits who had supported the papal policy toward Philip and the League. In December an attempt was made upon the king's life by a supporter of the League who had been under the tuition of some Jesuits. He was torn to death by four horses, two Jesuits were hanged, and the order was banished from the realm. Clement VIII was alarmed, for he feared that Henry IV might set up a national and schismatic church as had been done in England. Absolution was granted to Henry in September, 1595, and he promised to accept the teachings of the Church as defined in the Council of Trent. Its disciplinary doctrines he maintained encroached upon the liberties of the Church in France and were not to be applied. Clement made a virtue of necessity and yielded, for he knew that Spain was in decline and that Philip's policy would soon terminate.

The war with Spain finally came to an end with the Treaty of Vervins (May, 1598). The League now vanished into history, its members making peace with Henry as best they could, some of them receiving honors and decorations. Henry's next step was the settlement of the religious question. On April 15 he signed the Edict of Nantes, which provided that adherents of the Reformed faith might worship freely in certain towns mentioned in previous edicts, in one town in each district (sénéchaussée and bailliage), and on the estates of nobles. It was stipulated that no one could be barred from public service because of Protestantism. Furthermore, as guarantee that the edict would be carried out, the Huguenots were permitted to place garrisons in seventy-five fortified places. Finally, Protestant judges were to sit with Catholics in order to ensure equal justice.

The religious settlement of Nantes was one of the most remarkable achievements of the century. It had formerly been a universal political dogma that unity of religion was necessary to the welfare of the state, but with the rise of Lutheranism and Anglicanism the principle of cuius regio eius religio became the normal solution of the religious question of the day. The maintenance of unity in opinion, however, proved a difficult task. Prosecution of religious minorities brought little result in France and England, and William of Orange set a noble example by advocating tolerance. But in France the effort to secure religious uniformity led to civil strife which ruined public welfare and threatened to dismember the state. The Politiques argued that it would be far better to tolerate heretics than to ruin the state in a futile attempt to extirpate them. Since this was also Henry's conviction, the Edict of Nantes was the result. National interests were regarded as supreme and were given precedence over religious questions. Henceforth Huguenots could be as good citizens as the Catholics. The Edict marks an important moment in the history of religious liberty, for whereas the Peace of Augsburg allowed no toleration to religious minorities, the Edict of Nantes permitted Calvinist Huguenots to live at peace with the rest of the realm.

Genealogical Tables

Table 1. List of Popes, 1294–1605

Boniface VIII, 1294–1303
Benedict XI, 1303–1304

THE AVIGNONESE PAPACY 1309–1377

Clement V, 1305–1314
John XXII, 1316–1334
Benedict XII, 1334–1342
Clement VI, 1342–1352
Innocent VI, 1352–1362
Urban V, 1362–1370
Gregory XI, 1371–1378

THE GREAT SCHISM, 1378–1415

POPES IN ROME	POPES IN AVIGNON
Urban VI, 1378–1389	Clement VII, 1378–1394
Boniface IX, 1389–1404	Benedict XIII, 1394–1424
Innocent VII, 1404–1406	
Gregory XII, 1406, resigned in 1415	

COUNCIL OF PISA, 1409

Deposed Gregory XII and Benedict XIII
elected Alexander V, 1409–1410
John XXIII, succeeded him, 1410, but was deposed
by the Council of Constance, 1415

Martin V, 1417–1431	Adrian VI, 1522–1523
Eugenius IV, 1431–1447	Clement VII, 1523–1534
(Felix V, 1439–1449, counterpope	Paul III, 1534–1549
elected by Council of Basel)	Julius III, 1550–1555
Nicholas V, 1447–1455	Marcellus II, April, 1555
Calixtus III, 1455–1458	Paul IV, 1555–1559
Pius II, 1458–1464	Pius IV, 1559–1565
Paul II, 1464–1471	Pius V, 1566–1572
Sixtus IV, 1471–1484	Gregory XIII, 1572–1585
Innocent VIII, 1484–1492	Sixtus V, 1585–1590
Alexander VI, 1492–1503	Urban VII, Sept., 1590
Pius III, Sept.–Oct., 1503	Gregory XIV, 1590–1591
Julius II, 1503–1513	Innocent IX, Oct.–Dec., 1591
Leo X, 1513–1521	Clement VIII, 1592–1605

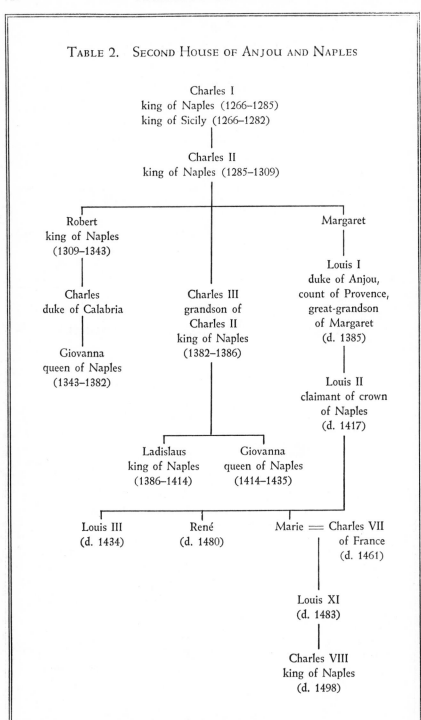

TABLE 2. SECOND HOUSE OF ANJOU AND NAPLES

Charles I
king of Naples (1266–1285)
king of Sicily (1266–1282)

Charles II
king of Naples (1285–1309)

Robert
king of Naples
(1309–1343)

Margaret

Charles
duke of Calabria

Charles III
grandson of
Charles II
king of Naples
(1382–1386)

Louis I
duke of Anjou,
count of Provence,
great-grandson
of Margaret
(d. 1385)

Giovanna
queen of Naples
(1343–1382)

Louis II
claimant of crown
of Naples
(d. 1417)

Ladislaus
king of Naples
(1386–1414)

Giovanna
queen of Naples
(1414–1435)

Louis III
(d. 1434)

René
(d. 1480)

Marie ══ Charles VII
of France
(d. 1461)

Louis XI
(d. 1483)

Charles VIII
king of Naples
(d. 1498)

TABLE 3. HOUSE OF ARAGON IN SICILY AND NAPLES

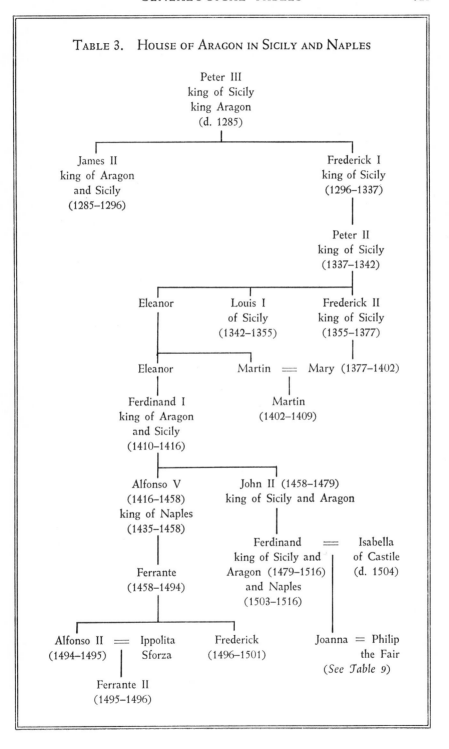

Peter III
king of Sicily
king Aragon
(d. 1285)

James II
king of Aragon
and Sicily
(1285–1296)

Frederick I
king of Sicily
(1296–1337)

Peter II
king of Sicily
(1337–1342)

Eleanor

Louis I
of Sicily
(1342–1355)

Frederick II
king of Sicily
(1355–1377)

Eleanor

Martin ═══ Mary (1377–1402)

Ferdinand I
king of Aragon
and Sicily
(1410–1416)

Martin
(1402–1409)

Alfonso V
(1416–1458)
king of Naples
(1435–1458)

John II (1458–1479)
king of Sicily and Aragon

Ferdinand ═══ Isabella
king of Sicily and   of Castile
Aragon (1479–1516)   (d. 1504)
and Naples
(1503–1516)

Ferrante
(1458–1494)

Alfonso II ═══ Ippolita
(1494–1495)   Sforza

Frederick
(1496–1501)

Joanna ═ Philip
the Fair
(*See Table 9*)

Ferrante II
(1495–1496)

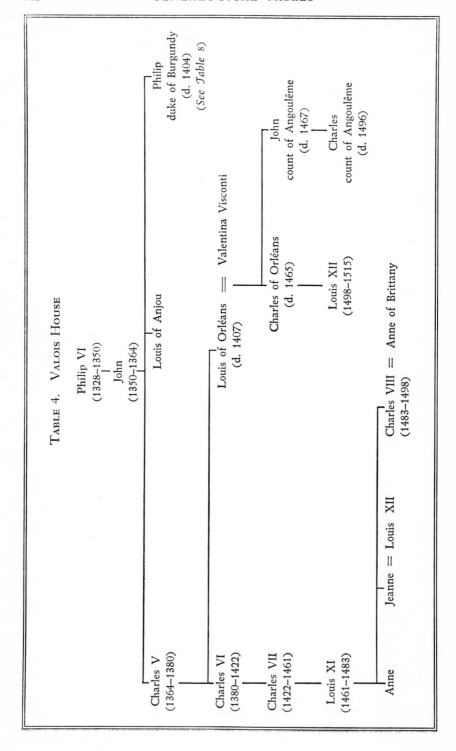

TABLE 4. VALOIS HOUSE

Philip VI
(1328–1350)

John
(1350–1364)

Charles V
(1364–1380)

Louis of Anjou

Philip
duke of Burgundy
(d. 1404)
(See Table 8)

Charles VI
(1380–1422)

Louis of Orléans
(d. 1407)
= Valentina Visconti

Charles VII
(1422–1461)

Charles of Orléans
(d. 1465)

John
count of Angoulême
(d. 1467)

Louis XI
(1461–1483)

Louis XII
(1498–1515)

Charles
count of Angoulême
(d. 1496)

Anne

Charles VIII = Anne of Brittany
(1483–1498)

Jeanne = Louis XII

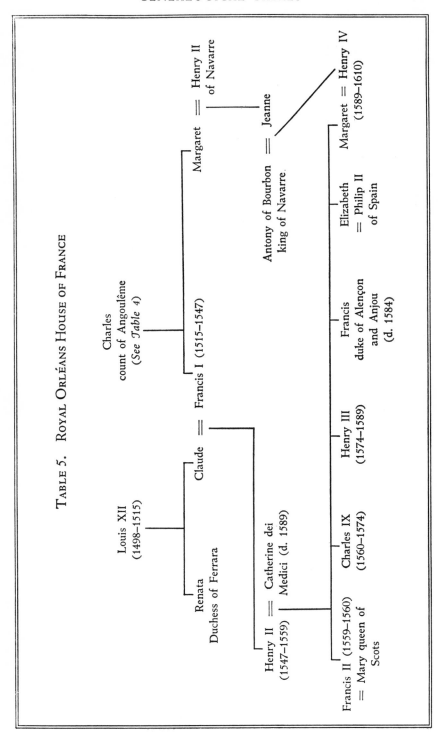

TABLE 5.   ROYAL ORLÉANS HOUSE OF FRANCE

Louis XII
(1498–1515)

Renata
Duchess of Ferrara

Claude = Francis I (1515–1547)

Charles
count of Angoulême
(*See Table 4*)

Margaret = Henry II
of Navarre

Jeanne

Antony of Bourbon = Jeanne
king of Navarre

Henry II = Catherine dei
(1547–1559)   Medici (d. 1589)

Francis II (1559–1560)
= Mary queen of
Scots

Charles IX
(1560–1574)

Henry III
(1574–1589)

Francis
duke of Alençon
and Anjou
(d. 1584)

Elizabeth
= Philip II
of Spain

Margaret = Henry IV
(1589–1610)

TABLE 6. RULING HOUSE OF SCOTLAND

Robert Bruce
(1306–1329)

David Bruce   Marjorie Bruce = Walter Stuart
(1329–1371)

Robert II
(1371–1390)

Robert III
(1390–1406)

James I
(b. 1394,
reign 1406–1437)

James II
(b. 1430,
reign 1437–1460)

James III
(b. 1451,
reign 1460–1488)

James IV   Henry VII of England
(b. 1473,
reign 1488–1513) = Margaret Tudor

Mary of Guise (Lorraine) = James V
(d. 1550)   (b. 1513,
reign
1528–1542)

(1) Francis II of France = Mary Stuart
(d. 1560)   (b. 1542,
(2) Henry Lord Darnley =   d. 1587)
(d. 1567)

James VI

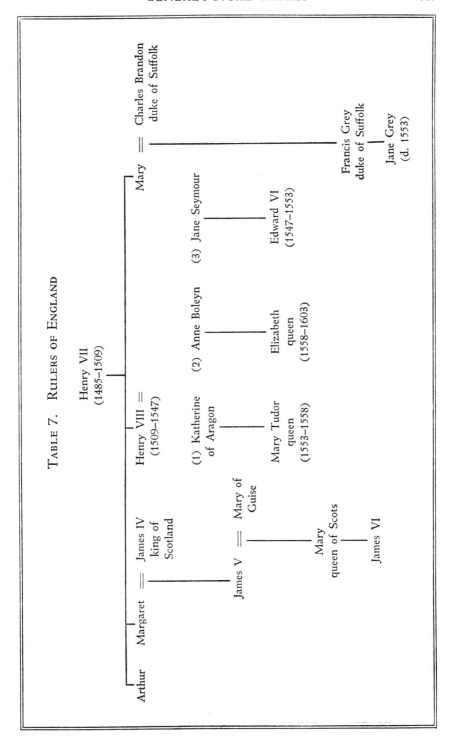

TABLE 7. RULERS OF ENGLAND

Henry VII
(1485–1509)

Arthur   Margaret = James IV   Mary = Charles Brandon
                        king of   duke of Suffolk
                        Scotland

          James V = Mary of
                      Guise

          Mary
          queen of Scots

          James VI

Henry VIII =
(1509–1547)

(1) Katherine   (2) Anne Boleyn   (3) Jane Seymour
    of Aragon

Mary Tudor   Elizabeth   Edward VI
queen   queen   (1547–1553)
(1553–1558)   (1558–1603)

Francis Grey
duke of Suffolk

Jane Grey
(d. 1553)

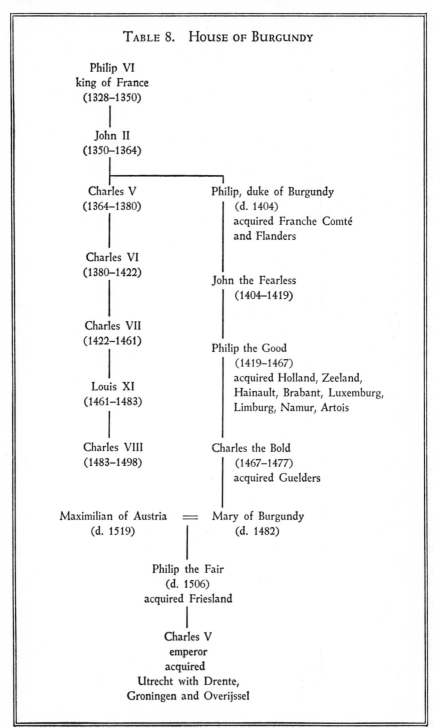

TABLE 8. HOUSE OF BURGUNDY

Philip VI
king of France
(1328–1350)

John II
(1350–1364)

Charles V
(1364–1380)

Charles VI
(1380–1422)

Charles VII
(1422–1461)

Louis XI
(1461–1483)

Charles VIII
(1483–1498)

Philip, duke of Burgundy
(d. 1404)
acquired Franche Comté
and Flanders

John the Fearless
(1404–1419)

Philip the Good
(1419–1467)
acquired Holland, Zeeland,
Hainault, Brabant, Luxemburg,
Limburg, Namur, Artois

Charles the Bold
(1467–1477)
acquired Guelders

Maximilian of Austria === Mary of Burgundy
(d. 1519)   (d. 1482)

Philip the Fair
(d. 1506)
acquired Friesland

Charles V
emperor
acquired
Utrecht with Drente,
Groningen and Overijssel

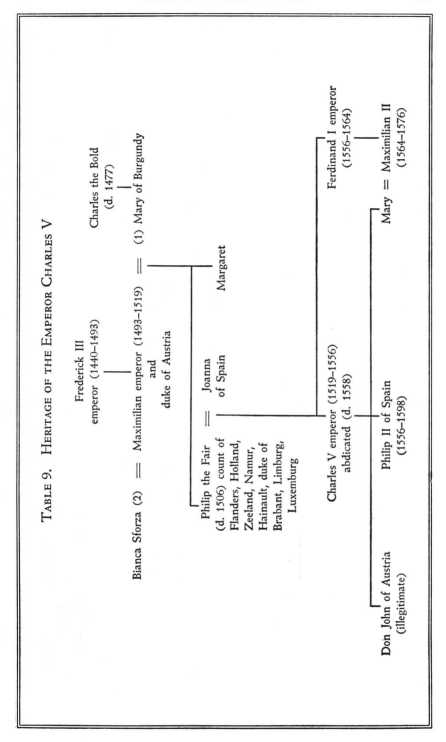

TABLE 9. HERITAGE OF THE EMPEROR CHARLES V

Frederick III
emperor (1440–1493)

Charles the Bold
(d. 1477)

Bianca Sforza (2) = Maximilian emperor (1493–1519) = (1) Mary of Burgundy
and
duke of Austria

Philip the Fair = Joanna
(d. 1506) count of of Spain
Flanders, Holland,
Zeeland, Namur,
Hainault, duke of
Brabant, Limburg,
Luxemburg

Margaret

Charles V emperor (1519–1556)
abdicated (d. 1558)

Ferdinand I emperor
(1556–1564)

Philip II of Spain
(1556–1598)

Mary = Maximilian II
(1564–1576)

Don John of Austria
(illegitimate)

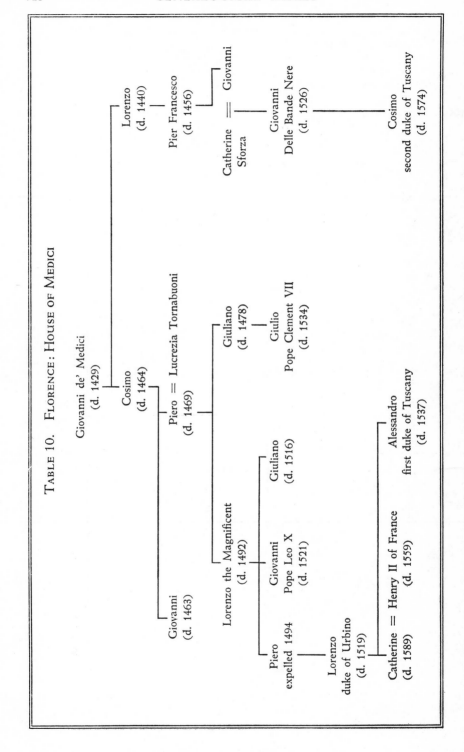

TABLE 10. FLORENCE: HOUSE OF MEDICI

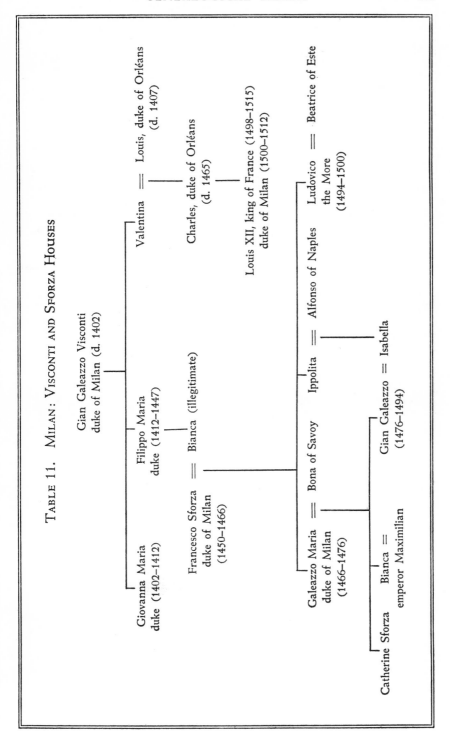

TABLE 11. MILAN: VISCONTI AND SFORZA HOUSES

Gian Galeazzo Visconti
duke of Milan (d. 1402)

Giovanna Maria
duke (1402–1412)

Filippo Maria
duke (1412–1447)

Valentina = Louis, duke of Orléans
(d. 1407)

Charles, duke of Orléans
(d. 1465)

Louis XII, king of France (1498–1515)
duke of Milan (1500–1512)

Francesco Sforza = Bianca (illegitimate)
duke of Milan
(1450–1466)

Galeazzo Maria = Bona of Savoy
duke of Milan
(1466–1476)

Ippolita = Alfonso of Naples

Ludovico = Beatrice of Este
the More
(1494–1500)

Catherine Sforza

Bianca =
emperor Maximilian

Gian Galeazzo = Isabella
(1476–1494)

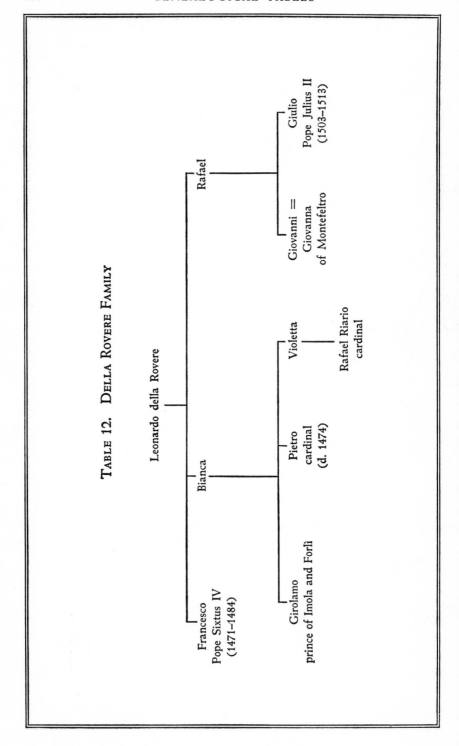

TABLE 12. DELLA ROVERE FAMILY

Leonardo della Rovere

Francesco
Pope Sixtus IV
(1471–1484)

Bianca

Rafael

Girolamo
prince of Imola and Forli

Pietro
cardinal
(d. 1474)

Violetta

Rafael Riario
cardinal

Giovanni =
Giovanna
of Montefeltro

Giulio
Pope Julius II
(1503–1513)

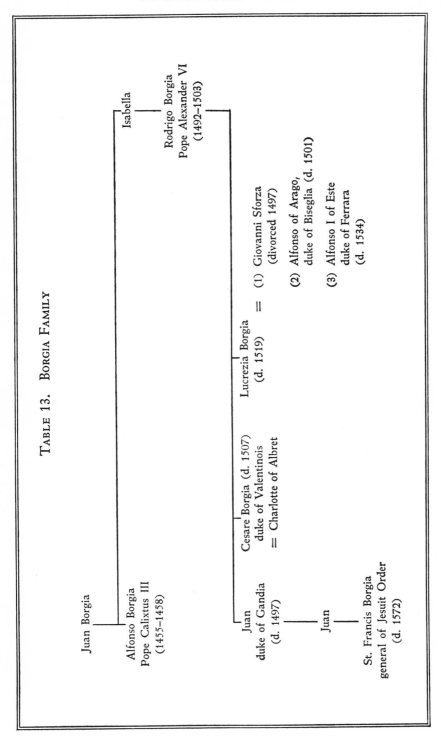

TABLE 13. BORGIA FAMILY

Juan Borgia

Alfonso Borgia
Pope Calixtus III
(1455–1458)

Isabella

Rodrigo Borgia
Pope Alexander VI
(1492–1503)

Cesare Borgia (d. 1507)
duke of Valentinois
= Charlotte of Albret

Lucrezia Borgia
(d. 1519)   =   (1) Giovanni Sforza
(divorced 1497)

(2) Alfonso of Arago,
duke of Biseglia (d. 1501)

(3) Alfonso I of Este
duke of Ferrara
(d. 1534)

Juan
duke of Gandia
(d. 1497)

Juan

St. Francis Borgia
general of Jesuit Order
(d. 1572)

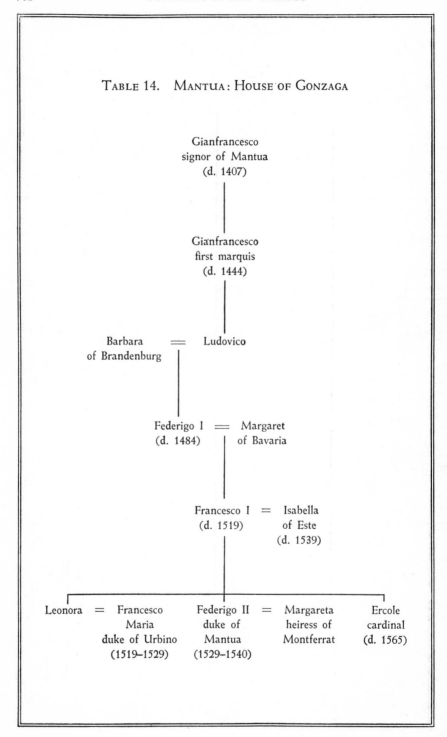

TABLE 14. MANTUA: HOUSE OF GONZAGA

Gianfrancesco
signor of Mantua
(d. 1407)

Gianfrancesco
first marquis
(d. 1444)

Barbara   ==   Ludovico
of Brandenburg

Federigo I == Margaret
(d. 1484)   of Bavaria

Francesco I = Isabella
(d. 1519)   of Este
                      (d. 1539)

Leonora = Francesco   Federigo II = Margareta   Ercole
                Maria   duke of   heiress of   cardinal
           duke of Urbino   Mantua   Montferrat   (d. 1565)
           (1519–1529)   (1529–1540)

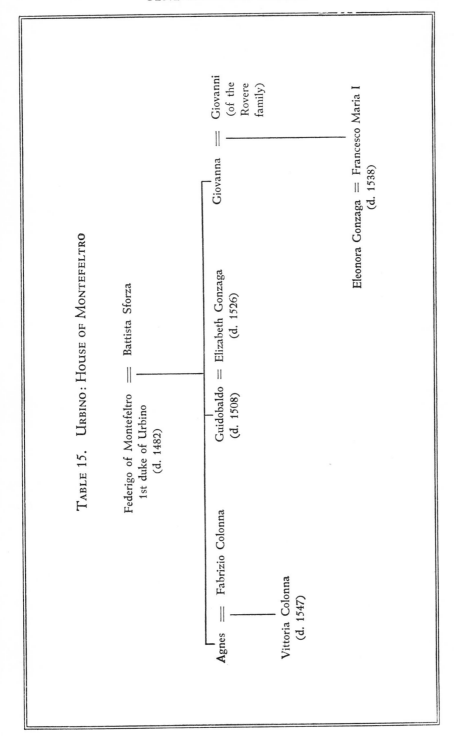

TABLE 15.   URBINO: HOUSE OF MONTEFELTRO

Federigo of Montefeltro = Battista Sforza
1st duke of Urbino
(d. 1482)

Agnes = Fabrizio Colonna

Vittoria Colonna
(d. 1547)

Guidobaldo = Elizabeth Gonzaga
(d. 1508)   (d. 1526)

Giovanna = Giovanni
                      (of the
                      Rovere
                      family)

Eleonora Gonzaga = Francesco Maria I
                              (d. 1538)

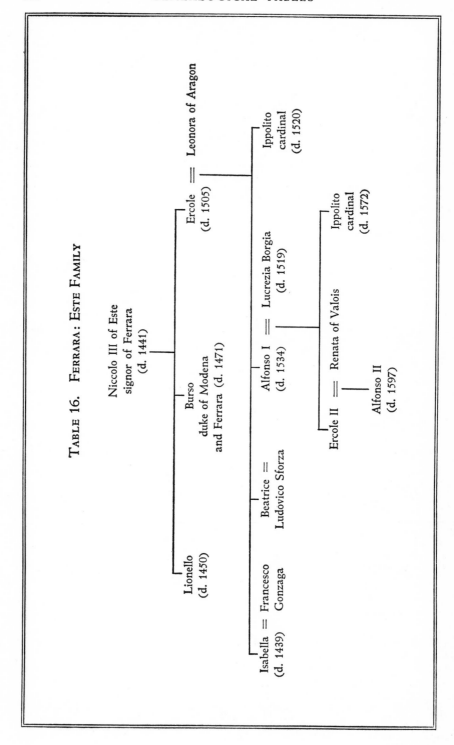

TABLE 16. FERRARA: ESTE FAMILY

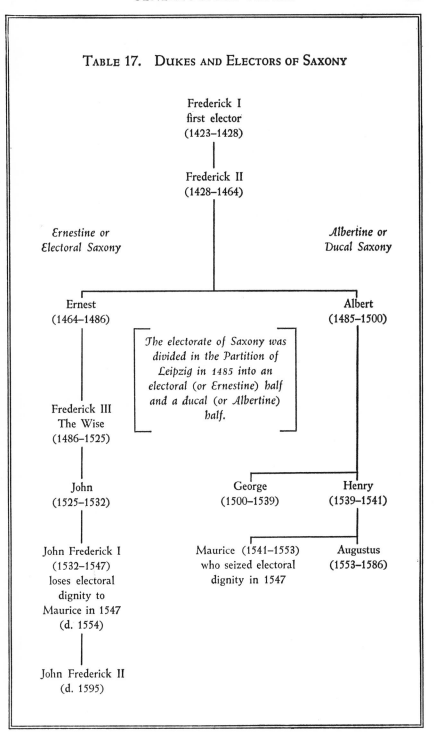

TABLE 17. DUKES AND ELECTORS OF SAXONY

Frederick I
first elector
(1423–1428)

Frederick II
(1428–1464)

Ernestine or
Electoral Saxony

Albertine or
Ducal Saxony

Ernest
(1464–1486)

Albert
(1485–1500)

The electorate of Saxony was divided in the Partition of Leipzig in 1485 into an electoral (or Ernestine) half and a ducal (or Albertine) half.

Frederick III
The Wise
(1486–1525)

John
(1525–1532)

George
(1500–1539)

Henry
(1539–1541)

John Frederick I
(1532–1547)
loses electoral
dignity to
Maurice in 1547
(d. 1554)

Maurice (1541–1553)
who seized electoral
dignity in 1547

Augustus
(1553–1586)

John Frederick II
(d. 1595)

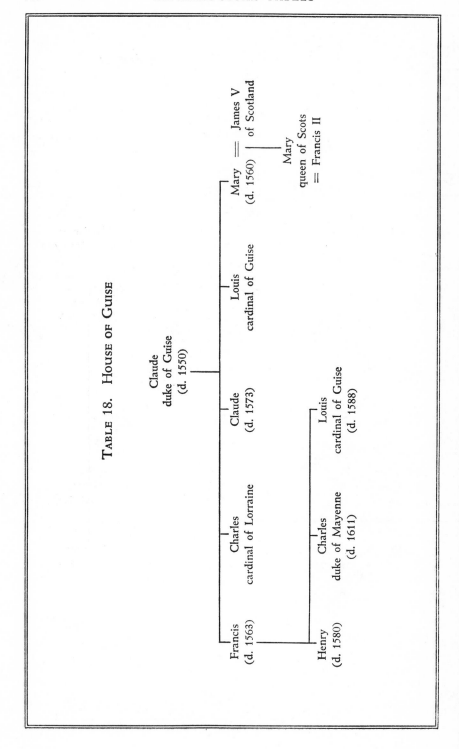

TABLE 18. HOUSE OF GUISE

Claude
duke of Guise
(d. 1550)

Francis
(d. 1563)

Charles
cardinal of Lorraine

Claude
(d. 1573)

Louis
cardinal of Guise

Mary = James V
(d. 1560) of Scotland

Mary
queen of Scots
= Francis II

Henry
(d. 1580)

Charles
duke of Mayenne
(d. 1611)

Louis
cardinal of Guise
(d. 1588)

Suggested Reference
Literature

GENERAL

Allgemeine Deutsche Biographie. For German topics.
Biographie Nationale. For Belgian subjects.
Catholic Encyclopedia. A general authority.
De Katholieke Encyclopaedie. Dutch and Belgian topics.
Der Grosse Brockhaus. For general information.
Dictionary of National Biography. For English topics.
Encyclopaedia Britannica, 14th ed. For articles on all subjects.
Enciclopedia Cattolica. Supplements the following.
Enciclopedia Italiana. Necessary for all Italian Renaissance subjects.
Enciclopedia Universal Illustrada Europeo-America. For Spanish matters.
Grand Dictionnaire Universel. Guide to French topics.
Schweizer Lexikon. For all Swiss matters.
Winkler Prins Encyclopaedia. Dutch and Belgian subjects.

BOOK ONE: THE RENAISSANCE

PART I: NEW SECULAR FOUNDATIONS

Boissonade, P., *Life and Work in Medieval Europe*, New York, 1927.
Cambridge Economic History of Europe, Vol. II.
Cambridge Mediaeval History, Vols. VII and VIII.
Chudoba, B., *Spain and the Emperor, 1519–1648*, Chicago, 1952.
Gras, N. S. B., *A History of Agriculture*, New York, 1925.
Gras, N. S. B., *An Introduction to Economic History*, New York, 1922.
Jamison, E. M., and others, *Italy Mediaeval and Modern*, Oxford, 1917.
Kerr, A. B., *Jacques Coeur Merchant Prince of the Middle Ages*, New York, 1921.
Lodge, R., *The Close of the Middle Ages, 1272–1494*, London, 1924.
New Cambridge Modern History, Vol. I, Cambridge, 1957.
Pirenne, H., *Economic and Social History of Medieval Europe*, New York, n.d.
Power, E., *Medieval People*, Boston, 1924.
Waugh, W. T., *History of Medieval and Modern Europe*, New York, 1932.

Part II: Spiritual Foundations of Late Medieval Culture

Baldwin, M. W., *The Medieval Church*, Ithaca, 1953.

Baldwin, M. W., *The Medieval Papacy in Action*, New York, 1940.

Boase, T. S. R., *Boniface VIII*, London, 1933.

Brezzi, P., *The Papacy*, Westminster, Md., 1955.

Cambridge Mediaeval History, Vols. VI, VII, and VIII.

Cranage, D., *The Home of the Monk*, Cambridge, 1926.

Creighton, M., *History of the Papacy*, 6 vols., London, 1897.

Locke, C., *The Age of the Great Western Schism*, New York, 1896.

Milman, H. H., *History of Latin Christianity*, 5 vols., London, 1855.

Mollat, G., *Les Papes d'Avignon*, Paris, 1924.

Pastor, L. von, *The History of the Popes*, Vols. I and II.

Paulus, N., *Indulgences as a Social Factor in the Middle Ages*, New York, 1922.

Sertillanges, A. D., *The Church*, London, 1922.

Ullman, W., *The Origins of the Great Schism*, London, 1948.

Vacandard, E., *The Inquisition*, New York, 1928.

Valois, N., *La France et le Schisme d'Occident*, Paris, 1896–1902.

Part III: Trials Confronting the Church

Baldwin, S., *The Organization of Medieval Christianity*, New York, 1929.

Betts, R. R., "English and Czech Influences on the Husite Movement," *Transactions of the Royal Historical Society*, 4th Series, XX (1939), 71–102.

Church, A. L., *Church and State in the Middle Ages*, Oxford, 1913.

Creighton, M., *History of the Papacy*, 6 vols., London, 1897.

Dufourcq, A., *L'Avenir du Christianisme*, Vol. VII.

Kitts, E., *Pope John the Twenty-Third and Master John Hus of Bohemia*, London, 1910.

Pastor, L. von, *The History of the Popes*, Vols. I and II.

Part IV: Late Medieval Chivalric Life and Letters

Bulfinch, T., *The Age of Chivalry*, Philadelphia, 1900.

Cowling, G. H., *Chaucer*, New York, 1927.

Froissart, J., *Chronicles* (Globe Edition).

Gesta Romanorum, London, 1905.

Gollancz, I., *The Pearl* (Everyman's Library).

Langland, W., *Piers Plowman* (Everyman's Library).

Lobeira, V., *Amadis of Gaul*, London, 1872.

Lull, R., *Ordre of Chyvalry*, London, 1926.

Malory, T., *Le Morte d'Arthur* (Everyman's Library).

Page, T. N., *Dante and His Influence*, New York, 1922.

Prestage, E., (ed.) *Chivalry*, London, 1928.

Rossetti, D. G., *Dante and His Circle*, London, 1908.

Specimens of the Pre-Shakespearean Drama, ed. by J. R. Manly, Boston, 1892.

Symonds, J. A., *An Introduction to the Study of Dante*, London, 1899.

Taylor, A. A., *An Introduction to Mediaeval Romance*, London, 1930.

Underhill, E., *Jacopone da Jodi, Poet and Mystic*, London, 1919.

Villon, F., *Poems* (Modern Library).

PART V: LATE MEDIEVAL PRACTICAL, PHILOSOPHICAL, AND ARTISTIC ACHIEVEMENT

Adamson, J., *A Short History of Education*, Cambridge, 1919.

Bruhns, L., *Von Eyck bis Holbein*, Vol. IV in *Die Meisterwerke*, Leipzig, 1928.

Cambridge Economic History of Europe, Vol. II, Cambridge, 1952.

Cartelliere, O., *The Court of Burgundy*, London, 1924.

Caxton, W., *Mirror of the World*, in *Early Eng. Jext Society*, London, 1950–1953.

Conway, W. M., *Early Juscan Art*, London, 1902.

Copleston, F., *A History of Philosophy*, Vols. I and II, London, 1950–1953.

Crombie, A. C., *Augustine to Galileo*, London, 1952.

Edgell, G. H., *A History of Sienese Painting*, New York, 1932.

Evans, J., *Life in Medieval France*, Oxford, 1925.

Fierens-Gevaert, *La Renaissance Septentrionale*, Brussels, 1905.

Germain, A., *Les Néerlandais en Bourgogne*, Brussels, 1909.

Gilson, E., *The Unity of Philosophical Experience*, New York, 1937.

Harvey, J. W., *Gothic England 1300–1550*, London, 1950.

Harvey, J. W., *The Gothic World*, London, 1947.

Huizinga, J., *The Waning of the Middle Ages*, London, 1924.

Kaftal, G., *Saint Catherine in Juscan Painting*, Oxford, 1948.

Kaftal, G., *St. Dominic in Early Juscan Painting*, Oxford, 1948.

Kaftal, G., *St. Francis in Italian Painting*, London, 1950.

Mâle, E., *L'art religieux*, Vols. I, II, and III.

Martin, H., *Les Joyaux de l'Enluminure*, Paris, 1928.

Moschetti, A., *The Scrovegni Chapel and the Frescoes Painted by Giotto Therein*, Florence, 1897.

Preuss, H., *Die Deutsche Frömmigkeit im Spiegel der bildende Kunst*, Berlin, 1926.

Wulf, M. de, *Philosophy and Civilization in the Middle Ages*, Princeton, 1922.

PART VI: THE EARLY RENAISSANCE

Boccaccio, G., *The Decameron* (Modern Library).

Burckhardt, J., *The Civilization of the Renaissance in Italy*, New York, 1929.

Cambridge Mediaeval History, Vols. VII and VIII.

Cosenza, M., *Francesco Petrarch and the Revolution of Cola de Rienzo*, Chicago, 1913.

Emerton, E., *Humanism and Jyranny*, Cambridge, 1925.

Geiger, L., *Renaissance und Humanismus*, Berlin, 1882.

Goetz, W., *"Mittelalter und Renaissance,"* in *Historische Zeitschrift*, Vol. XCVIII.

Holway-Calthrop, H., *Petrarch, His Life and Times*, London, 1907.

Jerrold, M., *Francesco Petrarch*, Cambridge, 1917.

Loomis, B., *The Great Renaissance in Italy*, in *Am. Historical Review*, Vol. XIII.

Monnier, P., *Le Quattrocento*, Paris, 1924.

Nolhac, P. de, *Pétrarque et l'Humanisme*, Paris, 1907.

Pastor, L. von, *History of the Popes*, Vols. I–V.

Petrarch, F., *Letters to Classical Authors*, tr. by M. Cosenza, Chicago, 1910.

Petrarch, F., *The Sonnets, Triumphs, and other Poems*, London, 1897.

Robinson, J. H., and Rolfe, R. W., *Petrarch the First Modern Scholar and Man of Letters*, New York, 1914.

Sellery, G. C., *The Renaissance, Its Nature and Origins*, Madison, 1950.

Symonds, J. A., *Renaissance in Italy: Age of Despots* (Modern Library).

Symonds, J. A., *Renaissance in Italy: The Revival of Learning* (Modern Library).

Part VII: Quattrocento Renaissance Culture Under Florentine Leadership

Ancona, P. d', *Umanesimo e Rinascimento*, Turin, 1948.

Anderson, W. J., *The Architecture of the Renaissance in Italy*, London, 1927.

Armstrong, E., *Lorenzo the Magnificent and Florence in Her Golden Age*, London, 1896.

Berenson, B., *The Italian Painters of the Renaissance*, London, 1933.

Brinton, S., *The Golden Age of the Medici (Cosimo, Piero, Lorenzo de' Medici), 1434–1494*, London, 1925.

Caggese, R., *Firenze della Decadenza di Roma al Risorgimento d'Italia*, Florence, 1913.

Ewart, K. D., *Cosimo de' Medici*, London, 1899.

Gilmore, M. P., *The World of Humanism, 1453–1517*, New York, 1954.

Hausenstein, W., *Fra Angelico*, London, 1928.

Horsburgh, E., *Lorenzo the Magnificent and Florence in the Fifteenth Century*, New York, 1908.

Hyett, F. A., *Florence, her History and Art to the Fall of the Republic*, London, 1913.

Marle, R. Van, *The Development of the Italian Schools of Painting*, Vols. I to XVI, The Hague, 1923–1938.

Mesnil, J., *Masaccio et les Débuts de la Renaissance*, The Hague, 1927.

Ormsby-Gore, W., *Florentine Sculptors of the Fifteenth Century*, London, 1930.

Phillipps, E. M., *The Frescoes in the Sistine Chapel*, London, 1907.

Ross, J., *Lives of the Early Medici*, London, 1910.

Schevill, F., *History of Florence*, New York, 1936.

Schevill, F., *The Medici*, New York, 1949.

Smeaton, W., *The Medici and the Italian Renaissance*, New York, 1901.

Symonds, J. A., *Renaissance in Italy: The Fine Arts* (Modern Library).

Tonks, O. S., *A History of Italian Painting*, New York, 1927.

Vasari, G., *Lives of the Most Eminent Painters, Sculptors, and Architects* (Everyman's Library).

Yriarte, C., *Florence, Its History, the Medici, the Humanists, Letters, Arts,* New York, 1882.

PART VIII: Quattrocento RENAISSANCE CULTURE OUTSIDE FLORENCE

Ady, C. M., *A History of Milan under the Sforzas,* London, 1907.

Berence, F., *Léonard de Vinci,* Paris, 1927.

Beyen, H. G., *Andrea Mantegna,* The Hague, 1931.

Brinton, S., *The Gonzaga Lords of Mantua,* London, 1927.

Chledowski, C., *Siena,* Berlin, 1923.

Coleman, C. B., *The Treatise of Lorenzo Valla or the Donation of Constantine,* New Haven, 1924.

Dennistoun of Dennistoun, J., *Memoires of the Dukes of Urbino Illustrating the Arms, Arts, and Literature of Italy,* New York, 1909.

Gardner, E., *Dukes and Poets of Ferrara,* New York, 1904.

Gardner, E., *The Painters of the School of Ferrara,* London, 1911.

Guicciardini, F., *The History of Italy,* London, 1763.

Hazlitt, W. C., *History of the Venetian Republic,* 2 vols., London, 1915.

Hutton, E., *Sigismondo Pandulfo Malatesta, Lord of Rimini,* London, 1906.

Klaczko, J., *Rome and the Renaissance: The Pontificate of Julius II, 1503–1515,* Paris, 1926.

Lucas, H., *Fra Girolamo Savonarola,* London, 1899.

McCurdy, E., *The Mind of Leonardo da Vinci,* New York, 1928.

McCurdy, E., *Leonardo da Vinci,* New York, 1923.

Muntz, E., *Raphael, his Life, Works and Times,* London, 1898.

Portigliotti, G., *The Borgias, Alexander VI, Caesar, Lucrezia,* London, 1928.

Symonds, J. A., *Life of Michael Angelo Buonarotti* (Modern Library).

PART IX: POLITICAL CRISES IN HIGH RENAISSANCE ITALY

Burchardus, J., *Pope Alexander VI and his Court,* New York, 1921.

Cambridge Modern History, Vol. I (first ed.).

Commines, P. de, *Memoires* (Bohn Library).

Creighton, M., *History of the Papacy,* Vols. IV, V, and VI, London, 1897.

Landucci, L., *A Florentine Diary from 1450 to 1516,* London, 1927.

Lodge, R., "Machiavelli's Il Principi," in *Transactions of the Royal Historical Society,* 4th Series, XIII (1930), 1–18.

Machiavelli, N., *The Prince* (Everyman's Library).

Machiavelli, N., *History of Florence* (Everyman's Library).

Machiavelli, N., *Discourses on the First Ten Books of Titus Livius and the Art of War,* in *The Historical, Political, and Diplomatic Writings of N. Machiavelli,* Vol. II, New York, 1891.

Morley, J., *Machiavelli,* Oxford, 1897.

Steinmann, E., *Rom in der Renaissance von Nicholas V bis auf Leo X*, Leipzig, 1908.

Villari, L., *Life and Times of Niccolò Machiavelli*, London, 1898.

Villari, L., *Life and Times of Girolamo Savonarola*, London, 1888.

Taylor, F. L., *The Art of War in Italy, 1494–1529*, Cambridge, 1921.

PART X: NOVEL CREATIONS OF THE HIGH RENAISSANCE

Ailly, P. d', *Ymago Mundi*, ed. by E. Buron, Paris, 1930.

Beazley, C. R., *Prince Henry the Navigator*, New York, 1908.

Biagi, G., *Men and Manners of Old Florence*, London, 1909.

Boulting, W., *Tasso and his Times*, London, 1907.

Cartwright, J., *Italian Gardens of the Renaissance*, London, 1914.

Cartwright, J., *Beatrice d'Este, Duchess of Milan, 1475–1497: A Study of the Renaissance*, London, 1913.

Cartwright, J., *Baldassare Castiglione, The Perfect Courtier, His Life and Letters*, New York, 1908.

Castiglione, B., *The Book of the Courtier* (Everyman's Library).

Cheyney, E. P., *The Dawn of a New Era 1250–1453*, New York, 1936.

Dampier-Whetham, W., *A History of Science and its Relations with Philosophy and Religion*, Cambridge, 1929.

Dennistoun of Dennistoun, J., *Memoirs of the Dukes of Urbino Illustrating the Arms, Arts, and Literature of Italy, 1440–1630*, New York, 1909.

Dickinson, R. E., and Hawarth, O. J., *The Making of Geography*, Oxford, 1933.

Dufourcq, A., "Les Origines de la Science Moderne d'après les Découvertes Récentes," in *Revue des Deux Mondes*, 6th Series, XVI, Paris, 1913, 349–379.

Duhem, P., *Études sur Léonard da Vinci: Ceux qu'il a Lus et Ceux qui l'ont Lu*, Paris, 1906–1909.

Duhem, P., "Un Précurseur Français de Copernic: Nicole Oresme" (1377), in *Revue Générale des Sciences Pures et Appliquées*, XX (1909), 866–73.

Dryer, J. L., *History of the Planetary Systems from Thales to Kepler*, Cambridge, 1906.

Gotheim, M. L., *A History of Garden Art*, New York, 1928.

Gray, E. F., *Leif Erikson Discoverer of America, A.D. 1003*, New York, 1930.

Hart, I., *Makers of Science: Mathematics, Physics, Astronomy*, Oxford, 1924.

Hart, I., *The Mechanical Investigations of Leonardo da Vinci*, London, 1925.

Hutton, E., *Pietro Aretino, the Scourge of Princes*, London, 1922.

Jerrold, M., *Vittoria Colonna with Some Account of her Friends and Her Times*, London, 1906.

Kennard, J. S., *The Italian Theatre from its Beginning to the Close of the Sixteenth Century*, New York, 1932.

Lenhart, J. M., *Pre-Reformation Printed Books*, in *Franciscan Studies*, No. 14, New York, 1935.

Lungo, I. del, *Women of Florence*, London, 1907.

Lybyer, A. H., "The Ottoman Turks and the Routes of Oriental Trade," in *English Historical Review*, XXX (1915).

Marco Polo, *The Book of Ser Marco Polo*, tr. and ed. by H. Yule, London, 1903.

New Cambridge Modern History, Vol. I, chaps. II, XV, XVI.

Pasolini, P. D., *Catherine Sforza*, New York, 1898.

Putnam, G., *Books and their Makers during the Middle Ages*, New York, 1896–1897.

Spingarn, J., *A History of Literary Criticism in the Renaissance*, New York, 1899.

PART XI: RENAISSANCE ART OUTSIDE ITALY

Bastelaer, R. van, *Les Étampes de Pieter Bruegel*, Brussels, 1908.

Bosschere, J., *La Sculpture Anversoise aux XVᵉ et XVIᵉ Siècles*, Brussels, 1909.

Chamberlain, R. B., *Hans Holbein the Younger*, New York, 1913.

Cust, L., *Albrecht Dürer, A Study of his Life and Work*, London, 1900.

Dieulafoy, M., *Art in France and Portugal*, New York, 1913.

Hind, A. M., *A History of Engraving and Etching from the 15th Century to the Year 1914*, London, 1923.

Holland, R. S., *Historic Inventions*, Philadelphia, 1911.

Hoogewerff, G. J., *Jan van Scorel, Peintre de la Renaissance Hollandaise*, The Hague, 1923.

Hourticq, L., *Art in France*, New York, 1911.

Hueffer, F. M., *Hans Holbein the Younger*, London, 1909.

Jackson, T. G., *The Renaissance of Roman Architecture*, Cambridge, 1922–1923.

Knackfuss, H., *Holbein*, London, 1899.

Ree, P., *Nuremberg and its Art to the End of the 18th Century*, New York, 1905.

Rooses, M., *Art in Flanders*, New York, 1914.

Segard, A., *Jean Gossart dit Mabuse*, Brussels, 1924.

Zype, G. van, *Bruegel*, Brussels, 1926.

PART XII: NORTHERN HUMANISM FROM ERASMUS TO MONTAIGNE

Allen, P. S., *The Age of Erasmus*, Oxford, 1904.

Brant, S., *The Ship of Fools*, tr. by E. H. Zeydel, New York, 1944.

Daly, W. A., *The Educational Psychology of Juan Luis Vives*, Washington, 1924.

Einstein, L., *The Italian Renaissance in England*, New York, 1916.

Emerton, E., *Desiderius Erasmus of Rotterdam*, New York, 1900.

Epistolae Obscurorum Virorum, tr. by F. G. Stokes, London, 1909.

Erasmus, D., *Ciceronianus*, New York, 1908.

Erasmus, D., *Complaint of Peace*, Chicago, 1917.

Erasmus, D., *Enchiridion Militis Christiani*, London, 1905.

Erasmus, D., *Familiar Colloquies*, London, 1900.

Erasmus, D., *In Praise of Folly*, Oxford, 1913.

Huizinga, J., *Erasmus*, New York, 1924.

Hyma, A., *The Christian Renaissance*, Grand Rapids, 1924.

Lee, S., *The French Renaissance in England*, London, 1910.

Margaret, Queen of Navarre, *The Heptameron* (Broadway Translations).

More, T., *Utopia* (Everyman's Library).

Montaigne, M., *Essays* (Everyman's Library).

Rabelais, F., *The Heroic Deeds of Gargantua and Pantagruel* (Everyman's Library).

Renaudet, A., *Préréforme et Humanisme à Paris pendant les premières Guerres d'Italie, 1494–1517*, Paris, 1916.

Renwick, W. A., *Edmund Spenser*, London, 1925.

Seebohm, F., *The Oxford Reformers* (Everyman's Library).

Sidney, P., *The Defense of Poesy*, Boston, 1890.

Smith, P., *Erasmus*, New York, 1923.

Smith, W. F., *Rabelais and his Writings*, Cambridge, 1918.

Strauss, D., *Ulrich von Hutten, his Life and Times*, London, 1874.

BOOK TWO: THE REFORMATION AND CATHOLIC REVIVAL

GENERAL

Bainton, R. H., *Bibliography of the Continental Reformation: Materials Available in English*, Chicago, 1935.

Bainton, R. H., *The Reformation of the Sixteenth Century*, Boston, 1952.

Hughes, P., *A Popular History of the Reformation*, New York, 1956.

Hulme, E. M., *The Renaissance, the Protestant Revolution, and the Catholic Reformation in Continental Europe*, New York, 1921.

Grimm, H. J., *The Reformation Era, 1500–1650*, New York, 1954. Contains an excellent biography.

Lindsay, T. M., *A History of the Reformation*, New York, 1914.

Smith, P., *The Age of the Reformation*, New York, 1923.

Whitney, J. P., *The History of the Reformation*, London, 1940.

Part I: Breakup of Religious Unity in Western Europe

Armstrong, E., *The Emperor Charles V*, London, 1892.

Bainton, R. H., *Here I Stand, A Life of Martin Luther*, New York, 1950.

Bergendoff, C., *Olavus Petri and the Ecclesiastical Transformation of Sweden, 1521–1552*, New York, 1929.

Betten, F., "The Cartoon in Luther's War against the Church," in *The Catholic Historical Review*, New Series, V (1925–1926), 252–64.

Boehmer, H., *Luther and the Reformation in the Light of Modern Research*, New York, 1931.

Butler, C. M., *The Reformation in Sweden*, New York, 1883.

Fife, R. H., *Luther and the Reformation in the Light of Modern Research*, New York, 1929.

Fèbure, L., *Martin Luther: A Destiny*, New York, 1929.
Fox, P., *The Reformation in Poland*, Baltimore, 1924.
Grisar, H., *Martin Luther: His Life and Work*, St. Louis, 1930.
Luther, M., *Works with Introduction and Notes*, Philadelphia, 1915–1932.

PART II: LUTHERANISM ASCENDANT

Cambridge Modern History, Vol. II.
Makinnon, J., *Luther and the Reformation*, London, 1925–1930.
Neve, J. L., *Introduction to Lutheran Symbolics*, Columbus, 1917.
Oman, C., "The German Peasant War," in *English Historical Review*, V (1890).
Reu, J. M., *Thirty-five Years of Luther Research*, Chicago, 1917.
Richard, J. W., *Philip Melanchthon, the Protestant Preceptor of Germany, 1497–1560*, New York, 1898.
Zeeden, E. W., *The Legacy of Luther*, London, 1954.

PART III: NOVEL PROTESTANT TEACHING

Dosker, H., *The Dutch Anabaptists*, Philadelphia, 1921.
Eekhof, A., *The Avondmaalsbrief van Cornelis Hoen (1525) in Facsimile*, The Hague, 1917.
Eells, H., *Martin Bucer*, New Haven, 1931.
Evans, A. P., *An Episode in the Struggle for Religious Freedom: the Sectaries of Nuremberg, 1524–1561*, New York, 1924.
Farner, O., *Zwingli the Reformer*, New York, 1952.
Horsch, J., *Mennonite History*, Vol. I: *Mennonites in Europe*, Scottdale, 1950.
Horsch, J., *Menno Simons. His Life, Labors, and Teachings*, Scottdale, 1916.
Hyma, A., *The Christian Renaissance*, Grand Rapids, 1924.
Jackson, S. M., *Huldreich Zwingli: The Reformer of German Switzerland, 1484–1531*, New York, 1900.
Kuhler, W., *Geschiedenis der Nederlandsche Doopsgesinden*, Haarlem, 1932.
Mennonitisches Lexikon, Frankfurt-am-Main, 1913. In progress.
Miller, E., and Scudder, J. W., *Wessel Gansfort: His Life and Teaching*, New York, 1917.
Vedder, H., *Balthasar Hubmaier*, New York, 1905.

PART IV: PROTESTANT MOVEMENTS IN ENGLAND, SPAIN, AND ITALY

Benrath, K., *Bernardino Ochino of Siena*, New York, 1877.
Brown, G. K., *Italy and the Reformation to 1550*, London, 1933.
Constant, G., *The Reformation in England: Henry VIII, 1509–1547*, New York, 1934.
Davis, E. J., "The Authorities for the Case of Richard Hunne 1514–1515," in *English Historical Review*, XXX (1915), 477–488.
Fletcher, J., *The Reformation in Northern England*, London, 1925.
Gairdner, J., "Mary and Anne Boleyn," in *English Historical Review*, VII (1898), 53–60.

Gee, H., and Hardy, W. J., *Documents Illustrative of English Church History*, London, 1914.

Hughes, P., *The Reformation in England*, London, 1950–1953.

Jacobs, H. E., *The Lutheran Movement in England during the Reigns of Henry VIII and Edward VI and its Literary Movements*, Philadelphia, 1894.

Pollard, A. F., *Henry VIII*, London, 1925.

Pollard, A. F., *Thomas Cranmer and the English Reformation, 1489–1556*, New York, 1904.

Pollard, A. F., *Wolsey*, London, 1929.

Part V: The Peace of Augsburg: An Epoch in Protestantism

Armstrong, E., *The Emperor Charles V*, London, 1892.

Cambridge Modern History, Vols. II and III.

Chudoba, B., *Spain and the Empire 1519–1643*, Chicago, 1952.

Johnson, A. J., *Europe in the Sixteenth Century 1494–1598*, London, 1925.

Lindsay, T. M., *A History of the Reformation*, Vol. I, New York, Chap. V.

Part VI: The Calvinist Revolt

Baird, H. M., *The History of the Rise of the Huguenots of France*, New York, 1900.

Baird, H. M., *Theodore Beza Counsellor of the French Reformation*, New York, 1899.

Batiffol, L., *The Century of the Renaissance*, New York, 1916.

Bower, H., *The Fourteen of Meaux*, London, 1894.

Breen, Q., *John Calvin: A Study in French Humanism*, Grand Rapids, 1931.

Buisson, E., *Sebastien Castellion sa Vie et son Oeuvre*, Paris, 1892.

Cambridge Modern History, Vol. III.

Calvin, J., *Institutes of the Christian Religion*, Edinburgh, 1845–1856.

Doumergue, E., *Jean Calvin, Les Hommes et les Choses de son Temps*, Lausanne, 1899–1927, 7 vols.

Eells, H., *Martin Bucer*, New Haven, 1931.

Giran, E., *Sebastien Castellion et la Réforme Calviniste*, Haarlem, 1913.

MacDonald, J. M., *History of France*, Vol. ii.

Walker, W., *John Calvin the Organizer of Reformed Protestantism 1509–1564*, New York, 1906.

Part VII: Leadership of Calvinist Thought in Protestantism

Armstrong, E., *The French Wars of Religion, their Political Aspect*, Cambridge, 1892.

Baird, H. M., *The History of the Rise of the Huguenots of France*, New York, 1902.

Blok, P. T., *A History of the People of the Netherlands*, New York, 1900, Vol. III.

Cambridge Modern History, Vol. III.

Cowan, H., *John Knox, the Hero of the Scottish Reformation*, New York, 1905.

Frere, W. H., *The English Church in the Reign of Elizabeth and James I, 1558–1625*, London, 1904.

Geyl, P., *The Revolt in the Netherlands 1556–1609*, New York, 1958.

Gossart, E., *Espagnols et Flamands au XVIᵉ Siècle: Charles Quint, Roi d'Espagne*, Brussels, 1910.

Harrison, F., *William the Silent*, London, 1907.

Hart, A. B., "John Knox as a Man of the World," in *The American Historical Review*, XIII (1908).

Philippson, M., *The Religious Wars*, Vol. XII of *A History of all Nations*.

Plummer, A., *English History to the Death of Archbishop Parker*, Edinburgh, 1905.

Vries, H. de, *Genève Pépinière du Calvinisme Hollandaise*, The Hague, 1918–1924.

Part VIII: Catholic Reform

Boehmer, H., *The Jesuits*, Philadelphia, 1928.

Brémond, H., *A Literary History of Religious Thought in France*, London, 1928–1930.

Broderich, J., *The Origin of the Jesuits*, New York, 1940.

Broderich, J., *The Progress of the Jesuits 1556–79*, New York, 1946.

Cambridge Modern History, Vol. III.

Capasso, C., *Paolo III, 1534–49*, Messina, 1925.

Clavière, M. de Maulde la, *Saint Cajetan*, New York, 1902.

Cuthbert, Father, *The Capuchins; A Contribution to the History of the Counter-Reformation*, New York, 1929.

Evennett, H., *The Cardinal of Louvaine and the Council of Trent*, Cambridge, 1930.

Figgis, J. N., "*Petrus Canisius and the German Counter-Reformation*" in *The English Historical Review*, London, 1909.

Froude, J. A., *Lectures on the Council of Trent*, New York, 1896.

Harney, M. P., *The Jesuits in History*, New York, 1941.

Hefele, C. J., *The Life of Cardinal Ximenes*, London, 1860.

Hughes, P., *Rome and the Counter-Reformation*, London, 1944.

Hulme, M. A., *Philip II of Spain*, London, 1911.

Kidd, B. J., *The Counter-Reformation 1555–1600*, London, 1933.

Littledale, A., *A Short History of the Council of Trent*, London, 1888.

Lucas, H. S., "Survival of the Catholic Faith in the Sixteenth Century," in *The Making of Modern Europe*, ed. by H. Ausubel, Vol. I, 1951.

Lyell, J., *Cardinal Ximenes*, London, 1917.

Mariejol, J. H., *Philip II, the First Modern King*, New York, 1933.

Pastor, L. von, *History of the Popes*, Vols. VIII to XIII.

Peers, E. A., *St. John of the Cross and Other Lectures and Addresses*, London, 1946.

Peers, E. A., *Spanish Mysticism*, London, 1924.

Peers, E. A., *Spirit of Flame. A Study of St. John of the Cross*, New York, 1915.

Peers, E. A., *Mother of Carmel. A Portrait of St. Teresa of Jesus*, New York, 1946.

Pollard, A. F., *The Jesuits in Poland*, Cambridge, 1902.

Ponelle, L., and Bordet, L., *St. Philip Neri and the Roman Society of his Times*, London, 1932.

Scheuber, J., *Kirche und Reformation*, Cologne, 1917.

Thompson, F., *Life of St Ignatius Loyola*, London, 1910.

PART IX: CATHOLIC POLITICAL REACTION

Baird, H. M., *The Huguenots of France*, New York, 1909.

Cambridge Modern History, Vols. I and II.

Geyl, P., *The Revolt in the Netherlands 1555–1609*, New York, 1958.

Lang, A., *The Mystery of Mary Stuart*, London, 1904.

Lavisse, E., ed., *Histoire de France*, Vol. VI.

Lavisse, E., and Rambaud, A., eds., *Histoire Generale*, Vol. V.

Lea, H. C., *The Moriscos of Spain*, Philadelphia, 1901.

MacCaffrey, J., *History of the Catholic Church from the Renaissance to the French Revolution*, Dublin, 1915.

Mumby, A. F., *The Fall of Mary Stuart*, London, 1921.

Neale, J. E., *Queen Elizabeth*, New York, 1934.

Pastor, L. von, *History of the Popes*, Vols. VIII to XIII.

Pollard, A. F., *The History of England from the Accession of Edward VI to the Death of Queen Elizabeth 1547–1603*, London, 1910.

Pollen, J. H., *Mary Queen of Scots and the Babington Plot*, Edinburgh, 1922.

Ranke, L. von, *The History of the Popes, their Church and State* (Bohn Library).

Turberville, A. S., *The Spanish Inquisition*, New York, 1932.

Whitney, J. P., *The History of the Reformation*, London, 1940.

Index

753

Set in Intertype Weiss
Format by Dorothy S. Kaiser
Manufactured by The Haddon Craftsmen, Inc.
Published by HARPER & ROW, *New York*